MARGARET THATCHER

MARGARET THATCHER

THE AUTOBIOGRAPHY

HARPER PERENNIAL

NEW YORK • LONDON • TORONTO • SYDNEY • NEW DELHI • AUCKLAND

HARPER ● PERENNIAL

HarperCollins books may be purchased for educational, business, or sales promotional use. For information, please write: Special Markets Department, HarperCollins Publishers, 10 East 53rd Street, New York, NY 10022.

First published by HarperCollins as *The Downing Street Years* in 1993 and *The Path to Power* in 1995.

This combined edition first published by HarperPress in the United Kingdom in 2010. Abridged by Kati Nicholl.

Many of the documents used in the writing of this book are now available online at www.margaretthatcher.org, the official Web site of the Margaret Thatcher Foundation.

FIRST EDITION

Library of Congress Cataloging-in-Publication data is available upon request.

ISBN 978-0-06-201234-0

13 14 RRD 10 9 8 7 6 5 4 3 2

CONTENTS

LIST OF ILLUSTRATIONS

My father
My mother
My father's shop in Grantham (*Express Newspapers*)
With my father
With my sister Muriel (*F/T, Camera Press, London*)
In the garden at the house of some friends
Muriel, father, mother and me
At Somerville College, Oxford (*By courtesy of the Principal and Fellows of Somerville College*)
At work as a research chemist (*Heute Magazine*)
With Denis on our wedding day (*Press Association Images*)
My 1951 election address
As MP for Finchley (*NI Syndication*)
With Ted Heath at the Conservative Party Conference (*Popperfoto/Getty Images*)
Visiting a primary school as Secretary of State for Education
With Denis, Carol and Mark (*NI Syndication/Arthur Steel*)

Meeting the press at Conservative Central Office (*Fox Photos*)
The State Opening of Parliament (*Getty Images*)
Delivering the 'Iron Lady' speech in Kensington (*Press Association Images*)
On a walkabout in Huddersfield (*Srdja Djukanovic*)
On the stairs at Central Office following the 1979 general election victory (*Lionel Chaerruault/Camera Press, London*)
With Denis outside No. 10 (*NI Syndication/Tony Eyles*)
At the funeral of Airey Neave (*Popperfoto/Getty Images*)
Presenting deeds in Milton Keynes (*Getty Images*)
Addressing the Conservative Party Conference in Brighton (*Press Association Images*)
Visiting my old school in Grantham (*NI Syndication/Arthur Edwards*)
HMS *Invincible* returning to Portsmouth at the end of the Falklands War (*Telegraph Syndication*)

EDITOR'S NOTE

The present edition is an abridged version of the original two volumes of Margaret Thatcher's memoirs. *The Downing Street Years*, describing the author's time as Prime Minister, was the first to appear, in 1993. *The Path to Power*, an account of her youth and early political career, was published two years later. The reverse chronological order was a response to the demands of the market and the relative interest of readers. But it had drawbacks.

This single, abridged volume sets them right. It begins at the beginning and ends at the – very dramatic – end. It excludes altogether the last section of *The Path to Power*, which was a series of essays on issues of the day. Also excluded, for brevity's sake, are the dedications, acknowledgements, many footnotes and most of the appendices, along with some discursive sections and travelogues that have lost immediate interest. That said, all the key moments, events, issues, exchanges and arguments are here. Arguably, the compression results in a stronger, sharper self-portrait of one of the twentieth century's towering figures.

ROBIN HARRIS

CHAPTER ONE

A Provincial Childhood

Grantham 1925–1943

MY FIRST DISTINCT MEMORY IS OF TRAFFIC. I was being pushed in a pram through the town to the park on a sunny day, and I must have encountered the bustle of Grantham on the way. The occasion stays in my mind as an exciting mixture of colour, vehicles, people and thunderous noise – yet, perhaps paradoxically, the memory is a pleasant one. I must have liked this first conscious plunge into the outside world.

As for indistinct memories, most of us probably recall our earliest years as a sort of blur. Mine was an idyllic blur in which the sun was always shining through the leaves of the lime tree into our living room and someone – my mother, my sister, one of the people working in the shop – was always nearby to cuddle me or pacify me with a sweet. Family tradition has it that I was a very quiet baby, which my political opponents might have some difficulty in believing. But I had not been born into a quiet family.

Four generations of the Roberts family had been shoemakers in Northamptonshire, at that time a great centre of the shoe industry. My father, who had wanted to be a teacher, had to leave school at thirteen because the family could not afford for him to stay on. He went instead to work at Oundle, one of the better public (i.e. private) schools. Years later, when I was answering questions in the House of Commons, Eric Heffer, a left-wing Labour MP and regular sparring partner of mine, tried to pull working-class rank by mentioning that his father had been a carpenter at Oundle. He was floored when I was able to retort that mine had worked in the tuck shop there.

My father had a number of jobs, most of them in the grocery trade, until in 1913 he was offered the post of manager of a grocery store in

Grantham. In later years he would say that of the fourteen shillings a week he received, twelve shillings paid for his board and lodging, one shilling he saved, and only then did he spend the remaining shilling. The First World War broke out a year later. My father, a deeply patriotic man, tried to enlist no fewer than six times, but was rejected on each occasion on medical grounds. His younger brother, Edward, did enlist, and died on active service in Salonika in 1917. Few British families escaped such a bereavement, and Remembrance Day after the war was observed throughout the country both strictly and intensely.

Four years after arriving in Grantham my father met my mother, Beatrice Ethel Stephenson, through the local Methodist church. She had her own business as a dressmaker. They were married in that church in May 1917 and my sister, Muriel, was born in 1921.

My mother was quite a saver too, and by 1919 they were able to take out a mortgage to buy their own shop in North Parade. Our home was over this shop. In 1923 my father opened a second shop in Huntingtower Road – opposite the primary school which I would later attend. On 13 October 1925 I was born over the shop at North Parade.

That same year, my father expanded his business further, taking in two adjoining buildings in North Parade. Our shop and house were situated at a busy crossroads and the main railway line – Grantham was an important junction – was just a hundred yards away. We could set our clocks by the 'Flying Scotsman' as it thundered through. What I most regretted was that we did not have a garden. Not until the end of the Second World War did my father buy a house with a long garden further along North Parade, on which the family had set our hearts some years previously.

Life 'over the shop' is much more than a phrase. It is something which those who have lived it know to be quite distinctive. For one thing, you are always on duty. People would knock on the door at almost any hour of the night or weekend if they ran out of bacon, sugar, butter or eggs. Everyone knew that we lived by serving the customer; it was pointless to complain – and so nobody did. These orders were, of course, on top of the regular ones. My father or his staff – we had three at North Parade and someone else at Huntingtower – would generally go out and collect these. But sometimes my mother would do so, and then she might take Muriel and me along too. My sister and I knew a lot of people in the town as a result.

There was, of course, no question of closing down the shop for long family holidays. We used to go to the local seaside resort, Skegness. But my father and mother had to take their holidays at different times, with my father taking a week off every year to play his favourite game, competing in the bowls tournament at Skegness. Living over the shop, children see far more of their parents than in most other walks of life. I saw my father at breakfast, lunch, high tea and supper. We had much more time to talk than some other families, for which I have always been grateful.

My father was a specialist grocer. He always aimed to supply the best-quality produce, and the shop itself suggested this. Behind the counter there were three rows of splendid mahogany spice drawers with sparkling brass handles, and on top of these stood large, black, lacquered tea canisters. One of the tasks I sometimes shared was the weighing out of tea, sugar and biscuits from the sacks and boxes in which they arrived into 1lb and 2lb bags. In a cool back room we called 'the old bake house' hung sides of bacon which had to be boned and cut up for slicing. Wonderful aromas of spices, coffee and smoked hams would waft through the house.

I was born into a home which was practical, serious and intensely religious. My father and mother were both staunch Methodists; indeed, my father was much in demand as a lay preacher in and around Grantham. He was a powerful preacher whose sermons contained a good deal of intellectual substance. But he was taken aback when I asked him why he put on a 'sermon voice' on these occasions. I don't think he realized that he did this. It was an unconscious homage to the biblical message, and quite different from the more prosaic tones in which he dispatched council business and current affairs.

Our lives revolved around Methodism. The family went to Sunday Morning Service at 11 o'clock, but before that I would have gone to morning Sunday School. There was Sunday School again in the afternoon; later, from about the age of twelve, I played the piano for the smaller children to sing the hymns. Then my parents would usually go out again to Sunday Evening Service.

On a few occasions I remember trying to get out of going. But when I said to my father that my friends were able to go out for a walk instead and I would like to join them, he would reply: 'Never do things just because other people do them.' This was one of his favourite expressions – used when I wanted to learn dancing, or sometimes when I wanted to go to the cinema. Whatever I felt at the time, the sentiment stood me in good stead, as it did my father.

My father's sense of duty, however, always had its gentler side. This was not true of everyone. Life for poor people in the years before the Second

World War was very difficult; and it was not much easier for those who had worked hard, accumulated a nest egg, and achieved a precarious respectability. They lived on a knife-edge and feared that if some accident hit them, or if they relaxed their standards of thrift and diligence, they might be plunged into debt and poverty. This precariousness often made otherwise good people hard and unforgiving. I remember a discussion between my father and a church-goer about the 'prodigal son' of a friend who, after running through his parents' savings, had turned up penniless and with a young family on their doorstep. The church-goer was clear: the boy was no good, would never be any good, and should be shown the door. My father's reply is vivid in my mind. No, he said. A son remained a son, and he must be greeted with all the love and warmth of his family when he turned to them. Whatever happens, you must always be able to come home.

As this suggests, my father was a man of firm principles – 'Your father always sticks to his principles,' my mother would say – but he did not believe in applying these principles in a way which made life wretched for everyone else. He showed this in his dealings as a local councillor and later alderman with the vexed question of what could be done on the Sabbath. In those days in Grantham and in most places cinemas were closed on Sundays, but during the war – adopting a utilitarian rather than a dogmatic approach – he supported Sunday opening because it gave the servicemen stationed near the town somewhere to go, without disturbing others who wanted a quieter, more contemplative Sabbath. At the same time he strongly (though in the end unsuccessfully) opposed the opening of the parks for the playing of games, which he felt would ruin other people's peace and quiet. He wanted to keep Sunday a special day, but he was flexible about how it should be done. For my own part, I was unpersuaded, even as a girl, of the need for these restrictions: but I can now appreciate how much this highly principled man was prepared to bend on the matter when circumstances made it sensible.

These upright qualities, which entailed a refusal to alter your convictions just because others disagreed or because you became unpopular, were instilled into me from the earliest days. In 1936, when I was eleven, I was given a special edition of *Bibby's Annual*. Joseph Bibby was a Liverpool food manufacturer who used part of his considerable self-made fortune to edit a religious magazine which was an odd combination of character building, homespun philosophy and religion; it also contained beautiful reproductions of great pictures. I was too young to know that the underlying approach was Theosophist* but the *Annual* was one of my most treasured possessions. Above all, it taught me some verses which I still use in off-the-cuff speeches because they came to embody for me so much of what I was brought up to feel.

> One ship drives East, and another drives West,
> By the self-same gale that blows;
> 'Tis the set of the sail, and not the gale,
> That determines the way she goes.
> ELLA WHEELER WILCOX

Or again:

> The heights by great men reached and kept
> Were not attained by sudden flight,
> But they, while their companions slept,
> Were toiling upward in the night.
> HENRY WADSWORTH LONGFELLOW

Whether it was that early exposure to *Bibby's Annual* or just a natural bent, I was soon fascinated by poetry. Aged ten, I was the proud winner of a prize at the Grantham Eisteddfod for reciting poetry. (I read John Drinkwater's 'Moonlit Apples' and Walter de la Mare's 'The Travellers'.) One day soon afterwards, when I called at a door to collect an order for groceries, I was given an edition of Milton by someone who knew how much poetry meant to me: I have treasured the book ever since. In the first years of the war I would go out as part of a concert party to the surrounding villages and recite from my *Oxford Book of English Verse* – another book which even now is never far from reach. Methodism itself, of course, has, in the form of the Wesley hymns, some really fine religious poetry.

Religious life in Grantham was very active and, in the days before Christian ecumenism, competitive. There were three Methodist chapels, St Wulfram's Anglican church – the sixth-highest steeple in England, according to local legend – and a Roman Catholic church just opposite our house. From a child's standpoint, the Catholics seemed to have the

---

* Theosophy was a mixture of mysticism, Christianity and the 'wisdom of the East', sense and nonsense.

most light-hearted time of all. I used to envy the young Catholic girls making their first communion, dressed in white, ribboned party dresses, and carrying baskets of flowers. The Methodist style was much plainer, and if you wore a ribboned dress an older chapel-goer would shake his head and warn against 'the first step to Rome'.

Even without ribbons, however, Methodism was far from dour. It placed great emphasis on the social side of religion and on music, both of which gave me plenty of opportunities to enjoy life, even if it was in what might seem a rather solemn way. Our friends from church would often come in to cold supper on Sunday evenings, or we would go to them. I always enjoyed the adults' conversation, which ranged far wider than religion or happenings in Grantham to include national and international politics. And one of the unintended consequences of the temperance side of Methodism was that Methodists tended to devote more time and attention to eating. 'Keeping a good table' was a common phrase, and many of the social occasions were built around tea parties and suppers. There was also a constant round of church events.

It was, I confess, the musical side of Methodism which I liked best. We sang special hymns on the occasion of Sunday School anniversaries. The Kesteven and Grantham Girls' School (KGGS) carol service – and the weeks of practice which preceded it – was something I always looked forward to. Our church had an exceptionally good choir. Every other year we would perform an oratorio: Handel's *Messiah*, Haydn's *Creation* or Mendelssohn's *Elijah*. We would have professionals from London to sing the more difficult solo parts. But what made an impression on me was the latent richness of musical talent which serious training and practice could develop. My family also belonged to a music society and three or four times a year there would be a chamber music concert.

We were a musical family. From the age of five my parents had me learn the piano: my mother played too. In fact, I turned out to be quite good, and I was fortunate enough to have excellent teachers and won several prizes at local music festivals. The piano on which I was taught was made by my great uncle, John Roberts, in Northampton. He also made church organs. When I was ten I visited him and was thrilled to be allowed to play one of the two he had built in a cavernous barn-like building in his garden. Sadly, at sixteen I found it necessary to stop music lessons when I was cramming for my university entrance, and I still regret that I never took the piano up again. At this time, however, it was I who played the piano at home, while my father (who had a good bass voice) and mother (a contralto) and sometimes friends sang the old favourites of an evening – 'The Holy City', 'The Lost Chord', Gilbert and Sullivan, etc.

Perhaps the biggest excitement of my early years was a visit to London when I was twelve years old. I came down by train in the charge of a friend of my mother's, arriving at King's Cross, where I was met by the Rev. Skinner and his wife, family friends who were going to look after me. The first impact of London was overwhelming: King's Cross itself was a giant bustling cavern; the rest of the city had all the dazzle of a commercial and imperial capital. For the first time in my life I saw people from foreign countries, some in the traditional native dress of India and Africa. The sheer volume of traffic and of pedestrians was exhilarating; they seemed to generate a sort of electricity. London's buildings were impressive for another reason; begrimed with soot, they had a dark imposing magnificence which constantly reminded me that I was at the centre of the world.

I was taken by the Skinners to all the usual sites. I fed the pigeons in Trafalgar Square; I rode the Underground – a slightly forbidding experience for a child; I visited the Zoo, where I rode on an elephant and recoiled from the reptiles – an early portent of my relations with Fleet Street; I was disappointed by Oxford Street, which was much narrower than the boulevard of my imagination; made a pilgrimage to St Paul's, where John Wesley had prayed on the morning of his conversion; and of course, to the Houses of Parliament and Big Ben, which did not disappoint at all; and I went to look at Downing Street, but unlike the young Harold Wilson did not have the prescience to have my photograph taken outside No. 10.

All this was enjoyable beyond measure. But the high point was my first visit to the Catford Theatre in Lewisham where we saw Sigmund Romberg's famous musical *The Desert Song*. For three hours I lived in another world, swept away as was the heroine by the daring Red Shadow – so much so that I bought the score and played it at home, perhaps too often.

I could hardly drag myself away from London or from the Skinners, who had been such indulgent hosts. Their kindness had given me a glimpse of, in Talleyrand's words, *'la douceur de la vie'* – how sweet life could be.

Our religion was not only musical and sociable – it was also intellectually stimulating. The ministers were powerful characters with strong views. The general political tendency among Methodists and other Nonconformists in our town was somewhat to the left wing and even pacifist. Methodists in Grantham were prominent in organizing the 'Peace Ballot' of 1935, circulating a loaded questionnaire to the electorate, which was then declared overwhelmingly to have 'voted for peace'. It is not recorded how far Hitler and Mussolini were moved by this result; we had our own views about that in the Roberts household. The Peace Ballot was a foolish idea which must take some of the blame nationally for delaying the rearmament necessary to deter and ultimately defeat the dictators. On this question and others, being staunchly Conservative, we were the odd family out. Our friend the Rev. Skinner was an enthusiast for the Peace Ballot. He was the kindest and holiest man, and he married Denis and me at Wesley's Chapel in London many years later. But personal virtue is no substitute for political hard-headedness.

The sermons we heard every Sunday made a great impact on me. It was an invited Congregationalist minister, the Rev. Childe, who brought home to me the somewhat advanced notion for those days that whatever the sins of the fathers (and mothers) they must never be visited on the children. I still recall his denunciation of the Pharisaical tendency to brand children born outside marriage as 'illegitimate'. All the town knew of some children without fathers; listening to the Rev. Childe, we felt very guilty about thinking of them as different. Times have changed. We have since removed the stigma of illegitimacy not only from the child but also from the parent – and perhaps increased the number of disadvantaged children thereby. We still have to find some way of combining Christian charity with sensible social policy.

When war broke out and death seemed closer to everybody, the sermons became more telling. In one, just after the Battle of Britain, the preacher told us that it is 'always the few who save the many': so it was with Christ and the apostles. I was also inspired by the theme of another sermon: history showed how it was those who were born at the depths of one great crisis who would be able to cope with the next. This was proof of God's benevolent providence and a foundation for optimism about the future, however dark things now looked. The values instilled in church were faithfully reflected in my home.

So was the emphasis on hard work. In my family we were never idle – partly because idleness was a sin, partly because there was so much work to be done, and partly, no doubt, because we were just that sort of people. As I have mentioned, I would help whenever necessary in the shop. But I also learned from my mother just what it meant to cope with a household so that everything worked like clockwork, even though she had to spend so many hours serving behind the counter. Although we had a maid before the war – and later a cleaning lady a couple of days a week – my mother did much of the work herself, and there was a great deal more than in a modern home. She showed me how to iron a man's shirt in the correct way and to press embroidery without damaging it. Large flat-irons were heated over the fire and I was let in on the secret of how to give a special finish to linen by putting just enough candle wax to cover a sixpenny piece on the iron. Most unusually for those times, at my second-ary school we had to study domestic science – everything from how to do laundry properly to the management of the household budget. So I was doubly equipped to lend a hand with the domestic chores. The whole house at North Parade was not just cleaned daily and weekly: a great annual spring clean was intended to get to all those parts which other cleaning could not reach. Carpets were taken up and beaten. The mahogany furniture – always good quality, which my mother had bought in auction sales – was washed down with a mixture of warm water and vinegar before being repolished. Since this was also the time of the annual stocktaking in the shop, there was hardly time to draw breath.

Nothing in our house was wasted, and we always lived within our means. The worst you could say about another family was that they 'lived up to the hilt'. Because we had always been used to a careful regime, we could cope with wartime rationing, though we used to note down the hints on the radio about the preparation of such stodgy treats as 'Lord Woolton's potato pie', an economy dish named after the wartime Minister for Food. My mother was an excellent cook and a highly organized one. Twice a week she had her big bake – bread, pastry, cakes and pies. Her home-made bread was famous, as were her Grantham gingerbreads. Before the war there were roasts on Sunday, which became cold cuts on Monday and disappeared into rissoles on Tuesday. With wartime, however, the Sunday roast became almost meatless stew or macaroni cheese.

Small provincial towns in those days had their own networks of private charity. In the run-up to Christmas as many as 150 parcels were made up in our shop, containing tinned meat, Christmas cake and pudding, jam and tea – all purchased for poorer families by one of the strongest social and charitable institutions in Grantham, the Rotary Club. There was always something from those Thursday or Sunday bakes which was sent out to elderly folk living alone or who were sick. As grocers, we knew something about the circumstances of our customers.

Clothes were never a problem for us. My mother had been a professional seamstress and made most of what we wore. In those days there were two very good pattern services, Vogue and Butterick's, and in the sales we could get the best-quality fabrics at reduced prices. So we got excellent value for money and were, by Grantham standards, rather fashionable. For my father's mayoral year, my mother made both her daughters new dresses – a blue velvet for my sister and a dark green velvet for me – and herself a black *moiré* silk gown. But in wartime the ethos of frugality was almost an obsession. Even my mother and I were taken aback by one of our friends, who told us that she never threw away her tacking cottons but re-used them: 'I consider it my duty to do so,' she said. After that, so did we. We were not Methodists for nothing.

I had less leisure time than other children. But I used to enjoy going for long walks, often on my own. Grantham lies in a little hollow surrounded by hills, unlike most of Lincolnshire which is very flat. I loved the beauty of the countryside and being alone with my thoughts in those surroundings. Sometimes I used to walk out of the town by Manthorpe Road and cut across on the north side to return down the Great North Road. I would also walk up Hall's Hill, where in wartime we were given a week off school to go and gather rose hips and blackberries. There was tobogganing there when it snowed.

I did not play much sport, though I learned to swim, and at school I was a somewhat erratic hockey player. At home we played the usual games, like Monopoly and Pit – a noisy game based on the Chicago Commodities Exchange. In a later visit to America I visited the Exchange; but my dabbling in commodities ended there.

It was, however, the coming of the cinema to Grantham which really brightened my life. We were fortunate in having among our customers the Campbell family who owned three cinemas in Grantham. They would sometimes invite me around to their house to play the gramophone, and I got to know their daughter Judy, later to be a successful actress who partnered Noël Coward in his wartime comedy *Present Laughter* and made famous the song 'A Nightingale Sang in Berkeley Square'. Because we knew the Campbells, the cinema was more acceptable to my parents than it might otherwise have been. They were content that I should go to 'good' films, a classification which fortunately included Fred Astaire and Ginger Rogers musicals, and the films of Alexander

Korda. They rarely went with me – though on a Bank Holiday we would go together to the repertory theatre in Nottingham or to one of the big cinemas there – so usually I would be accompanied by friends of my own age. Even then, however, there were limits. Ordinarily there was a new film each week; but since some of these did not sustain enough interest to last six days, another one was shown from Thursday. Some people would go along to the second film, but that was greatly frowned on in our household.

Perhaps that was a fortunate restraint; for I was entranced with the romantic world of Hollywood. For 9d you had a comfortable seat in the darkness while the screen showed first the trailer for forthcoming attractions, then the British Movietone News with its chirpy optimistic commentary, after that a short public service film on a theme like *Crime Does Not Pay*, and finally the Big Picture. These ran the gamut from imperialistic adventures like *The Four Feathers* and *Drum*, to sophisticated comedies like *The Women* (with every female star in the business), to the four-handkerchief weepies like Barbara Stanwyck in *Stella Dallas* or Ingrid Bergman in anything. Nor was I entirely neglecting my political education 'at the pictures'. My views on the French Revolution were gloriously confirmed by Leslie Howard and lovely Merle Oberon in *The Scarlet Pimpernel*. I saw my father's emphasis on the importance of standing up for your principles embodied by James Stewart in *Mr Smith Goes to Washington*. I rejoiced to see Soviet communism laughed out of court when Garbo, a stern Commissar, was seduced by a lady's hat in *Ninotchka*.

And my grasp of history was not made more difficult by the fact that William Pitt the Younger was played by Robert Donat and, in *Marie Walewska*, Napoleon was played by the great French charmer Charles Boyer.

I often reflect how fortunate I was to have been born in 1925 and not twenty years earlier. Until the 1930s, there was no way that a young girl living in a small English provincial town could have had access to this extraordinary range of talent, dramatic form, human emotion, sex appeal, spectacle and style. To a girl born twenty years later these offerings were commonplace and taken much more for granted. Grantham was a small town, but on my visits to the cinema I roamed to the most fabulous realms of the imagination. It gave me the determination to roam in reality one day.

For my parents the reality which mattered was here and now. Yet it was not really a dislike of pleasure which shaped their attitude. They made a very important distinction between mass and self-made entertainment, which is just as valid in the age of constant soap operas and game shows – perhaps more so. They felt that entertainment that demanded something of you was preferable to being a passive spectator. At times I found this irksome, but I also understood the essential point.

When my mother, sister and I went on holiday together, usually to Skegness, there was always the same emphasis on being active, rather than sitting around day-dreaming. We would stay in a self-catering guesthouse, much better value than a hotel, and first thing in the morning I went out with the other children for PT exercises arranged in the public gardens. There was plenty to keep us occupied and, of course, there were buckets and spades and the beach. In the evening we would go to the variety shows and reviews, with comedians, jugglers, acrobats, 'old tyme' singers, ventriloquists and lots of audience participation when we joined in singing the latest hit from Henry Hall's *Guest Night*. My parents considered that such shows were perfectly acceptable, which in itself showed how attitudes changed: we would never have gone to the variety while Grandmother Stephenson, who lived with us till I was ten, was still alive.

That may make my grandmother sound rather forbidding. Again, not at all. She was a warm presence in the life of myself and my sister. Dressed in the grandmotherly style of those days – long black sateen-beaded dress – she would come up to our bedrooms on warm summer evenings and tell us stories of her life as a young girl. She would also make our flesh creep with old wives' tales of how earwigs would crawl under your skin and form carbuncles. Her death at the age of eighty-six was the first time I had ever encountered death. As was the custom in those days, I was sent to stay with friends until the funeral was over and my grandmother's belongings had all been packed away. In fact, life is very much a day-to-day experience for a child, and I recovered reasonably quickly. But Mother and I went to tend her grave on half-day closing days. I never knew either of my grandfathers, who died before I was born, and I saw Grandmother Roberts only twice, on holidays down to Ringstead in Northamptonshire. She was a bustling, active little old lady who kept a fine garden. I remember particularly that she kept a store of Cox's orange pippins in an upstairs room from which my sister and I were invited to select the best.

My father was a great bowls player, and he smoked (which was very bad for him because of his weak chest). Otherwise, his leisure and entertainment always seemed to merge into duty. We had no alcohol in the house until he became mayor at the end of the war, and then only sherry and cherry brandy, which for some mysterious reason was considered more respectable than straight brandy, to entertain visitors. (Years of electioneering also later taught me that cherry brandy is very good for the throat.)

Like the other leading businessmen in Grantham, my father was a Rotarian. The Rotary motto, 'Service Above Self', was engraved on his heart. He spoke frequently and eloquently at Rotary functions, and we could read his speeches reported at length in the local paper. The Rotary Club was constantly engaged in fund raising for the town's different charities. My father would be involved in similar activity, not just through the church but as a councillor and in a private capacity. One such event which I used to enjoy was the League of Pity (now NSPCC) Children's Christmas party, which I would go to in one of the party dresses beautifully made by my mother, to raise money for children who needed help.

Apart from home and church, the other centre of my life was, naturally enough, school. Here too I was very lucky. Huntingtower Road Primary School had a good reputation in the town and by the time I went there I had already been taught simple reading by my parents. Even when I was very young I enjoyed learning. Like all children, I suspect, these days remain vividly immediate for me. I remember a heart-stopping moment at the age of five when I was asked how to pronounce W-R-A-P; I got it right, but I thought 'They always give me the difficult ones.' Later, in General Knowledge, I first came across the mystery of 'proverbs'. I already had a logical and indeed somewhat literal mind – perhaps I have not changed much in this regard – and I was perplexed by the metaphorical element of phrases like 'Look before you leap'. I thought it would be far better to say 'Look before you cross' – a highly practical point given the dangerous road I must traverse on my way to school. And I triumphantly pointed out the contradiction between that proverb and 'He who hesitates is lost'.

It was in the top class at primary school that I first came across the work of Kipling, who died that January of 1936. I immediately became fascinated by his poems and stories and asked my parents for a Kipling book at Christmas. His poems gave a child access to a wider world – indeed, wider worlds – of the Empire, work, English history and the animal kingdom. Like the Hollywood films later, Kipling offered glimpses into the romantic possibilities of life outside Grantham. By now I was probably reading more widely than most of my classmates, doubtless through my father's influence, and it showed on occasion. I can still recall writing an essay about Kipling and burning with indignation at being accused of having copied down the word 'nostalgia' from some book, whereas I had used it quite naturally and easily.

From Huntingtower Road I went on to Kesteven and Grantham Girls' School. It was in a different part of town, and what with coming home for lunch, which was more economical than the school lunch, I walked four miles a day back and forth. Our uniform was saxe-blue and navy and so we were called 'the girls in blue'. (When Camden Girls' School from London was evacuated to Grantham for part of the war they were referred to as 'the girls in green'.) The headmistress was Miss Williams, a petite, upright, grey-haired lady, who had started the school as head-mistress in 1910, inaugurated certain traditions such as that all girls however academic had to take domestic science for four years, and whose quiet authority by now dominated everything. I greatly admired the special outfits Miss Williams used to wear at the annual school fête or prize-giving, when she appeared in beautiful silk, softly tailored, looking supremely elegant. But she was very practical. The advice to us was never to buy a low-quality silk when the same amount of money would purchase a good-quality cotton. 'Never aspire to a cheap fur coat when a well-tailored wool coat would be a better buy.' The rule was always to go for quality within your own income.

My teachers had a genuine sense of vocation and were highly respected by the whole community. The school was small enough – about 350 girls – for us to get to know them and one another, within limits. The girls were generally from middle-class backgrounds; but that covered a fairly wide range of occupations from town and country. My closest friend came in daily from a rural village about ten miles distant, where her father was a builder. I used to stay with her family from time to time. Her parents, no less keen than mine to add to a daughter's education, would take us out for rural walks, identifying the wild flowers and the species of birds and birdsongs.

I had a particularly inspiring History teacher, Miss Harding, who gave me a taste for the subject, which, unfortunately, I never fully developed. I found myself with absolute recall remembering her account of the Dar-danelles campaign so many years later when, as Prime Minister, I walked over the tragic battlegrounds of Gallipoli.

But the main academic influence on me was undoubtedly Miss Kay, who taught Chemistry, in which I decided to specialize. It was not unusual – in an all-girls' school, at least – for a girl to concentrate on science, even before the war. My natural enthusiasm for the sciences was whetted by reports of breakthroughs in the splitting of the atom and the development of plastics. It was clear that a whole new scientific world was opening up. I wanted to be part of it. Moreover, as I knew that I would have to earn my own living, this seemed an exciting way to do so.

As my father had left school at the age of thirteen, he was determined to make up for this and to see that I took advantage of every educational opportunity. We would both go to hear 'Extension Lectures' from the University of Nottingham about current and international affairs, which were given in Grantham regularly. After the talk would come a lively question time in which I and many others would take part: I remember, in particular, questions from a local RAF man, Wing-Commander Millington, who later captured Chelmsford for Common Wealth – a left-wing party of middle-class protest – from the Churchill coalition in a by-election towards the end of the war.

My parents took a close interest in my schooling. Homework always had to be completed – even if that meant doing it on Sunday evening. During the war, when the Camden girls were evacuated to Grantham and a shift system was used for teaching at our school, it was necessary to put in extra hours at the weekend. My father, in particular, who was an all the more avid reader for being a self-taught scholar, would discuss what we read at school. On one occasion he found that I did not know Walt Whitman's poetry; this was quickly remedied, and Whitman is still a favourite author of mine. I was also encouraged to read the classics – the Brontës, Jane Austen and, of course, Dickens: it was the latter's *A Tale of Two Cities*, with its strong political flavour, that I liked best. My father also used to subscribe to the *Hibbert Journal* – a philosophical journal. But this I found heavy going.

Beyond home, church and school lay the community which was Grantham itself. We were immensely proud of our town; we knew its history and traditions; we were glad to be part of its life. Grantham was established in Saxon times, though it was the Danes who made it an important regional centre. During the twelfth century the Great North Road was re-routed to run through the town, literally putting Grantham on the map. Communications were always the town's lifeblood. In the eighteenth century the canal was cut to carry coke, coal and gravel into Grantham and corn, malt, flour and wool out of it. But the real expansion had come with the arrival of the railways in 1850.

Our town's most imposing structure I have already mentioned – the spire of St Wulfram's Church, which could be seen from all directions. But most characteristic and significant for us was the splendid Victorian Guildhall and, in front of it, the statue of Grantham's most famous son, Sir Isaac Newton. It was from here, on St Peter's Hill, that the Remembrance Day parades began to process en route to St Wulfram's. I would watch from the windows of the Guildhall Ballroom as (preceded by the Salvation Army band and the band from Ruston and Hornsby's locomotive works) the mayor, aldermen and councillors with robes and regalia, followed by Brownies, Cubs, Boys' Brigade, Boy Scouts, Girl Guides, Freemasons, Rotary, Chamber of Commerce, Working Men's Clubs, trade unions, British Legion, soldiers, airmen, the Red Cross, the St John's Ambulance and representatives of every organization which made up our rich civic life filed past. It was also on the green at St Peter's Hill that every Boxing Day we gathered to watch the pink coats of the Belvoir Hunt hold their meet (followed by the traditional tipple) and cheered them as they set off.

Nineteen thirty-five was a quite exceptional and memorable year for the town. We celebrated King George V's Silver Jubilee along with Grantham's Centenary as a borough. Lord Brownlow, whose family (the Custs) with the Manners family (the Dukes of Rutland) were the most distinguished aristocratic patrons of the town, became mayor. The town itself was heavily decorated with blue and gold waxed streamers – our local colours – across the main streets. Different streets vied to outdo one another in the show they put on. I recall that it was the street with some of the poorest families in the worst housing, Vere Court, which was most attractively turned out. Everyone made an effort. The brass bands played throughout the day, and Grantham's own 'Carnival Band' – a rather daring innovation borrowed from the United States and called 'The Grantham Gingerbreads' – added to the gaiety of the proceedings. The schools took part in a great open-air programme and we marched in perfect formation under the watchful eye of the wife of the headmaster of the boys' grammar school to form the letters 'G-R-A-N-T-H-A-M'. Appropriately enough, I was part of the 'M'.

My father's position as a councillor, Chairman of the Borough Finance Committee, then alderman* and finally, in 1945–46, mayor meant that I

---

* Aldermen were indirectly elected council members – elected to serve a fixed term by the directly elected element in the council; a highly honoured position which has since been abolished.

heard a great deal about the town's business and knew those involved in it. Politics was a matter of civic duty and party was of secondary importance. The Labour councillors we knew were respected and, whatever the battles in the council chamber or at election time, they came to our shop and there was no partisan bitterness. My father understood that politics has limits – an insight which is all too rare among politicians. His politics would perhaps be best described as 'old-fashioned liberal'. Individual responsibility was his watchword and sound finance his passion. He was an admirer of John Stuart Mill's *On Liberty*. Like many other business people he had, as it were, been left behind by the Liberal Party's acceptance of collectivism. He stood for the council as a ratepayer's candidate. In those days, before comprehensive schools became an issue and before the general advance of Labour politics into local government, local council work was considered as properly non-partisan. But I never remember him as anything other than a staunch Conservative.

I still recall with great sorrow the day in 1952 when Labour, having won the council elections, voted my father out as an alderman. This was roundly condemned at the time for putting party above community. Nor can I forget the dignity with which he behaved. After the vote in the council chamber was taken, he rose to speak: 'It is now almost nine years since I took up these robes in honour, and now I trust in honour they are laid down.' And later, after receiving hundreds of messages from friends, allies and even old opponents, he issued a statement which said: 'Although I have toppled over I have fallen on my feet. My own feeling is that I was content to be in and I am content to be out.' Years later, when something not too dissimilar happened to me, after my father was long dead, I tried to take as an example the way he left public life.

But this is to anticipate. Perhaps the main interest which my father and I shared while I was a girl was a thirst for knowledge about politics and public affairs. We read the *Daily Telegraph* every day, *The Methodist Recorder*, *Picture Post* and *John O'London's Weekly* every week, and when we were small we took *The Children's Newspaper*. Occasionally we read *The Times*.

And then came the day my father bought our first wireless – a Philips of the kind you sometimes now see in the less pretentious antique shops. I knew what he was planning and ran much of the way home from school in my excitement. I was not disappointed. It changed our lives. From then on it was not just Rotary, church and shop which provided the rhythm of our day: it was the radio news. And not just the news. During the war after the 9 o'clock news on Sundays there was *Postscript*, a short talk on a topical subject, often by J.B. Priestley, who had a unique gift of cloaking left-wing views as solid, down-to-earth, Northern homespun philosophy, and sometimes an American journalist called Quentin Reynolds who derisively referred to Hitler by one of his family names, 'Mr Schicklgruber'. There was *The Brains Trust*, an hour-long discussion of current affairs by four intellectuals, of whom the most famous was Professor C.E.M. Joad, whose answer to any question always began 'It all depends what you mean by . . .' On Friday evenings there were commentaries by people like Norman Birkett in the series called *Encounter*. I loved the comedy *ITMA* with its still serviceable catchphrases and its cast of characters like the gloomy charlady 'Mona Lott' and her signature line 'It's being so cheerful as keeps me going.'

As for so many families, the unprecedented immediacy of radio broadcasts gave special poignancy to great events – particularly those of wartime. I recall sitting by our radio with my family at Christmas dinner and listening to the King's broadcast in 1939. We knew how he struggled to overcome his speech impediment and we knew that the broadcast was live. I found myself thinking just how miserable he must have felt, not able to enjoy his own Christmas dinner, knowing that he would have to broadcast. I remember his slow voice reciting those famous lines:

> And I said to the man who stood at the gate of the year: 'Give me a light that I may tread safely into the unknown.'
> And he replied: 'Go out into the darkness and put your hand into the Hand of God. That shall be to you better than light and safer than a known way.'*

I was almost fourteen by the time war broke out, and already informed enough to understand the background to it and to follow closely the great events of the next six years. My grasp of what was happening in the political world during the thirties was less sure. But certain things I did take in. The years of the Depression – the first but not the last economic catastrophe resulting from misguided monetary policy – had less effect on Grantham itself than on the surrounding agricultural communities, and of course much less than on Northern towns dependent on heavy indus-

---

* From *God Knows*, by Minnie Louise Haskins.

try. Most of the town's factories kept going – the largest, Ruston and Hornsby, making locomotives and steam engines. We even attracted new investment, partly through my father's efforts: Aveling-Barford built a factory to make steamrollers and tractors. Our family business was also secure: people always have to eat, and our shops were well run. The real distinction in the town was between those who drew salaries for what today would be called 'white collar' employment and those who did not, with the latter being in a far more precarious position as jobs became harder to get. On my way to school I would pass a long queue waiting at the Labour Exchange, seeking work or claiming the dole. We were lucky in that none of our closest friends was unemployed, but we knew people who were. We also knew – and I have never forgotten – how neatly turned out the children of those unemployed families were. Their parents were determined to make the sacrifices that were necessary for them. The spirit of self-reliance and independence was very strong in even the poorest people of the East Midlands towns and, because others quietly gave what they could, the community remained together. Looking back, I realize just what a decent place Grantham was.

So I did not grow up with the sense of division and conflict between classes. Even in the Depression there were many things which bound us all together. The monarchy was certainly one. And my family like most others was immensely proud of the Empire. We felt that it had brought law, good administration and order to lands which would never other-wise have known them. I had a romantic fascination for out-of-the-way countries and continents and what benefits we British could bring to them. As a child, I heard with wonder a Methodist missionary describing his work in Central America with a tribe so primitive that they had never written down their language until he did it for them. Later, I seriously considered going into the Indian Civil Service, for to me the Indian Empire represented one of Britain's greatest achievements. (I had no interest in being a civil servant in Britain.) But my father said, all too perceptively as it turned out, that by the time I was ready to join it the Indian Civil Service would probably not exist.

As for the international scene, I recall when I was very young my parents expressing unease about the weakness of the League of Nations and its failure to come to the aid of Abyssinia when Italy invaded it in 1935. We had a deep distrust of the dictators.

We did not know much about the ideology of communism and fascism at this time. But, unlike many conservative-minded people, my father was fierce in rejecting the argument that fascist regimes had to be backed as the only way to defeat communists. He believed that the free society was the better alternative to both. This too was a conviction I quickly made my own. Well before war was declared, we knew just what we thought of Hitler. On the cinema newsreels I would watch with distaste and incomprehension the rallies of strutting brownshirts, so different from the gentle self-regulation of our own civic life. We also read a good deal about the barbarities and absurdities of the Nazi regime.

But none of this meant, of course, that we viewed war with the dictators as anything other than an appalling prospect, which should be avoided if possible. In our attic there was a trunk full of magazines showing, among other things, the famous picture from the Great War of a line of British soldiers blinded by mustard gas walking to the dressing station, each with a hand on the shoulder of the one in front to guide him. Hoping for the best, we prepared for the worst. As early as September 1938 – the time of Munich – my mother and I went out to buy yards of black-out material. My father was heavily involved in organizing the town's air raid precautions. As he would later say, 'ARP' stood for 'Alf Roberts' Purgatory', because it was taking up so much time that he had none to spare for other things.

The most pervasive myth about the thirties is perhaps that it was the Right rather than the Left which most enthusiastically favoured appeasement. Not just from my own experience in a highly political right-wing family, but from my recollection of how Labour actually voted against conscription even after the Germans marched into Prague, I have never been prepared to swallow this. But it is important to remember that the atmosphere of the time was so strongly pacifist that the practical political options were limited.

The scale of the problem was demonstrated in the general election of 1935 – the contest in which I cut my teeth politically, at the age of ten. It will already be clear that we were a highly political family. And for all the serious sense of duty which underlay it, politics was fun. I was too young to canvass for my father during council elections, but I was put to work folding the bright red election leaflets extolling the merits of the Conservative candidate, Sir Victor Warrender. The red came off on my sticky fingers and someone said, 'There's Lady Warrender's lipstick.' I had no doubt at all about the importance of seeing Sir Victor returned. On election day itself, I was charged with the responsible task of running back and forth between the Conservative committee room and the polling station (our school) with information about who had voted. Our candidate won, though with a majority down from 16,000 to 6,000.

I did not grasp at the time the arguments about rearmament and the League of Nations, but this was a very tough election, fought in the teeth of opposition from the enthusiasts of the Peace Ballot and with the Abyssinian war in the background. Later, in my teens, I used to have fierce arguments with other Conservatives about whether Baldwin had culpably misled the electorate during the campaign in not telling them the dangers the country faced. In fact, had the National Government not been returned at that election there is no possibility that rearmament would have happened faster, and it is very likely that Labour would have done less. Nor could the League have ever prevented a major war.

We had mixed feelings about the Munich Agreement of September 1938, as did many people. At the time, it was impossible not to be pulled in two directions. We knew by now a good deal about Hitler's regime and probable intentions – something brought home to my family by the fact that Hitler had crushed Rotary in Germany, which my father always considered one of the greatest tributes Rotary could ever be paid. Dictators, we learned, could no more tolerate Burke's 'little platoons' – the voluntary bodies which help make up civil society – than they could individual rights under the law. Dr Jauch, of German extraction and probably the town's best doctor, received a lot of information from Germany which he passed on to my father, and he in turn discussed it with me.

I knew just what I thought of Hitler. Near our house was a fish and chip shop where I was sent to buy our Friday evening meal. Fish and chip queues were always a good forum for debate. On one occasion the topic was Hitler. Someone suggested that at least he had given Germany some self-respect and made the trains run on time. I vigorously argued the opposite, to the astonishment and doubtless irritation of my elders. The woman who ran the shop laughed and said: 'Oh, she's always debating.'

My family understood clearly Hitler's brutal treatment of the Jews. At school we were encouraged to have foreign penfriends. Mine was a French girl called Colette: alas, I did not keep up contact with her. But my sister, Muriel, had an Austrian Jewish penfriend called Edith. After the Anschluss in March 1938, when Hitler annexed Austria, Edith's father, a banker, wrote to mine asking whether we could take his daughter, since he very clearly foresaw the way events were leading. We had neither the time nor the money to accept such a responsibility alone; but my father won the support of the Grantham Rotarians, and Edith came to stay with each of our families in turn until she went to live with relatives in South America. She was seventeen, tall, beautiful, well-dressed, and spoke good English. She told us what it was like to live as a Jew under an anti-semitic regime. One thing Edith reported particularly stuck in my mind: the Jews, she said, were being made to scrub the streets.

We wanted to see Hitler's wickedness ended, even by war if that proved necessary. From that point of view Munich was nothing to be proud of. We knew too that by the Munich Agreement Britain had complicity in the great wrong that had been done to Czechoslovakia. When fifty years later as Prime Minister I visited Czechoslovakia I addressed the Federal Assembly in Prague and told them: 'We failed you in 1938 when a disastrous policy of appeasement allowed Hitler to extinguish your independence. Churchill was quick to repudiate the Munich Agreement, but we still remember it with shame.' British foreign policy is at its worst when it is engaged in giving away other people's territory.

But equally we all understood the lamentable state of unpreparedness in Britain and France to fight a major war. Also, unfortunately, some were taken in by the German propaganda and actually believed that Hitler was acting to defend the Sudeten Germans from Czech oppression. If we had gone to war at that point, moreover, we would not have been supported by all of the Dominions. It was the Germans' subsequent dismemberment of what remained of Czechoslovakia in March 1939 that finally convinced almost everyone that war would soon be necessary to defeat Hitler's ambitions. Even then, as I have pointed out, Labour voted against conscription the following month. There was strong anti-war feeling in Grantham too: many Methodists opposed the official recruiting campaign of May 1939, and right up to the outbreak of war and beyond pacifists were addressing meetings in the town.

In any case, the conflict was soon upon us. Germany invaded Poland on 1 September 1939. When Hitler refused to withdraw by 11 a.m. on Sunday 3 September in accordance with Britain's ultimatum we were waiting by the radio, desperate for the news. It was the only Sunday in my youth when I can remember not attending church. Neville Chamberlain's fateful words, relayed live from the Cabinet Room at No. 10, told us that we were at war.

It was natural at such times to ask oneself how we had come to such a pass. Each week my father would take two books out of the library, a 'serious' book for himself (and me) and a novel for my mother. As a result, I found myself reading books which girls of my age would not generally read. I soon knew what I liked – anything about politics and international affairs. I read, for instance, John Strachey's *The Coming Struggle for Power*, which had first appeared in 1932. The contents of this fashionable communist analysis, which predicted that capitalism was shortly to be superseded by socialism, seemed to many of my generation exciting and new.

But both by instinct and upbringing I was always a 'true blue' Conservative. No matter how many left-wing books I read or left-wing commentaries I heard, I never doubted where my political loyalties lay. Such an admission is probably unfashionable. But though I had great friends in politics who suffered from attacks of doubt about where they stood and why, and though of course it would take many years before I came to understand the philosophical background to what I believed, I always knew my mind. I can see now that I was probably unusual. For the Left were setting the political agenda throughout the thirties and forties, even though the leadership of Churchill concealed it during the years of the war itself. This was evident from many of the books which were published at about this time. The Left had been highly successful in tarring the Right with appeasement, most notably in Victor Gollancz's Left Book Club, the so-called 'yellow books'. One in particular had enormous impact: *Guilty Men*, co-authored by Michael Foot, which appeared under the pseudonym 'Cato' after Dunkirk in 1940.

Robert Bruce Lockhart's best-selling *Guns or Butter?* appeared in the autumn of 1938, after Munich. Lockhart's travels through Europe led him to Austria (now Nazi-controlled) and then to Germany itself at the height of Hitler's triumph. There the editor of a German national newspaper is reported as telling him that 'Germany wanted peace, but she wanted it on her own terms.' The book ends with Lockhart, woken by 'the tramp of two thousand feet in unison', looking out of his window onto a misty dawn, where 'Nazi Germany was already at work'.

A more original variation on the same theme was Douglas Reed's *Insanity Fair*. This made a deep impression on me. Reed witnessed the persecution of the Jews which accompanied the advance of Nazi influence. He described the character and mentality – alternately perverted, unbalanced and calculating – of the Nazi leaders. He analysed and blisteringly denounced that policy of appeasement by Britain and France which paved the way for Hitler's successes. Written on the eve of the Anschluss, it was powerfully prophetic.

Out of the Night by Jan Valtin – pen name for the German communist Richard Krebs – was lent to my father by our future MP Denis Kendall. It was such strong meat that my father forbade me to read it – but when he went out to meetings I would take it down and read its spine-chilling account of totalitarianism in action. It is full of scenes of sadistic violence whose authenticity makes them still more horrifying. The appalling treatment by the Nazis of their victims is undoubtedly the most powerful theme. But underlying it is another, just as significant. For it describes how the communists set out in cynical alliance with the Nazis to subvert the fragile democracy of Germany by violence in the late twenties and early thirties. That same alliance against democracy would, of course, be replicated in the Nazi-Soviet pact of 1939 to 1941 which destroyed Poland, the Baltic States and Finland and plunged the world into war. The book undoubtedly contributed to my growing belief that Nazism (national socialism) and communism (international socialism) were but two sides of the same coin.

A book which had a particular influence on me was the American Herbert Agar's *A Time for Greatness*, which appeared in 1944. This was a powerful analysis of how the West's moral failure allowed the rise of Hitler and the war which had followed. It urged a return to western liberal democratic values and – though I liked this less – a fair amount of left-wing social engineering. For me the important message of Agar's book was that the fight against Hitler had a significance for human destiny which exceeded the clash of national interests or spheres of influence or access to resources or any of the other – doubtless important – stuff of power politics.

Agar also wrote of the need, as part of the moral regeneration which must flow from fighting the war, to solve what he called 'the Negro problem'. I had never heard of this 'problem' at all. Although I had seen some coloured people on my visit to London, there were almost none living in Grantham. Friends of ours once invited two American servicemen – one black, one white – stationed in Grantham back to tea and had been astonished to detect tension and even hostility between them. We were equally taken aback when our friends told us about it afterwards. This sort of prejudice was simply outside our experience or imagination.

Like many other young girls in wartime, I read Barbara Cartland's *Ronald Cartland*, the life of her brother, a young, idealistic Conservative MP, who had fought appeasement all the way and who was killed at Dunkirk in 1940. It was a striking testament to someone who had no doubt that the war was not only necessary but right, and whose thinking throughout his short life was 'all of a piece', something which I always admired. But the sense that the war had a moral significance which underlay the fear and suffering – or in our family's case in Grantham the material dreariness and mild deprivation – which accompanied it, was perhaps most memorably conveyed by Richard Hillary's *The Last Enemy*. The author – a young pilot – portrays the struggle which had claimed the lives of so many of his friends, and which would claim his own less than a year later, as one which was also being fought out in the human heart. It was a struggle for a better life in the sense of simple decency.

A generation which, unlike Richard Hillary, survived the war felt this kind of desire to put things right with themselves, their country and the world. As I would come to learn when dealing with my older political colleagues, no one who fought came out of it quite the same person as went in. Less frequently understood, perhaps, is that war affected deeply people like me who, while old enough to understand what was happening in the conflict, were not themselves in the services. But we all see these great calamities with different eyes, and so their impact upon us is different. It never seemed to me, for example, as it apparently did to many others, that the 'lesson' of wartime was that the state must take the foremost position in our national life and summon up a spirit of collective endeavour in peace as in war.

The 'lessons' I drew were quite different. The first was that the kind of life that the people of Grantham had lived before the war *was* a decent and wholesome one, and its values were shaped by the community rather than by the government. Second, since even a cultured, developed, Christian country like Germany had fallen under Hitler's sway, civilization had constantly to be nurtured, which meant that good people had to stand up for the things they believed in. Third, I drew the obvious political conclusion that it was appeasement of dictators which had led to the war, and that had grown out of wrong-headed but decent impulses, like the pacifism of Methodists in Grantham, as well as out of corrupt ones. And, finally, I had the patriotic conviction that, given great leadership of the sort I heard from Winston Churchill in the radio broadcasts to which we listened, there was almost nothing that the British people could not do.

Our life in wartime Grantham – until I went up to Oxford in 1943 – must have been very similar to that of countless other families. There was always voluntary work to do of one kind or another in the Service canteens and elsewhere. Our thoughts were at the front; we devoured voraciously every item of available news; and we ourselves, though grateful for being more or less safe, knew that we were effectively sidelined. But there were twenty-one German air raids on the town, and seventy-eight people were killed. The town munitions factory – the British Manufacturing and Research Company (BMAR Co., or 'British Marcs' as we called it) – was an obvious target, as was the junction of the Great North Road and the Northern Railway Line – the latter within a few hundred yards of our house. My father was frequently out in the evenings on air raid duty. During air raids we would crawl under the table for shelter – we had no outside shelter for we had no garden – until the 'all clear' sounded. After bombs fell on the town in January 1941 I asked my father if I could walk down to see the damage. He would not let me go. Twenty-two people died in that raid. We were also concerned for my sister Muriel, who was working in the Orthopaedic Hospital in Birmingham: Birmingham was, of course, very badly bombed.

In fact, Grantham itself was playing a more dramatic role than I knew at the time. Bomber Command's 5 Group was based in Grantham, and it was from a large house off Harrowby Road that much of the planning was done of the bombing raids on Germany. The Dambusters flew from near Grantham – my father met their commander, Squadron Leader Guy Gibson. I always felt that Bomber Harris – himself based in Grantham in the early part of the war – had not been sufficiently honoured. I would remember what Winston Churchill wrote to him at the end of the war:

> For over two years Bomber Command alone carried the war to the heart of Germany, bringing hope to the peoples of Occupied Europe and to the enemy a foretaste of the mighty power which was rising against him . . .
>
> All your operations were planned with great care and skill. They were executed in the face of desperate opposition and appalling hazards. They made a decisive contribution to Germany's final defeat. The conduct of these operations demonstrated the fiery gallant spirit which animated your air crews and the high sense of duty of all ranks under your command. I believe that the massive achievements of Bomber Command will long be remembered as an example of duty nobly done.
>
> WINSTON S. CHURCHILL

In Grantham, at least, politics did not stand still in the war years. Hitler's invasion of the Soviet Union in June 1941 sharply altered the attitudes of the Left to the war. Pacifist voices suddenly became silent. Anglo-

Soviet friendship groups sprouted. We attended, not without some unease, Anglo-Soviet evenings held at the town hall. It was the accounts of the suffering and bravery of the Russians at Stalingrad in 1942–43 which had most impact on us.

Although it can now be seen that 1941 – with Hitler's attack on Russia in June and the Japanese bombing of Pearl Harbor which brought America into the war in December – sowed the seeds of Germany's ultimate defeat, the news was generally bad, especially so in early 1942. This almost certainly contributed to the outcome of the by-election held in Grantham on 27 February 1942, after Victor Warrender was elevated to the Lords as Lord Bruntisfield, to become an Admiralty spokesman. Denis Kendall stood as an Independent against our Conservative candidate, Sir Arthur Longmore. Kendall fought an effective populist campaign in which he skilfully used his role as General Manager of British Marcs to stress the theme of an all-out drive for production for the war effort and the need for 'practical' men to promote it. To our great surprise, he won by 367 votes. Then and later the Conservative Party was inclined to complacency. A closer analysis of the limited number of by-elections should have alerted us to the likelihood of the Socialist landslide which materialized in 1945.

Unusually, I took little part in the campaign because I was preparing for examinations which I hoped would get me into Somerville College, Oxford. In particular, my evenings were spent cramming the Latin which was required for the entrance exam. Our school did not teach Latin. Fortunately, our new headmistress, Miss Gillies, was able to arrange Latin lessons for me from a teacher at the boys' grammar school, and to lend me her own books, including a textbook written by her father. The hard work helped keep my mind off the ever more dismal news about the war. In particular, there was a series of blows in the Far East – the loss of Malaya, the sinking of the *Prince of Wales* and *Repulse*, the fall of Hong Kong and then Singapore, the retreat through Burma and the Japanese threat to Australia. One evening in the spring of 1942 when I had gone for a walk with my father I turned and asked him when – and how – it would all end. He replied very calmly: 'We don't know how, we don't know when; but we have no doubt that we *shall* win.'

In spite of my efforts to get into Somerville, I failed to win the scholarship I wanted. It was not too surprising, for I was only seventeen, but it was a blow. If I was not able to go up in 1943 I would not be allowed to do more than a two-year 'wartime degree' before I was called up for national service at the age of twenty. But there was nothing I could do about it, and so at the end of August 1943 I entered the third-year sixth and became Joint Head of School. Then a telegram arrived offering me a place at Somerville in October. Someone else had dropped out. And so it was that I suddenly found myself faced with the exciting but daunting prospect of leaving home, almost for the first time, for a totally different world.

CHAPTER TWO

Gowns-woman

Oxford 1943–1947

O XFORD DOES NOT SET OUT TO PLEASE. Freshmen arrive there for the Michaelmas term in the misty gloom of October. Monumental buildings impress initially by their size rather than their exquisite architecture. Everything is cold and strangely forbidding. Or so it seemed to me.

It had been at Somerville during bitterly cold mid-winter days that I had taken my Oxford entrance exams. But I had seen little of my future college before I arrived, rather homesick and apprehensive, to begin my first term. In fact, Somerville always takes people by surprise. Many incurious passers-by barely know it is there, for the kindest thing to say of its external structure is that it is unpretentious. But inside it opens up into a splendid green space onto which many rooms face. I was to live both my first and second years in college, and in due course, a picture or two, a vase and finally an old armchair brought back from Grantham allowed me to feel that the rooms were in some sense mine. In my third and fourth years I shared digs with two friends in Walton Street.

Both Oxford and Somerville were strongly if indirectly affected by the war. For whatever reason, Oxford was not bombed, but like everywhere else, both town and university were subject to the blackout ('dim-out' from 1944) and much affected by wartime stringencies. Stained-glass windows were boarded up. Large static water tanks stood ready for use in case of fire. Most of our rations were allocated direct to the college which provided our unexciting fare in hall, though on rare occasions I would be asked out to dinner. There were a few coupons left over for jam and other things. One of the minor benefits to my health and figure of such austerities was that I ceased having sugar in my tea – though only many years later would I deny my ever-sweet tooth the pleasure of sugared coffee (not that there was over-much coffee for some time either). There were tight controls over the use of hot water. For example, there must be no more than five inches of water in the bath and of course I rigidly observed this, though coming from a family where the relationship between cleanliness and Godliness was no laughing matter. Not that we ever felt like complaining. After all, we were the lucky ones.

I was the first Roberts to go to Oxbridge and I knew that, however undemonstrative they might be, my parents were extremely proud of the fact. Before I went up to Oxford, I had a less clear idea of what the place would be like than did many of my contemporaries. But I regarded it as being quite simply the best, and if I was serious about getting on in life that is what I should always strive for. So, excellent as it was, particularly in the sciences, I was never tempted to opt for Nottingham, our 'local' university. Another aspect of Oxford which appealed to me then – and still does – is the collegiate system. Oxford is divided into colleges, though it also has some central university institutions, such as the Bodleian Library. In my day, life centred on the college (where you ate and slept and received many of your tutorials) and around other institutions – church and societies – which had more or less a life of their own. My experience of college life contributed to my later conviction that if you wish to bring the best out of people they should be encouraged to be part of smaller, human-scale communities rather than be left to drift on a sea of impersonality.

Perhaps the most obvious way in which wartime conditions affected the 'feel' of university life was the fact that so many of us were very young – only seventeen or just eighteen. From 1944, the feel of Oxford changed again as older people, invalided out, started coming back from the services either to complete a shortened wartime degree or to begin a full degree course. They had been through so much more than we had. As Kipling wrote (in 'The Scholars') of young naval officers returning to Cambridge after the Great War to continue their studies:

> Far have they steamed and much have they known, and most
>   would they fain forget;
> But now they are come to their joyous own with all the world in
>   their debt.

By the time I left I found myself dealing with friends and colleagues who had seen much more of the world than I had. And I gained a great deal from the fact that Oxford at the end of the war was a place of such mixed views and experience.

I began by keeping myself to myself, for I felt shy and ill at ease in this quite new environment. I continued to take long walks on my own, around Christ Church Meadow, through the university parks and along the Cherwell or the Thames, enjoying my own company and thoughts. But I soon started to appreciate Oxford life. I was a member of a Methodist Study Group which gave and attended tea parties. My mother would send me cakes through the post and on a Saturday morning I would join the queue outside the 'cake factory' in north Oxford for an hour or so to buy the sustenance for tea that Sunday. I joined the Bach Choir, conducted by Sir Thomas Armstrong (by a nice coincidence Robert Armstrong's father), whose repertoire was wider than its name suggested. I especially remember our performance of the *St Matthew Passion* in the Sheldonian Theatre, which Wren might have designed for the purpose. We also sang *Prince Igor*, Constant Lambert's *Rio Grande*, and Holst's *Hymn of Jesus*. Sometimes I went to listen rather than to sing: I heard Kathleen Ferrier in Elgar's *Dream of Gerontius*.

With the end of the war and the return of the servicemen, the pace of entertainment quickened. Eights Week was revived and I went down to the river to watch the races. It was at this time that I first went out to dances and even on occasion drank a little wine (I had previously only tasted sherry and did not like it; nor do I now). I smoked my first cigarettes. I did not like them much either, though I knew I would get the taste if I persisted. I decided not to, to save the money and buy *The Times* every day instead. I now went to my first commem ball, and, like the girl in the song, danced all night. I saw Chekhov and Shakespeare at the Playhouse and the New Theatre. (Christopher Fry's first plays were being performed at that time.) And I saw a wonderful OUDS (Oxford University Dramatic Society) production performed in a college garden and featuring Kenneth Tynan, Oxford's latest dandy. I cannot remember the play, partly because it was always difficult to distinguish Ken Tynan on stage from Ken Tynan in everyday life.

I might have had a more glittering Oxford career, but I had little money to spare and would have been hard put to make ends meet if it had not been for a number of modest grants secured for me from the college at the instance of my ever-helpful tutor, the chemist Dorothy Hodgkin. I was also assisted by some educational trusts. I might have been able to supplement my income further from such sources if I had been prepared to give an undertaking to go into teaching. But I knew I had no such calling; and I did and do believe that good teachers need a vocation. In fact, I did teach science for one vacation at a school in Grantham in the summer of 1944: this earned the money for that luxury in Grantham but near-necessity in Oxford – a bicycle. It was while I was teaching there that Paris was liberated. The headmaster called the school together, announced that Paris was free again and told us how the brave Resistance fighters had helped the Allies by rising up against the German occupiers.

It was a thrilling moment. The war was evidently being won; I felt somehow less guilty for not being able to play a larger part; and I shared the joy of the British people that the French Resistance had restored French honour and pride. We may have had an exaggerated view in those days of the universality of resistance – we told each other stories of how the customers of a café would tap out 'V for Victory' in morse code on their glasses when a German soldier entered the café – but we had no doubt that every true Frenchman wanted to be free.

I threw myself into intensely hard work. In Dorothy Hodgkin the college was fortunate to have a brilliant scientist and a gifted teacher, working in the comparatively new field of X-ray crystallography. Mrs Hodgkin was a Fellow of the Royal Society and later made a decisive contribution towards discovering the structure of penicillin, the first antibiotic, for which she won the Nobel Prize in 1964. In my fourth and final year (1946–47) I worked with a refugee German scientist, Gerhard Schmidt, under Dorothy Hodgkin's direction, on the simple protein Gramicidin B as the research project required to complete Part II of my chemistry course. Through the Cosmos Club and the Scientific Club I also came across other budding young scientists and heard many well-known scientists speak, including J.D. Bernal. His politics were very left wing, as indeed were those of many other scientists at that time. But they would never have dreamt of carrying their politics over into their professional relationships with their students.

Religion also figured large in my Oxford life. There are many tales of young people entering university and, partly through coming into contact with scepticism and partly for less wholesome reasons, losing their faith. I never felt in any danger of that. Methodism provided me with an anchor of stability and, of course, contacts and friends who looked at the world as I did. I usually attended the Wesley Memorial Church on Sundays. There was, as in Grantham, a warmth and a sober but cheerful social life which I found all the more valuable in my initially somewhat strange surroundings. The church had a very vigorous Students' Fellowship. After Sunday Evening Service there was usually a large gathering over coffee in the minister's house, where there would be stimulating discussion of religious and other matters. Occasionally I would go to the University Church of St Mary the Virgin to listen to a particularly interesting university sermon and sometimes I would go to the college chapel, especially when I knew that Miss Helen Darbishire, who was Principal and a distinguished scholar of Milton and Wordsworth when I first went up to Somerville, was preaching.

Generally speaking, though, I did not go to Anglican churches. But oddly enough – or perhaps not so oddly when one considers the great impact he had on so many of my generation – it was the religious writing of that High Anglican C.S. Lewis which had most impact upon my intellectual religious formation. The power of his broadcasts, sermons and essays came from a combination of simple language with theological depth. Who has ever portrayed more wittily and convincingly the way in which Evil works on our human weaknesses than he did in *The Screwtape Letters*? Who has ever made more accessible the profound concepts of Natural Law than he did in *The Abolition of Man* and in the opening passages of *Mere Christianity*? I remember most clearly the impact on me of *Christian Behaviour* (republished in *Mere Christianity*, but originally appearing as radio talks). This went to the heart of the appalling disparity between the way in which we Christians behave and the ideals we profess. One of C.S. Lewis's messages was that the standards of Christianity are not just binding on the saints. As he put it:

> Perfect behaviour may be as unattainable as perfect gear-changing when we drive; but it is a necessary ideal prescribed for all men by the very nature of the human machine just as perfect gear-changing is an ideal prescribed for all drivers by the very nature of cars.

Similarly, I was helped by what he wrote of the application of that sublime principle of Christian charity which seems to most of us so impossible of fulfilment. Lewis did not for a moment contest or diminish the sublimeness; but he very helpfully set out what charity is *not*.

> . . . what [does] loving your neighbour as yourself [mean?] I have to love him as I love myself. Well, how exactly do I love myself? Now that I come to think of it, I have not exactly got a feeling of

fondness or affection for myself, and I do not even always enjoy my own society. So apparently 'Love your neighbour' does not mean 'feel fond of him' or 'find him attractive' . . . I can look at some of the things I have done with horror and loathing. So apparently I am allowed to loathe and hate some of the things my enemies do . . . Consequently, Christianity does not want us to reduce by one atom the hatred we feel for cruelty and treachery . . . Even while we kill and punish we must try to feel about the enemy as we feel about ourselves – to wish that he were not bad, to hope that he may, in this world or another be cured: in fact, to wish his good.

Such words had a special poignancy, of course, at this time.

The main contribution one can make as a student to one's country in peace or wartime is to study hard and effectively. But we all also tried to do something more directly. For my part, I would serve one or two evenings a week at the Forces canteen in Carfax. British soldiers and American airmen from the nearby bases at Upper Heyford were among our main customers. It was hot, sticky and very hard on the feet, but also good fun, with plenty of company and wisecracking humour.

Reports of the D-day landings in July 1944, though, brought both apprehension and anxiety. The deadly struggle on those exposed beaches made us deeply uneasy. For perhaps the only time I wondered whether I was right to be at Oxford.

In fact we were now within a year of the end of the war in Europe. There were still the Battle of the Bulge and the tragedy of Arnhem to come. But slowly the emphasis came to be on preparing for peace. And among the peacetime activities which began to take an increasing amount of my time was politics.

Almost as soon as I came up to Oxford I had joined the Oxford University Conservative Association (OUCA), which was founded in the 1920s under the inspiration of a don at Christ Church – Keith Feiling, the historian of the Tory Party and later biographer of Neville Chamberlain. Although the national agreement to suspend party political electoral contests for the duration of the war had no direct implications for politics at the universities, in practice political life in Oxford was a good deal quieter than it had been in the 1930s. But, for all that, OUCA activities quickly became a focus for my life. In those days the Oxford Union, in which star speakers would come to debate issues of the highest importance as well as ones of unbelievable triviality, did not admit women to its membership, though I used sometimes to listen to debates. But I would never have excelled in the kind of brilliant, brittle repartee which the Union seemed to encourage. I preferred the more serious forensic style of our discussions in OUCA and of the real hustings. OUCA also provided a further network of acquaintance and friendship. It was, indeed, an effective forum for matchmaking, as a number of my OUCA colleagues demonstrated.

Oxford politics was a nursery for talent. I made friends in university politics who, as in the novels of Anthony Powell, kept reappearing in my life as the years passed by. Much the closest was Edward Boyle who, though he moved easily in a sophisticated social and political world which I had only glimpsed, shared with me a serious interest in politics. At this time Edward, the wealthy and cultivated son of a Liberal MP, was himself a classical liberal whose views chimed in pretty well with my own provincial middle-class conservatism. Although we were later to diverge politically, we remained dear friends until his tragically early death from cancer.

William Rees-Mogg, whom I knew in my final year, was a distinguished editor of *The Times* from a very early age. I was never as close to William as I was to Edward, but one sensed that he was marked out for higher things.

Robin Day was a prominent Liberal. Like Edward he was a leading light in the Oxford Union, and we later met as lawyers in the same chambers. One sometimes wondered what career would be open to the brilliant wits of the Union, until Robin Day invented a new one by pioneering television interviewing – after which our paths and our swords crossed frequently.

Another star was Tony Benn, at that time still rattling his full complement of syllables as the Hon. Anthony Wedgwood Benn. From start to finish he and I have rarely agreed on anything, but he was always a courteous and effective debater, an English patriot, and as time has made socialism more and more a thing of the past, even a traditional figure. But perhaps we enjoy a sympathy based on our religious roots. When Tony became President of the Union I was invited to a celebration, attended by his father Viscount Stansgate, which, true to Tony's Nonconformist principles, was teetotal.

Kenneth Harris was another leading debater, who along with Edward Boyle and Tony Benn spent several months touring the United States giving demonstration debates. He subsequently had a distinguished career in political journalism. We met again many times, notably when he wrote my biography.

As an officer in OUCA I was naturally taken up with the 1945 general election campaign. In Oxford I was busy campaigning for the city's MP Quintin Hogg until term ended, when I returned to Grantham to work for Squadron Leader Worth in his attempt to dislodge the sitting Independent Member, Denis Kendall.

In retrospect, we should all have known what to expect. By some mysterious but inexorable law, wars always seem to advance state control and those who advocate it. My husband Denis's view was that in the services people from totally different backgrounds mix in an unprecedented way and that the result is an acute twinge of social conscience and a demand for the state to step in and ameliorate social conditions. But, in any case, the Conservatives had done uniformly badly in the limited number of wartime electoral contests, and there was a general tendency for our share of the vote to fall. Nobody paid much attention to opinion polls then: but they too told the same story. As I have noted, the Left were extremely effective after Dunkirk in portraying the Conservatives as exclusively responsible for appeasement, and managed to distance Churchill from the party he led. Nor did people remember that Labour had opposed even the limited rearmament carried out by Baldwin and Chamberlain.

But there were also other influences at work. The command economy required in wartime conditions had habituated many people to an essentially socialist mentality. Within the Armed Forces it was common knowledge that left-wing intellectuals had exerted a powerful influence through the Army Education Corps, which as Nigel Birch observed was 'the only regiment with a general election among its battle honours'. At home, broadcasters like J.B. Priestley gave a comfortable yet idealistic gloss to social progress in a left-wing direction. It is also true that Conservatives, with Churchill in the lead, were so preoccupied with the urgent imperatives of war that much domestic policy, and in particular the drawing up of the agenda for peace, fell largely to the socialists in the Coalition Government. Churchill himself would have liked to continue the National Government at least until Japan had been beaten and, in the light of the fast-growing threat from the Soviet Union, perhaps beyond then. But the Labour Party understandably wished to come into its own collectivist inheritance.

In 1945, therefore, we Conservatives found ourselves confronting two serious and insuperable problems. First, the Labour Party had us fighting on their ground and were always able to outbid us. Churchill had been talking about post-war 'reconstruction' for some two years, and as part of that programme Rab Butler's Education Act was on the Statute Book. Further, our manifesto committed us to the so-called 'full employment' policy of the 1944 Employment White Paper, a massive house-building programme, most of the proposals for National Insurance benefits made by the great Liberal social reformer Lord Beveridge and a comprehensive National Health Service. Moreover, we were not able effectively to take the credit (so far as this was in any case appropriate to the Conservative Party) for victory, let alone to castigate Labour for its irresponsibility and extremism, because Attlee and his colleagues had worked cheek by jowl with the Conservatives in government since 1940. In any event, the war effort had involved the whole population.

I vividly remember sitting in the student common room in Somerville listening to Churchill's famous (or notorious) election broadcast to the effect that socialism would require 'some sort of Gestapo' to enforce it, and thinking, 'He's gone too far.' However logically unassailable the connection between socialism and coercion was, in our present circumstances the line would not be credible. I knew from political argument on similar lines at an election meeting in Oxford what the riposte would be: 'Who's run the country when Mr Churchill's been away? Mr Attlee.' And such, I found, was the reaction now.

Back in Grantham, I was one of the 'warm-up' speakers for the Conservative candidate at village meetings. In those days, many more people turned out to public meetings than today, and they expected their money's worth. I would frequently be speaking at half a dozen meetings an evening. Looking back at the reports in the local newspapers of what I said at the time, there is little with which I would disagree now. Germany must be disarmed and brought to justice. There must be co-operation with America and (somewhat less realistically) with the Soviet Union. The British Empire, the most important community of peoples that the world had ever known, must never be dismembered. (Perhaps not very realistic either – but my view of Britain's imperial future was not uncommon in the aftermath of victory.) The main argument I advanced for voting Conservative was that by doing so we would keep Winston Churchill in charge of our foreign policy. And perhaps if Churchill had been able to see through the July 1945 Potsdam Conference the post-war world might have looked a little different.

Like many other members of OUCA, I had received lessons in public speaking from Conservative Central Office's Mrs Stella Gatehouse. Her emphasis was on simplicity and clarity of expression and as little jargon as possible. In fact, at election meetings, when you never knew how long you would have to speak before the candidate arrived, a touch more long-windedness would have been very useful. Most valuable of all for me personally, however, was the experience of having to think on my feet when answering questions from a good-humoured but critical audience. I recall a point made by an elderly man at one such meeting that had a lasting effect on my views about welfare: 'Just because I've saved a little bit of money of my own, "Assistance" won't help me. If I'd spent everything, they would.' It was an early warning of the hard choices that the new Welfare State would shortly place before politicians.

Three weeks after polling day, by which time the overseas and service votes had been returned, I went to the election count at Sleaford. As we waited for the Grantham result, news trickled in of what was happening elsewhere. It was bad, and it became worse – a Labour landslide with Tory Cabinet ministers falling one after the other. Then our own candidate lost too. I simply could not understand how the electorate could do this to Churchill. On my way back home I met a friend, someone who I had always thought was a staunch Conservative, and said how shocked I was by the terrible news. He said he thought the news was rather good. Incomprehension deepened. At the time I felt that the British electorate's treatment of the man who more than anyone else secured their liberty was shameful. But was it not Edmund Burke who said: 'A perfect democracy is the most shameless thing in the world'? In retrospect, the election of the 1945–51 Labour Government seems the logical fulfilment of the collectivist spirit that came to dominate wartime Britain. It was to be about thirty-five years before this collectivism would run its course – shaping and distorting British society in the process, before it collapsed in 1979's Winter of Discontent.

At the time, it was clear to everyone that fundamental reassessment of Conservative principles and policies was required. We felt this as much in Oxford as anywhere else. It lay behind the preparation of a report of the OUCA Policy Sub-Committee which I co-authored in Michaelmas term 1945 with Michael Kinchin-Smith and Stanley Moss. The report contained no more profound insights than any other Tory undergraduate paper. And its two themes we have heard many times since – more policy research and better presentation.

Perhaps the main problem as regards what we would now call the 'image' of the Conservative Party was that we seemed to have lost our way and our policies seemed to be devised for the wealthy rather than for ordinary people. As our OUCA paper put it: 'Conservative policy has come to mean in the eyes of the public little more than a series of administrative solutions to particular problems, correlated in certain fields by a few unreasoning prejudices and the selfish interests of the moneyed classes.' The accusation was, of course, unfair. If the Conservatives had won in 1945 we would still have had a Welfare State – doubtless with less immediate public expenditure and certainly with greater scope for private and voluntary initiative. But the idea that Conservatism was simply that – conserving the interests of the status quo against change and reform – was immensely powerful at this time.

In March 1946 I became Treasurer of OUCA and later that month went as one of the Oxford representatives to the Federation of University Conservative and Unionist Associations (FUCUA) Conference at the Waldorf Hotel in London. It was my first such conference and I enjoyed it hugely. When I spoke it was in support of more involvement by people from working-class backgrounds in university Conservative politics. I felt that we had to get away from the perception of Conservatism as stuffy and frivolous. It was not so much that I wanted a classless society, as the socialists (somewhat disingenuously) said they did, but rather that I could not see that class was important. Everyone had something unique to offer in life and their responsibility was to develop those gifts – and heroes come from all backgrounds. As I put it to the FUCUA Conference: 'We have heard all about this being the age of the common man – but do not forget the need for the uncommon man.' Or, I suppose I might have added, 'woman'.

In October 1946 I was elected President of OUCA – the third woman to hold the position. I had done my final exams that summer and was now beginning the research project which constituted the fourth and last year of the Chemistry degree, so I had a little more time to spend on politics. For example, I attended my first Conservative Party Conference, held that year in Blackpool. I was entranced. So often in Grantham and in Oxford it had felt unusual to be a Conservative. Now suddenly I was with hundreds of other people who believed as I did and who shared my insatiable appetite for talking politics.

The Conference had a most extraordinary atmosphere. From my humble position as a 'representative', I had the sense that the Party leadership – with the notable exception of the Party Leader – had arrived at Blackpool prepared to reconcile itself and Conservatism to the permanence of socialism in Britain. A perceptive observer of the 1946 Conference, Bertrand de Jouvenal, wrote of our Front Bench: 'These great, intelligent thoroughbreds, trained from their earliest years to prudent administration and courteous debate, were in their hearts not far from accepting as definitive their electoral defeat in 1945.'*

This was decidedly not what the rank and file wanted to hear. Indeed, there was open dissent from the floor. A request on the first day for a general debate on questions of philosophy and policy was refused by the chairman. There was a lukewarm reaction to the consensus approach of speeches from the platform, though these became notably tougher the longer the Conference went on, as Shadow ministers perceived our discontent. My instincts were with the rank and file, though I had not yet fully digested the strong intellectual case against collectivism, as I was to do in the next few years.

Back in Oxford I had organized a very full programme of speakers. Lord Dunglass (Alec Douglas-Home) urged support for Ernest Bevin's foreign policy – support we readily gave. Bob Boothby – a wonderful speaker, with great style – declaimed against the 'revolutionary totalitarian absolutism of Moscow'. David Maxwell-Fyfe, whose daughter Pamela was at Oxford at the time, attacked nationalization and urged a property-owning democracy. Peter Thorneycroft put forward what seemed the very advanced views of the 'Tory Reform' wing in a debate with the University Labour Club at the Union. Lady (Mimi) Davidson told us how it felt to be the only Conservative woman Member of the House of Commons. Anthony Eden charmed and impressed us all over sherry. Each term we had a lively debate with the other political clubs at the Oxford Union, particularly the Labour Club, which at the time was very left wing and included some famous names like Anthony Crosland – who even in those days could condescend to a Duchess – and Tony Benn. Generally, however, OUCA met in the Taylorian Institute on a Friday evening, entertaining the speaker to dinner beforehand at the Randolph Hotel. So it was there that I first rubbed shoulders with the great figures of the Tory Party.

The most powerful critique of socialist planning and the socialist state which I read at this time, and to which I have returned so often since, F.A. Hayek's *The Road to Serfdom*, is dedicated famously 'To the socialists of all parties'.

---

* *Problems of Socialist England* (1947).

I cannot claim that I fully grasped the implications of Hayek's little masterpiece at this time. It was only in the mid-1970s, when Hayek's works were right at the top of the reading list given me by Keith Joseph, that I really came to grips with the ideas he put forward. Only then did I consider his arguments from the point of view of the kind of state Conservatives find congenial – a limited government under a rule of law – rather than from the point of view of the kind of state we must avoid – a socialist state where bureaucrats rule by discretion. At this stage it was the (to my mind) unanswerable criticisms of socialism in *The Road to Serfdom* which had an impact. Hayek saw that Nazism – national socialism – had its roots in nineteenth-century German social planning. He showed that intervention by the state in one area of the economy or society gave rise to almost irresistible pressures to extend planning further into other sectors. He alerted us to the profound, indeed revolutionary, implications of state planning for Western civilization as it had grown up over the centuries.

Nor did Hayek mince his words about the monopolistic tendencies of the planned society that professional groups and trade unions would inevitably seek to exploit. Each demand for security, whether of employment, income or social position, implied the exclusion from such benefits of those outside the particular privileged group – and would generate demands for countervailing privileges from the excluded groups. Eventually, in such a situation everyone will lose. Perhaps because he did not come from a British Conservative background and did not ever consider himself a Conservative at all, Hayek had none of the inhibitions which characterized the agonized social conscience of the English upper classes when it came to speaking bluntly about such things.

I was in Blackpool visiting my sister (who had gone there from the Birmingham Orthopaedic Hospital) when I learned from the radio news on that fateful 6 August 1945 that an atomic bomb had been dropped on Hiroshima. My academic study and the fascination exerted on me by issues relating to the practical application of science probably meant that I was better informed than most about the developments lying behind the manufacture of the atomic bomb. The following year I was able to read (and largely understand) the very full account contained in *Atomic Energy for Military Purposes* published by the United States. Yet – cliché as it may be – I was immediately aware on hearing the preliminary reports of Hiroshima that with the advent of the A-bomb 'somehow the world had changed'. Or as Churchill himself would put it in his majestic memoirs *The Second World War*: 'Here then was a speedy end to the Second World War, and perhaps to much else besides.'

The full scientific, strategic and political implications of the nuclear weapon would take some years to assess. But the direct human and environmental consequences of the use of atomic weapons were more quickly grasped. Yet neither on that first evening reflecting on the matter in the train home from Blackpool, nor later when I read accounts and saw the pictures of the overwhelming devastation, did I have any doubt about the rightness of the decision to use the bomb. I considered it justified primarily because it would avoid the losses inevitable if Allied forces were to take by assault the main islands of Japan. The Japanese still had 2½ million men under arms. We had already seen the fanatical resistance which they had put up during the Battle of Okinawa. Only the scale of the Allies' technological military superiority, demonstrated first at Hiroshima and then at Nagasaki, could persuade the Japanese leadership that resistance was hopeless. And so one week after Hiroshima, and after a second bomb had been dropped on Nagasaki, the Japanese surrendered.

Britain had, of course, been closely involved in the development of the bomb, though because of the breakdown of Anglo-American nuclear co-operation after the war it was not till 1952 that we ourselves were able to explode one. Churchill and Truman, as we now know, were duped by Stalin at Potsdam when the American President 'broke the news' of the bomb to the Soviet leader, who knew about it already and promptly returned to Moscow to urge his own scientists to speed up their atomic programme. But the fact remains, as I used to remind the Soviets when I became Prime Minister, that the most persuasive proof of the essential benevolence of the United States was that in those few crucial years when it alone possessed the military means to enforce its will upon the world, it refrained from doing so.

The greatest transformation affecting Britain at the time – and the one which would have a great impact on my political life – was the change of the Soviet Union from comrade in arms to deadly enemy. It is important to stress how little understanding most people in the West had at this time of conditions within the USSR. I was never tempted to sympathize with communism. But my opposition to it was at this time more visceral than intellectual. It was much later that I thought and read more deeply about the communist system and saw precisely where its weaknesses and wickednesses lay. And it is interesting to note that when Hayek came to write a new preface to *The Road to Serfdom* in 1976 he, too, felt that he had 'under-stressed the significance of the experience of communism in Russia'.

By the time I left Oxford with a second-class degree in Chemistry under my belt, I knew a great deal more about the world and particularly about the world of politics. My character had not changed; nor had my beliefs. But I had a clearer idea of where I stood in relation to other people, their ambitions and opinions. I had, in short, grown up. And I had discovered what I really wanted to do with my life.

Shortly before my university days came to an end I went back to Corby Glen, a village some ten miles from Grantham, to a dance. Afterwards a few of us gathered for coffee and a sandwich in the kitchen of the house where I was staying. Not unusually, I was talking about politics. Something I said, or perhaps the way I said it, prompted one of the men to remark: 'What you really want to do is to be an MP, isn't it?' Almost without thinking I said: 'Yes: that really *is* what I want to do.' I had never said it before – not even to myself. When I went to bed that night I found that I had a lot on my mind.

CHAPTER THREE

House Bound

Marriage, family, law and politics 1947–1959

I F GOING UP TO OXFORD is one sort of shock, coming down is quite another. I had made many like-minded friends at Oxford, I had enjoyed my adventures in chemistry and I was passionately interested in university politics. It was a wrench to leave all that behind.

The newly created Oxford University Appointments Committee, which helped new graduates to find suitable jobs, arranged several interviews for me, including one at a Northern ICI plant. We hopefuls were interviewed by several managers whose written comments were passed on to the general manager, who gave us our final interview. The remarks on me were lying on the table at the interview, and I could not resist using my faculty for reading upside down. They were both encouraging and discouraging; one manager had written: 'This young woman has much too strong a personality to work here.' In fact, I had three or four interviews with other companies and eventually I was taken on by BX Plastics at Manningtree just outside Colchester to work in their research and development section. BX produced a full range of plastics both for industrial use and consumer use, including for films.

It had been understood when we originally discussed the position that it would involve my being in effect Personal Assistant to the Research and Development Director. I had been looking forward to this because I thought it would allow me to get to know more of how the company as a whole operated and also to use the talents I had, over and above my knowledge of chemistry. But on my arrival it was decided that there was not enough to do in that capacity and so I found myself donning my white coat again and immersing myself in the wonderful world of plastics. By the time Christmas 1947 was approaching I had made one or two friends and the Section moved into a separate and rather pleasant house in nearby Lawford. Like many others at the company, I lived in Colchester – a town which I increasingly came to like and where I had found comfortable lodgings. A bus took us all out to Lawford every day.

And, as always with me, there was politics. I immediately joined the Conservative Association and threw myself into the usual round of Party activities. In particular, I thoroughly enjoyed what was called the '39–45' discussion group, where Conservatives of the war generation met to exchange views and argue about the political topics of the day. I also kept in touch with friends like Edward Boyle, who was later adopted for a Birmingham seat in the 1950 election. It was as a representative of the Oxford University Graduate Conservative Association (OUGCA) that I went to the Llandudno Conservative Party Conference in October 1948.

It had originally been intended that I should speak at the Conference, seconding an OUGCA motion deploring the abolition of university seats. At that time universities had separate representation in Parliament, and graduates had the right to vote in their universities as well as in the constituency where they lived. (I supported separate university representation, but not the principle that graduates should have more than one vote; my view was that graduates should be able to choose to vote in one or the other constituency.) It would have been my first Conference speech, but in the end the seconder chosen was a City man, because the City seats were also to be abolished.

My disappointment at this was very quickly overcome in a most unexpected way. After one of the debates, I found myself engaged in one of those speculative conversations which young people have about their future prospects. An Oxford friend, John Grant, said he supposed that one day I would like to be a Member of Parliament. 'Well, yes,' I replied, 'but there's not much hope of that. The chances of my being selected are just nil at the moment.' I might have added that with no private income of my own there was no way I could have afforded to be an MP on the salary then available. I had not even tried to get on the Party's list of approved candidates.

Later in the day, John Grant happened to be sitting next to the Chairman of the Dartford Conservative Association, John Miller. The Association was in search of a candidate. I learned afterwards that the conversation went something like this: 'I understand that you're still looking for a candidate at Dartford?' (In fact, Conservative Central Office was becoming exasperated at Dartford's failure to pick someone to fight the seat in an election that had to take place in 1950 and might be called before then.)

'That's right. Any suggestions?'

'Well, there's a young woman, Margaret Roberts, that you might look at. She's very good.'

'Oh, but Dartford is a real industrial stronghold. I don't think a woman would do at all.'

'Well, why not just look at her?'

And they did. I was invited to have lunch with John Miller and his wife, Phee, and the Dartford Women's Chairman, Mrs Fletcher, on the Saturday on Llandudno Pier. Presumably, and in spite of any reservations about the suitability of a woman candidate for their seat, they liked what they saw. I certainly got on well with them. The Millers were to become close friends and I quickly developed a healthy respect for the dignified Mrs Fletcher. After lunch we walked back to the Conference Hall in good time for a place to hear Winston Churchill give the Party Leader's speech. It was the first we had seen of him that week, because in those days the Leader did not attend the Conference itself, appearing only at a final rally on the Saturday. Foreign affairs naturally dominated his speech – it was the time of the Berlin blockade and the western airlift – and his message was sombre, telling us that only American nuclear weapons stood between Europe and communist tyranny and warning of 'what seems a remorselessly approaching third world war'.

I did not hear from Dartford until December, when I was asked to attend an interview at Palace Chambers, Bridge Street – then housing Conservative Central Office – not far from Parliament itself. With a large number of other hopefuls I turned up on the evening of Thursday 30 December for my first Selection Committee. Very few outside the political arena know just how nerve-racking such occasions are. The interviewee who is not nervous and tense is very likely to perform badly: for, as any chemist will tell you, the adrenaline needs to flow if one is to perform at one's best. I was lucky in that at Dartford there were some friendly faces around the table.

I found myself short-listed, and was asked to go to Dartford itself for a further interview. Finally, I was invited to the Bull Hotel in Dartford on Monday 31 January 1949 to address the Association's Executive Committee of about fifty people. As one of five would-be candidates, I had to give a fifteen-minute speech and answer questions for a further ten minutes.

It was the questions which were more likely to cause me trouble. There was a good deal of suspicion of women candidates, particularly in what was regarded as a tough industrial seat like Dartford. This was quite definitely a man's world into which not just angels feared to tread. There was, of course, little hope of winning it for the Conservatives, though this is never a point that the prospective candidate even in a Labour seat as safe as Ebbw Vale would be advised to make. The Labour majority was an all but unscalable 20,000. But perhaps this turned to my favour. Why not take the risk of adopting the young Margaret Roberts? There was not much to lose, and some good publicity for the Party to gain.

The most reliable sign that a political occasion has gone well is that you have enjoyed it. I enjoyed that evening at Dartford, and the outcome justified my confidence. I was selected. Afterwards I stayed behind for drinks and something to eat with the officers of the Association. The candidate is not the only one to be overwhelmed by relief on these occasions. The selectors too can stop acting as critics and start to become friends. The happy, if still slightly bewildered young candidate, is deluged with advice, information and offers of help. Such friendly occasions provide at least part of the answer to that question put to all professional politicians: 'Why on earth do you do it?'

My next step was to be approved by the national Party. Usually Party approval precedes selection, but when I went to Central Office the day after to meet the Women's Chairman, Miss Marjorie Maxse, I had no difficulties. A few weeks afterwards I was invited to dinner to meet the Party Chairman Lord Woolton, his deputy J.P.L. Thomas, Miss Maxse and the Area Agent, Miss Beryl Cook. Over the next few years Marjorie Maxse and Beryl Cook proved to be strong supporters and they gave me much useful advice.

After selection comes adoption. The formal adoption meeting is the first opportunity a candidate has to impress him or herself on the rank and file of the Association. It is therefore a psychologically important occasion. It is also a chance to gain some good local publicity, for the press are invited too. Perhaps what meant most to me, however, was the presence of my father. For the first time he and I stood on the same platform to address a meeting. He recalled how his family had always been Liberal, but that now it was the Conservatives who stood for the old Liberalism. In my own speech I too took up a theme which was Gladstonian in content if not quite style (or length), urging that 'the Government should do what any good housewife would do if money was short – look at their accounts and see what's wrong'.

After the adoption meeting at the end of February I was invited back by two leading lights of the Association, Mr and Mrs Soward, to a supper party they had arranged in my honour. Their house was at the Erith end of the constituency, not far from the factory of the Atlas Preservative Company, which made paint and chemicals, where Stanley Soward was a director. His boss, the Managing Director, had been at my adoption meeting and was one of the dinner guests: and so it was that I met Denis.

It was clear to me at once that Denis was an exceptional man. He knew at least as much about politics as I did and a good deal more about economics. His professional interest in paint and mine in plastics may seem an unromantic foundation for friendship, but it also enabled us right away to establish a joint interest in science. And as the evening wore on I discovered that his views were no-nonsense Conservatism.

After the evening was over he drove me back to London so that I could catch the midnight train to Colchester. It was not a long drive at that time of night, but long enough to find that we had still more in common. Denis is an avid reader, especially of history, biography and detective novels. He seemed to have read every article in the *Economist* and the *Banker*, and we found that we both enjoyed music – Denis with his love of opera, and me with mine of choral music.

From then on we met from time to time at constituency functions, and began to see more of each other outside the constituency. He had a certain style and dash. He had a penchant for fast cars and drove a Jaguar and, being ten years older, he simply knew more of the world than I did. At first our meetings revolved around political discussion. But as we saw more of each other, we started going to the occasional play and had dinner together. Like any couple, we had our favourite restaurants, small pasta places in Soho for normal dates, the wonderful White Tower in Fitzrovia, the Ecu de France in Jermyn Street and The Ivy for special occasions. I was very flattered by Denis's attentions, but I first began to suspect he might be serious when the Christmas after my first election campaign at Dartford I received from him a charming present of a crystal powder bowl with a silver top, which I still treasure.

We might perhaps have got married sooner, but my passion for politics and his for rugby football – Saturdays were never available for a date – both got in the way. He more than made up for this by being an immense help in the constituency – problems were solved in a trice and all the logistics taken care of. Indeed, the fact that he had proposed to me and that we had become engaged was one final inadvertent political service, because unbeknown to me Beryl Cook leaked the news just before election day to give my campaign a final boost.

When Denis asked me to be his wife, I thought long and hard about it. I had so much set my heart on politics that I really hadn't figured marriage in my plans. I suppose I pushed it to the back of my mind and simply assumed that it would occur of its own accord at some time in the future. I know that Denis too, because a wartime marriage had ended in divorce, only asked me to be his wife after much reflection. But the more I considered, the surer I was. More than forty years later I know that my decision to say 'yes' was one of the best I ever made.

I had in any case been thinking of leaving BX Plastics and Colchester for some time. It was my selection for Dartford that persuaded me I had to look for a new job in London. I had told the Selection Committee that I would fight Dartford with all the energy at my disposal, and I meant it. Nor was I temperamentally inclined to do otherwise. So I began to look for a London-based job which would give me about £500 a year – not a princely sum even in those days, but one which would allow me to live comfortably if modestly. I went for several interviews, but found that they were not keen to take on someone who was hoping to leave to take up a political career. I was certainly not going to disguise my political ambitions, so I just kept on looking. Finally, I was taken on by J. Lyons in Hammersmith as a food research chemist and moved into lodgings in the constituency.

Dartford became my home in every sense. The families I lived with fussed over me and could not have been kinder, their natural good nature undoubtedly supplemented by the fact that they were ardent Tories. The Millers also took me under their wing. After evening meetings I would regularly go back to their house to unwind over a cup of coffee. It was a cheerful household in which everyone seemed to be determined to enjoy themselves after the worst of the wartime stringencies were over. We regularly went out to political and non-political functions, and the ladies made an extra effort to wear something smart. John Miller's father – a widower – lived with the family and was a great friend to me: whenever there was a party he would send me a pink carnation as a buttonhole.

I also used to drive out to the neighbouring North Kent constituencies: the four Associations – Dartford, Bexley Heath (where Ted Heath was the candidate), Chislehurst (Pat Hornsby-Smith) and Gravesend (John Lowe) – worked closely together and had a joint President in Morris Wheeler. From time to time he would bring us all together at his large house, 'Franks', at Horton Kirby.

Of the four constituencies, Dartford was by far the least winnable, and therefore doubtless in the eyes of its neighbours – though not Dartford's – the least important. But there is always good political sense in linking safe constituencies with hopeless cases. If an active organization can be built up in the latter there is a good chance of drawing away your opponents' party workers from the political territory you need to hold. This was one of the services which Central Office expected of us to help Ted Heath in the winnable seat of Bexley.

It was thus that I met Ted. He was already the candidate for Bexley, and Central Office asked me to speak in the constituency. Ted was an established figure. He had fought in the war, ending up as a Lieutenant-Colonel; his political experience went back to the late 1930s when he had supported an anti-Munich candidate in the Oxford by-election; and he had won the respect of Central Office and the four Associations. When we met I was struck by his crisp and logical approach – he always seemed to have a list of four aims, or five methods of attack. Though friendly with his constituency workers, he was always very much the man in charge, 'the candidate', or 'the Member', and this made him seem, even when at his most affable, somewhat aloof and alone.

Pat Hornsby-Smith, his next-door neighbour at Chislehurst, could not have been a greater contrast. She was a fiery, vivacious redhead and perhaps the star woman politician of the time. She had brought the Tory Conference to its feet with a rousing right-wing speech in 1946, and was always ready to lend a hand to other young colleagues. She and I became great friends, and had long political talks at her informal supper parties.

Well before the 1950 election we were all conscious of a Conservative revival. This was less the result of fundamental rethinking within the Conservative Party than of a strong reaction both among Conservatives and in the country at large against the socialism of the Attlee Government.

The 1950 election campaign was the most exhausting few weeks I had ever spent. Unlike today's election campaigns, we had well-attended public meetings almost every night, and so I would have to prepare my speech some time during the day. I also wrote my letters to prospective constituents. Then, most afternoons, it was a matter of doorstep canvassing and, as a little light relief, blaring out the message by megaphone. I was well supported by my family: my father came to speak and my sister to help.

Before the election Lady Williams (wife of Sir Herbert Williams, veteran tariff reformer and a Croydon MP for many years) told candidates that we should make a special effort to identify ourselves by the particular way we dressed when we were campaigning. I took this very seriously and spent my days in a tailored black suit and a hat which I bought in Bourne and Hollingsworth in Oxford Street specially for the occasion. And, just to make sure, I put a black and white ribbon around it with some blue inside the bow. Quite whether these precautions were necessary is another matter. How many other twenty-four-year-old girls could be found standing on a soapbox in Erith Shopping Centre? In those days it was not often done for women candidates to canvass in factories. But I did – inside and outside. There was always a lively if sometimes noisy reception. The socialists in Dartford became quite irked until it turned out that their candidate – the sitting MP Norman Dodds – would have had the same facilities extended to him if they had thought of asking. It was only the pubs that I did not like going into, and indeed would not do so alone. Some inhibitions die hard.

I was lucky to have an opponent like Norman Dodds, a genuine and extremely chivalrous socialist of the old school. He knew that he was going to win, and he was a big enough man to give an ambitious young woman with totally different opinions a chance. Soon after I was adopted he challenged me to a debate in the hall of the local grammar school and, of course, I eagerly accepted. He and I made opening speeches, there were questions and then we each wound up our case. Each side had its own supporters, and the noise was terrific. Later in the campaign there was an equally vigorous and inconclusive re-run. What made it all such fun was that the argument was about issues and facts, not personalities. On one occasion, a national newspaper reported that Norman Dodds thought a great deal of my beauty but not a lot of my election chances – or of my brains. This perfect socialist gentleman promptly wrote to me disclaiming the statement – or at least the last part.

My own public meetings were also well attended. It was not unusual for the doors of our hall to be closed twenty minutes before the meeting was due to start because so many people were crowding in. Certainly, in those days one advantage of being a woman was that there was a basic courtesy towards us on which we could draw – something which today's feminists have largely dissipated. So, for example, on one occasion I arrived at a public meeting to find the visiting speaker, the former Air Minister Lord Balfour of Inchrye, facing a minor revolution from hecklers in the audience – to such an extent indeed that the police had been sent for. I told the organizers to cancel the request, and sure enough once

I took my place on the platform and started to speak the tumult subsided and order – if not exactly harmony – was restored.

I was also fortunate in the national and indeed international publicity which my candidature received. At twenty-four, I was the youngest woman candidate fighting the 1950 campaign, and as such was an obvious subject for comment. I was asked to write on the role of women in politics. My photograph made its way into *Life* magazine, the *Illustrated London News* where it rubbed shoulders with those of the great men of politics, and even the West German press where I was described as a '*junge Dame mit Charme*' (perhaps for the last time).

The slogans, coined by me, gained in directness whatever they lacked in subtlety – 'Vote Right to Keep What's Left' and, still more to the point, 'Stop the Rot, Sack the Lot'.

I felt that our hard work had been worthwhile when I heard the result at the count in the local grammar school. I had cut the Labour majority by 6,000. It was in the early hours at Lord Camrose's *Daily Telegraph* party at the Savoy Hotel – to which candidates, MPs, ministers, Opposition figures and social dignitaries were in those days all invited – that I experienced the same bittersweet feeling about the national result, where the Conservatives had cut Labour's overall majority from 146 to 5 seats. But victory it was not.

I should recall, however, one peculiar experience I had as candidate for Dartford. I was asked to open a Conservative fête in Orpington and was reluctantly persuaded to have my fortune told while I was there. Some fortune tellers have a preference for crystal balls. This one apparently preferred jewellery. I was told to take off my string of pearls so that they could be felt and rubbed as a source of supernatural inspiration. The message received was certainly optimistic: 'You will be great – great as Churchill.' Most politicians have a superstitious streak; even so, this struck me as quite ridiculous. Still, so much turns on luck that anything that seems to bring a little with it is more than welcome. From then on I regarded my pearls as lucky. And, all in all, they seem to have proved so.

As I have said, the 1950 result was inconclusive. After the initial exhilaration dies away such results leave all concerned with a sense of anti-climax. There seemed little doubt that Labour had been fatally wounded and that the *coup de grâce* would be administered in a second general election fairly shortly. But in the meantime there was a good deal of uncertainty nationally and if I were to pursue my political career further I needed to set about finding a winnable seat. But I felt morally bound to fight the Dartford constituency again. It would be wrong to leave them to find another candidate at such short notice. Moreover, it was difficult to imagine that I would be able to make the kind of impact in a second campaign that I had in the one just concluded. I was also extremely tired and, though no one with political blood in their veins shies away from the excitement of electioneering, another campaign within a short while was not an attractive prospect.

I had also decided to move to London. I had found a very small flat in St George's Square Mews, in Pimlico. Mr Soward (Senior) came down from Dartford to help me decorate it. I was able to see a good deal more of Denis and in more relaxing conditions than in the hubbub of Conservative activism in Dartford.

I also learned to drive and acquired my first car. My sister, Muriel, had a pre-war Ford Prefect which my father had bought her for £129, and I now inherited it. My Ford Prefect became well known around Dartford, where I was re-adopted, and did me excellent service until I sold it for about the same sum when I got married.

The general election came in October 1951. This time I shaved another 1,000 votes off Norman Dodds's majority and was hugely delighted to discover when all the results were in that the Conservatives now had an overall majority of seventeen.

During my time at Dartford I had continued to widen my acquaintanceship with senior figures in the Party. I had spoken as proposer of a vote of thanks to Anthony Eden (whom I had first met in Oxford) when he addressed a large and enthusiastic rally at Dartford football ground in 1949. The following year I spoke as seconder of a motion applauding the leadership of Churchill and Eden at a rally of Conservative Women at the Albert Hall, to which Churchill himself replied in vintage form. This was a great occasion for me – to meet in the flesh and talk to the leader whose words had so inspired me as I sat with my family around our wireless in Grantham. In 1950 I was appointed as representative of the Conservative Graduates to the Conservative Party's National Union Executive, which gave me my first insight into Party organization at the national level.

The greatest social events in my diary were the Eve of (parliamentary) Session parties held by Sir Alfred Bossom, the Member for Maidstone, at his magnificent house, No. 5 Carlton Gardens.

Several marquees were put up, brilliantly lit and comfortably heated, in which the greatest and the not so great – like one Margaret Roberts –

would mingle convivially. Sir Alfred Bossom would cheerily describe himself as the day's successor to Lady Londonderry, the great Conservative hostess of the inter-war years. You would hardly have guessed that behind his amiable and easygoing exterior was a genius who had devised the revolutionary designs of some of the first skyscrapers in New York. He was specially kind and generous to me. It was his house from which I was married, and there that our reception was held; and it was he who proposed the toast to our happiness.

I was married on a cold and foggy December day at Wesley's Chapel, City Road. It was more convenient for all concerned that the ceremony take place in London, but it was the Methodist minister from Grantham, our old friend the Rev. Skinner, who assisted the Rev. Spivey, the minister at City Road. Then all our friends – from Grantham, Dartford, Erith and London – came back to Sir Alfred Bossom's. Finally, Denis swept me off to our honeymoon in Madeira, where I quickly recovered from the bone-shaking experience of my first and last aquatic landing in a seaplane to begin my married life against the background of that lovely island.

On our return from Madeira I moved into Denis's flat in Swan Court, Flood Street in Chelsea. It was a light, sixth-floor flat with a fine view of London. It was also the first time I learned the convenience of living all on one level. As I would find again in the flat at 10 Downing Street, this makes life far easier to run. There was plenty of space – a large room which served as a sitting room and dining room, two good-sized bedrooms, another room which Denis used as a study and so on. Denis drove off to Erith every morning and would come back quite late in the evening. We quickly made friends with our neighbours; one advantage of living in a block of flats with a lift is that you meet everyone.

People felt that after all the sacrifices of the previous twenty years, they wanted to enjoy themselves, to get a little fun out of life. Although I may have been perhaps rather more serious than my contemporaries, Denis and I enjoyed ourselves quite as much as most, and more than some. We went to the theatre, we took holidays in Rome and Paris (albeit in very modest hotels), we gave parties and went to them, we had a wonderful time.

But the high point of our lives at that time was the coronation of Queen Elizabeth in June 1953. Those who had televisions – we did not – held house parties to which all their friends came to watch the great occasion. Denis and I, passionate devotees of the monarchy that we were, decided the occasion merited the extravagance of a seat in the covered stand erected in Parliament Square just opposite the entrance to Westminster Abbey. The tickets were an even wiser investment than Denis knew when he bought them, for it poured all day and most people in the audience were drenched – not to speak of those in the open carriages of the great procession. The Queen of Tonga never wore *that* dress again. Mine lived to see another day.

Pleasant though married life was in London, I still had time enough after housework to pursue a long-standing intellectual interest in the law. As with my fascination with politics, it was my father who had been responsible for stimulating this interest. Although he was not a magistrate, as Mayor of Grantham in 1945–46 my father would automatically sit on the Bench. During my university vacations I would go along with him to the Quarter Sessions (where many minor criminal offences were tried), at which an experienced lawyer would be in the chair as Recorder. On one such occasion my father and I lunched with him, a King's Counsel called Norman Winning. I was captivated by what I saw in court, but I was enthralled by Norman Winning's conversation about the theory and practice of law. At one point I blurted out: 'I wish I could be a lawyer; but all I know about is chemistry and I can't change what I'm reading at Oxford now.' But Norman Winning said that he himself had read physics for his first degree at Cambridge before changing to law as a second degree. I objected that there was no way I could afford to stay on all those extra years at university. He replied that there was another way, perfectly possible but very hard work, which was to get a job in or near London, join one of the Inns of Court and study for my law exams in the evenings. And this in 1950 is precisely what I had done. Now with Denis's support I could afford to concentrate on legal studies without taking up new employment. There was a great deal to read, and I also attended courses at the Council of Legal Education.

I had decided that what with running a home and reading for the Bar I would have to put my political ambitions on ice for some time to come. At twenty-six I could afford to do that and I told Conservative Central Office that such was my intention. But as a young woman candidate I still attracted occasional public attention. For example, in February 1952 an article of mine appeared in the *Sunday Graphic* on the position of women 'At the Dawn of the New Elizabethan Era'. I was also on the list of sought-after Party speakers and was invited to constituencies up and down the country. In any case, try as I would, my fascination for politics got the better of all contrary resolutions.

I talked it over with Denis and he said that he would support me all the way. So in June I went to see Beryl Cook at Central Office and told her: 'It's no use. I must face it. I don't like being left out of the political stream.' As I knew she would, 'Auntie Beryl' gave me her full support and referred me to John Hare, the Party Vice-Chairman for Candidates. In the kindest possible way, he told me about the pressures which membership of the House of Commons placed on family life, but I said that Denis and I had talked it through and this was something we were prepared to face. I said that I would like to have the chance of fighting a marginal or safe seat next time round. We both agreed that, given my other commitments, this should be in London itself or within a radius of thirty miles. I promptly asked to be considered for Canterbury, which was due to select a candidate. I left Central Office very pleased with the outcome – though I did not get Canterbury.

The question which John Hare had raised with me about how I would combine my home life with politics was soon to become even more sensitive. For in August 1953 the twins, Mark and Carol, put in an appearance. Late one Thursday night, some six weeks before what we still called 'the baby' was due, I began to have pains. I had seen the doctor that day and he asked me to come back on the Monday for an X-ray because there was something he wanted to check. Now Monday seemed a very long way away, and off I was immediately taken to hospital. I was given a sedative which helped me sleep through the night. Then on Friday morning the X-ray was taken and to the great surprise of all it was discovered that I was to be the mother of twins. Unfortunately, that was not the whole story. The situation required a Caesarean operation the following day. The two tiny babies – a boy and a girl – had to wait a little before they saw their father. For Denis, imagining that all was progressing smoothly, had very sensibly gone to the Oval to watch the Test Match and it proved quite impossible to contact him. On that day he received two pieces of good but equally surprising news. England won the Ashes, and he found himself the proud father of twins.

I had to stay in hospital for over a fortnight: this meant that after the first few uncomfortable days of recovery I found myself with time on my hands. The first and most immediate task was to telephone all the relevant stores to order two rather than just one of everything. Oddly enough, the very depth of the relief and happiness at having brought Mark and Carol into the world made me uneasy. The pull of a mother towards her children is perhaps the strongest and most instinctive emotion we have. I was never one of those people who regarded being 'just' a mother or indeed 'just' a housewife as second best. Indeed, whenever I heard such implicit assumptions made both before and after I became Prime Minister it would make me very angry indeed. Of course, to be a mother and a housewife is a vocation of a very high kind. But I simply felt that it was not the whole of my vocation. I knew that I also wanted a career. A phrase that Irene Ward, MP for Tynemouth, and I often used was that 'while the home must always be the centre of one's life, it should not be the boundary of one's ambitions'. Indeed, I needed a career because, quite simply, that was the sort of person I was. And not just any career. I wanted one which would keep me mentally active and prepare me for the political future for which I believed I was well suited.

So it was that at the end of my first week in hospital I came to a decision. I had the application form for my Bar finals in December sent to me. I filled it in and sent off the money for the exam, knowing that this little psychological trick I was playing on myself would ensure that I plunged into legal studies on my return to Swan Court with the twins, and that I would have to organize our lives so as to allow me to be both a mother and a professional woman.

This was not as difficult as it might sound. The flat was large enough, though being on the sixth floor, we had to have bars put on all the windows. And without a garden, the twins had to be taken out twice a day to Ranelagh Gardens. But this turned out to be good for them because they became used to meeting and playing with other children – though early on, when we did not know the rules, we had our ball confiscated by the Park Superintendent. Usually, however, it was the nanny, Barbara, who took Mark and Carol to the park, except at weekends when I took over. Barbara turned out to be a marvellous friend to the children.

Not long after I had the twins, John Hare wrote to me from Central Office:

> I was delighted to hear that you had had twins. How very clever of you. How is this going to affect your position as a candidate? I have gaily been putting your name forward; if you would like me to desist, please say so.

I replied thanking him and noting:

> Having unexpectedly produced twins – we had no idea there were two of them until the day they were born – I think I had better not

consider a candidature for at least six months. The household needs considerable reorganization and a reliable nurse must be found before I can feel free to pursue such other activities with the necessary fervour.

So my name was, as John Hare put it, kept 'in cold storage for the time being'. It was incumbent on me to say when I would like to come onto the active list of candidates again.

My self-prescribed six months of political limbo were quickly over. I duly passed my Bar finals. I had begun by considering specializing in patent law but it seemed that the opportunities there were very limited and so perhaps tax law would be a better bet. In any case, I would need a foundation in the criminal law first. So in December 1953 I joined Frederick Lawton's Chambers in the Inner Temple for a six months' pupillage. Fred Lawton's was a common law Chambers. He was, indeed, one of the most brilliant criminal lawyers I ever knew. He was witty, with no illusions about human nature or his own profession, extraordinarily lucid in exposition, and a kind guide to me.

In fact, I was to go through no fewer than four sets of Chambers, partly because I had to gain a grounding in several fields before I was competent to specialize in tax. So I witnessed the rhetorical fireworks of the Criminal Bar, admired the precise draftsmanship of the Chancery Bar and then delved into the details of company law. But I became increasingly confident that tax law could be my forte. It was a meeting point with my interest in politics; it offered the right mixture of theory and practical substance; and of one thing we could all be sure – there would never be a shortage of clients desperate to cut their way out of the jungle of overcomplex and constantly changing tax law.

Studying, observing, discussing and eventually practising law had a profound effect on my political outlook. In this I was probably unusual. Familiarity with the law usually breeds if not contempt, at least a large measure of cynicism. For me, however, it gave a richer significance to that expression 'the rule of law' which so easily tripped off the Conservative tongue.

When politics is in your blood, every circumstance seems to lead you back to it. Whether pondering Dicey,* poring over the intricacies of tax law or discussing current issues with other members of the Inns of Court

---

* A.V. Dicey, jurist (1835–1922).

Conservative Society, political questions insisted on taking centre stage in my imagination. So when in December 1954 I heard that there was a vacancy for the Conservative candidature in Orpington – which of course, being next to my old constituency of Dartford, I knew, and which was not too far from London – I telephoned Central Office and asked to have my name put forward. I was interviewed and placed on the short-list. Sitting just outside the selection meeting with Denis, I heard Donald Sumner, the local candidate (and Association Chairman), advancing in his speech the decisive argument that in Orpington what they really needed was 'a Member who really knows what is going on in the constituency – who knows the state of the roads in Locksbottom'. Denis and I roared with laughter. But Donald Sumner got the seat.

I was naturally disappointed by the decision, because Orpington would have been an ideal constituency for me. It seemed extremely unlikely now that a similarly suitable seat would become available before what looked like an increasingly imminent general election. So I wrote to John Hare to say that I would now 'continue at the Bar with no further thought of a parliamentary career for many years'. Knowing me better than I knew myself perhaps, he wrote back urging me at least to recon-sider if a winnable seat in Kent became available. But I was adamant, though I made it clear that I would always be available to speak in constituencies and would of course be active in the general election campaign.

Although I was in general a loyal Conservative, I had felt for some time that the Government could have moved further and faster in dismantling socialism and installing free enterprise policies. But it had not been easy for them to persuade popular opinion – or indeed themselves – that a somewhat stronger brew would be palatable. In fact, by 1955 a good deal of modest progress had been made as regards the removal of controls and, even more modestly, returning nationalized industries to the private sector.

In April 1955 Churchill resigned as Prime Minister to be succeeded by Anthony Eden, and there was in quick succession a snap general election, a new Conservative Government, the débâcle of Suez and the arrival at No. 10 of Harold Macmillan, the wizard of change.

During the general election campaign of May 1955 I spoke in a number of constituencies. But for me it was generally a dull affair. Once you have been a candidate everything else palls. Moreover, there was very little doubt of the outcome on this occasion. Sure enough, the Conservatives won an overall majority of fifty-eight. But the Eden administration's political honeymoon turned out to be a short one. It quickly appeared that Rab Butler's pre-election budget had been too loose, and there followed a much tighter emergency budget in October, which badly damaged Butler's reputation – he was replaced as Chancellor by Harold Macmillan six months later – and seriously dented the Government's. But it was, of course, to be foreign affairs which would be Eden's real undoing.

The background to the Suez crisis of July to November 1956 has been much discussed. The general feeling, at least among Conservatives, was that Britain was a great power which should not be pushed around by Nasser's Egypt and that the latter needed to be taught a lesson, not least *pour encourager les autres.* Many of the details, for example the degree of collusion between Britain and France on the one hand and Israel on the other, were not available to the wider public at the time. To us, therefore, it appeared almost incomprehensible that first Anthony Nutting and then my old friend Edward Boyle should resign from the Government in protest at the intervention. Now their actions are more understandable, though even all these years later I could not endorse them.

Politically, the failure of the Suez operation came as a body blow. Although it took many years for the full picture to emerge, it was immediately clear that the Government had been incompetent, and that its incompetence had been exposed in the most humiliating fashion. For a Conservative Government – particularly one led by someone whose reputation was founded on the conduct of foreign affairs – the outcome was particularly damaging. There was a mood of dismay bordering on despair among Conservative supporters. Denis's reaction, as an ex-officer in the Royal Artillery, was sharpened by anger that our troops had been let down when the operation was halted close to completion. As he said to me: 'You never announce a cease-fire when your troops are out on patrol.' I would remember this: politicians must never take decisions in war without full consideration of what they mean to our forces on the ground.

We also blamed harshly the conduct of the United States, and the fact that anti-Americanism lingered on in some generally right-wing circles when I was Prime Minister must be in part attributed to this. I too felt that we had been let down by our traditional ally – though at the time, of course, I did not realize that Eisenhower felt equally let down by the Anglo-French decision to launch military operations on the eve of a Presidential election in which he was running on a peace ticket. But in any case I also felt that the 'special relationship' with our transatlantic cousins had foundations too solid to be eroded by even such a crisis as Suez. Some people argued that Suez demonstrated that the Americans were so hostile to Britain's imperial role, and were now so much a superpower that they could not be trusted and that closer European integration was the only answer. But there was an alternative – and quite contrary – conclusion. This was that British foreign policy could not long be pursued without ensuring for it the support of the United States. Indeed, in retrospect I can see that Suez was an unintended catalyst in the peaceful and necessary transfer of power from Britain to America as the ultimate upholder of western interests and the liberal international economic system.

After the fiasco of Suez it was clear that Anthony Eden could not remain as Prime Minister. He fell ill during the crisis and resigned in January 1957. There was much speculation in the circles in which I moved as to who would succeed – in those days, of course, Conservative Leaders 'emerged' rather than being elected. My Conservative friends in Chambers were convinced that Rab Butler would never be summoned by the Queen because he was too left wing. By contrast, the Chancellor of the Exchequer at the time of Suez, Harold Macmillan, was considered to be the right-wing candidate. All of which shows how little we knew of the past and present convictions of both men – particularly the brilliant, elusive figure who was shortly to become Prime Minister.

Harold Macmillan had the strengths and weaknesses of the consummate politician. He cultivated a languorous and almost antediluvian style which was not – and was not intended to be – sufficiently convincing to conceal the shrewdness behind it. He was a man of masks. It was impossible to tell, for instance, that behind the cynical Edwardian façade was one of the most deeply religious souls in politics.

Harold Macmillan's great and lasting achievement was to repair the relationship with the United States. This was the essential condition for Britain to restore her reputation and standing. Unfortunately, he was unable to repair the damage inflicted by Suez on the morale of the British political class – a veritable 'Suez syndrome'. They went from believing that Britain could do anything to an almost neurotic belief that Britain could do nothing. This was always a grotesque exaggeration. At that time we were a middle-ranking diplomatic power after America and the Soviet Union, a nuclear power, a leading member of NATO, a permanent member of the UN Security Council and the centre of a great Commonwealth.

Macmillan's impact on domestic affairs was mixed. Under his leadership there was the 1957 decontrol of private sector rents – which greatly reduced the scope of the rent control that had existed in one form or another since 1915 – a necessary, though far from popular move. Generally, however, Macmillan's leadership edged the Party in the direction of state intervention, a trend which would become much more marked after 1959.

Even at the time some developments made me uneasy. When Peter Thorneycroft, Enoch Powell and Nigel Birch – Macmillan's entire Treasury team – resigned over a £50 million increase in public expenditure in January 1958, Macmillan talked wittily of 'little local difficulties'. I felt in no position to judge the rights and wrongs of the dispute itself. But the husbanding of public money did not strike me as an ignoble cause over which to resign. The first steps away from the path of financial rectitude always make its final abandonment that much easier. And that abandonment brings its own adverse consequences. Such was the case in the years that followed.

It was not until the late summer of 1958 that the Conservatives caught up with Labour in the opinion polls. By the time of the 1959 general election the two main parties were unashamedly competing to appeal to the nation's desire for material self-advancement. The Conservative manifesto bluntly stated: 'Life's better with the Conservatives, don't let Labour ruin it.' It went on to promise a doubling of the British standard of living in a generation. As for Labour, a few days into the campaign the Party Leader Hugh Gaitskell promised that there would be no rise in income tax in spite of all the extra spending Labour planned – even in that political climate of optimism, a fatally incredible pledge.

Well before this I myself had re-entered the fray. In February 1956 I wrote to Donald Kaberry, the Party Vice-Chairman in charge of candidates:

> For some time now I have been feeling the temptation to return to active politics. I had intended, when I was called to the Bar, to concentrate entirely on legal work but a little experience at the Revenue Bar, and in Company matters, far from turning my attention from politics has served to draw my attention more closely to the body which is responsible for the legislation about which I have come to hold strong views.

I went to see Donald Kaberry the following month. There was no problem in my being put back on the list of candidates – this time to be considered for safe, Conservative-held seats only. I was all the more delighted because I found in Donald Kaberry a constant and dependable source of wise advice and friendship – no small thing for an aspiring candidate.

I was less fortunate in the reception I received from Selection Committees. It had begun at Orpington in 1954. It was the same at Beckenham, Hemel Hempstead and then Maidstone in 1957 and 1958. I would be short-listed, would make what was generally acknowledged to be a good speech – and then the questions, most of them having the same purpose, would begin. With my family commitments, would I have time enough for the constituency? Did I realize how much being a Member of Parliament would keep me away from home? And sometimes more bluntly still: did I really think that I could fulfil my duties as a mother with young children to look after and as an MP?

I felt that Selection Committees had every right to ask me these questions. I explained our family circumstances and that I already had the help of a first-class nanny. I also used to describe how I had found it possible to be a professional woman and a mother by organizing my time properly. What I resented, however, was that beneath some of the criticism I detected a feeling that the House of Commons was not really the right place for a woman anyway. Perhaps some of the men at Selection Committees entertained this prejudice, but I found then and later that it was the women who came nearest to expressing it openly.

I was hurt and disappointed by these experiences. They were, after all, an attack on me not just as a candidate but as a wife and mother. But I refused to be put off by them. I was confident that I had something to offer in politics. I knew that many others who had crossed my political path very much wanted me to get into the House. And most important of all, Denis never had any doubts. He was always there to comfort and support me.

In April 1958 I had another long talk with Donald Kaberry and I spoke frankly about the difficulties I had faced as a woman with the Selection Committees. Unfortunately, this is not one of the topics on which even the wisest male friend can give very useful counsel. But Donald Kaberry did give me advice on what to wear on these sensitive occasions – something smart but not showy. In fact, looking me up and down he said he thought the black coat dress with brown trim which I was wearing would be just fine. His sartorial judgement would soon be put to the test. For I now entered my name for – and in July was called to interview at – the safe Conservative seat of Finchley, North London, whose MP was retiring.

I was one of a 'long list' of some 150 applicants, which contained a number of my future colleagues in the House. I was also one of those called for preliminary interview by the Constituency Selection Committee. I could tell that I had a good deal of support, but being the most popular person on these occasions can sometimes be less important than being the least unpopular person. If, as the weaker candidates are eliminated, all their support goes to your opponent it is quite possible to fall at the last fence – and we were barely out of the paddock.

It was arranged that the final four of us – three men and myself – should go before the Executive Council of the Association and I was pretty sure that I could expect some fierce opposition; it would be a fight.

I prepared myself as best I could. I felt reasonably confident that I knew the constituency. I had no doubt that I could cope with even quite abstruse questions of economic or foreign policy, for I had voraciously read the newspapers and all the briefing I could obtain. I prepared my speech until it was word perfect, and I had mastered the technique of talking without notes. Equally important was that I should put myself in the right state of mind – confident but not too confident. And I wore the black coat dress. I saw no harm, either, in courting the fates: so I wore not just my lucky pearls but also a lucky brooch which had been given to me by my Conservative friends in Dartford.

There was, however, one piece of thoroughly bad luck. This was that on the date of the meeting – Monday 14 July – it was quite impossible for Denis to come with me. Indeed, so quick was the whole selection process that he knew nothing whatever about it. Every year he would go away on a foreign sales tour for a month or so, and at this point his whereabouts were only 'somewhere in Africa'. By contrast, the other candidates were accompanied by their spouses. So as I entered the packed meeting on that warm July evening I felt very much alone.

But as soon as I was on my feet the inhibitions fell away. As always, I quickly became too taken up with the thrust of my argument to worry too much about what other people were thinking. The applause when I sat down seemed warm and genuine. It was at questions that the trouble began.

Could a mother with young children really effectively represent Finchley? What about the strains on my family life? I gave my usual answers, and as usual too a section of the audience was determinedly unconvinced. And doubtless it was easier for them because poor Denis was absent. I rejoined the other candidates and their wives, where the tension was only relieved by that over-polite inconsequential small talk which such occasions always seem to generate. Once the last of us had performed, it seemed an endless wait until one of the officers came through to tell us the result. And when he did, it was to me that he spoke. There was no time to feel relief, pleasure or even exhaustion, because it was now necessary to return to receive the congratulations of the Executive.

It was only afterwards that I knew the precise result. The first round of voting gave me thirty-five votes as against thirty-four for my nearest rival. On the second round, when the two other candidates had dropped out, I had forty-six against his forty-three. It was then expected that, for form's sake and to show that there was no ill feeling, the Executive should unanimously vote to select me as their candidate. Unfortunately, some of those who opposed my candidature had no such intentions. So I inherited an Association which I would have to unite behind me, and this would mean winning over people who had not disguised their disapproval.

But that was for tomorrow. First I must break the good news to my family back in Grantham. Denis was entirely incommunicado, blissfully unaware of what I had been through at Finchley. I had written him a letter some time before about the prospects, but he never received it. A couple of days later he was on his way from Johannesburg to Lagos via Kano in northern Nigeria. On changing planes he picked up a copy of the London *Evening Standard* which someone had left behind, and as he leafed through it he discovered the astonishing news that his wife had been selected for the safe seat of Finchley. I always seemed to be giving him surprises.

My first opportunity to impress myself on the Finchley Association as a whole was at the Adoption Meeting early the following month. This time I again appeared in a plain black outfit with a small black hat. I received what I afterwards learned was an almost embarrassingly glowing introduction from Bertie Blatch, the constituency chairman, who was to be a great patron and protector. (It was an added advantage then and later that Bertie owned the most important local newspaper, the *Finchley Press*.) As I entered the hall, I was met with warm applause. I used the occasion to speak at some length about both international and domestic affairs. I pulled out every stop. I knew that though I was the only duly selected candidate, this adoption meeting was not, as it should have been, a mere formality. There was still some die-hard opposition to my candidature, centred on one woman and her little *coterie*, who were trying to have the contest re-run. I was determined to overcome this. There were no problems in dealing with the three questions from the body of the hall. As Conservatives do on such occasions, they gave me a terrific reception. But at the end – and contrary to the newspaper report of the occasion – a few of those present refused to vote for my adoption, which was overwhelming but not (that magic word) 'unanimous'. I left the meeting knowing that I had secured my candidature and confident of the loyalty of the great majority of the Association, but aware too that some were still determined to make life as difficult as possible.

I went as far as to write to Ted Heath, then Chief Whip, about the problems I was having. Partly as a result of his assistance, and partly because I used my own personal contacts, I managed to attract a distinguished field of speakers to come and speak on my behalf between my adoption and election day. Iain Macleod, Keith Joseph, Peter Thorneycroft and John Boyd-Carpenter – all people around whom my future political life would soon revolve – were among them. Denis's belated but extremely welcome arrival on the scene also helped in a rather different way. Bertie Blatch gave me constant and unstinting support.

Finchley had been run with a degree of gentlemanly disengagement that was neither my style nor warranted by political realities. I intended to work and then campaign as if Finchley were a marginal seat, and I hoped and expected that others would follow my lead. From now on I was in the constituency two or three times a week and regularly went out canvassing in each of the wards, returning afterwards to get to know the Party activists over a drink in the local pub or someone's house.

By the time I arrived as candidate, there was a good deal of concern that the Liberals in Finchley were becoming strongly entrenched. They were always excellent campaigners, particularly effective in local government elections. A few years before, there had been a famous local scandal over the barring of Jews from membership of Finchley Golf Club, in which a number of local Conservatives had been involved: the Liberals never missed an opportunity to remind people of it. I simply did not understand anti-semitism myself, and I was upset that the Party should have been tainted by it. I also thought that the potential Conservative vote was not being fully mobilized because of this. So I set out to make it absolutely clear that we wanted new members, especially Jewish Conservatives, in our branch organizations. Though I did not know it at the time, I was subsequently to find some of my closest political friends and associates among Jews. What was clear was that the potential Conservative vote was not being fully exploited, and that however many feathers might be ruffled in the process it was vital to strengthen our branch organization. I also put a good deal of effort into strengthening the Young Conservative organization in the constituency: I was sure that it was by attracting energetic young people that we could most surely resist the challenge of activist Liberals. By the time the election was called in September 1959 the constituency organization was looking in better shape, and I had begun to feel very much at home.

My first general election polling day in Finchley in October 1959 was very much to set the pattern for the nine such polling days which would succeed it. Soon after the opening of the poll I would vote in my own home constituency – Orpington in 1959, Chelsea and Westminster in later elections – and then drive up to Finchley with Denis. I visited each of the polling stations and our committee rooms, breaking for lunch with Bertie Blatch and others in a hotel. There I rigorously paid just for my own food and drink, to avoid the accusation of 'treating' electors, terror of which is instilled by Conservative Central Office into all our candidates. From 5 o'clock I carefully avoided visiting committee rooms, which should all be sending out workers to summon our supporters to the polls, just dropping into a polling station or two to show the flag. Then at close of poll Denis and I went to the Blatches' for something to eat, visited the constituency offices to catch the latest largely anecdotal news, and finally attended the count – on this occasion at Christ's College, though later all nine constituency counts would be held at Barnet Town Hall.

At the school, I found that each of the candidates had been allocated a room where he or she with a select band of supporters could get something to eat and drink and where we had access to that miracle of modern political life – a television. The 1959 campaign had, in fact, been the first in which television played a serious part. I divided my time between watching the growing piles of ballot papers, candidate by candidate, on the long tables in the body of the hall, and slipping back to my room to catch the equally satisfactory results coming in across the country as a whole.

At about 12.30 a.m. I was told that the Finchley results were shortly to be announced, and was asked to join the Electoral Returning Officer with the other candidates on the platform. Perhaps some people in a safe seat when the Tories were on course for a national victory would have been confident or even complacent. Not me. Throughout my time in politics, whether from some sixth sense or perhaps – who knows? – from mere superstition, I have associated such attitudes with imminent disaster. So I stood by the side of Denis with a fixed smile and tried not to look as I felt.

The Returning Officer began: 'Deakins, Eric Petro: thirteen thousand, four hundred and thirty-seven.' (Labour cheers.) 'Spence, Henry Ivan: twelve thousand, seven hundred and one.' (Liberal cheers.) And finally we reached: 'Thatcher, Margaret Hilda: twenty-nine thousand, six hundred and ninety-seven.' I was home and dry – and with a majority of 16,260, almost 3,500 more than my predecessor. The cheers rose. I made my short speech of acceptance, thanked all my splendid helpers, received a warm hug from Denis and walked down from the platform – the elected Member for Finchley.

In an unguarded moment, shortly after I had been selected for Finchley, I had told the twins that once I became an MP they could have tea on the terrace of the House of Commons. From then on the plaintive request had been: 'Aren't you there yet, Mummy? It's taking a long time.' I had known the feeling. It had seemed so very long for me too. But I now knew that within weeks I would take my seat on the green leather benches of the House of Commons.

It was the first step.

CHAPTER FOUR

The Outer Circle

Backbencher and junior minister 1959–1964

B Y NOW MY FAMILY AND I were comfortably installed in a large-ish detached house at Farnborough in Kent. We had decided to buy 'Dormers', which we saw advertised in *Country Life*, after rent decontrol threatened to make it a good deal more expensive to continue renting our flat in Swan Court. In any event, we felt the children needed a garden to play in.

The one and a half acres of garden were heavily overgrown but I enjoyed setting to work to improve things. When my parents finally moved to a house with a garden – very long but narrow – I was no longer living at home. So the garden at 'Dormers' was my first real opportunity to don thick gardening gloves and rip out brambles, trundle barrows of leaf-mould from the nearby wood to improve the soil, and plant out flowerbeds. Luckily, in Bertie Blatch I had a constituency chairman who doubled as horticulturist: but for all his tips my roses never quite resembled his.

For the twins, 'Dormers' was a seventh heaven. There was the new experience of their own garden, neighbours with children and all the excitement of a wood to walk in – though not alone. The house was part of an estate, so there was no through-traffic and it was safe for the children. I eliminated right at the beginning the dreadful possibility of their falling in the pond by having it filled with earth and turned into a rose bed.

Mark and Carol were six when I became an MP, old enough to get into plenty of trouble if not firmly handled. Nor was Denis at home as much as he would have liked, since his job took him abroad a good deal.

Because my parliamentary duties meant that I was not always back before the twins went to bed, I insisted on full family attendance at breakfast. We also had the advantage of the long parliamentary recess and indeed the long parliamentary weekends. But I owe a debt of gratitude to Barbara, the children's nanny until she married a local horticulturist who advised me on the garden – and to Abby who replaced her and who in due course became a close family friend. They kept the children in order and I always telephoned from the House shortly before six each evening to see that all was well and to give the children a chance to tell me that it wasn't.

Although there were often constituency duties, the weekends provided the opportunity to sort out the house and usually to do a large bake, just as we had done at home in Grantham. In the summer months Denis and I and the children would work – or in their case play at working – in the garden. But on Saturdays in the rugby season Denis would probably be refereeing or watching a match – an arrangement which from the earliest days of our marriage had been solemnly set down in tablets of stone. Sometimes if he was refereeing an important game I would go along as well, though my concentration on the game was frequently disturbed by the less than complimentary remarks which English crowds are inclined to exchange about the conduct of referees. On Sundays we took the twins to the Family Service at the Farnborough parish church. Denis was an Anglican, and we both felt that it would be confusing for the children if we did not attend the same church. The fact that our local church was Low Church made it easier for the Methodist in me to make the transition. Anyway, John Wesley regarded himself as a member of the Church of England to his dying day. I did not feel that any great theological divide had been crossed.

Weekends, therefore, provided me with an invaluable and invigorating tonic. So did family holidays. I remembered what I had enjoyed – and not enjoyed – about my own holidays at Skegness. My conclusion was that for young children nothing beats buckets and spades and plenty of activity. So we used to take a house on the Sussex coast for a month right by the side of the beach, and there always seemed to be other families with small children nearby. Later we went regularly to a family hotel at Seaview on the Isle of Wight or rented a flat in the village. Crossing the Solent by ferry seemed a great adventure to the children who, like all twins, had a degree of (usually) playful rivalry. On the way down to the coast in the car we always passed through a place called 'Four Marks'. I was never able to answer Mark's question about who these four were. Nor could I think up a satisfactory response to Carol who thought that it was all unfair and that there should also be a 'Four Carols'. Not to be outdone, Mark pointed out that it was no less unfair that Christmas carols had no male equivalent.

It is hard to know whether one worries more about one's children when they are within reach or far away. I wanted the twins to be at home when they were young, but unfortunately, the nearby day school to which Mark went had to close in 1961, and Denis persuaded me that it was best that he should go to Belmont Preparatory School. At least Belmont was just on the edge of Finchley, so I could take him out to lunch. Also I knew he was not too far away in case of emergencies. But not to be left out, Carol decided that she wanted to go to boarding school as well. The house seemed empty without them.

By now there was another emptiness in my life which could never be filled, and that was the loss of my mother, who died in 1960. She had been a great rock of family stability. She managed the household, stepped in to run the shop when necessary, entertained, supported my father in his public life and as Mayoress, did a great deal of voluntary social work for the church, displayed a series of practical domestic talents such as dress-making and was never heard to complain. Like many people who live for others, she made possible all that her husband and daughters did. Her life had not been an easy one. Although in later years I would speak more readily of my father's political influence on me, it was from my mother that I inherited the ability to organize and combine so many different duties of an active life. Her death was a great shock, even though it had not been entirely unexpected. Even young children have a keen sense of family grief. After my mother's funeral, my father came back to stay with us for a while at 'Dormers'. That evening when I turned back the coverlet of his bed, I found a little note from Mark on the pillow: 'Dear Grandad I'm so sorry Granny died.' It was heartbreaking.

I was very glad, however, that both my parents had seen their daughter enter the Palace of Westminster as a Member of Parliament – quite liter-ally 'seen', because the press contained flattering photographs of me in my new hat on the way to the House. My first real contact with the Conserva-tive Parliamentary Party was when on the day before Parliament opened I went along as a member of the 1922 Committee – the Party committee to which all Conservative backbench MPs belong – to discuss the ques-tion of the Speakership of the House. I knew only a relatively small number of the several hundred faces packed into that rumbustious, smoky committee room, but I immediately felt at home.

Everyone in those early days was immensely kind. The Chief Whip would give new Members a talk about the rules of the House and the whipping system. Old-stagers gave me useful hints about dealing with correspondence. They also told me that I should not just concentrate on the big issues like foreign affairs and finance, but also find one or two less popular topics on which I could make a mark. Another piece of good practical advice was to find myself a 'pair', which I promptly did in the form of Charlie Pannell, the Labour MP for Leeds West.* I had met him years earlier when he lived in Erith, in my old Dartford constituency. He was exactly the sort of good-humoured, decent Labour man I liked.

The Palace of Westminster seems a bewildering labyrinth of corridors to the uninitiated. It was some time before I could find my way with ease around it. There were modestly appointed rooms set apart for the twenty-five women Members – the 'Lady Members' Rooms' – where I would find a desk to work at. Neither taste nor convention suggested my entering the Smoking Room. My formidably efficient secretary, Paddi Victor Smith, had a desk in a large office with a number of other secretaries where we worked on constituency correspondence. But the heart of the House of Commons was, even more than now, the Chamber itself. Early on, I was advised that there was no substitute for hours spent there. Finance and Foreign Affairs Committee meetings might be more informative. The weekly 1922 Committee meetings might be more lively, but it was only by absorbing the atmosphere of the House until its procedures became second nature and its style of debate instinctive that one could become that most respected kind of English politician, a 'House of Commons man' (or woman).

So I took my pre-arranged place in the fourth row back below the gangway – where thirty-one years later I chose to sit again after I resigned as Prime Minister. The House itself was – and still is – a very masculine place. This manifested itself above all, I found, in the sheer volume of noise. I was used to university debates and questions at the general election hustings, yet my brief previous visits to the Visitors' Gallery of the House had never prepared me for this. But when I remarked on it to a colleague he just laughed and said, 'You should have heard it during Suez!' Masculinity, I soon found, however, did not degenerate into male

---

* 'Pairing' is an informal arrangement by which pairs of MPs from opposing parties agree to abstain in parliamentary votes when one or other of them wishes to be absent from the House of Commons. The arrangement does not usually apply to crucial votes.

prejudice. In different ways I had on occasion been made to feel small because I was a woman in industry, at the Bar and indeed in Tory constituency politics. But in the House of Commons we were all equals; and woe betide ministers who suggest by their demeanour or behaviour that they consider themselves more equal than the rest. I soon saw with appreciation that sincerity, logic and technical mastery of a subject could earn respect from both sides of the House. Shallowness and bluff were quickly exposed. Perhaps every generation of young men and women considers that those it once regarded as great figures had a stature lacked by their equivalents in later years. But I would certainly be hard put now to find on the backbenches the extraordinary range of experience and talents which characterized the House of Commons then. Almost whatever the subject, there would be some figure on either side of the House who would bring massive, specialized knowledge and obvious intuition to bear on it – and be listened to with respect by front and backbenches alike.

As it happens, I had very little opportunity during my first few months as an MP for the relaxed acquisition of experience of the House. With 310 other Members I had entered the Commons ballot for the introduction of Private Members' Bills. Never previously having so much as won a raffle, I was greatly astonished to find myself drawn second. Only the first few Private Members' Bills have any chance of becoming legislation, and even then the Government's attitude towards them is crucial.

I had only given the most general consideration to the topic I would choose, but I now had just a week to make up my mind, for the Bill had to be tabled by 11 November.

As a result of an industrial dispute in the printing industry, which began in July 1958, a number of Labour-controlled councils in big cities had denied normal reporting facilities to journalists working on provincial newspapers involved in the dispute. This had highlighted a loophole in the law which many councils used to conceal information from the general public about their activities. The press had a statutory right of admission only to meetings of the full council, not to its committees. By the device of resolving to go into committee, councils could therefore exclude the press from their deliberations. And besides these 'committees of the whole council' there were many other committees which were closed. Large sums of ratepayers' money could be spent – or mis-spent – without outside scrutiny. Nor did members of the public themselves have the right to attend any council or council committee meetings.

My own interest in the question stemmed partly from the fact that it had come to a head because of socialist connivance with trade union power, partly because I knew from Nottingham, not far from Grantham, what was going on, and partly because the present situation offended against my belief in accountability by government for the spending of people's money. The 1959 Conservative manifesto had contained a promise 'to make quite sure that the press have proper facilities for reporting the proceedings of local authorities'. Having read this, I imagined that a Bill to do just that would be welcome to the Government. I was swiftly disillusioned by the whips. Apparently, nothing more than a code of practice on the subject had been envisaged. This seemed to me extremely feeble, and so I decided to go ahead.

It quickly became clear that the objection to a measure with teeth came not from ministers at the Ministry of Housing and Local Government but rather from officials, who in turn were doubtless echoing the fierce opposition of the local authorities to any democratic check on their powers. Henry Brooke, the Cabinet minister in charge, was consistently sympathetic. Each Private Member's Bill is placed under the supervision of a junior minister who either helps or hinders its progress. My Bill was given to Sir Keith Joseph, and it was in examination of the tedious technical intricacies of the measure that I first got to know Keith.

I learned a great deal in a very short time from the experience of devising, refashioning and negotiating for my Bill. Partly because the issue had been a live one for a number of years, but partly also because of senior Members' kindness towards a new Member, I was able to rely on invaluable assistance from backbench colleagues. Sir Lionel Heald, a former Attorney-General, gave me the benefit of his great legal experience. I learned from him and others the techniques of legal draftsmanship, which were generally the preserve of the parliamentary draftsmen.

I also witnessed the power of pressure groups. The influence of the local authority lobby made itself felt in a hundred ways, and not only through the Labour Party. I therefore learned to play pressure group against pressure group and made the most of the help offered to me by the Newspaper Editors' Guild and other press bodies.

In the end, however, there is no substitute for one's own efforts. I wanted to get as many MPs as possible to the House on a Friday (when most MPs have returned to their constituency) for the Bill's Second Reading – this was the great hurdle. I have always believed in the impact of a personal handwritten letter – even from someone you barely know.

So just before Second Reading I wrote 250 letters to Government back-benchers asking them to attend and vote for my measure.

By the time I rose to deliver my speech on Friday 5 February 1960, I knew the arguments by heart. As a result, I could speak for almost half an hour without notes to hand – though not without nerves. The three women members of the Government – Pat Hornsby-Smith, Mervyn Pike and Edith Pitt – showed moral support from the front bench, and the House was very full for a Friday. I was delighted that nearly 200 Members voted, and we won handsomely. I was also genuinely moved by the comments that different MPs made to me personally – particularly Rab Butler, the Leader of the House and a master of ambiguous compliments, whose congratulations on this occasion, however, were straightforward, generous and very welcome to a new Member.

It was clear from the press next day that the speech had been a success and that I was – for the present at least – a celebrity. 'A new star was born in Parliament', thrilled the *Daily Express*. 'Fame and Margaret Thatcher made friends yesterday', shrieked the *Sunday Dispatch*. 'A triumph', observed the *Daily Telegraph* evenly. Feature articles appeared about me and my family. I was interviewed on television. The cameras came down to 'Dormers', and in an unguarded moment in answer to one of the more preposterous questions I told a journalist that 'I couldn't even consider a Cabinet post until my twins are older.' But apart from this gaffe it was roses, roses all the way.

Excessive praise? I had no doubt myself that it was. And I was slightly nervous that it might excite the jealousy of colleagues. My speech had been a competent performance, but it was not an epic.

But was it, however, a portent? Some time before the general election I had read John Buchan's *The Gap in the Curtain*. I had not thought more about it until I considered these somewhat overstated headlines. John Buchan's tale concerns a group of men, including several politicians, who spend Whitsun at a friend's house where they are enabled by another guest, a mysterious and fatally ill physicist of world renown, to glimpse the contents of a page of *The Times* one year later. Each sees something affecting his own future. One, a new Conservative MP, reads a brief obituary of himself which notes that he had delivered a brilliant maiden speech that had made him a national figure overnight. And so it turns out. The speech is outstanding, praised and admired on all sides; but after that, deprived of the self-confidence which knowledge of the future gave him, he fails totally and sinks into oblivion, waiting for the end. I shuddered slightly and reached for my lucky pearls.

But my Bill – with the significant addition that members of the general public should have the same rights as the press to attend council meetings, and with committees (apart from committees of the whole council) excluded from its provisions – duly passed into law; and, though my seven-day stardom faded somewhat, I had learned a lot and gained a good deal of confidence.

Life on the backbenches was always exciting – but so hectic that on one occasion, to the consternation of my male colleagues, I fainted in the Members' Dining Room. I spent as much time as I could in the House and at backbench committees. I also regularly attended the dining club of new Tory Members to which the great figures of the Party – Harold Macmillan, Rab Butler, Iain Macleod and Enoch Powell – and brilliant young Tory journalists like Peter Utley would come to speak.

The natural path to promotion and success at this time lay in the centre of politics and on the left of the Conservative Party. Above all, the up-and-coming Tory politician had to avoid being 'reactionary'. Nothing was likely to be so socially and professionally damaging as to bear that label. Conservatism at this time lacked fire. Even though what are now widely seen as the damaging moral, social and economic developments of the sixties mainly belong to the period of Labour government after 1964, the first years of the decade also were ones of drift and cynicism, for which Conservatives must be held in large part responsible.

The odd thing is, looking back, that Conservatives in the sixties, though increasingly and obsessively worried about being out of touch with contemporary trends and fashions, were beginning to lose touch with the instincts and aspirations of ordinary conservative-minded people. This was true on issues as different as trade unions and immigration, law and order and aid to the Third World. But it was also and most directly important as regards management of the economy.

It was not so much inflation, which was zero throughout the winter of 1959–60 and did not reach 5 per cent until the summer of 1961, but rather the balance of payments that was seen as the main economic constraint on growth. And the means adopted to deal with the problems at this time – credit controls, interest rate rises, the search for international credit to sustain the pound, tax rises and, increasingly, prototype incomes policies – became all too familiar over the next fifteen years.

The rethinking that produced first 'Selsdon Man' and later Thatcherism was barely in evidence.

The more I learned about it, the less impressed I was by our management of the economy. I listened with great care to the speeches of the Tory backbencher Nigel Birch, which were highly critical of the Government's failure to control public spending. The Government's argument was that increases could be afforded as long as the economy continued to grow. But this in turn edged us towards policies of injecting too much demand and then pulling back sharply when this produced pressures on the balance of payments or sterling. This is precisely what happened in the summer of 1961 when the Chancellor of the Exchequer Selwyn Lloyd introduced a deflationary budget and our first incomes policy, the 'pay pause'. Another effect, of course, was to keep taxation higher than would otherwise be necessary. Chancellors of the Exchequer, wary of increases in basic income tax, laid particular importance on checking tax avoidance and evasion, repeatedly extending Inland Revenue powers to do so. Both as a tax lawyer and from my own instinctive dislike of handing more power to bureaucracies, I felt strongly on the matter and helped to write a critical report by the Inns of Court Conservative Society.

I felt even more strongly that the fashionable liberal tendencies in penal policy should be sharply reversed. So I spoke – and voted – in support of a new clause which a group of us wanted to add on to that year's Criminal Justice Bill which would have introduced birching or caning for young violent offenders. In the prevailing climate of opinion, this was a line which I knew would expose me to ridicule from the self-consciously high-minded commentators. But my constituents did not see it that way, and nor did a substantial number of us on the right. Although the new clause was defeated, sixty-nine Tory backbenchers voted against the Government and in support of it. It was the biggest Party revolt since we came to power in 1951, and the Whips' Office were none too pleased. It was also the only occasion in my entire time in the House of Commons when I voted against the Party line.

The summer of 1961 was a more than usually interesting time in politics. I retained my close interest in foreign affairs, which were dominated by the uneasy developing relationship between Kennedy and Khrushchev, the building by the Soviets of the Berlin Wall and, closer to home, by the beginning of negotiations for Britain to join the Common Market. There was also speculation about a reshuffle. In spite of my slightly blotted copybook, I had some reason to think that I might be a beneficiary of it. I had remained to a modest degree in the public eye, and not just with my speech on corporal punishment. I gave a press conference with Eirene

White, the Labour MP for East Flint, on the lack of provision being made for the needs of pre-school children in high-rise flats, a topic of growing concern at this time when so many of these badly designed monstrosities were being erected. But the main reason why I had hopes of benefiting from the reshuffle was very simple. Pat Hornsby-Smith had decided to resign to pursue her business interests, and it was thought politically desirable to keep up the number of women in the Government.

That said, I did not try to conceal my delight when the telephone rang and I was summoned to see the Prime Minister. Harold Macmillan was camping out in some style at Admiralty House while 10 Downing Street was undergoing extensive refurbishment. I had already developed my own strong impressions of him, not just from speeches in the House and to the 1922 Committee, but also when he came to speak to our New Members' Dining Club – on which occasion he had strongly recommended Disraeli's *Sybil* and *Coningsby* as political reading. But Disraeli's style was too ornate for my taste, though I can see why it may have appealed to Harold Macmillan. It is now clear to me that Macmillan was a more complex and sensitive figure than he appeared; but appearance did seem to count for a great deal. Certainly, whether it was striking a bargain and cementing a friendship with President Kennedy, or delivering a deliciously humorous put-down to a ranting Khrushchev, Harold Macmillan was a superb representative of Britain abroad.

I sorted out my best outfit, this time sapphire blue, to go and see the Prime Minister. The interview was short. Harold Macmillan charmingly greeted me and offered the expected appointment. I enthusiastically accepted. I wanted to begin as soon as possible and asked him how I should arrange things with the department. Characteristically, he said: 'Oh well, ring the Permanent Secretary and turn up at about 11 o'clock tomorrow morning, look around and come away. I shouldn't stay too long.'

So it was the following morning – rather before eleven – that I arrived at the pleasant Georgian house in John Adam Street, just off the Strand, which was at that time the headquarters of the Ministry of Pensions and National Insurance. In a gesture which I much appreciated – and which I myself as a Cabinet minister always emulated – John Boyd-Carpenter, my minister, was there at the front door to meet me and take me up to my new office. John was someone it was easy to like and admire for his personal kindness, grasp of detail and capacity for lucid exposition of a complex case. And he was an excellent speaker and debater. All in all, a good model for a novice Parliamentary Secretary to follow.

The first step was to re-read the original Beveridge Report in which the philosophy of the post-war system of pensions and benefits was clearly set out. I was already quite well acquainted with its main aspects and I strongly approved of them. At the centre was the concept of a comprehensive 'social insurance scheme', which was intended to cover loss of earning power caused by unemployment, sickness or retirement. This would be done by a single system of benefits at subsistence level financed by flat-rate individual contributions. By the side of this there would be a system of National Assistance, financed out of general taxation, to help those who were unable to sustain themselves on National Insurance benefits, either because they had been unable to contribute, or had run out of cover. National Assistance was means tested and had been envisaged as in large part a transitional system, whose scope would diminish as pensions or personal savings rose.

It is easy in retrospect to poke fun at many of Beveridge's assumptions and predictions. But Beveridge had sought to guard against the very problems which later governments more or less ignored and which have now returned to plague us, in particular the debilitating effects of welfare dependency and the loss of private and voluntary effort. Whatever the effects in practice, the Beveridge Report's rhetoric has what would later be considered a Thatcherite ring to it:

> ... The State should offer security for service and contribution. The State in organizing security should not stifle incentive, opportunity, responsibility; in establishing a national minimum, it should leave room and encouragement for voluntary action by each individual to provide more than that minimum for himself and his family. [Paragraph 9]

> ... The insured persons should not feel that income for idleness, however caused, can come from a bottomless purse. [Paragraph 22]

Much of our time at the Ministry was taken up both with coping with the effects of and finding remedies to the difficulties which flowed from the gap between Beveridge's original conception and the way in which the system – and with it public expectations – had developed. So, for example, in those days before inflation took hold and benefits were annually up-rated to cope with it, there were cries of disapproval when National Insurance pensions were increased and National Assistance, which made up your income to a certain level, was not. People also increasingly came to expect something better than a subsistence-level pension to retire upon, but the contribution levels or financing from general taxation which this would require seemed prohibitive. This lay behind John Boyd-Carpenter's idea of the 'graduated pensions' scheme, whereby the payment of higher contributions could secure a somewhat higher pension, and provision was made for the encouragement of private occupational pension schemes. Another constant source of difficulty for which we found no ultimate (affordable) answer was the 'earnings rule' whereby pensioners who worked would at a certain level of income lose part or all of their pension payments. It was the impact of this on pensioner widows which caused me most difficulty and not a little heart-searching.

Apart from the Beveridge Report and other general briefing from the department, it was the case work – that is the investigation of particular people's problems raised in letters – which taught me most about the Social Security system. I was not prepared to sign a reply if I did not feel that I properly understood the background. Consequently, a stream of officials came in and out of my office to give me the benefit of their matchless knowledge of each topic. I adopted a similar approach to parliamentary questions, which would be shared out between the ministers. I was not content to know the answer or the line to take. I wanted to know *why*.

Having served as a junior minister to three different ministers in the same department I was interested to see that the advice tendered to the ministers by civil servants differed, even though it was on the same topic. So I complained when both Niall Macpherson and Richard Wood received policy submissions proposing approaches that I knew had not been put to their predecessor, John Boyd-Carpenter. I remember saying afterwards: 'That's not what you advised the previous minister.' They replied that they had known that he would never accept it. I decided then and there that when I was in charge of a department I would insist on an absolutely frank assessment of all the options from any civil servants who would report to me. Arguments should be from first principles.

I also learned another lesson. There was a good deal of pressure to remove the earnings rule as regards widowed mothers. I sympathized with it strongly. Indeed, this was one of the issues upon which, as a new MP, I had publicly stated my position. I thought that if a woman who had lost her husband but still had children to support decided to try to earn a little more through going out to work she should not lose pension for doing so. Perhaps as a woman I had a clearer idea of what problems widows faced. Perhaps it was my recollection of the heartbreaking sight of a recently widowed mother eking out her tiny income buying bruised fruit at my father's shop. But I found it almost impossible to defend the Government line against Opposition attack. I raised the matter with officials and with my minister. On one occasion, I even raised it with Alec Douglas-Home as Prime Minister when he came to speak to a group of junior ministers. But although he seemed sympathetic, I never got anywhere.

The argument from officials in the department was always that ending the earnings rule for even this most deserving group would have 'repercussions' elsewhere. And, of course, they were logically correct. But how I came to hate that word 'repercussions'.

Ministers were wrong to take such arguments at face value and not to apply political judgement to them. It was no surprise to me that one of the first acts of the incoming Labour Government in 1964 was to make the change for which I had been arguing, and to get the credit too. The moral was clear to me: bureaucratic logic is no substitute for ministerial judgement. Forget that as a politician, and the political 'repercussions' will be on you.

I retained my taste for the Chamber of the Commons, developed during my two years on the backbenches. We faced no mean opponents on the Labour benches. Dick Crossman had one of the finest minds in politics, if also one of the most wayward, and Douglas Houghton a formidable mastery of his brief. I liked both of them, but I was still determined to win any argument. I enjoyed the battle of facts and figures when our policies were under fire at Question Time and when I was speaking in debates – though sometimes I should have trod more warily. One day at the Dispatch Box I was handed a civil service note giving new statistics about a point raised in the debate. 'Now,' I said triumphantly, 'I have the latest red hot figure.' The House dissolved into laughter, and it took a moment for me to realize my *double entendre*.

As luck would have it, at Pensions we were due to answer questions on the Monday immediately after the notorious Cabinet reshuffle in July 1962 which became known as 'The Night of the Long Knives'. John Boyd-Carpenter departed to become Chief Secretary to the Treasury and Niall Macpherson had not yet replaced him at Pensions. Since most of the questions on the Order Paper related to my side of the department's

activities, rather than War Pensions, I would have to answer in the place
of the senior minister for nearly an hour. That meant another nerve-
racking weekend for me and for the officials I had to pester. The Labour
Party was in rumbustious mood, but I got through, saying when asked
about future policy that I would refer the matter to my minister – 'when
I had one'.

But would the Government get through? As I was to experience myself
many years later, every Cabinet reshuffle contains its own unforeseen
dangers. But no difficulties I ever faced – even in 1989 – matched the
appalling damage to the Government done by 'The Night of the Long
Knives', in which one third of the Cabinet, including the Lord Chancellor
and the Chancellor of the Exchequer, were dispatched and a new generation including Reggie Maudling, Keith Joseph and Edward Boyle found
themselves in the front line of politics. One of the lessons I learned from
the affair was that one should try to bring in some younger people to the
Government at each reshuffle so as to avoid a log-jam. The handling of
the changes was badly botched by Macmillan, whose standing never
really recovered.

Above all, out in the country there had grown up a detectable feeling
that the Conservatives had been in power too long and had lost their way.
That most dangerous time for a government had arrived when most
people feel, perhaps only in some vague way, that it is 'time for a change'.
Later in the autumn of 1962 the Government ran into squalls of a different kind. The Vassall spy case, the flight of Philby to the Soviet Union,
confirming suspicions that he had been a KGB double-agent since the
1930s, and in the summer of 1963 the Profumo scandal – all served to
enmesh the Government in rumours of sleaze and incompetence. These
might have been shrugged off by a government in robust health. But the
significance attached to these embarrassments was the greater because of
the general malaise.

Europe was one of the main reasons for that malaise. In October 1961
Ted Heath had been entrusted by Harold Macmillan with the difficult
negotiations for British membership of the European Economic
Community. Not least because of Ted's tenacity and dedication, most of
the problems, such as what to do about Britain's agriculture and about
trade links with the Commonwealth, seemed eminently soluble. Then in
January 1963 General de Gaulle vetoed our entry. No great popular
passions about Europe were aroused at this time in Britain. There was a
general sense, which I shared, that in the past we had underrated the

potential advantage to Britain of access to the Common Market, that neither the European Free Trade Association (EFTA) nor our links with the Commonwealth and the United States offered us the trading future we needed, and that the time was right for us to join the EEC. I was an active member of the European Union of Women – an organization founded in Austria in 1953 to promote European integration – and sat on its 'Judicial Panel' which debated issues relating to law and the family. But I saw the EEC as essentially a trading framework – a Common Market – and neither shared nor took very seriously the idealistic rhetoric with which 'Europe' was already being dressed in some quarters. In fact, it is now clear to me that General de Gaulle was much more perceptive than we were at this time when, to our great chagrin, he noted:

> England in effect is insular, she is maritime, she is linked through her exchanges, her markets, her supply lines to the most diverse and often the most distant countries; she pursues essentially industrial and commercial activities, and only slight agricultural ones . . . In short, the nature, the structure, the very situation that are England's differ profoundly from those of the Continentals . . .

But he also said:

> If the Brussels negotiations were shortly not to succeed, nothing would prevent the conclusion between the Common Market and Great Britain of an accord of association designed to safeguard exchanges, and nothing would prevent close relations between England and France from being maintained, nor the pursuit and development of their direct cooperation in all kinds of fields . . .

If this is what de Gaulle was indeed offering, it would have been a better reflection of British interests than the terms of British membership that were eventually agreed a decade later. We may have missed the best European bus that ever came along. At the time, however, so much political capital had been invested by Harold Macmillan in the European venture that its undignified collapse contributed to the impression that the Government had lost its sense of direction.

The Labour Party had suffered a tragedy when Hugh Gaitskell died young in January 1963. Harold Wilson was elected as Leader. Though lacking the respect which Gaitskell had won, Wilson was a new and deadly threat to the Government. He was a formidable parliamentary debater with a rapier wit. He knew how to flatter the press to excellent effect. He could coin the kind of ambiguous phrase to keep Labour united (e.g. 'planned growth of incomes' rather than 'incomes policy'), and he could get under Harold Macmillan's skin in a way Hugh Gaitskell never could. While Gaitskell was more of a statesman than Wilson, Wilson was an infinitely more accomplished politician.

As a result of all these factors, the Conservatives' standing in the polls fell alarmingly. In July 1963, Labour were some 20 per cent ahead. In early October at the Labour Party Conference Harold Wilson's brilliant but shallow speech about the 'white heat' of scientific revolution caught the imagination of the commentators. And then just a few days later – a bombshell – a resignation statement from Harold Macmillan's hospital bed was read out by Alec Douglas-Home to the Party Conference at Blackpool, which was immediately transformed into a kind of gladiatorial combat by the leadership candidates.

But the real battle for the Conservative leadership was taking place elsewhere. The subtlest process of all was the way in which Harold Macmillan let it be known that he favoured Quintin Hogg over Rab Butler, thus stopping any bandwagon for the latter and preparing the ground for the 'emergence' of Alec Douglas-Home.

The Monday following the Conference I received a phone call from the Whips' Office to gauge my views on the leadership. I first told them that I would support Rab over Quintin, because he was simply the more qualified of the two. I was then asked my view of Alec. This opened up a possibility I had not envisaged. 'Is it constitutionally possible?' I asked. Assured that it was, I did not hesitate. I replied: 'Then I am strongly in favour of Alec.'

When Alec Douglas-Home became Foreign Secretary in June 1960 I had expressed doubts to Betty Harvie Anderson (MP for Renfrewshire East). I thought that there surely ought to be a suitable candidate for the post among the ministers in the Commons. Anthony Eden had, I recalled, ostensibly refused to give the Foreign Secretaryship to Lord Salisbury on these grounds. But Betty told me that Alec was quite outstanding and deserved the job. So I decided to read the new Foreign Secretary's first speech in Hansard. It was a masterly survey of East-West relations, which emphasized the need for deterrence as well as negotiation with the Soviets and stressed the importance of our relationship with the United States. Alec now and later managed, most unusually, to combine skill in diplomacy with clarity of vision and he had the charm, polish and eye for detail of the perfect negotiator.

Moreover, Alec Douglas-Home was a manifestly good man – and goodness is not to be underrated as a qualification for those considered for powerful positions. He was also, in the best possible way, 'classless'. You always felt that he treated you not as a category but as a person. And he actually listened – as I found when I took up with him the vexed question of the widowed mothers' allowance.

But the press were cruelly and almost unanimously against him. He was easy to caricature as an out-of-touch aristocrat, a throwback to the worst sort of reactionary Toryism. Inverted snobbery was always to my mind even more distasteful than the straightforward self-important kind. By 1964 British society had entered a sick phase of liberal conformism passing as individual self-expression. Only progressive ideas and people were worthy of respect by an increasingly self-conscious and self-confident media class. And how they laughed when Alec said self-deprecatingly that he used matchsticks to work out economic concepts. What a contrast with the economic models with which the technically brilliant mind of Harold Wilson was familiar. No one stopped to question whether the weaknesses of the British economy were fundamentally simple and only superficially complex. In fact, if politicians had been compelled to use more honest language and simple illustrations to ensure that people understood their policies, we might well have avoided Britain's slither into relative decline.

For all that – in spite of the media criticism, in spite of the chaotic end of the Macmillan Government, in spite of the correct but appallingly timed abolition of Retail Price Maintenance which so offended small-business support for the Conservatives – we very nearly won the 1964 general election. This recovery was not because of any economic improvement, for inflation worsened and the balance of payments deficit yawned. In part it was because the closer one looked at the Labour Party's programme and its Leader, the less substantial they seemed. But mainly the credit for our political recovery should go to Alec.

There had been some press speculation that I might not hold Finchley. The Liberals began predicting another Orpington. They had secured a tight grip on the old Finchley council, though in May 1964 they had done rather less well in the elections for the new Barnet borough council. The Liberals' new, energetic candidate, John Pardoe, campaigned principally on local issues while I mainly stuck to national ones – above all, how to secure prosperity without inflation.

I am always anxious on election day; but in 1964 my anxieties were, in spite of the predictions of my defeat at the start of the campaign, much greater for the Party nationally than for me in Finchley.

The results bore this out. I found myself with a majority over John Pardoe of almost 9,000. But I had seen the last of the Ministry at John Adam Street, for Labour had secured an overall majority of four seats. Thirteen years of Conservative government were over and a period of fundamental rethinking of Conservative philosophy was about to begin – alas, not for the last time.

CHAPTER FIVE

A World of Shadows

Opposition 1964–1970

T HE CONSERVATIVE PARTY has never been slow to shoot the pianist as a substitute for changing its tune. So it proved in the wake of our narrow 1964 election defeat. Anyone seriously thinking about the way forward for Conservatism would have started by examining whether the established tendency to fight on socialist ground with corporatist weapons had not something to do with the Party's predicament. Then and only then – after a more or less inevitable second election defeat, for there was a general sense in the country that Labour needed a larger working majority if it were to carry out its programme – would have been the time to consider a leadership change. I had hoped and indeed naively expected that the Party would soldier on under Alec Douglas-Home. I later heard that the supporters of Ted Heath and others anxious to oust Alec had been busy behind the scenes; but I was unaware of these mysterious cabals until it was too late. I was stunned and upset when Alec told the 1922 Committee that he intended to stand down; I was all the more distressed by his evident unhappiness. I kept on saying to people, 'Why didn't he let his supporters know? We might have been able to help.'

Reggie Maudling and Ted Heath were generally accepted as the only two figures in serious contention for the leadership, which for the first time would be decided by a ballot of MPs. Reggie was thought to have the better chance. Although his performance as Chancellor of the Exchequer had incurred serious and in some ways justified criticism, there was no doubting his experience, brilliant intellect and command of the House. His main weakness was a certain laziness – something which is a frequent temptation to those who know that they are naturally and effortlessly cleverer than those around them.

Ted had a very different character. He was methodical, forceful and, at least on the one question which mattered to him above all others – Europe – a man of unyielding determination. As Shadow Chancellor he had the opportunity to demonstrate his capabilities in attacking the 1965 Finance Bill, which in those days was taken on the floor of the House. Ted was regarded as being somewhat to the right of Reggie, but they were both essentially centrists in Party terms. Something could be made of the different approaches they took to Europe, with Reggie regarding EFTA more favourably and Ted convinced that membership of the EEC was essential. But their attitudes to specific policies hardly affected the question of which to support.

I knew Reggie as a neighbouring MP for Barnet and I liked his combination of laid-back charm and acute intellect. Ted's character seemed to me in many ways admirable. But he was not charming – nor, to be fair, did he set out to be. He was probably more at ease talking to men than women. But it was not just women who found him difficult to get on with. I felt that though I had known him for years, there was a sense in which I did not know him at all. I was not conscious at this time of any hostility, simply of a lack of human warmth. I did not either then or later regard amiability as an indispensable or even particularly important attribute of leadership. Yet, all things considered, I thought that I would vote for Reggie Maudling.

It was Keith Joseph who persuaded me to change my mind. By now Keith was a friend. We worked together, though with him very much as the senior partner, on pensions policy in 1964–65. Like everyone else who came to know him, I was deeply impressed by the quality of his mind and the depth of his compassion. Keith had gone into politics for the same reason that many on the left had done so – he wanted to improve the lot of ordinary people, particularly those he saw living deprived, unfulfilled lives. Many jokes would be made – and the best of them by Keith himself – about the way in which he changed his mind and reversed his policies on matters ranging from housing to health to social benefits. But the common thread was his relentless search for the right answer to the practical problems of human suffering. So I took him very seriously when he telephoned to say that while he knew I was currently intending to vote for Reggie, I should think again. Keith understood Reggie's weaknesses. But it was Ted's strengths that he wanted to speak about. He summed them up:

'Ted has a passion to get Britain right.' And, of course, so did Keith, and so did I.

This was decisive for me. To the disappointment of Reggie Maudling and his PPS, Neil Marten, I told them that Ted Heath would be getting my vote. Sufficient numbers thought similarly. Ted emerged with a clear majority on the first ballot, Reggie withdrawing to make a second ballot unnecessary.

I was not displeased to be given a different portfolio by the new Leader, exchanging my role as Shadow spokesman on Pensions for that of Housing and Land under my old boss, John Boyd-Carpenter. I would always regard my knowledge of the Social Security system as one of the most important aspects of what turned out to be my training to become Prime Minister. Now that we were in Opposition, however, it was not easy to oppose the large pension and benefit increases which the Labour Government was making: only later would the full financial implications of this spending spree become evident. So it was a relief to me to be moved to Housing and Land.

As was widely expected, Harold Wilson called an early snap election at the end of March 1966. The result – a Conservative rout and an overall Labour majority of ninety-seven – was equally expected. We fought an uninspiring campaign on the basis of a flimsy manifesto entitled *Action not Words*, which accurately summed up Ted's impact on politics. This was widely seen as a completion of Wilson's 1964 victory, and Ted was not blamed. I was not displeased to keep a healthy majority of 9,464, this time over the Labour Party which had beaten the Liberals into third place. But it was a depressing time. Denis knew my mood and went out to buy me an eternity ring to cheer me up.

I received a further fillip when Ted Heath made me Treasury spokesman on Tax under the Shadow Chancellor, Iain Macleod. There had been some speculation in the press that I would be promoted to the Shadow Cabinet myself. But I was not expecting it. I now know, having read Jim Prior's memoirs,* that I was indeed considered but that Ted, rather presciently, decided against it because if they got me in 'they would never get [me] out again'. As a tax lawyer I already knew my way around my new brief. Although I had no formal training in economic theory, I felt naturally at ease with the concepts and I had always had strong convictions about the

---

* *A Balance of Power* (1986), p.42.

way in which public money should be handled. As I had found when junior minister responsible for pensions, I was lucky enough to have the sort of mind to grasp technical detail and understand quite complex figuring fairly easily. None of which meant, however, that I could afford to relax.

I not only felt well-suited to my new job: it was also an exciting time to begin it. The incoherence and irresponsibility of socialist economic management had become apparent. The optimistic projections of George Brown's National Plan, published in September 1965, were an albatross to hang around Labour's neck, as forecasts of economic growth were not met. Labour's pre-election promises of 'no severe increases in taxation' were broken with the announcement in the budget of May 1966 that a new Selective Employment Tax (SET) would be introduced, in effect a payroll tax falling particularly heavily on service industries: it was a major part of my brief to oppose it. The Labour Government's reliance on its alleged special relationship with the trade unions to secure voluntary incomes restraint as a means of controlling inflation had already lost credibility with the failure of the Government-TUC joint *Declaration of Intent*, which had first been proclaimed amid fanfares in December 1964. In July 1966 the 'voluntary' approach was jettisoned. It was announced that there would be a six months' wage freeze followed by six months of 'severe restraint'. Prices would be frozen for a year, and a plea was made for limits to be applied to dividends over the same period. The National Board of Prices and Incomes, which Labour had established, was given powers to require one month's advance notification of any price and wage increases and powers to delay increases by Order in Council for up to three months. The Government might take power to direct that specified price and wage increases should not be made. Fighting this policy in general and, under Iain Macleod's leadership, opposing the 'Standstill orders' which came before the House of Commons, were the other important aspects of my brief.

In preparing myself for my first major Commons speech in my new role, I got out from the House of Commons Library every budget speech and Finance Bill since the war and read them. I was thus able to demonstrate to a somewhat bemused Jim Callaghan, then Chancellor of the Exchequer, and Jack Diamond, his Chief Secretary, that this was the only budget which had failed to make even a minor concession in the social services area. Then I sank my teeth into the SET. It was riddled with absurdities which I took great pleasure in exposing. The attempt to distinguish between manufacturing and service industries, shifting the tax burden onto the second and handing the money back as subsidies to the first, was a demonstrably inefficient, anomaly-ridden procedure. As I put it in the House: 'Whatever the payroll tax is, it is thoroughly bad administration . . . I only wish that Gilbert and Sullivan were alive today so that we could have an opera about it.'

Our side of the House liked it. I got a good press, the *Daily Telegraph* observing that 'it has taken a woman . . . to slam the faces of the Government's Treasury ministers in the mud and then stamp on them'. Iain Macleod himself wrote some generous lines about the performance in another paper.

He did the same after my speech that autumn to the Party Conference in Blackpool. I put a special effort into it – though the nine hours of work I did would have seemed culpable idleness compared with the time I took for Conference speechwriting as Party Leader. That autumn, however, I spoke from notes, which gives extra spontaneity and the flexibility to insert a joke or jibe on the spur of the moment. Although the debate I was answering was on taxation, the cheers came in response to what I said about the way in which the Government was undermining the rule of law by the arbitrary powers it had taken through incomes policy and tax policy. With more than a touch of hyperbole, it must be admitted, I said: 'All this is fundamentally wrong for Britain. It is a step not merely towards socialism but towards communism.' The new and still left-of-centre *Sun* noted: 'A Fiery Blonde Warns of the Road to Ruin'.

In October 1967 Ted made me front-bench spokesman on Fuel and Power and a member of the Shadow Cabinet. It may be that my House of Commons performances and perhaps Iain Macleod's recommendation overcame any temperamental reluctance on Ted's part. My first task was to read through all the evidence given to the inquiry about the causes of the terrible Aberfan disaster the previous year, when 116 children and 28 adults were killed by a slag tip which slipped onto a Welsh mining village. Many of the parents of the victims were in the gallery for the debate, and I felt for them. Very serious criticisms had been made of the National Coal Board and as a result someone, I thought, should have resigned, though I held back from stating this conclusion with complete clarity in my first speech to the House as Shadow spokesman. What was revealed by the report made me realize how very easy it is in any large organization to assume that someone else has taken the requisite action and will assume responsibility. This is a problem which, as later tragedies have demonstrated, industrial civilization has yet to solve.

Outside the House, my main interest was in trying to find a framework for privatization of electricity generation. To this end I visited power stations and sought all the advice I could from business contacts. But it turned out to be a fruitless enterprise, and I had not come up with what I considered acceptable answers by the time my portfolio was changed again – to Transport – in October 1968. Parliament had just passed a major Transport Bill reorganizing the railways, nationalizing the bus companies, setting up a new National Freight Authority – in effect, implementing most of the Government's transport programme in one measure. I argued our case against nationalization of the ports. But, all in all, Transport proved a brief with limited possibilities.

As a member of the Shadow Cabinet I attended its weekly discussions, usually on a Wednesday, in Ted's room in the House. Discussion was generally not very stimulating. We would begin by looking ahead to the parliamentary business for the week and agreeing who was to speak and on what line. There might be a paper from a colleague which he would introduce. But, doubtless because we knew that there were large divisions between us, particularly on economic policy, issues of principle were not usually openly debated.

For my part, I did not make a particularly important contribution to Shadow Cabinet. Nor was I asked to do so. For Ted and perhaps others I was principally there as the statutory woman whose main task was to explain what 'women' – Kiri Te Kanawa, Barbara Cartland, Esther Rantzen, Stella Rimington and all the rest of our uniform, undifferentiated sex – were likely to think and want on troublesome issues. I had, of course, great affection for Alec Douglas-Home, then Shadow Foreign Secretary, and got on perfectly well with most of my colleagues, but I had only three real friends around the table – Keith Joseph, Peter Thomas and Edward Boyle. And Edward by now was very much on the opposite wing of the Party from me.

The atmosphere at our meetings was certainly made more difficult by the fact that the most senior figures now had somewhat tense relations with each other. Ted was settling into the role of Party Leader with determination, but without any real assurance. Reggie Maudling, Deputy Leader, had never really recovered from his defeat for the leadership. Iain Macleod was the most politically acute of us, but though a superb public orator he was a rather private and reserved character. He was also growing out of sympathy with his old friend Enoch Powell, who was increasingly concerned about immigration, a topic about which Iain felt equally strongly on the other side. Undoubtedly, Enoch was our finest intellect – classicist, historian, economist and biblical scholar. In a quite different way from Iain, he was a powerful public orator and able to command the House of Commons, or indeed any audience, with his remorseless logic and controlled passion. But as regards the Shadow Cabinet, by this stage he had largely withdrawn into himself. He was disliked and probably feared by Ted Heath.

On Monday 26 February 1968 Shadow Cabinet discussed the Government's Commonwealth Immigrants' Bill to introduce the new immigration controls. A statement had been issued the previous week setting out the principles on which we would judge the measure. Ted Heath said that it was now up to Shadow Cabinet to decide whether the Bill came sufficiently within those terms. In fact, it did some of the things which we advocated. But it did not provide for registration of dependants, nor for appeal by those refused entry, nor for financial help for voluntary repatriation. It was decided to support the Bill, but also to move amendments where appropriate. Iain Macleod said that he would vote against the Bill, and was as good as his word.

On Wednesday 10 April Shadow Cabinet discussed the other side of the Government's policy, the Race Relations Bill. Ted opened the discussion. He said that though the Bill itself appeared to have many faults he thought that some legal machinery would be necessary to help improve the prospects for coloured immigrants in Britain. Quintin Hogg, the Shadow Home Secretary, outlined his own views. He thought that legislation was necessary, but that we should move amendments. However, he noted that our backbenchers were very hostile to the Bill. Reggie Maudling agreed with Quintin on both points. In the discussion which followed, in which I did not participate, the main point in dispute was whether, flawed as the Bill was, to vote against it at Second Reading would be misinterpreted as racist. Shadow Cabinet's view was that the best assurance for good race relations was confidence that future numbers of immigrants would not be too great and that the existing law of the land would be upheld. In the end it was decided that a reasoned amendment would be drafted and there would be a two-line whip. Keith Joseph, Edward Boyle and Robert Carr, on the liberal wing, reserved their positions until they had seen the terms of the amendment. In the event they all supported it.

On Sunday 21 April 1968 – two days before the debate – I woke up to find the front pages of the newspapers dominated by reports of a speech

Enoch Powell had made in Birmingham on immigration the previous afternoon. It was strong meat, and there were some lines which had a sinister ring about them. But I strongly sympathized with the gravamen of his argument about the scale of New Commonwealth immigration into Britain. I too thought this threatened not just public order but also the way of life of some communities, themselves already beginning to be demoralized by insensitive housing policies, Social Security dependence and the onset of the 'permissive society'. I was also quite convinced that, however selective quotations from his speech may have sounded, Enoch was no racist.

At about 11 o'clock the telephone rang. It was Ted Heath. 'I am ringing round all the Shadow Cabinet. I have come to the conclusion that Enoch must go.' It was more statement than enquiry. But I said that I really thought that it was better to let things cool down rather than heighten the crisis. 'No, no,' he said. 'He absolutely must go, and most people think he must go.' In fact, I understood later that several members of the Shadow Cabinet would have resigned if Enoch had not gone.

The longer-term consequences of Enoch's departure on this issue and under these circumstances extended far beyond immigration policy. He was free to develop a philosophical approach to a range of policies, uninhibited by the compromises of collective responsibility. This spanned both economic and foreign affairs and embraced what would come to be called 'monetarism', deregulation, denationalization, an end to regional policy, and culminated in his opposition to British membership of the Common Market. Having Enoch preaching to such effect in the wilderness carried advantages and disadvantages for those of us on the right in the Shadow Cabinet and later the Cabinet. On the one hand, he shifted the basis of the political argument to the right and so made it easier to advance sound doctrines without being accused of taking an extreme position. On the other hand, so bitter was the feud between Ted and Enoch that querying any policy advanced by the leadership was likely to be branded disloyalty. Moreover, the very fact that Enoch advanced all his positions as part of a coherent whole made it more difficult to express agreement with one or two of them. For example, the arguments against prices and incomes policies, intervention and corporatism might have been better received if they had not been associated with Enoch's views about immigration or Europe.

At this time, as it happens, other Conservatives were moving independently in the same direction, with the notable exception of Europe, and Ted gave me an opportunity to chart this way ahead. The annual Conservative Political Centre lecture is designed to give some intellectual meat to those attending the Tory Party Conference. The choice of speaker is generally reserved to the Party Leader. It was doubtless a pollster or Party adviser who suggested that it might be a good idea to have me talk about a subject which would appeal to 'women'. Luckily, I was free to choose my subject, and I decided on something that might appeal to thinking people of both sexes: I spoke on 'What's Wrong With Politics?'

I began by listing the reasons why there was so much disillusionment with politics. Some of these really consisted of the growth of a critical spirit through the effects of education and the mass media. But others were the fault of the politicians themselves. Political programmes were becoming dominated by a series of promises whose impact was all the greater because of the growth of the Welfare State. This led me on to what I considered the main cause of the public's increasing alienation from political parties – too much government. The competition between the parties to offer ever higher levels of economic growth and the belief that government itself could deliver these had provided the socialists with an opportunity massively to extend state control and intervention. This in turn caused ordinary people to feel that they had insufficient say in their own and their families' lives. The Left claimed that the answer was the creation of structures which would allow more democratic 'participation' in political decisions. But the real problem was that politics itself was intruding into far too many decisions that were properly outside its scope. Alongside the expansion of government had developed a political obsession with size – the notion that large units promoted efficiency. In fact, the opposite was true. Smaller units – small businesses, families and ultimately individuals – should once again be the focus of attention.

Apart from these general reflections, my CPC lecture also contained a section about prices and incomes policy. Although I stuck to the Shadow Cabinet line of condemning a compulsory policy while avoiding the issue of a voluntary one, I included a passage which reads:

> We now put so much emphasis on the control of incomes that we have too little regard for the essential role of government which is *the control of the money supply* and management of demand [emphasis added]. Greater attention to this role and less to the outward detailed control would have achieved more for the economy. It would mean, of course, that the government had to

exercise itself some of the disciplines on expenditure it is so anxious
to impose on others. It would mean that expenditure in the vast
public sector would not have to be greater than the amount which
could be financed out of taxation plus genuine saving.

In retrospect, it is clear to me that this summed up how far my understanding of these matters had gone – and how far it still needed to go. I
had come to see that the money supply was central to any policy to
control inflation. But I had not seen either that this made any kind of
incomes policy irrelevant or that monetary policy itself was the way in
which demand should be managed.

By now (1968) the left-of-centre consensus on economic policy was
being challenged and would continue to be. But the new liberal consensus on moral and social matters was not. That is to say that people in
positions of influence in government, the media and universities
managed to impose metropolitan liberal views on a society that was still
largely conservative morally. The 1960s saw in Britain the beginning of
what has become an almost complete separation between traditional
Christian values and the authority of the state. Some politicians regarded
this as a coherent programme. But for the great majority, myself
included, it was a matter of reforms to deal with specific problems, in
some cases cruel or unfair provisions.

So it was that I voted in 1966 for Leo Abse's Bill proposing that homosexual conduct in private between consenting adults over twenty-one
should no longer be a criminal offence. In the same year I voted for David
Steel's Bill to allow abortion if there was substantial risk that a child
would suffer from such physical or mental abnormalities as to be seriously handicapped, or 'where the woman's capacity as a mother would be
severely overstrained'. On both these issues I was strongly influenced by
my own experience of other people's suffering. For example, when I was
a barrister I had been moved by the humiliation I had seen inflicted in the
dock on a man of considerable local standing who had been found engaging in homosexual conduct.

On the other hand, some aspects of the liberal agenda seemed to me to
go too far. Divorce law reform was such a case. I had talked in my
constituency surgeries to women subjected to a life of misery from their
brutal husbands and for whom marriage had become a prison from
which, in my view, they should be released. In these circumstances
divorce might be the only answer. But if divorce became too easy it might

undermine marriages simply going through a bad patch. If people can withdraw lightly from their responsibilities they are likely to be less serious about entering into the initial obligation. I was concerned about the spouse who was committed to make the marriage work and was deserted. I was also very concerned about what would become of the family of the first marriage when the man (or woman) chose to start a second family. So in 1968 I was one of the minority who voted against a Bill to make divorce far easier. Divorce would be possible where it was judged that there had been an 'irretrievable breakdown', broadly defined, in the marriage. I also supported two amendments, the first of which made available a special form of marriage that was indissoluble (except by judicial separation). The second would seek to ensure that in any conflict of interest between the legal wife and children of the first marriage and a common-law wife and her children, the former should have priority.

Similarly, I voted against Sydney Silverman's Bill to abolish the death penalty for murder in 1965. Like all the other measures listed above this was passed by Parliament, but subject to a Conservative amendment to the effect that the Act was to expire at the end of July 1970 unless Parliament determined otherwise. I then voted against the motion in December 1969 to make the Act permanent.

I believed that the state had not just a right but a duty to deter and punish violent crime and to protect the law-abiding public. However sparingly it is used, the power to deprive an individual of liberty, and under certain circumstances of life itself, is inseparable from the sovereignty of the state. I never had the slightest doubt that in nearly all cases the supreme deterrent would be an influence on the potential murderer. And the deterrent effect of capital punishment is at least as great on those who go armed on other criminal activities, such as robbery. To my mind, the serious difficulty in the issue lay in the possibility of the conviction and execution of an innocent man – which has certainly happened in a small number of cases. Against these tragic cases, however, must be set the victims of convicted murderers who have been released after their sentence was served only to be convicted of murder a second time – who have certainly numbered many more. I believe that the potential victim of the murderer deserves that highest protection which only the existence of the death penalty gives.

As regards abortion, homosexuality, and divorce reform it is easy to see that matters did not turn out as was intended. For most of us in Parliament – and certainly for me – the thinking underlying these changes was that they dealt with anomalies or unfairnesses which occurred in a minority of instances, or that they removed uncertainties in the law itself. Or else they were intended to recognize in law what was in any case occurring in fact. Instead, it could be argued that they have paved the way towards a more callous, selfish and irresponsible society. Reforming the law on abortion was primarily intended to stop young women being forced to have back-street abortions. It was not meant to make abortion simply another 'choice'. Yet in spite of the universal availability of artificial contraception the figures for abortion have kept on rising. Homosexual activists have moved from seeking a right of privacy to demanding social approval for the 'gay' lifestyle, equal status with the heterosexual family and even the legal right to exploit the sexual uncertainty of adolescents. Divorce law reform has contributed to – though it is by no means the only cause of – a very large increase in the incidence of marriage breakdown which has left so many children growing up without the continual care and guidance of two parents.

Would I have voted differently on any of these measures? I now see that we viewed them too narrowly. As a lawyer, I felt that the prime considerations were that the law should be enforceable and its application fair to those who might run foul of it. But laws also have a symbolic significance: they are signposts to the way society is developing – and the way the legislators of society envisage that it should develop. Moreover, taking all of the 'liberal' reforms of the 1960s together they amount to more than their individual parts. They came to be seen as providing a radically new framework within which the younger generation would be expected to behave.

Although Britain gave a distinctive gloss to these trends, the affluent consumer society to which they catered was above all to be found in the United States. I had made my first visit to the USA in 1967 on one of the 'Leadership' programmes run by the American Government to bring rising young leaders from politics and business over to the US. For six weeks I travelled the length and breadth of the United States. The excitement which I felt has never really subsided. At each stopover I was met and accommodated by friendly, open, generous people who took me into their homes and lives and showed me their cities and townships with evident pride. The high point was my visit to the NASA Space Center at Houston. I saw the astronaut training programme which would just two years later help put a man on the moon. As a living example of the 'brain drain' from which over-regulated, high-taxed Britain was suffering, I met someone from my constituency of Finchley who had gone to NASA to make full use of his talents. I saw nothing wrong with that, and indeed was glad that a British scientist was making such an important contribution. But there was no way Britain could hope to compete even in more modest areas of technology if we did not learn the lessons of an enterprise economy.

I travelled to Moscow with the amiable Paul Channon and his wife. We had a full schedule including not just the sights of Moscow but also Leningrad (formerly, and now once again, St Petersburg) and Stalingrad (Volgograd). But though the name might vary, the propaganda was the same. It was relentless, an endless flow of statistics proving the industrial and social superiority of the Soviet Union over the West. Outside an art gallery I visited there was a sculpture of a blacksmith beating a sword with a hammer. 'That represents communism,' my guide proudly observed. 'Actually, it doesn't,' I replied. 'It's from the Old Testament – "And they shall beat their swords into ploughshares, and their spears into pruning-hooks".' Collapse of stout aesthete. Methodist Sunday School has its uses.

Yet, behind the official propaganda, the grey streets, all but empty shops and badly maintained workers' housing blocks, Russian humanity peeped out. There was no doubt about the genuineness of the tears when the older people at Leningrad and Stalingrad told me about their terrible sufferings in the war. The young people I talked to from Moscow University, though extremely cautious about what they said in the full knowledge that they were under KGB scrutiny, were clearly fascinated to learn all they could about the West. And even bureaucracy can prove human. When I visited the manager of the Moscow passenger transport system he explained to me at great length how decisions about new development had to go from committee to committee in what seemed – as I said – an endless chain of non-decision-making. I caught the eye of a young man, perhaps the chairman's assistant, standing behind him and he could not repress a broad smile.

On my return to London I was moved to the Education portfolio in the Shadow Cabinet. Edward Boyle was leaving politics to become Vice-Chancellor of the University of Leeds. There was by now a good deal of grassroots opposition at Party Conferences to what was seen as his weakness in defence of the grammar schools. Although our views had diverged, I was sorry to see him go and I would miss his intellect, sensitivity and integrity. But for me this was definitely a promotion, even though, as I have since learned, I was in fact the reserve candidate, after Keith Joseph: I got the job because Reggie Maudling refused to take over Keith's job as Trade and Industry Shadow.

I was delighted with my new role. I had risen to my present position as a result of free (or nearly free) good education, and I wanted others to have the same chance. Socialist education policies, by equalizing downwards and denying gifted children the opportunity to get on, were a major obstacle to that. I was also fascinated by the scientific side – the portfolio in those days being to shadow the Department of Education *and* Science.

Education was by now one of the main battlegrounds of politics. Since their election in 1964 Labour had been increasingly committed to making the whole secondary school system comprehensive, and had introduced a series of measures, to make local education authorities (LEAs) submit plans for such a change. (The process culminated in legislation, introduced a few months after I took over as Education Shadow.) The difficulties Edward had faced in formulating and explaining our response soon became clear to me.

The Shadow Cabinet and the Conservative Party were deeply split over the principle of selection in secondary education and, in particular, over the examination by which children were selected at the age of eleven, the 11-Plus. To oversimplify a little: first, there were those who had no real interest in state education because they themselves and their children went to private schools. This was a group all too likely to be swayed by arguments of political expediency. Second, there were those who, themselves or their children, had failed to get into grammar school and had been disappointed with the education received at a secondary modern. Third, there were those Conservatives who had absorbed a large dose of the fashionable egalitarian doctrines of the day. Finally, there were people like me who had been to good grammar schools, were strongly opposed to their destruction and felt no inhibitions at all about arguing for the 11-Plus.

But by the time I took on the Education portfolio, the Party's policy group had presented its report and the policy itself was largely established. It had two main aspects. We had decided to concentrate on improving primary schools. And in order to defuse as much as possible the debate about the 11-Plus, we stressed the autonomy of local education authorities in proposing the retention of grammar schools or the introduction of comprehensive schools.

The good arguments for this programme were that improvements in the education of younger children were vital if the growing tendency towards illiteracy and innumeracy was to be checked and, secondly, that in practice the best way to retain grammar schools was to fight centralization. There were, however, arguments on the other side. There was not much point in spending large sums on nursery and primary schools and the teachers for them, if the teaching methods and attitudes were wrong. Nor, of course, were we in the long run going to be able to defend grammar schools – or, for that matter, private schools, direct grant schools and even streamed comprehensive schools – if we did not fight on grounds of principle.

Within the limits which the agreed policy and political realities allowed me, I went as far as I could. This was a good deal too far for some people, as I learned when, shortly after my appointment, I was the guest of the education correspondents at the Cumberland Hotel in London. I put the case not just for grammar schools but for secondary moderns. Those children who were not able to shine academically could in fact acquire responsibilities and respect at a separate secondary modern school, which they would never have done if in direct and continual competition and contact with the more academically gifted. I was perfectly prepared to see the 11-Plus replaced or modified by testing later in a child's career, if that was what people wanted. I knew that it was quite possible for late developers at a secondary modern to be moved to the local grammar school so that their abilities could be properly stretched. I was sure that there were too many secondary modern schools which were providing a second-rate education – but this was something which should be remedied by bringing their standards up, rather than grammar school standards down. Only two of those present at the Cumberland Hotel lunch seemed to agree. Otherwise I was met by a mixture of hostility and blank incomprehension. It opened my eyes to the dominance of socialist thinking among those whose task it was to provide the public with information about education.

There were still some relatively less important issues in Conservative education policy to be decided. I fought hard to have an unqualified commitment to raising the school leaving age to sixteen inserted into the manifesto, and succeeded against some doubts from the Treasury team. I also met strong opposition from Ted Heath when, at our discussions at Selsdon Park in early 1970, I argued that the manifesto should endorse the proposed new independent University of Buckingham. I lost this battle but was at least finally permitted to make reference to the university in a speech.

Quite why Ted felt so passionately against it I have never fully understood.

The Selsdon Park policy weekend at the end of January and beginning of February was a success, but not for the reasons usually given. The idea that Selsdon Park was the scene of debate which resulted in a radical rightward shift in Party policy is false. The main lines of policy had already been agreed and incorporated into a draft manifesto which we spent our time considering in detail. Our line on immigration had also been carefully spelt out. Our proposals for trade union reform had been published in *Fair Deal at Work.* On incomes policy, a rightward but somewhat confused shift was in the process of occurring. Labour had effectively abandoned its own policy. There was no need, therefore, to enter into the vexed question of whether some kind of 'voluntary' incomes policy might be pursued. But it was clear that Reggie Maudling was unhappy that we had no proposals to deal with what was still perceived as 'wage inflation'. In fact, the manifesto, in a judicious muddle, avoided either a monetarist approach or a Keynesian one and said simply: 'The main causes of rising prices are Labour's damaging policies of high taxation and devaluation. Labour's compulsory wage control was a failure and we will not repeat it.'

This led us into some trouble later. During the election campaign the fallacious assertion that high taxes caused inflation inspired a briefing note from Central Office. This note allowed the Labour Party to claim subsequently that we had said that we would cut prices 'at a stroke' by means of tax cuts.

Thanks to the blanket press coverage of Selsdon Park, we seemed to be a serious alternative Government committed to long-term thinking about the policies for Britain's future. We were also helped by Harold Wilson's attack on 'Selsdon Man'. It gave us an air of down-to-earth right-wing populism which countered the somewhat aloof image conveyed by Ted. Above all, both Selsdon Park and the Conservative manifesto, *A Better Tomorrow*, contrasted favourably with the deviousness, inconsistency and horse trading which by now characterized the Wilson Government, especially since the abandonment of *In Place of Strife* under trade union pressure.*

Between our departure from Selsdon Park and the opening of the general election campaign in May, however, there was a reversal of the

---

* *In Place of Strife* was the – in retrospect ironically chosen – title of a Labour White Paper of 1969 which proposed a range of union reforms. The proposals had to be abandoned due to internal opposition within the Cabinet and the Labour Party, led by Jim Callaghan.

opinion poll standing of the two parties. Quite why this turnaround had occurred (or indeed how real it actually was) is hard to know. With the prospect of a general election there is always a tendency for disillusioned supporters to resume their party allegiance. But it is also true – and it is something that we would pay dearly for in government – that we had not seriously set out to win the battle of ideas against socialism during our years in Opposition. And indeed, our rethinking of policy had not been as fundamental as it should have been.

The campaign itself was largely taken up with Labour attacks on our policies. We for our part, like any Opposition, highlighted the long list of Labour's broken promises – 'steady industrial growth all the time', 'no stop-go measures', 'no increase in taxation', 'no increase in unemployment', 'the pound in your pocket not devalued', 'economic miracle' and many more. This was the theme I pursued in my campaign speeches. But I also used a speech to a dinner organized by the National Association of Head Teachers in Scarborough to outline our education policies.

It is hard to know just what turned the tide. Paradoxically perhaps, the Conservative figures who made the greatest contribution were those two fierce enemies, Ted Heath and Enoch Powell. No one could describe Ted as a great communicator, but as the days went by he came across as a decent man, someone with integrity and a vision – albeit a somewhat technocratic one – of what he wanted for Britain. It seemed, to use Keith's words to me five years earlier, that he had 'a passion to get Britain right'. This was emphasized in Ted's powerful introduction to the manifesto in which he attacked Labour's 'cheap and trivial style of government' and 'government by gimmick' and promised 'a new style of government'. Ted's final Party Election Broadcast also showed him as an honest patriot who cared deeply about his country and wanted to serve it. He had fought a good campaign. For his part, Enoch Powell made three powerful speeches on the failures of the Labour Government, urging people to vote Conservative. There is some statistical evidence that Enoch's intervention helped tip the balance in the West Midlands.

My own result was announced to a tremendous cheer at Hendon College of Technology – I had increased my majority to over 11,000 over Labour. Then I went down to the *Daily Telegraph* party at the Savoy, where it quite soon became clear that the opinion polls had been proved wrong and that we were on course for an overall majority.

Friday was spent in my constituency clearing up and writing the usual thank-you letters. I thought that probably Ted would have at least one

woman in his Cabinet, and that since he had got used to me in the
Shadow Cabinet I would be the lucky girl. On the same logic, I would
probably get the Education brief.

On Saturday morning the call from the No. 10 Private Secretary came
through. Ted wanted to see me. When I went in to the Cabinet Room I
began by congratulating him on his victory. But not much time was spent
on pleasantries. He was as ever brusque and businesslike, and he offered
me the job of Education Secretary, which I accepted.

I went back to the flat at Westminster Gardens with Denis and we
drove to Lamberhurst.*

Sadly my father was not alive to share the moment. Shortly before his
death in February, I had gone up to Grantham to see him. My stepmother,
Cissy, whom he had married several years earlier and with whom he had
been very happy, was constantly at his bedside. While I was there, friends
from the church, business, local politics, the Rotary and bowling club,
kept dropping in 'just to see how Alf was'. I hoped that at the end of my
life I too would have so many good friends.

I understand that my father had been listening to me as a member of a
panel on a radio programme just before he died. He never knew that I
would become a Cabinet minister, and I am sure that he never imagined
I would eventually become Prime Minister. He would have wanted these
things for me because politics was so much a part of his life and because
I was so much his daughter. But nor would he have considered that political power was the most important or even the most effective thing in life.
In searching through my papers to assemble the material for this volume
I came across some of my father's loose sermon notes slipped into the
back of my sixth-form chemistry exercise book.

> Men, nations, races or any particular generation cannot be saved
> by ordinances, power, legislation. We worry about all this, and our
> faith becomes weak and faltering. But all these things are as old as
> the human race – all these things confronted Jesus 2,000 years
> ago . . . This is why Jesus had to come.

My father lived these convictions to the end.

---

* We had bought 'The Mount', a mock-Tudor house with a large garden in Lamberhurst,
near Tunbridge Wells, in 1965. In 1972 we sold it, and bought the house in Flood Street
(Chelsea) which would be my home until in 1979 I moved into 10 Downing Street.

CHAPTER SIX

Teacher's Pest

The Department of Education 1970–1974

O N MONDAY 22 JUNE 1970 I arrived at the Department of Education and Science (DES) in its splendid old quarters in Curzon Street. I was met by the Permanent Secretary, Bill (later Sir William) Pile and the outgoing Permanent Secretary, Sir Herbert Andrew. They gave me a warm greeting and showed me up to my impressive office. It was all too easy to slip into the warm water of civil service respect for 'the minister', but I was very conscious that hard work lay ahead. I was generally satisfied with the ministerial team I had been allotted: one friendly, one hostile and one neutral. My old friend Lord Eccles, as Paymaster-General, was responsible for the Arts. Bill Van Straubenzee, a close friend of Ted's, dealt with Higher Education. Lord Belstead answered for the department in the Lords. I was particularly pleased that David Eccles, a former Minister of Education, was available, though installed in a separate building, to give me private advice based on his knowledge of the department.

My difficulties with the department, however, were not essentially about personalities. Nor did they stem from the opposition between my own executive style of decision-making and the more consultative style to which they were accustomed. Indeed, by the time I left I was aware that I had won a somewhat grudging respect because I knew my own mind and expected my decisions to be carried out promptly and efficiently. The real problem was – in the widest sense – one of politics.

The ethos of the DES was self-righteously socialist. For the most part, these were people who retained an almost reflex belief in the ability of central planners and social theorists to create a better world. There was nothing cynical about this. Years after many people in the Labour Party had begun to have their doubts, the educationalists retained a sense of mission. Equality in education was not only the overriding good, irrespective of the practical effects of egalitarian policies on particular schools; it was a stepping stone to achieving equality in society, which was itself an unquestioned good. It was soon clear to me that on the whole I was not among friends.

My difficulties with the civil service were compounded by the fact that we had been elected in 1970 with a set of education policies which were perhaps less clear than they appeared. During the campaign I had hammered away at seven points:

- a shift of emphasis onto primary schools
- the expansion of nursery education (which fitted in with Keith Joseph's theme of arresting the 'cycle of deprivation')
- in secondary education, the right of local education authorities to decide what was best for their areas, while warning against making 'irrevocable changes to any good school unless . . . the alternative is better'
- raising the school leaving age to sixteen
- encouraging direct grant schools and retaining private schools*
- expanding higher and further education
- holding an inquiry into teacher training

But those pledges did not reflect a clear philosophy. Different people and different groups within the Conservative Party favoured very different approaches to education, in particular to secondary education and the grammar schools. On the one hand, there were some Tories who had a commitment to comprehensive education which barely distinguished them from moderate socialists. On the other, the authors of the so-called *Black Papers* on education had started to spell out a radically different approach, based on discipline, choice and standards (including the retention of existing grammar schools with high standards).

On that first day at the department I brought with me a list of about fifteen points for action which I had written down over the weekend in an

---

* Direct grant schools, which included some of the most famous and successful secondary schools in Britain, entry to which was often highly competitive, were funded direct from the DES and were outside local control.

old exercise book. After enlarging upon them, I tore out the pages and gave them to Bill Pile. The most immediate action point was the withdrawal of Tony Crosland's Circular 10/65, under which local authorities were required to submit plans for reorganizing secondary education on completely comprehensive lines, and Circular 10/66, issued the following year, which withheld capital funding from local education authorities that refused to go comprehensive.

The department must have known that this was in our manifesto – but apparently they thought that the policy could be watered down, or its implementation postponed. I, for my part, knew that the pledge to stop pressuring local authorities to go comprehensive was of great importance to our supporters, and that it was important to act speedily in order to end uncertainty. Consequently, even before I had given Bill Pile my fifteen points, I had told the press that I would immediately withdraw Labour's Circulars. I even indicated that this would have happened by the time of the Queen's Speech. The alarm this provoked seems to have made its way to No. 10, for I was reminded that I should have Cabinet's agreement to the policy, though of course this was only a formality.

More seriously, I had not understood that the withdrawal of one Circular requires the issue of another. My civil servants made no secret of the fact that they considered that a Circular should contain a good deal of material setting out the department's views on its preferred shape for secondary education in the country as a whole. This might take for ever, and in any event I did not see things that way. The essence of our policy was to encourage variety and choice rather than 'plan' the system. Moreover, to the extent that it was necessary to lay down from the centre the criteria by which local authorities' reorganization proposals would be judged, this could be done now in general terms, with any further elaboration taking place later. It was immensely difficult to persuade them that I was serious. I eventually succeeded by doing an initial draft myself: they quickly decided that co-operation was the better part of valour. And in the end a very short Circular – Circular 10/70 – was issued on Tuesday 30 June: in good time for the Education Debate on the Queen's Speech on Wednesday 8 July.

I now came under fierce attack from the educational establishment because I had failed to engage in the 'normal consultation' which took place before a Circular was issued. I felt no need to apologize. As I put it in my speech in the House, we had after all 'just completed the biggest consultation of all', that is, a general election. But this carried little weight with those who had spent the last twenty-five years convinced that they knew best. Ted Short, Labour's Education spokesman, a former schoolmaster, even went so far as to suggest that, in protest, teachers should refuse to mark 11-Plus exam papers. A delegation from the NUT came to see me to complain about what I had done. Significantly, the brunt of their criticism was that I had 'resigned responsibility for giving shape to education'. If indeed that had been my responsibility, I do not think the NUT would have liked the shape I would have given it.

In fact, the policy which I now pursued was more nuanced than the caricatures it attracted – though a good deal could have been said for the positions caricatured. Circular 10/70 withdrew the relevant Labour Government Circulars and then went on: 'The Secretary of State will expect educational considerations in general, local needs and wishes in particular and the wise use of resources to be the main principles determining the local pattern.' It also made it clear that the presumption was basically against upheaval: 'where a particular pattern of organization is working well and commands general support the Secretary of State does not wish to cause further change without good reason'.

Strange though it may seem, although local education authorities had been used to sending in general plans for reorganization of all the schools under their control, neither these nor the Secretary of State's comments on them had any legal standing. The law only entered the picture when the notices were issued under Section 13 of the 1944 Education Act. This required local education authorities to give public notice – and notice to the department – of their intention to close or open a school, significantly alter its character, or change the age range of its pupils. Locally, this gave concerned parents, school governors and residents two months in which to object. Nationally, it gave me, as Secretary of State, the opportunity to intervene. It read: 'Any proposals submitted to the Secretary of State under this section may be approved by him after making such modifications therein, if any, as appear to him desirable.'

The use of these powers to protect particular good schools against sweeping reorganization was not only a departure from Labour policy; it was also a conscious departure from the line taken by Edward Boyle, who had described Section 13 as 'reserve powers'. But as a lawyer myself and as someone who believed that decisions about changing and closing schools should be sensitive to local opinion, I thought it best to base my policy on the Section 13 powers rather than on exhortation through Circulars. I was very conscious that my actions were subject to the scrutiny of the courts and that the grounds on which I could intervene were limited. And by the time I made my speech in the debate I was in a position to spell out more clearly how this general approach would be implemented.

My policy had a further advantage. At a time when even Conservative education authorities were bitten with the bug of comprehensivization, it offered the best chance of saving good local grammar schools. The administrative disadvantage was that close scrutiny of large numbers of individual proposals meant delays in giving the department's response. Inevitably, I was attacked on the grounds that I was holding back in order to defer the closure of more grammar schools. But in this the critics were unjust. I took a close interest in speeding up the responses. It was just that we were deluged.

For all the political noise which arose from this change of policy, its practical effects were limited. During the whole of my time as Education Secretary we considered some 3,600 proposals for reorganization – the great majority of them proposals for comprehensivization – of which I rejected only 325, or about 9 per cent. In the summer of 1970 it had seemed possible that many more authorities might decide to reverse or halt their plans. For example, Conservative-controlled Birmingham was one of the first education authorities to welcome Circular 10/70. A bitter fight had been carried on to save the city's thirty-six grammar schools. But in 1972 Labour took control and put forward its own plans for comprehensivization. I rejected sixty of the council's 112 proposals in June 1973, saving eighteen of the city's grammar schools.

Similarly, Richmond Council in Surrey had refused to come forward with a scheme under the Labour Government's Circular 10/65, but in September 1970 voted by a large majority to end selection. I had no choice but to give my approval to the change the following year.

Perhaps the most awkward decisions I had to make related to Barnet. The Conservative-controlled Barnet Council decided to go comprehensive in October 1970, having conducted a survey of parents in which 79 per cent apparently favoured ending selection. There was fierce opposition to Barnet's scheme, and in January 1971 I received 5,400 letters of protest. The following month I approved a scheme which ended two grammar schools, but I saved a third on the grounds that the proposed merger would lead to an inconvenient divided-site school. In April I saved another grammar school and in June blocked two more schemes, thus saving a good secondary modern and another grammar school. The Conservative Party locally was split and I was censured by the local

council. Most of the borough's secondary schools in fact went comprehensive that September. The local authority kept reformulating its plans.
Christ's College and Woodhouse Grammar Schools were the main bones
of contention. They were still grammar schools when I became Leader of
the Opposition in 1975; they only became part of a comprehensive system
(in Woodhouse's case, a sixth-form college) in 1978 after Labour's 1976
Education Act scrapped Section 13 and attempted to impose a comprehensive system from the centre on England and Wales.

In retrospect, it is clear that a near obsessive concern with educational
structures characterized the 1960s and '70s. It is not that structures are
unimportant. But educational theorists manifest a self-confidence which
events have done nothing to justify when they claim that there is one
system which in all circumstances and for all individuals is better than
another.

In one respect at least, the Department of Education was an excellent
preparation for the premiership. I came under savage and unremitting
attack that was only distantly related to my crimes.

I have described the arguments about grammar schools and compre-
hensives. Yet these caused me only limited trouble, partly because many
people – and not just Conservatives – agreed with me and partly because
I was the bringer of good tidings in other matters. For example, I was
hailed in a modest way as the saviour of the Open University. In Opposition both Iain Macleod and Edward Boyle had committed themselves in
public against it. And although its abolition was not in the manifesto,
many people expected it to perish. But I was genuinely attracted to the
concept of a 'University of the Airwaves', because I thought that it was an
inexpensive way of giving wider access to higher education, because I
thought that trainee teachers in particular would benefit from it, because
I was alert to the opportunities offered by technology to bring the best
teaching to schoolchildren and students, and above all because it gave
people a second chance in life. On condition that I agreed to reduce the
immediate intake of students and find other savings, my Cabinet
colleagues allowed the Open University to go ahead.

There were more discussions of public expenditure that autumn of
1970. The Treasury had its little list of savings for the education budget –
including charges for libraries, museums, school meals and school milk. I
persuaded the Cabinet to drop the proposed library charges, while reluctantly accepting entry charges for museums and galleries. (We kept one

free day.) But pressure for more cuts was maintained, and I had to come up with a list of priority targets.

Savings on school meals and school milk were, I had to admit, an obvious candidate. There seemed no reason why families who could afford to do so should not make a larger contribution to the cost of school meals. I thought that I could defend such cuts if I could demonstrate that some of the money saved would go towards meeting the priority which we had set, namely the primary school building programme. And within the Department of Education budget it seemed logical that spending on education should come before 'welfare' spending, which should in principle fall to Keith Joseph's department, Social Services.

As for milk, there were already mixed views on health grounds about the advantage of providing it. By 1970 very few children were so deprived that school milk was essential for their nourishment. Tony Barber, who became Chancellor in July 1970, after the death of Iain Macleod, wanted me to abolish free school milk altogether. But I managed to hold the line at an increased price for school meals and the withdrawal of free milk from primary school children over the age of seven. These modest changes came with safeguards: children in need of milk for medical reasons continued to receive it until they went to secondary school. All in all, I had defended the education budget effectively.

Nor was this lost on the press. The *Daily Mail* said that I had emerged as a 'new heroine'. The *Daily Telegraph* drew attention to my plans to improve 460 of the oldest primary schools. The *Guardian* noted: 'School meals and milk were the main casualties in a remarkably light raid on the education budget. Mrs Thatcher has won her battle to preserve a high school-building programme and turn it to the replacement of old primary schools.'

It was pleasant while it lasted.

The trouble was, it didn't last long. Six months later we had to introduce a Bill to remove the legal duty for local education authorities to provide free milk and allow them discretion to make it available for a small charge. This gave Labour the parliamentary opportunity to cause havoc.

Even before that, however, the newspapers had unearthed the potential in stories about school meals. One report claimed that some local education authorities were going to charge children who brought sandwiches to school for their lunch. 'Sandwich Kids In "Fines" Storm' was how the *Sun* put it. I introduced a circular to prevent the practice. But that story in turn restored attention to the increase in school meal charges. Overnight the number of children eating such meals became a politically sensitive indicator. The old arguments about the 'stigma' of means-tested benefits, which I had come to know so well as a Parliamentary Secretary in the 1960s, surfaced again. It was said that children from families poor enough to be entitled to free school meals would be humiliated when better-off classmates paid for their own. Probably unwisely, I came up with a suggestion in a television programme that this could be avoided if mothers sent dinner money to schools in envelopes. The teachers could put the change back in the envelope. A poor child entitled to free meals would bring an envelope with coins that would just be put back again by the teacher. This just added a new twist to the story.

In any case, it was not long before the great 'milk row' dwarfed debate about meals. Newspapers which had congratulated me on my success in protecting the education budget at the expense of cuts in milk and meals suddenly changed their tune. The *Guardian* described the Education (Milk) Bill as 'a vindictive measure which should never have been laid before Parliament'. The *Daily Mail* told me to 'think again'. The *Sun* demanded to know: 'Is Mrs Thatcher Human?' But it was a speaker at the Labour Party Conference who seems to have suggested to the press the catchy title 'Mrs Thatcher, milk snatcher'.

When the press discover a rich vein they naturally exhaust it. So it seemed as if every day some variant of the theme would emerge. For example, a Labour council was discovered to be considering buying its own herd of cows to provide milk for its children. Local education authorities sought to evade the legislation by serving up milky drinks but not milk. Councils which were *not* education authorities took steps to provide free milk for children aged seven to eleven under powers contained in the Local Government Act 1963. Only in Scotland and Wales did the action of councils involve a breach of the law, and it was for my Cabinet colleagues in the Scottish and Welsh departments to deal with the consequences of that rather than for me. But there was no doubt where the blame for it all was felt to lie. The campaign against me reached something of a climax in November 1971 when the *Sun* voted me 'The Most Unpopular Woman in Britain'.

I learned a valuable lesson. I had incurred the maximum of political odium for the minimum of political benefit. I and my colleagues were caught up in battles with local authorities for months, during which we suffered constant sniping in the media, all for a saving of £9 million which could have been cut from the capital budget with scarcely a ripple. In future if I were to be hanged, it would be for a sheep, not a lamb, still less a cow.

The image which my opponents and the press had painted of me as callously attacking the welfare of young children was one which, as someone who was never happier than in children's company, I found deeply wounding. But any politician who wants to hold high office must be prepared to go through something like this. Some are broken by it, others strengthened. Denis, always the essence of common sense, came through magnificently. If I survived, it was due to his love and support. I later developed the habit of not poring over articles and profiles in the newspapers about myself. I came to rely instead on briefings and summaries. If what the press wrote was false, I could ignore it; and if it was true, I already knew it.

Throughout 1971 as the assault on me was being mounted over the issue of school milk, I was locked in battle within the Cabinet on public spending. It was politically vital to my argument about school meals and milk that the primary school building programme should go ahead as envisaged. So within the department I rejected early suggestions of compromise with the Treasury budget cutters. In a note to Bill Pile in April 1971 I laid down our last-ditch position: 'We cannot settle for less than last year in real terms.'

I could not reach agreement with Maurice Macmillan, then Chief Secretary, and so appealed, as any Cabinet minister has a right to do, to Cabinet. But I was then irritated to learn that No. 10 had decided that I would not be allowed to put in a paper. I wrote a sharply worded letter to Ted pointing out the pressures I was under to announce the 1973/74 school building programme.

I won his agreement to put in my paper in June 1971 – and I got my way. At Cabinet later that month I succeeded in obtaining almost everything that I wanted for the school building programme. It was just in time to announce to the annual conference of the Association of Education Committees in Eastbourne and prompted such headlines as 'Record Programme to Improve Old Primary Schools'.

On my arrival at the DES, that really had been *the* priority for me. Because of it, I had to make (or at least accept) spending decisions which made life extraordinarily difficult. I felt that in the 1970s it was wrong for schools still to have leaky roofs, primitive equipment and outside lavatories. Moreover, now that the demographic 'bulge' of primary-school-age children had more or less been accommodated – the peak was in 1973 – there was some financial leeway to improve the quality of the often very old and gloomy schools which had been kept in use.

Whether or not the acclaim for my defence of the primary school building programme was justified, it soon faded away as a new agitation over the financing of student unions got under way. Unlike the controversy over school milk, this was largely a campaign organized by the hard Left. It was, therefore, less politically dangerous. But it was very vicious. Nor was it just directed against me. My daughter Carol, reading Law at University College, London, also had a hard time.

In both Europe and the United States this was the height of the period of 'student revolution'. Looking back, it is extraordinary that so much notice should have been taken of the kindergarten Marxism and egocentric demands which characterized it. In part, it was a development of that youth cult of the 1960s whereby the young were regarded as a source of pure insight into the human condition. In response, many students accordingly expected their opinions to be treated with reverence.

The Left had managed to gain control of many student unions, and therefore of the public money which financed them, using this position to mount campaigns of disruption which infuriated ordinary taxpayers and even many students who simply wanted to study. There were two aspects: first, the financing of student bodies, and second what those bodies did. On the first, the main source of money for student unions was subscriptions out of mandatory grants received from their local education authorities. Union membership was normally obligatory and the union subscription was then paid direct to the student union. Some student unions took advantage of this to spend the revenue on partisan purposes, often in defiance of both their constitution and the wishes of their members.

In July 1971 I put proposals to the Home and Social Affairs Committee of the Cabinet (HS) for reform. I proposed that in future the union subscription should not be included in the fees payable to colleges and universities. The student maintenance grant would be increased slightly to enable students to join particular clubs or societies on a voluntary basis. Responsibility for providing student union facilities would then be placed on each academic institution. The facilities of each union would be open to all students, whether or not they were members of the union. Besides dealing with the question of accountability for public money, these changes would also abolish the closed-shop element in student unions which I found deeply objectionable on grounds of principle. HS was not prepared to go along with my proposals immediately, but I came back to the argument, fully recognizing how controversial they would be, and gained the Committee's approval.

Bill Van Straubenzee was the minister directly responsible for dealing with consultations on the proposals. But I was the one immediately marked down as the hate-figure to be targeted for them. In early November in Leeds, where I was laying a stone to mark the construction of new buildings, about 500 students tried to shout me down. Later that month 2,000 screaming students tried to prevent my presenting the designation document of the South Bank Polytechnic at the Queen Elizabeth Hall. A dozen mounted police had to protect my car. In December the student protesters found time from their studies to organize a nationwide day of protest. My effigy was burnt at various universities.

By now many of the Vice-Chancellors and college authorities were giving tacit approval to the protests. Edward Boyle even addressed a mass meeting of students at Leeds to declare his opposition to my proposals. Since these had only been put out for consultation it was perfectly possible to allow tempers to cool and to delay action, which I did. The main problem was that until university authorities themselves were prepared to uphold the values of a university and exert some authority, no proposal for reform was likely to succeed. This was also the time when freedom of speech began to be denied by groups of students, who were then indulged by nervous university authorities. University intolerance was at its most violent in the early seventies. But, less visible and more institutionalized, the same censorship continues today.

Nineteen seventy-one had been a crucial year for the Government and for me personally. The pressures which mounted were all the more intolerable because they were cumulative. As I shall describe, the Government's self-confidence broke in early 1972. Somehow, although under greater strain than at any time before or since, my own held.

But a number of commentators, with varying mixtures of relish and regret, thought that I was done for. On my return after the Christmas holiday at Lamberhurst, I was able to read my fate openly discussed in the newspapers. One described me as 'The Lady Nobody Loves'. Another published a thoughtful article entitled 'Why Mrs Thatcher is so Unpopular'. But I pushed the stuff aside and concentrated on my red boxes.

In fact, it was not long before the tide – for me personally, though not for the Government – began to turn. The far more serious issues of 1972 were now upon us – the miners' strike and the various elements of the U-turn – and these dwarfed the personal campaign against me. And, of course, I was evidently not going to buckle or depart – at least voluntarily. But I owe a debt of gratitude to Ted Heath as well.

Ted asked me and my officials down to Chequers on Wednesday 12 January to have a general discussion about education. I took with me an *aide-mémoire* summing up the situation and looking ahead. In spite of all the difficulties, there was only one pre-election commitment which still remained to be implemented: the expansion of nursery education. More money was needed if something substantial was to be achieved. The other area was secondary school organization. There the problem was, as I put it, 'many of our own local councils are running with the comprehensive tide. The question is what sort of balance should be struck between defending existing grammar schools and leaving local education authorities free to make their own decisions?' We discussed both these points at Chequers. Ted was keen on nursery education; he had been pressing for action on student unions; and he very reasonably asked whether we could not use educational arguments in justifying our policy on selection, rather than just resting on the arguments about local authority autonomy.

From my point of view, however, at least as important as the discussion was the fact that by inviting me down with my officials Ted implied that there was no intention to move me from Education in the foreseeable future. This was a vital reinforcement for my authority. Ted went on a few days later in the House to list my achievements. Why did he give me such strong support? Some felt that he needed a woman in the Cabinet and it was difficult to find a credible alternative candidate. But I like to think that it also showed Ted's character at its admirable best. He knew that the policies for which I had been so roundly attacked were essentially policies which I had reluctantly accepted under pressure from the Treasury and the requirements of public finance. He also knew that I had not tried to shift the blame onto others. However unreliable his adherence to particular policies, he always stood by people who did their best for him and his Government. This was one of the better reasons why his Cabinet reciprocated by remaining united behind him.

From the spring of 1972 the chilly political climate in which I had been living began noticeably to thaw.

It was, however, the Education White Paper, published in December 1972, which restored the fortunes of our education policy. The decision to publish it stemmed from discussions of the three Programme Analysis and Review (PAR) Reports which we had prepared in the department.* *Education: A Framework for Advance* was the original suggested title but, in a change which appears in retrospect to be all too typical of these over-ambitious, high-spending years, this became *Education: A Framework for Expansion*. The White Paper set out a ten-year plan for higher spending and better provision.

The White Paper received a disconcertingly rapturous reception. The *Daily Telegraph*, although making some criticisms about the lack of proposals for student loans or vouchers, said that the White Paper established me 'as one of our most distinguished reforming – and spending – Ministers of Education'. The *Daily Mail* described it as a 'Quiet Revolution' and commented, 'there has been nothing like it since the war'. More unsettling was the *Guardian*'s praise for a 'progressive programme' and the comment – I hoped tongue in cheek – that 'apart from not mandatorily ending 11-Plus segregation, Mrs Thatcher is more than halfway towards a respectably socialist education policy'.

With the exception of some vigorous exchanges with Labour's new and highly articulate Education spokesman, Roy Hattersley, about the rate of increase of education expenditure, the early months of 1973 were as near as any at the DES to being quiet. But the consequences of the Government's fiscal and monetary policies were shortly to catch up with us. The first instalment was in May – a round of public expenditure cuts designed to cool the overheated economy. Capital spending in education, particularly the less politically sensitive area of higher education, was an obvious target. The reduction in the DES budget for 1974/75 was £182 million – out of £1,200 million total cuts in public spending. But I did manage for the time being to salvage the nursery school programme and also building programmes for special schools.

By now, however, my mind was fast focusing on the cataclysmic events overtaking the Government. It was not long before I would have to mount my soapbox and defend the policies I had pursued in my years at Education. I found no difficulty in doing so, for on almost every front the record was one of advance. And if the measures by which 'advance' at this time was assessed – resources committed rather than results achieved –

---

* The PAR system was a characteristic innovation of the Heath Government – an ambitious attempt to review existing departmental programmes with the professed intention of radically reducing the role of government, but with little or no effect.

are accepted, it was also a record of genuine improvement. Nearly 2,000 out-of-date primary schools in England and Wales were replaced or improved. There was a substantial expansion of nursery education. I pushed through the raising of the school leaving age, which the Labour Party had had to postpone. Fewer pupils were now taught in very large classes. There were more qualified teachers and more students in higher education. But too much of my time at Education had been spent arguing about structures and resources, too little in addressing the crucial issue of the *contents* of education.

Equally, it was clear by the time of the general election that both the figures and, more fundamentally, the approach of *A Framework for Expansion* had been bypassed by events. There was no way that a programme of universal nursery education was affordable. Schools would have to make do with leaky roofs for many more years, until declining pupil numbers and school closures allowed resources to be better used. The Robbins Report principle – that 'courses of higher education should be available for all those qualified by ability and attain-ment to pursue them' (paragraph 31) – would have to take second place to the demands of financial stringency.

However frustrating it was to watch the shrinkage of my cherished plans and programmes, I can now see that it was unavoidable. And it may have had the side effect of forcing us to think creatively about how to get the best value from our suddenly limited resources. In the economic sphere, the crises of 1973 to 1976 led to a deep scepticism about the value of Keynesian demand management and to a new appreciation of the clas-sical liberal economic approach of balanced budgets, low taxes and free markets. Similarly, in education and in other areas of social policy too, the realization that remedies must be found other than increased public expenditure opened up a whole new world. Fundamental questions began to be asked about whether the education system in its present form could deliver the results expected of it. Did it not in practice largely exist for the benefit of those who ran it, rather than those who received it? Was the state doing too much, rather than too little? What did the – often superior – results of other countries' education systems and methods have to teach us? It was becoming necessary to rethink these policies; and we were shortly to be granted plenty of time to think.

CHAPTER SEVEN

No End of a Lesson

The Heath Government 1970–1974

S HORTLY BEFORE 11 O'CLOCK on Tuesday 23 June 1970 my new ministerial car dropped me in Downing Street, where with other colleagues I ran the gauntlet of press and television outside No. 10. The hubbub in the ante-room was of enthusiasm and laughter. There was a spring in our step as we filed into the Cabinet Room where Ted Heath, with the Cabinet Secretary Sir Burke Trend beside him, awaited us. I found my place at the Cabinet table, but my mind was at least as much on the department as on the large strategic issues before the Government. It remained there – perhaps excessively so. But I felt an exhilaration which was prompted by more than the fact that this was my first ever Cabinet meeting: I felt, as I suspect we all did, that this was a decisive moment in the life of the country.

It was an impression which Ted himself did everything to justify. Speaking with the same intensity which had suffused his introduction to the manifesto on which we had just fought the election, he announced his intention of establishing a new style of administration. The emphasis was to be upon deliberation and the avoidance of hasty or precipitate reactions. There was to be a clean break and a fresh start and new brooms galore.

The tone was just what we would all have expected from Ted. He had a great belief in the capacity of open-minded politicians to resolve fundamental problems if the processes and structures of government were right and advice of the right technical quality was available and properly used. This was the approach which would lie behind the decision that autumn to set up the Central Policy Review Staff under Victor

Rothschild, to reconstruct the machinery of government on more 'rational' lines (including the setting up of the mammoth Department of the Environment) and the establishment of the PAR system. More generally, it inspired what turned out to be an excessive confidence in the Government's ability to shape and control events.

Inevitably, this account contains a large measure of hindsight. I was not a member of the key Economic Policy Committee (EPC) of the Cabinet, though I would sometimes attend if teachers' pay or spending on schools was an issue. More frequently, I attended Terence Higgins's sub-committee on pay when the full rigours of a detailed statutory prices and incomes policy – the policy our manifesto pledged us to avoid – were applied, and made some contributions there. And, naturally, I was not a member of Ted's inner circle where most of the big decisions originated. The role of the Cabinet itself was generally of reduced importance after the first year of the Heath Government until its very end.

This, however, is said in explanation not exculpation. As a member of the Cabinet I must take my full share of responsibility for what was done under the Government's authority. Reviewing the events of this period with the benefit of two decades' hindsight I can see more clearly how Ted Heath, whether right or wrong, took the course he did. And as time went on, he *was* wrong, not just once but repeatedly. His errors – our errors, for we went along with them – did huge harm to the Conservative Party and to the country. But it is easy to comprehend the pressures upon him.

It is also important to remember that the policies Ted pursued between the spring of 1972 and February 1974 were urged on him by most influential commentators and for much of the time enjoyed a wide measure of public support. There were brave and far-sighted critics who were proved right. But they were an embattled, isolated group. Although my reservations steadily grew, I was not at this stage among them.

But some of us (though never Ted, I fear) learned from these mistakes. I can well understand how after I became Leader of the Conservative Party Enoch Powell, who with a small number of other courageous Tory backbenchers had protested at successive U-turns, claimed that: 'If you are looking for somebody to pick up principles trampled in the mud, the place to look is not among the tramplers.'

But Enoch was wrong. In Rudyard Kipling's words, Keith Joseph and I had 'had no end of a lesson':

Let us admit it fairly, as a business people should;
We have had no end of a lesson; it will do us no end of good.*

In this sense, we owed our later successes to our inside knowledge and to our understanding of the earlier failures. The Heath Government showed, in particular, that socialist policies pursued by Tory politicians are if anything even more disastrous than socialist policies pursued by Labour politicians. Collectivism, without even the tincture of egalitarian idealism to redeem it, is a deeply unattractive creed.

How did it happen? In spite of the acclaim for the Selsdon Park manifesto, we had thought through our policies a good deal less thoroughly than appeared. In particular that was true of our economic policy. We had no clear theory of inflation or the role of wage settlements within it. And without such a theory we drifted into the superstition that inflation was the direct result of wage increases and the power of trade unions. So we were pushed inexorably along the path of regulating incomes and prices.

Ted was also impatient. I share this characteristic. I am often impatient with people. But I knew that, in a broader sense, patience is required if a policy for long-term change is to work. This is especially true if, like Ted's Government in 1970 and mine in 1979, you are committed to a non-interventionist economic policy that relies on setting a framework rather than designing a plan. Sudden shifts of direction, taken because the results are too long in appearing, can have devastating effects in undermining the credibility of the strategy. And so a government which came to power proud of its principle and consistency left behind it, among other embarrassing legacies, a host of quips about 'the U-turn'. Ted's own words in his introduction to the 1970 manifesto came back to haunt him:

> Once a decision is made, once a policy is established, the Prime Minister and his colleagues should have the courage to stick to it. Nothing has done Britain more harm in the world than the endless backing and filling which we have seen in recent years.

At another level, however – the level of day-to-day human experience in government – the explanation of what happened is to be found in the forces which buffeted us and in our reactions to them. We thought we

---

* 'The Lesson' (1902). The lesson in question was the Boer War, in which Britain had suffered many military reverses.

were well enough prepared to face these. But we were not. Little by little we were blown off course until eventually, in a fit of desperation, we tore up the map, threw the compass overboard and, sailing under new colours but with the same helmsman, still supremely confident of his navigational sense, set off towards unknown and rock-strewn waters.

The squalls began early. Within weeks of taking office the Government had been forced to declare a State of Emergency* as a national docks strike began to bite. At the same time a Court of Inquiry was set up to find an expensive solution. Although the strike evaporated within a fortnight, it was an ambiguous triumph.

The following month the crisis was international. On Sunday 6 September terrorists from the Popular Front for the Liberation of Palestine (PFLP) hijacked four aircraft (none of them British) and demanded that they be flown to Jordan. Three of the hijacks were successful, but on the fourth – an Israeli plane en route to London – the hijackers were overpowered by security men. The surviving terrorist, Leila Khalid, was arrested at Heathrow.

The PFLP demanded her release, and just before Cabinet met on Wednesday 9 September they hijacked a British aircraft in order to bring more pressure to bear. The plane was flying to Beirut as we met. It was explained to Cabinet that we had already acquiesced in an American suggestion to offer the release of Leila Khalid in return for the freedom of the hostages. Over the next few weeks Cabinet discussed the question many times as negotiations ran on. Meanwhile, Jordan fell into a state of civil war as King Hussein fought the Palestinians for control of his country and the Syrians invaded and occupied much of the north. Ted resisted any British involvement on the King's side and was certain that we were right to negotiate with the PFLP. Though it went against the grain to release Khalid, in the end the deal was made. In due course all the hostages were released, though the hijacked aircraft were blown up by the terrorists, and King Hussein survived the events of 'Black September' – barely but triumphantly.

---

* A State of Emergency may be proclaimed by the Crown – effectively by ministers – whenever a situation arises which threatens to deprive the community of the essentials of life by disrupting the supply and distribution of food, water, fuel or light, or communications. It gives Government extensive powers to make regulations to restore these necessities. Troops may be used. If Parliament is not sitting when the proclamation is made, it must be recalled within five days. A State of Emergency expires at the end of one month, but may be extended.

But by then the Government had already suffered a blow from which, perhaps, we never fully recovered. In mid-July Iain Macleod had gone into hospital for a small abdominal operation. It had been a success and he had returned to No. 11 for a few days' rest. At about midnight on Monday 20 July my telephone rang. It was Francis Pym, the Chief Whip. Iain had suffered a heart attack that evening and had just died. He was only fifty-six.

I felt the blow personally, for Iain had always been a generous and kind man for whom to work. But I also immediately recognized that we had lost our shrewdest political intellect and best communicator. How Iain would have performed as Chancellor I do not know. But if one accepts that the worst mistakes of economic policy derived from Ted's overruling the Treasury, it is reasonable to suppose that matters might have turned out better if Iain had lived. He was succeeded by Tony Barber, a man of considerable intellectual ability, who by and large had an unhappy time at the Treasury. The economic problems of the next few years were founded in this transition.

The Cabinet which met after Iain Macleod's death was a sombre one. Around the Cabinet table already sat nearly all of those who would be my colleagues over the next four and a half years. Their personal qualities would be severely tested. Tony Barber was an old if not particularly close friend from the Bar, an able tax lawyer, but not someone to stand up against Ted. Reggie Maudling, Home Secretary until his resignation over the Poulson affair in 1972,* was still interested in and had strong views about economic policy. By contrast, he was less than fascinated by his new brief. He was unlikely to oppose any shift back towards a more interventionist economic policy, which indeed he had always favoured.

Alec Douglas-Home had returned effortlessly to his old Foreign Office brief where, however, plenty of effort was soon required in giving effect to our promises made in Opposition to lift the arms embargo on South Africa and in trying to devise an affordable way of retaining a British military presence east of Suez. He was unlikely to take much part in domestic political affairs now. Quintin Hailsham had found his ideal role as Lord Chancellor, beginning a long spell in that office under Ted and then me, where he managed to combine his old sense of mischief and

---

* John Poulson was an architect convicted in 1974 of making corrupt payments to win contracts. A number of local government figures also went to jail. Reggie Maudling had served on the board of one of Poulson's companies.

theatre with the sedate traditions of the Upper House. Peter Carrington was Defence Secretary, a post for which he was well suited and which he filled with aplomb. I knew that he was close to Ted. He doubtless became still closer when later as Party Chairman and Energy Secretary he had a crucial role in dealing with the final miners' strike which precipitated the general election of February 1974. He was one of Ted's 'inner circle'.

Keith Joseph, by contrast, though a senior Cabinet figure and someone whose views had always to be taken seriously, was certainly not part of that circle and was never, so far as I know, invited to join it. Having been appointed to be Secretary of State for Social Services, Keith's compassionate, social reforming side had become uppermost at the expense of his more conservative economic convictions, though he retained a profound distrust of corporatism in all its forms. His passion became the need to tackle the problem of the 'cycle of deprivation' which condemned successive generations to poverty. Like me, Keith had been given a high-spending 'social' department, and there was a natural opposition between what he (also like me) wanted for his own preferred programmes and the requirements of tight public expenditure control. Whether by chance or calculation, Ted had ensured that the two most economically conservative members of his Cabinet were kept well out of economic decision-making, which was left to those over whom he could wield maximum influence.

John Davies, the former Director-General of the Confederation of British Industry (CBI) (who knew nothing of politics when he was summoned after Iain Macleod's death to become Minister of Technology), certainly fell into that category. John was someone I liked, but his warmest admirer would have been hard put to make a case for his handling of the turbulent industrial politics which would now become his responsibility. John also represented 'business', a concept which Ted, with his latent corporatism, considered had some kind of 'role' in government.

With Tony Barber and John Davies, Robert Carr was, as Employment Secretary, the third key figure responsible for economic strategy under Ted. He was a good deal senior to me and we had different views and temperaments. He was a decent, hard-working though not a colourful personality. But he had a difficult, arguably impossible, brief in trying to make the flawed Industrial Relations Act work. His reputation as a left winger in Conservative terms was less useful than some might have expected; trade unionists used to regard left-wing Conservatives not as more compassionate but merely as less candid. As Employment Secretary at the time of the first (1972) miners' strike and Home Secretary at the time of the second (1974), few people faced greater difficulties during these years.

One who did was Willie Whitelaw as, successively, Leader of the House, Northern Ireland Secretary and finally Employment Secretary at the time of the three-day week. We seemed to have little in common and neither of us, I am sure, suspected how closely our political destinies would come to be linked. Since Education was not a department requiring at this time a heavy legislative programme, our paths rarely crossed. But I was already aware of Willie as a wise, reassuring figure whose manner, voice and stature made him an excellent Leader of the House. Willie's bluff public persona, however, concealed a shrewd political intelligence and instinct for managing men.

After Iain Macleod's untimely death, Geoffrey Rippon was given responsibility for negotiating the terms of our entry into the European Economic Community. Although we had superficially similar backgrounds, Geoffrey and I were never close. It always seemed to me that he tried to overwhelm opponents with the force of his personality rather than with the force of his argument. This may have been because Ted had given him the task of getting the best deal he could in negotiations with the EEC – and that deal was not always in our best long-term interests.

My impression was that the two members of Cabinet Ted trusted most were Jim Prior and Peter Walker. Both had proved their loyalty, Jim as Ted's PPS in Opposition, and Peter as organizer of his 1965 leadership campaign. Jim was Agriculture minister, a post which his farming background and rubicund features helped him make his own, before becoming Deputy Chairman of the Party under Peter Carrington in April 1972. Peter Walker's thirst for the 'modernization' of British institutions must have helped draw him closer to Ted. He soon became Secretary of State for the huge new Department of the Environment, where he embarked with vigour upon the most unpopular local government reforms until my own Community Charge – and at the cost of far greater bureaucracy. Later he would go to the other conglomerate, the Department of Trade and Industry (DTI). Jim and, still more so, Peter were younger than me, but both had far more influence over the general direction of government. Although their political views were very different from mine, I respected their loyalty to Ted and their political effectiveness.

The other members of Cabinet – Gordon Campbell at Scotland, George Jellicoe as Lord Privy Seal and Leader of the Lords, Peter Thomas, a close parliamentary neighbour and friend, as Secretary of State for Wales and Party Chairman, and Michael Noble briefly at Trade – did not figure large in discussions. I therefore found myself with just one political friend in Cabinet – Keith.

But for all the difficulties which were quickly upon us that summer and autumn of 1970, such melancholy reflections were still far from our thoughts. Indeed, Ted Heath, Tony Barber, Robert Carr and John Davies set out on the course of radical reform with impressive zeal; and the rest of us in the Cabinet were enthusiastic cheerleaders.

First, the Government embarked with a will on cutting public spending. Discussions began at the end of July. A target was agreed of £1,700 million net reduction in planned spending by 1974/75, and Ted circulated a paper on the economy to show his commitment to the strategy. The cuts were to fall most heavily on industrial spending, though as already noted I had my own departmental spending battles at Education. Investment grants were ended. The Industrial Re-organization Corporation (IRC) would be closed down. Aircraft and space projects would be subject to the closest scrutiny. Even with the reprieve of the hugely expensive Concorde project, largely on European policy grounds, it was an impressive free-market economic programme. And it made possible a tax-cutting budget in October, which reduced the standard rate of income tax by 6d, down from 8s.3d in the pound (just over 41p), and made reductions in corporation tax to take effect at the beginning of the next financial year.

Nor was there any delay in bringing forward the other key feature of our economic programme – the Industrial Relations Bill. The framework of the Bill was already familiar: this was one of the areas of policy most thoroughly worked out in Opposition and we had published our proposals in 1968. The main principles were that collective bargaining agreements should be legally enforceable unless the parties to them agreed otherwise, and that the unions' historic immunities from civil action should be significantly narrowed and confined to those whose rule books met certain minimum standards ('registered unions').

Cases brought under this legislation would be dealt with by a new system of industrial courts and tribunals, headed by a branch of the High Court – the National Industrial Relations Court (NIRC). The Bill also gave new powers to the Secretary of State for Employment, when negotiation had failed, to apply to the NIRC either for an order deferring industrial action for up to sixty days – a 'cooling off' period – or for one requiring a secret ballot of the workers involved before a strike.

There was a good deal in the Bill that actively favoured trade unionism, for all the hostility it encountered on the Left. For the first time in English law there would be a legally enforceable right to belong (or not to belong) to a trade union. There would be statutory protection against unfair dismissal. Finally, the Bill would repeal provisions that made it a criminal offence for gas, water and electricity workers to strike during the lifetime of their contracts.

At the time I was a strong supporter of the Bill, although I had doubts about particular parts, such as the measure on essential services. We were all conscious that the previous Labour Government had backed off from its *In Place of Strife* proposals for trade union reform under a mixture of union and Party pressure. We were, therefore, doubly determined to make the changes required.

In retrospect, the philosophy of the Bill was muddled. It assumed that if the unions were in general confirmed in their powers they would discipline their members industrially, reducing wildcat strikes for instance, and use their industrial strength in a regulated and orderly fashion. But it also contained provisions to strengthen the powers of individuals against the unions. So the Bill was in part corporatist and in part libertarian.

Finally, we naively assumed that our opponents would play by the same rules as we did. In particular, we imagined that there would not be either mass opposition to laws passed by a democratically elected government or mass infringement of the criminal law, as in the miners' strike of 1972. We did not recognize that we were involved in a struggle with unscrupulous people whose principal objectives lay not in industrial relations but in politics. It was later, as Leader of the Opposition, that I realized how far the extreme Left had penetrated into trade union leaderships and why that 'giant's strength', of which the Tory pamphlet had spoken in the late 1950s, was now being used in such a ruthless manner. The communists knew that they could not be returned to Parliament, so they chose to advance their cause by getting into office in the trade union movement. And the fact that both the Wilson and Heath Governments had stood up to the unions and then lost, increased their influence more than if we had not challenged their power in the first place.

But at this early stage we pressed ahead. The TUC was told by Robert Carr in October 1970 that the central aspects of the Industrial Relations Bill were not negotiable. The Bill had its Second Reading in December. February and March 1971 saw mass protests and strikes against it. Labour used every device to fight the Bill, but in August 1971 it duly reached the

Statute Book. The TUC Congress passed a resolution instructing unions to de-register. It therefore remained to be seen, when the Act came into force at the end of February 1972, what its practical effects would be – revolution, reform or business as usual. We were soon to find out.

Meanwhile other problems preoccupied us. It is sometimes suggested – and was at the time by Enoch Powell – that the Government's decision in February 1971 to take control of the aerospace division of Rolls-Royce marked the first U-turn. This is not so. Shortly before the company told the Government of the impossible financial problems it faced (as a result of the escalating cost of the contract with Lockheed to build the RB-211 engine for its Tri-star aircraft), a constituent of mine had told me that he was worried about the company. So I asked Denis to look at the figures. I arrived home late one evening to find him surrounded by six years' accounts. He told me that Rolls-Royce had been treating research and development costs as capital, rather than charging it to the profit and loss account. This spelt real trouble.

A few days later I was suddenly called to a Cabinet meeting and found Fred Corfield, the Aviation Minister, waiting in the Cabinet ante-room. 'What are you here for, Fred?' I asked. He replied gloomily: 'Rolls-Royce.' His expression said it all. At the meeting itself we heard the full story. To the amazement of my colleagues I confirmed the analysis, based on what Denis had told me. We decided without much debate to let the company itself go into liquidation but to nationalize the aerospace division. Over the next few months we renegotiated the original contract with Lockheed, which was then itself in financial difficulties. One could argue – and people did – about the terms and the sum which needed to be provided. But I do not think any of us doubted that on defence grounds it was important to keep an indigenous aircraft engine capability. And in the long term, of course, this was one 'lame duck' which eventually found the strength to fly away again into the private sector, when I was Prime Minister.

It was to be a year before the serious economic U-turns – reflation, subsidies to industry, prices and incomes policy – occurred, and began the alienation of the Conservative right in Parliament and of many Tory supporters outside it. The failure of these U-turns to deliver success divided the Party still further and had other consequences. It created an inflationary boom which caused property prices to soar and encouraged a great deal of dubious financial speculation, tarnishing capitalism, and, in spite of all the disclaimers, the Conservative Party with it. I shall return to the economic developments which led to all this shortly. But it is important not to underrate the impact on the Party of two non-economic issues – Europe and immigration.

I was wholeheartedly in favour of British entry into the EEC, and General de Gaulle's departure from the Elysée Palace in April 1969 had transformed the prospects. His successor, Georges Pompidou, was keen to have Britain in; and no one on our side of the Channel was keener than the new Prime Minister, Ted Heath. Many people across the political spectrum opposed it. These included some of the most effective parliamentarians such as Michael Foot, Peter Shore and Enoch Powell. But the worlds of business, the media and fashionable opinion generally were strongly in favour.

Talks formally opened in Brussels at the end of October 1970, with Geoffrey Rippon reporting back to Ted and a Cabinet Committee and, on occasion, to the rest of us in full Cabinet. There was no doubt that the financial cost of entry would be high. It was estimated that the best we could hope for would be a gross British contribution of 17 per cent of total EEC expenditure, with a five-year transition, and three years of so-called 'correctives' after that (to hold it at 17 per cent). To defuse the inevitable criticism, Geoffrey Rippon also hoped to negotiate a special review provision which we could invoke at any time if the burden of our net contributions to the budget threatened to become intolerable; but he seemed to attach little significance to it, and assumed that we could reopen the question whether there was a formal review mechanism or not.

At the time Ted resolved discussion about the costs of entry by saying that no one was arguing that the burden would be so intolerable that we should break off negotiations. But this whole question of finance should have been considered more carefully. It came to dominate Britain's relations with the EEC for more than a decade, and it did not prove so easy to reopen. Though the Community made a declaration during the entry negotiations that 'should an unacceptable situation arise within the present Community or an enlarged Community, the very survival of the Community would demand that the Institutions find equitable solutions', the net British contribution quickly grew. The Labour Government of 1974–79 made no progress in reducing it. It was left to me to do so later.

Cabinet discussed the matter again in early May 1971, by which time the talks were reported to be 'deadlocked'. There were difficulties outstanding on preferential arrangements for New Zealand products (butter and lamb) and Commonwealth sugar, and shadow-boxing by the French about the role of sterling as an international currency. But the budget was still the real problem. We had an idea what deal might be on offer: promises to cut the cost of the Common Agricultural Policy and the creation of a Regional Development Fund from which Britain would benefit disproportionately. It was still not the settlement we would have wanted – promises are not bankable – but at the time none of us foresaw how large the burden would turn out to be. Ted ended the discussion by telling us that he was planning a summit with President Pompidou in Paris to cut through the argument.

Ted spent two days talking to the French President. In view of all the past difficulties with the French, the summit was seen as a veritable triumph for him. Negotiations were completed rapidly afterwards – other than for the Common Fisheries Policy, which took years to resolve – and the terms approved by Cabinet the following month. Parliamentary approval could not be assumed, for both parties were deeply split and Labour had reversed its former support for British entry. In the end, the Government decided that there would be a free vote on the Conservative side on the principle of entry. This embarrassed Labour, especially when sixty-nine Labour MPs ignored their own party whip and voted in favour, giving a majority of 112 for entry. But when it came to the terms rather than the principle of entry, the argument was far from won. The Second Reading of the European Communities Bill in February 1972 was only passed by 309 to 301.

The dog that barely barked at the time was the issue of sovereignty – both national and parliamentary – which, as the years have gone by, has assumed ever greater importance. There was some discussion of the question in Cabinet in July 1971, but only in the context of the general presentation of the case for entry in the White Paper. The resulting passages of the document – paragraphs 29–32 – can now be read in the light of events, and stand out as an extraordinary example of artful confusion to conceal fundamental issues. In particular, two sentences are masterpieces:

> There is no question of any erosion of essential national sovereignty; what is proposed is a sharing and an enlargement of individual national sovereignties in the general interest.

And:

> The common law will remain the basis of our legal system, and our
> Courts will continue to operate as they do at present.

I can claim to have had no special insight into these matters at the
time. It then seemed to me, as it did to my colleagues, that the arguments
about sovereignty advanced by Enoch Powell and others were theoretical
points used as rhetorical devices.

In the debate on Clause 2 of the Bill, Geoffrey Howe, as Solicitor-
General, gave what appeared to be satisfactory assurances on the matter
in answer to criticisms from Derek Walker-Smith, saying that 'at the end
of the day if repeal [of the European Communities Act], lock, stock and
barrel, was proposed, the ultimate sovereignty of Parliament must remain
intact'. Asking himself the question: 'What will happen if there is a future
Act of Parliament which inadvertently, to a greater or lesser extent, may
be in conflict with Community law?' Geoffrey said: 'The courts
would . . . try in accordance with the traditional approach to interpret
Statute in accordance with our international obligations.' But what if they
could not be reconciled? He went on, elliptically:

> One cannot do more than that to reconcile the inescapable and
> enduring sovereignty of Parliament at the end of the road with the
> proposition that we should give effect to our treaty obligations to
> provide for the precedence of Community law . . . If through
> inadvertence any such conflict arose, that would be a matter for
> consideration by the Government and Parliament of the day . . .*

It was not, however, this question which was to make the Common
Market such a difficult issue for the Government. The main political
error was to overplay the advantages due to come from membership. As
regards the Government itself, this tendency led ministers to adopt and
excuse unsound policies. In order to 'equip' British industry to meet the
challenges of Europe, subsidies and intervention were said to be necessary
– reasoning endorsed in the 1972 budget speech. Still worse, loose monetary and fiscal policies were justified on the grounds that high levels of
economic growth – of the order of 5 per cent or so – were now sustainable
within the new European market of some 300 million people. It was also
suggested that competition from Europe would compel the trade unions

---

* *Hansard*, 13 June 1972; Volume 838, columns 1319–20.

to act more responsibly. As regards the general public, expectations of the benefits of membership rose – and then were sharply dashed as economic conditions deteriorated and industrial disruption worsened.

The success of the negotiations for British entry and their ratification by Parliament seemed to have a psychological effect on Ted Heath. His enthusiasm for Europe had already developed into a passion. As the years went by it was to become an obsession – one increasingly shared by the great and the good. The argument became less and less about what was best for Britain and more and more about the importance of being good Europeans.

January and February 1972 saw three events which tried the Government's resolve and found it wanting – the miners' strike, the financial problems of Upper Clyde Shipbuilders (UCS) and the unemployment total reaching one million. It is always a shock when unemployment reaches a new high figure, especially one as dramatic as a million. But the rise of unemployment in 1971 was in fact the consequence of Roy Jenkins's tight fiscal and monetary policies of 1969–70. Since monetary policy had already been significantly eased in 1971, largely as a result of financial decontrol, we could have sat tight and waited for it to work through in lower unemployment from 1972 onwards. In fact, Ted never bought this analysis, and he greatly underestimated the stimulating effects of removing credit controls. He felt that emergency fiscal measures were necessary to boost demand and reduce unemployment. And this conviction influenced his decisions across the board. Ironically, because it led to higher inflation whose main effects were suffered under the following Labour Government, and because inflation destroys jobs rather than preserves them, it ultimately led to higher unemployment as well.

In particular, the approach of the Government to Upper Clyde Shipbuilders flowed from fear of the consequences of higher unemployment. But it was also seen as caving in to the threats of left-wing militants. When we first discussed the company's problems in December 1970 the Cabinet agreed that existing government support for the UCS Group would not be continued, though there was a lifeline: we would continue with credit guarantees so long as the management agreed to close the Clydebank yard and separate Yarrow Shipbuilders from the rest of the group. Yarrow – an important Royal Navy supplier – seemed salvageable. But by June 1971 the UCS Group was insolvent and its liquidation was announced. There followed a protest strike on Clydeside. In July trade unionists occupied the four UCS shipyards.

There was further discussion in Cabinet in the autumn of 1971, and the Government allowed itself to be sucked into talks with the trade unions, who it was believed might be able to influence the militant shop stewards behind the occupation. The Economic Committee of the Cabinet had agreed that money should be provided to keep open the yards while the liquidator sought a solution, but only on condition that the unions gave credible undertakings of serious negotiations on new working practices. There was strong criticism of this from some of my colleagues, rightly alert to the danger of seeming to give in on the basis of worthless undertakings. But the money was provided and negotiations went ahead.

It was the unemployment prospect rather than the prospects for shipbuilding which by now were undisguisedly foremost. In November Ted Heath affirmed in a Party Political Broadcast that the 'Government is committed completely and absolutely to expanding the economy and bringing unemployment down'. The fateful one-million mark was passed on 20 January 1972. On 24 February at Cabinet we heard that the Economic Committee had agreed to provide £35 million to keep three of the four yards open. John Davies openly admitted that the new group had little chance of making its way commercially and that if the general level of unemployment had been lower and the economy reviving faster, he would not have recommended this course. There was tangible unease, but Cabinet endorsed it and at the end of February John announced the decision. It was a small but memorably inglorious episode. I discussed it privately with Jock Bruce-Gardyne, who was scathing about the decision. He regarded it as a critical, unforgivable U-turn. I was deeply troubled.

But by now we all had other things to worry about. In framing the Industrial Relations Act we had given too much emphasis to achieving the best possible legal framework and not enough to how the attacks on our proposals were to be repelled. The same mentality prevailed as regards the threat which the National Union of Mineworkers (NUM) posed to the Government and the country. We knew, of course, that the miners and the power workers held an almost unbeatable card in pay negotiations, because they could turn off the electricity supply to industry and people. Industrial action by the power workers in December 1970 had been settled after the setting up of a Court of Inquiry under Lord Wilberforce which recommended a large increase in February the following year. Within the NUM, however, there was a large militant faction at least as interested in bringing down the Conservative Government as in flexing industrial muscle to increase miners' earnings. The NUM held a strike ballot in October 1970 and narrowly turned down an offer from the National Coal Board (NCB). Fearing unofficial action, Cabinet authorized the NCB to offer a productivity bonus to be paid in mid-1971. The NUM again turned the offer down, following which Derek Ezra, the NCB Chairman, without consulting ministers, offered to pay the bonus at once and without strings attached to productivity. Cabinet accepted this *fait accompli*. Perhaps John Davies and other ministers continued to monitor events. If they did I heard nothing about it.

Only in early December 1971 did the issue of miners' pay surface at Cabinet, and then in what seemed a fairly casual way. The NUM's annual conference that year had significantly revised the rules which provided for an official strike, so that now only a 55 per cent, as opposed to a two-thirds, majority was required. The NUM ballot, which was still going on, had, it was thought, resulted in a 59 per cent majority vote for strike action. Yet nobody seemed too worried. We were all reassured that coal stocks were high.

Such complacency proved unwarranted. At the last Cabinet before Christmas Robert Carr confirmed to us that the NUM was indeed calling a national strike to begin on 9 January 1972. There was more trouble over pay in the gas and electricity industries. And we only needed to glance outside to know that winter was closing in, with all that meant for power consumption. But there was no real discussion and we all left for the Christmas break.

There was still some suggestion over Christmas that the strike might not be solid, but two days after it began it was all too clear that the action was total. There was then discussion in Cabinet about whether we should use the 'cooling off' provisions of the Industrial Relations Act. But it was said to be difficult to satisfy the legal tests involved – 'cooling off' orders would only be granted by the courts if there was a serious prospect that they would facilitate a settlement, which in this case was doubtful. The possibility of using the ballot provisions of the Act remained. But there was no particular reason to think that a ballot forced on the NUM would lead to anything other than a continuation of the strike. It was an acutely uncomfortable demonstration of the fragility of the principal weapons with which the Act had equipped us. Moreover, important parts of the Act had yet to come into force, and we were also aware that there was a good deal of public sympathy with the miners.

The pressure on the Government to intervene directly now increased. Looking back, and comparing 1972 with the threatened miners' strike of 1981 and the year-long strike of 1984–85, it is extraordinary how little attention we gave to 'endurance' – the period of time we could keep the power stations and the economy running with limited or no coal supplies – and how easily Cabinet was fobbed off by assurances that coal stocks were high, without considering whether those stocks were in the right locations to be usable, i.e. actually at the power stations. The possibility of effective mass picketing, which would prevent coal getting to power stations, was simply not on the agenda. Instead, our response was to discuss the prospects for conciliation by Robert Carr and the use of 'emergency powers' which would allow us to conserve power station stocks a few weeks longer by imposing power cuts. There was a great deal of useless talk about 'keeping public opinion on our side'. But what could public opinion do to end the strike? This was one more thing I learned from the Heath years – and anyway, on the whole public opinion *wasn't* on our side. A further lesson from this period – when no fewer than five States of Emergency were called – was that for all the sense of urgency and decision that the phrase 'emergency powers' conveys they could not be relied upon to change the basic realities of an industrial dispute.

The crunch came on the morning of Thursday 10 February when we were all in Cabinet. A State of Emergency had been declared the previous day. It was John Davies who dropped the bombshell. He told us that picketing had now immobilized a large part of the remaining coal stocks, and that the supplies still available might not even suffice beyond the end of the following week. Electricity output would fall to as little as 25 per cent of normal supply, drastic power cuts were inevitable, and large parts of industry would be laid off. The Attorney-General reported that the provisions of the Industrial Relations Act against secondary boycotts, blacking of supplies and the inducement of other workers to take action resulting in the frustration of a commercial contract, would not come into force until 28 February. He thought that most of the picketing which had taken place was lawful. As regards the criminal law, some arrests had been made but, as he put it, 'the activities of pickets confronted the police with very difficult and sensitive decisions'.

This was something of an understatement. The left-wing leader of the Yorkshire miners, Arthur Scargill, who was to organize the politically motivated miners' strike I faced in 1984–85, was already busy winning his militant's spurs. In the course of Cabinet a message came through to the

Home Secretary, Reggie Maudling. The Chief Constable of Birmingham had asked that the West Midlands Gas Board's Saltley Coke Depot be closed because lorries were being prevented from entering by 7,000 'pickets' who were facing just 500 police.

There was no disguising that this was a victory for violence.

Ted now sounded the retreat. He appointed a Court of Inquiry under the ubiquitous Lord Wilberforce. By now the power crisis had reached such proportions that we sat in Cabinet debating whether we had time to wait for the NUM to ballot its members on ending a strike; a ballot might take over a week to organize. There was therefore no inclination to quibble when Wilberforce recommended a massive pay increase, way beyond the level allowed for in the 'n-1' voluntary pay policy already in force.

But we were stunned when the militant majority on the NUM Executive rejected the court's recommendation, demanding still more money and a ragbag of other concessions.

Ted summoned us all on the evening of Friday 18 February to decide what to do. The dispute simply had to be ended quickly. If we had to go an additional mile, so be it. Later that night Ted called the NUM and the NCB to No. 10 and persuaded the union to drop the demand for more money, while conceding the rest. The NUM Executive accepted, and just over a week later so did the miners in a ballot. The dispute was over. But the devastation it had inflicted on the Government and indeed on British politics as a whole lived on.

The combination of the rise in unemployment, the events at Upper Clyde Shipbuilders and the Government's humiliation by the miners resulted in a fundamental reassessment of policy. I suspect that this took place in Ted's own mind first, with other ministers and the Cabinet very much second. It was not so much that he jettisoned the whole Selsdon approach, but rather that he abandoned some aspects of it, emphasized others and added a heavy dose of statism which probably appealed to his temperament and his continental European sympathies.

None of this pleased me. But our inability to resist trade union power was now manifest. The Industrial Relations Act itself already seemed hollow: it was soon to be discredited entirely. Like most Conservatives, I was prepared to give at least a chance to a policy which retained some of the objectives we had set out in 1969/70. I was even prepared to go along with a statutory prices and incomes policy, for a time, to try to limit the damage inflicted by the arrogant misuse of trade union power. But I was wrong. State intervention in the economy is not ultimately an answer to over-mighty vested interests: for it soon comes to collude with them.

It is unusual to hold Cabinets on a Monday, and I had a long-standing scientific engagement for Monday 20 March 1972, so I was not present at the Cabinet which discussed the budget and the new Industry White Paper. Both of them signalled a change in strategy, each complementing the other. The budget was highly reflationary, comprising large cuts in income tax and purchase tax, increased pensions and social security benefits, and extra investment incentives for industry. It was strongly rumoured that Tony Barber and the Treasury were very unhappy with the budget and that it had been imposed on them by Ted. The fact that the budget speech presented these measures as designed to help Britain meet the challenge opened up by membership of the EEC in a small way confirms this. It was openly designed to provide a large boost to demand, which it was argued would not involve a rise in inflation, in conditions of high unemployment and idle resources. Monetary policy was mentioned, but only to stress its 'flexibility'; no numerical targets for monetary growth were set.

On Wednesday 22 March John Davies published his White Paper on *Industry and Regional Development*, which was the basis for the 1972 Industry Act. This was seen by our supporters and opponents alike as an obvious U-turn. Keith and I and probably others in the Cabinet were extremely unhappy, and some of this found its way into the press. Should I have resigned? Perhaps so. But those of us who disliked what was happening had not yet worked out an alternative approach. Nor, realistically speaking, would my resignation have made a great deal of difference. I was not senior enough for it to be other than the littlest 'local difficulty'. All the more reason for me to pay tribute to people like Jock Bruce-Gardyne, John Biffen, Nick Ridley and, of course, Enoch Powell who did expose the folly of what was happening in Commons speeches and newspaper articles.

There is also a direct connection between the policies pursued from March 1972 and the very different approach of my own administration later. A brilliant, but little-known, monetary economist called Alan Walters resigned from the Central Policy Review Staff (CPRS) and delivered not only scathing criticism of the Government's approach but also accurate predictions of where it would lead.[*]

---

[*] Alan Walters became my economic adviser as Prime Minister 1981–84 and again in 1989.

One more blow to the approach we adopted in 1970 had still to fall. This was the effective destruction of the Industrial Relations Act. It had never been envisaged that the Act would result in individual trade unionists going to jail. Of course, no legal provisions can be proof against some remote possibility of that happening if troublemakers are intent on martyrdom. It was a long-running dispute between employers and dockers about 'containerization' which provided the occasion for this to happen. In March 1972 the National Industrial Relations Court (NIRC) fined the Transport and General Workers' Union (TGWU) £5,000 for defying an order to grant access to Liverpool Docks. The following month the union was fined £50,000 for contempt on the matter of secondary action at the docks. The TGWU maintained that it was not responsible for the action of its shop stewards, but the NIRC ruled against this in May. Then, out of the blue, the Court of Appeal reversed these judgments and ruled that the TGWU was *not* responsible, and so the shop stewards themselves were personally liable. This was extremely disturbing, for it opened up the possibility of trade unionists going to jail. The following month three dockers involved in blacking were threatened with arrest for refusing to appear before the NIRC; 35,000 trade unionists were now on strike. At the last moment the Official Solicitor applied to the Court of Appeal to prevent the dockers' arrest. But then in July another five dockers were jailed for contempt.

The Left were merciless. Ted was shouted down in the House. Sympathetic strikes spread, involving the closure of national newspapers for five days. The TUC called a one-day general strike. On 26 July, however, the House of Lords reversed the Court of Appeal decision and confirmed that unions were accountable for the conduct of their members. The NIRC then released the five dockers.

This was more or less the end of the Industrial Relations Act, though it was not the end of trouble in the docks. A national dock strike ensued and another State of Emergency was declared. This only ended – very much on the dockers' terms – in August. In September the TUC General Congress rubbed salt into the wound by expelling thirty-two small unions which had refused, against TUC instructions, to de-register under the Act. Having shared to the full the Party's enthusiasm for the Act, I was appalled.

In the summer of 1972 the third aspect – after reflation and industrial intervention – of the new economic approach was revealed to us. This was the pursuit of an agreement on prices and incomes through 'tripartite' talks with the CBI and the TUC. Although there had been no explicit pay policy, we had been living in a world of 'norms' since the autumn of 1970 when the 'n-1' was formulated in the hope that there would be deceleration from the 'going rate' figure in successive pay rounds. The miners' settlement had breached that policy spectacularly, but Ted drew the conclusion that we should go further rather than go back. From the summer of 1972 a far more elaborate prices and incomes policy was the aim, and more and more the centre of decision-making moved away from Cabinet and Parliament. I can only, therefore, give a partial account of the way in which matters developed. Cabinet simply received reports from Ted on what policies had effectively been decided elsewhere, though individual ministers became increasingly bogged down in the details of shifting and complicated pay negotiations. This almost obsessive interest in the minutiae of pay awards was matched by a large degree of impotence over the deals finally struck. In fact, the most important result was to distract ministers from the big economic issues and blind us with irrelevant data when we should have been looking ahead to the threats which loomed.

The period of the tripartite talks with the TUC and the CBI from early July to the end of October did not get us much further as regards the Government's aim of controlling inflation by keeping down wage demands. It did, however, move us down other slippery slopes. In exchange for the CBI's offer to secure 'voluntary' price restraint by 200 of Britain's largest firms, limiting their price increases to 5 per cent during the following year, we embarked on the costly and self-defeating policy of holding nationalized industry price increases to the same level, even though this meant that they continued to make losses. The TUC, for its part, used the role it had been accorded by the tripartite discussions to set out its own alternative economic policy. In flat contradiction to the policies we had been elected to implement, they wanted action to keep down council rents (which would sabotage our Housing Finance Act – intended to bring them closer to market levels). They urged the control of profits, dividends and prices, aimed at securing the redistribution of income and wealth (in other words, the implementation of socialism), and the repeal of the Industrial Relations Act. These demands were taken sufficiently seriously by Ted for him to agree studies of methods by which the pay of low-paid workers could be improved without entailing proportionate increases to other workers. We had, in other words, moved four-square onto the socialist ground that 'low pay' – however that might be defined

– was a 'problem' which it was for government rather than the workings of the market to resolve. In fact, the Government proposed a £2 a week limit on pay increases over the following year, with the CBI agreeing maximum 4 per cent price increases over the same period and the extension of the Government's 'target' of 5 per cent economic growth.

It was not enough. The TUC was not willing – and probably not able – to deliver wage restraint. At the end of October we had a lengthy discussion of the arguments for proceeding to a statutory policy, beginning with a pay freeze. It is an extraordinary comment on the state of mind that we had reached that, as far as I can recall, neither now nor later did anyone at Cabinet raise the objection that this was precisely the policy we had ruled out in our 1970 general election manifesto. Only with the greatest reluctance did Ted accept that the TUC were unpersuadable. And so on Friday 3 November 1972 Cabinet made the fateful decision to introduce a statutory policy beginning with a ninety-day freeze of prices and incomes. No one ever spoke a truer word than Ted when he concluded by warning that we faced a troubled prospect.

The change in economic policy was accompanied by a Cabinet reshuffle. Maurice Macmillan – Harold's son – had already taken over at Employment from Robert Carr in July 1972, when the latter replaced Reggie Maudling at the Home Office. Ted now promoted his younger disciples. He sent Peter Walker to replace John Davies at the DTI and promoted Jim Prior to be Leader of the House. Geoffrey Howe, an instinctive economic liberal, was brought into the Cabinet but given the poisoned chalice of overseeing prices and incomes policy.

For a growing number of backbenchers the new policy was a U-turn too far. When Enoch Powell asked in the House whether the Prime Minister had 'taken leave of his senses', he was publicly cold-shouldered, but many privately agreed with him. Still more significant was the fact that staunch opponents of our policy like Nick Ridley, Jock Bruce-Gardyne and John Biffen were elected to chairmanships or vice-chairmanships of important backbench committees, and Edward du Cann, on the right of the Party and a sworn opponent of Ted, became Chairman of the 1922 Committee.

As the freeze – Stage 1 – came to an end we devised Stage 2. This extended the pay and price freeze until the end of April 1973; for the remainder of 1973 workers could expect £1 a week and 4 per cent, with a maximum pay rise of £250 a year – a formula designed to favour the low-paid. A Pay Board and a Prices Commission were set up to administer the policy. Our backbench critics were more perceptive than most commentators, who considered that all this was a sensible and pragmatic response to trade union irresponsibility. In the early days it seemed that the commentators were right. A challenge to the policy by the gas workers was defeated at the end of March. The miners – as we hoped and expected after their huge increase the previous year – rejected a strike (against the advice of their Executive) in a ballot on 5 April. The number of working days lost because of strikes fell sharply. Unemployment was at its lowest since 1970. Generally, the mood in government grew more relaxed. Ted clearly felt happier wearing his new collectivist hat than he ever had in the disguise of Selsdon.

Our sentiments should have been very different. The effects of the reflationary budget of March 1972 and the loose financial policy it typified were now becoming apparent. The Treasury, at least, had started to worry about the economy, which was growing at a clearly unsustainable rate of well over 5 per cent. The money supply, as measured by M3 (broad money), was growing too fast – though the (narrower) M1, which the Government preferred, less so.* The March 1973 budget did nothing to cool the overheating and was heavily distorted by the need to keep down prices and charges so as to support the 'counter-inflation policy', as the prices and incomes policy was hopefully called. In May modest public expenditure reductions were agreed. But it was too little, and far too late. Although inflation rose during the first six months of 1973, Minimum Lending Rate (MLR) was steadily cut and a temporary mortgage subsidy was introduced. The Prime Minister also ordered that preparations be made to take statutory control of the mortgage rate if the building societies failed to hold it down when the subsidy ended. These fantastic proposals only served to distract us from the need to tackle the growing problem of monetary laxity. Only in July was MLR raised from 7.5 per cent, first to 9 per cent and then to 11.5 per cent. We were actually ahead of Labour in the opinion polls in June 1973, for the first time since 1970. But in July the Liberals took Ely and Ripon from us at by-elections. Economically and politically we had already begun to reap the whirlwind.

Over the summer of 1973 Ted held more talks with the TUC, seeking their agreement to Stage 3. The detailed work was done by a group of

---

* M1 comprised the total stock of money held in cash and in current and deposit accounts at a particular point in time; M3 included the whole of M1, with the addition of certain other types of bank accounts, including those held in currencies other than sterling.

ministers chaired by Ted, and the rest of us knew little about it. Nor did I know that close attention was already being given to the problem which might arise with the miners. Like most of my colleagues, I imagine, I believed that they had had their pound of flesh already and would not come back for more.

I hope, though, that I would have given a great deal more attention than anyone seems to have done to building up coal stocks against the eventuality, however remote, of another miners' strike. The miners either had to be appeased or beaten. Yet, for all its technocratic jargon, this was a government which signally lacked a sense of strategy. Ted apparently felt no need of one since, as we now know, he had held a secret meeting with the miners' President, Joe Gormley, in the garden of No. 10 and thought he had found a formula to square the miners – extra payment for 'unsocial hours'. But this proved to be a miscalculation. The miners' demands could not be accommodated within Stage 3.

In October Cabinet duly endorsed the Stage 3 White Paper. It was immensely complicated and represented the high point – if that is the correct expression – of the Heath Government's collectivism. All possible eventualities, you might have thought, were catered for. But as experience of past pay policies ought to have demonstrated, you would have been wrong.

My only direct involvement in the working of this new, detailed pay policy was when I attended the relevant Cabinet Economic Sub-Committee, usually chaired by Terence Higgins, a Treasury Minister of State. Even those attracted by the concept of incomes policy on grounds of 'fairness' begin to have their doubts when they see its provisions applied to individual cases. My visits to the Higgins Committee were usually necessitated by questions of teachers' pay.

On one sublime occasion we found ourselves debating the proper rate of pay for MPs' secretaries. This was the last straw. I said that I hadn't come into politics to make decisions like this, and that I would pay my secretary what was necessary to keep her. Other ministers agreed. But then, they knew their secretaries; they did not know the other people whose pay they were deciding.

In any case, reality soon started to break in. Two days after the announcement of Stage 3 the NUM rejected an NCB offer worth 16.5 per cent in return for a productivity agreement. The Government immediately took charge of the negotiations. (The days of our 'not intervening' had long gone.) Ted met the NUM at No. 10. But no progress was made.

In early November the NUM began an overtime ban. Maurice Macmillan told us that though an early strike ballot seemed unlikely and, if held, would not give the necessary majority for a strike, an overtime ban would cut production sharply. The general feeling in Cabinet was still that the Government could not afford to acquiesce in a breach of the recently introduced pay code. Instead, we should make a special effort to demonstrate what was possible within it. The miners were not the only ones threatening trouble. The firemen, electricians and engineers were all in differing stages of dispute.

Admittedly, the threatened oil embargo and oil price rises resulting from the Arab-Israeli war that autumn made things far worse. As the effects of the miners' industrial action bit deeper, the sense that we were no longer in control of events deepened. Somehow we had to break out. This made a quick general election increasingly attractive. Quite what we would have done if we had been re-elected is, of course, problematic. Perhaps Ted would have liked to go further towards a managed economy. Others would probably have liked to find a way to pay the miners their Danegeld. Keith and I and a large part of the Parliamentary Conservative Party would have wanted to discard the corporatist and statist trappings with which the Government was now surrounded and try to get back to the free market approach from which we had allowed ourselves to be diverted in early 1972.

At Cabinet on Tuesday 13 November it was all gloom as the crisis accelerated on every front. Tony Barber told us that the October trade figures that day would show another large deficit.

One shrewd move on Ted's part at the beginning of December was to bring Willie Whitelaw back from Northern Ireland to become Employment Secretary in place of Maurice Macmillan. Willie was both conciliatory and cunning, a combination of qualities particularly necessary if some way were to be found out of the struggle with the miners. The Government's hand was also strengthened by the fact that, perhaps surprisingly, the opinion polls were now showing us with a clear lead over Labour as the public reacted indignantly to the miners' actions. In these circumstances, all but the most militant trade unionists would be fearful of a confrontation precipitating a general election.

On Thursday 13 December Ted announced the introduction of a three-day working week to conserve energy. He also gave a broadcast that evening. This gave an impression of crisis which polarized opinion in the country. At first industrial output remained more or less the same, itself an indication of the inefficiency and overmanning of so much of British industry. But we did not know this at the time. Nor could we know how long even a three-day week would be sustainable. I found strong support among Conservatives for the measures taken. There was also understanding of the need for the £1.2 billion public spending cuts, which were announced a few days later.

At this stage we believed that we could rely on business leaders. Shortly before Christmas, Denis and I went to a party at a friend's house in Lamberhurst. There was a power cut and so night lights had been put in jam jars to guide people up the steps. There was a touch of wartime spirit about it all. The businessmen there were of one mind: 'Stand up to them. Fight it out. See them off. We can't go on like this.' It was all very heartening. For the moment.

There still seemed no honourable or satisfactory way out of the dispute itself. The Government offer of an immediate inquiry into the future of the mining industry and miners' pay if the NUM went back to work on the basis of the present offer was turned down flat.

It was clear that, if and when we managed to come through the present crisis, fundamental questions would need to be asked about the Government's direction. The miners, backed in varying degrees by other trade unions and the Labour Party, were flouting the law made by Parliament. The militants were clearly out to bring down the Government and to demonstrate once and for all that Britain could only be governed with the consent of the trade union movement. This was intolerable not just to me as a Conservative Cabinet minister but to millions of others who saw the fundamental liberties of the country under threat. Denis and I, our friends and most of my Party workers, felt that we now had to pick up the gauntlet and that the only way to do that was by calling and winning a general election. From now on, this was what I urged whenever I had the opportunity.

I was, though, surprised and frustrated by Ted Heath's attitude. He seemed out of touch with reality, still more interested in the future of Stage 3 and in the oil crisis than he was in the pressing question of the survival of the Government. Cabinet discussions concentrated on tactics and details, never the fundamental strategy. Such discussions were perhaps taking place in some other forum; but I rather doubt it. Certainly, there was a strange lack of urgency. I suspect it was because Ted was secretly desperate to avoid an election and did not seriously wish to think about the possibility of one. In the end, perhaps – as some of us speculated – because his inner circle was split on the issue, Ted finally did ask some of us in to see him, in several small groups, on Monday 14 January in his study at No. 10.

By this stage we were only days away from the deadline for calling a 7 February election – the best and most likely 'early' date. At No. 10 in our group John Davies and I did most of the talking. We both strongly urged Ted to face up to the fact that we could not have the unions flouting the law and the policies of a democratically elected government in this way. We should have an early election and fight unashamedly on the issue of 'Who governs Britain?' Ted said very little. He seemed to have asked us in for form's sake. I gathered that he did not agree, though he did not say as much. I went away feeling depressed. I still believe that if he had gone to the country earlier we would have scraped in.

The following Wednesday, 30 January, with the strike ballot still pending, an emergency Cabinet was called. Ted told us that the Pay Board's report on relativities had now been received. The question was whether we should accept the report and set up new machinery to investigate 'relativities' claims. The miners had always claimed to be demanding an improvement in their relative pay – hence their rejection of Ted's 'unsocial hours' provision, which applied to *all* shift workers. The Pay Board report might provide a basis for them to settle within the incomes policy – all the more so because it specifically endorsed the idea that changes in the relative importance of an industry due to 'external events' could also be taken into account when deciding pay. The rapidly rising price of oil was just such an 'external event'.

We felt that the Government had no choice but to set up the relativities machinery. Not to do so – having commissioned the relativities report in the first place – would make it seem as if we were actively trying to prevent a settlement with the miners. And with an election now likely we had to consider public opinion at every step.

An election became all but certain when, on Tuesday 5 February, we learned that 81 per cent of those voting in the NUM ballot had supported a strike. Election speculation reached fever pitch from which there was no going back. Ted told us at Cabinet two days later that he had decided to go to the country. The general election would take place on Thursday 28 February.

Willie proposed formally to refer the miners' claim to the Pay Board for a relativities study. He couched his argument for this course entirely in terms of it giving us something to say during the election in reply to the inevitable question: How will you solve the miners' dispute if you win? Cabinet then made the fateful decision to agree to Willie's proposal.

Because of the emergency nature of the election, I had not been involved in the early drafts of even the education section of the manifesto, which was now published within days. There was little new to say, and the dominant theme of the document – the need for firm and fair government at a time of crisis – was clear and stark. The main new pledge was to change the system whereby Social Security benefits were paid to strikers' families.

During most of the campaign I was reasonably confident that we would win. Conservative supporters who had been alienated by the U-turns started drifting back to us. Indeed, their very frustrations at what they saw as our past weaknesses made them all the more determined to back us now that we had decided, as they saw it, to stand up to trade union militancy. Harold Wilson set out Labour's approach in the context of a 'social contract' with the unions. Those who longed for a quiet life could be expected to be seduced by that. But I felt that if we could stick to the central issue summed up by the phrase 'Who governs?' we would win the argument, and with it the election.

I felt victory – almost tangibly – slip away from us in the last week. I just could not believe it when I heard on the radio of the leak of evidence taken by the Pay Board which purported to show that the miners could have been paid more within Stage 3, with the implication that the whole general election was unnecessary. The Government's attempts to deny this – and there did indeed turn out to have been a miscalculation – were stumbling and failed to carry conviction. From now on it was relentlessly downhill.

Two days later, Enoch Powell urged people to vote Labour in order to secure a referendum on the Common Market. I could understand the logic of his position, which was that membership of the Common Market had abrogated British sovereignty and that the supreme issue in politics was therefore how to restore it. But what shocked me was his manner of doing it – announcing only on the day the election was called that he would not be contesting his Wolverhampton seat and then dropping this bombshell at the end of the campaign. It seemed to me that to betray one's local supporters and constituency workers in this way was heartless. I suspect that Enoch's decision had a crucial effect.

Then three days later there was another blow. Campbell Adamson, the Director-General of the CBI, publicly called for the repeal of the Industrial Relations Act. It was all too typical of the way in which Britain's industrial leaders were full of bravado before battle was joined, but lacked the stomach for a fight.

By polling day my optimism had been replaced by unease.

That sentiment grew as I heard from Finchley and elsewhere around the country of a surprisingly heavy turn-out of voters to the polls that morning. I would have liked to think that these were all angry Conservatives, coming out to demonstrate their refusal to be blackmailed by trade union power. But it seemed more likely that they were voters from the Labour-dominated council estates who had come out to teach the Tories a lesson.

The results quickly showed that we had nothing to be cheerful about. We lost thirty-three seats. It would be a hung Parliament. Labour had become the largest party with 301 seats – seventeen short of a majority; we were down to 296, though with a slightly higher percentage of the vote than Labour; the Liberals had gained almost 20 per cent of the vote with fourteen seats, and smaller parties, including the Ulster Unionists, held twenty-three. My own majority in Finchley was down from 11,000 to 6,000, though some of that decline was the result of boundary changes in the constituency.

On Friday afternoon we met, a tired and downcast fag-end of a Cabinet, to be asked by Ted Heath for our reactions as to what should now be done. There were a number of options. Ted could advise the Queen to send for Harold Wilson as the leader of the largest single party. Or the Government could face Parliament and see whether it could command support for its programme. Or he could try to do a deal with the smaller parties for a programme designed to cope with the nation's immediate difficulties. Having alienated the Ulster Unionists through our Northern Ireland policy, this in effect meant a deal with the Liberals – though even that would not have given us a majority. There was little doubt from the way Ted spoke that this was the course he favoured.

My own instinctive feeling was that the party with the largest number of seats in the House of Commons was justified in expecting that they would be called to try to form a government. But Ted argued that with the Conservatives having won the largest number of votes, he was duty bound to explore the possibility of coalition. So he offered the Liberal Leader Jeremy Thorpe a place in a coalition government and promised a Speaker's conference on electoral reform. Thorpe went away to consult his party. Although I wanted to remain Secretary of State for Education, I did not want to do so at the expense of the Conservative Party's never forming a majority government again. Yet that is what the introduction of proportional representation, which the Liberals would be demanding, might amount to. I was also conscious that this horse-trading was making us look ridiculous. The British dislike nothing more than a bad loser. It was time to go.

When we met again on Monday morning Ted gave us a full account of his discussions with the Liberals. They had not been willing to go along with what Jeremy Thorpe wanted. A formal reply from him was still awaited. But it now seemed almost certain that Ted would have to tender his resignation. The final Cabinet was held at 4.45 that afternoon. By now Jeremy Thorpe's reply had been received. From what Ted said, there were clues that his mind was already turning to the idea of a National Government of all parties, something which would increasingly attract him. It did not, of course, attract me at all. In any case, the Liberals were not going to join a coalition government with us. There was nothing more to say.

I left Downing Street, sad but with some sense of relief. I had given little thought to the future. But I knew in my heart that it was time not just for a change in government but for a change in the Conservative Party.

CHAPTER EIGHT

Seizing the Moment

The October 1974 general election and the
campaign for the Tory Leadership

I T IS NEVER EASY to go from government to opposition. But for several reasons it was particularly problematical for the Conservatives led by Ted Heath. First, of course, we had up until almost the last moment expected to win. Whatever the shortcomings of our Government's economic strategy, every department had its own policy programme stretching well into the future. This now had to be abandoned for the rigours of Opposition. Secondly, Ted himself desperately wanted to continue as Prime Minister. He had been unceremoniously ejected from 10 Downing Street and for some months had to take refuge in the flat of his old friend and PPS Tim Kitson, having no home of his own – from which years later I drew the resolution that when my time came to depart I would at least have a house to go to. Ted's passionate desire to return as Prime Minister lay behind much of the talk of coalitions and Governments of National Unity which came to disquiet the Party. The more that the Tory Party moved away from Ted's own vision, the more he wanted to see it tamed by coalition. Thirdly, and worst of all perhaps, the poisoned legacy of our U-turns was that we had no firm principles, let alone much of a record, on which to base our arguments. And in Opposition argument is everything.

I was glad that Ted did not ask me to cover my old department at Education but gave me the Environment portfolio instead. I was convinced that both rates and housing – particularly the latter – were issues which had contributed to our defeat. The task of devising and presenting sound and popular policies in these areas appealed to me.

There were rumblings about Ted's own position, though that is what they largely remained. This was partly because most of us expected an early general election to be called in order to give Labour a working majority, and it hardly seemed sensible to change leaders now. But there were other reasons. Ted still inspired nervousness, even fear among many of his colleagues. In a sense, even the U-turns contributed to the aura around him. For he had single-handedly reversed Conservative policies and had gone far, with his lieutenants, in reshaping the Conservative Party. Paradoxically too, both those committed to Ted's approach and those – like Keith and me and many on the backbenches – who thought very differently agreed that the vote-buying policies which the Labour Party was now pursuing would inevitably lead to economic collapse. Just what the political consequences of that would be was uncertain. But there were many Tory wishful thinkers who thought that it might result in the Conservative Party somehow returning to power with a 'doctor's mandate'. And Ted had no doubt of his own medical credentials.

He did not, though, make the concessions to his critics in the Party which would have been required. He might have provided effectively against future threats to his position if he had changed his approach in a number of ways. He might have shown at least some willingness to admit and learn from the Government's mistakes. He might have invited talented backbench critics to join him as Shadow spokesmen and contribute to the rethinking of policy. He might have changed the overall complexion of the Shadow Cabinet to make it more representative of parliamentary opinion.

But he did none of these things. He replaced Tony Barber – who announced that he intended to leave the Commons though he would stay on for the present in the Shadow Cabinet without portfolio – with Robert Carr, who was even more committed to the interventionist approach that had got us into so much trouble. He promoted to the Shadow Cabinet during the year those MPs like Michael Heseltine and Paul Channon who were seen as his acolytes, and were unrepresentative of backbench opinion of the time. Only John Davies and Joe Godber, neither of whom was ideologically distinct, were dropped. Above all, he set his face against any policy rethinking that would imply that his Government's economic and industrial policy had been seriously flawed. When Keith Joseph was not made Shadow Chancellor, he said he wanted no portfolio but rather to concentrate on research for new policies – something which would prove as dangerous to Ted as it was fruitful for the Party. Otherwise, these were depressing signals of 'more of the same' when the electorate had clearly demonstrated a desire for something different. Added to this, the important Steering Committee of Shadow Ministers was formed even more in Ted's image. I was not invited to join it, and of its members only Keith and perhaps Geoffrey Howe were likely to oppose Ted's wishes.

Between the February and October 1974 elections most of my time was taken up with work on housing and the rates. I had an effective housing policy group of MPs working with me. Hugh Rossi, a friend and neighbouring MP, was a great housing expert, with experience of local government. Michael Latham and John Stanley were well versed in the building industry. The brilliant Nigel Lawson, newly elected, always had his own ideas. We also had the help of people from the building societies and construction industry. It was a lively group which I enjoyed chairing.

The political priority was clearly lower mortgage rates. The technical problem was how to achieve these without open-ended subsidy. In government we had introduced a mortgage subsidy, and there had been talk of taking powers to control the mortgage rate. The Labour Government quickly came up with its own scheme, devised by Harold Lever, to make large cheap short-term loans to the building societies. Our task was to devise something more attractive.

As well as having an eye for a politically attractive policy, I had always believed in a property-owning democracy and wider home ownership. It is cheaper to assist people to buy homes with a mortgage – whether by a subsidized mortgage rate, or by help with the deposit, or just by mortgage interest tax relief – than it is to build more council houses or to buy up private houses through municipalization. I used to quote the results of a Housing Research Foundation study which observed: 'On average each new council house now costs roughly £900 a year in subsidy in taxes and rates (including the subsidy from very old council houses)... Tax relief on an ordinary mortgage, if this be regarded as a subsidy, averages about £280 a year.' My housing policy group met regularly on Mondays. Housing experts and representatives from the building societies gave their advice. It was clear to me that Ted and others were determined to make our proposals on housing and possibly rates the centrepiece of the next election campaign, which we expected sooner rather than later. For example, at the Shadow Cabinet on Friday 3 May we had an all-day discussion of policies for the manifesto. I reported on housing and was authorized to set up a rates policy group. But this meeting was more significant for another reason. At it Keith Joseph argued at length but in vain for a broadly 'monetarist' approach to dealing with inflation.

The question of the rates was a far more difficult one than any aspect of housing policy, and I had a slightly different group to help me. Reform, let alone abolition, of the rates had profound implications for the relations between central and local government and for the different local authority services, particularly education. I drew on the advice of the experts – municipal treasurers proved the best source, and gave readily of their technical advice. But working as I was under tight pressure of time and close scrutiny by Ted and others who expected me to deliver something radical, popular and defensible, my task was not an easy one.

The housing policy group had already held its seventh meeting and our proposals were well developed by the time the rates group started work on 10 June. I knew Ted and his advisers wanted a firm promise that we would abolish the rates. But I was loath to make such a pledge until we were clear about what to put in their place. Anyway, if there was to be an autumn election, there was little chance of doing more than finding a sustainable line to take in the manifesto.

Meanwhile, throughout that summer of 1974 I received far more publicity than I had ever previously experienced. Some of this was inadvertent. The interim report of the housing policy group which I circulated to Shadow Cabinet appeared on the front page of *The Times* on Monday 24 June. On the previous Friday Shadow Cabinet had spent the morning discussing the fourth draft of the manifesto. By now the main lines of my proposed housing policy were agreed. The mortgage rate would be held down to some unspecified level by cutting the composite rate of tax paid by building societies on depositors' accounts, in other words by subsidy disguised as tax relief. A grant would be given to first-time buyers saving for a deposit, though again no figure was specified. There would be a high-powered inquiry into building societies; this was an idea I modelled on my earlier James Inquiry into teachers' training. I hoped it might produce a long-term answer to the problem of high mortgage rates and yet save us from an open-ended subsidy.

The final point related to the right of tenants to buy their council houses. Of all our proposals this was to prove the most far-reaching and the most popular. The February 1974 manifesto had offered council tenants the chance to buy their houses, but retained a right of appeal for the council against sale, and had not offered a discount. We all wanted to go further than this; the question was how far. Peter Walker constantly pressed for the

'Right to Buy' to be extended to council tenants at the lowest possible prices. My instinct was on the side of caution. It was not that I underrated the benefits of wider property ownership. Rather, I was wary of alienating the already hard-pressed families who had scrimped to buy a house on one of the new private estates at the market price and who had seen the mortgage rate rise and the value of their house fall. These people were the bedrock Conservative voters for whom I felt a natural sympathy. They would, I feared, strongly object to council house tenants who had made none of their sacrifices suddenly receiving what was in effect a large capital sum from the Government. We might end up losing more support than we gained. In retrospect, this argument seems both narrow and unimaginative. And it was. But there was a lot to be said politically for it in 1974 at a time when the value of people's houses had slumped so catastrophically.

In the event, the October 1974 manifesto offered council tenants who had been in their homes for three years or more the right to buy them at a price a third below market value. If the tenant sold again within five years he would surrender part of any capital gain. Also, by the time the manifesto reached its final draft, we had quantified the help to be given to first-time buyers of private houses and flats. We would contribute £1 for every £2 saved for the deposit up to a given ceiling. (We ducked the question of rent decontrol.)

It was, however, the question of how low a maximum mortgage interest rate we would promise in the manifesto that caused me most trouble. When I was in the car on the way from London to Tonbridge on Wednesday 28 August in order to record a Party Political Broadcast the bleeper signalled that I must telephone urgently. Ted wanted a word. Willie Whitelaw answered the phone and it was clear that the two of them, and doubtless others of the inner circle, were meeting. Ted came on the line. He asked me to announce on the PPB the precise figure to which we would hold down mortgages, and to take it down as low as I could. I said I could understand the psychological point about going below 10 per cent. That need could be satisfied by a figure of 9½ per cent, and in all conscience I could not take it down any further. To do so would have a touch of rashness about it. I was already worried about the cost. I did not like this tendency to pull figures out of the air for immediate political impact without proper consideration of where they would lead. So I stuck at 9½ per cent.

It was a similar story on the rates. When we had discussed the subject at our Shadow Cabinet meeting on Friday 21 June I had tried to avoid any firm pledge. I suggested that our line should be one of reform to be established on an all-party basis through a Select Committee. Even more than housing, this was not an area in which precipitate pledges were sensible. Ted would have none of this and said I should think again.

In July Charles Bellairs at the Conservative Research Department and I worked on a draft rates section for the manifesto. We were still thinking in terms of an inquiry and an interim rate relief scheme. I went along to discuss our proposals at the Shadow Cabinet Steering Committee. I argued for the transfer of teachers' salaries – the largest item of local spending – from local government onto the Exchequer. Another possibility I raised was the replacement of rates with a system of block grants, with local authorities retaining discretion over spending but within a total set by central government. Neither of these possibilities was particularly attractive. But at least discussion revealed to those present that 'doing something' about the rates was a very different matter from knowing what to do.

On Saturday 10 August I used my speech to the Candidates' Conference at the St Stephen's Club to publicize our policies. I argued for total reform of the rating system to take into account individual ability to pay, and suggested the transfer of teachers' salaries and better interim relief as ways to achieve this. It was a good time of the year – a slack period for news – to unveil new proposals, and we gained some favourable publicity.

It seemed to me that this proved that we could fight a successful campaign *without* being more specific; indeed, looking back, I can see that we were *already* a good deal too specific because, as I was to discover fifteen years later, such measures as transferring the cost of services from local to central government do not in themselves lead to lower local authority rates.

I had hoped to have a pleasant family holiday at Lamberhurst away from the demands of politics. It was not to be. The telephone kept ringing, with Ted and others urging me to give more thought to new schemes. Then I was called back for another meeting on Friday 16 August. Ted, Robert Carr, Jim Prior, Willie Whitelaw and Michael Wolff from Central Office were all there. It was soon clear what the purpose was – to bludgeon me into accepting a commitment in the manifesto to abolish the rates altogether within the lifetime of a Parliament. I argued against this for very much the same reason that I argued against the '9½ per cent' pledge on the mortgage rate. But so shell-shocked by their unexpected defeat in February were Ted and his inner circle that in their desire for re-election they were clutching at straws, or what in the jargon were described as manifesto 'nuggets'.

There were various ways to raise revenue for expenditure on local purposes. We were all uneasy about moving to a system whereby central government just provided block grants to local government. So I had told Shadow Cabinet that I thought a reformed property tax seemed to be the least painful option. But in the back of my mind I had the additional idea of supplementing the property tax with a locally collected tax on petrol. Of course, there were plenty of objections to both, but at least they were better than putting up income tax.

What mattered to my colleagues was clearly the pledge to abolish the rates, and at Wilton Street Ted insisted on it. I felt bruised and resentful to be bounced again into policies which had not been properly thought out. But I thought that if I combined caution on the details with as much presentational bravura as I could muster I could make our rates and housing policies into vote-winners for the Party. This I now concentrated my mind on doing.

It was at a press conference on the afternoon of Wednesday 28 August that I delivered the package of measures – built around 9½ per cent mortgages and the abolition of the rates – without a scintilla of doubt, which as veteran *Evening Standard* reporter Robert Carvel said, 'went down with hardened reporters almost as well as the sherry' served by Central Office. We dominated the news. It was by general consent the best fillip the Party had had since losing the February election. The Building Societies' Association welcomed the proposals for 9½ per cent mortgages but questioned my figures about the cost. As I indignantly told them, it was their sums which were wrong and they subsequently retracted. Some on the economic right were understandably critical, but among the grassroots Conservatives that we had to win back the mortgage proposal was extremely popular. So too was the pledge on the rates. The Labour Party was rattled and unusually the party-giving Tony Crosland was provoked into describing the proposals as 'Margaret's midsummer madness'. All this publicity was good for me personally as well. Although I was not to know it at the time, this period up to and during the October 1974 election campaign allowed me to make a favourable impact on Conservatives in the country and in Parliament without which my future career would doubtless have been very different.

* * *

Although it was my responsibilities as Environment spokesman which took up most of my time and energy, from late June I had become part of another enterprise which would have profound consequences for the Conservative Party, for the country and for me. The setting up of the Centre for Policy Studies (CPS) is really part of Keith Joseph's story rather than mine. Keith had emerged from the wreckage of the Heath Government determined on the need to rethink our policies from first principles. If this was to be done, Keith was the ideal man to do it. He had the intellect, the integrity and not least the humility required. He had a deep interest in both economic and social policy. He had long experience of government. He had an extraordinary ability to form relationships of friendship and respect with a wide range of characters with different viewpoints and backgrounds. Although he could, when he felt strongly, speak passionately and persuasively, it was as a listener that he excelled. Moreover, Keith never listened passively. He probed arguments and assertions and scribbled notes which you knew he would go home to ponder. He was so impressive because his intellectual self-confidence was the fruit of continual self-questioning. His bravery in adopting unpopular positions before a hostile audience evoked the admiration of his friends, because we all knew that he was naturally shy and even timid. He was almost too good a man for politics – except that without a few good men politics would be intolerable.

I could not have become Leader of the Opposition, or achieved what I did as Prime Minister, without Keith. But nor, it is fair to say, could Keith have achieved what he did without the Centre for Policy Studies and Alfred Sherman. Apart from the fact of their being Jewish, Alfred and Keith had little in common, and until one saw how effectively they worked together it was difficult to believe that they could co-operate at all.

Alfred had his own kind of brilliance. He brought his convert's zeal (as an ex-communist), his breadth of reading and his skills as a ruthless polemicist to the task of plotting out a new kind of free market Conservatism. He was more interested, it seemed to me, in the philosophy behind policies than the policies themselves. He was better at pulling apart sloppily constructed arguments than at devising original proposals. But the force and clarity of his mind, and his complete disregard for other people's feelings or opinion of him, made him a formidable complement and contrast to Keith. Alfred helped Keith to turn the Centre for Policy Studies into the powerhouse of alternative Conservative thinking on economic and social matters.

I was not involved at the beginning, though I gathered from Keith that he was thinking hard about how to turn his Shadow Cabinet responsibilities for research on policy into constructive channels. In March Keith had won Ted's approval for the setting up of a research unit to make comparative studies with other European economies, particularly the so-called 'social market economy' as practised in West Germany. Ted had Adam Ridley put on the board of directors of the CPS (Adam acted as his economic adviser from within the Conservative Research Department), but otherwise Keith was left very much to his own devices. Nigel Vinson, a successful entrepreneur with strong free enterprise convictions, was made responsible for acquiring a home for the Centre, which was found in Wilfred Street, close to Victoria. It was at the end of May 1974 that I first became directly involved with the CPS. Whether Keith ever considered asking any other members of the Shadow Cabinet to join him at the Centre I do not know: if he had, they certainly did not accept. His was a risky, exposed position, and the fear of provoking the wrath of Ted and the derision of left-wing commentators was a powerful disincentive. But I jumped at the chance to become Keith's Vice-Chairman.

The CPS was the least bureaucratic of institutions. Alfred Sherman has caught the feel of it by saying that it was an 'animator, agent of change, and political enzyme'. The original proposed social market approach did not prove particularly fruitful and was eventually quietly forgotten, though a pamphlet called *Why Britain Needs a Social Market Economy* was published.

What the Centre then developed was the drive to expose the follies and self-defeating consequences of government intervention. It continued to engage the political argument in open debate at the highest intellectual level. The objective was to effect change – change in the climate of opinion and so in the limits of the 'possible'. In order to do this, it had to employ another of Alfred's phrases, to 'think the unthinkable'. It was not long before more than a few feathers began to be ruffled by that approach.

Keith had decided that he would make a series of speeches over the summer and autumn of 1974 in which he would set out the alternative analysis of what had gone wrong and what should be done. The first of these, which was also intended to attract interest among potential fund-raisers, was delivered at Upminster on Saturday 22 June. Alfred was the main draftsman. But as with all Keith's speeches – except the fateful Edgbaston speech which I shall describe shortly – he circulated endless drafts for comment. All the observations received were carefully considered and the language pared down to remove every surplus word. Keith's speeches always put rigour of analysis and exactitude of language above style, but taken as a whole they managed to be powerful rhetorical instruments as well.

The Upminster speech infuriated Ted and the Party establishment because Keith lumped in together the mistakes of Conservative and Labour Governments, talking about the 'thirty years of socialistic fashions'. He said bluntly that the public sector had been 'draining away the wealth created by the private sector', and challenged the value of public 'investment' in tourism and the expansion of the universities. He condemned the socialist vendetta against profits and noted the damage done by rent controls and council housing to labour mobility. Finally – and, in the eyes of the advocates of consensus, unforgivably – he talked about the 'inherent contradictions [of the] . . . mixed economy'. It was a short speech but it had a mighty impact, not least because people knew that there was more to come.

From Keith and Alfred I learned a great deal. I renewed my reading of the seminal works of liberal economics and conservative thought. I also regularly attended lunches at the Institute of Economic Affairs where Ralph Harris, Arthur Seldon, Alan Walters and others – in other words all those who had been right when we in government had gone so badly wrong – were busy marking out a new non-socialist economic and social path for Britain. I lunched from time to time with Professor Douglas Hague, the economist, who would later act as one of my unofficial economic advisers.

At about this time I also made the acquaintance of a polished and amusing former television producer called Gordon Reece, who was advising the Party on television appearances and who had, it seemed to me, an almost uncanny insight into that medium. In fact, by the eve of the October 1974 general election I had made a significant number of contacts with those on whom I would come to rely heavily during my years as Party Leader.

Keith delivered a further speech in Preston on Thursday 5 September. After some early inconclusive discussion in Shadow Cabinet of Keith's various ideas, Ted had refused the general economic re-evaluation and discussion which Keith wanted. Keith decided that he was not prepared to be either stifled or ignored, and gave notice that he was intending to make a major speech on economic policy. Ted and most of our colleagues were desperate to prevent this. Geoffrey Howe and I were accordingly dispatched to try to persuade Keith not to go ahead, or at least to tone down what he intended to say. In any case, Keith showed me an early draft. It was one of the most powerful and persuasive analyses I have ever read. I made no suggestions for changes. Nor, as far as I know, did Geoffrey. The Preston speech must still be considered as one of the very few which have fundamentally affected a political generation's way of thinking.

It began with the sombre statement: 'Inflation is threatening to destroy our society.' At most times this would have seemed hyperbole, but at this time, with inflation at 17 per cent and rising, people were obsessed with its impact on their lives. That only made more explosive Keith's admission that *successive* governments bore the responsibility for allowing it to get such a grip. He rejected the idea embraced by the Shadow Cabinet that inflation had been 'imported' and was the result of rocketing world prices. In fact, it was the result of excessive growth of the money supply. Explaining as he did that there was a time lag of 'many months, or even as much as a year or two' between loose monetary policy and rising inflation, he also implicitly – and accurately – blamed the Heath Government for the inflation which was now beginning to take off and which would rise to even more ruinous levels the following year. He also rejected the use of incomes policy as a means of containing it. The analysis was subtle, detailed and devastating.

Keith then put his finger on the fundamental reason why we had embarked on our disastrous U-turns – fear of unemployment. It had been when registered unemployment rose to one million that the Heath Government's nerve broke. But Keith explained that the unemployment statistics concealed as much as they revealed because they included 'frictional unemployment' – that is, people who were temporarily out of work moving between jobs – and a large number of people who were more or less unemployable for one reason or another. Similarly, there was a large amount of fraudulent unemployment, people who were drawing benefit while earning. In fact, noted Keith, the real problem had been labour shortages, not surpluses. He said that we should be prepared to admit that control of the money supply to beat inflation would temporarily risk some increase in unemployment. But if we wanted to bring down inflation (which itself destroyed jobs, though this was an argument to which Keith and I would subsequently have to return on many occasions), monetary growth had to be curbed. Keith did not argue that if we got the money supply right, everything else would be right. He specifically said that this was not his view. But if we did *not* achieve monetary control, we would never be able to achieve any of our other economic objectives.

The Preston speech was, of course, highly embarrassing for Ted and the Party establishment. Some still hoped that a combination of dire warnings about socialism, hints of a National Government and our new policies on mortgages and the rates would see us squeak back into office – an illusion fostered by the fact that on the very day of Keith's speech an opinion poll showed us two points ahead of Labour. The Preston speech blew this strategy out of the water, for it was clear that the kind of reassessment Keith was advocating was highly unlikely to occur if the Conservatives returned to government with Ted Heath as Prime Minister. Keith himself discreetly decided to spend more time at the CPS in Wilfred Street than at Westminster, where some of his colleagues were furious. For my part, I did not think that there was any serious chance of our winning the election. In the short term I was determined to fight as hard as I could for the policies it was now my responsibility to defend. In the longer term I was convinced that we must turn the Party around towards Keith's way of thinking, preferably under Keith's leadership.

The Conservative Party manifesto was published early, on Tuesday 10 September – about a week before the election was announced – because of a leak to the press. I was taken by surprise by a question on it when I was opening the Chelsea Antiques Fair. The release of the manifesto in this way was not a good start to the campaign, particularly because we had so little new to say.

I had never had so much exposure to the media as in this campaign. The Labour Party recognized that our housing and rates proposals were just about the only attractive ones in our manifesto, and consequently they set out to rubbish them as soon as possible. On Tuesday 24 September Tony Crosland described them as 'a pack of lies'. (This was the same press conference at which Denis Healey made his notorious claim that inflation was running at 8.4 per cent, calculating the figure on a three-month basis when the annual rate was in fact 17 per cent.) I immediately issued a statement rebutting the accusation, and in order to keep the argument going, for it would highlight our policies, I said at Finchley that evening that the cut in mortgage rates would be among the first actions of a new Conservative Government. Then, in pursuit of the same goal, and having consulted Ted and Robert Carr, the Shadow Chancellor, I announced at the morning press conference at Central Office on Friday that the mortgage rate reduction would occur 'by Christmas' if we won. The main morning papers led with the story the following day – 'Santa Thatcher' – and it was generally said that we had taken the initiative for the first time during the campaign. On the following Monday I described this on a Party Election Broadcast as a 'firm, unshakeable promise'. And the brute political fact was that, despite my reservations about the wisdom of the pledge, we would have had to honour it at almost any cost.

It was at this point that the way in which I was presenting our housing and rates policies first began to run up against the general approach Ted wanted to take in the campaign. At his insistence I had made the policies I was offering as hard and specific as possible. But the manifesto, particularly in the opening section, deliberately conveyed the impression that the Conservatives might consider some kind of National Government and would therefore be flexible on the policies we were putting forward.

At the Conservative press conference on Friday 2 October Ted stressed his willingness as Prime Minister to bring non-Conservatives into a government of 'all the talents'. This tension between firm pledges and implied flexibilities was in danger of making nonsense of our campaign and dividing Shadow ministers.

On Thursday I continued when campaigning in the London areas with the vigorous defence of our housing policies and combined this with attacks on 'creeping socialism' through municipalization. In the evening I was asked to come and see Ted at Wilton Street. His advisers had apparently been urging him to actually start talking about the possibility of a Coalition Government. Because I was known to be firmly against this for both strategic and tactical reasons, and because I was due to appear on the radio programme *Any Questions* in Southampton the following evening, I had been called in to have the new line spelt out to me. Ted said that he was now prepared to call for a Government of National Unity which, apparently, 'the people' wanted. I was extremely angry. He had himself, after all, insisted on making the housing and rates policies I had been advocating as specific as possible: now, at almost the end of the campaign, he was effectively discarding the pledges in the manifesto because that seemed to offer a better chance of his returning to Downing Street.

Why he imagined that he himself would be a Coalition Government's likely Leader quite escaped me. Ted at this time was a divisive figure, and although he had somehow convinced himself that he represented the 'consensus', this accorded with neither his record, nor his temperament, nor indeed other people's estimation. For myself, I was not going to retreat from the policies which at his insistence I had been advocating. I went away highly disgruntled.

The last few days of the campaign were dominated by all the awkward questions which talk of coalitions brings. But I stuck to my own brief, repeating the manifesto pledges sitting alongside Ted Heath at the last Conservative press conference on Tuesday 7 October. The general election result two days later suggested that in spite of the natural desire of electors to give the minority Labour Government a chance to govern effectively, there was still a good deal of distrust of them. Labour finished up with an overall majority of three, which was unlikely to see them through a full term. But the Conservative result – 277 seats compared with Labour's 319 – though it might have been worse, was hardly any kind of endorsement for our approach.

Though my majority fell a little in Finchley, I was thought to have had a good campaign. Talk of my even possibly becoming Leader of the Party, a subject which had already excited some journalists a great deal more than it convinced me, started to grow. I felt sorry for Ted Heath personally. He had his music and a small circle of friends, but politics was his life. That year, moreover, he had suffered a series of personal blows. His yacht, *Morning Cloud*, had sunk and his godson had been among those lost. The election defeat was a further blow.

Nonetheless, I had no doubt that Ted now ought to go. He had lost three elections out of four. He himself could not change and he was too defensive of his own past record to see that a fundamental change of policies was needed. So my reluctance to confirm suggestions that I might myself become Leader had little to do with keeping Ted in his present position. It had everything to do with seeing Keith take over from him. Indeed, by the weekend I had virtually become Keith's informal campaign manager. Accordingly I discouraged speculation about my own prospects.

Then, on Saturday 19 October, Keith spoke at Edgbaston in Birmingham. It was not intended as part of the series of major speeches designed to alter the thinking of the Conservative Party, and perhaps for this reason had not been widely circulated among Keith's friends and advisers: certainly, I had no inkling of the text. The Edgbaston speech is generally reckoned to have destroyed Keith's leadership chances. It was the section containing the assertion that 'the balance of our population, our human

stock, is threatened', and going on to lament the high and rising proportion of children being born to mothers 'least fitted to bring children into
the world', having been 'pregnant in adolescence in social classes 4 and 5',
which did the damage. Ironically, the most incendiary phrases came not
from Keith's own mouth, but from passages taken from an article by two
left-wing sociologists published by the Child Poverty Action Group. This
distinction, however, was lost upon the bishops, novelists, academics,
socialist politicians and commentators who rushed to denounce Keith as
a mad eugenicist.

The speech was due to be given on Saturday night, and so the text was
issued in advance with an embargo for media use. But the *Evening Standard* broke the embargo and launched a fierce attack on Keith, distorting
what he said. I read its version on Waterloo Station and my heart sank.
Afterwards Keith himself did not help his cause by constantly explaining,
qualifying and apologizing.

Doubtless as a result of all this, Ted felt a good deal more secure. He
even told us in Shadow Cabinet the following Tuesday that the election
campaign had been 'quite a good containment exercise and that the
mechanics had worked well'. A strange unreality pervaded our discussions. Everyone except Ted knew that the main political problem was the
fact that he was still Leader.

Ted was now locked in a bitter battle with the 1922 Executive. In reply
to their demands for a leadership contest – and indeed for reform of the
leadership election procedure – he disputed their legitimacy as representatives of the backbenches on the grounds that they had been elected
during the previous Parliament and must themselves first face re-election
by Tory MPs. Ted and his advisers hoped that they might be able to have
his opponents thrown off the Executive and replaced by figures more
amenable to him. As part of a somewhat belated attempt to win over
backbenchers, Ted also proposed that extra front-bench spokesmen
should be appointed from among them and that officers of the Parliamentary Committees might speak from the front bench on some occasions. It was also widely rumoured that there would shortly be a reshuffle
of the Shadow Cabinet.

Not for the first time, I found the press more optimistic about my
prospects than I was. The *Sunday Express* and the *Observer* on 3 November ran stories that I was to be appointed Shadow Chancellor. This was a
nice thought and I would have loved the job; but I regarded it as
extremely unlikely that Ted would give it to me. That was more or less

confirmed by stories in the *Financial Times* and the *Daily Mirror* on the Monday that said that I would get a top economic job, but not the Shadow Chancellorship. And so indeed it turned out. I was appointed Robert Carr's deputy with special responsibility for the Finance Bill and also made a member of the Steering Committee. Some of my friends were annoyed that I had not received a more important portfolio. But I knew from the years when I worked under Iain Macleod on the Finance Bill that this was a position in which I could make the most of my talents. What neither Ted nor I knew was just how important that would be over the next three months. The reshuffle as a whole demonstrated something of the weakness of Ted's political standing. Edward du Cann refused to join the Shadow Cabinet, which was therefore no more attractive to the right of the Party, some of whom at least Ted needed to win over. Tim Raison and Nicholas Scott who did come in were more or less on the left and, though able, not people who carried great political weight.

The re-election of all the members of the 1922 Executive, including Edward du Cann, on the day of the reshuffle – Thursday 7 November – was bad news for Ted. A leadership contest could no longer be avoided. He wrote to Edward saying that he was now willing to discuss changes to the procedure for electing the Party Leader. From now on it was probably in Ted's interest to have the election over as soon as possible, before any alternative candidate could put together an effective campaign.

At this time I started to attend the Economic Dining Group which Nick Ridley had formed in 1972 and which largely consisted of sound money men like John Biffen, Jock Bruce-Gardyne, John Nott and others. Above all, I buried myself in the details of my new brief. It was a challenging time to take it up, for on Tuesday 12 November Denis Healey introduced one of his quarterly budgets. It was a panic reaction to the rapidly growing problems of industry and consisted of cuts in business taxation to the tune of £775 million (£495 million of new business taxes having been imposed only six months before) and some curbs on subsidies to nationalized industries. Ted's reply – in which, against the background of an audible gasp from Tory backbenchers, he criticized the Chancellor for allowing nationalized industry prices to rise towards market levels – did him no good at all.

My chance came the following Thursday when I spoke for the Opposition in the Budget Debate. I had done my homework and I set about contrasting the Labour Government's past statements with its present actions. Some of the speech was quite technical and detailed, as it had to be. But it was my answers to the interruptions that had the backbenchers roaring support. I was directly answering Harold Lever (without whom Labour would have been still more economically inept) when he interrupted early in my speech to put me right on views I had attributed to him. Amid a good deal of merriment, not least from Harold Lever himself, a shrewd businessman from a wealthy family, I replied: 'I always felt that I could never rival him [Lever] at the Treasury because there are four ways of acquiring money. To make it. To earn it. To marry it. And to borrow it. He seems to have experience of all four.'

At another point I was interrupted by a pompously irate Denis Healey when I quoted the *Sunday Telegraph* which reported him as saying: 'I never save. If I get any money I go out and buy something for the house.' Denis Healey was most indignant, so I was pleased to concede the point, saying (in reference to the fact that like other socialist politicians he had his own country house): 'I am delighted that we have got on record the fact that the Chancellor is a jolly good saver. I know that he believes in buying houses in good Tory areas.'

No one has ever claimed that House of Commons repartee must be subtle in order to be effective. This performance boosted the shaky morale of the Parliamentary Party and with it my reputation.

Meanwhile, Alec Douglas-Home, now returned to the Lords as Lord Home, had agreed to chair a review of the procedure for the leadership election. On Wednesday 20 November I received a note from Geoffrey Finsberg, a neighbouring MP and friend, which said: 'If you contest the leadership you will almost certainly win – for my part I hope you will stand and I will do all I can to help.' But I still could not see any likelihood of this happening. It seemed to me that for all of the brouhaha caused by his Edgbaston speech Keith must be our candidate.

The following afternoon I was working in my room in the House, briefing myself on the Finance Bill, when the telephone rang. It was Keith to check I was there because he had something he wanted to come along and tell me. As soon as he entered, I could see it was serious. He told me: 'I am sorry, I just can't run. Ever since I made that speech the press have been outside the house. They have been merciless. Helen [his wife] can't take it and I have decided that I just can't stand.'

His mind was quite made up. I was on the edge of despair. We just could not abandon the Party and the country to Ted's brand of politics. I heard myself saying: 'Look, Keith, if you're not going to stand, I will, because someone who represents our viewpoint *has* to stand.'

There was nothing more to say. My mind was already a whirl. I had no idea of my chances. I knew nothing about leadership campaigns. I just tried to put the whole thing to the back of my mind for the moment and concentrate on the Finance Bill. Somehow or other the news got out and I started to receive telephone calls and notes of support from MP friends. Late that night I went back to Flood Street and told Denis of my intention.

'You must be out of your mind,' he said. 'You haven't got a hope.' He had a point. But I never had any doubt that he would support me all the way.

The following day Fergus Montgomery, my PPS, telephoned me, and I told him that Keith was not going to stand but that I would. I wondered how best to break the news to Ted. Fergus thought I should see him personally.

I arranged to see Ted on Monday 25 November. He was at his desk in his room at the House. I need not have worried about hurting his feelings. I went in and said: 'I must tell you that I have decided to stand for the leadership.' He looked at me coldly, turned his back, shrugged his shoulders and said: 'If you must.' I slipped out of the room.

Monday was, therefore, the first day I had to face the press as a declared contender for the Tory leadership. I was glad to be able to rely on the help and advice of Gordon Reece, who had now become a friend and who sat in on some of my early press interviews, which went quite well. It was, of course, still the fact that I was a woman that was the main topic of interest.

Ted's *coterie* and, I believe, at least one Central Office figure had, in any case, alighted on something which they hoped would destroy me as effectively as had happened to Keith. In the interview I had given to *Pre-Retirement Choice* more than two months before I had given what I considered to be practical advice to elderly people trying to make ends meet in circumstances where food prices were rising sharply. I said that it made sense to stock up on tinned food. This was precisely the sort of advice I myself had been given as a girl. Any good housewife shops around and buys several items at a time when prices are low, rather than dashing out at the last minute to buy the same thing at a greater cost.

To my horror the press on Wednesday 27 November was full of stories of my 'hoarding' food. Someone had clearly used this obscure interview in order to portray me as mean, selfish and above all 'bourgeois'. In its way it was cleverly done. It allowed the desired caricature to be brought out to the full. It played to the snobbery of the Conservative Party, because the unspoken implication was that this was all that could be expected of a grocer's daughter. It reminded the public of all that had been said and written about me as the 'milk snatcher' at Education.

A veritable circus of indignation was now staged. Pressure groups were prompted to complain. A deputation of housewives was said to be travelling from Birmingham to urge me to give them the tins. Food chemists gave their views about the consequences of keeping tinned food too long in the larder. Martin Redmayne, the former Chief Whip, reliable Party establishment figure and now Deputy Chairman of Harrods, appeared on television to say that 'any sort of inducement to panic buying was ... against the public interest' – although Lord Redmayne's larder probably contained something more enticing than a few tins of salmon and corned beef. There was nothing for it but to invite the cameramen in and have them check the contents of my Flood Street larder and cupboards. This may have convinced some of the Tory hierarchy that my and my family's tastes and standards were not at all what should be expected from someone who aspired to lead their party. But it certainly showed that the 'hoarding' allegation was malicious nonsense.

Finally, in order to keep the dying story alive my opponents went too far. On Friday 29 November I was in John Cope's South Gloucestershire constituency when my secretary, Alison Ward, telephoned to say that the radio was now broadcasting that I had been seen in a shop on the Finchley Road buying up large quantities of sugar. (There was a sugar shortage at the time.) Alison had already checked and discovered that in fact no such shop existed. It was a straightforward lie. A firm denial prevented its circulation in the press and marked the effective end of this surreal campaign.

At the time, however, I was bitterly upset by it. Sometimes I was near to tears. Sometimes I was shaking with anger. But as I told Bill Shelton, the MP for Streatham and a friend: 'I saw how they destroyed Keith. Well, they're not going to destroy me.'

What had happened made me all the more determined to throw my hat into the ring. But there was also much talk of Edward du Cann's putting himself forward as a candidate. As Chairman of the 1922 Committee – and a man – he might reasonably be expected to command more support than me.

One of Edward du Cann's chief supporters, Airey Neave, the MP for Abingdon and a colleague of Edward's on the 1922 Executive, was someone I knew quite well. As barristers we had shared the same Chambers, and he had been a neighbour at Westminster Gardens.

Airey was a man of contrasts. His manner was quiet yet entirely self-assured. As a writer and a war hero who escaped from Colditz there was an air of romance about him. He had seen much more of the world than most MPs, and suffered a good deal too. He had the benefit, in Diana, of a marvellous political wife. He had briefly been a junior minister in the late 1950s but had to resign because of ill-health, and I understand Ted had unfeelingly told him that that was the end of his career. It was difficult to pin down Airey's politics. I did not consider him, ideologically, a man of the right. He probably did not look at the world in those terms. We got on well and I was conscious of mutual respect, but we were not yet the close friends we were to become.

Airey had come to see me shortly after my decision to stand was known. He hoped to persuade Edward du Cann to stand, but Edward himself remained undecided. Excluded by Ted from high office, he had devoted himself to a City career he was now reluctant to give up.

A new factor that weakened Ted and strengthened his potential rivals was the announcement of the Home Committee's conclusions on Tuesday 7 December. There would be annual elections for the Tory Leader, challengers needed only a proposer and a seconder to put themselves forward, and the majority required to win on the first ballot was significantly increased to 50 per cent plus 15 per cent of those eligible to vote. It was in effect an incentive to challengers, since it meant that a Leader in difficulties needed to retain the confidence of a super-majority of those voting.

Still, Christmas at Lamberhurst that year was less festive than on some other occasions.

On Wednesday 15 January Edward du Cann made it publicly known that he would not run for the leadership. The way was therefore open for me. It was now vitally necessary to have an effective campaign team.

That same afternoon I was leading for the Opposition on the Committee Stage of the Finance Bill. Fergus had just learned that he would have to go on a parliamentary visit to South Africa, though he still thought (wrongly as it turned out) that he would be back in time for the leadership first ballot. He therefore asked Bill Shelton, when they met in the Division Lobby, to run my campaign in his absence, and Bill agreed. I was delighted when Bill told me, for I knew he was loyal and would be a skilful campaigner. Then, as I learned later, in the course of a subsequent vote Airey approached Bill and said: 'You know that I have been running Edward du Cann's campaign? Edward is withdrawing. If we could come to some agreement I will bring Edward's troops behind Margaret.' In fact, the 'agreement' simply consisted of Airey taking over the running of my campaign with Bill assisting him.

When I began to make suggestions to Airey about people to contact, he told me firmly not to bother about any of that, to leave it to him and to concentrate on my work on the Finance Bill. This was good advice, not least because both in the upstairs Committee Room and on the floor of the Chamber I had every opportunity to show my paces. It was, after all, the members of the Parliamentary Conservative Party who would ultimately make the decision about the Conservative leadership, and they were just as likely to be impressed by what I said in debate as by anything else. The campaign team began as a small group of about half a dozen, though it swelled rapidly and by the second ballot had become almost too large, consisting of as many as forty or fifty. Canvassing was done with great precision, and MPs might be approached several times by different people in order to verify their allegiances. Airey and his colleagues knew that there was no short cut to this process, and day after day it went on, with Bill Shelton crossing off names and keeping the tally.

Meanwhile, dealings with the media were suddenly becoming important. In these Gordon Reece was invaluable.

In fact, the attitude towards my candidature was tangibly changing. I spoke on Tuesday 21 January to a lunch in St Stephen's Tavern of the Guinea Club, consisting of leading national and provincial newspaper journalists. By this time as a result of the soundings Airey had taken I was actually beginning to feel that I was in with a chance. I said to them wryly at one point: 'You know, I really think you should begin to take me seriously.' By the weekend articles had begun to appear reappraising my campaign in a different light.

Nor were my prospects harmed by another exchange in the Commons the following day with the ever-obliging Denis Healey. In bitter but obscure vein he described me as the '*La Pasionaria* of privilege'. I jotted down a reply and delivered it a few moments later with relish: 'Some Chancellors are microeconomic. Some Chancellors are fiscal. This one is just plain cheap.' The Tory benches loved it.

With just a week to go, Airey, Keith and Bill came round to Flood Street on Sunday 26 January to discuss the latest position. The number of pledges – mine at around 120 and Ted's less than eighty – looked far too optimistic. People would need to be revisited and their intentions re-examined. Presumably the Heath campaign, in which Peter Walker and Ted's PPSs Tim Kitson and Ken Baker were the main figures, was receiving equally or even more optimistic information; but they made the mistake of believing it. In marked contrast to Airey's public demeanour, they were loudly predicting a large victory on the first ballot.

At Flood Street it was agreed that I should address my core campaigners in Committee Room 13 on Monday night. I could not tell them anything about campaigning. They had forgotten far more about political tactics and indeed political skulduggery than I would ever know. So instead I spoke and answered questions on my vision of a Conservative society from 10.30 till midnight. It was marvellous to be able to speak from the heart about what I believed, and to feel that those crucial to my cause were listening.

The Heath camp now changed the direction of their campaign. Ridicule had failed. Instead, the accusation became that the sort of Conservatism I represented might appeal to the middle-class rank and file supporters of the Party, particularly in the South, but would never win over the uncommitted. My article in the *Daily Telegraph*, which appeared on Thursday 30 January, took this head-on:

> I was attacked [as Education Secretary] for fighting a rearguard action in defence of 'middle-class interests'. The same accusation is levelled at me now, when I am leading Conservative opposition to the socialist Capital Transfer Tax proposals. Well, if 'middle-class values' include the encouragement of variety and individual choice, the provision of fair incentives and rewards for skill and hard work, the maintenance of effective barriers against the excessive power of the state and a belief in the wide distribution of individual *private* property, then they are certainly what I am trying to defend . . .

This theme – the return to fundamental Conservative principles and the defence of middle-class values – was enormously popular in the Party. I repeated it when speaking to my Constituency Association the following day. I rejected the idea that my candidature was representative of a faction. I emphasized that I was speaking up for all those who felt let down by recent Conservative Governments. I was also prepared to accept my share of the blame for what had gone wrong under Ted.

> But [I added] I hope I have learned something from the failures and mistakes of the past and can help to plan constructively for the future . . . There is a widespread feeling in the country that the Conservative Party has not defended [Conservative] ideals explicitly and toughly enough, so that Britain is set on a course towards inevitable socialist mediocrity. That course must not only be halted, it must be reversed.

I knew from my talks with Conservative MPs that there were many contradictory factors which would influence their votes. Some would support Ted simply because he was the Leader *in situ*. Many would not dare go against him because, even after two successive election defeats, he inspired fear that there would be no forgiveness for mutiny. Moreover, many thought that I was inexperienced – and as I had publicly admitted, there was more than a little truth in that. There was also some suspicion of me as too doctrinaire and insensitive. And then, of course, there was the rather obvious fact that I was a woman.

As a result of these conflicting considerations, many MPs were undecided. They wanted to be able to talk to me, to find out what I was like and where I stood. Airey and his team would send these Members along to see me in the room of Robin Cooke – one of our team – in the House where, singly or in small groups, over a glass of claret or a cup of tea, I would try to answer their points as best I could. Ted, by contrast, preferred lunch parties of MPs where, I suspect, there was not much straight talking – at least not from the guests. Doubtless his campaign team marked them down as supporters, which many were not.

The press on Monday 3 February was full of the fact that the National Union of the Party had reported that 70 per cent of Constituency Associations favoured Ted Heath and that the great majority of Conservative supporters agreed with them. We were not surprised by this. The Conservative Associations, nudged by Central Office, were understandably loyal to the existing Leader and the opinion poll results reflected the fact that I was a relatively unknown quantity outside the House of Commons. But obviously it did not help, and it certainly boosted confidence in the Heath camp. Indeed, there was evidence of a late surge of support for Ted among MPs. Airey's and Bill's final canvass returns suggested that I was

neck and neck with Ted, with the third candidate, the gallant and tradi-
tionalist Hugh Fraser, picking up a few right-wing misogynist votes. But I
was told that I came over quite well on the *World in Action* television
programme that night.

On Tuesday 4 February, the day of the first ballot, I was up early to
prepare Denis's breakfast and see him off to work before driving from
Flood Street to the House of Commons, exhibiting what I hoped was a
confident smile and a few friendly words for the press gathered outside.
For me it was another day on the Finance Bill Committee, while in
another House of Commons Committee Room the voting for the leadership took place. The ballot was due to close at 3.30. I went up to Airey
Neave's room to await the result. Bill Shelton represented me at the count
and Tim Kitson represented Ted. I believe that even after they had heard
the sombre news of the outcome of that day's voting the Heath camp had
hoped that the proxy votes, counted last, would see Ted through. But
most of the proxies also went to me. I was trying to concentrate on
anything other than the future when the door opened and Airey came in.
Softly, but with a twinkle in his eye, he told me: 'It's good news. You're
ahead in the poll. You've got 130 votes to Ted's 119.' Hugh Fraser had
sixteen.

I could barely believe it. Although I was thirty-one votes short of the
required margin to win outright on the first ballot – 50 per cent plus a
lead of 15 per cent of those eligible to vote – and therefore there would
have to be a second round, I was decisively ahead. I had no doubt that if I
had failed against Ted that would have been the end of me in politics. As
it was, I might be Leader. Who knows? I might even be Prime Minister.

My own surprise at the result was as nothing compared to the shat-
tering blow it had delivered to the Conservative establishment. I felt no
sympathy for them. They had fought me unscrupulously all the way.
But I did feel sorry for Ted, who quickly announced his decision to
resign as Leader and not to contest the second ballot. Willie Whitelaw
now put his name forward and immediately became the favourite. I
myself thought that Willie had a very good chance of winning; and
though I could not seriously imagine him changing the direction of the
Party as I wished, it did please me to think that between us there would
be none of the bitterness which had soured my relations with Ted. Jim
Prior, John Peyton and Geoffrey Howe also entered the contest. I was a
little worried about Geoffrey's candidature because he held similar
views to mine and might split the right-wing vote, which in a close

contest could be crucial. Hugh Fraser withdrew and urged his supporters to vote for Willie.

In fact, without knowing it, I had what the Americans call 'momentum'. I had always reckoned that a substantial number of those voting for me in the first round would only do so as a tactical way of removing Ted and putting in someone more acceptable but still close to his way of thinking, such as Willie. But in fact my support actually hardened.

Certainly, many people in the Party at Westminster and outside it were now desperately anxious to bring the whole process to a swift end. The very circumstances which had counted against me in the first ballot now assisted me as the leading candidate in the second. The *Daily Telegraph*, an important barometer of Tory grassroots feeling, swung decisively onto my side.

Willie and I both attended the Young Conservative Conference at Eastbourne on Saturday 8 February. One woman on the platform was dressed in funereal black and glowering. I was rather concerned and asked her whether anything was wrong. 'Yes,' she said. 'I'm in mourning for Mr Heath.' There were few other mourners present. Willie and I were photographed as we kissed for the cameras. I remarked: 'Willie and I have been friends for years. I've done that to Willie many times and he to me. It was not that difficult for him to do it, I think.' Willie replied: 'I've kissed her often. But we have not done it on a pavement outside a hotel in Eastbourne before.' It was all good fun and the atmosphere lightened.

I used my own speech to the Conference to give a full-blooded rendering of my views. I said:

> You can get your economic policies right, and still have the kind of society none of us would wish. I believe we should judge people on merit and not on background. I believe the person who is prepared to work hardest should get the greatest rewards and keep them after tax. That we should back the workers and not the shirkers: that it is not only permissible but praiseworthy to want to benefit your own family by your own efforts.

Conservatives had not heard this sort of message for many years, and it went down well.

On Tuesday the second ballot took place. Again I waited nervously in Airey's room. And again it was Airey who came to give me the news. He smiled and said: 'You are now Leader of the Opposition.' I had obtained

146 votes to Willie's seventy-nine. The other candidates were out of the picture.*

I now had to hurry down to the Grand Committee Room, off Westminster Hall, where the press were waiting. I told them: 'To me it is like a dream that the next name in the lists after Harold Macmillan, Sir Alec Douglas-Home, Edward Heath, is Margaret Thatcher. Each has brought his own style of leadership and stamp of greatness to his task. I shall take on the work with humility and dedication.'

Then it was off for the Leader's traditional first visit to Conservative Central Office. On entering, I could not help remembering how hard some of the people there had worked to stop my becoming Leader.

Then I was driven back to Bill Shelton's house in Pimlico for a celebration with my friends. Denis was there. I had tried to telephone the news through to him myself, but somehow the Press Association beat me to it. Mark learned the news while he was at work as a trainee accountant. As for Carol, she could not be disturbed until she had finished the solicitors' exam she was taking that afternoon.

Only much later that night, after I had returned from dinner with the Chief Whip, Humphrey Atkins, could all of the family celebrate the good news. It was wonderful to be together. I suspect that they knew, as I did, that from this moment on our lives would never be quite the same again.

Nor would the Conservative Party.

---

* Jim Prior and Geoffrey Howe had nineteen votes each and John Peyton eleven.

CHAPTER NINE

A Bumpy Ride

Leader of the Opposition February 1975–March 1977

MY FIRST TASK was to compose the Shadow Cabinet. I met Humphrey Atkins, the Chief Whip, in the Leader of the Opposition's room in the House of Commons where we had an excellent dinner prepared by his wife Maggie. Humphrey Atkins had, of course, been Ted's appointment, and occupying the position he did had not declared his support for one side or the other in the leadership contest. But he was amiable and amenable and, as Chief Whip, was possessed of the unique fund of knowledge and gossip so essential when making high political appointments. I told Humphrey that although there were some people, like Keith Joseph and Airey Neave, to whom I felt a special obligation, I did not want to make a clean sweep of the existing team. After the bitterness of the contest with Ted there had to be sufficient continuity to keep the Party together.

The more we talked, however, the clearer it became to both of us that all the other dispositions depended upon Ted. If he wished to serve under my leadership – and I had publicly committed myself to offering him the opportunity during the leadership campaign – he might decide that he wanted one of the three main Shadow posts, or possibly a post without portfolio. I privately hoped that he would not take up my offer at all. Although none of us knew how enduring his sense of injury would be, it was already hard to imagine Ted behaving like Alec Douglas-Home and fitting in as a loyal and distinguished member of his successor's team. In any case, the newspapers were saying that Ted had no intention of serving. But I had to know for myself. Having sounded Ted out and received the impression that the speculation about his intentions was accurate, Humphrey reported back to me. But I had said I would make the offer, and the following morning I was driven to Ted's house in Wilton Street to do it in person.

Tim Kitson, Ted's PPS, showed me into the downstairs study. Ted was sitting at his desk. He did not get up; and I sat down without waiting to be asked. There was no point in pleasantries. I could guess what he thought about recent events and about me. Without offering a specific post, I asked him whether he would join the Shadow Cabinet. He said no, he would stay on the backbenches. The interview was effectively at an end. I knew that it must be painful and probably humiliating for him. But I also knew that if I walked out of Wilton Street past the assembled press after just a few minutes, the lunchtime news would be dominated by stories of snubs and splits. So I spun things out a little by asking his views about Labour's promised referendum on Britain's continuing membership of the European Economic Community and, in particular, whether he would lead the Conservative campaign. Again, he said no. I had done all I decently could to keep Ted within the fold and to ensure the meeting did not end too abruptly. But only five minutes or so had elapsed when I left Ted's study. So Tim Kitson (who was equally aware of the risk of bad publicity) and I talked inconsequentially for another quarter of an hour to fill out the time before I left the house. Respecting, as I thought, Ted's confidence, I did not even tell Airey Neave, who was setting up my office, the details of what had transpired. I made it public later only in order to set the record straight. I returned to the House of Commons and told Humphrey Atkins that Ted would indeed not be in the Shadow Cabinet.

Next, Robert Carr, who had been acting Leader of the Party during the leadership campaign, wanted to see me. He had, of course, been close to Ted and I could well understand if he did not relish the prospect of serving under me. In fact, when I saw him he made it quite clear that the only post he would accept was that of Shadow Foreign Secretary. I said that I could not promise him that. Not only was I unwilling to have my hands tied before I had properly considered the shape of the team as a whole: I was not convinced that Robert Carr would have a place in it.

By contrast, Willie Whitelaw definitely had. He had demonstrated his popularity in the leadership election. He was immensely experienced and his presence would be a reassuring guarantee to many on the backbenches that evolution rather than revolution was the order of the day. Perhaps both of us already sensed that we could form a strong political partnership, our strengths and weaknesses complementing one another's. Although I could not as yet offer him a particular portfolio, I asked Willie to be Deputy Leader of the Party, and he accepted. But his loyalty was not contingent on that; he was loyal from the first.

That evening I chaired the Shadow Cabinet for the first time. The meeting had a slightly unreal atmosphere since none of those present had yet been formally reappointed, and some would not be. Quintin Hailsham congratulated me on the Shadow Cabinet's behalf and pledged their loyalty and co-operation. I felt that he at least probably meant it. I said that Willie had agreed to be Deputy Leader and that Ted had turned down my offer of a place in the Shadow Cabinet. Willie then said that he had accepted the Deputy Leadership at once and looked forward to serving in this capacity. The formalities thus indicated a kind of armed truce between the competing views and personalities.

The following evening, I made my first appearance as Leader at the 1922 Committee meeting. My relations with the wider Parliamentary Party were much easier than with the Shadow Cabinet. As I entered, everyone rose to their feet. Edward du Cann presented me with an unsigned Valentine card (a day early) which would join the other Valentines and roses that accumulated at Flood Street.

In the next few days my time was taken up in meeting journalists, discussing arrangements for my office and fulfilling long-standing constituency engagements. There were few opportunities to sit down with Humphrey and Willie to discuss Shadow Cabinet membership. In any case, I wanted the weekend to make my final decisions. But the delay encouraged speculation. According to the press a battle was under way to prevent Keith Joseph becoming Shadow Chancellor. In fact, he did not ask for the position nor did I offer it.

Willie was the first to come in. I gave him a roving brief which included the issue of devolution – which already spelt political difficulties that he, as both a former Chief Whip and a Scot representing an English seat, might be able to tackle. Then I saw Keith Joseph, whom I asked to continue with his Shadow Cabinet responsibility for policy and research. In a sense, Willie and Keith were the two key figures, one providing the political brawn and the other the policy-making brains of the team. I also felt that Keith must continue his intellectual crusade from the Centre for Policy Studies for wider understanding and acceptance of free enterprise economics. I was under no illusion that my victory in the leadership election represented a wholesale conversion.

My next visitor was Reggie Maudling. I suspect that, although he had made it clear publicly that he was willing to serve, he was as surprised as the press when I made him Shadow Foreign Secretary. Though widely praised at the time, this was not a good appointment.

Still less of a soulmate was Ian Gilmour. He had been a strong partisan of Ted, and he lacked the support or standing which might have made him politically costly to dispense with. But I valued his intelligence. I felt that he could make a useful contribution as long as he was kept out of an economic post, to which neither his training nor his aptitudes suited him. I asked him to be Shadow Home Secretary.

Michael Heseltine, who now came in to see me, had a much more flamboyant personality than Ian's, although they shared many of the same views. I asked him to stay on as Shadow Industry Secretary. It was a portfolio which gave full scope to his talent for Opposition, since it fell to him to fight the Labour Government's main nationalization proposals. What I did not fully grasp at this time was how ideologically committed he was to an interventionist approach in industry which I could not accept.

I asked Peter Carrington to stay on as Leader of the House of Lords. Again, I had no illusions about Peter's position in the Tory Party's political spectrum: he was not of my way of thinking. He had, of course, been in Ted's inner circle making the political decisions about the miners' strike and the February 1974 election. But since we lost office he had proved an extremely effective Opposition Leader in the Upper House, and as a former Defence Minister and an international businessman he had wide experience of foreign affairs. Admittedly, he was likely in Shadow Cabinet to be on the opposite side to me on economic policy. But he never allowed economic disagreements to get in the way of his more general responsibilities. He brought style, experience, wit and – politically incorrect as the thought may be – a touch of class.

Geoffrey Howe had his own droll wit. But in most other ways he was a very different politician from my other appointments that day. I would in any case have felt obliged to give Geoffrey a Shadow Cabinet post, simply because he was a candidate against me and I wished to unify the Party as much as possible. But it was a calculated gamble to make him Shadow Chancellor. Geoffrey was to have a difficult time both trying to resolve our divisions on economic policy and in defending our case in the House. I would be put under a good deal of pressure to remove him and find someone better able to take on the Chancellor, Denis Healey. But I knew that Geoffrey's difficulties, like mine, were more the result of circumstances than lack of native talent. By the time our period in Opposition was approaching its end he had become indispensable.

After careful thought I decided to keep Jim Prior as Shadow Employment Secretary. This was rightly taken as a signal that I had no immediate plans for a fundamental reform of trade union law. It was Jim's strong conviction that our aim should be to establish both that we accepted the existing trade union law, with perhaps a few alterations, and that we saw the union leaders as people with whom we could deal. Such an approach made more sense at the beginning of the period in Opposition than at the end of it.

Airey Neave had already privately told me that the only portfolio he wanted was that of Shadow Northern Ireland Secretary. His intelligence contacts, proven physical courage and shrewdness amply qualified him for this testing and largely thankless task. The other appointments were less strategically crucial. Two offers of Shadow Cabinet posts were turned down – one to John Biffen, who would in fact join later, and the other to Edward du Cann, whose early campaign team had provided the nucleus of mine. Edward stayed on as Chairman of the 1922 Committee, which was probably far more useful to me.

The next day (Tuesday) I had some less pleasant business to transact. At 10.30 Peter Walker came in. There was no personal warmth between us. He had been one of the most effective members of Ted's inner circle, and he opposed with vigour and eloquence the approach which Keith and I were committed to adopt. He clearly had to go.

I confirmed in a discussion with Geoffrey Rippon, who now came into my room, that he did not wish to serve: that suited us both. I then saw Nicholas Scott, who had shadowed Housing. He too was on the left of the Party. The conversation was made slightly easier by the fact that I had absorbed the Housing portfolio into the wider Environment one. His job had been shot from under him.

I left to last the interview with Robert Carr. I told him that I had given the Shadow Foreign Secretary post to Reggie Maudling, which he presumably knew already. Perhaps he had just bid too high, or perhaps he might have been persuaded to stay in another capacity. But I was not keen to have another strong opponent in any position on the team.

The published Shadow Cabinet list (to which Peter Thorneycroft as Party Chairman and Angus Maude as Chairman of the Conservative Research Department would later be added) was rightly seen as a compromise. As such, it annoyed the left of the Party who disliked my dropping of Robert Carr, Peter Walker and Nicholas Scott: it also disappointed the right who worried about Reggie Maudling's return, the fact that Geoffrey and not Keith was Shadow Chancellor and the lack of any new right-wing faces from the backbenches. In fact, given the fragility as yet of my position and the need to express a balance of opinion in the Shadow Cabinet to bring the Party together, it was a relatively successful operation. It created a Treasury team that shared my and Keith's views on the free market economy, shifted the balance of opinion within the Shadow Cabinet as a whole somewhat in my direction and yet gave grounds for loyalty to those I had retained from Ted's regime. I felt I could expect support (within limits) from such a team, but I knew I could not assume agreement – even on basic principles.

Airey Neave and I decided that there would have to be changes at Conservative Central Office. Constitutionally, Central Office is the Leader of the Party's office: events during the leadership campaign had convinced me that it would be very difficult for some of those there to act in that capacity under me.

At Central Office I wanted as Chairman an effective administrator, one preferably with business connections, who would be loyal to me. I had always admired Peter Thorneycroft and in retrospect I thought that his courageous resignation on the issue of public expenditure in 1958 had signalled a wrong turning for the post-war Conservative Party. As part of that older generation which had been leading the Party when I first entered Parliament, and as chairman of several large companies, Peter seemed to me to fit the bill. But how to persuade him? It turned out that Willie Whitelaw was related to him, and Willie persuaded him to take the job. It would have taxed the energy of a much younger man, for the Party Chairman has to keep up morale even in the lowest periods, of which there would be several. Peter had the added problem that at this stage most of the Party in the country accepted my leadership only on sufferance. This would gradually change after the 1975 Party Conference. But it took a good deal longer – and some painful and controversial personnel changes – before I felt that the leading figures at Central Office had any real commitment to me. Peter gradually replaced them with loyalists; I never enquired how.

Alistair McAlpine's arrival as Party Treasurer certainly helped. Although a staunch Tory from a family of Tories, Alistair had to turn himself into something of a politician overnight. I told him that he would have to give up his German Mercedes for a British Jaguar and he immediately complied. But I had not prepared him for the host of minor but irritating examples of obstructive behaviour which confronted him at Central Office, nor for the great difficulties he would encounter in trying to persuade businessmen that in spite of the years of Heathite corporatism we were still a free enterprise Party worth supporting.

Some people expected me to make even more substantial changes at the Conservative Research Department. The CRD was in theory a department of Central Office, but largely because of its geographical separateness (in Old Queen Street) and its intellectually distinguished past, it had a specially important role, particularly in Opposition. In a sense, the Centre for Policy Studies had been set up as an alternative to the Research Department. Now that I was Leader, however, the CRD and the CPS would have to work together. The Director of the Research Department, Chris Patten, I knew to be on the left of the Party. Much bitterness and rivalry had built up between the CRD and the CPS. In the eyes of many on the right it was precisely the consensus-oriented, generalist approach epitomized by the CRD which had left us directionless and – in the words of Keith Joseph – 'stranded on the middle ground'. I decided to replace Ian Gilmour with Angus Maude as Chairman of the Research Department, who would work with Keith on policy, but leave Chris Patten as Director and Adam Ridley, Ted's former economic adviser, as his deputy. These were good decisions.

Meanwhile, Airey Neave and I had to assemble a small personal staff who would run my office. A flood of letters followed my becoming Leader, sometimes 800 a day. Girls would come across from Central Office to help sort out the post, but usually this was the task of my four secretaries, who sat on the floor in the main room opening envelopes and categorizing the letters. They did their best, but it was hopelessly unsystematic. Then Alistair McAlpine suggested that I ask David Wolfson to take charge of the correspondence section. Alistair thought that if David, as the man responsible for the mail-order section of Great Universal Stores, could not bring order out of this chaos no one could. In fact, both in Opposition and then at 10 Downing Street, David's talents were put to a good deal wider use than sorting the mail: he gave insights into what business was thinking, provided important contacts and proved particularly adept at smoothing ruffled political feathers.

But I also needed a full-time head of my office, who had to be industrious, dependable and, with the number of speeches, articles and letters to draft, above all literate. It was my old friend and colleague, providentially translated to the editorship of the *Daily Telegraph*, Bill Deedes who suggested Richard Ryder, then working on Peterborough, the *Telegraph*'s respectable gossip column.

A month after Richard's arrival Gordon Reece, on secondment from EMI for a year, joined my full-time staff to help in dealing with the press and much else. Gordon was a godsend. An ebullient former TV producer whose good humour never failed, he was able to jolly me along to accept things I would have rejected from other people. His view was that in getting my message across we must not concentrate simply on heavy-weight newspapers, *The Times* and the *Daily Telegraph*, but be just as concerned about the mid-market populars, the *Daily Mail* and the *Daily Express* and – the real revolution – about the *Sun* and the *News of the World*. Moreover, he believed that even newspapers which supported the Labour Party in their editorial line would be prepared to give us fair treatment if we made a real attempt to provide them with interesting copy. He was right on both counts. The *Sun* and the *News of the World* were crucial in communicating Conservative values to traditionally non-Conservative voters. The left-wing *Sunday Mirror* also gave me fair and full coverage, however critical the comments. Gordon regularly talked to the editors. But he also persuaded me that the person they really wanted to see and hear from was me. So, whatever the other demands on my diary, when Gordon said that we must have lunch with such-and-such an editor, that was the priority.

Gordon also performed another invaluable service. Every politician has to decide how much he or she is prepared to change manner and appearance for the sake of the media. It may sound grittily honourable to refuse to make any concessions, but such an attitude in a public figure is most likely to betray a lack of seriousness about winning power or even, paradoxically, the pride that apes humility. When Gordon suggested some changes in my style of hair and clothes in order to make a better impression, he was calling upon his experience in television. 'Avoid lots of jewellery near the face. Edges look good on television. Watch out for background colours which clash with your outfit.' It was quite an education.

There was also the matter of my voice. In the House of Commons one has to speak over the din to get a hearing. This is more difficult the higher the pitch of one's voice, because in increasing its volume one automatically goes up the register. This poses an obvious problem for most women. Somehow one has to learn to project the voice without shrieking.

Even outside the House, when addressing an audience my voice was naturally high-pitched, which can easily become grating and I had deliberately tried to lower its tone. The result, unfortunately, was to give me a sore throat – an even greater problem for a regular public speaker. Gordon found me an expert who knew that the first thing to do was to get your breathing right, and then to speak not from the back of the throat but from the front of the mouth. She was a genius. Her sympathetic understanding for my difficulties was only matched by that for her ailing cat. Unfortunately, the cat would sometimes fall sick just before my lesson and force its cancellation. Fortunately, I too like cats. And so we finished the course.

On one occasion Gordon took me to meet Sir Laurence Olivier to see whether he had any tips. He was quite complimentary, telling me that I had a good gaze out to the audience, which was important, and that my voice was perfectly all right, which – no thanks to the cat – it now probably was.

Getting all these things right took me several months. But all in all the general system never let me down. The real political tests of Opposition leadership, however, still lay ahead.

My first real experience of the *public* aspects of being Leader of the Opposition came when I visited Scotland on Friday 21 February. From the time that I stepped off the aircraft at Edinburgh Airport, where a waggish piper played 'A man's a man for a' that', I received an enthusiastic Scottish welcome.

I could always be sure of a friendly reception from grassroots Scottish Tories, whose embattled position seems to sharpen their zeal. More generally, however, the honeymoon did not last long and ordinary political life resumed with a vengeance. The opinion polls, which in February had given the Conservatives a 4 percentage point lead over Labour, showed a 2 per cent Labour lead just a month later – not statistically significant perhaps, but a check on any premature tendency to euphoria. It also soon became clear that powerful elements in the Party were out to make trouble for me. In early April Harold Macmillan and Ted Heath made speeches to a conference of Young Conservatives, warning against shifting the Conservative Party to the right. The European referendum campaign placed the focus on European issues, and this in turn gave a fillip to advocates of coalition government. All this created more difficulties for me.

My first major parliamentary performance, in which I crossed swords with Harold Wilson, in a debate on the economy on Thursday 22 May, was heavily and justly criticized for not spelling out convincingly the Conservative alternative. The difficulty was that at this point we *had* no credible alternative to offer. Imprisoned by the requirement of defending the indefensible record of the Heath Government, we were unable as yet to break through to a proper free market alternative.

Even so, on this and several other occasions I did not make a good speech. Leading for the Opposition in set-piece debates, one is not able to make a wide-ranging speech on the basis of a few notes, something which I was good at. The root of all our problems, however, lay in the unresolved contradictions of policy.

In March 1975 we discussed a paper from Keith and Angus on policy-making. They proposed involving both backbench committees and sympathetic outside experts; and this was accepted. The number of policy groups continued to multiply. They were generally chaired by the relevant front-bench spokesmen. Geoffrey Howe's Economic Reconstruction Group was the main forum for hashing over economic policy. From time to time, there would be whole-day Shadow Cabinet policy discussions, which I myself would chair. The full Shadow Cabinet approved, rather than devised, policy on the basis of papers put to it by the chief Shadow spokesmen and their policy groups.

The Centre for Policy Studies and a range of outside advisers, particularly on economic matters, fed in ideas and suggestions to Keith and me (Keith also had a number of lunchtime meetings with other Shadow Cabinet colleagues on policy). And on top of all that I would sometimes advance a new policy in a speech or interview – not always to the applause of my colleagues.

As a system of decision-taking the structure had a somewhat ramshackle feel to it. But then, no amount of institutional neatness could resolve the fundamental questions we had to decide. The fact that by the time we took office in May 1979 so many of the big issues had been satisfactorily resolved, and Shadow ministers had as clear an idea of their priorities as any incoming post-war British Government, shows that in the most important sense this policy-making system 'worked'.

The foremost policy issue was how to deal with inflation, which soared to 26.9 per cent in August 1975 before beginning to fall, going below 10 per cent in January 1978. Discussion of how inflation was caused and cured also necessarily involved making a judgement about the Heath Government. If inflation was the result of an increase in the money supply, which takes approximately eighteen months to work through in the form of higher prices, then the prime responsibility for the high inflation during the first eighteen months or so of the Labour Government should be laid at the door of the Conservatives. If, however, the cause of high inflation was excessive wage awards after the collapse of the previous Conservative Government's incomes policy and Labour's abdication of authority to the trade unions, then political life in Opposition would be easier. We might not have any credible solutions to offer, but we could at least blame everything on the Government. This approach was likely to be favoured by those of my colleagues who prided themselves on being sceptics about all kinds of economic theory. In fact, the case that the Heath Government's monetary incontinence was to blame for inflation seemed to me convincingly argued by Alan Walters, whose devastating indictment and predictions were circulated by Keith as background for a discussion with Shadow Cabinet colleagues in March 1975. But if I had publicly accepted this it would have provoked even more trouble from Ted Heath and his supporters.

Our failure to be explicit about the overriding importance of monetary policy did, however, open up our flank to attack on incomes policy. For if wage rises were the cause of inflation, then how would we in government be able to contain such rises?

The October 1974 Conservative manifesto had committed the Party to seek a voluntary policy for prices and incomes, with the qualification that it might be necessary to move to a statutory policy if voluntary support were not achieved. I could only gradually wean the Party away from this position. My task was made more difficult both by the fact that wages and prices were soaring alarmingly, and by Ted Heath and Peter Walker putting me under heavy public pressure to support successive stages of the Labour Government's incomes policy. In an interview with Robin Day in May 1975 I said that under some circumstances a pay freeze might be necessary, but not as a prelude to a permanent statutory incomes policy. Wages had, after all, been growing at some 30 per cent a year since Labour took office. But I never saw even a short wage freeze as having more than a transitional role in any realistic strategy to bring down inflation, which must be based on control of the money supply and government borrowing. In fact, there were already some early signs that the Government had woken up to the need for some financial discipline. The April 1975 budget announced cuts in planned spending levels and raised the basic rate of income tax by two pence – to 35 per cent – in order to reduce the swelling deficit which was expected to reach £9,000 million in 1975/76.

If public expenditure was one aspect of the debate about counter-inflation policy, trade union power was another. On this matter, the line-up in the Shadow Cabinet over these years was slightly different from that on the question of voluntary/statutory incomes policy versus 'free collective bargaining'. Geoffrey Howe was the most consistently hawkish on trade unions. Right from the beginning he emphasized in our discussions the need to shift the balance of power in industrial relations: indeed, I suspect that he would ideally have liked to get back to the Industrial Relations Act framework which he had devised. Keith Joseph and I shared that approach, though I remained extremely wary about committing ourselves to more changes than we could deliver. Jim Prior and most of the other Shadow Cabinet members could be found in the opposite camp.

On incomes policy, however, Geoffrey and Jim, supported by Ian Gilmour, were the strongest advocates of some kind of national understanding with the trade unions. Geoffrey's view was that we should seek to emulate the alleged successes of the West German approach of 'concerted action', whose purpose was to educate 'both sides' of industry in the realities of the state of the economy and win some kind of consent to limit wages. This did not in itself involve a renunciation of monetarism, to which Geoffrey, in contrast with Jim and Ian, was increasingly committed. But it did involve a large element of corporatism and centralized economic decision-making, to which Keith was fiercely opposed and which I too disliked.

The most convinced opponent of monetarism and all its works was Reggie Maudling who, when he put his mind to it, actually had the grasp of economics to give his arguments weight. Reggie was the most ardently committed to a statutory incomes policy. As he put it in a dissenting paper to the Shadow Cabinet in May: 'To the economic purist, no doubt, prices are only a symptom of inflation, but to us as politicians they are the real problem, because it is rising prices that are breaking the country in half.' With such divisions in our midst it is not surprising that for much of the time our economic policies were felt to lack coherence.

The difficulties I had faced in the Economic Debate on Thursday 22 May – when for these reasons I had not been able to present a coherent alternative to government policy – persuaded me of the urgent need to sort out our position. Further public differences confirmed this. In June I spoke to the Welsh Party Conference in Aberystwyth, expressing strong

reservations about statutory wage controls: the same day Reggie
Maudling spoke in Chislehurst implying that we might support a statutory policy. A few days later Keith made a speech casting severe doubt on
the value of even a wage freeze, suggesting that it would be used as an
excuse for not cutting public spending and taking the other necessary
economic steps. On the same day Peter Walker called for a statutory pay
policy – and was himself rebutted by Keith, who said bluntly that wage
freezes did not work. Not surprisingly, Conservative splits figured large in
the press. The fact that these divisions were more than replicated on the
Government side was of only limited comfort.

I found from my own soundings that Conservative opinion in the
country was strongly opposed to employers having to bear the brunt of
anti-inflation measures. Our supporters wanted us to be tough on
Labour. The following day the Backbench Finance Committee met and
Bill Shelton reported to me their concerns. While very few wanted us to
vote against the Government's package outright, there was widespread
anxiety lest by supporting it we would also be endorsing a continuation
of the socialist programme.

At Shadow Cabinet on Monday 7 July, Jim Prior and Keith Joseph
argued their conflicting cases. But the crucial question was still which
Division Lobby the Party should enter, if any. By now the safest, if least
glorious, course appeared to be to abstain. The risk was that such a tactic
would dismay both wings of the Parliamentary Party and we could find
ourselves with a three-way split.

Whatever the tactics to employ, I also needed to be clear in my own
mind whether the Healey measures were a genuine step towards financial discipline or a smokescreen. So the day after the Shadow Cabinet
discussion I had a working supper in my room in the House with Willie,
Keith, Geoffrey, Jim and a number of economists and City experts,
including people like Alan Walters, Brian Griffiths, Gordon Pepper and
Sam Brittan who were in regular touch with me and on whose opinions
I set a high value.* Although we would have to look at the package as a

---

* Alan Walters was then Cassel Professor at the London School of Economics. He left the
following year for the United States to work for the World Bank. As already noted, he was
my economic adviser as Prime Minister, 1981–84 and in 1989. Brian Griffiths (later Head
of my Policy Unit at No. 10) was then a lecturer at the London School of Economics; he
became a professor at the City University the following year. Gordon Pepper was an
economic analyst at Greenwell & Co., and an expert on monetary policy. Sam Brittan was
Principal Economic Commentator on the *Financial Times*.

whole, especially the monetary and fiscal side, as Geoffrey said at the start of the evening, I came away feeling still less inclined to lend support to flimsy and possibly harmful proposals.

The White Paper, containing the details, was published on Friday 11 July. It was, as expected, a curate's egg, containing measures like cash limits which we approved but not matching these with any real public expenditure cuts. The centrepiece was a £6 limit on pay increases for the coming year. The most astonishing omission was that the Government refused to publish the draft Bill it claimed to have drawn up which would introduce statutory controls if the voluntary limits were ignored. By the time it came to a vote, backbench and Shadow Cabinet opinion favoured abstention and this was now agreed. My own speech in the debate did not go particularly well – unsurprisingly, given the protean case I had to present. That might have been awkward, but Ted bailed me out by regretting that we were not supporting the Government and then refusing to back our critical amendment.

If one good thing came out of these travails, it was that the Shadow Cabinet was pushed towards an agreed line on incomes policy. This was that the conquest of inflation required that all economic policies must be pulling in the same anti-inflationary direction, in particular public spending and monetary policy. An incomes policy might play a useful part as one of a comprehensive package of policies, but was not to be considered as an alternative to the others, and could not be expected to achieve much on its own. While hardly qualifying as an original (or even true) economic insight, this at least provided a temporary refuge.

In any case, the Government's July package was rightly judged to be insufficient to deal with the looming economic crisis. Inflation that summer reached an all-time high of 26.9 per cent.

We fled to Brittany in August for a holiday canal-cruising. I was still away when Harold Wilson launched the incomes policy in a television broadcast asking people to give 'a year for Britain' by sticking to the £6 limit. In my absence, Willie Whitelaw replied the following evening giving this nonsense a rather warmer welcome than I could have been persuaded to do.

In spite of the difficulties I had faced in the months since I became Leader, I approached that autumn's Party Conference in reasonably good spirits. Ted and his friends seemed likely to continue being as difficult as possible, but my foreign visits had boosted my own standing. The

Government's economic policy was in ruins. The Conservatives were 23 per cent ahead of Labour, according to a pre-Conference opinion poll. The task at Blackpool was to consolidate all this by showing that I could command the support of the Party in the country.

The Leader's speech at a Party Conference is quite unlike the Conference speeches of other front-bench spokesmen. It has to cover a sufficiently wide number of subjects to avoid the criticism that one has 'left out' some burning issue. Yet each section of the speech has to have a thematic correspondence with all the other sections. Otherwise, you finish up with what I used to call a 'Christmas tree', on which pledges and achievements are hung and where each new topic is classically announced by the mind-numbing phrase 'I now turn to . . .'

I told my speech writers that I was not going to make just an economic speech. The economy had gone wrong because something else had gone wrong spiritually and philosophically. The economic crisis was a crisis of the spirit of the nation. But when I discussed the kind of draft I wanted with Chris Patten and others from the Research Department, I felt they were just not getting the message I wanted to dispatch. So I sat down over the weekend and wrote out sixty pages of my large handwriting. I found no difficulty: it flowed and flowed. But was it a speech? I was redrafting on Sunday morning when Woodrow Wyatt – a former Labour MP turned entrepreneur, author, sympathizer and close friend – telephoned. I told him what I was doing and he suggested I come round to his house for supper so that he could look at it. The experienced journalist's eye saw all that I had not. So the two of us began to cut and shape and reorganize. By the time I arrived in Blackpool I had the beginnings of a Conference speech. I also found that Chris Patten and others had written new material. We married the two and a first draft was accordingly produced.

In between receptions and visits to the debates I would go in to see how the speech writers were proceeding. But by Wednesday it was clear to me that none of those working away in my suite was what in the jargon is known as a 'wordsmith'. We had the structure, the ideas and even the foundations for some good jokes. But we needed someone with a feel for the words *themselves* who could make the whole text flow along. Gordon suggested that the playwright Ronnie Millar, who had drafted material in the past for Ted's broadcasts, was the man to help. So the whole text was urgently sent to Ronnie to be (what I would always later describe as) 'Ronniefied'. It came back transformed. More precisely, it came back a speech. Then there was more cutting and retyping throughout Thursday night. It was about 4.30 on Friday morning when the process was complete and I felt I could turn in for an hour or so's sleep.

Earlier on Thursday evening, when I was reading through the latest draft, I had been called to the telephone to speak to Willie Whitelaw. Willie told me that Ted had arrived and was staying at the same hotel (the Imperial). His suite was a couple of floors below mine. For several months a number of Ted's friends had been urging him to bury the hatchet. Willie explained to me that pride was involved in these matters and Ted could not really come and see me. Would I therefore come and see him? I replied that of course I would. Willie said that that was 'absolutely splendid' and that he would ring me back to confirm. Meanwhile, I plunged back into the draft. About an hour and a half went by with no telephone call. Since it was now about 10 o'clock, I thought that we must really get on with our 'reconciliation'. So I rang Willie and asked what was happening. I was told that Ted had had second thoughts. The hatchet would evidently remain unburied.

The climax of the Conservative Conference creates a special electricity at Blackpool. For my part, though I had had almost no sleep, I was confident of my text and resolved to put everything into its delivery.

Reading it through almost twenty years later, there is nothing substantial that I would change – least of all the section about my personal creed and convictions.

> Let me give you my vision: a man's right to work as he will, to spend what he earns, to own property, to have the state as servant and not as master – these are the British inheritance . . . We must get private enterprise back on the road to recovery – not merely to give people more of their own money to spend as they choose, but to have more money to help the old and the sick and the handicapped . . . I believe that, just as each of us has an obligation to make the best of his talents, so governments have an obligation to create the framework within which we can do so . . . We can go on as we have been doing, we can continue down. Or we can stop and with a decisive act of will we can say 'Enough'.

I was relieved when, as I got into my speech, I began to be interrupted by applause and cheers. The representatives on the floor were hearing their own opinions expressed from the platform and they responded with great enthusiasm. I picked up some of their excitement in turn. On both the floor and the platform there was a sense that something new was happening.

But would it play outside the Empress Ballroom? I hoped, and in my heart believed, that the *Daily Mail*'s leader comment on the contents of the speech was correct: 'If this is "lurching to the right", as her critics claim, 90 per cent of the population lurched that way long ago.'

By the end of that first year as Leader of the Opposition I felt that I had found my feet. I still had difficulties adjusting to my new role in the House of Commons. But I had established a good rapport with the Party in Parliament and in the country. I was pleased with the way my little team in the office were working together. I only wished the Shadow Cabinet could be persuaded to do likewise.

I reshuffled the pack on 15 January 1976. Reshuffles in Opposition had strong elements of farce. The layout of the Leader of the Opposition's suite of rooms in the Commons was such that it was almost impossible to manage the entrances and exits of fortunate and unfortunate colleagues with suitable delicacy. Embarrassing encounters were inevitable. But on this occasion there was not too much blood on the carpet.

I was delighted that John Biffen was now prepared to join the Shadow Cabinet as Energy spokesman. He had been perhaps the most eloquent and effective critic on the backbenches at the time of the Heath Government U-turn and I welcomed his presence. And the promotion of Douglas Hurd, one of Ted's closest aides, to be Party spokesman on Europe, showed that whatever Ted himself might feel, I had no grudges against those who had served him. I made Willie Shadow Home Secretary in place of Ian Gilmour, whom I moved to Defence where he proved an extremely robust and effective Shadow spokesman; if he had limited himself to that, life would have been easier for all concerned.

More important, our occasional victories did not seem to lead anywhere. The Government remained insecurely in place. On Wednesday 11 February (on the first anniversary of my becoming Leader) we won a division on a motion to reduce the Industry Secretary Eric Varley's salary by £1,000 – a formal means of expressing rejection of policies. Then, in the midst of the sterling crisis of March 1976, the Government was defeated as a result of a left-wing revolt on a vote on its public expenditure plans. As one does on these occasions, I demanded that the Prime Minister should resign. I never imagined that he would. But the following Tuesday Harold Wilson did just that, letting me know of his decision in a note I received just before the announcement was made.

I can say little in favour of either of Harold Wilson's terms as Prime Minister. Doubtless he had principles, but they were so obscured by artful dodging that it was difficult for friends and opponents alike to decide what they might be. Yet I had always liked him personally; I had appreciated his sense of humour, and was aware of his many kindnesses. He was a master of Commons repartee, and I usually scored nothing better than a draw against him in the House. This would continue to be the case with his successor, Jim Callaghan. He adopted in the House a manner that appeared avuncular, was in fact patronizing and made it hard for me to advance serious criticism of government policy without appearing to nag. In a larger sense, Mr Callaghan in those years was a sort of moderate disguise for his left-wing party and its trade union backers. As a result, he articulated views and attitudes – on education, family policy, law and order etc. – which were never embodied in government policy. Tactically brilliant, he was strategically unsuccessful – until eventually in the Winter of Discontent the entire house of cards that was Labour moderation collapsed.

Meanwhile, the state of the economy was worsening. In February 1976 the Government had announced spending cuts of £1,600 million for 1977/78 and £3,000 million for 1978/79 (in today's terms the equivalent of £6,000 million and £11,500 million). Impressive though this might sound, it amounted to no more than a modest cut in large planned increases. In December 1975 the International Monetary Fund had granted an application for stand-by credit to tide over Britain's finances. Even so, in March there was a full-scale sterling crisis. The pound came under heavy pressure yet again in June, and more international stand-by credit had to be obtained, repayable in six months, failing which Britain agreed to apply again to the IMF. Inflation was falling by then, but large negative interest rates, combined with the failure to make real cuts in public spending and borrowing, prevented the Government from getting to grips with its underlying financial and economic problems. The new sterling crisis in September, which would lead to the humiliating abdication of control over our economy to the IMF, was the final result of an entirely justified loss of confidence by international markets in the Labour Government's handling of the economy.

It might be expected that all of this would make an Opposition's life easier, no matter how bad it was for the country. But that was not so.

We were expected to support the Labour Government's hesitant and belated moves to apply financial discipline. That was fair enough. But we were also under a more general pressure to be 'responsible' in dealing with the Labour Government's self-contrived tribulations. However commendable, this inevitably cramped my attacking style.

All in all, the regular Party politics of 1976 were frustrating and inconclusive.

The Right Approach, which we published on the eve of the 1976 Conference, gave a persuasive account of the new Conservatism. Indeed, it still reads well and, stylistically at least, ranks with *Change is Our Ally* as one of the best-written documents produced by the post-war Conservative Party. The credit for this must go to Chris Patten and Angus Maude who, with Keith Joseph, Geoffrey Howe and Jim Prior, drafted it.

It was helped by the fact that a truce had been reached in the internal arguments about where we all stood on incomes policy. A speech by Geoffrey Howe to the Bow Group (a Conservative ginger group) in May 1976 provided an agreed 'line to take' which was broadly followed in *The Right Approach*. The document pointed out that prices and incomes policies did not offer a long-term solution to inflation, while noting that it would be unwise 'flatly and permanently' to reject the idea, and nodding favourably in the direction of the West German system of 'concerted action'. It was a fudge – but temporarily palatable.

But it was the fact that *The Right Approach* concentrated on the big general arguments, restating what differentiated our approach from that of socialism, that made it the success it was. It received a good press, not least because I and my colleagues put in considerable effort to explain it to the editors beforehand.

The success of *The Right Approach* illustrates an important paradox about the whole of this period. For a variety of reasons, we were not a particularly successful Opposition in the ordinary sense of the word. Differences kept on emerging between us. We were usually unsuccessful in the House of Commons. We found it difficult to capitalize on the Government's mistakes. Yet on the higher plane of belief, conviction and philosophy we were extremely effective. We were winning the battle of ideas which was the necessary preliminary not just to winning the election but to winning enduring popular support for the change of direction we wanted to make. Keith Joseph's speeches continued to put over the powerful themes he developed in the CPS. In March he delivered a speech in Harrow which took head-on the Government's claim that high public expenditure was necessary for high levels of employment. In fact, as Keith pointed out:

> Government overspending is a major and continued cause of
> unemployment. Immediate cuts in runaway state expenditure are
> essential if we are to save the economy now, and eventually restore
> a high and stable level of employment . . . Several Peters go on the
> dole for every Paul kept in a protected job.

I wrote the introduction to the published version of Keith's Stockton
Lecture, entitled *Monetarism is Not Enough*, which appeared a few
months later. Since monetarism was far from accepted by most members
of the Shadow Cabinet, this title was a deliberately bold way of expressing
an important truth. It was 'not enough' to exert monetary control alone;
if we also failed to cut public expenditure and public borrowing, the
whole burden of disinflation would then be placed on the wealth-creating
private sector.

Alfred Sherman, who had assisted Keith with his Stockton Lecture,
helped me draft the speech I made to the Zurich Economic Society on
Monday 14 March 1977. Although delivered in Switzerland, it was aimed
very much at the domestic audience. Alfred and I worked particularly
hard on the text, which took an optimistic view of Britain's future,
arguing that:

> The tide is beginning to turn against collectivism . . . and this turn
> is rooted in a revulsion against the sour fruit of socialist experi-
> ence. The tide flows away from failure. But it will not automatically
> float us to our desired destination . . . It is up to us to give intellec-
> tual content and political direction . . . If we fail, the tide will be
> lost. But if it is taken, the last quarter of our century can initiate a
> new renaissance matching anything in our island's long and
> outstanding history.

There was a growing crisis of confidence in Labour, and the polls
showed us more than ten points ahead. By-election victories at Walsall
North and Workington with big swings to us would shortly confirm the
picture. It was at this juncture that talk of a coalition began again among
those Conservatives determined at all costs to snatch defeat for me from
the jaws of victory.

Harold Macmillan went on television to call for a 'Government of
National Unity'. Nor, it seemed, was there much doubt in his mind about
who should be called back to lead it. I thought that I had better go and

talk to him to see what he really thought, and it was arranged that we should meet in Maurice Macmillan's house in Catherine Place. I arrived early and waited upstairs in the sitting room. I heard Maurice's father arrive and say to him: 'Has the call come?' Maurice said: 'No, not quite.' He had to make do with me. Our meeting was pleasantly inconclusive, with Macmillan urging me not to be too critical of the Government at a time of crisis. And the only call was that eventually made to the IMF.

I now decided to make some changes of my own. Reggie Maudling's performance as Shadow Foreign Secretary had long been a source of embarrassment. He did not agree with my approach to either the economy or foreign affairs; he was increasingly unwilling to disguise his differences with me; and he was laid back. But when I told him that he had to go, he summoned up enough energy to be quite rude.

I also wanted to move Michael Heseltine out of Industry and replace him with John Biffen. When not overreacting, Michael was an effective scourge of the Government, and he was certainly passionately interested in his brief at Industry. The trouble was that his outlook was completely different from anything recognizably Conservative. For example, in January 1976 he made a speech criticizing Labour ministers for failing to meet sufficiently often 'to agree and develop an industrial strategy for this nation'. His real criticism seemed to be that the Labour Party intervened in industry and picked losers whereas he would intervene and pick winners. The notion that the state did not and could not know who *would* win or lose, and that in intervening to back its own judgement with taxpayers' money it was impoverishing the economy as a whole, seemed never to have occurred to him. Again, however, when I asked Michael to leave Industry and go to Environment, he said that he preferred not to. I sent my PPS, John Stanley, who knew him well, off to negotiate, and Michael reluctantly agreed to make way for John Biffen on the under-standing that he would not have to be Secretary of State for the Environment once we were in power. That settled, the rest of the changes could now go ahead. I asked John Davies to take over from Reggie on Foreign Affairs, where until illness tragically struck him down, he worked hard and effectively.

It was important to have an energetic and effective front-bench team because there seemed a growing likelihood that we might soon be asked to become a government. On Wednesday 15 December Denis Healey introduced a further mini-budget. He announced deep cuts in public spending and borrowing, and targets for the money supply (though expressed in terms of domestic credit expansion), as part of the deal agreed with the IMF. It was, in fact, a monetarist approach of the sort which Keith Joseph and I believed in, and it outflanked on the right those members of my own Shadow Cabinet who were still clinging to the outdated nostrums of Keynesian demand management. True to the tactic of not opposing measures necessary to deal with the crisis, we abstained in the vote on the measures. The IMF-imposed package was a turning point, for under the new financial discipline the economy began to recover. In party political terms this was a mixed blessing. On the one hand, discontent with the Government's economic stewardship would diminish and support was likely to swing back towards Labour. On the other, we could now argue that socialism as an economic doctrine was totally discredited and that even the socialists were having to accept that reality was Conservative.

The political uncertainty made everyone jittery. The Government no longer had an overall majority. No one knew how members of the smaller parties might vote on any particular issue. It was frustrating enough even for those of us who were kept informed of the changing parliamentary arithmetic by the whips. But it was all but incomprehensible to Conservative supporters in the country, who could not understand why we were unable to inflict a fatal defeat and bring about a general election. In fact, on Tuesday 22 February 1977 the Government was defeated on a guillotine on the Scotland and Wales Bill. The end of any immediate hope of achieving devolution in Scotland and Wales caused the Scottish and Welsh Nationalists to withdraw their support from the Government. A new parliamentary crisis – one in which the Government had ceased to have even a working majority – was upon us.

Ted had originally committed the Conservatives to devolution at the Scottish Party Conference in May 1968, following a surge in support for the Scottish Nationalist Party (SNP) – a short-lived surge, as it turned out. Ted's 'Perth Declaration' came as a shock to most Conservatives, including those in Scotland. I was never happy with the policy and there was little enthusiasm for it among English Tories generally.

After the general election, Ted became convinced that the Party should offer devolution to Scotland as a way of winning back lost support and appointed Alick Buchanan-Smith as Shadow Scottish Secretary with a brief to do so. Anxieties about the way in which the Party had been bounced into the new policy had never been far below the surface.

This was the situation I inherited as Leader. Ted had impaled the Party on an extremely painful hook from which it would be my unenviable task to set it free. As an instinctive Unionist, I disliked the devolution commitment. But I realized that so much capital had by now been invested in it that I could not change the policy immediately. Had I done so, there would have been resignations which I simply could not afford. For the moment I would have to live with the commitment.

The Government's White Paper which proposed directly elected Assemblies for both Scotland and Wales was published in November 1975. But the Shadow Cabinet was deeply divided as to how to deal with it.

The arguments continued in 1976. I now began to harden our opposition. In November, when the Bill was published, I had dinner with a constitutional lawyer, Professor Yardley of Birmingham, to discuss its details. I also saw a good deal of the constitutional scholar Nevil Johnson. The more I heard and the more closely I read the Bill, the more dangerous it appeared to the Union. It was a prescription for bureaucracy and wrangling, and the idea that it would appease those Scots who wanted independence was becoming ever more absurd. Moreover, a private poll conducted for the Party in November 1976 confirmed my suspicion of the electoral arguments for devolution. Scottish opinion was highly fragmented: the Government's devolution plans had only 22 per cent support – less than our own (26 per cent), and less even than 'no change' (23 per cent). Only 14 per cent favoured independence. A far-reaching constitutional change required much more public support than that.

In November/December 1976, with the Bill about to come before the House for Second Reading, there were four long discussions in Shadow Cabinet about whether or not to impose a three-line whip against it. Our position could be fudged no longer. In addition to the overwhelming majority of our backbenchers, most Shadow ministers were by now opposed to devolution, at least on any lines similar to those contained in the White Paper. But there was a rooted belief among its supporters that devolution was the only way of heading off independence, and even some of those who disliked it intensely were wary of appearing to be anti-Scottish or of being seen to overrule the Scottish Tory leaders. In the end, in a marathon meeting ending in the early hours of Thursday 2 December we decided – with a significant dissenting minority including Alick Buchanan-Smith – that we would oppose the Bill on a three-line whip.

Alick Buchanan-Smith duly resigned as Shadow Scottish Secretary, along with Malcolm Rifkind. Four other front-benchers wanted to go, but

I refused their resignations and even allowed one of them to speak against our line in the debate and vote with the Government. No Party leader could have done more. To replace Alick Buchanan-Smith I moved Teddy Taylor, whose robust patriotism and soundness had long impressed me, from Trade to become Shadow Scottish Secretary.

It is generally an unnerving experience to have to speak from the front bench when you know that the debate, and in all probability the vote, will expose divisions on your own side. But the speech I had to give on Monday 13 December at the Bill's Second Reading debate was exactly the sort of forensic operation that I enjoyed. I said as little as possible about our proposals, making only minimal reference to our residual commitment to an Assembly in Scotland, and saying a great deal about the internal contradictions and inconsistencies of the legislation. At the end of the debate twenty-seven Conservatives, including Ted Heath and Peter Walker, abstained. Five voted with the Government, including Alick Buchanan-Smith, Malcolm Rifkind and Hamish Gray. But Labour were also divided: twenty-nine Labour MPs abstained and ten voted with us. The forty-five-vote majority at Second Reading thus concealed great unhappiness on the Labour side as well as our own over the issue, which was to resurface. In the course of the debate the Prime Minister hinted that the Government would concede a referendum in Scotland and Wales – a commitment that in the end proved fatal to the whole devolution enterprise.

Precisely what would happen now was far from clear. On Thursday 17 March 1977 the Government refused to contest our motion to adjourn the House following a debate on public expenditure, for fear of a defection of left-wing Labour MPs. I promptly described this almost unheard-of breach of orderly procedure as 'defeat with dishonour'. We tabled, as we had to, a Motion of No Confidence in the Government. If it succeeded, there would be a general election. In spite of my natural caution, I thought that it would. I used the speech I made to the Central Council at Torquay that Saturday to put the Party on the alert for an imminent campaign.

These were days of intense manoeuvring between the parties and their whips. But I refused to engage in it. David Steel, the Liberal Party Leader, had already indicated that he might be prepared to keep Labour in power if the terms and conditions were judged right. Legislation for direct elections to the European Assembly on a proportional representation basis, 'industrial democracy' and tax reform were the topics publicly mentioned, but no one believed that the Liberals' decision as to whether or not to support the Labour Government would be determined by secondary issues. For the Liberals there were two large questions they had to answer. Would they be blamed for keeping an unpopular government in power? Or would they be credited with moderating its policies? I did not myself believe that they would sign up to a pact with the Government – certainly not unless there was a formal coalition with several Liberals as Cabinet ministers, which it was difficult to imagine the left of the Labour Party being prepared to tolerate.

My calculation of the political equation was broadly correct; but I left out the crucial element of vanity. Although the Lib-Lab Pact did the Liberals a good deal of harm, while doing Jim Callaghan no end of good, it did allow Liberal Party spokesmen the thrilling illusion that they were important.

I was told some hours before I was due to propose the No Confidence Motion in the House that the Liberals would support the Government. The pact would apparently last initially for the rest of the parliamentary session. The Liberals would not be members of the Government, but would liaise with individual ministers and send representatives to a joint consultative committee chaired by Michael Foot, the Leader of the House. The Government gave undertakings on direct elections to the European Assembly and devolution (accepting free votes on PR), promised to find time for a Liberal Bill on homelessness and agreed to limit the scope of planned legislation on local authority direct-labour organizations. It was a lacklustre shopping list. But, knowing that we were looking at certain defeat, with all the recriminations which would follow from the press and our supporters, it drained me of inspiration.

Angus Maude had helped me with the drafting of the speech. We decided to make it very short. In fact, it was too short. Moreover, it had been drafted when it seemed that we might be facing an immediate general election, so that positive statements of our policies had appeared preferable to detailed attacks on the Government's. It received the worst press of any speech I have given. Of course, if I had read out the Westminster telephone directory and we had won at the end of the day no one would have bothered. But in politics, as in life, the 'ifs' offer no consolation. As I drove back to Flood Street later that night it was not my poor reception in the House or even the Government's majority of twenty-four which most depressed me. It was the fact that after all our efforts the chance to begin turning Britain round seemed no nearer than before.

CHAPTER TEN

━━━◆━━━

Détente or Defeat?

Foreign policy and visits 1975–1979

THE FIRST MAJOR POLITICAL CHALLENGE I faced on becoming Leader was the referendum on Britain's membership of the European Economic Community, promised by Labour in Opposition as a way of keeping their party together. I would have preferred a challenge on some other topic. Europe was very much Ted's issue. He considered that his greatest achievement was to take Britain into the EEC and, now that he had lost the leadership, it was only natural that he would engage even more passion in the cause. As had become evident during the leadership campaign, there was some suspicion that I was less enthusiastic. Compared with Ted, perhaps, that was true. But I did genuinely believe that it would be foolish to leave the Community; I thought it provided an economic bond with other western European countries, which was of strategic significance; and above all I welcomed the larger opportunities for trade which membership gave. I did not, however, see the European issue as a touchstone for everything else. It did not seem to me that high-flown rhetoric about Britain's European destiny, let alone European identity, was really to the point, though I had on occasion to employ a little on public platforms. For all these reasons, I was more than happy for Ted to take the leading public role on our side in the referendum campaign and for Willie to be the Conservative Vice-President of 'Britain in Europe' – the 'Yes' campaign organization which was set up in co-operation with pro-European Labour MPs and the Liberals, and of which Con O'Neill and later Roy Jenkins was President.

The Commons passed the proposal for a referendum by 312 votes to 248. But it was the outcome of the debate on Wednesday 9 April on the substantive issue of continued EEC membership which was a foretaste of things to come: Ayes 396, Noes 170. From now on until Thursday 5 June, the day set for the referendum, the formidable power of business, the leaderships of both parties and the wider, respectable establishment combined to extol the merits of Community membership, to elaborate fears of job losses, to warn of a third world war originating in intra-European conflict and to ridicule the odd combination of Labour left-wingers and Tory reactionaries which constituted the 'No' lobby. The 'Yes' campaign was well organized and very well funded – not least as a result of the efforts of Alistair McAlpine, whom I would shortly recruit to be Conservative Party Treasurer. For all the talk of a 'great debate' it was really a contest between David and Goliath, which Goliath won. The substantial issues often went by default.

Most distasteful of all to me was the patent opportunism of the Labour leadership. The 'renegotiation' of Britain's terms of entry, which had been concluded in March at the Dublin European Council where a special 'Financial Mechanism' had been agreed to prevent Britain shouldering too heavy a financial burden, was simply not serious: the mechanism was never triggered and so never yielded a penny piece. Yet the booklet distributed to all households by the Government abandoned all of the Euro-sceptical rhetoric which Labour, particularly the Foreign Secretary Jim Callaghan, had employed at the general election.

I duly launched the Conservative pro-Market campaign at the St Ermin's Hotel, at a press conference presided over by Ted Heath, even describing myself as 'the pupil speaking before the master'. I spoke in my constituency and elsewhere. I contributed an article on the eve of poll to the *Daily Telegraph*. I felt that I did my share of campaigning. But others did not see it that way. There was criticism in the press – the *Sun*, for example, commenting:

> Missing: one Tory Leader. Answers to the name of Margaret Thatcher. Mysteriously disappeared from the Market Referendum Campaign eleven days ago. Has not been seen since. Will finder kindly wake her up and remind her she is failing the nation in her duty as Leader of the Opposition?

The referendum result itself was no surprise, with 67 per cent voting 'Yes' and 33 per cent 'No'. Less predictable were the effects on the political scene as a whole. The result was a blow to the left of the Labour Party; and

Harold Wilson, whose cunning tactical ploy the whole exercise had been, used it to move Tony Benn from Industry, where he had proved a political liability, to Energy where his scope for mischief was more limited. For the Conservatives, it was naturally Ted and his friends who won most of the plaudits; I myself paid tribute to him in the House. He made no response. That came later.

Soon the press was full of accounts of Ted's earlier meeting with me at Wilton Street, but given in such a way as to suggest that I had not made a serious offer to him to join the Shadow Cabinet. These stories were accompanied by suggestions that he now intended to use the position gained through the referendum campaign to make his way back – presumably at my expense – to power. Ted's ambitions were his own affair. But at least the real facts about the Wilton Street meeting should be known. Consequently, I told them to George Hutchinson of *The Times* – not a supporter of mine, but a journalist of great integrity – and the account duly appeared.

No doubt Ted's hopes were buoyed up by two other things. First, I could not fail to be aware that all sorts of well-informed commentators were predicting that my tenure of the leadership would not last; indeed, that I would be gone by Christmas. Secondly, the deepening economic crisis into which a combination of the Heath Government's earlier financial irresponsibility and the Wilson Government's present anti-enterprise policies were plunging Britain might conceivably lead to that National Government on which Ted's prospects were deemed to ride. And perhaps too, the introduction of proportional representation might keep a centrist coalition in power – and people like me out of it – permanently.

In fact, the chances of any of this happening were less than the commentators imagined. It was not just that I had no intention of relinquishing the leadership, nor even that Tory backbenchers were unprepared to tolerate Ted's return. Neither was there any prospect of a shrewd, self-assured politician like Harold Wilson stepping aside gracefully to allow the sort of self-important figures he despised a free hand to sort Britain's problems out. If he went he would do so on his terms and at his timing: this of course is what subsequently occurred.

One of the first foreign statesmen I met after becoming Leader was Henry Kissinger, President Gerald Ford's Secretary of State. Over the years my respect for Dr Kissinger steadily grew and – though starting from different perspectives – our analysis of international events increasingly converged. At this time, however, I was uneasy about the direction of western policy towards the Soviet Union, of which he was acknowledged to be the impresario.

I did indeed recognize the importance of the 'opening to China' achieved under Richard Nixon in the power play with the Soviets. It was a crucial element of victory in the Cold War to detach China permanently from the Soviet Union. As for 'linkage' – that is to recognize the links between one issue and another in bilateral relations between states, in Henry Kissinger's own words 'to create a network of incentives and penalties to produce the most favourable outcome'* – I took the view that its prospects had been undermined by President Nixon's domestic weakness induced by Watergate. But I had serious doubts about the strategy of détente.

My gut instinct was that this was one of those soothing foreign terms which conceal an ugly reality that plain English would expose. It was difficult to see any difference between appeasement and détente as it began to evolve under the conditions of American paralysis after the election of a post-Watergate Congress dominated by ultra-liberal Democrats and the collapsing position in South Vietnam. Although so many obeisances had been paid to the concept that it was not prudent to attack it directly, I came as near as I could. This was not just a reflection of my preference for plain speaking: it was also the result of my conviction that too many people in the West had been lulled into believing that their way of life was secure, when it was in fact under mortal threat.

The first condition for meeting and overcoming that threat was that the Alliance should perceive what was happening; the second and equally important condition was that we should summon up the will to change it. Even in Britain's parlous economic state we still had the resources to fight back, as part of NATO and under the leadership of the United States. But we could not assume that that would always be so. At some point decline – not just relative but absolute and not just limited to one sphere but in every sphere, economic, military, political and psychological – might become irreversible. Urgent action was required and urgency entails risks. Accordingly, my first major foreign affairs speech was a risk.

Events continued to confirm my analysis. In March the Labour Government's Defence White Paper announced sharp cuts in the defence

---

* Henry Kissinger, *Diplomacy* (New York, 1994), p. 717. This is, of course, an oversimplified description of the concept. *Diplomacy* contains a fuller, masterly account of Dr Kissinger's thinking.

budget, £4,700 million over the next ten years. In the same month Alexander Shelepin, previously head of the KGB and now in charge of the Soviet Union's 'trade unions', arrived in Britain as a guest of the TUC. The following month saw the fall of Saigon to the North Vietnamese communists amid scenes of chaos, adding to America's woes. Cuban 'advisers' were beginning to arrive to support the communist MPLA faction in Angola. It was, however, what I heard and read about the preparations for the Helsinki summit that triggered my decision to speak.

The idea for Helsinki had come from the Soviets, was warmly welcomed by Chancellor Brandt's West Germany as a contribution to *Ostpolitik*, and was then accepted on to the Nixon Administration's agenda. The West wanted the Soviets to enter into talks to reduce their military superiority in Europe – Mutual Balanced Force Reductions (MBFR) – and to respect the human rights of their subject peoples. But what did the Soviets want? This was by far the most interesting question, since even if, as the sceptics suggested, they would not honour their agreements anyway, they still would not have taken this trouble unless something important for them would result. Respectability could be the only answer. If the Soviet Union and its satellites – particularly the more potentially fragile regimes in eastern Europe – could receive the international seal of approval they would feel more secure.

But did we want them to feel more secure? Arguably, one of the most exploitable weaknesses of totalitarian dictatorships is the paranoid insecurity which flows from the lack of consent to the regime itself and which results in inefficiency and even paralysis of decision-taking. If the Soviets felt more secure, if their new-found respectability gave them greater access to credit and technology, if they were treated with tolerant respect rather than suspicious hostility, how would they use these advantages?

If I was to challenge the accepted wisdom on these matters I needed expert help. But most of the experts had jumped aboard the Sovietology gravy train which ran on official patronage, conferences with 'approved' Soviet academics, visa journalism and a large dose of professional complacency. I had, however, through John O'Sullivan of the *Daily Telegraph*, heard about Robert Conquest, a British historian and fearless critic of the USSR. I asked him to help me and together we wrote the speech which I delivered on Saturday 26 July 1975 in Chelsea. The occasion itself was only arranged a few days in advance. I did not speak to Reggie Maudling or anyone else in the Shadow Cabinet about it beforehand, because I knew that all I would receive were obstruction and warnings, which would doubtless be leaked afterwards – particularly if things went wrong.

I began by setting the large military imbalance between the West and the Soviet Union against the background of the retreat of western power. I drew particular attention to the Soviet naval build-up, describing the Soviet navy as a global force with more nuclear submarines than the rest of the world's navies put together and more surface ships than could possibly be needed to protect the USSR's coast and merchant shipping. I argued that nothing was more important to our security than the American commitment to Europe, adding that an isolationist Britain would encourage an isolationist America.

I then dealt with the imminent Helsinki summit. I did not attack détente directly, indeed I called for a 'real' détente. But I quoted Leonid Brezhnev speaking in June 1972 to illustrate the Soviets' true intentions. Brezhnev had affirmed that peaceful coexistence 'in no way implies the possibility of relaxing the ideological struggle. On the contrary we must be prepared for this struggle to be intensified and become an even sharper form of confrontation between the systems.'

I also drew attention to the importance of human rights as a further measure of the nature of the regime with which we were dealing:

> When the Soviet leaders jail a writer, or a priest, or a doctor or a worker for the crime of speaking freely, it is not only for humanitarian reasons that we should be concerned. For these acts reveal a country that is afraid of truth and liberty; it dare not allow its people to enjoy the freedoms we take for granted, and a nation that denies those freedoms to its own people will have few scruples in denying them to others.

Human rights would, we already knew, be the subject of far-reaching verbal undertakings in the so-called 'Basket Three' of the Helsinki package – 'Co-operation in humanitarian and other fields'. But I placed no trust in the Soviets' good faith: indeed, since their whole system depended upon repression, it was difficult to see how they could comply. I suspected that for many of those present at Helsinki – and not just on the communist side – the undertakings about human rights would be regarded as uplifting rhetoric rather than clear conditions to be rigorously monitored. So I noted:

We must work for a real relaxation of tension, but in our negotiations with the Eastern bloc we must not accept words or
gestures as a substitute for genuine détente. No flood of words
emanating from a summit conference will mean anything unless
it is accompanied by some positive action by which the Soviet
leaders show that their ingrained attitudes are really beginning to
change.

That is why we so strongly support all those European and
American spokesmen, who have insisted that no serious advance
towards a stable peace can be made unless some progress at least is
seen in the free movement of people and of ideas.

The reaction to this speech confirmed that I was the odd woman out.
The Helsinki Agreement was widely welcomed. I could imagine the
shaking of wise heads at my impulsive imprudence. Reggie Maudling
came round at once to see me in Flood Street to express both his anger at
my delivering such a speech without consulting him and his disagreement with its content. I gave no ground. Indeed, Mr Brezhnev's evident
satisfaction at what Helsinki achieved helped convince me that I must
return to the subject: he described it as 'a necessary summing up of the
political outcome of the Second World War'. In other words he regarded
it – not least perhaps the commitment not to alter European borders
except 'by peaceful means and by agreement' – as recognizing and legit-
imizing the Soviet hold on eastern Europe which they had obtained by
force and fraud at the end of the war.

The Helsinki summit of 1975 is now viewed in a favourable light
because the dissidents in the Soviet Union and eastern Europe used its
provisions as a programme for which to fight in their long struggle with
the communist State. And indeed by making human rights a matter of
treaty obligations rather than domestic law it gave the dissidents leverage
which they employed to the full. Their bravery would have been of little
account, however, without the subsequent western, particularly American, renewal of resolve and defence build-up. These halted the expansion
that had given Soviet communism the psychological prestige of historical
inevitability, exerted an external pressure on communist regimes that
diverted them from domestic repression, and gave heart to the burgeon-
ing resistance movements against communism. This pincer movement –
the revived West and the dissidents – more than countered the advantages
that the Soviets received from Helsinki in the form of increased legiti-

macy and western recognition. Without that, Helsinki would have been just one more step on the road to defeat.

Undoubtedly, the most important foreign tour I made in 1975 – probably the most significant during my time as Leader of the Opposition – was to the United States in September. I already, of course, knew something of the States; and I liked and admired most of what I knew. This, however, was my first opportunity to meet all the leading political figures, and do so on something approaching equal terms. I was guaranteed plenty of media attention, if largely for the depressing reason that Britain's stock had rarely fallen lower. American newspapers, magazines and television programmes were concentrating on the precipitous decline of the British economy, the advance of trade union power, the extension of the socialist state and what was perceived to be a collapse of national self-confidence. Aside from the *schadenfreude*, also evident was a nagging worry that America, itself suffering a deep but different crisis in the wake of the fall of Vietnam and the trauma of Watergate, might suffer the same fate.*

Gordon Reece flew on ahead of me to New York in order to set up the media arrangements. Just before I left London he telephoned to say that expectations of my visit were now so high that I should make the first speech I was to deliver – to the Institute of Socio-Economic Studies in New York – a blockbuster rather than, as planned, a low-key performance with the main speech coming later in Washington. I began by taking head-on the American comments on the sorry state of contemporary Britain and treating them seriously. I then drew attention to what I called 'the progressive consensus, the doctrine that the state should be active on many fronts in promoting equality: in the provision of social welfare and in the redistribution of wealth and incomes'. There followed a detailed analysis of its effects in the form of over-taxation, the discouragement of enterprise, the squeeze on profits, the defrauding of savers by inflation

---

* Typical of the coverage was an article from the *Wall Street Journal* (20 August 1975) I found in my briefing papers. It began: 'Hardly anyone needs to be told now that Great Britain is the sick country of Europe. Everywhere you look the evidence abounds.' The article described our position – falling output, runaway inflation, declining industries, a falling (and relatively low) standard of living. Its author reflected: 'It is all very curious. For Britain has not been brought to this state by defeat in war, by earthquakes, plagues, droughts or any natural disasters. Britain's undoing is its own doing. It has been brought to this by the calculated policies of its Government and by their resigned acceptance by the people.'

and negative interest rates and the apparently inexorable growth of the public sector and public spending.

I was promptly attacked back home by the Labour Government for running Britain down abroad. In fact, the message I was bringing to America about Britain was essentially one of hope, namely that the nation's potential was great enough to withstand even the effects of socialism. The criticism from the Foreign Secretary, Jim Callaghan, who quaintly criticized me later for putting 'argumentative passages' into my American speeches, found a faithful echo in the British Embassy where I was staying. A senior member of the embassy staff briefed the American press against me. Gordon Reece quickly discovered what was happening, and there was a sharp exchange of letters on the subject between me and Jim Callaghan when I returned to England.

Aware of the attempt to try to cast me in this light, I used my speech to the National Press Club in Washington to point out that if the present socialist policies were abandoned, Britain had underlying strengths which would ensure its swift recovery. A shift of popular opinion against the far Left, the extent of our energy reserves and the strength of our scientific potential – shown by seventy-two Nobel Prizes, more than France, Italy, the Netherlands and Belgium put together – all justified long-term optimism.

> Now, slowly, we are finding our way. It is true that the reports about Britain still reflect a serious situation, and they are right to do so. But a change is coming over us . . . I see some signs that our people are ready to make the tough choice, to follow the harder road. We are still the same people who have fought for freedom, and won. The spirit of adventure, the inventiveness, the determination are still strands in our character. We may suffer from a British sickness now, but our constitution is sound and we have the heart and the will to win through.

In the course of my American visit I met the key figures in the Ford Administration. Dr Kissinger I knew already. But this was the first time that I had met Bill Simon, the free-market-minded Treasury Secretary, who had jettisoned the wage and price controls imposed under President Nixon, and the immensely experienced James Schlesinger, the Defense Secretary, the Administration's principal internal opponent to détente.

I was also received by President Ford himself. He was a large, friendly man, unexpectedly precipitated into high office who, perhaps to his own surprise as well as that of others, had started to relish it. He had assembled or inherited a talented team around him and had already demonstrated to the Europeans America's continued commitment to their security, in spite of all the upheavals of domestic politics. He had, in fact, both the strengths and weaknesses of what in current political parlance is described as 'a safe pair of hands'. He was not the kind of man to challenge accepted orthodoxies, which I increasingly believed ought to be challenged. But he was a reassuring and steady figure who helped America heal the self-inflicted wounds of Watergate. After a rocky period in the wake of his pardon for Richard Nixon, his Administration's fortunes appeared to be improving, and his undeclared bid for the Republican nomination was proceeding against a genially effective campaign by a certain Governor Ronald Reagan. President Ford's prospects for re-election appeared good. I came away hoping that he would succeed.

I found on my return to London that the coverage given to my American tour had transformed my political standing. Even the Labour Party's simulated outrage helped. For the more attention was paid to my arguments, the more seriously they were taken. I was soon conscious also of a change of attitude within the upper echelons of the Conservative Party. People who had regarded my accession to the leadership as an irritating but temporary fluke had to think again. Not only was I evidently being treated seriously by some of the most powerful figures in the free world; the warnings I had given in my Helsinki speech looked ever less eccentric and more prescient.

In late September the Cubans, acting as Soviet surrogates, began to pour troops into Angola. In December the US Senate overturned President Ford's policy of providing assistance to the anti-communist forces there and resistance to the MPLA collapsed. I thought and read more about these things over Christmas and decided that I would make a further speech.

On this occasion I stuck to the conventions and told Reggie Maudling of my decision. It was perhaps a testimony to his unease at the prospect that Reggie went so far as to offer me a draft. Unfortunately, as Denis might have said, 'It was so weak it wouldn't pull the skin off a rice pudding.' Bob Conquest had now departed for the Hoover Institution in California, so I asked Robert Moss to help me. The editor of the *Economist*'s Foreign Report, an expert on security and strategic matters, one of the founders of the National Association for Freedom set up to combat overweening trade union power, and destined to be a best-selling novelist, Robert turned out to be an ideal choice.

The speech, which I delivered on Monday 19 January at Kensington Town Hall, covered similar ground to the previous year's Chelsea speech, but concentrated more on defence and contained even stronger language about the Soviet menace. It accused the Labour Government of 'dismantling our defence at a moment when the strategic threat to Britain and her allies from an expansionist power is graver than at any moment since the end of the last war'.

I warned of the imbalance between NATO and Warsaw Pact forces in central Europe, where the latter outnumbered us by 150,000 men, nearly 10,000 tanks and 2,600 aircraft. But I emphasized that the West's defence could not be ensured in Europe alone: NATO's supply lines had also to be protected. This meant that we could not ignore what Soviet-backed forces were doing in Angola. If they were allowed their way there, they might well conclude that they could repeat the performance elsewhere.

The reaction to the speech, particularly in the more thoughtful sections of the British press, was much more favourable than to the Chelsea speech. The *Daily Telegraph* entitled its editorial comment 'The Truth About Russia'. *The Times* admitted that 'there has been complacency in the West'. Nor was the Soviet reaction long in coming. The Soviet Embassy wrote a letter to Reggie Maudling, and the ambassador called on the Foreign Office to protest in person. A stream of crude invective flowed from the different Soviet propaganda organs. But it was some apparatchik in the office of *Red Star*, the Red Army newspaper, his imagination surpassing his judgement, who coined the description of me as 'The Iron Lady'.

It is one of the few defences which free societies have against totalitarian propaganda that totalitarians are inclined to see the western mind as a mirror image of their own. They are consequently capable from time to time of the most grotesque misjudgements. This was one of them. When Gordon Reece read on the Press Association tapes what *Red Star* had said he was ecstatic and rushed into my office to tell me about it. I quickly saw that they had inadvertently put me on a pedestal as their strongest European opponent. They never did me a greater favour.

The election of Jimmy Carter as President of the United States at the end of 1976 brought to the White House a man who put human rights at the top of his foreign policy agenda. One could at least be sure that he would not make the mistake of his predecessor, who had refused to meet Solzhenitsyn for fear of offending the Soviet Union.

President Carter was soon to be tested. In January 1977 the text of 'Charter 77', the manifesto of the Czech dissidents, was smuggled into West Germany and published. The following month Jimmy Carter wrote personally to Professor Andrei Sakharov, the Soviet nuclear scientist and leading dissident. This change of tone was reassuring.

But I soon became worried about other aspects of the Carter Administration's approach to foreign policy. President Carter had a passionate commitment to disarmament, demonstrated both by his early cancellation of the B1 strategic bomber and the renewed impetus he gave to SALT II (Strategic Arms Limitation Talks), which President Ford had initiated with the Soviets. Ironically, therefore, President Carter found that he could only take action to improve human rights against countries linked to the West, not against countries that were hostile and strong enough to ignore him.

As for the SALT II negotiations, it was possible to argue about the particular formulae, but the really important strategic fact was that the Soviet Union had in recent years been arming far faster than the Americans. Any mere 'arms limitation' agreement was bound to stabilize the military balance in such a way as to recognize this. Only deep arms *cuts* on the one hand, or a renewed drive for stronger American defences on the other, could reverse it. When I visited the United States again in September 1977, the Carter Administration was still enjoying its political honeymoon. President Carter had brought a new informal style to the White House, which appeared to accord with the mood of the times. Although there was unease about some of his appointments, this was largely put down to Washington resentment against outsiders. In Cyrus Vance, his Secretary of State, and Zbigniew Brzezinski, his National Security Adviser, he had two remarkable assistants, whose differences of outlook were not yet apparent.

I had met Jimmy Carter himself in London in May when he attended the G7 summit. In spite of my growing doubts about his foreign policy, I liked him and looked forward to meeting him again. At our discussion in the White House the President was most keen to explain and justify his recently launched initiative for a comprehensive nuclear test ban. Although he had clearly mastered the details and was a persuasive advocate, I was not convinced. Believing as I did in the vital importance of a credible nuclear deterrent, and knowing that nuclear weapons had to be tested in order to be credible, I could not go along with the policy. Equally, I was unable to agree with President Carter, or indeed Cyrus Vance and Andrew Young, the US Ambassador to the United Nations, on their preferred approach to settling the Rhodesian question. The Americans were insisting that the Rhodesian security forces be dismantled. But I knew that would never be acceptable to the white population – who still enjoyed military superiority over the 'armed struggle' – without some real guarantee of peace. The Americans were also toying with the idea of imposing sanctions against South Africa, which seemed to me equally ill-judged considering that they needed to have the South African Government on their side if they were to persuade Ian Smith to compromise.

At least on this occasion I did not have to contend with hostile briefing from the embassy, which was ironic considering that the new ambassador, Peter Jay, was Jim Callaghan's son-in-law. There had been loud accusations of nepotism when this appointment had been announced. But I liked and admired Peter Jay personally. His understanding of monetary economics would have made him a welcome recruit to the Shadow Cabinet.

Meanwhile, uncertainties about the direction of American policy and the extent of Soviet ambitions had increasingly focused attention on those countries which were balanced uneasily between the two blocs. Of these, Yugoslavia had a special significance. Since Marshal Tito's break with Stalin in 1948, Yugoslavia had been in an anomalous but important position.

The fragility of Yugoslavia was both symbolized by and depended upon the state of Tito's own health. It was an open question whether the Soviets would try to reassert control in the chaos which was widely expected to follow his death. At eighty-five, he was still in control of events, but ailing. I had wanted to visit Yugoslavia for some time, but my visit was twice postponed because Tito was not well enough to receive me. On a bitter early December day in 1977, however, in the company of Sir Fitzroy Maclean, a comrade in arms and old friend of the Yugoslav President from the Second World War, I arrived in Belgrade.

We visited Tito at his Belgrade home. His was a powerful personality, retaining some of the outward panache of his flamboyant partisan past, but leaving no doubt about the inner steel that explained his post-war dominance. We discussed and broadly agreed about the Soviet threat. The looming question of his legacy did not figure in our talks. Perhaps he had already concluded, for all the elaborate constitutional safeguards, that it would indeed be the *déluge*.

Before I departed for Yugoslavia, Alfred Sherman had asked me to raise with Tito the case of Milovan Djilas, Tito's former friend and colleague and for many years most insistent domestic critic. Djilas had been one of a number of political prisoners recently freed but was, I understood, the object of continuing harassment. It seemed likely that he would soon disappear back into prison. I decided on a shot across Tito's bows. I said with studied innocence how pleased I was that Djilas had been released. Tito glowered.

'Yes, he's out,' the President said, 'but he's up to his old tricks. And if he goes on upsetting our constitution he will go straight back to jail.'

'Well,' I replied, 'a man like Djilas will do you far more harm in prison than out of it.'

Fitzroy Maclean chipped in, 'She's right, you know.' Tito gave me a hard look. There was a pause in the conversation before he turned to other matters. As far as I know, Djilas stayed out of jail – only to suffer more harassment for his independent thinking under the brutal regime of Serbian President Slobodan Milosevic.

In fact, though I did not know it at the time, three developments were opening up the long-term prospect of turning back the Soviet advance. The first, paradoxically, was that they had become too arrogant. It is a natural and often fatal trait of the totalitarian to despise opponents. The Soviets believed that the failure of western politicians signified that western peoples were resigned to defeat. A little more subtlety and fore-thought might have secured the Soviet leaders far greater gains. As it was, particularly through the invasion of Afghanistan in 1979, they provoked a western reaction which finally destroyed the Soviet Union itself.

The second development was the election in September 1978 of a Polish Pope. John Paul II would fire a revolution in eastern Europe which shook the Soviet Empire to its core.

Finally, there was the emergence of Ronald Reagan as a serious contender for the American Presidency. I had met Governor Reagan shortly after my becoming Conservative Leader in 1975. Even before then, I knew something about him because Denis had returned home one evening in the late 1960s full of praise for a remarkable speech Ronald Reagan had just delivered at the Institute of Directors. I read the text myself and quickly saw what Denis meant. When we met in person I was immediately won over by his charm, sense of humour and directness. In the succeeding years I read his speeches, advocating tax cuts as the root to wealth creation and stronger defences as an alternative to détente. I also read many of his fortnightly broadcasts to the people of California, which his Press Secretary sent over regularly for me. I agreed with them all. In November 1978 we met again in my room in the House of Commons.

In the early years Ronald Reagan had been dismissed by much of the American political elite, though not by the American electorate, as a right-wing maverick who could not be taken seriously. (I had heard that before somewhere.) Now he was seen by many thoughtful Republicans as their best ticket back to the White House. Whatever Ronald Reagan had gained in experience, he had not done so at the expense of his beliefs. I found them stronger than ever. When he left my study I reflected on how different things might look if such a man were President of the United States. But in November 1978 such a prospect seemed a long way off.

ABOVE My mother as a young woman.

LEFT My father.

BELOW My father's shop in Grantham, where I grew up.

ABOVE With my father.

RIGHT With my sister Muriel.
I am on the right of the picture.

BELOW In the garden at the house
of some friends during the summer
of 1935, aged ten.

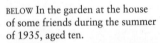

Muriel, father, mother and me on the day
my father became mayor of Grantham.

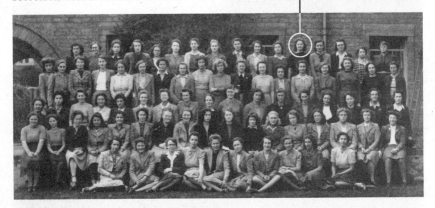

RIGHT AND BELOW At Somerville College, Oxford, with the 1943 intake.

BOTTOM At work as a research chemist.

With Denis on our wedding day.

GENERAL ELECTION
1951

DARTFORD
CONSTITUENCY

Polling Day
Thursday, 25th October
7 a.m.—9 p.m.

PEACE

COST OF
LIVING

HOMES

FUEL

GO AND
HEAR

MARGARET
ROBERTS

The Conservative Candidate

ABOVE My 1951 election address.

RIGHT As MP for Finchley in 1962.

ABOVE With Ted Heath at the Conservative Party Conference in 1970.

BELOW Visiting a primary school as Secretary of State for Education.

With Denis, Carol and Mark.

ABOVE Meeting the press at Conservative Central Office,
11 February 1975, the day I became Leader of the Conservative Party.

BELOW The State Opening of Parliament in 1976. Seated on the front
bench, from l-r: Geoffrey Howe, Keith Joseph, Willie Whitelaw,
myself, Jim Prior, Francis Pym, Humphrey Atkins.

LEFT Delivering the 'Iron Lady' speech in Kensington Town Hall in January 1976.

BELOW On a walkabout in Huddersfield during the 1979 election campaign.

ABOVE On the stairs at Central Office following the election victory, with Peter Thorneycroft, Denis, Carol and Mark.

RIGHT With Denis outside No. 10 on the day I became Prime Minister.

ABOVE With Denis at the funeral of Airey Neave in April 1979.

BELOW Presenting the deeds to one of the first tenants to buy their home under the Government's new 'right to buy' scheme in September 1979.

RIGHT Addressing the Conservative Party Conference in Brighton, on 10 October 1980, when I delivered the famous line 'The lady's not for turning'.

BELOW Visiting my old school in Grantham.

LEFT HMS *Invincible* returning to Portsmouth at the end of the Falklands War.

BELOW On the steps of St Paul's Cathedral following the memorial service for the Falklands War, July 1982, with Lord Lewin, Chief of Defence Staff, standing beside me.

OPPOSITE Presenting medals on board HMS *Hermes*, 21 July 1982.

ABOVE With Cecil Parkinson at Central Office on the night of our victory in the 1983 general election.

BELOW At my desk in No. 10.

CHAPTER ELEVEN

—————◆—————

Apprenticeship for Power

Leader of the Opposition March 1977–March 1979

THE LIB-LAB PACT did none of the things subsequently claimed for it by its exponents. It did not halt, let alone reverse, the advance of socialism: indeed, it kept the Labour Government in office and enabled it to complete the nationalization of the aircraft and shipbuilding industries. Nor was it responsible for the frail but real economic recovery which gradually improved the Labour Party's political standing in 1977/78: that was the result of the financial measures imposed by the IMF several months before the Pact was agreed. It did not help Mr Callaghan to marginalize and defeat the Left; indeed, the Left emerged strong enough to take over the Labour Party within a few years.

The real benefits were quite different and completely unintended. First, the fact that the Liberal Party demonstrated the closeness of its approach to that of Labour gave a salutary warning to potential Conservatives who, for whatever reason, flirted with the idea of voting Liberal as a more civilized alternative to socialism. The Pact therefore hardened our support. Secondly, I can see now that in March 1977 we were not yet ready to form the kind of government which could have achieved a long-term shift away from the policies which had led to Britain's decline. Neither the Shadow Cabinet, nor the Parliamentary Party, nor in all probability the electorate, would have been prepared to take the necessary but unpalatable medicine, because they had not witnessed how far the disease had spread. It took the strikes of the winter of 1978/79 to change all that. Finally, the Government's survival was a real, if well-disguised, blessing for me. I benefited greatly from the next two gruelling years as Leader of the Opposition. I learned more about how to achieve what I wanted, even though I always felt in a minority in the Shadow Cabinet. I also became a more effective debater, public speaker and campaigner, all of which would stand me in good stead as Prime Minister. Above all, perhaps, I had the opportunity to demonstrate both to myself and to others that I had that elusive 'instinct' for what ordinary people feel – a quality which, I suspect, one is simply born with or not, but which is sharpened and burnished through adversity.

But just as the political reality was never as bad as it seemed at the time of the agreement of the Lib-Lab Pact, so we were now in truth facing far more serious problems than even the commentators understood. Our popularity largely reflected widespread reaction against the Government's manifest failures. Now that some order was being restored to the public finances, we would be under more pressure to spell out our own alternative. We would have to set out clearly and persuasively an alternative analysis and set of policies. For my part, I was keen to do just that. But I knew that on such central questions as trade union power, incomes policy and public spending there was still no agreement in Shadow Cabinet between the minority of us who fundamentally rejected the approach pursued between 1970 and 1974 and the majority who more or less wished to continue it. All of the damaging divisions which plagued us over these years, and which we desperately tried to minimize by agreeing on 'lines to take', stemmed from that basic problem. Ultimately, it was not one which was amenable to the techniques of political management, only to the infinitely more difficult process of clarifying thoughts and changing minds.

So it was that what came to be known as the 'Grunwick affair' burst onto the political scene. This was a clear case of the outrageous abuse of trade union power. Paradoxically, it proved almost as politically damaging to us, whom the unions regarded with undisguised hostility, as to the Labour Party, who were their friends and sometime clients.

Grunwick was a medium-sized photographic processing and printing business in north-west London run by a dynamic Anglo-Indian entrepreneur, George Ward, with a largely immigrant workforce. A dispute in the summer of 1976 resulted in a walkout of a number of workers and their subsequent dismissal. This escalated into a contest between the management and the APEX trade union, which had subsequently signed up the dismissed workers and demanded 'recognition'. That would have given the union the right to negotiate on behalf of its members working for the company. APEX consequently demanded the reinstatement of those who had been dismissed.

For its part, Grunwick established in the courts that the dismissals had been perfectly legal – even under Labour's new union legislation, which the unions had virtually written themselves. None of those who had been dismissed could be taken back under existing law unless *all* were taken back, and in a number of cases there was simply too much bad blood. Grunwick argued too that the behaviour of APEX in other firms suggested that it was out to impose a closed shop. Finally, secret ballots conducted by MORI and Gallup showed that the great majority of the Grunwick workforce – over 80 per cent – did not want to join APEX, or any other union.

A left-wing coalition emerged to support APEX and punish Grunwick. Every part of the socialist world was represented: the local Brent Trades Council, trade union leaders and 'flying pickets', the Socialist Workers Party, and leading members of the Labour Party itself, among them Cabinet ministers Shirley Williams and Fred Mulley, and the Minister for Sport, Denis Howell, who dusted off their donkey jackets and joined the Grunwick picket line for a short time, a couple of weeks before the picketing turned violent. Someone called it 'the Ascot of the Left'.

The National Association for Freedom (NAFF) took up the case of George Ward as part of its campaign against abuses of individual freedom resulting from overweening trade union power. NAFF had been launched in December 1975, shortly after the IRA's murder of someone who would have been one of its leading lights – Ross McWhirter, whom I had known (along with his twin brother Norris) from Orpington days.* NAFF's Chairman was Bill De L'Isle and Dudley, the war hero and the MP who had spoken to us at Oxford attacking Yalta when I was an undergraduate.

The mass picketing began at the end of June 1977 and continued day after day with terrifying scenes of mob violence, injuries to police and pickets. At times thousands of demonstrators crowded the narrow suburban streets around the Grunwick factory, to waylay the coaches laid on by the firm to bring their employees through. So I asked my PPS, Adam Butler, and Jim Prior's number two, Barney Hayhoe, to join the employees on one of their morning coach journeys through the hail of missiles

---

* His death had a particular significance for me, quite apart from the loss of a courageous friend: within days I was assigned a team of personal detectives who have been with me ever since.

and abuse. Adam reported back to me on the fear – and the courage – of the people he had been with.

During this period a strange reticence gripped the Government. The Shadow Cabinet organized a number of Private Notice Questions to force ministers to declare their position on the violence. We issued a statement demanding that the Prime Minister state categorically that the police had the Government's backing in carrying out their duties. But as I wrote to John Gouriet, one of NAFF's directors, at the time: 'we feel that the scenes of wild violence portrayed on television plus the wild charges and allegations being thrown about in certain quarters, are enough in themselves to put most of the public on the side of right and are doing more than hours of argument'.

Although the scenes outside the factory seemed to symbolize the consequences of giving trade unions virtually unlimited immunity in civil law, it was in fact the criminal law against violence and intimidation which was being breached. No matter how many new legal provisions might be desirable, the first duty of the authorities was to uphold the existing law. All the more so because the violence at Grunwick was part of a wider challenge posed by the far Left to the rule of law; and no one quite knew how far that challenge would ultimately go.

It was also at this time that a new shamelessness on the part of the Left became apparent. Until the early 1970s, Transport House banned members of certain 'proscribed organizations' on the far Left from being members of the Labour Party. The lifting of this ban, long sought by the Left, was a very significant landmark in Labour's drift to extremism. Hard-left Labour MPs saw less reason to conceal their links with communist organizations. The warmth of fraternal relations between trade union leaders and socialist politicians on the one hand and the Soviet bloc on the other was undisguised. High-ranking Soviet visitors were received by both the TUC and the Labour Party. Trotskyist organizations, such as the Militant Tendency, began to gain a grip on Labour Party constituencies. There was an almost tangible sense that, whatever the IMF or Prime Minister Jim Callaghan might think, it was the extreme Left whose programme represented Labour's future, and that whether the tactics employed to achieve it were violent or peaceful was the only question at issue. In such an atmosphere, the scenes at Grunwick suggested – and not only to the Left itself – that perhaps the revolution had begun.

Grunwick came to symbolize the closed shop, under which employees had effectively been compelled to join a union if they wished to obtain or keep a job. This was because NAFF was also vigorously campaigning against the closed shop. Also APEX clearly wished to coerce Grunwick's employees, probably with a view ultimately to achieving a closed shop in the industry. More broadly, the closed shop represented a secure redoubt of trade union power from which further assaults on liberty could be mounted.

Yet, for all that, Grunwick was not limited to the closed shop; it was about the sheer power of the unions. Appalled as I was by what was happening at Grunwick, I did not believe that the time was yet ripe to depart from the cautious line about trade union reform (which I had agreed with Jim Prior) in order to mount a radical attack on the closed shop. We had to consider a much wider raft of questions, ranging from the unions' immunity under civil law, to violence and intimidation which only escaped the criminal law because they came under the guise of lawful picketing. Until we had begun to solve some of these problems, we could not effectively outlaw the closed shop.

For Jim Prior, I suspect, it was a practical question rather than a moral one: the important thing was to be realistic and accept that the trade unions could not be tamed by law. Any reform would need their co-operation. By contrast, Keith Joseph was an unswerving opponent of what he saw as a breach of human rights resulting from collectivist bullying. Jim's and Keith's opposing views, expressed in public statements on the Scarman Report on the Grunwick dispute, brought all this out into the open. At the time, I thought that Keith's criticisms of Lord Scarman were too sharp, though the Scarman Report itself was anything but a judicial document and had no legal force. Moreover Jim, not Keith, was the spokesman on these matters. Either I sacked Jim, or I moved him (neither of which I could afford to do), or I had to go along with his approach.

That was what I did. In retrospect, Jim and I were wrong and Keith was right. What the whole affair demonstrated was that our careful avoidance of any kind of commitment to changing the law on industrial relations, though it might make sense in normal times, would be weak and unsustainable in a crisis. But I took the decision to support Jim in part because, as yet, the climate was still not right to try to harden our policy. But some time soon the nettle would have to be grasped.

In reflecting on all this, I came back to the idea of a referendum. On my return from America I knew that I would be pressed hard by Brian Walden, who was making his debut as interviewer on the television programme *Weekend World*, on what a Conservative Government would do if it were faced with an all-out confrontation with the trade unions. I had to have a convincing answer: and there was not much hope that any amount of discussion within Shadow Cabinet would arrive at one. So on the programme I argued that although such a confrontation was unlikely, yet if such an emergency was reached, then a referendum might be necessary. The suggestion was well received both in the press and – most significantly – got public backing from both wings of the Party. (It helped perhaps that Jim was expecting a rough ride at the Conservative Party Conference over the closed shop.) I set up a Party Committee under Nick Edwards to report on referenda and their possible uses. But, of course, though the suggestion of a referendum bought us vital time, it was not in itself an answer to the problem of trade union power. Assuming that we won a referendum, so demonstrating that the general public backed the Government against the militants, it would still be necessary to frame the measures to reduce trade union power. And so far we had not seriously considered what those measures should be.

The argument about trade union power remained linked to that about incomes policies. At this time the Government's own incomes policy was looking increasingly fragile. No formal policy could be agreed with the unions after the end of the second year of 'restraint', though the TUC exhorted its members not to seek more than one increase in the next twelve months and the Chancellor of the Exchequer pleaded for settlements to be below 10 per cent (backed as before with the threat of sanctions against employers who paid more). But, of course, whatever difficulties the Labour Government had in agreeing incomes policy with the trade unions were likely to pale into insignificance by comparison with ours. Unfortunately, we were committed to produce a document on economic policy, including incomes policy, before the 1977 Party Conference. David Howell, an able journalist of monetarist persuasions and also a front-bench spokesman, was the principal draftsman. And Geoffrey Howe, remorselessly seeking some kind of consensus between the conflicting views in his Economic Reconstruction Group, had by now become thoroughly convinced of the merits of German-style 'concerted action' within some kind of economic forum.

I could see trouble coming down the track and I expressed my unease about all of this. Geoffrey tried to convince me of the system's merits by sending me a paper on how the Germans did it, but I wrote back: 'This paper frightens me to death even more. We really must avoid some of this terrible jargon. Also we should recognize that the German talking shop works because it consists of Germans.'

Work on the document continued, but among the front-bench economic spokesmen rather than the Shadow Cabinet. By contrast with the Grunwick/closed shop issue, Keith, who shared my misgivings about the 'forum', was prepared to compromise more than I would have done. And in the end, the document appeared under the signatures of Keith, Geoffrey, Jim Prior, David Howell and Angus Maude; it was not formally endorsed by the Shadow Cabinet.

I never felt much affection for *The Right Approach to the Economy*. Unlike *The Right Approach* of 1976, it made little impact either on the outside world or on the policy we would pursue as a government. I was careful to ensure that 'concerted action' – apart from within the limited framework of the NEDC – never saw the light of day.

So it was that we more or less successfully papered over the policy cracks up to the 1977 Party Conference at Blackpool. On the face of it, the Blackpool Conference was a success. Colleagues generally stuck to the agreed lines on controversial issues. Embarrassing splits were avoided. Somewhat in the same spirit was my own speech. It contained many good lines but, for all the spit and polish, it was essentially a rollicking attack on Labour that lacked positive substance. Although the immediate reception was good, it was soon clear that it left the large questions about our policies unanswered; and I was not satisfied with it. My instincts proved correct. Having entered the Conference season several points ahead of Labour in the opinion polls, we finished it running neck and neck. A 'good' Conference never avoids rows at the expense of issues.

In any case, January 1978 saw the spotlight turn back onto just those difficult, important issues which the Party managers considered best avoided. Geoffrey Howe, speaking in Swindon, delivered a sharp and comprehensive attack on the role of trade unions in Britain and was met by a barrage of abuse from the union leaders and scarcely concealed irritation from some colleagues. I agreed with Geoffrey and strongly defended him in public. But I was still basically sticking with the Prior line and so I dissuaded him from making a second such speech, noting on the draft: 'Geoffrey: this is not your subject. Why go on with it? The press will crucify you for this.'

Oddly enough, just a few days later I found myself on the receiving end of almost equally sharp criticism. I had determined to use a speech to a conference of Scottish industrialists in Glasgow to break away from the qualification and obfuscation into which I felt we had been manoeuvred over incomes policy. I said:

> The counterpart of the withdrawal of government from interfer-
> ence in prices and profits in the private sector which both we and
> you want to see, is inevitably the withdrawal of government from
> interference in wage bargaining. There can be no selective return
> to personal responsibility.

This was attacked by, among others, the *Economist* under the timid headline: 'Mrs Thatcher Takes the Tories into Dangerous Water'.

I was soon to offend against Party political wisdom still more funda-mentally. Ever since Enoch Powell's Birmingham speech in April 1968 it had been the mark of civilized high-mindedness among right-of-centre politicians to avoid speaking about immigration and race at all, and if that did not prove possible, then to do so in terms borrowed from the left of the political spectrum, relishing the 'multi-cultural', 'multi-racial' nature of modern British society. This whole approach glossed over the real problems that immigration sometimes caused and dismissed the anxieties of those who were directly affected as 'racist'. I had never been prepared to go along with it. It seemed both dishonest and snobbish.

Nothing is more colour-blind than the capitalism in which I placed my faith for Britain's revival. It was part of my credo that individuals were worthy of respect *as individuals*, not as members of classes or races; the whole purpose of the political and economic system I favoured was to liberate the talents of those individuals for the benefit of society. I felt no sympathy for rabble rousers, like the National Front, who sought to exploit race. I found it deeply significant that such groups were just as much socialist as they were nationalist. All collectivism is always conducive to oppression: it is only the victims who differ.

At the same time, large-scale New Commonwealth immigration over the years had transformed large areas of Britain in a way that the indige-nous population found hard to accept. It is one thing for a well-heeled politician to preach the merits of tolerance on a public platform before returning to a comfortable home in a tranquil road in one of the more respectable suburbs, where house prices ensure him the exclusiveness of apartheid without the stigma. It is quite another for poorer people, who cannot afford to move, to watch their neighbourhood changing and the value of their house falling.

Policy work on immigration had been proceeding under Willie Whitelaw's direction for some time by January 1978. But it had not progressed very far – certainly not as far as many of our supporters wished. This was only partly because Willie himself was instinctively liberal-minded on Home Office matters. The problem was that it was very difficult to see what scope existed to cut down on present and potential future immigration.

Closing loopholes, tightening up administration and some new controls on primary and secondary immigration – all of these offered opportunities to reduce the inflow. But I knew that the single most important contribution we could make to good race relations was to reduce the uncertainties about the future. It was fear of the unknown which threatened danger. Willie Whitelaw shared that basic analysis, which is why he had pledged us at the 1976 Party Conference 'to follow a policy which is clearly designed to work towards the end of immigration as we have seen it in these post-war years'.

Although I had not planned any specific announcement on immigration, I was not surprised when I was asked in an interview on *World in Action* about the subject. I had been giving it a good deal of thought, having indeed expressed myself strongly in other interviews. I said:

> People are really rather afraid that this country might be rather swamped by people with a different culture . . . So, if you want good race relations you have got to allay people's fears on numbers . . . We do have to hold out the prospect of an end to immigration, except, of course, for compassionate cases. Therefore we have got to look at the numbers who have a right to come in . . . Everyone who is here must be treated equally under the law and that, I think, is why quite a lot of them too are fearful that their position might be put in jeopardy, or people might be hostile to them, unless we cut down the incoming numbers.

Even I was taken aback by the reaction to these extremely mild remarks. What it quickly showed was the degree to which politicians had become isolated from people's real worries. I was denounced as 'appallingly irresponsible' by David Steel, the Liberal Party Leader, who later added that my remarks were 'really quite wicked'. Denis Healey spoke of my 'cold-blooded calculation in stirring up the muddy waters of racial prejudice . . . to spread fear and hatred among peaceful communities'. The

Home Secretary, Merlyn Rees, accused me of 'making respectable racial hatred'. The bishops joined in. Fifteen years later, this reaction to ideas which were later embodied in legislation and are all but universally accepted seems hysterical.

Even at the time, the reaction in the country, undoubtedly sharpened by the exaggerated rhetoric of critics who imagined they had finally sunk me, was completely different. Before my interview, the opinion polls showed us level-pegging with Labour. Afterwards, they showed the Conservatives with an eleven-point lead. This unintended effect of a spontaneous reply to an interviewer's question had important political consequences. Whatever Willie in his heart of hearts and my other colleagues felt about it, it provided a large and welcome boost at an extremely difficult time. It also sharpened up the discussion within Shadow Cabinet of our proposals. Within weeks we had a comprehensive and agreed approach which satisfied all but the diehard advocates of repatriation and which would see us through the general election.*

The whole affair was a demonstration that I must trust my own judgement on crucial matters, rather than necessarily hope to persuade my colleagues in advance; for I could expect that somewhere out in the country there would be a following and perhaps a majority for me.

Quite apart from the immigration issue, 1978 had all the makings of a politically difficult year for the Opposition. As a result of the financial measures introduced under pressure from the IMF, the economic situation improved. In January 1978 inflation fell below 10 per cent for the first time since 1974 and it continued to fall. Unemployment was also falling gradually from its peak in August 1977; although there were sharp increases during the summer of 1978, 1.36 million were registered unemployed by that December, 120,000 fewer than the year before. We succeeded, with support from the Liberals, in forcing a cut of one penny

---

* Our manifesto pledged us to introduce a British Nationality Act defining British citizenship and the right to abode, to set up a register of dependants from Commonwealth countries who had the right of settlement under existing legislation (whose numbers were uncertain) and to establish a quota system to restrict the rate of entry for settlement from non-EC countries. In the event, only the first of these measures was passed into law. During the 1980s primary immigration – the admission of heads of household in their own right – fell significantly, diminishing the number of future dependants with a right of settlement and reducing the overall total below 50,000 in most years, compared to 82,000 in 1975 and 69,000 in 1979.

in the basic rate of income tax: but that in itself would probably reduce the gloom about the economy which had played such an important part in Labour's unpopularity and which had worked to our advantage.

Our assumption was that Jim Callaghan hoped to coast along on these gradual improvements towards an election in the autumn on a platform of 'safety first'. One large obstacle in his way was that the Liberals now recognized that the Lib-Lab Pact had been politically disastrous for them. But their anxiety to bring it to an end was modified by their reluctance to face the electoral consequences of having sustained Labour in power at all. As for the opinion polls, Labour had drawn almost level with us by the summer and though we pulled away from them in August/September, during October and November (after a difficult Conservative Conference) they were around 5 per cent ahead, with the Liberals not even in double figures.

In these circumstances, I commissioned work on a draft manifesto. It was drawn together by Chris Patten and the Research Department on the basis of Shadow spokesmen's drafts. When I read it in July I was unimpressed. The large, simple themes had become obscured by lists of costly promises designed to appeal to interest groups. I said that the next draft must put the main emphasis on a few central objectives, like tax cuts and strengthening the country's internal and external defences. The fulfilment of all other spending pledges was conditional on meeting these pledges first. In truth, I was disagreeably reminded of what little real progress in analysis or policy we had made in Opposition over the last three years. If we continued thinking in these terms, how would we ever manage to turn the country round?

More encouraging, however, was the change which had come over the Party's publicity. Gordon Reece had returned to become Director of Publicity at Central Office. It was through Gordon that Tim Bell and Saatchi & Saatchi were made responsible for the Party's advertising. This was a significant departure in our political communications. But I needed no persuading that it was right to obtain the best professionals in their field to put across our message. Politicians should resist the temptation to consider themselves experts in fields where they have no experience.

Saatchis put new life into the tired format of Party Political Broadcasts. There were the inevitable accusations of frivolity or over-simplification. But PPBs should not be judged on the basis of the comments of the Party faithful, but rather by whether the casual, unpolitical viewer actually chooses to watch them, rather than turning to another channel, and whether he gains a sympathetic impression. On this score, the change was a great improvement.

Most significant, however, was the 'Labour Isn't Working' poster campaign in the summer of 1978. Tim, Gordon and Ronnie Millar came down to Scotney* on a Saturday in June 1978 to get my agreement for a campaign on this theme. Again, it would break new ground. Unemployment, which would be depicted both by the wording and by a picture of a dole queue, though it had risen to almost 1.5 million, was traditionally a 'Labour issue'. That is to say, it was a topic which we would not normally make a campaign priority because, like the Welfare State, it was one where the Labour Party was generally regarded as stronger than us. The poster would also break with the notion that in party propaganda you should not mention your opponent directly. Saatchis, however, understood – and convinced me – that political advertising of the sort proposed could ignore such considerations. It was designed to undermine confidence in our political opponents, and so it should limit itself to a simple, negative message.

Generally, governments do well during the summer recess because the political temperature drops. The planned campaign would keep it high and doubtless provoke strong reactions. So, after much discussion, I agreed that the campaign should go ahead.

As expected, it evoked a response. Denis Healey launched a bombardment. But the more it was condemned by the Labour Party, the greater publicity it got. Simply in order to explain what the controversy was about, the newspapers had to print pictures of the poster, thus multiplying the effect. So successful was it that a further series was developed on other topics, on each of which Labour was 'not working'. Partly as a result of all this, we came through to the autumn of 1978 in better political shape than might have been expected – and in August-September we were strengthening. That in turn may have been of some significance, insofar as it affected the Prime Minister's decision on whether to call an election.

Only Jim Callaghan can say precisely why he did not call a general election that autumn. Certainly, I expected that he would, particularly after his speech to the TUC Conference which ended improbably with him

---

* We had moved into the old dower flat in Scotney Castle at Lamberhurst in 1975. Denis had officially retired from Burmah and the twins, now aged twenty-two, were living very much their own lives. Flood Street remained our London home.

bursting into song: 'There was I, waiting at the church . . .' – a teasing refusal to tell them what he was going to do. Then, just two days later, on Thursday 7 September while I was on a visit to Birmingham, the news was telephoned through to me from Downing Street that in the Prime Ministerial broadcast that evening Jim Callaghan would announce that there would not in fact be an election.

I shared the general sense of anti-climax which the Prime Minister's announcement caused. But I knew that others, who had been working night and day to place the Party on a war footing in what had every sign of being a closely contested struggle, would feel the let-down even more.

Would we have won a general election in the autumn of 1978? I believe that we might have scraped in with a small overall majority. But it would only have needed one or two mistakes in our campaign to have lost. And even if we had just won, what would have happened next? The Labour Government's pay policy was now clearly coming apart. The TUC had voted against a renewal of the Social Contract – and the following month's Labour Party Conference would vote to reject all pay restraint – so even that fig leaf would be removed. A strike of Ford car workers already looked impossible to settle within the Government's 5 per cent 'pay norm'. The distortions and frustrations of several years of prices and incomes policy were unwinding, as they had under the Heath Government, amid bitterness and upheaval.

If we had been faced with that over the winter of 1978/79 it might have broken us, as it finally broke the Labour Government. First, I would have had to insist that all the talk about 'norms' and 'limits' should be dropped immediately. For reasons I shall explain, that would have been very unpopular and perhaps unacceptable to most of the Shadow Cabinet! Secondly, even had we tried to use cash limits in the public sector and market disciplines in the private sector, rather than some kind of pay policy, there would have been a high risk of damaging strikes. Rather than giving us a mandate to curb trade union power, as they would in the following year, these would probably only have confirmed in the public mind the impression left by the three-day week in 1974 that Conservative Governments meant provoking and losing confrontations with the trade unions. Appalling as the scenes of the winter of 1978/79 turned out to be, without them and without their exposure of the true nature of socialism, it would have been far more difficult to achieve what was done in the 1980s.

But in any case, we could afford to wait. Although I cannot claim to have foreseen what followed, I was convinced that the Labour Party's basic approach was unsustainable. In exchange for agreement with the trade union leaders on pay limits, the Labour Government had pursued policies which extended state control of the economy, reduced the scope for individual enterprise and increased trade union power. At some point such a strategy would collapse. The trade union leaders and the left of the Labour Party would find their power so strengthened that they would no longer have an interest in delivering pay restraint. Nor would union members respond to calls for sacrifice in pursuit of policies that had plainly failed. The effects of socialist policies on the overall performance of the economy would be that Britain would lag further and further behind its competitors on productivity and living standards. Beyond a certain point this could no longer be concealed from the general public – nor from the foreign-exchange markets and foreign investors. Assuming that the basic structures of a free political and economic system were still operating, socialism must then break down. And that, of course, is exactly what happened that winter.

The Conservative Party Conference at Brighton was always likely to be difficult. The opinion polls showed us falling behind Labour. Above all, the controversy over the Government's rapidly disintegrating pay policy focused even more attention on our approach, and that was itself threatened with disintegration.

A couple of weeks before the Conference Jim Prior had unwisely made remarks in a radio interview which seemed to offer Conservative backing for the Government's 5 per cent policy, and not only made clear his support for the principle of a statutory incomes policy but actually revealed that he thought a Conservative Government would be forced to introduce one: 'I think that may well happen under certain circumstances.' In my own interviews, I tried to shift the emphasis back towards the link between pay, profits and output and away from norms. Although I made it clear that I was not supporting the Ford strike, I equally blamed the Government's 5 per cent pay norm for what was happening and said that a statutory policy was not a practical possibility. I was widely interpreted as having called for a return to free collective bargaining, an interpretation I did not seek to deny.

Ted Heath now intervened on the other side. Speaking in the Conference economic debate, while I watched from the platform, he warned of the risks of dogmatism and said of the Government's 5 per cent policy: 'It is not yet clear to what extent it has broken down. But if it has broken down, there is nothing here for gloating, nothing for joy. We should grieve for our country.' Geoffrey Howe made a strong closing speech, handling Ted's intervention with aplomb and saying that a future Conservative Government would return to 'realistic, responsible collective bargaining, free from government interference'. But later that evening Ted appeared on television and went further. He warned that 'free collective bargaining produces massive inflation', and when asked if the Conservative Party should support the Government's pay policy at a general election, he replied: 'If the Prime Minister says he is going to the country and expresses the view that we cannot have another roaring inflation or another free-for-all, I would say I agree with that.'

This was a thinly veiled threat. An open split between the two of us during the general election would cause enormous damage. The question of Ted's role during an election had long worried the Party, and Peter Thorneycroft had met him quietly to discuss his plans earlier in the year. Humphrey Atkins had also received messages from several MPs close to Ted who told him that he was proving amenable to an approach to help. Arrangements were made to liaise with his office during the campaign. Ted's intervention had blown all that out of the water.

Moreover, in substance Ted's view seemed to me entirely misconceived. There was no point in backing a policy which was beyond repair, even if it had been beneficial (which, in anything except the very short term, it was not). Moreover, although opposition to centrally imposed pay policies meant that we would find ourselves with strange bedfellows, including the more extreme trade union militants, the revolt against centralization and egalitarianism was basically healthy. As Conservatives, we should not frown on people being well rewarded for using sharp wits or strong arms to produce what the customer wanted. Of course, when such an approach was described, even by those allegedly on our own side, as being opportunist – and when it was accompanied by open disagreements as now between Shadow ministers like Jim Prior and Keith Joseph – it was difficult to have the analysis taken seriously. But in fact it was an essential part of my political strategy to appeal directly to those who had not traditionally voted Conservative, but who now wanted more opportunities for themselves and their families. So I addressed much of my Conference speech directly to trade unionists.

> You want higher wages, better pensions, shorter hours, more government spending, more investment, more – more – more –

more. But where is this 'more' to come from? There is no more. There can be, but there will not be, unless we all produce it. You can no more separate pay from output than you can separate two blades of a pair of scissors and still have a sharp cutting edge. And here, let me say plainly to trade union leaders, you are often your own worst enemies. Why isn't there more? Because too often restrictive practices rob you of the one thing you have to sell – your productivity.

Restrictive practices are encrusted like barnacles on our industrial life. They have been there for almost a century. They were designed to protect you from being exploited, but they have become the chief obstacle to your prosperity . . . I understand your fears. You're afraid that producing more goods with fewer people will mean fewer jobs, and those fears are naturally stronger at a time of high unemployment. But you're wrong. The right way to attack unemployment is to produce more goods more cheaply, and then more people can afford to buy them . . .

We shall do all that a government can to rebuild a free and prosperous Britain. We believe in realistic, responsible, collective bargaining, free from government interference. Labour does not. We believe in encouraging competition, free enterprise, and profits in firms large and small. Labour does not. We believe in making substantial cuts in the tax on your pay packet. Labour does not. We will create conditions in which the value of the money you earn and the money you save can be protected.

Over the next six months this strategy would be successful. But in the short term it was a liability, because the Party was not united on it and because opinion polls suggested that the public wanted us to support the Government against the unions. And not surprisingly we found ourselves at the end of the Conference season five and a half percentage points behind the Labour Party.

The removal of the prospect of an immediate election, after everyone's nerves had been screwed up to fight one, led to a breakdown in the ordinary disciplines in both parties. In the Labour Party this focused on economics. With us it boiled over on Rhodesia, first at the Party Conference and then in the House of Commons.

But Labour's time was running out. Jim Callaghan had been dealt a bad hand by history and Harold Wilson in 1976. Like a brilliant poker player, he had employed skill, gamesmanship and simple bluff to spin out his defeat as long as possible on the chance that an ace or two might suddenly appear from up his sleeve. As 1978 became 1979, however, a succession of deuces tumbled forth. On Tuesday 12 December trade unions representing National Health Service and local authority workers rejected the 5 per cent pay limit and announced that they would strike in the New Year. At the end of December the elements conspired to create more trouble, with heavy snow, gales and floods. On Wednesday 3 January the TGWU called the lorry drivers out on strike in pursuit of a 25 per cent pay rise. Some two million workers faced being laid off. Hospital patients, including terminally ill cancer patients, were denied treatment. Gravediggers went on strike in Liverpool. Refuse piled up in Leicester Square. With government compliance, trade union shop stewards dispensed permits to allow lorry drivers to transport 'essential' goods across picket lines. In short, Britain ground to a halt. What was more damaging even than this to the Labour Government, however, was that it had handed over the running of the country to local committees of trade unionists.

Would we be able to grasp the opportunities this provided? That might depend in part on an operation which had been proceeding in fits and starts, under conditions of the greatest secrecy, since the summer of 1977 and which went under the umbrella title of 'Stepping Stones'. It was the brainchild of John Hoskyns, an able ex-soldier who had set up one of the first computer software companies, which he had built up and then sold to concentrate on public affairs. John had been in contact with Keith Joseph at the Centre for Policy Studies for some time before we were introduced. Together with his colleague Norman Strauss, he had a refreshingly if sometimes irritatingly undisguised scorn for the *ad hoc* nature of political decision-making in general and the decision-making of the Shadow Cabinet in particular. The two of them argued that we could never succeed unless we fitted all our policies into a single strategy in which we worked out in advance the order in which actions had to be taken – hence the title. The first time I heard all this I was not very impressed. We met over Sunday lunch at Flood Street and the session ended by my remarking on the fact that they had eaten a whole joint of roast beef and I wasn't sure what I had gained from it all. Alfred Sherman quipped that next time they would bring sandwiches. But under different circumstances, when long-term thinking was concerned, I came to appreciate the depth and quality of John Hoskyns's analysis.

What rejuvenated the Stepping Stones initiative, after ministerial objection had effectively halted it, was the collapse of the Government's 5 per cent pay policy that autumn. Immediately after the Labour Conference rejected the policy, Keith Joseph came to see Willie Whitelaw and me, expressing his disappointment that we had not got on further. At various times people had suggested that the only way forward was to shift Jim Prior, but now there was obviously an opportunity to move on without taking such a strong step. Accordingly, I arranged another meeting of the Stepping Stones Steering Group for mid-November.

At this and at a later meeting, however, Jim was still able to block proposals for a vigorous campaign on the union question that winter. Peter Thorneycroft gave him strong support. Peter had never been a friend of Stepping Stones: at one point he actually suggested that every copy of the Stepping Stones report should be recalled to Central Office and burned. Even though Party opinion had begun to shift in my direction, no amount of discussion between Shadow ministers, advisers and MPs would have sufficed to persuade the Shadow Cabinet of the need to think seriously about trade union reform, had it not been for the industrial chaos of the Winter of Discontent.

Even then they would require a lead. This was an area in which we had made little or no advance since 1975. As Shadow Employment spokesman, Jim Prior had been well placed to veto the development of new policy on union reform. Although just before Christmas 1978 we managed to persuade him to accept an extension of our policy of providing state funds for unions voluntarily holding secret ballots – we would offer cash to cover the cost of pre-strike ballots as well as union elections – this really amounted to very little. Indeed, to the average voter our policy on secret ballots would have been hard to distinguish from Labour's: in November 1978 the Prime Minister was offering to legislate on secret ballots if the unions wanted it.

In December Keith Joseph had tried to reopen the question of benefits paid to strikers' families. I had agreed to the summoning of a new Policy Group to consider this question, but when it met, Jim Prior's opposition had prevented any progress.

I spent Christmas and New Year anxiously and reflectively at Scotney, watching the crisis build up. As it had at Christmas 1974, the bad weather discouraged us from our usual walks, and besides I had plenty to do. I read through the various Policy Group papers on union questions and I had brought down a bulging file of briefing from the press and interested outsiders; I spent many hours studying a textbook on industrial relations law and went back to the original Acts of Parliament, reading through the most important legislation since 1906. Every time I turned on the radio or the television the news was worse. I came back to London determined on one thing: the time had come to toughen our policy on union reform.

There was no difficulty in finding a platform. I had agreed before Christmas to be interviewed on Sunday 14 January by Brian Walden on *Weekend World*; the date was brought forward a week to 7 January. When I came back to London in the New Year, I saw Alfred Sherman, Gordon Reece and a few other close advisers to continue my briefing. The industrial situation was changing so fast that it was becoming more and more difficult to keep up to date, but over the next few weeks having the very latest facts to hand gave me vital advantages.

On Wednesday 3 January Jim Prior intervened to prevent a change in policy. Interviewed by Robin Day on radio, he firmly rejected compulsory strike ballots ('not something that you can make compulsory in any way'), rejected legislation on strikers' benefits, and commented on the closed shop: 'we want to take this quite quietly . . . it is better in these matters to play a quiet game rather than to shout too much'. Asked what he thought of recent criticism of the trade union leadership by David Howell and Michael Heseltine, he said: 'I don't think they are being fair to trade union leaders who at the moment are trying to give good advice to the rank and file, and the rank and file is quite often rejecting it.'

On *Weekend World* I struck rather a different note. 'Every power implies responsibility, every liberty a duty. The unions have [had] tremendous power over the years . . . [And] this is what the debate has got to be about – how unions use their power. I'm a parliamentarian, I am not in Parliament to enable them to have a licence to inflict harm, damage and injury on others and be immune from the law, and if I see it happening, then I've got to take action.'

Although I was careful not to commit us firmly to individual measures before they had received proper consideration, I ran through with Brian Walden a shopping list of possible changes, which naturally moved them higher on the agenda than some of my colleagues really wanted. I reaffirmed Jim Prior's announcement that we would make funds available for secret ballots before strikes as well as for union elections. But I hinted at compulsion if needed, holding out the possibility of legislation to refuse Social Security benefits unless there had been a strike ballot. I also mentioned the possibility of restricting strikes in essential services, announced that we would subject short-term Social Security benefits to taxation and made the case for a right of appeal to the courts for people excluded from a union, who faced losing their jobs where there was a closed shop.

On television the following day Jim Prior replied to my interview. He said that nothing had been agreed between us on Social Security benefits for strikers and that he was against compulsory secret ballots. Thankfully, others reacted more positively. I had broken ranks. People could see that I was going to fight. Offers of support, information and new ideas began to flow into my office.

The strong support that I received for what I said in my *Weekend World* interview was in marked contrast to the reaction to Jim Callaghan's remarks on his arrival back three days later from the Guade-loupe summit. His absence from the country at such a critical time had itself been politically damaging, helping to strengthen the impression that the Government was paralysed in the face of the strikes. The press coverage of the summit itself had not helped him; the sight of the Prime Minister sitting with the other leaders in the Caribbean sun, casually dressed, was a dangerous contrast to events at home. But the final disaster was the impression he left with the press when he flew into Heathrow. Although he never did use those precise words – 'Crisis? What Crisis?' – the myth faithfully represented his attempt to play down the scale of the problem. His image of unflappability and competence was never restored.

What should be our next move? Parliament was due to return on Monday 15 January. I wrote to the Prime Minister demanding a full statement and a debate on the industrial situation. We had a slot already arranged for a PPB on Wednesday 17 January and work began on a script.

The preparations I made for my speech in the debate were perhaps the most thorough I had ever made for an appearance in the Commons. My original idea had been to make a hard-hitting but essentially conventional speech from the Opposition benches – hammering the Government and demanding that they change course. But at Scotney over the weekend of 13–14 January and on Monday back in London several people urged a different approach. Peter Utley and Peter Thorneycroft sent me suggestions for a speech offering support for the Government if it was prepared to introduce the kind of legislative changes necessary to break the union stranglehold. Ronnie Millar and Chris Patten – working on the PPB script – were urging the same idea.

My own immediate inclination was to avoid offers of co-operation, for several reasons. First, unlike the more coalition-minded of my colleagues, I believed that the job of Oppositions is generally to oppose. We had a fundamentally different approach from that of the Government and our main duty was to explain it and persuade the country of its merits. Secondly, it was dangerous to make an offer of co-operation without having thought through clearly in advance whether we actually wanted it accepted or not. Probably nothing which went to the heart of the problem would – or indeed could – be accepted by Jim Callaghan's Government. There was, therefore, a risk that in order to make a credible offer of support, we would have to set our sights too low as regards measures of reform. And if the Government then *did* accept the offer, we would have thrown away, for the time being at least, the opportunity of forcing it out of office. Moreover, reforms in trade union law alone would not suffice to deal with Britain's underlying economic problems: that would need a much more comprehensive strategy to which the socialists could never agree.

That evening – Monday 15 January – I called a Steering Committee meeting. Most of my senior colleagues favoured the idea of a conditional offer and by this stage I had come round to the idea myself. Reforms were essential; and if the Government were prepared to introduce the necessary measures, how could we oppose them? By offering help we enhanced our moral authority. I believed – as did most of the supporters of the idea – that the offer should be set at a level which, though abundantly justified by events, would be unlikely to be accepted by the Government. This was a difficult matter to judge in detail: the Labour Party might just be persuaded to agree to the negotiation of no-strike agreements in essential services, the payment by the taxpayer of the cost of secret ballots in trade unions and even a code of practice to end secondary picketing – though the last was doubtful. Equally, I was clear that if the Government did accept, we were honour-bound to keep our side of the bargain. For me, however, there was an additional and very important consideration. By agreeing to offer co-operation with the Government on selected measures, Jim Prior and his supporters would find it impossible to refuse support to those same measures if and when a Conservative Government introduced them.

The upshot was that the Steering Committee agreed that the Government could rely on Conservative support if it took firmer action on picketing (to get essential supplies moving), legislated to outlaw secondary picketing and to encourage secret ballots for union elections, and if it made efforts to negotiate non-strike agreements in essential industries. Events are a powerful advocate.

I opened the debate the following day. I began by describing the crisis. Transport of goods by road was widely disrupted, in many cases due to secondary picketing of firms and operators not involved in the actual disputes. British Rail had issued a brief statement: 'There are no trains today.' The CBI had reported that many firms were being strangled, due to shortage of materials and inability to move finished goods. There was trouble at the ports, adding to the problems of exporters. At least 125,000 people had been laid off already and the figure was expected to reach a million by the end of the week. The food industry, in particular, was in a shambolic state, with growing shortages of basic supplies like edible oils, yeast, salt and sugar. And all this on top of a winter of strikes – strikes by tanker drivers, bakers, staff at old people's homes and hospitals; strikes in the press and broadcasting, airports and car plants; a strike of gravediggers.

I reminded the arch-moderate Shirley Williams that she had joined the Grunwick picket line. I made the conditional offer of support agreed in the Steering Committee, and I also made it a condition of co-operation that the Government should act on the closed shop; I felt too strongly on this subject not to include it.

The Prime Minister began his reply in a surprising way:

> I congratulate the Right Honourable lady on a most effective parliamentary performance. It was in the best manner of our debates and the style in which it was delivered was one of which the Right Honourable lady can be proud.

It was a good start. But all that the Prime Minister then had to offer in the body of his speech were further concessions to the unions – exemptions from the 5 per cent pay limit, tighter price controls and extension of the principle of 'comparability' under which public sector workers could expect more money. All these were intended as inducements to the unions to sign up to a new pay policy. But he signally failed to address what everyone except the far Left considered the main problem, excessive trade union power.

To my offer the Prime Minister made no direct reply. He had clearly been wrong-footed. The question now was whether I should repeat the offer the following evening in our Party Political Broadcast – or limit myself to attacking the Government's paralysis and pledging that a Conservative Government would reform trade union law.

I was still uneasy, and toughened the script when I saw it the following day. But after all, the offer had already been made, and the higher the profile we gave it, the more tightly it would bind reluctant colleagues and the more public support we would gain. So we went ahead, filming it in my room at the House of Commons. Again, the Government made no direct reply.

But now Banquo's ghost came back to haunt the Labour Government. Devolution, which they had embraced solely as a means of staying in power with support from the Scottish and Welsh Nationalists, returned to grimace and gibber at Jim Callaghan at his lowest point. Following the defeat of the Scotland and Wales Bill in early 1977 Labour had reintroduced devolution legislation in the form of separate Bills for Scotland and Wales, with provision for referenda in each country before they came into effect. Backbench dissent on their own side led to the passage of a number of amendments, including the crucial additional requirement that a minimum of 40 per cent of those eligible to vote had to support devolution in each case. Although I had not publicly campaigned for a 'No' vote in the referenda in Scotland and Wales, that was the result I wanted. When the vote took place on 1 March 1979 in Scotland a bare majority of those voting was in favour – well below the required 40 per cent of the total electorate – and in Wales a large majority of those who voted rejected the proposal. For the moment, devolution was dead: I did not mourn it.

From this point on it seemed likely that the Government would be unable to continue in office; but the circumstances under which a general election would occur were far from predictable. The Prime Minister sought desperately to spin out discussion about devolution rather than go ahead immediately with the repeal of the Devolution Acts. But his potential allies were preparing to desert. The SNP now had no reason to keep Labour in office and wanted an early confidence motion. The Liberals were keen on an early election, even though their standing in the opinion polls was weak; this was principally in order to avoid the embarrassment of the forthcoming trial of their former Leader, Jeremy Thorpe, on a charge of conspiracy to murder, of which he was later acquitted. Admittedly, the Welsh Nationalists, who were more of a socialist party than their Scottish equivalents, might still be persuadable.

That meant that the Northern Irish MPs – ten Ulster Unionists, one member of the Social Democratic and Liberal Party (SDLP) and one Independent Republican – were likely to be decisive.

On Thursday 22 March the Prime Minister made a last effort to keep devolution alive and win over the SNP, making a parliamentary statement offering yet more talks and following it with a Prime Ministerial broadcast that evening. He never had any real chance of success, and when assurances of SNP and Liberal support for our motion seemed to be forthcoming – though there was none from the Welsh Nationalists – I agreed that it should be tabled, which was done a little before 7 p.m. The Conservative whips now went all out to persuade the minority parties to see that their less reliable members actually joined us in the lobbies. Equally important, of course, was ensuring that there was a full turn-out of Conservative MPs. Luckily, none was seriously ill – though one Member's car overturned on the motorway as he was driving down and another insisted on voting for us though he had been shattered by the death of his wife the previous day.

Amid clamour and confusion we began to file into the lobbies. Having voted, I returned to my place by the side of Willie, Francis and Humphrey and waited to learn our fate. Humphrey had sought to ensure that I had some advance notice of the result. He asked John Stradling Thomas, one of the senior whips, to go through our lobby very quickly and then stand at the exit of the other one. For some reason, not just when they are in a minority, Conservative MPs go through the lobby more quickly than the Labour Party. As soon as we were all through, the message as to what our numbers were would be given to John Stradling Thomas, who meanwhile was listening to the other (government) lobby being counted out. As soon as they had finished, he would know whether we had won or not. If we had *not* won he would come back, and just stand next to the Speaker's chair. If we *had* won, he would put up a finger so that Humphrey could tell me. Only later was I let into the secret code. I just saw John Stradling Thomas return – and then Humphrey leaned across to me and with a stage whisper said: 'We've won!'

The announced figures bore it out. 'Ayes, 311. Noes, 310.' So at last I had my chance, my only chance. I must seize it with both hands.

Two days later I was attending a function in my constituency – a fund-raising event organized by Motability, which provided disabled people with special cars at a modest price. I was to make the presentation. My mind was at least half on the Party Election Broadcast I was due to make that evening, when Derek Howe approached me to say: 'I think you ought to know that a bomb has gone off in the precincts of the House of Commons, in the garage they think. At least one person has been very seriously injured, but we don't know who.'

A hundred possibilities – though not the correct one – went through my mind as we drove down to the BBC studios in Portland Place. When I got there, and before I went in to be made up, one of the producers took me aside into a private room and told me who it was. It was Airey Neave. He was critically injured. The Irish National Liberation Army – a break-away faction from the IRA – had placed a bomb under his car and it had exploded when he drove up the ramp from the House of Commons car park. It was very unlikely that he would survive – indeed, by the time I heard the news he may well have been dead. There was no way I could bring myself to broadcast after that. I telephoned the Prime Minister and explained. I felt only stunned. The full grief would come later. With it came also anger that this man – my friend – who had shrugged off so much danger in his life should be murdered by someone worse than a common criminal.

CHAPTER TWELVE

Just One Chance . . .

The 1979 general election campaign

A COMPARISON BETWEEN THE MANIFESTO DRAFT of August 1978 and the final text published in April 1979 illustrates both the extent and the limits of the changes which – in varying combinations – Keith Joseph, Geoffrey Howe, my advisers and I secured. The passage on trade unions, of course, was the real test. In 1978 I was prepared to go along with almost everything that Jim Prior suggested, including the promise that we would be 'even-handed in our approach to industrial problems'. The 1979 text was significantly different. Now we promised to strike 'a fair balance between the rights and duties of the trade union movement'. Furthermore, we challenged directly the idea that the law had no useful role to play in this area: 'Labour claim that industrial relations in Britain cannot be improved by changing the law. We disagree. If the law can be used to confer privileges it can and should also be used to establish obligations.'

I had disliked both the tone and the intellectual confusion which characterized Jim Prior's suggested manifesto passages on the general role of trade unions in the spring of 1978. But I objected still more strongly to Jim's suggestions on the closed shop. Although Jim wanted us to say that we were 'opposed to the closed shop in principle', he wanted to add that 'experience has shown that a number of managements and unions consider it a convenient method of conducting their negotiations'. The contrast in the same sentence between the requirements of 'principle' and 'convenience' struck me as particularly distasteful. There are, of course, many freedoms which it would be 'convenient' for powerful groups to suppress: but most of us reckon that 'principle' requires that those freedoms should be defended. Jim also wanted us to promise a 'code of practice' which would regulate the closed shop. If the code of practice was not honoured 'it could result (as at present) in workers losing their livelihood without compensation or redress from either employer or union. In this event we would be prepared to legislate to protect their rights.'

Even in 1978 I had felt that we could do better than this. I had insisted that there must be a right of appeal to the courts if someone was unfairly excluded or expelled from their union. But in 1979 we went significantly further by dropping the formula about the closed shop being objectionable but inevitable and making a clear commitment to change the law. Existing employees and 'those with personal conviction' (a weasel phrase but still unavoidable in the circumstances) 'must be adequately protected, and if they lose their jobs as a result of the closed shop they must be entitled to adequate compensation'. The manifesto also promised an inquiry into the coercive recruitment practices of the SLADE printing union. Additionally we made it clear that the code of practice would have statutory force.

But the main change of substance related to picketing. In 1978 I had gone along with what Jim Prior wanted, which was not very much: 'In consultation with all parties, we must find acceptable means to regulate the conduct of picketing. The strict arrangements adopted by the NUM in February 1974 could provide a sensible basis for this.'

There was no mention even of a code of practice, let alone legislation. It was also, in retrospect, not particularly wise to remind voters directly of the occasion when the previous Conservative Government had been broken by the miners' strike. Thankfully, the shocking scenes of the Winter of Discontent ensured that this feeble approach was now out of touch with reality and people's expectations. We now promised to make secondary picketing unlawful and to review trade union immunities. Moreover, there was the clear suggestion that we would be prepared to take further legislative steps if these proved necessary: 'We shall also make any further changes that are necessary so that a citizen's right to work and to go about his or her lawful business free from intimidation or obstruction is guaranteed.'

Two other new provisions were inserted between the 1978 and 1979 texts: one was the promise to 'seek to conclude no-strike agreements in a few essential services' (which in fact came to nothing), and the other to 'ensure that unions bear their fair share of the cost of supporting those of their members who are on strike', which we later implemented. Together with the limited proposals to ease the effects of the closed shop and equally modest proposals to finance postal ballots for union elections and other important issues, these constituted our package of trade union reform. I was very happy with it: indeed, it would turn out that I was far more confident not just in its practicality but also its popularity than some of my colleagues.

By contrast with my victory over the position on trade unions, I scored no better than a draw on incomes policy. On this question, of course, I could not place my usual reliance on Geoffrey Howe who had developed a fatal attraction for the so-called 'forum'. In 1978 I had argued that we should be clearer about our intention to break away from incomes policies, suggesting that instead of asserting (as proposed) that 'the return to flexibility will take time, but it cannot be postponed for ever', the last phrase should be replaced by 'but it must start without delay'. And I did not even win this small point.

In 1979 the manifesto contained, indeed, a somewhat more explicit allusion to the 'forum', even mentioning the German model. But this I could live with. Of more practical importance, there was a strongly worded promise to avoid incomes policies in the private sector: 'Pay bargaining in the private sector should be left to the companies and workers concerned. At the end of the day, no one should or can protect them from the results of the agreements they make.'

That left one particularly thorny aspect of incomes policy to be grasped in the public sector. The Prime Minister's offer in January 1979 of new machinery to establish 'comparability' between the public and private sectors led to the setting up of a commission under Professor Hugh Clegg to take evidence and make recommendations which, of course, the Government committed itself to honour – after the election. Inevitably, when the election campaign began we were pressed to define our attitude. The question, in effect, was whether we would agree to pick up the bill (size unknown) for Labour's efforts to buy off the public sector unions.

Our policy for public sector pay had always been based on the strict application of cash limits. Geoffrey Howe and I did our best to stick to that, but there was intense pressure from colleagues and the Party, frankly concerned not to lose vital votes. And so finally we yielded and pledged ourselves to implement Professor Clegg's recommendations. It was an expensive but unavoidable commitment.

In general, however, I was happy with the manifesto, both as regards contents and style. It contained a coherent philosophy and a limited number of clearly defined pledges. And it passed the most important final test, namely that at no stage in the campaign did we have to modify or retreat from it.

I was to fight three general elections as Leader of the Conservative Party; and each one was different. The 1983 campaign was perhaps the easiest; the 1987 campaign was certainly the most emotionally fraught; but the general election of 1979 was the most challenging both for me and the Party. I never had any illusion that if we lost or even if we failed to win an overall majority I would be given another chance. I accepted this and was even prepared to speak about it openly. Personally, I had little doubt that it was also a watershed for the Conservative Party and for Britain.

The 1979 campaign was also different in a number of other ways. It was the first time that the Conservative Party had ever fought so clearly on the theme that it was 'time for a change'. Implicit in this approach was that Britain had been in retreat for much more than the years since 1974; the 1970–74 Conservative Government, however bravely it had started out, had been part of that retreat. I therefore believed that we should be bold in explaining precisely what had gone wrong and why radical action was required to put it right. I was soon to be aware, however, that this was not how Peter Thorneycroft and Central Office in general saw things. Their belief was that we should at all costs avoid 'gaffes', which meant in practice almost anything controversial – in particular, attacks on trade union power – in the belief that the Labour Party was already sufficiently discredited to lose the election. In fact, with a few concessions, I insisted on doing it my way. But this led to tensions.

It also led to an odd reversal of roles between Government and Opposition. From the very beginning of their campaign, Labour more or less ignored their own manifesto – with the exception of vote-buying promises like free television licences for pensioners – and offered only limited excuses for their record. Instead, they concentrated on attacking real and alleged Conservative policies. Jim Callaghan largely discarded his image of avuncular *bonhomie* and led an extremely effective but wholly negative campaign. This was carried on at three levels. First, the media were fed with a daily diet of scare stories – ranging from the doubling of Value Added Tax to large cuts in the National Health Service – which would allegedly occur if we were elected. Secondly, doubt was cast on the credibility of our promises, particularly the pledge to cut income tax. Thirdly, there was an attempt to portray me as a dangerous right-wing ideologue, unsuited to the complex and demanding tasks of the premiership.

Labour's strategy presented us with a fundamental dilemma. Should we reply to their attacks? Or should we stick to our own message and our own ground? We only ever partly solved this dilemma.

It is always difficult to co-ordinate the different aspects of an election campaign. The best-laid plans unravel and in no time at all the morning press conferences are concentrating on one message, the Party Leader's speeches a second, Shadow ministers a third, and briefing for candidates something else again. In spite of the serious difference I had with Peter Thorneycroft over tactics, Peter and the team which worked with him were extremely capable.

Two important tactical questions had to be addressed before the campaign got under way. The first was whether I should agree to take part in televised debates with Jim Callaghan. Discussions had been going on with the broadcasters since the summer of 1978 when the BBC (on behalf of both networks) had approached my office and the Prime Minister's simultaneously.

Shortly before the actual campaign began, ITV revived the idea, proposing two debates on successive Sundays at the end of the campaign with Brian Walden as chairman. This time I was inclined to accept. It was not just that I had always been a natural debater; I believed that Jim Callaghan was greatly overrated and I wanted the chance to expose that fact.

There were, however, still powerful arguments on the other side which persuaded Gordon Reece, Peter Thorneycroft and Willie Whitelaw to argue against. When the possibility had first been mooted, we were neck-and-neck with the Labour Party in the opinion polls. But by the time the decision had to be made we had a substantial lead of probably 10 per cent. This meant that we might hope to win *without* the risks of a televised confrontation. And those risks were certainly large. I might make a mistake which it would be hard to obliterate. Jim Callaghan was usually a polished performer on television and he would certainly have no hesitation in using his authority and experience to patronize me. The fact that in the early tentative discussions we learned that he would wish to have the first debate on foreign affairs, where he would be able to deploy all those strengths, caused me to reconsider my earlier enthusiasm.

So I was persuaded to turn down the invitation to debate. It was not worth the risks. In any case, as I wrote in my published reply to ITV's invitation: 'Personally, I believe that issues and policies decide elections, not personalities. We should stick to that approach. We are not electing a president, we are choosing a government.' It was the right decision and the criticism it provoked in some quarters quickly dissipated.

The other tactical question concerned the morning press conferences. Gordon Reece would have liked to dispense with these altogether. In terms of media impact, he was right. Very rarely did anything which happened at the press conference – other perhaps than egregious slip-ups, which were thankfully absent during this campaign – make its way into the day's main news. But the morning press conference does provide the press with opportunities to ask awkward questions, and this in turn provides an opportunity for politicians to show what they are made of. The morning press conferences are therefore an opportunity to win the respect of seasoned journalists whose judgement will influence the coverage they give throughout the campaign.

For some reason, the Conservative Party always starts campaigning later and builds up more slowly than the Labour Party. Labour on this occasion, however, had an even freer run than usual between the Dissolution and the launch of our manifesto on Wednesday 11 April – largely because the political colleagues to whom I left the public appearances and statements were not very effective. This was, indeed, a difficulty throughout the campaign. With the exception of Michael Heseltine, always relishing a headline, they seemed to behave more like ministers-in-waiting than politicians – which meant, of course, that they risked waiting a good deal longer than they expected. It also ensured that even more of the focus was on me, which even I felt was a mixed blessing. In all campaigns there should ideally be a balance of tones and personalities.

Labour used this period to some effect in order to begin attacking policies which we had not yet published. But the trade union leaders managed, before they were muzzled by Labour Party managers, to play into our hands by adopting tones reminiscent of the Winter of Discontent. Sid Weighell, leader of the National Union of Railwaymen, threatened that with free collective bargaining and a Conservative Government, he would 'say to the lads, come on get your snouts into the trough'. Bill Keays, leader of the print union SOGAT, promised 'confrontation' if the country was 'foolish enough to elect the Tory Party'. David Basnett, leader of the General and Municipal Workers, also predicted industrial conflict. It was the same old tune which had played well for Labour in the past, but which was out of harmony with what voters were now prepared to tolerate.

Nor had I been entirely silent. On Thursday 5 April I had addressed the candidates (including Conservative MPs standing for re-election) at a meeting at Central Hall, Westminster. This was not my – or probably anyone else's – favourite place for a public meeting, since it was then rather drab and characterless. There was a special difficulty this year because the candidates expected to hear from me the main themes of a manifesto which was still unpublished. I had to give them some idea of what was coming without revealing the details. So I concentrated heavily on income tax cuts to give greater incentives for wealth-creation and on the need for trade union reform. An audience composed entirely of speakers is not the easiest to address. But their enthusiasm confirmed my instinct that we had chosen the right battleground.

On Wednesday 11 April the manifesto itself was launched at the first Conservative press conference which I chaired, joined by Willie Whitelaw, Keith Joseph, Geoffrey Howe, Peter Carrington, Jim Prior, Humphrey Atkins, Peter Thorneycroft and Angus Maude. The manifesto's tone was modest and practical and Chris Patten and Angus Maude had dressed our ideas in language which was simple and jargon-free.*

It went down well in the following day's press. But the heat at the hugely overcrowded press conference was almost unbearable.

The following day was Maundy Thursday. Because Easter fell during the campaign, four days of electioneering were lost. So my first day of serious campaigning was on Monday 16 April – what in the election agents' jargon was D-17 ('D-day' of course was polling day itself). We had decided to begin in Wales. Having flown down from Gatwick, I met the election battle bus at Swansea Airport, visited an NHS hospital and went on to the local Conservative Club, where I was to give regional television and radio interviews. I was aware of a fair amount of background noise at

---

* Our proposals were distilled into five tasks:

1. To restore the health of our economic and social life, by controlling inflation and sinking a fair balance between the rights and duties of the trade union movement.
2. To restore incentives so that hard work pays, success is rewarded and genuine new jobs are created in an expanding economy.
3. To uphold Parliament and the rule of law.
4. To support family life, by helping people to become home-owners, raising the standards of their children's education, and concentrating welfare services on the effective support of the old, the sick, the disabled and those who are in real need.
5. To strengthen Britain's defences and work with our allies to protect our interests in an increasingly threatening world.

the club. But I only learned afterwards that a huge row, which finished up with fisticuffs, had arisen when the club authorities had tried to keep women reporters out of those rooms reserved for male members only.

Then I went on to Cardiff for the first of the major rallies of the campaign. It was an appropriate place to start. This was very much the heart of enemy territory since Mr Callaghan's constituency was Cardiff South East. So it was a good thing that Cardiff City Hall had a pleasant feel, the right acoustics and an enthusiastic audience. I also had an extremely powerful speech to deliver. It was an uncompromising statement of how socialism had debilitated Britain and of the need for a fundamental change of direction – though not towards some experiment with Utopia but rather back to principles from which we had mistakenly departed.

> ... In politics, I've learned something you in Wales are born knowing: if you've got a message, preach it. I am a conviction politician. The Old Testament prophets didn't merely say: 'Brothers, I want consensus.' They said: 'This is my faith and vision. This is what I passionately believe. If you believe it too, then come with me.' Tonight I say to you just that. Away with the recent bleak and dismal past. Away with defeatism. Under the twin banners, choice and freedom, a new and exciting future beckons the British people.

The audience loved it and so did I. But my cunning adversary, Jim Callaghan, successfully used it to awaken all of the old fear in the Tory Party establishment about the unnerving figure leading them in an uncomfortable, unfamiliar direction. From now on a gap opened up between the way in which Central Office wished to campaign and the direction I insisted on taking.

Such problems were not, however, immediately evident to me.

By Thursday 19 April much agonizing had taken place back in London about the implications of my Cardiff speech for the 'positioning' of the Party and our campaign. Peter Thorneycroft had persuaded himself that we had made a strategic error which should not be repeated. And since nothing that Central Office or my colleagues did seemed to get much publicity, he decided to involve himself in the drafting of my speeches. Oblivious to all this, I spent that Thursday morning visiting a Leicester textile factory, where I put my childhood training to good effect by stitching overall pockets amid a chaotic crowd of journalists and an astonished workforce.

It was, however, just before the bus arrived at the Cadbury factory in Bournville that I learned that Peter Thorneycroft was insisting that a strong passage on trade unions, drafted by Paul Johnson, one of Britain's leading journalists, an historian and a convert from socialism, should be removed from that evening's speech in Birmingham – the second major rally of the campaign. Peter thought it too provocative. He had also apparently intervened to stop Keith Joseph speaking on the same subject. I did not agree with Peter's assessment. But being away from London I felt insufficiently sure of my judgement to substitute it for his. So I angrily tore out the relevant pages of my draft speech and inserted some more innocuous passages. I contented myself with the knowledge that the last section of the speech, with which I had been helped by Peter Carrington, contained some extremely strong stuff on defence and foreign affairs, deliberately adopting the tone and some of the language of my earlier Kensington Town Hall speech.

The Birmingham speech was a great success – not just the passages on East-West relations and the communist threat, but also those on law and order, on which I pledged to 'place a barrier of steel' against the socialist path to lawlessness. Afterwards we drove back to London where the following day's (Friday 20 April) constituency visits would take place.

Saturday 21 April was a day of regular campaigning which began at a factory producing highly sophisticated electrical components in Milton Keynes. I was excited by the technology, about which I had been thoroughly briefed, and soon found myself giving a detailed exposition of it to a group of slightly bemused pressmen. I was then wired up and tested on a heart monitoring machine. With all the dials pointing in the right direction I was shown to be in good working order: 'Solid as a rock,' as I remarked – something which also reflected my judgement about how our campaign as a whole was going. For one of the oddest characteristics of the 1979 general election campaign was the wide and growing difference of perceptions between those of us who were out in the field and those who were back at the centre. Of course, politicians, like everyone else, are susceptible to self-delusion. But, far more than in 1983 and 1987 when security considerations loomed so large, I was confident that I *did* have a real sense of what the electorate felt and that their hearts were with us. I was also convinced that this change had come about largely because of the events of the winter of 1978/79 and that therefore undue caution on the issue of trade union power was bad tactics. But it was clear from discussion at the strategy meeting I held in Flood Street on Sunday 22 April that not everyone saw matters this way. Although the opinion polls were still varied – one showing a 20 per cent and another a 5.5 per cent Conservative lead – there had not been much movement during the campaign. Peter Thorneycroft's view was that we should more or less carry on as we were. As he put it in a paper for that Sunday's meeting: 'We should not embark on any high-risk initiatives. We are in the lead.' This seemed to me fair enough as far as it went. But it begged two questions. First, had we not gained our lead in the first place by taking some quite high-risk initiatives, such as my interventions in the Winter of Discontent? Secondly, what now constituted a 'high risk'? Measures to curb union power? Or the absence of them? In any case, one of the greatest dangers in a campaign where you have started out with a significant lead is complacency. Exciting the voters, as long as it is not on some issue on which they disagree with you, is an indispensable part of winning elections.

My campaigning that week would take me to the North of England, before going on to Scotland. After the Monday morning press conference, I flew to Newcastle where the photo-opportunity was at a tea factory.

Outside the factory a crowd had gathered, among which was a large, formidable woman who was pouring out a torrent of abuse in my direction. The police advised me to stay away. But I felt that if she had something to say she had better do so to my face rather than my back, and so I walked over to talk to her. I took her arm and told her quietly just to say what was wrong. Her manner changed completely. She had the usual grumbles and worries. But the real cause of her anger was a conviction that politicians were just not people who listened. I tried to answer as best I could and we parted amicably. As I walked away I heard her unmistakable tones telling a friend: 'I told you she wasn't half so bad.' My experience of campaigning over the years is that there are very few irredeemably hostile electors. It is one of the tragedies of the terrorist threat that politicians nowadays have so few opportunities to convince themselves of that fact.

After the Wednesday 25 April morning press conference and radio interviews I had lunch at Central Office before flying to Edinburgh in the afternoon. I was beginning to become tired of the standard speech I made to audiences around the country, which drew heavily on the texts prepared for Cardiff and Birmingham with extra pieces slotted in that would go out as press releases. As a result, I performed inadvisably radical surgery on the material I took with me to Scotland. Just minutes before I was due to speak, I was on my knees in the Caledonian Hotel applying scissors and Sellotape to a speech which spread from one wall to the other and back again.

It was a marvellous audience, and from the first few cheers my spirits lifted and I gave of my best.

We went on to the hotel at Glasgow Airport to have a late supper and then turn in before another day of Scottish campaigning. I was buoyed up with that special excitement which comes of knowing you have given a good speech. Although the opinion polls suggested that Labour might be closing on us, the gap was still a healthy one and my instincts were that we were winning the argument. Labour's campaign had a distinctly tired feel about it.

They reiterated so frequently the theme that Tory policies could not work, or would work only at the cost of draconian cuts in public services, that they slipped imperceptibly into arguing that nothing could work, and that Britain's problems were in essence insoluble. This put Labour in conflict with the people's basic instinct that improvement *is* possible and ought to be pursued. We represented that instinct – indeed, Labour was giving us a monopoly on it. I felt that things were going well.

Denis, Carol and Ronnie Millar were with me at the hotel and we exchanged gossip and jokes. My old friend and now Deputy Chairman of the Party, Janet Young, was also travelling with us and had slipped out during the meal. She now returned with a serious expression to tell me that Peter Thorneycroft – or 'the Chairman' as she insisted on calling him – felt that things were not too good politically and that Ted Heath should appear on the next Party Election Broadcast.

I exploded. It was about as clear a demonstration of lack of confidence in me as could be imagined. If Peter Thorneycroft and Central Office had not yet understood that what we were fighting for was a reversal not just of the Wilson-Callaghan approach but of the Heath Government's approach they had understood nothing. I told Janet Young that if she and Peter thought that, then I might as well pack up. Ted had lost three elections out of four and had nothing to say about an election fought on this kind of manifesto. To invite him to deliver a Party Political for us was tantamount to accepting defeat for the kind of policies I was advancing.

It was perhaps unfair of me to blame Janet in part for conveying Peter's message. But this was the closest I came in the campaign to being really upset. I told her that I would not even hear of it. She conveyed a doubtless censored version of my response to 'the Chairman' and, still seething, I went to bed.

* * *

It can well be imagined that there was some unseasonal frost in the April air when I came for my briefing at Central Office before the Friday morning press conference. I was also rather too sharp with a journalist at it on the subject of the impact of technology on employment. Then a television interviewer, whom I had been told would be sympathetic, turned out to be very much the opposite. It was that point in an election campaign when everybody's nerves have become frayed with tiredness. And the pressure was still building. I knew I had further important media interviews, the last PEB to record and big speeches at Bolton and the final Conservative Trade Unionists' rally. Moreover, the opinion polls now seemed to suggest that our lead was being eroded. The Central Office view was that it had fallen from about 10 per cent to about 6 per cent. Unfortunately, there was no reason to give any more credence to the internal Party opinion polling – which was on the optimistic side of the median – than to other polls. I had to cancel my visit to the Fulham constituency that afternoon in order to work on the PEB text and the CTU speech. But someone told the press that the real cause was that my voice was failing, which was used to paint an exaggerated picture of a 'battle-worn Maggie' trying to stop the election slipping away. In fact, my voice was in remarkably good order but I now had to risk real strain by raising it so as to convince interviewers and audiences that my larynx was alive and well.

Saturday morning's *Daily Express* carried a MORI poll showing our lead down to just 3 per cent. There was evidence of a mild case of the jitters affecting Conservative Central Office. Peter Thorneycroft wrote to candidates saying: 'Whatever happens, I ask for no complacency and no despair.' It was not a very encouraging message and perhaps indicated all too accurately the feeling of its author and his advisers that the way to win elections was by doing nothing wrong rather than by doing something right. For myself, I publicly shrugged off the polls, noting that: 'Always as you get up to an election the lead narrows.' In fact, I had decided that by far the best course now was to shut the opinion polls out of my mind and put every ounce of remaining energy into the decisive final days of the campaign. I had a good morning of campaigning in London, including my own Finchley constituency, returning home to Flood Street in the afternoon for discussion of the Election Broadcast.

Sunday 29 April would be crucial. The opinion polls were all over the place. I ignored them. I had my hair done in the morning and then after lunch was driven to the Wembley Conference Centre for the Conservative

Trade Unionists' rally. Harvey Thomas, drawing on his experience of Billy Graham's evangelical rallies, had pulled out every stop. A galaxy of actors and comedians livened up the proceedings. Ignoring previous instructions from perhaps over-serious Party officials concerned about the dignity of 'the next Prime Minister', Harvey played the campaign song 'Hello Maggie' when I entered. And dignity certainly went by the board as everyone joined in. I had never known anything quite like it – though compared with Harvey's extravaganzas of future years this came to seem quite tame.

The speech itself was short and sharp. And the reception was terrific. Then I went on to Saatchi & Saatchi to record the final Election Broadcast. From 4 o'clock in the afternoon Gordon, Ronnie, Tim and I worked and reworked the text. Then there was an apparently endless succession of 'takes', each of which – until the final one – seemed not quite right to at least one of us. At last, well after midnight, we were satisfied.

The main event of my campaign on Monday was the *Granada 500* programme, when each of the three party leaders was questioned by an audience from what was deemed to be the most representative seat in the country, Bolton East. (For many years Bolton East had been won by the party which formed the next government, but in 1979, dazzled perhaps by national attention, the electors got it wrong.) I enjoyed these occasions, feeling more at ease than when interviewed on a one-to-one basis. Somehow the fact that these were 'real' people with real worries helped me to relax. Judging by the 'clapometer' reading I won the contest.

But the following (Tuesday) morning there was a further opinion poll by NOP which showed Labour 0.7 per cent ahead. There was only one real question on people's lips at that morning's press conference: how would I react to the poll? I just brushed it aside, saying that I hoped it would stir Conservative Party supporters to go out and vote on the day. Not only did this line serve me at a difficult moment: I suspect it was a correct judgement. For if anything really threatened our victory it was complacency, and from this moment there was no chance of that. I went on to campaign in the North-West, finishing up, of course, by addressing a rally in Bolton, where the comedian Ken Dodd appeared on stage with a blue feather-duster to greet me. After Ken Dodd's message from Knotty Ash – which he made sound a pretty true blue constituency – any speech would have seemed over-serious. But there was only one real message for this stage of the campaign, which was that those who wished to throw the

Labour Party out of government must not fritter their votes away on minor parties, but rather vote Conservative.

Moreover, the same message had to be repeated insistently until polling day. It was my theme at the final press conference on Wednesday (2 May). I returned to it as I went around the London constituencies, finishing up at Woodhouse School in Finchley – where I had to push my way through protesting feminists chanting: 'We want women's rights, not a right-wing woman.' As I drove back to Flood Street I felt the tiredness flow over me. I had had my chance and had taken it. It was oddly satisfying to know that whatever happened now was out of my hands. For the first time in many nights Denis and I had a full six hours' sleep.

I woke on election day to learn from the radio news that all of that morning's opinion polls showed the Conservatives with a lead ranging from 2 per cent to 8 per cent. Denis and I went out to vote at 9 o'clock in Chelsea before driving on to Finchley, where, as was my wont, I toured the committee rooms followed by photographers. I went back to Flood Street for a light supper and to try to have some rest before what I knew would be a long evening. At the Finchley count in Barnet Town Hall, where I arrived shortly after midnight, I kept out of the way in a side room, equipped with a television and supplied with coffee and sandwiches, where I could listen to the results as they came in. Roger Boaden was with me, supplementing the television reports with early information telephoned through from Central Office. I kept a running tally, referring to the detailed briefing which Keith Britto had prepared for me. The first few results suggested that we had won, though among them was the upsetting news that Teddy Taylor had lost Glasgow Cathcart. The projections of our majority steadily began to mount. Local councillors, my Constituency Chairman and his wife, my agent and others came in and out looking more and more cheerful. But I deliberately suppressed any inclinations to premature euphoria: calculation, superstition and above all the knowledge that it is easiest to cope with bad news when you are not expecting good entered into this. In the end, however, not even I could remain non-committal. It was clear to everyone by the time I went out to hear the results of my own count that we would form the next Government.

The scale of the victory took everyone – or almost everyone – by surprise. It was not just that we had won an election: we had also won a new kind of mandate for change. As the psephologists and commentators mulled over the detailed results, the pattern of our success bore this out.

The 5.6 per cent national swing from Labour to the Conservatives was the largest achieved by either – and our 7 per cent lead over Labour was also the largest – since 1945.

Equally significant, the biggest swing to us was among the skilled workers; and over a third of that lead had apparently built up during the campaign. These were precisely the people we had to win over from their often-lifelong socialist allegiances. They were confronted in a particularly acute form by the fundamental dilemma which faced Britain as a whole: whether to accept an ever greater role for government in the life of the nation, or to break free in a new direction. For these people, above all, it was a severely practical matter of choosing whether to rely on the comforting security of state provision or to make the sacrifices required to win a better life for themselves and their families. They had now decided to take the risk (for it was a risk) of voting for what I offered – for what, in a certain sense, I knew that I now personified. I would always try to keep faith with them.

CHAPTER THIRTEEN

Over the Shop

First days and early decisions as Prime Minister

W E KNEW WE HAD WON by the early hours of Friday 4 May, but it was not until the afternoon that we gained the clear majority of seats we needed – 43 as it eventually turned out.

There were many friends with me as we waited for the results to come in during those long hours in Conservative Central Office. But I can remember an odd sense of loneliness as well as anticipation when I received the telephone call which summoned me to the Palace. I was anxious about getting the details of procedure and protocol right; it is extraordinary how on really important occasions one's mind often focuses on what in the cold light of day seem to be mere trivia. But I was haunted by tales of embarrassing episodes as one Prime Minister left and his successor entered office and I could not help feeling sorry for James Callaghan, who just a little earlier had conceded victory in a short speech, both dignified and generous. Whatever our past and indeed future disagreements, I believed him to be a patriot with the interests of Britain at heart, whose worst tribulations had been inflicted by his own party.

At about 2.45 p.m the call came. I walked out of Central Office through a crowd of supporters and into the waiting car, which drove Denis and me to the Palace on my last journey as Leader of the Opposition.

The Audience at which one receives the Queen's authority to form a government comes to most Prime Ministers only once in a lifetime. The authority is unbroken when a sitting Prime Minister wins an election, and so it never had to be renewed throughout the years I was in office. All audiences with the Queen take place in strict confidence – a confidentiality vital to the working of both government and constitution. I was to have such audiences with Her Majesty once a week, usually on a Tuesday, when she was in London and sometimes elsewhere when the royal family was at Windsor or Balmoral.

Anyone who imagines that these meetings are confined to social niceties is quite wrong; they are quietly businesslike and Her Majesty brings to bear a formidable grasp of current issues and breadth of experience. And, although the press could not resist the temptation to suggest disputes between the Palace and Downing Street, I always found the Queen's attitude towards the work of the Government absolutely correct.

Of course, stories of clashes between 'two powerful women' were just too good not to make up. In general, more nonsense was written about the so-called 'feminine factor' during my time in office than about almost anything else. I was always asked how it felt to be a woman Prime Minister. I would reply: 'I don't know: I've never experienced the alternative.'

After the audience, Sir Philip Moore, the Queen's Secretary, took me to his office down what are called 'the Prime Minister's stairs'. I found my new principal private secretary, Ken Stowe, waiting there, ready to accompany me to Downing Street. Ken had come to the Palace with the outgoing Prime Minister, James Callaghan, barely an hour before. As we drove out through the Palace gates, Denis noticed that this time the Guards saluted me. In those innocent days before security had to become so much tighter for fear of terrorism, crowds of well-wishers, sightseers, press and camera crews were waiting for us in Downing Street itself. The crowds extended all the way up Downing Street and out into Whitehall. Denis and I got out of the car and walked towards them. This gave me the opportunity to run through in my mind what I would say outside No. 10.

When we turned to the cameras and reporters, the cheers were so deafening that no one in the street could hear what I was saying. Fortunately, the microphones thrust in front of me picked it up and carried it over the radio and television.

I quoted a famous prayer attributed to St Francis of Assisi, beginning, 'Where there is discord, may we bring harmony.' Afterwards a good deal of sarcasm was expended on this choice, but the rest of the quotation is often forgotten. The prayer goes on: 'Where there is error, may we bring truth. Where there is doubt, may we bring faith. And where there is despair, may we bring hope.' The forces of error, doubt and despair were so firmly entrenched in British society, as the Winter of Discontent had just powerfully illustrated, that overcoming them would not be possible without some measure of discord.

Inside No. 10 all the staff had turned out to welcome us. I am assured that in the days before television there was a good practical reason for this ceremony, in that everyone in the building has to be able to recognize the Prime Minister personally, both for security reasons and for the smooth running of the many different services which are provided there. It is also true that within No. 10 there is almost a family atmosphere. The number of staff is relatively small – between seventy or eighty, though because of the shift system not all will be there at one time. That figure comprises those working in the Private Office, including the duty clerks who ensure that No. 10 is able to operate round the clock; the Press Office, where someone is also always on call; the 'garden room girls', who do the secretarial and paperwork; 'confidential filing', which sorts and files the enormous accumulations of documents; the parliamentary section which deals with Parliamentary Questions, Statements and Debates; the correspondence section where some four to seven thousand letters are received every week; the sections which deal with Church matters and with honours; the Political Office and the Policy Unit; and the messengers and other staff who keep the whole extended family supplied with tea and coffee and – above all – information from the outside world. It is an extraordinary achievement, and it requires people of unusual qualities and commitment.

The Prime Minister's private secretaries, headed by the principal private secretary, are crucial to the effective conduct of government. They are the main channel of communication between the Prime Minister and the rest of Whitehall, and they bear a heavy burden of responsibility. I was fortunate to have a succession of superb principal private secretaries over the years. Other private secretaries, specializing in economic or foreign affairs, also quickly acquired judgement, expertise and a knowledge of my thinking which allowed me to rely on them. Bernard Ingham, my press secretary, who arrived five months after I became Prime Minister, was another indispensable member of the team. I was told that Bernard's politics had been Labour, not Conservative; but the first time we met I warmed to this tough, blunt, humorous Yorkshireman. Bernard's outstanding virtue was his total integrity. He never let me down.

The hours at No. 10 are long. I never minded this. There was an intensity about the job of being Prime Minister which made sleep seem a luxury. In any case, over the years I had trained myself to do with about four hours a night. The Private Office too would often be working till 11 o'clock at night. We were so few that there was no possibility of putting work on someone else's desk. This sort of atmosphere helps to produce a remarkably happy team, as well as a formidably efficient one. People are under great pressure, and there is no time for trivia. Mutual respect and friendly relations are often the result. This feature of No. 10 shapes people's attitudes not only towards each other but towards the Prime Minister whom they all directly or indirectly serve. The cheers and clapping when a new Prime Minister arrives may perhaps be a traditional formality. But the tears and regrets when the outgoing Prime Minister makes his or her final departure are usually genuine.

Number 10 is more than an office: it is intended to serve as the Prime Minister's home. I never had any doubt that when the Callaghans had left I would move into the Prime Minister's small flat at the top of the building. As we used to say, harking back to my girlhood in Grantham, I liked living over the shop but I was not able to move out of the house in Flood Street until the first week of June.

The flat at No. 10 quickly became a refuge from the rest of the world, though on occasion a good deal of business was done there too. It was right at the top of the building – but that was an advantage, for the stairs provided me with about the only real exercise I got.

Denis and I decided that we would not have any living-in domestic help. No housekeeper could possibly have coped with the irregular hours. When I had no other engagement, I would go up to the flat for a quick lunch of salad or poached egg on Bovril toast. But usually it was 10 or 11 o'clock at night when I would go into the kitchen and prepare something – we knew every way in which eggs and cheese could be served and there was always something to cut at in the fridge – while Denis poured me a night-cap.

Prime Minister or not, I never forgot that I was also MP for Finchley; nor, indeed, would I have wanted to. My monthly surgeries in the constituency and the correspondence which was dealt with from within No. 10 by my secretary, Joy Robilliard (who had been Airey Neave's secretary until his death), kept me directly in touch with people's worries. I always had the benefit of a first-class constituency agent and a strongly supportive constituency chairman, which as any MP knows makes a world of difference. I also kept up my own special interests which had been developed as a result of constituency work, for example as patron of the North London Hospice.

I could never have been Prime Minister for more than eleven years without Denis at my side. Always a powerful personality, he was a fund of shrewd advice and penetrating comment. And he very sensibly saved these for me rather than the outside world, always refusing to give interviews. He never had a secretary or public relations adviser but answered between thirty and fifty letters every week in his own hand. With the appearance of the 'Dear Bill' letters in *Private Eye*, he seemed to become half the nation's favourite correspondent.

Being Prime Minister is a lonely job. In a sense, it ought to be: you cannot lead from the crowd. But with Denis there I was never alone. What a man. What a husband. What a friend.

In some ways 10 Downing Street is an unusual sort of home. Portraits, busts and sculptures of one's Prime Ministerial predecessors remind one of the nearly 250 years of history into which one has stepped.

Outside the flat I had displayed my own collection of porcelain, which I had built up over the years. I also brought with me a powerful portrait of Churchill from my room in the House of Commons. It looked down on those who assembled in the antechamber to the Cabinet Room. When I arrived, this area looked rather like a down-at-heel Pall Mall club, with heavy and worn leather furniture; I changed the whole feel by bringing in bookcases, tables and chairs from elsewhere in the building. There might be some difficult times to come in the Cabinet Room itself, but there was no reason why people should be made to feel miserable while they were waiting to go in.

Although it was not until I had been there some ten years that I had the most important redecorations done, I tried from the start to make the rooms seem more lived in. The official rooms had very few ornaments and when we arrived Downing Street had no silver. Whenever there was an official dinner the caterers had to bring in their own. Lord Brownlow lent me silver from his collection at Belton House: it sparkled and transformed the No. 10 dining room. One particular piece had a special meaning for me – a casket containing the Freedom of the Borough of Grantham, of which both the previous Lord Brownlow and later my father had been Mayor. The gardeners who kept St James's Park brought in flowers and I also had the study repapered at my own expense. Its unappealing sage-green damask flock wallpaper was replaced by a cream stripe, which was a much better background for some fine pictures.

I felt that Downing Street should have some works by contemporary British artists and sculptors, as well as those of the past. I had met Henry Moore when I was Secretary of State for Education and much admired his work. The Moore Foundation let No. 10 borrow one of his smaller sculptures which fitted perfectly in an alcove in the main hallway. Behind the sculpture was hung a Moore drawing, which was changed every three months; among my favourites were scenes of people sleeping in the London underground during the Blitz.

I was conscious of being the first research scientist to become Prime Minister – almost as conscious as I was of being the first woman Prime Minister. So I had portraits and busts of some of our most famous scientists placed in the small dining room, where I often lunched with visitors and colleagues on less formal occasions.

On this first evening, though, I could do little more than make a brief tour of the main rooms of the building. Then I entered the Cabinet Room where I was greeted by more familiar faces – among them my daughter Carol. There was Richard Ryder who would continue for a time as my political secretary, responsible for keeping me in touch with the Conservative Party in the country; David Wolfson (now Lord Wolfson) who acted as my Chief of Staff, bringing to bear his charm and business experience on the problems of running No. 10; Caroline Stephens (later to become Caroline Ryder) who became my diary secretary; Alison Ward (later Alison Wakeham) my constituency secretary; and Cynthia Crawford – known to all of us as 'Crawfie' – who acted as my personal assistant and who has stayed with me ever since. We did not waste much time in conversation. They were anxious to sort out who was to go to which office. I had exactly the same task in mind: the choice of my Cabinet.

Choosing a Cabinet is undoubtedly one of the most important ways in which a Prime Minister can exercise power over the whole conduct of government. But it is not always understood how real are the constraints under which the choices take place. By convention, all ministers must be members of either the Commons or the Lords, and there must not generally be more than three Cabinet members in the Lords, thus limiting the range of potential candidates for office. In addition one has to achieve distribution across the country – every region is easily convinced it has been left out. You must also consider the spectrum of Party opinion.

Even so, the press expect the Cabinet of some twenty-two ministers to be appointed and the list to be published within about 24 hours – otherwise it is taken as a sure sign of some sort of political crisis. So I do not think that any of us at No. 10 relaxed much that day, which turned out to be a long one. I received the usual detailed security briefing which is given to incoming Prime Ministers. Then I went upstairs to the study accompanied by Willie Whitelaw and our new Chief Whip, Michael Jopling. We began to sift through the obvious and less obvious names and slowly this most perplexing of jigsaws began to take shape, and Ken Stowe sought to contact those involved to arrange for them to come in the next day.

I knew that the hardest battles would be fought on the ground of economic policy. So I made sure that the key economic ministers would be true believers in our economic strategy. Geoffrey Howe had by now thoroughly established himself as the Party's chief economic spokesman. Geoffrey was regularly bullied in debate by Denis Healey. But by thorough mastery of his brief and an ability to marshal arguments and advice from different sources, he had shown that beneath a deceptively mild exterior he had the makings of the fine Chancellor he was to become. Some of the toughest decisions were to fall to him. He never flinched. In my view these were his best political years.

After becoming Leader in 1975, I had considered appointing Keith Joseph as Shadow Chancellor. Keith had done more than anyone else to spell out in his speeches and pamphlets what had gone wrong with Britain's economic performance and how it could be transformed. He is an original thinker, and combines humility, open-mindedness and unshakeable principle and is genuinely sensitive to people's misfortunes. Although he had no doubt of the rightness of the decisions which we were to make, he knew that they meant unviable firms would collapse and overmanning become unemployment, and he cared about those who were affected – far more than did all our professionally compassionate critics. But such a combination of personal qualities may create difficulties in the cruel hurly-burly of political life which Chancellors above all must endure. So Keith took over at Industry, where he did the vital job of altering the whole philosophy which had previously dominated the department. Keith was – and remains – my closest political friend.

John Biffen I appointed Chief Secretary to the Treasury. He had been a brilliant exponent in Opposition of the economic policies in which I believed, but he proved rather less effective than I had hoped in the grueling task of trying to control public expenditure. His later performance as Leader of the House where the qualities required were acute political sensitivity, good humour and a certain style was far happier. John Nott became Secretary of State for Trade. He, too, had a clear understanding of and commitment to our policies of monetary control, low taxes and free enterprise. But John is a mixture of gold, dross and mercury. No one was better at analysing a situation and prescribing a policy to deal with it. But he found it hard, or perhaps boring, to stick with the policy once it had been firmly decided. His vice was second thoughts.

It seemed prudent in the light of our effective performance in Opposition and the election campaign to maintain a high degree of continuity between Shadow Cabinet and Cabinet posts. Willie Whitelaw became Home Secretary, and in that capacity and later as Leader of the Lords he provided me personally and the Government as a whole with shrewd advice based on massive experience. People were often surprised that the two of us worked so well together, given our rivalry for the leadership and our different outlook on economics. But Willie is a big man in character as well as physically. He wanted the success of the Government which from the first he accepted would be guided by my general philosophy. Once he had pledged his loyalty, he never withdrew it. He was an irreplaceable Deputy Prime Minister – an office which has no constitutional existence but is a clear sign of political precedence – and the ballast that helped keep the Government on course.

But some changes in portfolios were required. I brought in the formidable Christopher Soames to be Leader of the House of Lords. Christopher was his own man, indeed excessively so, and thus better suited to solo performances than to working in harmony with others. Peter Carrington, who had led the Lords skilfully in Opposition, became Foreign Secretary. Peter had great panache and the ability to identify immediately the main points in any argument; and he could express himself in pungent terms. We had disagreements, but there were never any hard feelings. We were an effective combination – not least because Peter could always tell some particularly intractable foreign minister that whatever he himself might feel about a particular proposition, there was no way in which his Prime Minister would accept it. I was determined, however, that at least one Foreign Office minister should have a good grounding in – and sound views on – economic policy. I had Peter bring in Nick Ridley.

Two other appointments excited more comment. To his surprise, I asked Peter Walker to be Minister of Agriculture. Peter had never made a secret of his hostility to my economic strategy. But he was both tough and persuasive, priceless assets in dealing with the plain absurdities of the European Community's Common Agricultural Policy.

And despite the divergences of opinion between Jim Prior and the rest of us during Opposition there was no doubt in my mind that we needed him at Employment. There was still the feeling in the country, and indeed in the Conservative Party, that Britain could not be governed without the tacit consent of the trade unions. It was to be some years before that changed.

By about 11 p.m. the list of Cabinet was complete and had been approved by the Queen. I went upstairs to thank the No. 10 telephonists who had had a busy time arranging all the appointments for the following day. Then I was driven home.

On Saturday I saw the future Cabinet one by one. It all went smoothly enough. Those who were not already Privy Councillors* were sworn in at Buckingham Palace. By Saturday afternoon the Cabinet was appointed and the names announced to the press. That gave every new minister the weekend to draft instructions to his department to put into effect the manifesto policies.

My last and best appointment was of Ian Gow as my Parliamentary Private Secretary (or PPS). Ian's combination of loyalty, shrewdness and an irrepressible sense of fun was to see us all through many difficult moments.

On Tuesday at 2.30 p.m. we held our first Cabinet meeting. It was 'informal': no agenda had been prepared by the Cabinet Secretariat and no minutes were taken. (Its conclusions were later recorded in the first 'formal' Cabinet which met on the customary Thursday morning.) Ministers reported on their departments and the preparations they had made for forthcoming legislation. We gave immediate effect to the pledges in our manifesto to see that both the police and the armed forces were properly paid. As a result of the crisis of morale in the police service, the fall in recruitment and talk of a possible police strike, the Labour Government had set up a committee on police pay under Lord Justice Edmund Davies. The committee had devised a formula to keep police pay in line with other earnings. We decided that the recommendations for pay increases due for implementation on 1 November should be brought forward. This was duly announced the following day. We similarly

---

* The Privy Council is one of the oldest of Britain's political institutions, with the most important of the Crown's advisers among its members, including by convention all Cabinet ministers. Its meetings – usually of a few ministers in the presence of the Queen – are now purely formal, but the oath taken by new members reinforces the obligation of secrecy in conducting government business, and the issue of 'Orders in Council' is still an important procedure for enacting the legislation not requiring the approval of Parliament.

decided that the full military salary recommended by the latest Report of the Armed Forces Pay Review Body should be paid in full, as from 1 April.

At that first informal Cabinet we began the painful but necessary process of shrinking down the public sector. We imposed an immediate freeze on all civil service recruitment, though this would later be modified and specific targets for reduction set. We started a review of the controls imposed by central on local government, though here, too, we would in due course be forced down the path of applying still tougher, financial controls, as the inability or refusal of councils to run services efficiently became increasingly apparent.

Pay and prices were an immediate concern. Professor Hugh Clegg's Commission on Pay Comparability had been appointed by the Labour Government as a respectable means of bribing public sector workers not to strike with postdated cheques due to be presented after the election. The Clegg Commission was a major headache, and the pain became steadily more acute as the cheques fell due.

As regards pay bargaining in the nationalized industries, we decided that the responsible ministers should stand back from the process as far as possible. Our strategy would be to apply the necessary financial discipline and then let the management and unions directly involved make their own decisions.

There would also have to be a fundamental overhaul of the way in which prices were controlled by such interventionist measures as the Price Commission, government pressure, and subsidy. We were under no illusion: price rises were a symptom of underlying inflation, not a cause of it. Inflation was a monetary phenomenon which it would require monetary discipline to curb. Artificially holding down increases merely reduced investment and undermined profits – both already far too low for the country's economic health – while spreading a 'cost plus' mentality through British industry.

At both Cabinets, I concluded by emphasizing the need for collective responsibility and confidentiality between ministers. I said I had no intention of keeping a diary of Cabinet discussions and I hoped that others would follow my example. Inconvenient as that may be for the authors of memoirs, it is the only satisfactory rule for government.

On the following day Members of Parliament assembled to take the oath. But Thursday was a day of more than ceremonial importance (indeed there was one ceremony which somehow got lost in the rush – Denis's birthday). It was on that day that Helmut Schmidt, the West

German Federal Chancellor, arrived in London on an official visit originally arranged with the Labour Government – the first head of a foreign government to visit me as Prime Minister.

I had met Herr Schmidt in Opposition and had soon developed the highest regard for him. He had a profound understanding of the international economy on which – although he considered himself a socialist – we were to find ourselves in close agreement. In fact, he understood a good deal better than some British Conservatives the importance of financial orthodoxy – the need to control the money supply and to restrain public spending and borrowing so as to allow room for the private sector to grow. But he had to be told straight away that although Britain wanted to play a vigorous and influential role in the European Community, we could not do so until the problem of our grossly unfair budgetary contribution had been resolved. I saw no reason to conceal our views behind a diplomatic smokescreen so I used every occasion to get the message across.

On Saturday I flew to Scotland to address the Scottish Conservative Conference, something I always enjoyed. Life is not easy for Scottish Tories. Unlike English Conservatives, they are used to being a minority party, with the Scottish media heavily slanted against them. But these circumstances gave Scottish Conservatives a degree of enthusiasm and a fighting spirit which I admired, and which also guaranteed a warm-hearted and receptive audience. Some leading Scottish Tories, a small minority, still hankered after a kind of devolved government, but the rest of us were deeply suspicious of what that might mean to the future of the Union. While reaffirming our decision to repeal Labour's Scotland Act, I indicated that we would initiate all-party talks 'aimed at bringing government closer to the people'. In the event we did so by rolling back the state rather than by creating new institutions of government.

My main message to the Conference was a deliberately sombre one, intended for Britain as a whole. That same day an inflation figure of 10.1 per cent had been published. It would rise further. I noted:

> The evil of inflation is still with us. We are a long way from restoring honest money and the Treasury forecast when we took over was that inflation was on an upward trend. It will be some considerable time before our measures take effect. We should not underestimate the enormity of the task which lies ahead. But little can

be achieved without sound money. It is the bedrock of sound government.

As our economic and political difficulties accumulated in the months ahead, no one could claim that they had not been warned.

We arrived back at RAF Northolt and drove to Chequers where I spent my first weekend as Prime Minister. I do not think anyone has stayed long at Chequers without falling in love with it. From the time of its first Prime Ministerial occupant, David Lloyd George, it has been assumed that the holders of that office would not necessarily have their own country estates. For that reason, Lord Lee's gift to the nation of his country house for the use and relaxation of Prime Ministers marks as much a new era as did the Reform Bills.

Chequers is an Elizabethan house, but has been substantially rebuilt over the years. The centre of the house is the great hall, once a courtyard, enclosed at the end of the last century, where in winter a log fire burns, giving a slight tang of woodsmoke through every room.

Thanks to the generosity of Walter Annenberg, US Ambassador to Britain from 1969–74, Chequers has a covered swimming pool. But in the years I was there it was only used in the summer. Early on I learned that it cost £5,000 a year to heat. By saving this money we had more which could be spent on the perpetual round of necessary repairs to the house.

The group which gathered for Sunday lunch just ten days after our election victory was fairly typical of a Chequers weekend. My family were there, Denis, Carol, Mark. Keith Joseph, Geoffrey and Elspeth Howe, the Pyms and Quintin Hailsham represented, as it were, the Government team. Peter Thorneycroft and Alistair McAlpine were present from Central Office. David Wolfson, Bryan Cartledge (my private secretary) with their wives, and our friends, Sir John and Lady Tilney, completed the party.

We were still in a mood to celebrate our election victory. We were away from the formality of No. 10. We had completed the initial task of getting the Government on the road. We still had that spirit of camaraderie which the inevitable disputes and disagreements of government were bound to sap. The meal was a light-hearted and convivial one. It was perhaps an instance of what a critic was later to call 'bourgeois triumphalism.'

But we were aware that there was a long road ahead. As my father used to say:

It's easy to be a starter, but are you a sticker too?

It's easy enough to begin a job, it's harder to see it through.

At 7 p.m. that evening Denis and I returned to London to begin my second full week as Prime Minister. Work was already piling up, with boxes coming to and from Chequers. I recall once hearing Harold Macmillan tell an eager group of young MPs, none more eager than Margaret Thatcher, that Prime Ministers (not having a department of their own) have plenty of spare time for reading. He recommended Disraeli and Trollope. I have sometimes wondered if he was joking.

CHAPTER FOURTEEN

Changing Signals

Domestic politics in the first six months
until the end of 1979

TO TURN FROM THE EUPHORIA of election victory to the problems
of the British economy was to confront the morning after the night
before. Inflation was speeding up; public sector pay was out of control;
public spending projections were rising as revenue projections fell; and
our domestic problems were aggravated by a rise in oil prices that was
driving the world into recession.

The temptation in these circumstances was to retreat to a defensive
redoubt: not to cut income tax when revenues were already threatening to
fall; not to remove price controls when inflation was already accelerating;
not to cut industrial subsidies in the teeth of a rising recession; and not to
constrain the public sector when the private sector seemed too weak to
create new jobs. And, indeed, these adverse economic conditions did slow
down the rate at which we could hope to regenerate Britain. But I
believed that was all the more reason to redouble our efforts. We were
running up the 'Down' escalator, and we would have to run a great deal
faster if we were ever to get to the top.

Our first opportunity to demonstrate to both friends and opponents that we
would not be deterred by the difficulties was the Queen's Speech. The first
Loyal Address of a new government sets the tone for its whole term of office.
If the opportunity to set a radical new course is not taken, it will almost
certainly never recur. I was determined to send out a clear signal of change.

By the end of the debates on the Address it was evident that the House
of Commons could expect a heavy programme, designed to reverse

socialism, extend choice and widen property ownership. There would be legislation to restrict the activities of Labour's National Enterprise Board and to begin the process of returning state-owned businesses and assets to the private sector. We would give council tenants the right to buy their homes at large discounts, with the possibility of 100 per cent mortgages. There would be partial deregulation of new private sector renting. (Decades of restrictive controls had steadily reduced the opportunities for those who wished to rent accommodation and thereby retarded labour mobility and economic progress.) We would repeal Labour's Community Land Act – this attempt to nationalize the gains accruing from development had created a shortage of land and pushed up prices. We removed the obligation on local authorities to replace grammar schools and announced the introduction of the Assisted Places Scheme, enabling talented children from poorer backgrounds to go to private schools. We would, finally, curb what were often the corrupt and wasteful activities of local government direct labour organizations (usually social-ist controlled).

When I spoke in the Queen's Speech debate, two points attracted particular attention: the abolition of price controls and the promise of trade union reform. Most people expected that we would keep price controls in some form, at least temporarily. After all, the regulation of prices, wages and dividends had been one of the means by which, throughout most of the western world, governments sought to extend their powers and influence and to alleviate the inflationary effects of their own financially irresponsible policies.

I was also keen to use my speech in the debate to put an authoritative stamp on our trade union reforms. Jim Prior's preferred strategy was one of consultation with the trade unions before introducing the limited reforms of trade union law which we had proposed in Opposi-tion. But it was vital to show that there would be no back-tracking from the clear mandate we had received to make fundamental changes. Initially, we proposed three reforms in the Queen's Speech. First, the right to picket – which had been so seriously abused in the strikes of the previous winter and for many years before – would be strictly limited to those in dispute with their employer at their own place of work. Second, we were committed to changing the law on the closed shop, which at that time covered some five million workers. Those who lost their jobs for refusing to join a union must in future be entitled to proper compensation. Third, public funds would be made available to finance postal ballots for union elections and other important union decisions: we wanted to discourage votes by show of hands and the sharp practice, rigging and intimidation which had become associated with 'trade union democracy'.

In retrospect it seems extraordinary that such a relatively modest programme was represented by most trade union leaders and the Labour Party as an outright attack on trade unionism. In fact, as time went by, it became increasingly clear to the trade union leaders and to the Labour Party that not only did we have huge public support for our policies, but that the majority of trade unionists supported them too, because their families were being damaged by strikes which many of them had not voted for. We were the ones in touch with the popular mood.

This was my first important parliamentary performance as Prime Minister, and I emerged unscathed. But it is Questions to the Prime Minister every Tuesday and Thursday which are the real test of your authority in the House, your standing with your party, your grip of policy and of the facts to justify it. No head of government anywhere in the world has to face this sort of regular pressure; no head of government, as I would sometimes remind those at summits, is as accountable as the British Prime Minister.

I always briefed myself very carefully for Questions and I would go through all the likely issues which might come up without any notice. This is because the questions on the Order Paper only ask about the Prime Minister's official engagements for that day. The real question is the supplementary whose subject matter may vary from some local hospital to a great international issue or to the crime statistics. Each department was, naturally, expected to provide the facts and a possible reply on points which might arise. It was a good test of the alertness and efficiency of the Cabinet minister in charge of a department whether information arrived late – or arrived at all; whether it was accurate or wrong, comprehensible or riddled with jargon. On occasion the results, judged by these criteria, were not altogether reassuring. Little by little I came to feel more confident about these noisy ritual confrontations, and as I did so my performance became more effective. Sometimes I even enjoyed them.

The next watershed in the Government's programme was the budget. Our general approach was well known. Firm control of the money supply was necessary to bring down inflation. Cuts in public expenditure and borrowing were needed to lift the burden on the wealth-creating private sector. Lower income tax, combined with a shift from taxation on earning to taxation on spending, would increase incentives. However, these broad objectives would have to be pursued against a rapidly worsening economic background at home and abroad.

No amount of advance preparation could change the unpleasant facts of finance or the budget arithmetic. The two crucial discussions on the 1979 budget took place on 22 and 24 May between me and the Chancellor. Geoffrey Howe was able to demonstrate that to reduce the top rate of income tax to 60 per cent (from 83 per cent), the basic rate to 30 per cent (from 33 per cent), and the Public Sector Borrowing Requirement (PSBR) to about £8 billion (a figure we felt we could fund and afford) would require an increase in the two rates of VAT of 8 per cent and 12.5 per cent to a unified rate of 15 per cent. I was naturally concerned that this large shift from direct to indirect taxation would add about four percentage points onto the Retail Price Index (RPI).

This would be a once and for all addition to prices (and so it would not be 'inflationary' in the correct sense of the term which means a continuing rise in prices). But it would also mean that the RPI would double in our first year of office.* I was also concerned that too many of the proposed public spending cuts involved higher charges for public services. These too would have a similar effect on the RPI. Rab Butler as Chancellor in 1951 had introduced his tax cuts gradually. Should we do the same? We went away to consider the question further.

At our second meeting we decided to go ahead. Income tax cuts were vital, even if they had to be paid for by raising VAT. The decisive argument was that such a controversial increase in indirect taxes could only be made at the beginning of a Parliament, when our mandate was fresh.

It was generally agreed to be a dramatic reforming budget even by those opposed to us, like the *Guardian* newspaper, which described it as 'the richest political and economic gamble in post-war parliamentary history'. Its main provisions followed closely our discussions at the end of May: a cut in the basic rate of income tax from 33 to 30 per cent (with the

---

* In order to try to give a better indication of the real effect of government policies on living standards, we published from 17 August 1979 a new 'Tax and Price Index' (TPI) which combined, in one figure, a measure both of the tax changes and the movements in retail prices. For those dependent on earned income, who constituted the bulk of the population, this provided a better indicator of changes in total household costs than the RPI. However, for purposes of wage bargaining, the circumstances of an individual enterprise should determine what could be afforded.

highest rate cut from 83 to 60 per cent), tax allowances increased by 9 per cent above the rate of inflation, and the introduction of a new, unified rate of VAT at 15 per cent.

Apart from the budget's big income tax cuts, however, we were able to reduce or remove controls on a number of areas of economic life. Pay, price and dividend controls had gone. Industrial Development Certificates, Office Development Permits and a range of circulars and unnecessary planning controls were also removed or modified.

I took greatest personal pleasure in the removal of exchange controls – that is the abolition of the elaborate statutory restrictions on the amount of foreign exchange British citizens could acquire. These had been introduced as an 'emergency measure' at the start of the Second World War and maintained by successive governments, largely in the hope of increasing industrial investment in Britain and of resisting pressures on sterling. The overwhelming evidence was that they no longer achieved either of their objectives – if in fact they ever had done. With sterling buoyant and Britain beginning to enjoy the economic benefits of North Sea oil, the time had come to abolish them entirely. They were duly removed in three stages though the legislation itself stayed on the Statute Book until 1987, but no further use was made of it. Not only did the ending of exchange controls increase the freedom of individuals and businesses; it encouraged foreign investment in Britain and British investment abroad, which has subsequently provided a valuable stream of income likely to continue long after North Sea oil runs out.

But not every capitalist had my confidence in capitalism. I remember a meeting in Opposition with City experts who were clearly taken aback at my desire to free their market. 'Steady on!' I was told. Clearly, a world without exchange controls in which markets rather than governments determined the movement of capital left them distinctly uneasy. They might have to take risks.

We had also been distracted throughout our budget discussions by the worrying level of public sector pay rises. Here we had limited freedom of manoeuvre. Hard, if distasteful, political calculations had led us to commit ourselves during the election campaign to honour the decisions of the Clegg Commission on those claims which had already been formally referred to it. The issue was now whether to refer the unsettled claims of other groups to Clegg, or to seek some new method of dealing with the problem.

In the end, it was not until August 1980 that we announced that Clegg would be abolished after its existing work had been completed. Its last report was in March 1981. The fact remains, however, that the momentum of public sector pay claims created by inflation, powerful trade unions and an over-large public sector was not going to be halted, let alone reversed, all at once.

Whatever the short-term difficulties, I was determined at least to begin work on long-term reforms of government itself. Since the early 1960s, the public sector had grown steadily.* Unlike the private sector, it actually tended to grow during recessions while maintaining its size during periods of economic growth; it was shielded from the normal economic disciplines which affect the outside world.

The size of the civil service reflected this. In 1961 the numbers in the civil service had reached a post-war low of 640,000; by 1979 they had grown to 732,000. Within days of taking office, as I have noted, we imposed a freeze in recruitment to help reduce the Government's pay bill by some 3 per cent and by 13 May 1980 I was able to lay before the House our long-term targets for reducing civil service numbers. The total had already fallen to 705,000. We would seek to reduce it to around 630,000 over the next four years. Since some 80,000 left the civil service by retirement or resignation every year, it seemed likely that our target could be achieved without compulsory redundancies. We were, in fact, able to do it.

But the corollary of this was that we should reward outstanding ability within the civil service appropriately. The difficulties of introducing pay rates related to merit proved immense; it took several years and a great deal of pushing and shoving.

Similarly, I took a close interest in senior appointments in the civil service from the first, because they could affect the morale and efficiency of whole departments.

I was enormously impressed by the ability and energy of the members of my Private Office at No. 10. I wanted to see people of the same calibre, with lively minds and a commitment to good administration, promoted to hold the senior posts in the departments. Indeed, during my time in government, many of my former private secretaries went on to head

* The proportion of the British workforce employed in the public sector crept inexorably upwards from 24 per cent in 1961 to reach almost 30 per cent by the time we came into office. By 1990 through privatization and other measures we had brought it down again to a level below that of 1961.

departments. In all these decisions, however, ability, drive and enthusiasm were what mattered; political allegiance was not something I took into account.

Over the years, certain attitudes and work habits had crept in that were an obstacle to good administration. I had to overcome, for instance, the greater power of the civil service unions (which in addition were increasingly politicized). The pursuit of new and more efficient working practices – such as the application of information technology – was being held up by union obstruction. In a department like Health and Social Security where we needed to get the figures quickly to pay out benefits, these practices were disgraceful. But eventually we overcame them. And some Permanent Secretaries had come to think of themselves mainly as policy advisers, forgetting that they were also responsible for the efficient management of their departments.

To see for myself, I decided to visit the main government departments and devoted most of a day to each department. In September 1979, for instance, I had a useful discussion with civil servants at the Department of Health and Social Security. I brought up the urgent need to dispose of surplus land held by the public sector. I was keen that where hospitals had land which they did not need they should be able to sell it and retain the proceeds to spend on improving patient care. There were arguments for and against this, but one argument advanced on this occasion, which was all too symptomatic of what had gone seriously wrong, was that this was somehow unfair on those hospitals which did not have the good fortune to have surplus land. We clearly had a long way to go before all the resources of the Health Service would be used efficiently for the benefit of patients. But this visit planted seeds that later grew into the Griffiths* reforms of NHS management and, later still, the internal market reforms of the Health Service in 1990.

Inevitably, my visits to government departments were not as long as I would have liked. There were other limits too on what I could learn on those occasions – particularly that senior civil servants might feel inhibited from speaking freely when their ministers were present. Consequently, I invited the Permanent Secretaries to dinner at No. 10 on the evening of Tuesday 6 May 1980. There were twenty-three Permanent Secretaries, Robin Ibbs (Head of the CPRS), Clive Whitmore, my prin-

---

* The Griffiths Report of 1983 was the basis for the introduction of general management in the NHS, without which the later reforms would not have been practicable.

cipal private secretary, David Wolfson and myself around the dining table.

I enjoy frank and open discussion, even a clash of temperaments and ideas, but such a menu of complaints and negative attitudes as was served up that evening was enough to dull any appetite I may have had for this kind of occasion in the future. The dinner took place a few days before I announced the programme of civil service cuts to the Commons, and that was presumably the basis for complaints that ministers had damaged civil service 'morale'.

What lay still further behind this, I felt, was desire for no change. But the idea that the civil service could be insulated from a reforming zeal that would transform Britain's public and private institutions over the next decade was a pipe dream. I preferred disorderly resistance to decline rather than comfortable accommodation to it. And I knew that the more able of the younger generation of civil servants agreed with me. So, to be fair, did a few of the Permanent Secretaries present that night. They were as appalled as I was. It became clear to me that it was only by encouraging or appointing individuals, rather than trying to change attitudes *en bloc*, that progress would be made. And that was to be the method I employed.*

Such an approach, however, would take years. We were dealing with crises on a weekly basis during the second half of 1979 as we scanned the figures on public spending and borrowing, against the background of an international economy slipping faster and faster into recession. Our first task was to make whatever reductions we could for the current financial year, 1979–80. Ordinarily, public spending decisions were made by Government during the summer and autumn of the previous year and announced in November. Even though we were several months into the current financial year, we had to begin by reopening the public expenditure plans we had inherited from the Labour Government. We would announce our new public expenditure plans with the budget. The scope for cuts was limited, partly because of this, partly because of our own

---

* It was only towards the end of my time in government that we embarked upon the radical reforms of the civil service which were contained in the 'Next Steps' programme. Under this programme much of the administrative – as opposed to policy-making – work of government departments is being transferred to agencies, staffed by civil servants and headed by chief executives appointed by open competition. The agencies operate within frameworks set by the departments, but are free of detailed departmental control. The quality of management within the public service promises to be significantly improved.

election pledges, and partly because some changes we wanted to make required legislation.

But I was determined that we should make as vigorous a start as possible and in the end we were able to announce £3.5 billion of economies along with Geoffrey's budget.

No sooner had we agreed savings for the current year, 1979–80, than the still more difficult task was upon us of planning public expenditure for 1980–81 and subsequent years. In July 1979, when the crucial decisions were being hammered out, we had a series of particularly testing (and testy) Cabinet discussions on the issue. Our goal was what it had been in Opposition, that is to bring public expenditure back to the 1977–78 level in real terms. But in spite of the reductions we had made, public expenditure was already threatening to run out of control.

Nonetheless there was strong opposition from some ministers to the cuts. Geoffrey Howe was superbly stolid in resisting this pressure. Later in July he set out for colleagues the precise implications of a failure to agree the £6.5 billion reductions he was proposing. He also dispelled some of the misunderstandings. Ministers had to recognize that we were not cutting to the bone, but merely reining in the increases planned by Labour and compensating for other increases that the deepening recession had made almost inevitable.

Labour's plans would have involved expenditure of a further £5 billion in 1980–81 to be financed out of growth that was not happening. Moreover, this overshoot had been aggravated by a rate of pay increase in the public sector which would cost another £4.5 billion. To offset these increasing obligations we had to make reductions of £6.5 billion in the expenditure plans for 1980–81, just to hold the PSBR in that year down to £9 billion. That figure was in itself too high. But the 'wets'* continued to oppose the cuts both in Cabinet and in the indecent obscurity of leaks to the *Guardian*.

Over the summer the economic situation worsened. In September we again returned to public spending. We not only had to publish the conclusions we had agreed in July, but also our plans for the years up to

---

* 'Wet' is a public schoolboy term meaning 'feeble' or 'timid', as in 'He is so wet you could shoot snipe off him.' The opponents of government economic policy in the early 1980s were termed 'wets' by their opponents because they were judged to be shrinking from stern and difficult action. As often happens with pejorative political labels (cf. Tory, which originally referred to Irish political bandits), 'wet' was embraced by the opponents of our economic strategy, who in turn named its supporters 'the dries'.

1983–84. And that meant more economies. We decided on a renewed drive to cut waste and reduce civil service numbers. We also agreed sharp increases in the price of electricity and gas (which had been artificially held down by Labour) that would come into effect in October 1980. Electricity would rise by 5 per cent, and gas by 10 per cent, over and above inflation.

The 1980–81 Public Expenditure White Paper was duly published on 1 November. These public spending plans honoured our pledges to provide more resources for defence, law and order and social security. They would also hold the public spending total for 1980–81 at the same level as 1979–80. In spite of the fact that this reduction of some £3.5 billion from Labour's plans was denounced as draconian, it really was not large enough. That was evident not only to me, but also to the financial markets, already concerned about excess monetary growth.

Here, too, we seemed to be running up the 'Down' escalator. On 15 November we accordingly raised Minimum Lending Rate (MLR – the successor to Bank Rate) to 17 per cent. (Measured by the RPI, inflation at this time was running at 17.4 per cent.) Other measures to help fund the PSBR were also announced.

Of course, the Opposition had a field day, attacking our whole strategy as misguided and incompetent. The fact of the matter was not that our strategy was wrong but that we had yet to apply it sufficiently rigorously and get a grip on public spending and borrowing. That in turn was increasing the pressure on the private sector through higher interest rates.

I knew that we had to break this vicious spiral, otherwise private enterprise would have to bear a crushing burden of public sector profligacy. Geoffrey and I accordingly decided that we had no alternative but to seek further spending reductions in 1980–81 and in subsequent years. He brought forward a paper proposing an extra £1 billion reduction in 1980–81, and £2 billion in each of the following years. From what I had seen of departmental ministers' fierce defence of their own budgets, I knew that this would provoke trouble. But I also knew that the great majority in the Party were determined to see the strategy succeed.

When Geoffrey Howe delivered his second budget on 26 March 1980, he was able to announce that we had found over £900 million in further savings in 1980–81 (though part of that was absorbed by an increase in the contingency reserve). Overall, at current prices this was over £5 billion less than Labour had planned to spend. In the circumstances, it was a formidable achievement, but also a fragile one. As the economy sank deeper into recession, there would be fresh demands, some difficult to resist, for higher public spending on programmes like social security and the loss-making nationalized industries. In a paper he wrote for me in June 1979, John Hoskyns, now head of my policy unit, had used a memorable phrase about governments 'trying to pitch [their] tent in the middle of a landslide'. As we moved into the 1980–81 public expenditure round and the forecasts worsened, I could hear the canvas strain and the ground rumble.

The second half of 1979, though dominated by economic policy and by the intense round of diplomatic activity, was also a time darkened by terrorism. Barely a fortnight after entering No. 10 I had delivered the address at the Memorial Service for Airey Neave. Not long afterwards, IRA terrorists struck another blow.

I was at Chequers for the Bank Holiday Monday of 27 August when I learnt of the shocking murder of Lord Mountbatten and, that same day, of eighteen British soldiers. Lord Mountbatten was killed by an explosion on board his boat off the coast at Mullaghmore, County Sligo. Three other members of his party were killed and three injured.

The murder of our soldiers was contemptible. Eighteen were killed and five injured in a double explosion triggered by remote-controlled devices at Narrow Water, Warrenpoint, near Newry, close to the border with the Republic. The IRA had exploded the first bomb and then waited for those who came by helicopter to rescue their comrades before detonating the second. Among those murdered by the second bomb was the Commanding Officer of the Queen's Own Highlanders.

I decided immediately that I must go to Northern Ireland to show the army, police and civilians that I understood the scale of the tragedy and to demonstrate our determination to resist terrorism. Having returned to London from Chequers, I stayed there on Tuesday to allow those involved to deal with the immediate aftermath while I held two meetings with colleagues to discuss the security requirements of the province. That evening I wrote personally to the families of the soldiers who had died; such letters are not easy to write. There were, alas, to be many more of them during my time in office.

I flew to Ulster on Wednesday morning. I went first to the Musgrave Park Hospital in Belfast and talked to the injured soldiers, then visited the Lord Mayor of Belfast at City Hall. I had insisted that I must meet the ordinary citizens of the city, and since the best way to do so was to walk through Belfast's shopping centre, that is where I went next. I shall never forget the reception I received. It is peculiarly moving to receive good wishes from people who are suffering and I formed then an impression I have never had reason to revise, that the people of Ulster will never bow to violence.

After a buffet lunch with soldiers of all ranks from 3 Brigade, I received a briefing from the army and then departed by helicopter to the 'bandit country' of South Armagh. Dressed in a camouflage jacket, I saw the bomb-battered Crossmaglen RUC station – the most attacked RUC-Army post in the province – before running back to the helicopter. It is too dangerous for either security force personnel or helicopters to remain stationary in these parts.

My final visit was to Gough barracks, the RUC base in Armagh. It is difficult to convey the courage of the security forces whose job it is to protect the lives of us all from terrorism. In particular, members of the UDR, who do their military duty living in the community where they and their families are always vulnerable, show a quiet, matter-of-fact heroism which I have never ceased to admire.

Back in London, there were two major questions. How were we to improve the direction and co-ordination of our security operations in the province? And how were we to get more co-operation in security matters from the Irish Republic? On the first, we decided that the difficulties of co-ordinating intelligence gathered by the RUC and the army would be best overcome by instituting a new high-level security directorate. On the second, we agreed that I would tackle the Irish Prime Minister, Jack Lynch, when he arrived for Lord Mountbatten's funeral.

Accordingly, we arranged a day's talks with Mr Lynch and his ministerial colleagues at No. 10 on the afternoon of Wednesday 5 September. The first session was a tête-à-tête between the two Prime Ministers; then we were joined by our respective ministers and officials.

Mr Lynch had no positive suggestions of his own to make at all. When I stressed the importance of extradition of terrorists from the Republic, he said that the Irish constitution made it very difficult. Mr Lynch pointed out that under Irish law terrorists could be tried in the Republic for offences committed in the UK. So I asked that RUC officers – who would have to amass the evidence for such prosecutions – be able to attend interrogations of terrorist suspects in the south. He said they would 'study' it. I knew what that meant: nothing doing.

We also lost no opportunity to use the revulsion the killings provoked in the US to inform public opinion there about the realities of life in

Ulster. The emotions and loyalties of millions of decent Irish-Americans are manipulated by Irish Republican extremists who have been able to give a romantic respectability to terrorism that its sordid reality belies. As a result, there has been a continuing flow of funds and arms which helps the IRA to continue its campaign, whereas in 1979 we were faced with the absurd situation that the purchase of 3,000 revolvers for the RUC was held up by a State Department review under pressure from the Irish Republican lobby in Congress.

I visited the province again on Christmas Eve. It made the troubles of a political life seem very trivial.

CHAPTER FIFTEEN

Into the Whirlwind

Foreign affairs during the first eighteen
months in 1979–1980

M Y FIRST EUROPEAN COUNCIL took place in Strasbourg on 21 and
22 June 1979.

I was confident that Chancellor Schmidt had taken away from our
earlier discussions a clear impression of my determination to fight for
large reductions in Britain's net budget contribution. I was hoping he
would pass the message on to President Giscard, who was to chair the
summit; both men were former Finance ministers and should be well able
to understand Britain's point of view. (I could not help noticing too that
they spoke to one another in English: but I was too tactful to remark on
it.)

The background to the British budget problem is quickly described,
though the precise details were extremely complicated. At the time of the
negotiations for Britain's accession we had received an assurance (as I
would continue to remind other member states) that:

> should an *unacceptable situation* arise within the present Commu-
> nity or an enlarged Community, the very survival of the Commu-
> nity would demand that the [Community] Institutions find
> equitable solutions. [my italics]

The reason why such an assurance had been necessary was that
Britain's unique trading pattern made her a very large net contributor to
the EC budget – so large that the situation was indeed unacceptable. We
traditionally imported far more from non-EC countries than did other

Community members, particularly of foodstuffs. This meant that we paid more into the Community budget in the form of tariffs than they did. By contrast, the Community budget itself is heavily biased towards supporting farmers through the Common Agricultural Policy (CAP): indeed when we came into office more than 70 per cent of the budget was spent in this way. The CAP was – and is – operated in a wasteful manner. The dumping of these surpluses outside the EC distorts the world market in foodstuffs and threatens the survival of free trade between the major economies. The British economy is less dependent on agriculture than that of most other Community countries and our farms are generally larger and more efficient than those of France and Germany; consequently we receive less in subsidy than they do. Britain traditionally received a fairer share of the receipts of the Community's non-agricultural programmes (such as the regional and social funds), but the growth of these programmes had been limited by the power of the farming lobby in Europe and by the international recession.

The previous Labour Government had made a great play of 'renegotiating' the terms of Britain's original entry. In 1975 a Financial Mechanism to limit our contribution had been worked out in principle: but it had never been triggered, and never would be, unless the originally agreed conditions were changed. As a result, there was no solid agreement to which we could hold our Community partners.

One other development had worsened the overall position: Britain's prosperity, relative to that of our European neighbours, had steadily declined. In spite of North Sea oil, by 1979 Britain had only the seventh highest GDP per head of population among the member states. Yet we were expected shortly to become the largest net contributor.

So from the first my policy was to seek to limit the damage and distortions caused by the CAP and to bring financial realities to bear on Community spending. But at the Council meeting in Strasbourg I also had two short-term objectives. First, I wanted to have the budget question raised now and to gain acceptance of the need for action. Second, I wanted to secure a firm undertaking that at the next Council meeting in Dublin the Commission would bring forward proposals to deal with the problem.

If the budget issue was to concentrate minds as I wished, it had to be raised on the first day, because the communiqué is always drafted by officials overnight, ready for discussion the following morning. Over lunch I spoke to President Giscard about what I wanted and gained a strong impression that we would be able to deal with the budget early on.

But when we resumed, it quickly became clear that he was intent on following his previous agenda. At least I was well briefed and took an active part in the discussion about energy and the world economy. I pointed out that Britain had not flinched from the hard decisions required to ride out these difficulties and that we were making large cuts in public spending. By twenty minutes to seven that evening, we had decided, if we could, to hold Community imports of oil between 1980 and 1985 at a level no higher than that of 1978. We had committed ourselves to keep up the struggle against inflation. Inevitably, I suppose, we had agreed to say something about 'convergence' between the economic performance of member states (a classic piece of Euro-jargon). In fact, we had done almost everything except what I most wanted us to do – tackle the budget issue.

Fortunately, I had been warned what might happen next. President Giscard proposed that as time was getting on and we needed to get ready for dinner, the matter of the budget should be discussed the following day. Did the Prime Minister of the United Kingdom not agree? And so at my very first European Council I had to say 'no'. As it turned out the lateness of the hour probably worked in my favour: conclusions are often easier to reach when time presses and minds are turning to the prospect of French *haute cuisine*. I spelt out the facts and it was agreed to include in the communiqué an instruction to the Commission to prepare proposals for the next Council to deal with the matter. So, a little late, we rose for dinner. Argument always gives one an appetite.

Strasbourg had one solid result: it had put the question of Britain's unfair budget contribution squarely on the agenda. I felt that I had made an impression as someone who meant business, and afterwards I learned that this feeling was correct. It was at Strasbourg, too, that I overheard a foreign government official make a stray remark that pleased me as much as any I can remember: 'Britain is back,' he said.

Many of the wider issues discussed at Strasbourg were raised again shortly afterwards in the still grander surroundings of the economic summit of the seven principal western industrial powers in Tokyo (the Group of Seven, or G7 for short). As soon as I had finished my report to the House of Commons on the Strasbourg Council, we drove out to Heathrow for the long flight to Japan. Oil prices and their effect on the economy would again be top of the agenda.

The previous G7 summit had been held in Bonn in 1978 when the doctrine of 'fine tuning demand' had still been fashionable. Germany had then been expected to act as the 'locomotive' for growth, pulling the world out of recession. As Chancellor Schmidt was to tell the summit leaders at Tokyo, the main result had been to put up German inflation: he would not go down that path again. At Bonn there had been no new heads of government present and the old nostrums prevailed. At Tokyo, by contrast, there were three newcomers – the Japanese Prime Minister and Conference Chairman, Mr Ohira, the new Prime Minister of Canada, Joe Clark, and myself. Apart from me, the strongest advocates of free market economics were Helmut Schmidt and, to an even greater extent, Count Otto von Lambsdorff, his Finance minister.

Soon after my arrival, I went to see President Carter at the United States Embassy where we talked over our approach to the issues which would arise, especially energy consumption, which posed a particular problem – and one with important political implications – for the US. It was impossible not to like Jimmy Carter. He was a deeply committed Christian and a man of obvious sincerity. He was also a man of marked intellectual ability with a grasp, rare among politicians, of science and the scientific method. But he had come into office as the beneficiary of Watergate rather than because he had persuaded Americans of the right-ness of his analysis of the world around them. And, indeed, that analysis was badly flawed. He had an unsure handle on economics and was there-fore inclined to drift into a futile *ad hoc* interventionism when problems arose. In foreign affairs, he was over-influenced by the doctrines then gaining ground in the Democratic Party that the threat from commu-nism had been exaggerated and that US intervention in support of right-wing dictators was almost as culpable. Hence he found himself surprised and embarrassed by such events as the Soviet invasion of Afghanistan and Iran's seizure of American diplomats as hostages. And in general he had no large vision of America's future so that, in the face of adversity, he was reduced to preaching the austere doctrine of limits to growth that was unpalatable, even alien, to the American imagination.

The meeting began, as usual, with a short general speech by each head of government. Chancellor Schmidt spoke before me in the first session, and after me in the second. We found ourselves stressing exactly the same points – the importance of the battle against inflation and the crucial role of the price mechanism in limiting energy consumption. My interven-tions appeared to be well received – not least by the Germans, as Count Lambsdorff subsequently told us. It was perhaps the nearest we ever came to an Anglo-German entente. I noted that many of our present difficulties stemmed from the pursuit of Keynesian policies with their emphasis on the deficit financing of public expenditure and I stressed the need to control the money supply in order to defeat inflation. There followed, after Mr Ohira and Chancellor Schmidt had taken a similar line, an extraordinary intervention by President Giscard in which he mounted a spirited defence of Lord Keynes and clearly rejected the basic free market approach as unnecessarily deflationary. Sig. Andreotti, Italy's Prime Minister, endorsed the French view. It was a revealing expression of the fundamental philosophical differences which divide the Community.

It would be difficult to claim too much for the quality of Japan's chairmanship of the proceeding. At one stage I intervened to clarify for the sake of the officials – the 'sherpas' as they are known – precisely which of the two alternative draft communiqués we were discussing. While we were entertained that evening at a banquet given by the Emperor of Japan, the sherpas began their work. At about 2 o'clock in the morning, still in my evening dress, I went to see how the communiqué drafters were getting on. I found them refining their earlier draft in the light of our discussions and setting out alternative forms of words where decisions would be required from the summit. I hoped we would be as businesslike as they evidently were.

The following day we met once again at the Akasaka Palace to go through the communiqué, always a tedious and lengthy process. There was some disagreement between the Americans and the Europeans about the base year from which to set our different targets for the reduction of oil imports. But for me perhaps the most revealing discussion concerned the Japanese target. Until almost the last moment it was far from clear whether Mr Ohira's advisers would allow him to give a figure at all. When in the end the Japanese did announce their figures no one had any idea what sort of reduction they constituted, if any; but President Carter warmly congratulated them all the same.

And so the communiqué was issued and the customary press conference held. The most important decision made had nothing to do with checking oil consumption. It was that, despite the inclinations of several G7 governments, we were not going to fall into the trap of trying to achieve a co-ordinated reflation of demand. It was a useful signal for the future.

From Tokyo I flew to Canberra. This was my third visit to Australia, though it was to be only a brief one. There was time to see my daughter, Carol, who was working as a journalist there, but my main purpose was to talk to Malcolm Fraser, the Australian Prime Minister. I briefed him on what had taken place at Tokyo. But even more important, we discussed the forthcoming Commonwealth Conference in Lusaka at which Rhodesia would inevitably be the main issue. Over the next eight months, Rhodesia was to take up a great deal of my time.

Rhodesia had been a long-standing source of grief to successive British governments, but the elections of April 1979 in Rhodesia fundamentally changed the whole position. Under the new constitution, Bishop Muzorewa was elected as head of a black majority government, in a 64 per cent turn-out of a black majority electorate. The 'Patriotic Front' parties – the guerrillas of Robert Mugabe and Joshua Nkomo – had not taken part in the elections. Viscount Boyd of Merton – a former Conservative Colonial Secretary – had attended as an observer and reported back to me, as Leader of the Opposition, that the elections had been fairly conducted.

However, I was well aware that what the people of Rhodesia needed above all was peace and stability. It was the war, relentlessly carried on by the guerrillas, which had forced the white minority government to make concessions: that war had to be ended. To bring peace we had either to win international acceptance for the new regime or bring about the changes which would win such acceptance.

The first and most immediate problem was the attitude of the neighbouring 'front line' African states. We sent Lord Harlech, another former Conservative minister and an ex-Ambassador to Washington, for talks with the Presidents of Zambia, Tanzania, Botswana, Malawi and Angola. He also went to Mozambique and Nigeria. I was not at all keen at this stage that he should talk to Mr Mugabe and Mr Nkomo: their forces had carried out atrocities which disgusted everyone and I was as keen to avoid dealings with terrorists abroad as I would be at home. However, Peter Carrington's view was that it was essential to secure the widest possible recognition for a Rhodesian regime, since that country held the key to the whole South African region.

Accordingly, Lord Harlech did see the Patriotic Front leaders and, in July, the Organization of African Unity (OAU) endorsed the Patriotic Front as the sole legitimate authentic representative of the people of Zimbabwe. Black African states insisted on viewing Bishop Muzorewa's Government as nothing more than a façade for continued white minority rule. The fact that this greatly underrated the change which the internal settlement had effected did nothing to reduce the consequences of their attitude for Rhodesia.

Yet the situation did offer opportunities, if we were able to grasp them. First, nearly everyone considered that it was Britain's responsibility to solve the problem, and even though this frequently made us the object of criticism it also gave us a relatively free hand if we knew how to use it. Second, there was a great weariness among the parties involved and not just the Rhodesians themselves. The surrounding African states were finding it costly, disruptive and dangerous to play host to the two guerrilla armies. Nkomo's forces in Zambia were said to outnumber Zambia's own army.

Our best chance of a breakthrough was likely to be at the forthcoming Commonwealth Conference in Lusaka. This would be the first regular Commonwealth Heads of Government Meeting held in Africa. Zambia adjoined the Rhodesian war zone. It was also land-locked, so that the Queen, who is traditionally present during the first days as Head of the Commonwealth (though she does not open or attend the meeting) could not use the Royal Yacht *Britannia*. There were, accordingly, some worries about Her Majesty's safety, on which it was my responsibility to advise. My feeling was that there was no reason why her visit should not go ahead, and she received an enormous welcome. I, by contrast, was far from being their favourite person, when, late in the evening of Monday 30 July, I arrived in Lusaka to face a hostile and demanding press conference.

Our strategy was to take full responsibility ourselves for reaching a settlement. The task in Lusaka was to persuade the Commonwealth leaders to accept this, and to acknowledge that the Rhodesian problem was not the responsibility of the Commonwealth as a whole. To obtain that result we had to make it clear that Britain would be ready to resume authority in Rhodesia and to hold fresh elections. We knew also that there would have to be significant changes to the present constitution of Rhodesia if, after elections, the new government was to receive international recognition and acceptance. Those changes could only be brought about by some kind of Constitutional Conference bringing together all sides. The decision whether or not to hold such a conference would very much depend on how matters went at Lusaka, where our host was President Kenneth Kaunda.

It had been agreed to hold back the debate on southern Africa until the Friday so that after it the heads of government could go straight to their customary informal weekend retreat for private discussions on Rhodesia's future. My task was to win the support of the key figures there. A small group was set up consisting of myself and Peter Carrington, Mr (now Sir) Sonny Ramphal, Secretary-General of the Commonwealth, President Kaunda of Zambia, President Nyerere of Tanzania, Messrs Fraser and Manley, the Prime Ministers of Australia and Jamaica and Mr Adefope, the representative of Nigeria. Sir Anthony Duff, who was part of my team, drafted the heads of agreement. Our meeting ended successfully at Sunday lunchtime and the full version of the agreement was to have been discussed and endorsed by the full conference on Monday morning. However, on Sunday afternoon Malcolm Fraser chose to brief the Australian press. This required some rapid and unconventional action.

That evening we all attended a Commonwealth service in Lusaka Cathedral, where we had the benefit of a long polemical sermon from the Archbishop. I had been told already that the press knew the substance of what had been decided. Sonny Ramphal and I were sitting together; he was to read the first lesson, and I the second. After he had read his I showed him a note I had received from Peter Carrington about Malcolm Fraser's intervention, suggesting that we must now brief the British press on what had taken place. On the back of my hymn sheet, while I was reading the second lesson, Mr Ramphal wrote an alternative suggestion. The heads of government had been invited to a barbecue that evening at Malcolm Fraser's conference villa: we could hold a meeting there and settle a communiqué to be issued at once. This seemed to me an excellent idea and so the meeting came about. I was none too pleased with Malcolm Fraser myself. But the conclusion was satisfactory. Indeed, most of us were relieved that it had all been so amicable and that our proceedings could therefore end a day early.

I returned home on Wednesday morning. I was well pleased with what had been achieved, so much of it by Peter Carrington and Tony Duff. Many had believed that we could not come out of Lusaka with an agreement on the lines we wanted. We had proved them wrong.

Britain accordingly called a Constitutional Conference for the interested parties at Lancaster House in London in September. Its purpose was emphasized as being not just to talk but to reach a settlement. Peter Carrington chaired the conference with great skill and took charge of its day-to-day work. My role lay outside it. The heads of the 'front line' states came to London in person or sent in High Commissioners to see me for a progress report. President Machel of Mozambique was especially helpful in putting pressure on Robert Mugabe. I also gave a dinner for President Nyerere, another strong backer of Mr Mugabe. His concern was how to blend the three separate armies – the two guerrilla armies and the

Rhodesian army – into one, a task which would fall to the British army to achieve.

Just after the conference concluded, all three rival leaders – Bishop Muzorewa, Robert Mugabe and Joshua Nkomo – came to see me together at No. 10. They were in contemplative mood, pondering the future. I had the clear impression that each of them expected to win. Perhaps that was just as well.

Probably the most sensitive aspect of our approach related to the transitional arrangements: it was clear to me that, both for constitutional and practical reasons, Britain must resume direct authority in Rhodesia until the elections were over. On 15 November a Bill was introduced to provide for the appointment of a Governor and for sanctions to be removed as soon as he arrived in Rhodesia. Christopher Soames accepted the post. The decision to send him, as Governor, to Salisbury on 12 December, even before the Patriotic Front had accepted the cease-fire proposals, certainly involved some risk and was much criticized at the time. But we were clear that the momentum had to be maintained. Moreover, not only did Christopher have the authority of a Cabinet minister and wide diplomatic experience, he and his wife, Mary, had precisely the right style to carry off this most delicate and demanding job. Heavy pressure from the US and the 'front line' states finally led the Patriotic Front to accept the proposals for the cease-fire on 17 December, and the agreement was finally initialled on 21 December.

The outcome of the elections is well known. Mr Mugabe's party, to most people's surprise, won an overwhelming victory. On 18 April Rhodesia, as the Republic of Zimbabwe, finally received its independence.

It was sad that Rhodesia/Zimbabwe finished up with a Marxist government in a continent where there were too many Marxists maladministering their countries' resources. But political and military realities were all too evidently on the side of the guerrilla leaders. With the Rhodesian question finally solved, Britain again played an effective role in dealing with other Commonwealth – and especially African – issues, including the pressing problem of the future of Namibia and the longer-term challenge of bringing peaceful change to South Africa. Britain had demonstrated her ability, by a combination of honest dealing and forceful diplomacy, to settle one of the most intractable disputes arising from her colonial past.

*   *   *

With the Lancaster House Conference still in progress, I had to turn my mind to the vexed question of how to negotiate a substantial reduction in Britain's net contribution to the European Community budget. Figures had at long last been put on the size of that contribution and henceforth it was difficult for anyone to deny the scale of the problem.

At the next Council – in Dublin at the end of November, the Irish having now assumed the European Community presidency – the issue of our budget contribution dominated the business. The security risk from the IRA required that I be lodged overnight in splendid isolation in Dublin Castle and the Irish press enjoyed the idea that I slept in the bed used by Queen Victoria in 1897 – though I had the advantage over her of a portable shower in my room. Indeed, I was very well looked after. The hospitality was perhaps the best feature of the visit, and contrasted strongly with the atmosphere at the meetings which was extremely and increasingly hostile.

The Council opened amicably enough in Phoenix Park at the Irish President's official residence where he hosted lunch. Back in the Council at Dublin Castle we got down to business. My opening speech set out the facts of our case in somewhat greater detail than at Strasbourg and I elaborated on them in the vigorous debate which followed. There was a good deal of argument about the figures, at the root of which was an obscure and complex issue – how to calculate the losses and gains resulting to individual states from the operation of the CAP. But whichever way one did the sums, there was no doubt that the UK was making a huge net contribution, and unless it was mitigated it was about to become the biggest.

We had put forward our own proposals on the budget. But the Commission had come up with some of its own and I was prepared to accept their basic approach as a starting point. First, they proposed that action be taken to shift the weight of Community expenditure programmes. The trouble was this would take too long – if it happened at all. Second, they proposed, in addition, specific spending on UK projects to boost our receipts. But there simply were not enough suitable projects. Finally, on the contribution side, the 1975 Correction Mechanism had so far failed to cut our payments. If it were reformed on the lines the Commission was proposing, it could help reduce our net contributions – but still not enough: we would still be contributing about the same as Germany and much more than France.

I made one other point which was to prove of some significance. I said that, 'The arrangement [must] last as long as the problem.' It seemed to me then, and even more so by the end of the Council, that we simply could not have these battles every year, all to establish what common sense and equity ought to have made self-evident from the beginning.

It quickly became clear that I was not going to make the other heads of government see matters like this. Some, for example the Dutch Prime Minister, Mr Andries Van Agt, were reasonable, but most were not. I had the strong feeling that they had decided to test whether I was able and willing to stand up to them. They were determined to keep as much of our money as they could. By the time the Council broke up Britain had been offered a refund of only £350 million, implying a net contribution of some £650 million. That refund was just not big enough and I was not going to accept it. I had agreed that there should be another Council to discuss the matter further, but I was not overoptimistic after what I had seen and heard in Dublin, and what I would not accept was the attitude that fairness as such did not seem to enter into the equation at all.

At the press conference after the Council, I gave a vigorous defence of our position. I said that the other states should not have 'expected me to settle for a third of a loaf'. I also refused to accept the *communautaire* language about 'own resources'. I continued to state without apology that we were talking about Britain's money, not Europe's. I said:

> I am only talking about our money, no one else's; there should be a cash refund of our money to bring our receipts up to the average level of receipts in the Community.

Most of the other heads of government were furious.

We used the period between the end of the Dublin meeting and the next European Council to press our case. On 25 February Helmut Schmidt came to London again. Our talks centred on the question of our budget contribution and on the German Chancellor's repeated wish to see sterling within the ERM, and – contrary to the usual misleading press reports – they were useful and quite jolly. On 27 and 28 March there was a full-scale Anglo-German summit in London. I sought once more to stress how seriously we felt about the British contribution. Subsequently, I learned that Helmut Schmidt had been telling other Community governments that if there were no solution there was a danger that we would withhold British contributions to the Community. I had created the desired impression. The European Council due for 31 March and 1 April had to be postponed because of a political crisis in Italy (not an unusual event), but we pressed for a new Council before the end of April and it was finally called for Sunday and Monday 27 and 28, to meet in Luxemburg.

The atmosphere in Luxemburg turned out to be a good deal better than in Dublin. But we did not get around to talking about the budget at all at our first session. Indeed, only after dinner, and the usual foreign affairs *tour de table*, did I obtain agreement that the official group should resume effective negotiation that evening. The French were the main stumbling block: the proposals their officials presented were much less helpful to us than President Giscard's had seemed to be. In the meantime, the Agriculture ministers of the other governments of the Community had agreed on a package of proposals which would have raised farm prices, increasing again the proportion of the Community budget devoted to agriculture (quite contrary to the proposals put forward in Dublin) and giving the French a sheep meat regime which was more or less all that they wanted. Against this – for us – distinctly unfavourable background, we received eventually the offer of a limit on our net contribution of about £325 million, applying only to the year 1980. Under a subsequent proposal our net contribution would have been limited to about £550 million for 1981 as well.

My reaction was that this was too little. But above all I was not prepared to have a settlement that only lasted for two years. Helmut Schmidt, Roy Jenkins (President of the Commission) and almost everyone else urged me to settle. But I was not willing to return the following year to face precisely the same problem and the attitude that went with it. So I rejected the offer.

In fact, we were a good deal closer to a settlement than was widely recognized. Great progress had already been made in winning agreement to substantial reductions in our contribution. What remained was to secure these reductions for the first two years with a reliable undertaking for the third. We had a number of powerful levers by which we could apply pressure to this end. The French were increasingly desperate to achieve their aims in the Agriculture Council. The Germans, too, were keen to see higher agricultural prices. Most important of all, the Community would, we thought, probably reach the limit of its financial resources in 1982. Its persistent overspending was catching up with it, and greater resources could only be made available with British agreement. Ultimately our negotiating position was a strong one.

It soon became clear that Luxemburg, following the clashes in Dublin, had had the desired effect. In spite of talk of the Luxemburg offer having now been 'withdrawn', there was evidence of a general desire to solve the budget issue before the next full European Council at Venice in June. The easiest way to achieve this appeared to be a meeting of the Community Foreign ministers.

Peter Carrington, having received his mandate from me, flew to Brussels on Thursday 29 May with Ian Gilmour. After a marathon eighteen-hour session they came back with what they considered an acceptable agreement, arriving at lunchtime on Friday to brief me at Chequers.

My immediate reaction was far from favourable. The deal involved a net budget contribution in 1980 higher than envisaged at Luxemburg. It appeared from Peter's figures that we would pay rather less under the new package in 1981, though to some extent this was sleight of hand, reflecting different assumptions about the size of that year's total budget. But the Brussels proposal had one great advantage: it now offered us a three-year solution. We were promised a major review of the budget problem by mid-1981 and if this had not been achieved (as proved to be the case) the Commission would make proposals along the lines of the formula for 1980–81 and the Council would act accordingly. The other elements of the Brussels package relating to agriculture, lamb and fisheries, were more or less acceptable. We had to agree a 5 per cent rise in farm prices. Overall, the deal marked a refund of two-thirds of our net contribution and it marked huge progress from the position the Government had inherited. I therefore decided to accept the offer.

Wider international affairs had not stood still while we were engaged in bringing Rhodesia to legal independence and negotiating a reduction in our Community budget contribution. In November 1979, forty-nine American diplomatic personnel had been taken hostage in Iran, a source of deep and growing humiliation to the greatest western power. In December at the invitation of President Carter I made a short visit to the United States – the first of many as Prime Minister. In a short speech at my reception on the White House lawn I went out of my way to reaffirm my support for American leadership of the West.

At the end of 1979, the world reached one of those genuine watersheds which take almost everyone by surprise: the Soviet invasion of Afghanistan. In April 1978, the Government of Afghanistan had been overthrown in a communist-inspired coup; a pro-Soviet government was established, which was met by widespread opposition and eventual rebellion. In September 1979 the new President, Taraki, was himself overthrown and killed by his deputy, Hafizullah Amin. On 27 December, Amin was overthrown and killed, to be replaced by Babrak Karmal, whose regime was supported by thousands of Soviet troops.

Perhaps I was less shocked than some by the invasion of Afghanistan. I had long understood that détente had been ruthlessly used by the Soviets to exploit western weakness and disarray. I knew the beast.

What had happened in Afghanistan was only part of a wider pattern. The Soviets had instigated Cubans and East Germans to advance their aims and ambitions in Africa. They had been working to further communist subversion throughout the Third World, and had built up armed forces far beyond their defensive needs. Whatever their precise motives now in Afghanistan, they must have known that they had threatened the stability of Pakistan and Iran and were within 300 miles of the Straits of Hormuz. Moreover, bad as the situation was in itself, it could be worse as a precedent. There were other areas of the world in which the Soviets might prefer aggression to diplomacy, if they now prevailed: for example, Marshal Tito was approaching the end of his life in Yugoslavia and there could be opportunities for Soviet intervention there. They clearly had to be punished for their aggression and taught that the West would not only talk about freedom, but was prepared to make sacrifices to defend it.

On Friday 28 December President Carter rang me at Chequers. What had happened was a bitter blow to him. Britain had not felt able to comply with all that the Americans had wanted of us in response to the hostage crisis: in particular, we were not willing (or indeed legally able) to freeze Iranian financial assets, which would have had a devastating effect on international confidence in the City of London as a world financial centre. However, I was determined that we should follow America's lead now in taking action against the USSR and its puppet regime in Kabul. We therefore decided on a range of measures, including the curtailment of visits and contacts, non-renewal of the Anglo-Soviet credit agreement and a tightening of the rules on technology transfer. I also sought to mobilize the governments of the European Community to support the Americans. But, like President Carter, I was sure that the most effective thing we could do would be to prevent the USSR using the forthcoming Moscow Olympics for propaganda purposes. Unfortunately, most of the British Olympic team decided to attend the Games, though we tried to persuade them otherwise: of course, unlike their equivalents in the Soviet Union, our athletes were left free to make up their own minds. At the UN our ambassador, Tony Parsons, helped to rally the 'non-aligned' countries to condemn the Soviet Union's aggression. In London, on 3 January, I saw the Soviet Ambassador to enlarge in vigorous terms on the contents of my exchanges by telegram with President Brezhnev.

From now on, the whole tone of international affairs began to change, and for the better. Hard-headed realism and strong defence became the order of the day. The Soviets had made a fatal miscalculation: they had prepared the way for the renaissance of America under Ronald Reagan.

But this was the future. America had still to go through the humiliating agony of the failed attempt to rescue the Iranian hostages. As I watched President Carter's television broadcast explaining what had happened, I felt America's wound as if it were Britain's own; and in a sense it was, for anyone who exposed American weakness increased ours. I was soon, though, in a position to demonstrate that there would be no flinching when it came to dealing with our own brand of Middle East terrorism.

I first learned of the terrorist attack on the Iranian Embassy at Prince's Gate in Knightsbridge on Wednesday 30 April during a visit I was making to the BBC. Several gunmen had forced their way into the Iranian Embassy and were holding twenty hostages – most of them Iranian staff, but also a policeman who had been on duty outside and two BBC journalists who had been applying for visas. The gunmen were threatening to blow up both the embassy and the hostages if their demands were not met. The terrorists belonged to an organization calling itself 'the Group of the Martyr'; they were Iranian Arabs from Arabistan, Iraqi-trained and bitterly opposed to the prevailing regime in Iran. They demanded that a list of 91 prisoners be set free by the Iranian Government, that the rights of Iranian dissidents should be recognized and a special aeroplane provided to take them and the hostages out of Britain. The Iranian Government had no intention of conceding these demands; and we, for our part, had no intention of allowing terrorists to succeed in their hostage taking. Though the group involved was a different one, this was no less an attempt to exploit perceived western weakness than was the hostage taking of the American Embassy personnel in Tehran. My policy would be to do everything possible to resolve the crisis peacefully, without unnecessarily risking the lives of the hostages, but above all to ensure that terrorism should be – and be seen to be – defeated.

Willie Whitelaw, as Home Secretary, took immediate charge of operations from the special emergency unit in the Cabinet Office. Throughout the crisis, Willie kept in regular contact with me. In turn the Metropolitan Police kept in touch with the terrorists by a specially laid telephone line. We also made contact with those who might be able to exert some influence over the gunmen. The latter wished to have an Arab country's ambassador act as intermediary. But there was a risk that the objective of such an intermediary would be different from our own. The Jordanians, whom we *were* prepared to trust, refused to become involved. A Muslim imam did talk to the terrorists, but without result. It was a stalemate.

The position began to deteriorate on Sunday afternoon. I was called back early from Chequers and we were driving back to London when a further message came over the car-phone. The hostages' lives were now at risk and Willie wanted my permission to send in the SAS. 'Yes, go in,' I said. Executed with the superb courage and professionalism the world now expects of the SAS, the assault took place in the full glare of the television cameras. Of the 19 hostages known to be alive at the time of the assault all were rescued. Four gunmen were killed; one was captured; none escaped. I breathed a sigh of relief when I learned that there were no police or SAS casualties. Later I went to the Regent's Park Barracks to congratulate our men. I was met by Peter de la Billière, the SAS commander, and then watched what had happened on television news, with a running commentary, punctuated by relieved laughter, from those involved in the assault. One of them turned to me and said, 'We never thought you'd let us do it.' Wherever I went over the next few days, I sensed a great wave of pride at the outcome; telegrams of congratulation poured in from abroad: we had sent a signal to terrorists everywhere that they could expect no deals and would extort no favours from Britain.

The Middle East continued to occupy my attention throughout the rest of 1980. At the European Council in Venice on 12 and 13 June the heads of government discussed Israel and the Palestinian question. The key issue was whether the Community governments were to call for the PLO to be 'associated with' the Middle East peace talks, or to 'participate in' them: I was very much against the latter course, for as long as the PLO did not reject terrorism. The final communiqué reaffirmed the right of all the states in the region – including Israel – to existence and security, but also demanded justice for all peoples, which implied recognition of the Palestinians' right to self-determination. So, of course, it pleased no one.

Then in September 1980 Iraq attacked Iran and we were once again in the throes of a new crisis, with potentially dangerous political and economic implications for western interests. Saddam Hussein had decided that the chaos in Iran provided him with a good opportunity to renounce the 1975 Algiers Settlement of the two countries' disputed claims to the Shatt-al-Arab waterway and seize it by force.

I was chiefly concerned to prevent the conflict spreading down the Gulf and involving the vulnerable oil-rich Gulf States, which had traditionally close links with Britain. I told Peter Carrington that I did not share the common view that the Iranians would quickly be beaten. They were fanatical fighters and had an effective air force with which they could attack oil installations. I was right: by the end of the year the Iraqis became bogged down and the war threatened both the stability of the Gulf and western shipping. But by this time we had put in the Armilla Patrol to protect our ships.

As I looked back on the international scene that Christmas of 1980 at Chequers, I reflected that the successes of British foreign policy had helped us through a particularly dark and difficult time in domestic, and particularly economic, affairs. But, as in economic matters, so in foreign affairs I knew that we were only starting the course. Tackling Britain's Community budget problem was only the first step to reforming the Community's finances. Bringing Rhodesia to legal independence was but a prelude to addressing the problem of South Africa. The West's response to the Soviet invasion of Afghanistan would have to be a fundamental rethinking of our relations with the communist bloc, and this had barely begun. The renewed instability in the Gulf as a result of Iraq's attack on Iran would ultimately require a new commitment by the western powers to the security of the region. All these issues were to dominate British foreign policy in the years ahead.

CHAPTER SIXTEEN

Not At All Right, Jack

The restructuring of British industry and
trade union reform in 1979–1980

I N THE YEARS SINCE THE WAR British politics had focused, above all,
on the debate about the proper role of the state in the operation of the
economy. By 1979 and perhaps earlier, optimism about the beneficent
effects of government intervention had largely disappeared. This change
of attitude, for which I had long worked and argued, meant that many
people who had not previously been Conservative supporters were now
prepared to give our approach at least the benefit of the doubt.

A sort of cynical disdain, often disguised as black humour, had come to
characterize many people's attitude to industry and unions. We all
enjoyed the film *I'm All Right, Jack*, but the problem was no laughing
matter.

British goods will only be attractive if they can compete with the best
on offer from other countries, and the truth is that too often British
industrial products were uncompetitive. This was not simply because the
strong pound was making it difficult to sell abroad, but because our
industrial reputation had steadily been eroded. In the end reputation
reflects reality. Nothing less than changing that reality – fundamentally
and for the better – would do.

The root of Britain's industrial problem was low productivity. British
living standards were lower than those of our principal competitors and
the number of well-paid and reasonably secure jobs was smaller because
we produced less per person than they did. The overmanning resulting
from trade union restrictive practices was concealed unemployment; and
beyond a certain point – certainly beyond the point we had reached in

1979 – overmanning would bring down businesses and destroy existing jobs. Outdated capacity and old jobs have to go to make the most of new opportunities. Yet the paradox, which neither British trade unions nor the socialists were prepared to accept, was that an increase in productivity is likely, initially, to reduce the number of jobs before creating the wealth that sustains new ones. Time and again we were asked when plants and companies closed, 'Where will the new jobs come from?' As the months went by, we could point to the expansion of self-employment and to industrial successes in aerospace, chemicals and North Sea oil. Increasingly we could also look to foreign investment, for example in electronics and cars. But the fact is that in a market economy government does not – and cannot – know where jobs will come from.

Because our analysis of what was wrong with Britain's industrial performance centred on low productivity and its causes – rather than on levels of pay – incomes policy had no place in our economic strategy. I was determined that the Government should not become enmeshed, as previous Labour and Conservative administrations had been, in the obscure intricacies of 'norms', 'going rates' and 'special cases'. Of course, pay rises at this time were far too high in large parts of British industry where profits were small or nonexistent, investment was inadequate, or market prospects looked poor. Judged by relative labour costs, our level of competitiveness in 1980 was some 40 to 50 per cent worse than in 1978: and around three-fifths of this was due to UK unit labour costs increasing at a faster rate than those abroad, with only two-fifths the result of exchange rate appreciation. There was little, if anything, we could do to influence the exchange rate, without allowing inflation to rise still further and faster. But there was a great deal which trade union negotiators had it in their power to do if they wished to prevent their own members and others being priced out of jobs; and as the scale of union irresponsibility grew apparent, talk of the need for a pay policy began to be heard.

So it was important that from the very beginning I stood firm against suggestions of pay policies. I had come to feel that all such talk was at best irrelevant and at worst misguided.

Some people offered what they thought of as the 'German model'. We were all conscious of Germany's economic success. Indeed, we had helped create the conditions for it after the war by introducing competition and restructuring their trade unions. There were those in Britain who said that we should copy the German corporatist tendency of making national economic decisions in consultation with business organizations and trade union leaders. However, what might work for Germany would not necessarily work for us. The German experience of hyperinflation between the wars meant that nearly everyone there was deeply conscious of the need to keep inflation down, even at the expense of a short-term rise in unemployment. German trade unions were also far more responsible than ours, and of course the German character is less individualistic and more regimented. So the 'German model' was inappropriate for Britain.

In any case, we already had the National Economic Development Council (NEDC) in which ministers, employers and trade unionists met from time to time. And so I was quite sure that we should not proceed further with the idea of a new 'forum'. In fact, I felt that the whole approach based on prices and incomes controls should be swept away. The Government would set the framework, but it was for businesses and workforces to make their own choices, and to face the consequences of their actions, good and bad. In the private sector rates of pay must be determined by what businesses could afford, depending on their profitability and productivity. In the public sector also affordability was the key – in this case meaning the scale of the burden it was right to ask the taxpayer and ratepayer to bear. Given that government was the ultimate owner and banker, however, the mechanism by which these disciplines could be made effective was bound to be less clear and direct than in the private sector.

The income tax cuts in our 1979 budget were intended to give more incentives to work. However, the most important aspect of the 1980 budget related to monetary policy rather than taxation. We announced in the budget our Medium Term Financial Strategy (quickly known as the MTFS), which was to remain at the heart of our economic policies throughout the period of their success and which was only relegated in importance in those final years, when Nigel Lawson's imprudence had already begun to steer us to disaster. A little historical irony is provided by the fact that Nigel himself, as Financial Secretary, signed the Financial Statement and Budget Report (FSBR), or 'Red Book', in which the MTFS first burst on an astonished world, and that he was its most brilliant and committed exponent.

The MTFS was intended to set the monetary framework for the economy over a period of years. The aim was to bring down inflation by decreasing monetary growth, while curbing borrowing to ensure that the pressure of disinflation did not fall solely on the private sector in the form of higher interest rates. The monetary figures for later years that we announced in 1980 were illustrative rather than firm targets – though this did not prevent commentators poking tiresome fun when the targets were altered or not met. The 1980 MTFS figures for the money supply were expressed in sterling M3 (£M3), though the Red Book noted that 'the way in which the money supply is defined for target purposes may need to be adjusted from time to time as circumstances change', an important qualification.*

A firm financial strategy was necessary to improve our economic performance: but we never believed that it would be sufficient. We also had to deal with the problem of trade union power, made worse by successive Labour Governments and exploited by the communists and militants who had risen to key positions within the trade union move- ment – positions which they ruthlessly exploited in the callous strikes of the winter of 1978–79.

The engineering industry dispute in 1979 provided a good demonstra- tion of how much poison excessive trade union power and privilege had injected into British industry – and not just the public but the private sector too. The engineering industry had every commercial reason to reduce costs so as to compete. Yet after a ten-week strike, the Engineering Employers' Federation (EEF) conceded a 39-hour week, increases of £13 a week for skilled men and an extra week's holiday phased over four years, all of this greatly increasing their costs. Because of the centralized system of pay bargaining, employers throughout the industry had also given in. The EEF had long accepted the closed shop as an unavoidable fact of life. So the unions' power over their members was more or less absolute.

On 14 May 1979, less than a fortnight after I formed the Government, Jim Prior wrote to me setting out his plans for trade union reform. There

---

* Notes and coins are included in all the monetary measures. But since the great majority of transactions in the economy are not conducted in cash, but in transferring claims on the banking system (e.g., writing cheques), most measures also include some part of total bank deposits. Wider measures often include the deposits of other financial institutions such as building societies. £M3 comprises notes and coins in circulation with the public, together with all sterling deposits (including certificates of deposit) held by UK residents in both public and private sectors. The argument about which is the best measure contin- ues, though a misplaced obsession with the exchange rate has since rather put such argu- ment into the shade.

was a certain amount that we could do at once. We could set up our promised inquiry into the coercive recruitment practices of the printing union SLADE – which would deal also with the activities of the NGA in the advertising industry. We could also make certain changes to employment legislation by Order in Council, with the aim of reducing the heavy burden placed – on small firms in particular – by the provisions on unfair dismissal and redundancy. But we would have to consult with employers and unions extensively about our main proposals.

Two weeks later Jim set out his proposals in a Cabinet paper. They covered three main areas: picketing, the closed shop and ballots. We planned to limit the specific immunities for picketing strictly to those who were themselves party to the dispute and who were picketing at the premises of their own employer. Where there was a closed shop, we proposed to give employees who might be dismissed for refusing to join a union the right to apply to an industrial tribunal for compensation. There would be a legal right of complaint for those arbitrarily expelled or excluded from union membership. We would extend the present protection for employees who objected to joining a union because of deeply held personal conviction. A new closed shop could in future only be established if an overwhelming majority of workers voted for it by secret ballot. A statutory code relating to the closed shop would be drawn up. Finally, the Secretary of State for Employment would be given power to reimburse trade unions for the postal and administrative costs of secret ballots.

These early proposals were as notable for what they did not contain as for what they did. At this stage they did not extend to the question of secondary action other than secondary picketing, nor did they deal with the wider question of trade union immunities. In particular, they left alone the crucial immunity which prevented action being taken by the courts against union funds. On secondary action we were awaiting the conclusions of the House of Lords in the important case of *Express Newspapers v. MacShane*. It is worth noting that the changes we made in all these areas were changes in the civil, not the criminal, law. In public discussion of subsequent strikes this distinction was often lost. The civil law could only change the way in which unions behaved if employers or, in some cases, workers were prepared to use it. They had to bring the case. By contrast, the criminal law on picketing had to be enforced by the police and the courts. Although the Government would make it clear that the police enjoyed its moral support, the constitutional limits on us in this area were real and sometimes frustrating.

As the summer wore on, it became obvious that although the TUC was prepared to talk to the Government about our proposals, it had no intention of actually co-operating with them. There was no willingness on their side to face economic facts or to try to understand the economic strategy we were pursuing.

In the last part of 1979 and the early months of 1980 we continued refining the Employment Bill and spent a good deal of time on the question of secondary action and immunities. We also discussed item by item measures to deal with the burdens which past Labour legislation had placed on industry.

But by far the most contested issue was that of trade union immunities. Our proposals on secondary picketing had already begun to address it. But we now took a further step. We had received the report of the inquiry set up earlier into the recruitment activities of the printing union SLADE, undertaken by Mr Andrew Leggatt QC.* In response, we decided to remove the immunity where industrial disruption was called or threatened by people other than those directly working for a particular firm with the intention of coercing its employees into joining a trade union.

We decided to go further, following the House of Lords decision in the *MacShane* case on 13 December. The *MacShane* case was important because it confirmed the wide scope of existing immunities in the case of secondary action. Most of the immunities then enjoyed by trade unions had their origin in the Trade Disputes Act (1906), which Labour extended significantly in October 1974. The *MacShane* case arose from a dispute that began in 1978 between the National Union of Journalists (NUJ) and a number of provincial newspapers. The provincial papers managed to keep going during the dispute by publishing stories supplied to them by the Press Association. The NUJ unsuccessfully attempted to prevent this, first, by direct appeal to NUJ members working for the Press Association and when that failed, by instructing its people on national newspapers to black Press Association material altogether. In response the *Daily Express* applied for an injunction against the NUJ. The Court of Appeal in December 1978 ruled in favour of the *Express* that the NUJ secondary

---

* The report was damning. SLADE had been using its strength in the printing industry to recruit among freelance artists, photographic studios and advertising agencies by threatening to 'black' the printing of their work unless they joined the union. The report concluded that the campaign 'was conducted without any regard whatever to the feelings, interests, or welfare of the prospective recruits'.

action had exceeded that which could be regarded as furthering the objectives of the dispute and therefore did not enjoy immunity. As a result of this decision, injunctions could be and were granted. However, when the case went to the House of Lords, the Appeal Court's ruling was overturned. Essentially, the Lords decided that for purposes of law an industrial action was 'in furtherance of a trade dispute', and therefore immune, if trade union officials genuinely believed it to be so. It meant that henceforth there would be virtually unlimited immunity for secondary industrial action.

The position was complicated by the outcome of two other court cases. One of these – *N.W.L. Limited v. Nelson Wood*, or the 'Nawala Case' – resulted from the attempts of the International Transport Workers' Federation to prevent the employment by a British shipping company of overseas seamen in British registered ships. The Federation's action threatened the future of the British shipping industry. Still more important, however, was the second case, which widened the scope for secondary action in the steel strike. The Iron and Steel Trades Confederation (ISTC) had called out its members in the private steel sector as part of its dispute with the British Steel Corporation, which had begun on 2 January 1980. Duport Steels, a private steel company, was granted an injunction by the Court of Appeal against Bill Sirs, General Secretary of the ISTC. The Court of Appeal ruled that immunity did not apply in this case because the ISTC's argument was essentially with the Government rather than BSC itself. But again, the House of Lords reversed this ruling, relying on broadly the same grounds as in the *MacShane* case. The practical result was that the strike spread once more to the private steel companies.

We were all agreed that the law as now interpreted by the courts must be changed. But we disagreed both about what immunity, if any, there should be for secondary action and about the timing of the introduction of the necessary change into the Employment Bill. Again and again, Jim Prior said that he did not want decisions about changes in the law to be linked with a particular dispute. But as the steel strike worsened, with none of our proposed legislation yet in force, the public criticism grew. I had the greatest sympathy with the critics, though I wished that some employers had earlier been rather more robust. Whenever those of us who felt that we ought to go faster put our case – and our number included Geoffrey Howe, John Nott, Keith Joseph, Angus Maude, Peter Thorneycroft and John Hoskyns – Jim Prior was always able to argue against 'hasty action' by reference to the cautious attitude of the CBI.

By this stage I did not share Jim's analysis of the situation at all. He really believed that we had already tried to do too much and that we should go no further, whether in the area of trade union law or general economic strategy. I, for my part, had begun bitterly to regret that we had not made faster progress both in cutting public expenditure and with trade union reform.

For all his virtues, Jim Prior was an example of a political type that had dominated and, in my view, damaged the post-war Tory Party. I call such figures 'the false squire'. They have all the outward show of a John Bull – ruddy face, white hair, bluff manner – but inwardly they are political calculators who see the task of Conservatives as one of retreating grace-fully before the Left's inevitable advance. Retreat as a tactic is sometimes necessary; retreat as a settled policy eats at the soul. In order to justify the series of defeats that his philosophy entails, the false squire has to persuade rank and file Conservatives that advance is impossible. His whole political life would, after all, be a gigantic mistake if a policy of positive Tory reform turned out to be both practical and popular. Hence the passionate and obstinate resistance mounted by the 'wets' to the fiscal, economic and trade union reforms of the early 1980s. These reforms had either to fail or be stopped. For if they succeeded, a whole generation of Tory leaders had despaired unnecessarily. It made Jim Prior timid and overcautious in his trade union policy. I had to stake out a more deter-mined approach.

Brian Walden interviewed me for *Weekend World* on Sunday 6 January. I used the occasion to say that we would be introducing a new clause in the Employment Bill to rectify the problem left by the *MacShane* judgment. I made it clear that we did not intend to remove the immunity enjoyed by trade unions as regards action intended to cause people to break their employment contracts, but would concentrate on the immunity relating to action designed to cause employers to break their commercial contracts. I also drew attention to the way in which trade union immuni-ties had combined with nationalized monopolies to give huge power to the trade unions in these industries. We needed to restrict the immunities and to break the monopolies by introducing competition.

All my instincts told me that we would have strong public support for further action to restrict union power, and the evidence supported me. An opinion survey in *The Times* on 21 January 1980 asked people the question:

'Do you think sympathy strikes and blacking are legitimate weapons to use in an industrial dispute, or should the new law restrict their use?' Seventy-one per cent of those who replied – and 62 per cent of trade unionists who did so – said that a new law should indeed restrict their use.

On the morning of Tuesday 5 February I had two meetings with industrialists. The first was with the CBI. Some of them said that the present Bill, as drafted, went as far as possible.

The second meeting that day was with the private sector steel producers. They complained that the private steel companies had been dragged into a dispute not of their making and in which they would be the only real victims. As a result of the strike they were losing about £10 million a week. It was clear that there was no real grievance on the part of private sector steel workers but the threat of losing union cards was the decisive factor in persuading private sector workers to join the strike. In these circumstances it is not surprising that the private sector steel companies wanted immediate legislation to outlaw secondary picketing.

Ministers now agreed to restore the law to what it had been understood to be before the *MacShane* judgment, adding further tests relating to the dispute to be applied by the courts. There would not, however, be a total ban on secondary action. There followed a short period for consultation and the new clause was introduced into the Employment Bill at the Report Stage in the House of Commons on 17 April 1980, limiting immunity for secondary action which broke or interfered with commercial contracts. Immunity would only exist when the action was taken – by employees of suppliers or customers of the employer in dispute – with the 'sole or principal purpose' of furthering the primary dispute and when the action was reasonably likely to succeed. Of great significance for the future was the fact that we announced the publication of a Green Paper on trade union immunities, which would appear later in the year and would look at the whole issue from a wider perspective.

The debate about trade union reform, both inside and outside government, was conducted under the shadow of industrial conflict: the issues of secondary action and immunities became inextricably entangled with the 1980 steel strike. But that strike also challenged our economic strategy directly and it is unlikely, once the strike had begun, that our economic policies would have survived if we had suffered defeat.

One of my first decisions about the nationalized industries was to agree to the closure of the Shotton steel works in North Wales. Measures aimed at providing new job opportunities in the area would be announced, but I knew that the closure would have a devastating effect on the steelmen and their families. I felt desperately sorry for them. They had done all that was expected. But it was not – and could not be – enough.

BSC exemplified not only the disadvantages of state ownership and intervention, but also the way that British trade unionism dragged down our industrial performance. At the Hunterston ore terminal on the Clyde BSC had built the largest deep-water jetty in Europe. It had been opened in June 1979, but could not be used until November because of a manning dispute between the Transport and General Workers' Union and the ISTC. For five months bulk ore carriers had to be diverted to the Continent, where their cargo was transferred to smaller vessels for shipment to Terminus Quay, Glasgow, and from there finally sent on to Ravenscraig.

Over the five years to 1979–80 more than £3 billion of public money had gone into BSC, which amounted to £221 for every family in the country. Yet still the losses accumulated. Keith Joseph and I were prepared to continue for the present to fund BSC's investment and redundancy programme; what we were not prepared to do was to fund losses which arose from excessive wage costs, unearned by higher productivity.

If we were serious about turning BSC round – with all the closures, job losses, and challenges to restrictive practices that would involve – we faced the risk of a very damaging steel strike. There was only one worse alternative: to allow the present situation to continue.

BSC's cash limit for 1980–81 was first set in June 1979: the aim was for it to break even by March 1980. This objective had been set by the previous Labour Government. But by 29 November 1979 BSC had announced a £146 million half-year loss. The crisis was fast approaching.

On 6 December Keith Joseph let me know that BSC could not afford any general wage increase from 1 January other than the consolidation of certain additional increases agreed the previous year – amounting to 2 per cent. Any further increase would be dependent on local negotiations and conditional on the equivalent improvements in productivity. The Corporation had told the unions the week before that 5 million tonnes of surplus capacity, over and above the closure of iron- and steel-making at Corby and Shotton, would have to be shut down. Already Bill Sirs was threatening a strike. I agreed with Keith that we must back the Corporation. We also agreed that BSC must win the support of public opinion

and bring home to the unions the harm which a strike would do to their
own members.

As the strike loomed, there was much disquiet about whether the
management of BSC had properly prepared its ground for it. The figures
used to justify the management's position were questioned, even by
Nicholas Edwards, the Secretary of State for Wales. He might have been
right. But I said that we must not attempt to substitute our judgement as
politicians for that of the industry. It was up to the management of BSC
– at last – to manage.

On 10 December the BSC Board confirmed that 52,000 steel jobs
would have to go. The business prospects for BSC were still worsening.
Indeed, when we looked at their figures for future steel demand we
thought that they were, if anything, slightly optimistic.

From the end of December I chaired regular meetings of a small group
of ministers and officials to monitor the steel situation and decide what
action needed to be taken. It was a frustrating and anxious time. The
details of the BSC offer were not well understood either by the steel
workers or by the public and allowed a bewildering array of different
figures to gain currency, pleasing no one: to the general public the figures
always seemed to be increasing, while to the unions they never seemed
sufficient.

It was against this background that I met first the unions at their
request and then the management of BSC on Monday 21 January at No.
10. The union leaders had seen Keith Joseph and Jim Prior the previous
Saturday. One difficulty we had was that the unions might have drawn the
wrong impression from widely reported remarks made by Jim, criticizing
the BSC management. I had been angry to read this. But, when a week
later I was asked about it by Robin Day on *Panorama*, my reply was
sweetly dismissive: 'We all make mistakes now and then. I think it was a
mistake, and Jim Prior was very, very sorry indeed for it, and very apolo-
getic. But you don't just sack a chap for one mistake.'

In my discussion with Mr Sirs and Mr Smith (the leaders respectively
of the ISTC and NUB), I said that the Government was not going to intervene in the dispute. I did not know enough about the steel industry to
become involved in the negotiations though, of course, I was keen to hear
their views. The unions wanted the Government to bring pressure on
BSC to make an increased offer. They wanted some 'new money', but I
pointed out that there is no such thing: money for the steel industry
could only come from other industries which were making a profit. The

real issue, I said, was productivity where – although Bill Sirs disputed the figures – it was generally accepted that BSC's performance lagged far behind. Luxemburg had reduced its steel workforce from 24,000 to 16,000 and substantially increased its productivity, with the result that it was now exporting railway lines to the UK. When I had heard this the previous autumn I had been cut to the quick, and I told him so.

That same afternoon I met Sir Charles Villiers and Bob Scholey, the Chairman and Chief Executive of BSC. They described to me precisely what was on offer and the very limited scope for flexibility. I gave them my full support.

The real problem was now arising in the private steel sector. Mass picketing at Hadfields raised the stakes. It had overtones of the kind of intimidation and violence which had led to the closure of the Saltley Coke Depot during the miners' strike in 1972: it was vital that we win through.

British business proved resourceful in meeting the strike: somehow, they got hold of the steel they needed.

Although it was now obvious that the unions had lost, the precise terms on which the Government and management had won remained in the balance. On 9 March BSC had held a 'ballot about a ballot', asking workers whether they wanted a ballot on pay, which the ISTC had hitherto denied them, and this had shown strong evidence of disenchantment with the ISTC's tactics and leadership. The union wanted a way out which would save face. BSC had formally proposed arbitration on 17 February and, although rejected, the offer had remained open. There was strong pressure for a Court of Inquiry into the strike which would propose a settlement. I would have preferred the involvement of ACAS (the Advisory, Conciliation and Arbitration Service). It seemed to me that if ACAS had any reason for existing at all, it should surely have a role in a situation such as this. In fact, we were condemned to watch while BSC and the unions agreed to the appointment of a three-man inquiry consisting of Lords Lever and Marsh (both former Labour Cabinet ministers) and Bill Keyes of SOGAT, which on 31 March recommended a settlement well above the figure originally offered by BSC but substantially below what the ISTC had demanded. The offer was accepted.

At its final meeting on 9 April my committee was told that all the BSC plants were back in operation. Production and steel deliveries were about 95 per cent of what they would have been without the dispute. The outcome, in spite of the size of the final settlement, was generally seen as a victory for the Government. The bills, however, kept on coming in.

This had been a battle fought and won not simply for the Government and for our policies, but for the economic well-being of the country as a whole. It was necessary to stand up to unions which thought that because they were in the public sector they should be allowed to ignore commercial reality and the need for higher productivity. In future, pay had to depend on the state of the employing industry, and not on some notion of 'comparability' with what other people received. But it was always going to be more difficult to induce such realism where the state was owner, banker, and at times tempted to be manager as well.

In many ways British Leyland presented a similar challenge to the Government as BSC, though in a still more acute and politically difficult form. Like BSC, BL was effectively state-owned and controlled, though technically it was not a nationalized industry. The company had become a symbol of Britain's industrial decline and of trade union bloody-mindedness. However, by the time I entered No. 10 it had also begun to symbolize the fightback by management. Michael Edwardes, BL's Chairman, had already demonstrated his grit in taking on the trade union militants who had brought the British car industry to its knees. I knew that whatever we decided to do about BL would have an impact on the psychology and morale of British managers as a whole, and I was determined to send the right signals. Unfortunately, it became increasingly clear that the action required to support BL's stand against trade union obstruction diverged from what was required on purely commercial grounds. This was a problem: but we had to back Michael Edwardes.

We had indicated in Opposition our hostility to the Ryder Plan for BL with its enormous cost, unmatched by sufficiently rigorous measures to increase productivity and earn profits.* My first direct experience as Prime Minister of BL's difficulties came in September 1979 when Keith Joseph informed me of BL's dreadful half-yearly results and of the measures the Chairman and Board intended to take. The new plan involved the closure of BL's Coventry plant. At least 25,000 jobs would be lost. Productivity would be increased. The development of BL's medium car range of models would be accelerated. The BL Board said that the company would require additional funds beyond the £225 million remaining of the £1 billion which Labour had in principle committed.

---

* The Ryder Plan, dating from 1975, proposed the investment by government in phases over seven years of £1.4 billion to modernize BL plant and introduce new models.

BL's workers were to be balloted on the Corporate Plan. If it received substantial majority support the Government would find it very difficult to turn down and, as quickly became apparent, the company would want a further £200 million above and beyond the final tranche of Ryder money. The ballot, of which the result would be announced on 1 November, seemed likely to go the company's way. But it might not; and that would present its own immediate problems. For if the ballot showed anything other than overwhelming support for the company's proposals there would be speculation about its future, with the prospect of BL's many small and medium-sized creditors demanding immediate payment and the large holders of loan stock adding to the pressure. BL might be forced precipitately into liquidation and the economic implications of such a collapse were appalling. One hundred and fifty thousand people were employed by the company in the UK; there were perhaps an equal number of jobs in the component and other supplying industries dependent on BL. It was suggested that complete closure would mean a net loss to the balance of trade of around £2,200 million a year, and according to the NEB it might cost the Government as much as £1 billion.

Closure would have some awful consequences, but we must never give the impression that it was unthinkable. If ever the company and workforce came to believe that, there would be no limit to their demands on the public purse. For this reason Keith and I decided not to agree to BL's request for the Government to issue an undertaking to honour the company's debt. They had wanted us to publish a letter to this effect even before the ballot result. In fact, 87.2 per cent of those voting supported BL's plan and BL immediately sought approval from the NEB to go ahead with it. A firm request for money was made to the Government.

Our consideration of the BL Corporate Plan was delayed by two other events. First, as a result of our (unconnected) decision to remove Rolls-Royce from the purview of the NEB, Sir Leslie Murphy and his colleagues resigned and a new Board had to be appointed under Sir Arthur Knight. Second, the Amalgamated Union of Engineering Workers (AUEW) now threatened the very survival of BL by calling a strike following the dismissal on 19 November of Derek Robinson, a notorious agitator, convenor of the shop stewards at Longbridge and chairman of the so-called 'Leyland Combine Trade Union Committee'. Robinson and others had continued to campaign against the BL plan even after its approval. The management had been right to sack him, pending the outcome of an inquiry by the AUEW.

We were now, though, put under pressure to approve the plan before the Christmas recess – without waiting for completion of BL's wage negotiations – in order to enable the company to sign a collaborative deal with Honda for a new middle-range car. I was not prepared to be bounced into a commitment. Past experience suggested to me that the plan would not in fact be fulfilled.

I, therefore, asked John Nott to go over BL's accounts with the company's Finance Director. Keith Joseph, John Biffen and others also went over the plan in detail with Michael Edwardes. Their conclusion was that there was only a small chance of BL surviving and that it was probable that the plan would fail, followed by a run-down or liquidation of the company. About a third of BL was thought to be saleable. But the final judgement had to be based on wider considerations. We reluctantly decided that people would simply not understand liquidation of the company at the very moment when its management was standing up to the unions and talking the language of hard commercial common sense. After much discussion, we agreed to endorse the plan and to provide the necessary financial support. Keith announced our decision to the House of Commons on 20 December.

But BL's ballot on their pay offer went badly wrong, partly because the question put to the workforce – 'Do you support your Negotiating Committee's rejection of the Company's wage and conditions offer?' – was confusing. Fifty-nine per cent of those taking part voted against the offer. Moreover, the AUEW inquiry found that Robinson had been unfairly dismissed by the company and an official strike was announced, to begin on 11 February. Michael Edwardes rightly refused to reinstate him or to improve on the pay offer. Contingency plans were made by the BL Board, assisted by Department of Industry and Treasury officials, to cope with the situation if the plan had to be withdrawn and the company put into liquidation. Michael Edwardes was unwilling to approach possible foreign buyers for a sell-off of BL, although he agreed to respond positively to any approaches potential buyers might make to him. Certainly, the workforce at BL could be in little doubt as to the seriousness of their position. BL's share of the market had fallen so low that in January Ford sold more of one model (the Cortina) than BL's total sales.

Michael Edwardes and the BL Board faced down the union threat. The strikers were told that unless they returned to work by Wednesday 23 April they would be dismissed. But much as I admired BL's tenacity, I was becoming increasingly unhappy about the Board's commercial approach.

As the summer wore on it became clear that the company's financial position was deteriorating even further. The company lost £93.4 million before interest and tax in the first half-year compared with a profit of £47.7 million for the same period the previous year. Michael Edwardes tried to get the Government to agree to fund the new BL medium-range car – known as the LM10 – separately and in advance of the 1981 Corporate Plan. Indeed, he wanted me to announce the Government's commitment to this at a dinner given by the Society of Motor Manufacturers and Traders (SMMT) on 6 October. I had no intention of agreeing; once again, I would not be bounced.

On 27 October BL's trade unions decided overwhelmingly to reject the company's offer of a pay increase of 6.8 per cent and recommended a strike. Michael Edwardes wrote to Keith Joseph to say that a strike would make it impossible to achieve the 1981 Corporate Plan submitted just a week before. To win support for the pay offer, he wanted to write to inform union officials of the key aspects of the 1981 Plan, including the funds required for 1981 and 1982 – a figure which he would put at £800 million. I reluctantly accepted his approach but only on the clear understanding that the Department of Industry would make it known that the Government was not committed in any way to finding these funds and that the matter had yet to be considered. In fact, on 18 November BL's union representatives backed down and finally decided to accept the company's offer. Almost the same thing had happened the previous year. The need to deal with an industrial relations crisis made it extremely difficult to avoid the impression that we were prepared to provide large amounts of extra public funding for the company. No matter how clear our disclaimers, inevitably people drew that conclusion.

On any rational commercial judgement, there were no good reasons for continuing to fund British Leyland. BL was still a high-cost, low-volume manufacturer of cars in a world where low cost and high volume were essential for success. But I knew that closure of the volume car business, with all that would mean for the West Midlands and the Oxford area, would not be politically acceptable, at least in the short term. It would also be a huge cost to the Exchequer – perhaps not very different from the sort of sums BL was now seeking. I was in favour of supporting the BL Plan – but on condition that BL disposed of its assets rapidly or arranged mergers with other companies.

But this was contentious. Michael Edwardes was not willing to sell Land Rover if BL were also required to go on trying to salvage the volume car business. He said that the Board's position would be quite impossible if a public deadline were to be set for its sale.

Political realities had to be faced. We agreed to accept BL's Corporate Plan, involving the division of the company into four more or less independent businesses. We settled the contingencies which would lead to the plan being abandoned. We set out the objectives for further collaboration with other companies. And – most painfully – we provided £990 million.

This was not, of course, the end of the story for BL. In due course, it would be shown that the changes in attitude and improvements in efficiency achieved were permanent. To that extent, the account of our policy in 1979–81 towards BL is one of success. But the huge extra sums of public money that we were forced to provide came from the taxpayer, or through higher interest rates needed to finance extra borrowing, from other businesses. And every vociferous cheer for higher public spending was matched by a silent groan from those who had to pay for it.

CHAPTER SEVENTEEN

Not for Turning

Politics and the economy in 1980–1981

A T 2.30 ON THE AFTERNOON of Friday 10 October 1980 I rose to address the Conservative Party Conference in Brighton. Unemployment stood at over two million and rising; a deepening recession lay ahead; inflation was far higher than we had inherited, though falling; and we were at the end of a summer of government leaks and rifts. The Party was worried, and so was I. Our strategy was the right one, but the price of putting it into effect was proving so high, and there was such limited understanding of what we were trying to do, that we had great electoral difficulties. However, I was utterly convinced of one thing: there was no chance of achieving that fundamental change of attitudes which was required to wrench Britain out of decline if people believed that we were prepared to alter course under pressure. I made the point with a line provided by Ronnie Millar:

> To those waiting with bated breath for that favourite media catch-
> phrase, the 'U-turn', I have only one thing to say. 'You turn if you
> want to. The lady's not for turning.' I say that not only to you, but
> to our friends overseas – and also to those who are not our friends.

The message was directed as much to some of my colleagues in the Government as it was to politicians of other parties. It was in the summer of 1980 that my critics within the Cabinet first seriously attempted to frustrate the strategy which we had been elected to carry out – an attack which reached its climax and was defeated the following year. At the time that I spoke many people felt that this group had more or less prevailed.

* * *

Battle was to be joined over the next two years on three related issues: monetary policy, public spending and trade union reform.

The most bitter Cabinet arguments were over public spending. In most cases those who dissented from the line which Geoffrey Howe and I took were not merely intent on opposing our whole economic strategy as doctrinaire monetarism; they were trying to protect their departmental budgets. It had soon become clear that the public expenditure plans announced in March 1980 had been far too optimistic. Local authorities, as usual, were overspending; and the recession was proving deeper than expected, increasing spending on unemployment and other benefits. Government borrowing for the first quarter of 1980 looked like being very large. In addition, Francis Pym, Defence Secretary, was pressing for an increase in the Ministry of Defence (MoD) cash limit.

The debate continued inside and outside government. The 'wets'' central message was always the same: spend and borrow more. They used to argue that we needed extra public spending on employment and industrial schemes, over and above what we had planned and were effectively forced to spend simply as a result of the recession. But this did not escape from the fact that extra public spending – whatever it was spent on – had to come from taxes levied on private individuals and industry; or borrowing, pushing up interest rates; or printing money, setting off inflation.

These basic differences between us came out clearly at the public spending Cabinet on 10 July 1980. Some ministers argued that the PSBR should be allowed to increase to accommodate the huge new requirements of the loss-making nationalized industries. But the PSBR was already far too high and the higher it went, the greater the pressure to raise interest rates in order to persuade people to lend the Government the necessary funds. At a certain point – if pushed too far – there would be the risk of a full-scale government funding crisis – that is, when you cannot finance your borrowing from the non-banking sector. We could not risk going further in that direction.

The defence budget was a special problem. We had already accepted the NATO commitment for annual 3 per cent real increases in our defence spending. This had the obvious merit of demonstrating to the Soviets our determination to prevent their winning the arms race on which they had embarked, but in other respects it was unsatisfactory. First, it meant that the MoD had little incentive to get value for money in the hugely expensive equipment it purchased. Second, the 3 per cent commitment meant that Britain, spending a substantially higher proportion of its GDP on defence than other European countries and going through a peculiarly deep recession, found herself bearing an unfair and increasing burden; and by the end of 1980 the MoD had overspent its cash limit because, with the depressed state of industry, suppliers had fulfilled government orders faster than expected.

As we moved into the winter of 1980 the economic difficulties accumulated and the political pressure built up. On Wednesday 3 September Geoffrey Howe and I met to discuss the monetary position. Measured in terms of £M3, the money supply had been rising much faster than the target we had set in the MTFS at the time of the March budget. It was hard to know how much of this was the result of our removing exchange controls in 1979 and our decision in June to remove the 'corset' – a device by which the Bank of England imposed limits on bank lending. Money analysts argued that both of these liberalizations had misleadingly bloated the £M3 figures.*

Of course, we never just looked at monetary figures to gauge what was happening. We also looked at the real world around us. And what we saw told a somewhat different tale from the high £M3 figures. Inflation had slowed down markedly, particularly prices in the shops where competition was intense. Sterling was very strong, averaging just below $2.40 during the second half of 1980. And here the crucial issue was whether the high exchange rate was more or less an independent factor bringing down inflation, or rather a result of the monetary squeeze being tighter than we intended and than the £M3 figures suggested.

Some of my closest advisers thought the latter. Professor Douglas Hague sent me a paper in which he described our policies as 'lopsided': first, they were bearing down more heavily on the private than the public sector (which I knew to be true), and second, they were putting too much emphasis on controlling the money supply and too little on controlling the PSBR, with the result that interest rates were higher than they should have been. (I also came to share this view over the next year.) In the summer of 1980 I consulted Alan Walters, who was to join me at the beginning of 1981 as my economic policy adviser at No. 10. Alan's view was that the monetary squeeze was too tight and that it was the narrowest definition of 'money', known as the monetary base, which was the best, indeed the only reliable, star to steer by.

---

* Higher interest rates caused people to increase the amount they held in interest-bearing financial assets and to reduce cash and non-interest-bearing assets in their current accounts.

If there was uncertainty about the monetary position at this time, there was none about the trend in public spending, which was inexorably upwards. In September, Geoffrey Howe sent me a note elaborating on the warning he had already given to Cabinet about public expenditure. The increases required for the nationalized industries, particularly BSC, would require larger cuts in programmes than those agreed in July in order to hold the total. To the extent that more was provided, as the Cabinet wished, for industrial support and employment, the corresponding cuts would need to be larger still. The fifth public expenditure round in sixteen months was bound to prompt squeals of indignation: and so it proved.

Geoffrey and I decided not to take the whole matter to Cabinet cold, as it were, so I called a meeting of key ministers to go into it first. The Chancellor described the position and outlined the arithmetic.

Our plan succeeded. Without too much grumbling, the Cabinet of 30 October endorsed the strategy and confirmed our objective of keeping public spending in 1981–82 and later years broadly at the levels set out in the March White Paper. This meant that it would be necessary to make cuts of the order of magnitude proposed by the Treasury – though even with these reductions we would be forced to increase taxes if we were to bring the PSBR down to a level compatible with lower interest rates.

Much stronger Cabinet opposition surfaced when we began to look at the decisions required to give effect to the strategy which had been endorsed. The 'wets' now claimed that they lacked sufficient information to judge whether the overall strategy was soundly based. In effect, spending ministers were trying to behave as if they were Chancellors of the Exchequer. It would be a recipe for complete absence of spending control and thus for economic chaos.

The Autumn Statement on 24 November 1980, therefore, contained some highly unpopular measures. Employees' National Insurance Contributions had to go up. Retirement pensions and other social security benefits would be increased by 1 per cent less than the rate of inflation next year if they turned out to have risen by 1 per cent more in the present year. There were cuts in defence and local government spending. It was announced that a new supplementary tax would be introduced on North Sea oil profits. However, there was some good news: further employment measures – and a 2 percentage point cut in the MLR.

* * *

Few members of the public are experts in the finer matters of economics – though most have a shrewd sense when promises do not add up. By the end of 1980 I began to feel that we risked forfeiting the public's confidence in our economic strategy. Unpopularity I could live with. But loss of confidence in our capacity to deliver our economic programme was far more dangerous. And the very last thing I could afford was well-publicized dissent from within the Cabinet itself. Yet this was what I now had to face.

The economic and public expenditure discussions of 1980 repeatedly found their way into the press; decisions came to be seen as victories by one side or the other and Bernard Ingham told me that it was proving quite impossible to convey a sense of unity and purpose in this climate. During 1980 the public was treated to a series of speeches and lectures by Ian Gilmour and Norman St John Stevas on the shortcomings of monetarism, which, according to them, was deeply un-Tory – though they usually took care to cover themselves against charges of disloyalty by including some fulsome remarks praising me and the Government's approach.

Industrial leaders helped worsen the general impression of disarray: in the same month the new Director-General of the CBI was promising 'a bare knuckle fight' over government policies, though when I met the CBI shortly afterwards I am glad to say that knuckles were not in evidence. Then in December Jim Prior was reported as urging us not to use the language of the 'academic seminar'. But perhaps the most astonishing remark was John Biffen's widely reported admission to the Conservative Party Parliamentary Finance Committee that he did not share the enthusiasm for the MTFS, which he – the Chief Secretary to the Treasury – was trying, with singularly little success, to apply in the field of public expenditure.

I decided that it was time to reshuffle the Cabinet. On Monday 5 January I made the changes, beginning with Norman St John Stevas, who left the Government. I was sorry to lose Norman. He had a first-class brain and a ready wit, but he turned indiscretion into a political principle. The other departure, Angus Maude, had employed his own sharp wit in my support but he felt that it was time to give up the job as Paymaster-General to return to writing. I moved John Nott to Defence to replace Francis Pym, convinced that someone with real understanding of finance and a commitment to efficiency was needed in this department. I moved John Biffen to replace John Nott at Trade, and at Geoffrey Howe's request appointed Leon Brittan as Chief Secretary. Leon was enormously intelligent and hard-working and he had impressed me with the sharpness of his mind. Two very talented new Ministers of State came into the Department of Industry to support Keith Joseph: Norman Tebbit and Kenneth Baker. Norman was totally committed to our policies, shared much of my own outlook and was a devastating Commons in-fighter. Ken was given special responsibility for Information Technology, a task in which he showed his talents as a brilliant presenter of policy. Francis Pym took over the task of disseminating government information, which he combined with the position of Leader of the House of Commons. But the first half of this appointment was to prove a source of some difficulty in the months ahead.

I shall never forget the weeks leading up to the 1981 budget. Hardly a day seemed to go by without the financial scene deteriorating in some way. Alan Walters, who had now joined me at No. 10, argued for a larger cut in the PSBR than Geoffrey Howe was proposing. He also believed that the way in which the monetary policy was conducted was defective. But the Treasury were not prepared to move to the system of monetary base control which Alan favoured and to which I was attracted.

And this was much more than a technical disagreement. Alan Walters, John Hoskyns and Alfred Sherman had suggested that Professor Jurg Niehans, a distinguished Swiss monetary economist, should prepare a study on our monetary policy for me. Professor Niehans's report had a clear message. It was that North Sea oil had probably not been a major factor in sterling's appreciation; rather, tight monetary policy had caused the pound to rise so high, imposing such pressure on British industry and deepening the recession. The report argued that we should use the monetary base rather than £M3 as the main monetary measure and suggested that we should allow it to rise in the first half of 1981. In short, Professor Niehans thought monetary policy was too tight and should quickly be loosened. Alan emphatically agreed with him.

My doubts at this time about the Treasury's conduct of monetary policy, however, were more than matched by the concern I felt at the steady growth in its estimates of the PSBR – the target by which we steered our fiscal policy. The trend of PSBR forecasts was upwards. The likelihood was that we would budget for too low a reduction in the PSBR, as we had in 1980–81. To repeat that mistake would either force us to introduce an additional budget in late summer or autumn, or put great strains on the funding of Government borrowing. In the last resort it might lead to a funding crisis, and it would certainly force us to increase interest rates, keeping sterling high and increasing the already severe squeeze on the private sector. We had to avoid such an outcome. What we needed was a budget for employment.

On Friday 13 February I had a further meeting with Geoffrey Howe. Alan Walters was also present. The latest forecast for the PSBR was between £13.5 billion and £13.75 billion. The tax increases Geoffrey was proposing would reduce it to something between £11.25 billion and £11.5 billion, but he did not believe it was politically possible to go below £11 billion. But Alan argued strongly that the PSBR should be lower still. He told us that a PSBR of, say, £10 billion would be no more deflationary than one of £11 billion because the latter would actually be worse for City expectations and for interest rates. Alan concluded by arguing that we had no alternative but to raise the basic rates of income tax by 1 or 2 per cent.

Alan was the economist. But Geoffrey and I were politicians. Geoffrey rightly observed that introducing what would be represented as a deflationary budget at the time of the deepest recession since the 1930s, via an increase in the basic rate, would make it a political nightmare. I went along with Geoffrey's judgement about the problems of raising income tax, but without much conviction, and as the days went by my unease grew.

When Geoffrey and I had our next budget meeting on 17 February, he said that he was now prepared to contemplate a basic rate increase. But his concern was whether it might not be better to raise the basic rate of income tax by 1 per cent and personal allowances by about 10 per cent, thus reducing the burden on people below average earnings. I confirmed that I was prepared to contemplate this, but I also told him that I was coming to the view that it was essential to get the PSBR below £11 billion.

My advisers – Alan Walters, John Hoskyns and David Wolfson – continued to argue for this much lower PSBR with great passion. Keith Joseph also strongly backed this view. Alan, who knew that he could always have access to me more or less when he wished – as in my view any really close adviser should if a Prime Minister is not to be the prisoner of his (or her) in-tray – came in to my study to have one last attempt to get me to change my mind about the budget. I know today that he went away still believing that I was not persuaded. Yet I knew in my heart of hearts that there was only one right decision, and that it now had to be made.

Geoffrey Howe and I, with Douglas Wass, the Treasury's Permanent Secretary, met for a further discussion of the budget on the afternoon of Tuesday 24 February. Geoffrey still envisaged a PSBR for 1981–82 of £11.25 billion. I said that I was dismayed by such a figure and that I doubted whether it would be possible to cut interest rates, which we badly needed to do, unless Government borrowing was reduced to a figure around £10.5 billion. I said that I was even prepared to accept a penny on the standard rate.

Geoffrey argued against a penny on income tax – on which I was not too difficult to persuade for I was horrified at the thought of reversing even some of the progress we had made on bringing down Labour's tax rates. But he also argued against the need to bring down the PSBR further, and on this last point I was not persuaded at all.

Early the following morning, Alan came in to see me. I told him that I had insisted on the lower PSBR he wanted. But I still did not know quite how Geoffrey would react. Then Geoffrey came in to see me. Having consulted his ministerial colleagues in the Treasury he had accepted that we should have a smaller PSBR, below £11 billion. Rather than increase the basic rate of income tax he proposed the less unpopular course of withholding any increase in tax thresholds – though this was still an extraordinarily bold move when inflation remained at 13 per cent. Our budget strategy was now set. And it looked as if we would be able to announce a reduction of 2 per cent in MLR in the budget the following Tuesday.

Unsurprisingly, the budget was very unpopular. In the eyes of our critics, the strategy was fundamentally wrong. If you believed, as they did, that increased Government borrowing was the way to get out of recession, then our approach was inexplicable. If, on the other hand, you thought, as we did, that the way to get industry moving again was above all to get down interest rates, then you had to reduce Government borrowing. Far from being deflationary, our budget would have the reverse effect: by cutting government borrowing and over time easing the monetary squeeze, it would allow interest rates and the exchange rate to fall, both of which had created severe difficulties for industry. I doubt that there has ever been a clearer test of two fundamentally different approaches to economic management.

The dissenters in the Cabinet had been stunned by the budget when they learned its contents at the traditional morning Cabinet on budget day. The press was soon full of leaks expressing their fury and frustration. They knew that the budget gave them a political opportunity. Because it departed so radically from post-war economic orthodoxy even some of our supporters would not wholly believe in the strategy until it started to yield results. That might not be for some time.

Thankfully, strikes occupied far less of our time during 1981 than they had in 1980, and the number of working days lost due to strike action was only a third of that in the previous year. But two disputes – one in the coal industry, which did not in the end result in a strike, and another in the civil service, which did* – were of great importance, both to budget decisions and to the overall political climate.

A foreigner unaware of the extraordinary legacy of state socialism in Britain would probably have found the threatened miners' strike in January 1981 quite incomprehensible: £2.5 billion of taxpayers' money had been invested in the coal industry since 1974; productivity at some of the new pits was high, and a slimmed-down and competitive coal industry could have provided employees with good, well-paid jobs. But this was possible only if uneconomic pits were closed. Moreover, the pits which the NCB was intent on closing were not just uneconomic but more or less exhausted. On 27 January the Energy Secretary, David Howell, told me about the closure plans. The following afternoon Sir Derek Ezra, NCB Chairman, visited Downing Street and briefed me in person. I agreed with him that with coal stocks piling up there was no alternative to speeding up the closure of uneconomic pits.

As in the cases of BSC and BL, it was the management which had to implement the agreed approach. The press was soon full of NCB plans to close 50 pits and a bitter conflict was predicted. The National Union of Mineworkers was pledged to fight closures and although Joe Gormley, its President, was a moderate, the powerful left-wing faction of the union was bound to exploit the situation and Arthur Scargill, the hard-left leader, was likely to succeed Mr Gormley as President in the near future.

At a meeting with the NUM on 11 February the NCB Board resisted pressure to publish a list of pits it was proposing to close and denied the

---

* The civil service strike began in March 1981 and lasted for five months. Union members struck selectively at crucial government installations, including computer staff involved in tax collection, costing the Government over £350 million in interest charges on money borrowed to cover delayed and lost tax revenue. Industrial action was also taken at GCHQ, the installation at the heart of Britain's signals intelligence, which led to our decision in January 1984 to ban trade unions there.

figure of 50. However, the Board failed to mention the idea of improved redundancy terms, which was already being discussed by the Government, and instead undertook to join the NUM in an approach to us seeking a lower level of coal imports, the maintenance of a high level of public investment and subsidies comparable to those allegedly being paid by other governments to coal industries abroad. The NCB Board was behaving as if it entirely shared the interests of the union representing its employees. The situation quickly deteriorated further.

On Monday 16 February I had a meeting with David Howell and others. Their tone had entirely changed. The department had suddenly been forced to look over the abyss and had recoiled. The objective had now become to avoid an all-out national strike at the minimum cost in concessions. David Howell would have to agree to a tripartite meeting with the NUM and the NCB to achieve this. The tone of the NCB Chairman had also changed in short order. I was appalled to find that we had inadvertently entered into a battle which we could not win. There had been no forward thinking in the Department of Energy. The coal stocks piled at the pit heads were largely irrelevant to the question of whether the country could endure a strike: it was the stocks at the power stations which were important, and these were simply not sufficient. It became very clear that all we could do was to cut our losses and live to fight another day, when – with adequate preparation – we might be in a position to win. Defeat in a coal strike would have been disastrous.

The tripartite meeting was due to take place on 23 February. On the morning of 18 February I met hurriedly with David Howell to agree on the concessions which would have to be offered to stave off a strike. There was still considerable confusion as to what the facts really were. Whereas the NCB had been reported to be seeking 50 or 60 pit closures, it now appeared that they were talking about 23. But the tripartite meeting achieved its immediate objective: the strike was averted. The Government undertook to reduce imports of coal, with David Howell indicating that we were prepared to discuss the financial implications with an open mind. Sir Derek Ezra said that in the light of this undertaking to review the financial constraints under which the NCB was operating, the Board would withdraw its closure proposals and re-examine the position in consultation with the unions.

The following day David Howell made a statement to the Commons to explain the outcome of the meeting. The press reaction was that the miners had won a major victory at the expense of the Government, but that we had probably been right to surrender. This was not, however, the end of our difficulties. It had emerged at the tripartite meeting on 25 February that the NCB was in far deeper financial trouble than we had known. They were likely to overrun their external financing limit (EFL), which had already been set at some £800 million, by between £450 and £500 million and were expecting to make a loss of £350 million. We would need to challenge these figures and examine them in detail, but we could not do this when the NUM knew almost as much about the NCB's financial position as we did. Therefore, our aim must be to draw a ring fence around the coal industry by arguing that coal was a special case rather than a precedent. Above all, we must prepare contingency plans in case the NUM sought a confrontation in the next pay round.

Having managed to ease the Government out of an impossible position – at what I knew to be a high political cost – I concentrated attention on limiting the financial consequences of our retreat and preparing the ground so that we would never be put in such an awful situation again.

The real question in my mind was whether we would be able to resist a strike that winter. It was evident from the NUM Conference which took place in July that the left wing of the union had become obsessed with the idea of taking on the Government and that Arthur Scargill, certain of the presidency, would make this his policy. Willie Whitelaw, as the minister in overall charge of civil contingency planning, sent me a report on 22 July, which concluded that a strike this year probably could not be withstood for more than 13–14 weeks. The calculations took account of the transfer of coal stocks which we had put in hand. In theory, endurance could be increased by power cuts or the use of troops to move coal to the power stations. But either option was fraught with difficulty. There would be huge political pressure to give in to a strike. The union might see what was up if we set about increasing oil stocks for power stations. We would have to rely on a judicious mixture of flexibility and bluff until the Government was in a position to face down the challenge posed to the economy, and indeed potentially to the rule of law, by the combined force of monopoly and union power in the coal industry.

Over the weekend of 10–12 April, riots broke out in Brixton, South London. Shops were looted, vehicles destroyed, and 149 police officers and 58 members of the public were injured. Two hundred and fifteen people were arrested. There were frightening scenes, reminiscent of riots in the United States during the 1960s and '70s. I accepted Willie

Whitelaw's suggestion that Lord Scarman, the distinguished Law Lord, should undertake an inquiry into the causes of what had happened and make recommendations.

There was a lull; then on Friday 3 July a battle in Southall between white skinheads and Asian youths erupted into a riot in which the police quickly became the main victims, attacked with petrol bombs, bricks and anything else to hand. The mob even turned on firemen and ambulancemen. Over the weekend, Toxteth in Liverpool was also the scene of violence: once again there were outbreaks of arson, looting and savage attacks on the police.

On 8 and 9 July it was the turn of Moss Side in Manchester to experience two days of serious disorder. Willie Whitelaw told me after his visits to Manchester and Liverpool that the Moss Side riots had taken the form of looting and hooliganism rather than direct confrontation with the police. In Liverpool, as I was to learn, racial tension and bitter hostility to the police – in my view encouraged by left-wing extremists – were more important.

The riots were, of course, a godsend to the Labour Opposition and the Government's critics in general. Here was the long-awaited evidence that our economic policy was causing social breakdown and violence. I found myself countering the argument that the riots had been caused by unemployment. This rather overlooked the fact that riots, football hooliganism and crime generally had been on the increase since the 1960s, most of that time under the very economic policies that our critics were urging us to adopt. Another argument – that racial minorities were reacting to police brutality and racial discrimination – we took more seriously. Following Lord Scarman's report we introduced a statutory framework for consultation between the police and local authorities, tightened the rules on stopping and searching suspects, and brought in other measures relating to police recruitment, training and discipline.

Whatever Lord Scarman might recommend, however, the immediate requirement was that law and order should be restored. I told Willie on Saturday 11 July that I intended to go to Scotland Yard and wished to be shown how they handled the difficulties on the ground.

After a briefing at Scotland Yard I was taken round Brixton, and on Monday 13 July I made a similar visit to Liverpool. Driving through Toxteth, the scene of the disturbances, I observed that for all that was said about deprivation, the housing there was by no means the worst in the city. I had been told that some of the young people involved got into trouble through boredom and not having enough to do. But you had only to look at the grounds around those houses with the grass untended, some of it almost waist high, and the litter, to see that this was a false analysis. They had plenty of constructive things to do if they wanted. Instead, I asked myself how people could live in such circumstances without trying to clear up the mess and improve their surroundings. What was clearly lacking was a sense of pride and personal responsibility – something which the state can easily remove but almost never give back.

The first people I talked to in Liverpool were the police. I also met councillors at Liverpool City Hall and then talked to a group of community leaders and young people. I was appalled by the latter's hostility to the Chief Constable and the police. But I listened carefully to what they had to say. They were articulate and talked about their problems with great sincerity.

The whole visit left me in no doubt that we faced immense problems in areas like Toxteth and Brixton. People had to find once again a sense of respect for the law, for the neighbourhood, and indeed for themselves. Despite our implementation of most of Scarman's recommendations and the inner-city initiatives we were to take, none of the conventional remedies relying on state action and public spending was likely to prove effective. The causes went much deeper; so must the cures.

The rioters were invariably young men, whose high animal spirits, usually kept in check by a whole range of social constraints, had been unleashed to wreak havoc. What had become of the constraints? A sense of community – including the watchful disapproval of neighbours – is the strongest such barrier. But this sense had been lost in the inner cities. Often those neighbourhoods were the artificial creation of local authorities which had uprooted people from genuine communities and decanted them into badly designed and ill-maintained estates where they did not know their new neighbours. Some of these new 'neighbourhoods', because of large-scale immigration, were ethnically mixed; on top of the tensions which might initially arise in any event, even immigrant families with a very strong sense of traditional values found those values undermined in their own children by messages from the surrounding culture. In particular, welfare arrangements encouraged dependency and discouraged a sense of responsibility. The results were a steadily increasing rise in crime (among young men) and illegitimacy (among young women).

All that was needed for these to flower into full-scale rioting was the decline of authority, and authority of all kinds – in the home, the school, the churches and the state – had been in decline for most of the post-war years. Hence the rise in football hooliganism, race riots and delinquency over that period. What perhaps aggravated the 1981 riots into a virtual saturnalia, however, was the impression given by television that rioters could enjoy a fiesta of crime, looting and rioting in the guise of social protest. These are precisely the circumstances in which young men riot, and riot again – and they have nothing whatever to do with £M3.

Once we had solved the problem of the British economy, we would need to turn to those deeper and more intractable problems. I did so in my second and third terms with the set of policies for housing, education, local authorities and social security that my advisers, over my objections, wanted to call 'Social Thatcherism'. But we had only begun to make an impact on these by the time I left office.

The 1981 budget continued to agitate the Cabinet. Some ministers were long-standing in their dissent. Others on whose support I had counted in the past began to fall away. The irony was that at the very time the opposition to the strategy was greatest, the trough of the recession had already been reached. Whereas in 1980 the dissenters in the Cabinet had refused to face up to the true seriousness of the economic situation and so had insisted on higher government spending than we could afford, in 1981 they made the opposite mistake by exaggerating the bleakness of the economic outlook and calling for even higher spending in a bid to reflate the economy out of recession. Surely there is something logically suspect about a solution which is always correct whatever the problem.

One of the myths perpetuated by the media at this time was that Treasury ministers and I were obsessively secretive about economic policy, seeking always to avoid debate in Cabinet. In view of past leaks that might have been an understandable approach, but it was never one we adopted. Geoffrey Howe was anxious to have three or four full economic discussions in Cabinet every year, in the belief that it would help us to win greater support for the policy; I doubted whether discussions of this sort would achieve a meeting of minds, but I went along with Geoffrey's suggestion as long as it generated practical results.

The arguments came to a head at the Cabinet discussion on Thursday 23 July. I had more than an inkling of what was coming. Indeed, that morning I had said to Denis that we had not come this far to go back now. I would not stay as Prime Minister unless we saw the strategy through. Spending ministers had submitted bids for extra expenditure of more than £6.5 billion, of which some £2.5 billion was demanded for the nationalized industries. But the Treasury urged reduced public spending for 1982–83, below the totals derived from the March White Paper. The result was one of the bitterest arguments on the economy, or any subject, that I can ever recall taking place at Cabinet during my premiership. Some argued for extra public spending and borrowing as a better route to recovery than tax cuts. There was talk of a pay freeze. Even those, like John Nott, who had been known for their views on sound finance, attacked Geoffrey Howe's proposals as unnecessarily harsh. All at once the whole strategy was at issue. I had thought that we could rely on these people when the crunch came and I was not interested in this kind of creative accounting that enabled fair-weather monetarists to justify an about-turn. Others, though, were as loyal as ever, notably Willie, Keith and, of course, Geoffrey himself who was a tower of strength at this time. And indeed it was their loyalty that saw us through.

I had said at the beginning of the Government 'Give me six strong men and true, and I will get through.' Very rarely did I have as many as six. So I responded vigorously in defence of the Chancellor. I was prepared to have a further paper on the issue of tax cuts versus public spending. But I warned of the effects on international confidence of public expenditure increases or any departure from the MTFS. I was determined that the strategy should continue. But when I closed the meeting I knew that there were too many in Cabinet who did not share that view.

Much of this bitter disagreement found its way into the press – and not simply in reports of what had been said in Cabinet derived from non-attributable ministerial comments. There were particularly embarrassing comments from Francis Pym and Peter Thorneycroft, who between them were meant to be responsible for the public presentation of our policies. At Francis's suggestion I had authorized the recreation of the 'Liaison Committee', at which ministers and Central Office were supposed to work together to achieve a coherent message. In August it became clear that these arrangements were actually being used to undermine the strategy.

Geoffrey Howe had said in the House of Commons that the CBI's latest Industrial Trends Survey provided evidence that we were now at the end of the recession – a remark which may have been slightly imprudent, but which was strictly true. The following weekend Francis Pym in the course of a lengthy speech observed: 'There are few signs yet of when an upturn will occur. And that recovery when it comes in due course may be slower and less pronounced than in the past.' This forecast would have been bold even from an economist; coming from Francis it verged on the visionary. Even Peter Thorneycroft, who had been a superb chairman of the Party in Opposition, joined the 'wet' chorus, describing himself as suffering from 'rising damp' and saying that 'there [was] no great sign of [the economy] picking up'. Given that these comments came from the two men in charge of presenting government policy, they were extremely damaging and easily seen (in that inevitable metaphor) as 'the tip of the iceberg'.

Trade union reform was another subject of Cabinet disagreement. We had issued a Green Paper on trade union immunities on which comments were to be received by the end of June 1981. When they came in, these showed a desire among businessmen for further radical action to bring trade unions fully under the rule of law. But Jim Prior and I disagreed about what should be done. I wanted further action to restrict trade union immunities, which would make union funds liable to court action. Jim's proposals would not have achieved this. In his reading, history showed that the unions could defeat any legislation if they wanted to. I believed that history showed nothing of the sort, but rather that governments in the past had failed the nation through lack of nerve – drawing back when the battle was nearly won. I was also convinced that on the issue of union reform there was a great reserve of public support on which we could draw.

The differences between Cabinet ministers over the economic strategy – and between myself and Jim Prior over trade union reform – were of fundamentals. So it was quite clear to me that a major reshuffle was needed if our economic policy were to continue, and perhaps if I were to remain Prime Minister.

I preferred to have a Cabinet reshuffle during the recess if possible, so that the ministers could get used to their departments before being questioned in the House. It was not, therefore, until September that I discussed the details with my closest advisers. Willie Whitelaw, Michael Jopling (the Chief Whip) and Ian Gow came over to Chequers on the weekend of 12–13 September. For part of the time Peter Carrington and Cecil Parkinson joined us. The reshuffle itself took place on the Monday.

I always saw first those who were being asked to leave the Cabinet. I began with Ian Gilmour and told him of my decision. He was – I can find no other word for it – huffy. He left Downing Street and denounced government policy to the television cameras as 'steering full speed ahead for the rocks' – altogether a flawless imitation of a man who has resigned on principle. Christopher Soames was equally angry – but in a grander way. I got the distinct impression that he felt that he was, in effect, being dismissed by his housemaid. Mark Carlisle, who had not been a very effective Education Secretary, also left the Cabinet – but he did so with courtesy and good humour. Jim Prior was obviously shocked to be moved from Employment. The press had been full of his threats to resign from the Government altogether if he were asked to leave his present position. I wanted this post for the formidable Norman Tebbit, so I called Jim's bluff, and offered him the post of Northern Ireland Secretary. After some agonizing and some telephoning he accepted my offer and became Secretary of State for Northern Ireland in place of the debonair Humphrey Atkins, who succeeded Ian Gilmour as the main Foreign Office minister in the Commons.

I moved David Howell from Energy to Transport. It gave me great pleasure to promote the immensely talented Nigel Lawson into the Cabinet to take his place.

Keith Joseph had told me that he wished to move from Industry. With his belief that there was an anti-enterprise culture that had harmed Britain's economic performance over the years, it was natural that Keith should now wish to go to Education where that culture had taken deep roots. Accordingly, I sent Keith to my old department to replace Mark Carlisle. Norman Fowler returned to take up Health and Social Security, the portfolio he had held in Opposition, replacing Patrick Jenkin who took over at Industry from Keith. Janet Young, a friend for many years, became Leader of the House of Lords, the first woman to hold the post, taking over Christopher Soames's responsibility for the civil service.

Perhaps the most important change was the promotion of Norman Tebbit to replace Jim Prior at Employment. Norman had been an official of the British Airline Pilots' Association and had no illusions about the vicious world of hard-left trade unionism, nor by contrast, any doubt about the fundamental decency of most trade union members. As a true believer in the kind of approach Keith Joseph and I stood for, Norman understood how trade union reform fitted into our overall strategy. Norman was also one of the Party's most effective performers in Parliament and on a public platform. The fact that the Left howled disapproval confirmed that he was just the right man for the job. He was someone they feared.

I had already agreed with Peter Thorneycroft that he should cease to be Party Chairman. I had been unhappy about some of Peter's actions in recent months. But I would never forget how much he did to help win the 1979 election and he remained a friend. I appointed Cecil Parkinson to succeed him – dynamic, full of common sense, a good accountant, an excellent presenter and, no less important, on my wing of the Party.

The whole nature of the Cabinet changed as a result of these appointments. After the new Cabinet's first meeting I remarked to David Wolfson and John Hoskyns what a difference it made to have most of the people in it on my side. This did not mean that we would always agree, but it would be a number of years before there arose an issue which fundamentally divided me from the majority of my Cabinet, and by then Britain's economic recovery, so much a matter of controversy in 1981, had been accepted – perhaps all too easily accepted – as a fact of life.

The 'wets' had been defeated, but they did not yet fully realize it and decided to make a last assault at the 1981 Party Conference in Blackpool that October.

The circumstances on the eve of the Conference were grim. Inflation remained stubbornly at between 11 and 12 per cent. Largely as a result of the US budget deficit, interest rates had been increased by 2 per cent in mid-September. Then, shortly after I arrived at Melbourne for the Commonwealth Conference on 30 September, I received a telephone call to say that we would have to make a second increase of 2 per cent. Interest rates now stood at an alarming 16 per cent.

Above all, unemployment continued its inexorable rise: it would reach the headline figure of three million in January 1982, but already in the autumn of 1981 it seemed almost inevitable that this would happen. Most people were unpersuaded, therefore, that recession was coming to an end and it was too soon for the new sense of direction in Cabinet to have had an effect on public opinion.

We were also in political difficulties for another reason. The weakness of the Labour Party had allowed the newly formed SDP to leap into political contention. In October the Liberals and SDP were standing at 40 per cent in the opinion polls: by the end of the year the figure was over 50 per cent. (At the Crosby by-election in the last week of November Shirley Williams was able to overturn a 19,000 Conservative majority to get back into the Commons.) On the eve of our Party Conference I was being described in the press as 'the most unpopular Prime Minister since polls began'.

In the Conference economic debate no less a figure than Ted Heath spearheaded the attack. He argued that there were alternative policies available but that we just refused to adopt them. In answer to Ted, Geoffrey Howe, who summed up our case with a cool, measured and persuasive speech, reminded the Conference of Ted's own words in his introduction to the 1970 Conservative manifesto:

> Nothing has done Britain more harm in the world than the endless backing and filling which we have seen in recent years. Once a policy has been established, the Prime Minister and his colleagues should have the courage to stick with it.

'I agree with every single word of that,' said Geoffrey. His speech won over some of the doubters and ensured that we had a comfortable win. Nevertheless, in my own speech later I felt the need to fasten down our victory by taking the arguments to Ted Heath and others head-on:

> Today's unemployment is partly due to the sharp increase in oil prices; it absorbed money that might otherwise have gone to increased investment or to buy in the things which British factories produce. But that is not all. Too much of our present unemployment is due to enormous past wage increases unmatched by higher output, to union restrictive practices, to overmanning, to strikes, to indifferent management, and to the basic belief that, come what may, the government would always step in to bail out companies in difficulty. No policy can succeed that shirks those basic issues.

Even though the 'wets' would continue to be sceptics for another six months, our policy had already begun to succeed. The early signs of recovery in the summer of 1981 were confirmed by statistics in the following quarter, which marked the start of a long period of sustained economic growth. Political recovery followed in the wake of these early signs of improvement, with better poll figures in the spring of 1982. We were about to find ourselves in the Falklands War, but we had already won the second Battle of Britain.

CHAPTER EIGHTEEN

The West and the Rest

The early reassertion of western – and British –
influence in international affairs in 1981–1982

W E WERE NOT TO KNOW IT AT THE TIME, but 1981 was the last year of the West's retreat before the axis of convenience between the Soviet Union and the Third World. The year began with Iran's release of US hostages in a manner calculated to humiliate President Carter and ended with the crushing, albeit temporarily, of Solidarity in Poland. The post-Vietnam drift of international politics, with the Soviet Union pushing further into the Third World with the help of Cuban surrogates, and the United States reacting with a nervous defensiveness, had settled into an apparently fixed pattern. Several consequences flowed from that. The Soviet Union was increasingly arrogant; the Third World was increasingly aggressive in its demands for international redistribution of wealth; the West was increasingly apt to quarrel with itself, and to cut special deals with bodies like OPEC; and our friends in Third World countries, seeing the fate of the Shah, were increasingly inclined to hedge their bets. Such countervailing trends as had been set in motion – in particular, the 1979 decision to deploy Cruise and Pershing in Europe – had not yet been given concrete effect or persuaded people that the tide had turned. In fact it had just begun to do so.

The election of Ronald Reagan as President of the United States in November 1980 was as much of a watershed in American affairs as my own election victory in May 1979 was in those of the United Kingdom, and a greater one in world politics. As the years went by, the British example steadily influenced other countries in different continents, particularly in economic policy. But Ronald Reagan's election was of immediate and fundamental importance, because it demonstrated that the United States, the greatest force for liberty that the world has known, was about to reassert a self-confident leadership in world affairs. From the first I regarded it as my duty to do everything I could to reinforce and further President Reagan's bold strategy to win the Cold War which the West had been slowly but surely losing.

I had met Governor Reagan twice when I was Leader of the Opposition. I had been immediately struck by his warmth, charm and complete lack of affectation – qualities which never altered in the years of leadership which lay ahead. Above all, I knew that I was talking to someone who instinctively felt and thought as I did; not just about policies but about a philosophy of government, a view of human nature, all the high ideals and values which lie – or ought to lie – beneath any politician's ambition to lead his country.

It was easy for lesser men to underrate Ronald Reagan. His style of work and decision-making was apparently detached and broad-brush – very different from my own. This was in part the result of our two very different systems of government rather than differences of temperament. He laid down clear general directions for his Administration, and expected his subordinates to carry them out at the level of detail. These objectives were the recovery of the American economy through tax cuts, the revival of American power by means of a defence build-up, and the reassertion of American self-confidence. Ronald Reagan succeeded in attaining these objectives because he not only advocated them; in a sense, he embodied them. He was a buoyant, self-confident, good-natured American who had risen from poverty to the White House – the American dream in action – and who was not shy about using American power or exercising American leadership in the Atlantic alliance. In addition to inspiring the American people, he went on later to inspire the people behind the Iron Curtain by speaking honest words about the evil empire that oppressed them.

At this point, however, President Reagan still had to face a largely sceptical audience at home and particularly among his allies. I was perhaps his principal cheerleader in NATO.

So I was delighted to learn that the new President wished me to be the first foreign head of government to visit the United States after he took office. When I arrived in Washington I was the centre of attention, not just because of my closeness to the new President but for another less flattering reason. As I left for America, US readers were learning from a long article in *Time* entitled 'Embattled but Unbowed' that my Government was beset with difficulties. The US press and commentators suggested that given the similarity of economic approach of the British and US Governments, the economic problems we were now facing – above all high and rising unemployment – would soon be faced in the US too. This in turn prompted some members of the Administration and others close to it to explain that the alleged failures of the 'Thatcher experiment' stemmed from our failure to be sufficiently radical. I took every occasion to explain the facts of the case both to the press and to the Senators and Congressmen whom I met. Unlike the US, Britain had to cope with the poisonous legacy of socialism – nationalization, trade union power, a deeply rooted anti-enterprise culture.

At one meeting, Senator Jesse Helms said that some of the US media were playing a requiem for my Government. I was able to reassure him that news of a requiem for my policies was premature. There was always a period during an illness when the medicine was more unpleasant than the disease, but you should not stop taking the medicine. I said that I felt there was a deep recognition among the British people that my policies were right.

I had successfully persuaded President Reagan in the course of our discussions in Washington of the importance of attending the Cancún summit which was held that October in Mexico. I felt that we should be present, both to argue for our positions and to forestall criticism that we were uninterested in the developing world. The whole concept of 'North-South' dialogue, which the Brandt Commission had made the fashion-able talk of the international community, was in my view wrong-headed. Not only was it false to suggest that there was a homogeneous rich North which confronted a homogeneous poor South: underlying the rhetoric was the idea that redistribution of world resources rather than the creation of wealth was the way to tackle poverty and hunger. Moreover, what the developing countries needed more than aid was trade, so our first responsibility was – and still is – to give them the freest possible access to our markets.

The conference's joint chairmen were President López-Portillo, our Mexican host, and Pierre Trudeau who had stepped in for the Chancellor of Austria, prevented by illness from attending. Twenty-two countries were represented. We were staying in one of those almost over-luxurious hotels which you so often seem to find in countries where large numbers of people are living in appalling poverty.

There is no immodesty in saying that Mrs Indira Gandhi and I were the two conference media 'personalities'. India had just received the largest loan yet given by the International Monetary Fund at less than the market rate of interest. She and others naturally wanted more cheap loans in the future. This was what lay behind the pressure, which I was determined to resist, to place the IMF and the World Bank directly under United Nations control. I engaged in a vigorous discussion with a group of heads of government who could not see why I felt so strongly that the integrity of the IMF and the World Bank would inevitably be compromised by such a move, which would do harm rather than good to those who were advocating it. In the end I put the point bluntly: I said that there was no way in which I was going to put British deposits into a bank which was totally run by those on overdraft. They saw the point.

While I was at Cancún I also had a separate meeting with Julius Nyerere, who was, as ever, charmingly persuasive, but equally misguided and unrealistic about what was wrong with his own country and, by extension, with so much of black Africa. He told me how unfair the IMF conditions for extending credit to him were: they had told him to bring Tanzania's public finances into order, cut protection and devalue his currency to the much lower level the market reckoned it worth. Perhaps at this time the IMF's demands were somewhat too rigorous: but he did not see that changes in this direction were necessary at all and in his own country's long-term interests. He also complained of the effects of droughts and the collapse of his country's agriculture – none of which he seemed to connect with the pursuit of misguided socialist policies, including collectivizing the farms.

The process of drafting the communiqué itself was more than usually fraught. An original Canadian draft was in effect rejected; and Pierre Trudeau left it largely to the rest of us, making clear that he thought our efforts rather less good than his own.

The summit was a success – though not really for any of the reasons publicly given. What mattered to me was that the independence of the IMF and the World Bank were maintained. Equally valuable, this was the last of such gatherings. The intractable problems of Third World poverty, hunger and debt would not be solved by misdirected international intervention, but rather by liberating enterprise, promoting trade – and defeating socialism in all its forms.

Before I left Mexico, I had one more item of business to transact. This was to sign an agreement for the building of a huge new steel plant by the British firm of Davy Loewy. Like other socialist countries, the Mexicans wrongly thought that large prestige manufacturing projects offered the best path to economic progress. However, if that was what they wanted, then I would at least try to see that British firms benefited. The ceremony required my going to Mexico City. I stayed at the residence of the British Ambassador, Crispin Tickell. While I was there at dinner the chandeliers started swinging and the floor moved. At first I thought that I must have been affected by the altitude, but I was reassured by our ambassador: 'No,' he said, 'it's just an earthquake.'

Other earthquakes were sending out tremors that year. Before I left for my international visits, I had been all too aware of the significance for the Cold War of the stationing of Cruise and Pershing missiles in Europe. If it went ahead as planned the Soviet Union would suffer a real defeat; if it was abandoned in response to the Soviet-sponsored 'peace offensive', there was a real danger of a decoupling of Europe and America. I saw it as Britain's task to put the American case in Europe since we shared their analysis but tended to put it in less ideological language. And this we did in the next few years.

But there was a second front in the Cold War – that between the West and the Soviet-Third World axis. My visits to India, Pakistan, the Gulf, Mexico and Australia for the Commonwealth Conference brought home to me how badly the Soviets had been damaged by their invasion of Afghanistan. It had alienated the Islamic countries *en bloc*, and within that bloc strengthened conservative pro-western regimes against radical states like Iraq and Libya. Traditional Soviet friends like India, on the other hand, were embarrassed. Not only did this enable the West to forge its own alliance with Islamic countries against Soviet expansionism; it also divided the Third World and so weakened the pressure it could bring against the West on international economic issues. In these circumstances, countries which had long advocated their own local form of socialism, to be paid for by western aid, suddenly had to consider a more realistic approach of attracting western investment by pursuing free market policies – a small earthquake as yet, but one that would transform the world economy over the next decade.

CHAPTER NINETEEN

The Falklands War: Follow the Fleet

The attempts by diplomacy and the sending of the task force
to regain the Falkland Islands – to the end of April 1982

NOTHING REMAINS MORE VIVIDLY in my mind, looking back on
my years in No. 10, than the eleven weeks in the spring of 1982 when
Britain fought and won the Falklands War. Much was at stake: what we
were fighting for eight thousand miles away in the South Atlantic was not
only the territory and the people of the Falklands, important though they
were. We were defending our honour as a nation, and principles of fundamental importance to the whole world – above all that aggressors should
never succeed and that international law should prevail over the use of
force. When I became Prime Minister I never thought that I would have
to order British troops into combat and I do not think I have ever lived so
tensely or intensely as during the whole of that time.

The first recorded landing on the Falklands was made in 1690 by British
sailors, who named the channel between the two principal islands 'Falkland's
Sound' in honour of the Treasurer of the Navy, Viscount Falkland. Britain,
France and Spain each established settlements on the islands at various times
during the eighteenth century. In 1770 a quarrel with Spain caused the British
Government of the day to mobilize the fleet and a naval task force was
prepared, though never sent: a diplomatic solution was found.

The islands had obvious strategic importance, possessing several good
harbours within 500 miles of Cape Horn. In the event that the Panama
Canal is ever closed their significance would be considerable. But the
Falklands were an improbable cause for a twentieth-century war.

The Argentine invasion of the Falklands took place 149 years after the
beginning of formal British rule there, and it seems that the imminence

of the 150th anniversary was an important factor in the plotting of the Argentine Junta. Since 1833 there has been a continuous and peaceful British presence on the islands. Britain's legal claim in the present day rests on that fact, and on the desire of the settled population – entirely of British stock – to remain British. The principle of 'self-determination' has become a fundamental component of international law, and is enshrined in the UN Charter. British sovereignty has strong legal foundations, and the Argentinians know it.

Some 800 miles to the south-east of the Falklands lies South Georgia, and 460 miles further out, the South Sandwich Islands. Here the Argentine claim is even more dubious. These islands are dependencies of the United Kingdom, administered from the Falklands. Their climate is severe and they have no settled population. No state claimed them before British annexation in 1908 and there has been continuous British administration since that time.

My first involvement with the Falklands issue came very early in the life of the 1979 Parliament. It was clear that there were only two ways in which the prosperity of the Falkland Islanders could be achieved. The more obvious and attractive approach was by promoting the development of economic links with neighbouring Argentina. Yet this ran up against the Argentine claim that the Falklands and the dependencies were part of their sovereign territory. Ted Heath's Government had signed an important Communications Agreement in 1971 establishing air and sea links between the islands and the mainland, but further progress had been blocked by the Argentinians unless sovereignty was also discussed. Consequently it was argued that some kind of accommodation with Argentina would have to be reached on the question of sovereignty. Arguments of this kind led Nick Ridley (the responsible minister) and his officials at the Foreign and Commonwealth Office (FCO) to advance the so-called 'lease-back' arrangement, under which sovereignty would pass to Argentina but the way of life of the islanders would be preserved by the continuation of British administration. I disliked this proposal, but Nick and I both agreed that it should be explored, subject always to the requirement that the islanders themselves should have the final word. Their wishes must be paramount.

There was, however, another option – far more costly. We could implement the recommendations of the long-term economic survey produced in 1976 by the former Labour minister, Lord Shackleton, and one recommendation in particular – the enlargement of the airport and lengthening of the runway. Such a commitment would have been seen as evidence of the British Government's determination to have no serious talks about sovereignty and it would have increased our capacity to defend the islands, since a longer runway would have allowed for rapid reinforcement by air. This in turn might have provoked a swift Argentine military response. Unsurprisingly, no government – Labour or Conservative – was prepared to act while there seemed any possibility of an acceptable solution and lease-back had become the favoured option.

However, as I rather expected, the islanders would have nothing to do with such proposals. They distrusted the Argentine dictatorship and more than that, they wanted to remain British. The House of Commons too was noisily determined that the islanders' wishes should be respected.

However, what all this meant for the future of the Falklands in the longer term was less clear. We were keen, if we could, to keep talking to the Argentinians, but diplomacy was becoming increasingly difficult. In 1976 the Argentinians had established and had maintained since a military presence on Southern Thule in the South Sandwich Islands, which the Labour Government did nothing to remove and which ministers did not even reveal to the House of Commons until 1978.

Then, in December 1981, there was a change of government in Buenos Aires. A new three-man military Junta replaced the previous military government, with General Leopoldo Galtieri as President. Galtieri relied on the support of the Argentine Navy, whose Commander-in-Chief, Admiral Anaya, held particularly hardline views on the Argentine claim to the 'Malvinas'.

There were talks in New York at the end of February 1982 which seemed to go well. But then the Argentinian line hardened abruptly. With hindsight this was a turning point. But it is important to remember how much aggressive rhetoric there had been in the past, none of it coming to anything. Moreover, based on past experience our view was that Argentina was likely to follow a policy of progressively escalating the dispute, starting with diplomatic and economic pressures. Contrary to what was said at the time, we had no intelligence until almost the last moment that Argentina was about to launch a full-scale invasion. Nor did the Americans: Al Haig later told me that they had known even less than we had.

A factor in all this was the American Administration's policy of strengthening ties with Argentina as part of its strategy of resisting Cuban-based communist influence in Central and South America, and the Argentinians had gained a wildly exaggerated idea of their importance to the

United States. They convinced themselves on the eve of the invasion that they need not take seriously American warnings against military action, and became more intransigent when diplomatic pressure was applied on them afterwards to withdraw.

Could they have been deterred? In order to take action to deter Argentina militarily, given the vast distance between Britain and the Falklands, we would have had to have some three weeks' notice. Further, to send down a force of insufficient size would have been to subject it to intolerable risk. Certainly, the presence of HMS *Endurance* – the lightly armed patrol vessel which was due to be withdrawn – was a military irrelevance. It would neither deter nor repel any planned invasion. (Indeed, when the invasion occurred I was very glad that the ship was at sea and not in Port Stanley: if she had been, she would have been captured or blown out of the water.) Most important perhaps is that nothing would have more reliably precipitated a full-scale invasion, if something less had been planned, than if we had started military preparations on the scale required to send an effective deterrent. Of course with the benefit of hindsight, we would always like to have acted differently. So would the Argentinians. This was the main conclusion of the Committee of Inquiry, chaired by Lord Franks, which we set up to examine the way we had handled the dispute in the run-up to the invasion. The committee had unprecedented access to government papers, including those of the intelligence services. Its report ends with the words: 'We would not be justified in attaching any criticism or blame to the present Government for the Argentine Junta's decision to commit its act of unprovoked aggression in the invasion of the Falkland Islands on 2 April 1982.'

It all began with an incident on South Georgia. On 20 December 1981 there had been an unauthorized landing on the island by what were described as Argentine scrap metal dealers; we had given a firm but measured response. The Argentinians subsequently left and the Argentine Government claimed to know nothing about it. I was more alarmed when, after the Anglo-Argentine talks in New York, the Argentine Government broke the procedures agreed at the meeting by publishing a unilateral communiqué disclosing the details of discussion, while simultaneously the Argentine press began to speculate on possible military action before the symbolically important date of January 1983. On 3 March 1982 I minuted on a telegram from Buenos Aires: 'we must make contingency plans' – though, in spite of my unease, I was not expecting anything like a full-scale invasion, which indeed our most recent intelligence assessment of Argentine intentions had discounted.

On 20 March we were informed that the previous day the Argentine scrap metal dealers had made a further unauthorized landing on South Georgia. The Argentine flag had been raised and shots fired. In answer to our protests the Argentine Government claimed to have no prior knowledge. We first decided that HMS *Endurance* should be instructed to remove the Argentinians, whoever they were. But we tried to negotiate with Argentina a way of resolving what still seemed to be an awkward incident rather than a precursor of conflict, so we withdrew our instructions to *Endurance* and ordered the ship to proceed instead to the British base at Grytviken, the main settlement on the island.

As March drew to a close with the incident still unresolved we became increasingly concerned. On Sunday evening, 28 March, I rang Peter Carrington to express my anxiety at the situation. He assured me that he had already made a first approach to Al Haig, the US Secretary of State, asking him to bring pressure to bear. The following morning Peter and I met at RAF Northolt on our way to the European Council at Brussels and agreed to send a nuclear-powered submarine to reinforce HMS *Endurance* and to make preparations to send a second submarine. I was not too displeased when news of the decision leaked. The submarine would take two weeks to get to the South Atlantic, but it could begin to influence events straight away. My instinct was that the time had come to show the Argentines that we meant business.

In the late afternoon of Tuesday 30 March I returned from Brussels. By that time Peter Carrington had already left on an official visit to Israel. The Foreign Office and the Ministry of Defence had been working to prepare up-to-date assessments and review the diplomatic and military options. The following day – Wednesday 31 March – I made my statement to the House reporting on the Brussels summit, but my mind was focused on what the Argentinians were intending and on what our response should be. The advice we received from intelligence was that the Argentine Government were exploring our reactions, but that they had not contrived the landing on South Georgia. By now I was deeply uneasy. Yet still I do not think that any of us expected an immediate invasion of the Falklands themselves.

I shall not forget that Wednesday evening. I was working in my room at the House of Commons when I was told that John Nott wanted an immediate meeting to discuss the Falklands. I called people together. Humphrey Atkins and Richard Luce attended from the Foreign Office, with FCO and MoD officials. (The Chief of Defence Staff was in New Zealand.) John was alarmed. He had just received intelligence that the Argentinian Fleet, already at sea, looked as if they were going to invade the islands on Friday 2 April. John gave the MoD's view that the Falklands could not be retaken once they were seized. This was terrible, and totally unacceptable: these were our people, our islands. I said instantly: 'If they are invaded, we have got to get them back.'

I asked the Chief of the Naval Staff, Sir Henry Leach, what we could do. He was quiet, calm and confident: 'I can put together a task force of destroyers, frigates, landing craft, support vessels. It will be led by the aircraft carriers HMS *Hermes* and HMS *Invincible*. It can be ready to leave in forty-eight hours.' He believed such a force could retake the islands. All he needed was my authority to begin to assemble it. I gave it him, and he left immediately. We reserved for Cabinet the decision as to whether and when the task force should sail.

Now my outrage and determination were matched by a sense of relief and confidence. Henry Leach had shown me that if it came to a fight the courage and professionalism of Britain's armed forces would win through. It was my job as Prime Minister to see that they got the political support they needed. But first we had to do everything possible to prevent the appalling tragedy.

Our only hope lay with the Americans – people to whom Galtieri, if he was still behaving rationally, should listen. We drafted and sent an urgent message to President Reagan asking him to press Galtieri to draw back from the brink. This the President immediately agreed to do.

At 9.30 on Thursday morning, 1 April, I held a Cabinet, earlier than usual so that a meeting of the Overseas and Defence Committee of the Cabinet (OD) could follow it before lunch. The latest assessment was that an Argentine assault could be expected about midday our time on Friday. We thought that President Reagan might yet succeed. However, Galtieri refused altogether at first to take the President's call. I was told of this outcome in the early hours of Friday morning and I knew then that our last hope had now gone.

At 9.45 on Friday morning Cabinet met again. I reported that an Argentine invasion was now imminent. We would meet later in the day to consider once more the question of sending a task force – though to my mind the issue by this stage was not so much whether we should act, but how.

Communications with the Falklands were often interrupted due to atmospheric conditions. On Friday morning the Governor of the Falklands – Rex Hunt – sent a message telling us that the invasion had begun, but it never got through. (Indeed, the first contact I had with him after the invasion was when he reached Montevideo in Uruguay, where the Argentinians flew him and a number of other senior people, on Saturday morning.) It was, in fact, the captain of a British Antarctic Survey vessel who intercepted a local Falkland Islands ham radio broadcast and passed on the news to the Foreign Office. My private secretary brought me final confirmation while I was at an official lunch.

By now discussion was taking place all over Whitehall about every aspect of the campaign and feverish military preparations were under way. The army was preparing its contribution. A naval task force was being formed, partly from ships currently at Gibraltar and partly from those in British ports. The Queen had already made it clear that Prince Andrew, who was serving with HMS *Invincible*, would be joining the task force: there could be no question of a member of the royal family being treated differently from other servicemen.

Cabinet met for the second time at 7.30 in the evening when the decision was made to send the task force. What concerned us most at this point was the time it would take to arrive. We believed, rightly, that the Argentinians would pile in men and materiel to make it as difficult as possible for us to dislodge them. And all the time the weather in the South Atlantic would be worsening as the violent storms of the southern winter approached.

More immediate and more manageable was the problem of how to deal with public opinion at home. Support for the dispatch of the task force was likely to be strong, but would it fall away as time went on? In fact, we need not have worried. Our policy was one which people understood and endorsed. Public interest and commitment remained strong throughout.

One particular aspect of this problem, though, does rate a mention. We decided to allow defence correspondents on the ships who reported back during the long journey. This produced vivid coverage of events. But there was always a risk of disclosing information which might be useful to the enemy. I also became very unhappy at the attempted 'even-handedness' of some of the comment, and the chilling use of the third-person – talk of 'the British' and 'the Argentinians' on our news programmes.

It was also on Friday 2 April that I received advice from the Foreign Office which summed up the flexibility of principle characteristic of that department. I was presented with the dangers of a backlash against the

British expatriates in Argentina, problems about getting support in the UN Security Council, the lack of reliance we could place on the European Community or the United States, the risk of the Soviets becoming involved, the disadvantage of being looked at as a colonial power. All these considerations were fair enough. But when you are at war you cannot allow the difficulties to dominate your thinking: you have to set out with an iron will to overcome them. And anyway what was the alternative? That a common or garden dictator should rule over the Queen's subjects and prevail by fraud and violence? Not while I was Prime Minister.

In the short term, we needed to win our case against Argentina in the UN Security Council and to secure a resolution denouncing their aggression and demanding withdrawal. On the basis of such a resolution we would find it far easier to win the support of other nations for practical measures to pressurize Argentina. But in the longer term we knew that we had to try to keep our affairs out of the UN as much as possible. With the Cold War still under way, there was a real danger that the Security Council might attempt to force unsatisfactory terms upon us. If necessary we could veto such a resolution, but to do so would diminish international support for our position. The second long-term goal was to ensure maximum support from our allies, principally the US, but also members of the EC, the Commonwealth and other important western nations. This was a task undertaken at head of government level, but an enormous burden fell on the FCO and no country was ever better served than Britain by our two key diplomats at this time: Sir Anthony Parsons, Britain's UN Ambassador and Sir Nicholas (Nico) Henderson, our ambassador in Washington.

At the UN Tony Parsons, on the eve of the invasion, was busy outmanoeuvring the Argentinians. The UN Secretary-General had called on both sides to exercise restraint: we responded positively, but the Argentinians remained silent. On Saturday 3 April, Tony Parsons managed a diplomatic triumph in persuading the Security Council to pass what became Security Council Resolution (UNSCR) 502, demanding an immediate and unconditional withdrawal by the Argentinians from the Falklands. It had not been easy. The debate was bitter and complex. We knew that the old anti-colonialist bias of the UN would incline some Security Council members against us, were it not for the fact that there had been a flagrant act of aggression by the Argentinians. I was particularly grateful to President Mitterrand who was among the staunchest of our friends and who telephoned me personally to pledge support on

Saturday. (I was to have many disputes with President Mitterrand in later years, but I never forget the debt we owed him for his personal support throughout the Falklands crisis.) France used her influence in the UN to swing others in our favour. I myself made a last-minute telephone call to King Hussein of Jordan, who also came down on our side. He is an old friend of Britain's and I did not have to go into lengthy explanations to persuade him to cast Jordan's vote on our side. He began the conversation by asking simply: 'What can I do for you, Prime Minister?' In the end we were delighted to have the votes we needed for the Resolution and to avoid a veto from the Soviet Union. But we had no illusions as to who would be left to remove the aggressor when all the talking was done: it would be us.

The debate in the House of Commons that Saturday is another very powerful memory.

The House was rightly angry that British territory had been invaded and occupied, and many Members were inclined to blame the Government for its alleged failure to foresee and forestall what had happened. My first task was to defend us against the charge of unpreparedness.

Far more difficult was my second task: convincing MPs that we would respond to Argentina's aggression forcefully and effectively.

My announcement that the task force was ready and about to sail was greeted with growls of approval. But I knew that some saw the task force as a purely diplomatic armada that would get the Argentinians back to the negotiating table. They never intended that it should actually fight, while I felt in my bones that the Argentinians would never withdraw without a fight and anything less than withdrawal was unacceptable to the country, and certainly to me. Others shared my view that the task force would have to be used, but doubted the Government's will and stamina.

That morning in Parliament I could keep the support of both groups by sending the task force out and by setting down our objectives: that the islands would be freed from occupation and returned to British administration at the earliest possible moment. I obtained the almost unanimous but grudging support of a Commons that was anxious to support the Government's policy, while reserving judgement on the Government's performance.

But I realized that even this degree of backing was likely to be eroded as the campaign wore on. I knew, as most MPs could not, the full extent of the practical military problems. I foresaw that we would encounter setbacks that would cause even some of a hawkish disposition to question whether the game was worth the candle. And how long could a coalition of opinion survive that was composed of warriors, negotiators and even virtual pacifists? For the moment, however, we received the agreement of the House of Commons for the strategy of sending the task force. And that was what mattered.

Almost immediately I faced a crisis in the Government. John Nott, who was under great strain, had delivered an uncharacteristically poor performance in his winding-up speech. He had been very harshly treated in the debate. He was held responsible by many of our backbenchers for what had happened because of the Defence Review which he had pioneered. This was unfair; but there was no doubt that the Party's blood was up: nor was it just John Nott they were after.

Peter Carrington defended the Government's position that morning in the House of Lords and had a reasonably good reception. But Peter and John then attended a packed and angry meeting of Tory backbenchers. Here, Peter was at a distinct disadvantage: as a peer he had struck up none of those friendships and understandings with backbenchers on which all of us have to rely when the pressure builds. As Ian Gow reported to me afterwards, it was a very difficult meeting, and feelings had boiled over.

The press over the weekend was very hostile. Peter Carrington was talking about resigning. I saw him on Saturday evening, Sunday morning and again in the evening. Both Willie Whitelaw and I did all that we could to persuade him to stay, but there seems always to be a visceral desire that a disaster should be paid for by a scapegoat. There is no doubt that Peter's resignation ultimately made it easier to unite the Party and concentrate on recovering the Falklands: he understood this.

John Nott also wished to resign. But I told him straight that when the fleet had put to sea he had a bounden duty to stay and see the whole thing through. He therefore withdrew his letter on the understanding that it was made public that his offer to resign had been rejected. Whatever issues might have to be faced later as a result of the full inquiry (which I announced on 8 April), now was the time to concentrate on one thing only – victory. Meanwhile, I had to find a new Foreign Secretary. The obvious choice was Francis Pym, who had had the requisite experience of Foreign Affairs in Opposition and Defence in Government. And so I appointed him, asking John Biffen to take over his former position as Leader of the House of Commons. Francis is in many ways the quintessential old-style Tory: a country gentleman and a soldier, a good tactician, but no strategist. He is the sort of man of whom people used to say that he would be 'just right in a crisis'. I was to have reason to question that judgement. Francis's appointment undoubtedly united the Party. But it heralded serious difficulties for the conduct of the campaign itself.

On Tuesday 6 April there was a long Cabinet discussion of the crisis. From the beginning, we were sure that the attitude of the United States would be a key element in the outcome. The Americans could do enormous damage to the Argentine economy if they wanted. I sent a message to President Reagan urging the US to take effective economic measures. But the Americans were not prepared to do this. Nico Henderson had his first discussions with Al Haig in which the main themes of their response over the next few weeks were already clear. They had stopped arms sales. But they would not 'tilt' too heavily against Argentina. They did not want Galtieri to fall and so wanted a solution that would save his face. There were clear signs that they were contemplating a mediation between the two sides. All of this was fundamentally misguided and Nico was very robust in his reply. But in practice the Haig negotiations almost certainly worked in our favour by precluding for a time even less helpful diplomatic intervention from other directions, including the UN. I should add, though, that from the first Caspar Weinberger, US Defense Secretary, was in touch with our ambassador, emphasizing that America could not put a NATO ally and long-standing friend on the same level as Argentina and that he would do what he could to help. America never had a wiser patriot, nor Britain a truer friend.

It was at this Cabinet that I announced we were setting up OD(SA), which became known to the outside world as 'the War Cabinet'. Formally, this was a sub-committee of OD, though several of its members did not serve on that committee. Its exact membership and procedure were influenced by a meeting I had with Harold Macmillan, who came to see me at the House of Commons after Questions on Tuesday 6 April to offer his support and advice as the country's and the Conservative Party's senior ex-Prime Minister. His main recommendation was to keep the Treasury – that is, Geoffrey Howe – off the main committee in charge of the campaign, the diplomacy and the aftermath. This was a wise course, but Geoffrey was upset. Even so I never regretted following Harold Macmillan's advice. We were never tempted to compromise the security of our forces for financial reasons. Everything we did was governed by military necessity. So the War Cabinet consisted of myself, Francis Pym,

John Nott, Willie Whitelaw as my deputy and trusted adviser, and Cecil Parkinson, who not only shared my political instincts but was brilliantly effective in dealing with public relations. Sir Terence (now Lord) Lewin, Chief of Defence Staff, always attended. So did Michael Havers, the Attorney-General, as the Government's legal adviser. Of course, we were constantly advised and supported by FCO and MoD officials and by the military. It met every day, and sometimes twice a day.

By the time of our first meeting the task force had already been dispatched with a speed and efficiency which astounded the world. Millions watched on television as the two carriers sailed from Portsmouth on Monday 5 April, and on that day and the following two they were joined by a force of eleven destroyers and frigates, three submarines, the amphibious assault ship HMS *Fearless* (crucial to the landings), and numerous naval auxiliaries. Merchantmen of all kinds were 'taken up from trade'. Three thousand troops were initially assigned to the operation – 3 Commando Brigade of the Royal Marines, the 3rd Battalion of the Parachute Regiment and a unit of the Air Defence Regiment. This first group left the UK, sailing on the cruise ship *Canberra*, on Friday 9 April. It was not always understood that to sail a large task force with troops halfway round the world, with the intention of making opposed landings, required an enormous logistical operation – both in the UK and at sea. In the end we sent over 100 ships, carrying more than 25,000 men.

The Commander-in-Chief, Fleet, was Admiral Sir John Fieldhouse; he took overall command of the task force from his base at Northwood in West London, choosing Rear Admiral Sandy Woodward as the operational commander of the surface ships in the force. (Our submarines were controlled directly from Northwood by satellite.) I had not yet met Sandy Woodward, but I knew of his reputation as one of the cleverest men in the navy. Admiral Fieldhouse's land deputy was Major-General Jeremy Moore of the Royal Marines who began the campaign in Northwood, departing for the South Atlantic in May. His deputy, who sailed with HMS *Fearless* in the first wave of ships, was Brigadier Julian Thompson, of 3 Commando Brigade. Brigadier Thompson was to have charge of our forces on the Falklands for a vital period after the landing until General Moore's arrival.

OD(SA) met twice on Wednesday 7 April. Throughout the war we were confronted with the problem of managing the intricate relationship between diplomatic and military requirements. I was determined that the needs of our servicemen should have priority over politics and it was on this day that we had to resolve our first problem of this kind. Our nuclear-powered submarines were due in the area of the Falklands within the next few days. We would therefore shortly be in a position to set up a 200-mile Maritime Exclusion Zone (MEZ*) for ships around the Falklands. Should we announce it now? Or should we postpone the announcement until after Al Haig's imminent visit the next day? For legal reasons we had to give several days' notice before the MEZ could come into effect.

In fact Al Haig's visit had to be postponed because of that day's Commons debate. At the War Cabinet which met at 7 o'clock that evening there was a classic disagreement between the MoD and the FCO on the timing of the announcement. We decided to go ahead straight away, informing Al Haig of the decision shortly in advance.

John Nott made the announcement when he wound up the debate in a speech which restored his standing and self-confidence. Not a voice was raised against the MEZ and Jim Callaghan was heard to say 'absolutely right'. It took effect in the early hours of Easter Monday morning, 12 April, by which time our submarines were in place to enforce it. It is worth noting that never during the Falklands operation did we say we would take action until we were in a position to do it. I was determined that we should never allow our bluff to be called.

All this time we were bringing as much pressure to bear on the Argentinians as we could through diplomatic methods. I had sent messages on 6 April to the heads of state and heads of government of European Community countries, the US, Japan, Canada, Australia and New Zealand. I asked them to support us against Argentina by banning arms sales, banning all or some imports, ending export credit cover for new commitments and giving no encouragement or incentive to their banks to lend to Argentina. It had been suggested at first that I should ask for a total import ban, but I thought it bad tactics to press for too much at once. The responses were now coming through. I have already mentioned those of the United States and of France, and our success in the UN Security Council. Helmut Schmidt assured me personally of West Germany's strong support. Not all the countries of the European Community were

---

* The MEZ was a circle with a 200-nautical-mile radius drawn around a point approximately at the centre of the Falkland Islands. From the time of its coming into effect Argentine warships and naval auxiliaries found in the zone would be treated as hostile and would be liable to be attacked by British forces.

as positive. There were close ties between Italy and Argentina. Though opposing the use of force, the Spanish continued to support the Argentine case and – no great surprise – the Irish caused us some concern. However, initially the EC gave us all that we asked for, imposing an embargo on Argentine imports from the middle of April for one month. When the embargo came up for renewal in mid-May there were considerable difficulties, but eventually a compromise was reached by which Italy and Ireland were able to resume links with Argentina while the other eight continued the embargo indefinitely.

The response of the Commonwealth, with the partial exception of India, had been very supportive. But we were disappointed by Japan's somewhat equivocal attitude. Predictably, the Soviet Union increasingly leaned towards Argentina and stepped up verbal attacks on our position.

Similarly, we were subject to a stream of vitriol from a number of Latin American countries – as was the US – though, because of its own long-standing disputes with Argentina, Chile was on our side. A number of others were quietly sympathetic, whatever their public stance. In this way action on the diplomatic front supported the objectives of our task force as it sailed further into the South Atlantic. And, of course, effective diplomacy would have been impossible without the dispatch of the task force. As Frederick the Great once remarked, 'Diplomacy without arms is like music without instruments.'

On Thursday 8 April Al Haig arrived in London for the first stage of his long and tiring diplomatic shuttle. I had an extremely accurate account from Nico Henderson of the propositions Mr Haig was likely to advance. We made it quite clear to him – and he accepted that this was the line we would take – that he was not being received in London as a mediator but as a friend and ally, here to discuss ways in which the United States could most effectively support us in our efforts to secure Argentine withdrawal from the Falklands. His team included Ed Streator from the US Embassy in London, General Vernon Walters, Mr Haig's special assistant – a powerful personality and someone I particularly liked and respected – and Thomas Enders who dealt with South American Affairs in the State Department. I was joined by Francis, John, Terry Lewin, Sir Antony Acland (head of the Foreign Office) and Clive Whitmore (my principal private secretary). The discussions were lively and direct, to use the diplomatic jargon: there was too much at stake for me to allow them to be anything else.

It was apparent from the beginning that, whatever might be said publicly, Al Haig and his colleagues had come to mediate. The Argentine

Foreign minister had indicated that they might accept Soviet assistance, which made the Americans extremely uncomfortable. In Al Haig's judgement the next seventy-two hours would be the best time for negotiation as far as the Argentinians were concerned. He told us that he had decided to visit Britain first because he did not wish to go to Buenos Aires without a full understanding of our approach.

I told Mr Haig that the issue was far wider than a dispute between the United Kingdom and Argentina. The use of force to seize disputed territory set a dangerous precedent. In that sense, the Falklands mattered to many countries – to Germany, for example, because of West Berlin, to France because of its colonial possessions, to Guyana, a large part of whose territory was claimed by Venezuela.

It became increasingly clear to me that Mr Haig was anxious not only to avoid what he described as '*a priori* judgements about sovereignty' but that he was aiming at something other than the British administration which I was publicly pledged to restore. The whole of his approach rested on trying to persuade the two sides to accept some kind of neutral 'interim administration' after Argentine withdrawal to run the islands while their long-term future was decided.

But Mr Haig agreed a common line with us. We would both say to the press that we wanted UNSCR 502 to be implemented as quickly as possible and had discussed how the United States could help. He had heard the British view of the situation and knew how strongly we felt, but he should not give the slightest impression that our position had changed in any way or that we were showing any flexibility.

In fact, Mr Haig may have looked back on our friendly disagreements in London with something like nostalgia when he got to Buenos Aires and began trying to negotiate with the Argentine Junta. It became evident that the Junta itself was deeply divided, and both General Galtieri and the Foreign minister, Sr Costa Mendez, seemed to alter their position from hour to hour. At one stage Mr Haig thought that he had won concessions, but as he was about to leave for England on Easter Sunday, 11 April – indeed, as he was boarding the aeroplane – Sr Costa Mendez handed him a paper which appeared to abrogate the concessions which, rightly or wrongly, he believed he had won.

By Easter Monday the first ships of the task force had begun arriving at Ascension Island, halfway to the Falklands. The American team returned to London on the morning of that day, 12 April.

Al Haig began by giving an oral account of his talks in Buenos Aires. He said that he had detected differences of view between the three Argentinian Armed Services. The navy were looking for a fight. However, the air force did not want a war, and the army were somewhere in between. He had worked out a set of proposals which he thought the Argentinians might be brought eventually to accept. There were seven main elements:

- First, both Britain and Argentina would agree to withdraw from the islands and a specified surrounding area within a two-week period.
- Second, no further military forces were to be introduced and forces withdrawn were to return to normal duties. The Argentinians had wanted an undertaking from us to keep our task force out of the South Atlantic altogether, but Al Haig said that he had told them that this was impossible and believed that they might be satisfied if the agreement provided for British units to return to normal duties.
- Third, there would be a Commission, in place of the Governor, made up of United States, British and Argentine representatives who would act together (whether by unanimity or majority was not specified) to ensure compliance with the agreement. For that purpose they would each need to have observers. Each member of the Commission could fly his flag at headquarters.
- Fourth, economic and financial sanctions against Argentina would be lifted.
- Fifth, the traditional local administration of the islands would be restored, including the re-establishment of the Executive and Legislative Councils, to which Argentine representatives from the tiny Argentine population in the Falklands would be added. The Argentinians were adamantly opposed to the return of our Governor.
- Sixth, the Commission would promote travel, trade and communications between the islands and Argentina, but the British Government would have a veto on its operations.
- Finally, negotiations on a lasting settlement would be pursued 'consistently with the Purposes and Principles of the United Nations Charter'. The United States had apparently insisted on this because of the references in it to the right of self-

determination. It seemed that the Argentinians would only
have been prepared to agree to this part of the proposals if
they contained a date for the conclusion of negotiations,
which was suggested as 31 December 1982.

At this time, I did not attempt to reply to Al Haig's proposals point by
point: I simply restated my belief in the principle of self-determination. If
the Falkland Islanders chose to join Argentina, the British Government
would respect their decision. But, equally, the Argentine Government
should be prepared to accept an expressed wish of the islanders to remain
British. The Americans then left us for ninety minutes, as we had agreed
in advance, while we discussed the proposals with the other members of
the War Cabinet.

Al Haig's proposals had some attractions. If we could really get the
Argentine forces off the islands by conceding what seemed a fairly power-
less commission, very limited Argentine representation on each council –
drawn from local residents and not nominated by the Junta – and an
Argentine flag flown alongside others at Headquarters there was something
to be said for these ideas. However, on closer inspection there were formidable difficulties. What security would there be for the islanders after the
interim period? Clearly, the United States would have to be asked to guarantee the islands against renewed invasion. Then there were the inescapable
geographical realities. The Argentinians would remain close to the Falklands; but if we had to withdraw to 'normal areas' where would our forces
be? We must have the right to be at least as close as the Argentine forces. In
spite of the general reference to the UN Charter, there was still nothing to
make it clear that the islanders' wishes must be paramount in the final
negotiations. There must also be no possibility of the Argentinians steadily
increasing the number of their people on the islands during the interim
period so as to become the majority – a serious worry, particularly if our
people started to leave, which they might well do in those circumstances.

At this point Francis Pym, John Nott and I rejoined Al Haig. I said that
I was very grateful for the tremendous amount of work which he had
done but that I had a number of questions. What did the Americans
envisage would happen if no final settlement had been reached by 31
December 1982? The answer was not entirely clear – nor did it become
clearer with the passage of time. I emphasized again the importance
attached by the House of Commons to the principle of self-determination for the islanders. We would have to have some specific reference to

Article 1(2) and Article 73 of the UN Charter on this matter, which enshrined the principle of self-determination. We recognized, however, that Argentina would place a different gloss upon the agreement from the British Government. Al Haig accepted this.

On the matter of their flag, I told Al Haig that wherever else it flew, it must not fly over the Governor's house. He said that for the Argentinians the governorship of the Falklands was a key issue: they wanted to keep the Governor they had appointed after the invasion on the island as a commissioner. I said that if they did that, the British Government would have to appoint Rex Hunt as our commissioner. I also raised the question of South Georgia where Britain had an absolute title. Al Haig saw no problem about this. (We regretted afterwards that we had ever put South Georgia into the first proposals. But at the time there seemed a possibility of getting the Argentines off without a battle and they had occupied the island shortly after their invasion of the Falklands themselves.)

However, the main issue was always bound to be the military one. I knew that the only reason the Argentinians were prepared to negotiate at all was because they feared our task force. I stressed that although British submarines in the proposed demilitarized zone would leave as the Argentine forces withdrew, the British task force must continue to proceed southwards, though it would not enter the demilitarized zone. This was essential: we could not afford to let the Argentinians invade a second time. One concession I might be prepared to make was that the task force could be stood off at a point no closer to the Falklands than Argentine forces were based. Anything less would be unacceptable to Parliament.

Our two teams met once more just before 6 p.m. Al Haig said that President Galtieri would not survive if after the Argentinians had committed themselves to withdrawing from the Falkland Islands in two weeks the British newspapers continued to report that the task force was proceeding south. The Americans were not asking for our fleet to be turned around: but they were asking for it to be halted once an agreement had been reached. I replied that I would not survive in the House of Commons if I stopped the task force before Argentine withdrawal had been completed. I was ready to let the troop ships proceed more slowly once an agreement had been signed. But the main task force must maintain its progress towards the Falkland Islands.

We argued until late into the evening. Argentina, starting from the Communications Agreement of 1971, wanted their citizens to have the same rights to reside on the islands, own property and so on, as the Falklanders. They wanted the commission positively to promote that state of affairs and to decide upon such matters. We fought the proposal down on the grounds that the interim administration must not change the nature of life on the islands. We finally agreed that we would pursue further negotiations on a somewhat woolly text. There were, however, some conditions which had to be made absolutely clear – the withdrawal zones, the fact that the one Argentine representative per council must be local, and that Argentinians on the islands must have the same qualifying period for voting as the Falklanders.

Just before 10 o'clock that night Al Haig telephoned me to say that Sr Costa Mendez had rung him to say that he saw no reason for the Secretary of State to go to Buenos Aires again unless any agreement about the Falkland Islands provided for the Governor to be appointed by the Argentine Government and for the Argentine flag to continue to be flown there. And if that was not possible, the Argentinians must have assurances that at the end of negotiations with Britain there would be a recognition of Argentine sovereignty over the Falkland Islands. Al Haig was shattered.

Having decided not to go on to Buenos Aires, the following morning the Americans sought another meeting with us. By this stage it was becoming obvious that the proposals the Americans had presented to us the previous day had no measure of Argentine approval. In fact, the status of all these proposals was doubtful. The more closely I questioned Al Haig on this point, the more uncertain it became. Since the proposals had not been agreed with the Argentinians, even if we accepted them, they might therefore not form the basis of a settlement.

This fact was made painfully clear at the meeting that morning when Mr Haig handed us a document embodying five points which he described as essential to the Argentine position.

I was becoming impatient with all this. I said that it was essentially an issue of dictatorship versus democracy. The question now was whether Galtieri could be diverted from his course by economic sanctions or, as I had suspected all along, only by military force. Mr Haig replied that he had made it abundantly clear to Argentina that if conflict developed the United States would side with Britain. But did we wish to bring the negotiations to an end today? He could say publicly that he was suspending his own efforts, making it clear that this was due to Argentine intransigence. But if he did so, other less helpful people might try to intervene.

Later that day events took another bizarre turn. Al Haig told Francis Pym of the contents of a further discussion he had had on the telephone with Sr Costa Mendez. Apparently, the Argentinians had now dropped their five demands and moved a considerable way from their previous position. Mr Haig thought there was a chance of a settlement on the lines we had been discussing, if we would agree to language about decolonization, subject to the wishes of islanders, with perhaps one or two small changes in addition to make the proposals more palatable still. It was to turn out that this talk of decolonization held its own particular danger, though we agreed to look at a draft. He also urged us not to be too rigid on the question of sovereignty. He had decided to return to Washington and would decide his next step there.

It was clear from all this that Mr Haig was very anxious to keep the negotiations going. But had there been a genuine change of heart on the part of the Argentinians?

Wednesday 14 April was the day scheduled for a further Commons debate on the Falklands. It was an opportunity for me to spell out our objectives in the negotiations and to demonstrate to the outside world the united support of the House of Commons.

While the debate was still in progress, Al Haig was on the telephone. The Argentinians were complaining that the United States was not being even-handed between Argentina and Britain and in particular that it was supplying military aid to Britain. He wanted to make a statement which would allow him to return to Buenos Aires to continue the negotiations, ending with these three sentences:

> Since the outset of the crisis the United States has not acceded to requests that would go beyond the scope of customary patterns of co-operation. That would continue to be its stand while peace efforts were under way. Britain's use of US facilities on Ascension Island had been restricted accordingly.

While the debate continued, I discussed it with Francis Pym and, half an hour later, rang Al Haig.

I was very unhappy about what he wanted to say and I told him so. Of course, a good deal was being done to help us. This was occurring within those 'customary patterns of co-operation' which applied between allies like the United States and Britain. But to link this with the use of Ascension Island was wrong and misleading. Moreover, to make such a statement would have a very adverse reaction on UK opinion.

I went on to point out that Ascension Island was our island, indeed the Queen's island. The Americans used it as a base – but, as the Secretary of State well knew, this was under an agreement which made it clear that sovereignty remained with us. I am glad to say that Mr Haig agreed to remove all mentions of Ascension Island from his statement.

The following day Al Haig flew to Buenos Aires for further talks. Back in London, the War Cabinet met that morning not in No. 10 but in the Ministry of Defence. We had important decisions to make. More troops were needed and had to be sent to join the task force. We had to look at the new draft we had agreed the previous day to consider. (Nothing came of it in the end.) We also had to prepare a message to the United States stressing the need for them to help enforce the agreement during that period and to ensure that when it ended the Argentinians did not attempt another invasion. I am afraid that we never got very far: the Americans were not keen to accept the role of guarantor.

Our main task on Friday 16 April was to consider and approve the rules of engagement which would apply for transit from Ascension Island, for the 200-mile zone around South Georgia and for the purposes of South Georgia's repossession. The rules of engagement are the means by which the politicians authorize the framework within which the military can be left to make the operational decisions. They have to satisfy the objectives for which a particular military operation is undertaken. They must also give the man on the spot reasonable freedom to react as is required and to make his decisions knowing that they will be supported by the politicians. So the rules have to be clear and to cover all possible eventualities. It was after very careful questioning and long discussion that they were approved.

I had received the day before a message from President Reagan who had been rung by Galtieri, who apparently said that he was anxious to avoid a conflict. There was no difficulty in replying to that. I told the President:

> I note that General Galtieri has reaffirmed to you his desire to avoid conflict. But it seems to me – and I must state this frankly to you as a friend and ally – that he fails to draw the obvious conclusion. It was not Britain who broke the peace but Argentina. The mandatory Resolution of the Security Council, to which you and we have subscribed, requires Argentina to withdraw its troops from the Falkland Islands. That is the essential first step which

must be taken to avoid conflict. When it has been taken, discussions about the future of the islands can profitably take place. Any suggestion that conflict can be avoided by a device that leaves the aggressor in occupation is surely gravely misplaced. The implications for other potential areas of tension and for small countries everywhere would be of extreme seriousness. The fundamental principles for which the free world stands would be shattered.

On Friday 17 April our two vital aircraft carriers HMS *Hermes* and HMS *Invincible* reached Ascension Island.

After a week of labyrinthine negotiations, I spent the weekend at Chequers. I found time to have a private lunch with friends and an artist who was going to paint a view of the house and its surroundings. However, I had to return to No. 10 briefly on Saturday evening to receive a telephone call from President Reagan – there is a direct line from Chequers to the White House, but there were technical problems that day. I was glad to have the chance to go over the issues with the President. Al Haig had found the Argentinians even more impossible than on his first visit. The White House had instructed him to tell the Junta that if they persisted in their intransigence this would lead to a breakdown of talks and the US Administration would make clear who was to blame.

On Sunday, far away in the Atlantic HMS *Hermes*, *Invincible*, *Glamorgan*, *Broadsword*, *Yarmouth*, *Alacrity* and the Royal Fleet Auxiliaries *Olmeda* and *Resource* left Ascension Island for the south.

It was on Monday that I first read the details of the proposals discussed by Al Haig and the Argentinians in Buenos Aires. They were quite unacceptable. The closer one looked the clearer it was that Argentina was still trying to keep what it had taken by force. They were intent on subverting the traditional local administration by insisting that two representatives of the Argentine Government should serve on each of the Island Councils. They wanted to flood the islands with their own people to change the nature of the population. Finally, they were not prepared to allow the islanders to choose if they wished to return to the British administration they had enjoyed before the invasion. The wording of their proposal was:

> December 31st 1982 will conclude the interim period during which the signatories shall conclude negotiations on modalities for the removal of the islands from the list of non-self-governing territo-

ries under Chapter XI of the United Nations Charter and on mutually agreed conditions for their definitive status, including due regard for the rights of the inhabitants and for the principle of territorial integrity applicable to this dispute . . .

The innocuous sounding reference to removing the islands from the list under Chapter XI ruled out a return to the *status quo ante* the invasion and so effectively denied the islanders the right to choose freely the form of government under which they were to live. A great many words to shroud the simple fact that the use of force would have succeeded, dictatorship would have prevailed and the wishes of the islanders would have been overridden. We told Al Haig that we saw no need for him to come to London from Buenos Aires and promised to let him have detailed comments on the text when he returned to Washington.

On the same day I received a telegram from Buenos Aires which confirmed that there was no apparent let-up in the Junta's determination to secure sovereignty over the islands. Every five minutes or so Argentine Radio would play the 'Malvinas song' which ran, 'I am your fatherland and may need you to die for me.' Soon that sentiment would be put to the test: it was on this day that the War Cabinet authorized the operation to repossess South Georgia – although the recovery was somewhat delayed because our ships arrived in a Force 11 gale which lasted for several days.

Al Haig asked that Francis Pym should go to Washington to discuss our views of the Argentine text and I agreed to this. Francis sent ahead our detailed comments and essential amendments to the Buenos Aires text. We agreed that he was to be guided by these counter-proposals during his visit. He was also to seek an American guarantee for the security of the islands. Unfortunately during questions on a Commons statement the following day, Francis gave the impression that force would not be used as long as negotiations were continuing. This was an impossible position for us to take up, enabling the Argentinians to string us along indefinitely, and he had to return to the House to make a short statement retracting the remark.

Also on Wednesday we notified Al Haig via Nico Henderson that a firm decision had been taken to recover South Georgia in the near future. Mr Haig expressed himself surprised and concerned. He asked whether our decision was final: I confirmed that it was. We were informing, not consulting him. Later he told our ambassador that he thought he would have to give the Argentine Junta advance notice of our intended operation. We were appalled. Nico Henderson persuaded him to think better of it.

That Thursday evening John Nott and the Chief of the Defence Staff came to Downing Street to give me urgent news. Our Special Forces had landed on the Fortuna glacier in South Georgia to carry out a reconnaissance. But the weather then rapidly worsened with a south-west wind gusting over 70 knots. Their exposed position on the glacier became intolerable and they sent a message to HMS *Antrim* asking for helicopters to take them off. The first helicopter came in and, blinded by the snow, crashed. A second suffered the same fate. The MoD did not know whether lives had been lost. It was a terrible and disturbing start to the campaign.

My heart was heavy as I changed for a charity dinner at the Mansion House at which I was to be the main speaker. How was I to conceal my feelings? But just as I reached the foot of the stairs at No. 10, Clive Whitmore, my principal private secretary, rushed out of his office with more news. A third helicopter had landed on the glacier and picked up all the SAS men and the other two helicopter crews. How that pilot managed it I do not know. Months later I met him – completely modest, quietly professional: his comment was that he had never seen so many people in his helicopter. As I carried on out of No. 10 and left for the dinner I walked on air. All our people had survived.

Francis Pym was now on his way back from the United States with new draft proposals.

Saturday 24 April was to be one of the most crucial days in the Falklands story and a critical one for me personally. Early that morning Francis came to my study in No. 10 to tell me the results of his efforts. I can only describe the document which he brought back as conditional surrender. I told Francis that the terms were totally unacceptable. They would rob the Falklanders of their freedom and Britain of her honour and respect. Francis disagreed. He thought that we should accept what was in the document. We were at loggerheads.

A meeting of the War Cabinet had been arranged for that evening and I spent the rest of that day comparing in detail all the different proposals which had been made up to that point. The closer I looked the clearer it was that our position was being abandoned and the Falklanders betrayed. I asked for the Attorney-General to come to No. 10 and go through them with me. But the message went astray and instead he went to the Foreign Office. Less than an hour before the War Cabinet, he at last received the message and came to see me, only to confirm all my worst fears.

It is important to understand that what might appear at first glance to the untutored eye as minor variations in language between diplomatic texts can be of vital significance, as they were in this case. There were four main texts to compare. There were the proposals which Al Haig discussed with us and took to Argentina on 12 April. Our own attitude towards these had been left deliberately vague; though he had discussed them in detail with us, we had not committed ourselves to accept them. Then there were the totally impossible proposals brought back by Mr Haig after his visit to Buenos Aires on 19 April. On 22 April we amended those proposals in ways acceptable to us and it was on this basis that Francis Pym had been instructed to negotiate. Finally, there was the later draft brought back by Francis from the United States, which now confronted me. The differences between the texts of 22 and 24 April went to the heart of why we were prepared to fight a war for the Falklands.

First, there was the question of how far and fast would our forces withdraw. Under the text Francis Pym had brought back our task force would have had to stand off even further than in the Buenos Aires proposals. Worse still, all of our forces would have to leave the defined zones within seven days, depriving us of any effective military leverage over the withdrawal process. What if the Argentinians went back on the deal? Nor was there any way of ensuring that Argentine troops kept to the provision that they be 'at less than 7 days' readiness to invade again' (whatever that meant).

Second, sanctions against Argentina were to be abandoned the moment the agreement was signed, rather than as in our counter-proposals on completion of withdrawal. Thus we lost the only other means we had to ensure that Argentine withdrawal actually took place.

Third, as regards the Special Interim Authority the text reverted to the Buenos Aires proposals for two representatives of the Argentine Government on the Islands' Councils, as well as at least one representative of the local Argentine population. Moreover, there was a return to the wording relating to Argentine residence and property which would effectively have allowed them to swamp the existing population with Argentinians.

Equally important was the wording relating to the long-term negotiations after Argentine withdrawal. Like the Buenos Aires document, Francis Pym's ruled out the possibility of a return to the situation enjoyed by the islanders before the invasion. We would have gone against our commitment to the principle that the islanders' wishes were paramount and would have abandoned all possibility of their staying with us. Did Francis realize how much he had signed away?

Despite my clear views expressed that morning, Francis put in a paper to the War Cabinet recommending acceptance of these terms. Shortly before 6 o'clock that evening ministers and civil servants began assembling outside the Cabinet Room. Francis was there, busy lobbying for their support. I asked Willie Whitelaw to come upstairs and told him that I could not accept these terms and gave him my reasons. As always on crucial occasions he backed my judgement.

The meeting began and Francis Pym introduced his paper, recommending that we concur in the plan. But five hours of preparation on my part had not been wasted. I went through the text clause by clause. What did each point actually mean? How come that we had now accepted what had previously been rejected? Why had we not insisted as a minimum on self-determination? Why had we accepted almost unlimited Argentine immigration and acquisition of property on an equal basis with the existing Falkland Islanders? The rest of the committee were with me.

It was John Nott who found the procedural way forward. He proposed that we should make no comment on the draft but ask Mr Haig to put it to the Argentinians first. If they accepted it we should undoubtedly be in difficulties: but we could then put the matter to Parliament in the light of their acceptance. If the Argentinians rejected it – and we thought that they would, because it is almost impossible for any military Junta to withdraw – we could then urge the Americans to come down firmly on our side, as Al Haig had indicated they would as long as we did not break off the negotiations. This is what was decided. I duly sent our message to Mr Haig.

Later that afternoon I learnt of our success in South Georgia. An audience was arranged with the Queen that evening at Windsor. I was glad to be able personally to give her the news that one of her islands had been recovered. I returned to Downing Street to await confirmation of the earlier signal and the release of the news. I wanted John Nott to have the opportunity of making the announcement and so I had him come to No. 10. Together, he, the MoD press officer and I drafted the press release and then went out to announce the good news.

A remark of mine was misinterpreted, sometimes wilfully. After John Nott had made his statement journalists tried to ask questions. 'What happens next Mr Nott? Are we going to declare war on Argentina Mrs Thatcher?' It seemed as if they preferred to press us on these issues rather than to report news that would raise the nation's spirits and give the Falklanders new heart. I was irritated. 'Just rejoice at that news and congratulate our forces and the marines . . . Rejoice.' I meant that they should rejoice in the bloodless recapture of South Georgia, not in the war itself. To me war is not a matter for rejoicing. But some pretended otherwise.

At home the apparent imminence of full-scale military conflict began to shake the determination of those whose commitment to retaking the Falklands had always been weaker than it appeared. Some MPs seemed to want negotiations to continue indefinitely.

Unfortunately, the cracks now appearing in the Labour Party were likely to be widened by what was happening at the United Nations. The Secretary-General of the UN started to become more involved. A low-key appeal from Sr Perez de Cuellar to both sides – which appeared to imply that we, like Argentina, had failed to comply with UNSCR 502 – was seized upon by Denis Healey and Michael Foot. I had a serious clash with Mr Foot during Prime Minister's Questions on Tuesday 27 April on the question of our returning to the United Nations. In fact, the Secretary-General very quickly took the point, but the damage was done. We ourselves had been exploring whether an offer from President López-Portillo of Mexico to provide a venue for negotiations might be productive. But Al Haig did not wish us to pursue this.

Al Haig had had his own share of diplomatic problems. The Argentine Foreign minister, furious at the retaking of South Georgia, had publicly refused to see him, though they had been in contact privately.

Mr Haig had again modified the proposals discussed with Francis Pym in Washington and now transmitted these to the Argentine Government. He told the Junta that no amendments were permissible and imposed a strict time limit for their reply, though he was subsequently unwilling to stick to this.

At Cabinet on Thursday 29 April we discussed the continuing uncertainty. The deadline given to the Argentinians for their answer had passed, but now Mr Haig was talking of the possibility of the Argentinians amending his proposals. Where would all this end?

After Cabinet I sent a message to President Reagan saying that in our view the Argentinians must now be regarded as having rejected the American proposals. In fact, later that day the Argentinians did formally reject the American text. President Reagan now replied to my message in these terms:

I am sure you agree that it is essential now to make clear to the world that every effort was made to achieve a fair and peaceful solution, and that the Argentine Government was offered a choice between such a solution and further hostilities. We will therefore make public a general account of the efforts we have made. While we will describe the US proposal in broad terms, we will not release it because of the difficulty that might cause you. I recognize that while you see fundamental difficulties in the proposal, you have not rejected it. We will leave no doubt that Her Majesty's Government worked with us in good faith and was left with no choice but to proceed with military action based on the right of self-defence.

Friday 30 April effectively marked the end of the beginning of our diplomatic and military campaign to regain the Falklands. The United States now came down clearly on our side. President Reagan told television correspondents that the Argentinians had resorted to armed aggression and that such aggression must not be allowed to succeed. Most important, the President also directed that the United States would respond positively to requests for military materiel. Unfortunately, they were not prepared to agree to place an embargo on imports from Argentina. However, the President's announcement constituted a substantial moral boost to our position.

It was on this day the TEZ came into force. And it is fair to say that from now on it was the military rather than the diplomatic which increasingly commanded our attention. At that morning's War Cabinet it was the Argentine aircraft carrier, the *25 de Mayo*, which concerned us. She could cover 500 miles a day and her aircraft a further 500. Her escorts carried Exocet missiles, supplied by France in the 1970s. The Exocet threat had to be taken seriously. It increased the danger which the Argentine carrier group posed to our ships and their supply lines. We therefore authorized an attack on the carrier, wherever she was, provided it was south of latitude 35 degrees and east of longitude 48, and outside the 12-mile limit of Argentine territorial waters. Such an attack would be based upon the right of self-defence and be within Article 51 of the UN Charter; in accordance with the notification which had been given on 23 April no further warning was required.

CHAPTER TWENTY

The Falklands: Victory

The battle for the Falklands in May and June 1982

F ROM THE BEGINNING OF MAY through to the recapture of the Falklands in mid-June military considerations loomed ever larger in my mind. But this did not mean that the pressure for negotiations eased – far from it. I was under an almost intolerable pressure to negotiate for the sake of negotiation and because so many politicians were desperately anxious to avoid the use of force – as if the Argentinians had not already used force by invading in the first place. And all this time there was constant, nagging fear of the unknown. Would we have sufficient air cover? Where were the Argentine submarines? Would we be able to reach the military and diplomatic position required for a successful landing within that narrow time-frame set by the onset of intolerable winter weather in the South Atlantic?

Over breakfast at Milton Hall in Stephen Hastings's constituency I received a telephone call to say that our Vulcans had bombed the runway of Port Stanley airport. Our naval task force was also bombarding Argentine positions elsewhere on the Falklands. There had so far been no British casualties but it would still be many hours before the Vulcans – after their marathon flight involving five mid-air refuellings – would be back at Ascension Island. In fact they all returned safely.

That day the Argentine Air Force mounted a major attack on our ships. The Argentinians were in a position to send photographs to the outside world, which we were not. They claimed that many of our aeroplanes had been shot down but in that famous broadcast Brian Hanrahan, the excellent BBC correspondent, put the record straight when he reported: 'I counted them all out and I counted them all back.' It was a great relief.

The next day, Sunday, which I spent at Chequers, was one of great – though often misunderstood – significance for the outcome of the Falklands War. The members of the War Cabinet, Chiefs of Staff and officials came to Chequers for lunch and discussion. On this occasion there was a special matter on which I needed an urgent decision.

I called together Willie Whitelaw, John Nott, Cecil Parkinson, Michael Havers, Terry Lewin, Admiral Fieldhouse and Sir Antony Acland. (Francis Pym was in America.) Admiral Fieldhouse told us that one of our submarines, HMS *Conqueror*, had been shadowing the Argentine cruiser, *General Belgrano*. The *Belgrano* was escorted by two destroyers. The cruiser itself had substantial firepower provided by 6 guns with a range of 13 miles and anti-aircraft missiles. We were advised that she might have been fitted with Exocet anti-ship missiles, and her two destroyer escorts were known to be carrying them. The whole group was sailing on the edge of the Exclusion Zone. There had been extensive air attacks on our ships the previous day and Admiral Woodward had every reason to believe that a full-scale attack was developing. The Argentine aircraft carrier, the *25 de Mayo*, had been sighted some time earlier and we had agreed to change the rules of engagement to deal with the threat she posed. However, our submarine had lost contact with the carrier and there was a strong possibility that *Conqueror* might also lose contact with the *Belgrano* group. From all the information available, Admiral Woodward concluded that the carrier and the *Belgrano* group were engaged in a classic pincer movement against the task force. It was clear to me what must be done to protect our forces. We therefore decided that British forces should be able to attack any Argentine naval vessel on the same basis as agreed previously for the carrier.

The necessary order conveying the change of rules of engagement was sent from Northwood to HMS *Conqueror* at 1.30 p.m but it was not until after 5 p.m. that *Conqueror* reported that she had received the order. The *Belgrano* was torpedoed and sunk just before 8 o'clock that evening. Our submarine headed away as quickly as possible. Wrongly believing that they would be the next targets, the *Belgrano*'s escorts seem to have engaged in anti-submarine activities rather than rescuing its crew, some 321 of whom were lost. The ship's poor state of battle readiness greatly increased the casualties. Back in London we knew that the *Belgrano* had been hit, but it was some hours before we knew that she had sunk.

A large amount of malicious and misleading nonsense was circulated about the reasons why we sank the *Belgrano*. These allegations have been demonstrated to be without foundation. The decision to sink the *Belgrano* was taken for strictly military not political reasons: the claim that we were trying to undermine a promising peace initiative from Peru will not bear scrutiny. Those of us who took the decision at Chequers did not at that time know anything about the Peruvian proposals, which in any case closely resembled the Haig plan rejected by the Argentinians only days before. There was a clear military threat which we could not responsibly ignore. Moreover, subsequent events more than justified what was done. As a result of the devastating loss of the *Belgrano*, the Argentine Navy – above all the carrier – went back to port and stayed there. The sinking of the *Belgrano* turned out to be one of the most decisive military actions of the war.

Both military and diplomatic pressure now mounted. On Tuesday 4 May the destroyer HMS *Sheffield* was hit by an Argentine Exocet missile with devastating effects. It was a terrible demonstration of the risks our forces faced. The *Sheffield* was a relatively old ship, with outdated radar: it was transmitting via satellite to London moments before the missile struck, interfering with its capacity to detect the attack sufficiently in advance to throw up chaff as a decoy. Also the fire doors were open and, as we learnt from the raging fire that followed the missile impact, there was too much aluminium in the structure. At first I was told that there were 20 casualties: then 40.

It was very difficult to know how to announce this sort of news. We would have liked to inform all next of kin first, and indeed sought to do so. But meanwhile the Argentinians would be putting out statements – some true, some false but all with a deliberate purpose – before we knew the real facts. As a result, wives and families spent some agonizing days and nights. That day we also lost one of our Harriers.

By this stage Francis Pym had returned from the United States. We did not like the US/Peruvian proposals he brought with him, but Al Haig would not accept our changes or pass them to the Peruvians because he believed that the Argentinians would reject them out of hand. I received a message from President Reagan urging us to make further compromise.

On the morning of Wednesday 5 May I called first the War Cabinet and then the full Cabinet to consider the US/Peruvian proposals. I was deeply unhappy about them and Cabinet did not like them much either. But we had to make some response. I wanted to ensure that any interim administration would consult the islanders and that their wishes should be respected in the long-term settlement. I also wanted South Georgia and the other Falklands dependencies to be outside the scope of the proposals. Cabinet was firm about these objectives. We agreed to seek changes to meet them and in this we were successful.

Tony Parsons defended Britain's position at the UN with great force and brilliance. The Argentinians were clearly determined to get the maximum propaganda advantage in the discussions sponsored by the UN Secretary-General, but I was not prepared to hold up military progress for negotiations. We were coming to a critical period. If we were to land and repossess the islands it would have to be done between 16 and 30 May. We could not leave it later because of the weather. That meant that negotiations at the UN must be completed within ten days or so. If they were successful and our principles and minimum requirements were met, well and good. If not, or they were still dragging on, then – if the Chiefs of Staff so advised – we would have to go ahead.

As the negotiations with the Argentinians in Washington continued it became ever more evident that they were not prepared to make the concessions we required. An ultimatum was obviously necessary.

We now had to stand firm against the pressure for making unacceptable compromises while avoiding the appearance of intransigence. Specific instructions went to Tony Parsons about our position on withdrawal distances, interim administration, the issue of immigration and the acquisition of property during the interim period and to ensure that the Argentinians did not get away with prejudging the issue on sovereignty. There were detailed discussions on the constitutional position of a United Nations administration of the islands. Our view was that the UN representative could only administer the law, not change it. We also continued to press for a United States military guarantee of the security of the islands – but with very limited success. The UN Secretary-General was somewhat taken aback by the firmness of our stance. But Tony Parsons impressed on him the basic facts of the dispute. It was not we who had committed the aggression; any arrangement which appeared to reward Argentine aggression would simply not be accepted in Britain.

Al Haig was now in Europe and his absence apparently gave those in the Administration who were favourable to the Argentinians an opportunity to persuade President Reagan that it was we who were being inflexible. President Reagan telephoned me at 6.40 that evening. He had gained the impression that the Argentinians and ourselves were now quite close in our negotiating positions. I had to tell him that unfortunately this was not the case. Major obstacles remained. President Reagan was also concerned that the struggle was being portrayed as one between David and Goliath – in which the United Kingdom was cast as Goliath. I pointed out that this could hardly be true at a distance of 8,000 miles. I reminded the President that he would not wish his people to live under the sort of regime offered by the military Junta and also of the length of time that many of the islanders had lived there, and the strategic significance of the Falkland Islands if, for example, the Panama Canal were ever closed. I finished by seeking to persuade him – I believe successfully – that he had been misinformed about the Argentinians' alleged concessions. It was a difficult conversation but on balance probably a useful one. The fact that even our closest ally could look at things in this way demonstrated the difficulties we faced.

That Sunday at Chequers was mainly spent in drafting our own final proposals, to be put to the Argentinians by the UN Secretary-General. The vital consideration was that we bring the negotiating process to an end – ideally, before the landings – but in such a way as to avoid appearing intransigent. It became clear that we would have to make a very reasonable offer. I accepted this because I was convinced that the Argentinians would reject it, and strictly on a take-it-or-leave-it basis: the Argentinians must accept the offer as a whole, or not at all, and once rejected, it would be withdrawn. We would set a time limit for their response.

Tony Parsons and Nico Henderson – back in Britain – were both closely involved in the drafting. We went over every point in detail, remodelling the draft clause by clause. At hand were voluminous refer-ence sources on the UN and the law relating to the administration of the Falklands. We hardened our terms in respect of interim administration, ensuring something close to self-government for the islanders and denying any role to the Argentine Government. We excluded South Georgia and the other dependencies from the proposals altogether. We made reference to Article 73 of the UN Charter, which implies self-deter-mination, to make it clear that the wishes of the islanders would be para-mount in long-term negotiations. The Argentine Government was required to give a response within 48 hours and there was to be no nego-tiation of the terms. This exercise also allowed me subsequently to explain each phrase to the House of Commons to allay their understandable fears that we might be prepared to yield too much.

* * *

On the morning of Tuesday 18 May the War Cabinet met with all the Chiefs of Staff. It was perhaps the crucial moment. We had to decide whether to go ahead with the landing on the Falklands; I asked each Service Chief to give his views. The difficulties were clear: we would be vulnerable on landing and, in particular, there were doubts whether we had enough air cover. We had not been able to knock out as many Argentine ships or aircraft as we would have liked in the weeks before the landing. And always there was the fact that we had not been able to locate their submarines.

But it was also clear that the longer the delay, the greater the risk of losses and the worse the condition of our troops when they had to fight. The troops could not remain on board ship indefinitely. The judgement was that the advantages of landing outweighed the risks of postponement. The rules of engagement had already been agreed. The attack would be by night.

None of us now doubted what must be done. We authorized the landing on the basis of the Force Commander's plan, subject to the Cabinet's final approval. It could be stopped any time until late on Thursday which would allow us thoroughly to consider any reply from the Argentinians to our proposals. Beyond that, the timing was for the Force Commander himself.

In fact, on the next day, Wednesday, we received the Argentine response, which was in effect a comprehensive rejection of our proposals. We had decided earlier – at Francis Pym's suggestion – that following Argentine rejection we would publish them, and we did so on 20 May. This was the first time during the whole of the diplomatic manoeuvring that either side had made public their actual negotiating position and our terms created a good international impression.

The Secretary-General made a last-minute attempt in messages to me and General Galtieri to put forward his own proposals. On Thursday morning (20 May) the War Cabinet met before the full Cabinet. Once again, Francis urged a compromise. He suggested that the Secretary-General's *aide-mémoire* was very similar to our own proposals and that it would not be understood if we now went ahead with military measures. But the fact was that Sr de Cuellar's proposals were sketchy and unclear; to have accepted would have put us right back at the beginning again. I summed up very firmly. There could be no question of holding up the military timetable. It could be fatal for our forces. The War Cabinet and later the full Cabinet agreed.

The Secretary-General had received no reply from the Argentinians about his *aide-mémoire* – on which we, in spite of all our reservations, had offered serious comments. He admitted the failure of his efforts to the Security Council. We published our proposals and I defended them in the House of Commons that afternoon. The debate went well and provided a good background for what now had to happen.

I had a full day of engagements in my constituency on Friday 21 May and I knew how important it was to carry on with business as usual.

Later that evening, while I was at a reception in Woodhouse School, still in the constituency, the news came over on the television. The Union Jack was flying in San Carlos: we had returned to the Falklands.

But I was desperately anxious about casualties.

Later that night I returned to No. 10 and John Nott brought me a full report. The actual landing had been achieved without a single casualty. But now it was daytime and fierce air attacks had begun. The frigate HMS *Ardent* was lost. Another frigate – HMS *Argonaut* – and the destroyer HMS *Brilliant* were badly damaged.

The main amphibious force had moved towards San Carlos Water, blessed with an overcast sky and poor visibility, while diversionary raids continued elsewhere on East Falkland. Under cover of naval gun fire, our troops had been taken ashore in landing craft, while helicopters moved equipment and stores. Five thousand men were safely landed, though we lost two helicopters and their crews. The beach-head had been established, though it would take several days for it finally to be secured.

At the Security Council, meeting in open session, Tony Parsons defended our position against predictable rhetorical attacks from Argentina's allies. At the end of the debate the Irish tabled a totally unacceptable resolution. It was the Africans who amended the Irish resolution to the point at which we could accept it. This became UNSCR 505, adopted unanimously on 26 May, giving the Secretary-General a mandate to seek an end to the hostilities and full implementation of UNSCR 502.

On Saturday afternoon I visited Northwood before going on to Chequers and spent some time getting up to date in the Operations Room. I did my best to seem confident, but when I left with Admiral Fieldhouse and we were out of earshot of anyone else, I could not help asking him: 'How long can we go on taking this kind of punishment?' He was no less worried. But he also had the ability of a great commander to see the other side of things. And, terrible as our losses had been, the fact was that we had landed our forces successfully and serious losses were being inflicted on the Argentine Air Force.

I should note here that we were assisted throughout by three important weaknesses in the Argentine air offensive, though in some ways these were the result of deliberate action on our part. First, the Argentinians concentrated their attacks – with the later tragic exception of the losses at Bluff Cove – on the naval escorts rather than the troop ships and aircraft carriers. Of course, in part that was because the escorts succeeded in shielding these units. Second, the Argentine aircraft were forced to fly at a very low level to escape our missiles, with the result that the bombs they dropped (fused for higher altitude) frequently failed to explode. (Sadly a bomb which lodged in HMS *Antelope* did go off, sinking the ship, when a brave bomb disposal expert was trying to defuse it.) Third, the Argentinians had only a limited number of French Exocet missiles. They made desperate attempts to increase their arsenal. There was evidence that arms from Libya and Israel were finding their way through South American countries to them. We for our part were equally desperate to interdict this supply. Later, on 29 May, I was to have a telephone conversation with President Mitterrand who told me that the French had a contract to supply Exocets to Peru, which he had already held up and which both of us feared would be passed on to Argentina. As always during the conflict, he was absolutely staunch.

The Americans too, however irritating and unpredictable their public pronouncements on occasion, were providing invaluable help such as 150,000 square yards of matting to create a makeshift airstrip. On 3 May Caspar Weinberger even proposed sending down the carrier USS *Eisenhower* to act as a mobile runway for us – an offer that we found more encouraging than practical.

I was working in my room at the House of Commons on the evening of Tuesday 25 May when John Nott came in to say that the destroyer HMS *Coventry* had been attacked by a wave of Argentine aircraft and she was sinking. She had, in fact, been one of the two warships on 'picket duty' outside the opening of Falkland Sound, providing early warning of air attack and an air defence screen for the supply ships unloading in San Carlos Water. She later capsized and sank. Nineteen members of her crew died in the attack. John had to appear on television within half an hour. Something of what had happened was already publicly known, although not the name of the ship. It was thought better not to reveal it until we had more details about the crew. Whether the decision was right or wrong I am still not sure: the effect of not announcing the name was that every navy family was full of anxiety.

Later the same evening I had more bad news. I had gone into the Private Office to find out the latest about *Coventry*, but instead, the No. 10 duty clerk told me that the 18,000-ton Cunard container ship *Atlantic Conveyor* had been hit by an Exocet missile; that the ship was on fire and that orders had been given to abandon it. *Atlantic Conveyor* was loaded with vital supplies for our forces on the Falklands. Four of those on board were killed and the captain was drowned, though I was told later that he survived the explosion and fires, and had been seen alive in the water. Thankfully, though, the great majority were saved.

I knew that the *Atlantic Conveyor* had been carrying nineteen more Harriers, sorely needed reinforcements. Had they still been on board?

If so, would we be able to carry on? The ship was also carrying helicopters which were vital to the movement of troops and supplies in the land campaign. Only one was saved. To add to our general dismay, there was also news, based on an Argentine claim, that HMS *Invincible* had been hit and damaged. And somewhere east of the Falklands was the *QE2*, carrying 3,000 troops. For me, this was one of the worst nights of the war.

Early next morning I learnt that the news was not quite so bleak. I was told of the remarkable rescue of most members of the crews of *Coventry* and the *Atlantic Conveyor*. The nineteen Harriers had previously been flown onto *Hermes* and *Invincible*. Relief flooded over me: we were not fatally wounded after all. Moreover, the news that *Invincible* had been hit was totally false.

Stores were still being unloaded at San Carlos. Some landing and supply craft were attacked and hit and there were unexploded bombs, most of which were defused. Our hospital centre at San Carlos was also hit, but the doctors carried on.

Somewhat to the dismay of the UN Secretary-General and Al Haig, we made it clear that having landed we were not now prepared to negotiate. We were put under continual pressure from Washington to avoid the final military humiliation of Argentina, which they now seemed to see as inevitable. I wish I could have been as confident. I knew, as they could not, how many risks and dangers still faced us in the campaign to recapture the islands.

This was amply demonstrated by the battle to retake Darwin and Goose Green. The Argentinians were well prepared and dug into strong defensive positions which had to be approached by our troops across the open ground of a narrow isthmus. They faced heavy enemy fire. As is well known, Colonel 'H' Jones, the commander of 2 Para, lost his life in securing the way forward for his troops. His second-in-command took over and eventually took the surrender. At one point a white flag was waved from the Argentine trenches, but when two of our soldiers advanced in response they were shot and killed. Finally, our commander sent two Argentinian POWs forward with a message to surrender, saying that they could have a parade if they liked but that they must lay down their arms. This proved acceptable. The Argentine officers harangued their men about the justice of their cause, but they surrendered all the same. The people of Goose Green, who had been imprisoned inside the community hall for three weeks, were now released. A famous battle had been won. Today there is a memorial to the Paras near Goose Green itself and a special memorial to 'H'.

The media had reported that our troops were about to take Goose Green the day before the attack. I had been furious when I learned of this – as, I believe, had 'H'. Too much talk was giving the Argentinians warning of what we intended, though the fault did not always lie with the media themselves but also with the media management at the MoD.

Unfortunately, the Americans now sought to revive diplomatic negotiation. I knew that we could not afford to alienate the United States, particularly at this stage. We kept in contact with Mr Haig both about the question of how to provide for and repatriate Argentine prisoners of war and more generally about our plans for the long-term future of the islands.

What would have been quite wrong was to snatch diplomatic defeat out of the jaws of military victory – as I had to tell President Reagan when he telephoned me late at night on Monday 31 May. It was not very satisfactory for either of us that I should not have had advance warning of what he was likely to say and as a result I was perhaps more forceful than friendly. I would have a further opportunity shortly to talk to President Reagan in person during the forthcoming G7 summit at Versailles.

In the meantime, we had to deal delicately with a five-point peace plan which had been advanced by the UN Secretary-General. The pressure for a cease-fire sponsored by the UN Security Council was growing. On Wednesday 2 June after the Secretary-General had announced that he had given up his own efforts, Spain and Panama, on behalf of Argentina, sought to press to the vote an apparently innocuous Draft Resolution on a cease-fire which would have had exactly the effect we were determined to avoid. It was touch and go whether the Spanish would even now manage to obtain the necessary nine votes which would force us to veto the resolution. We ourselves lobbied as hard as possible. The vote was postponed until Friday.

At noon that day I flew to Paris for the G7. My first and most important meeting was, of course, with President Reagan who was staying at the US Embassy. We talked alone. I thanked him for the great help we had received from the United States. I asked him what the Americans could do to help repatriate the Argentine POWs. I also requested that the American vote should support us at the Security Council.

The mood at Versailles seemed very different from that which was now prevailing at the UN in New York. The heads of government were staying in the Petit Trianon. After dinner we had a long discussion about the Falklands and the response was generally sympathetic and helpful. Later the British delegation and I withdrew to the sitting room which we had been allocated. We had been talking for about fifteen minutes when a message came through from the Foreign Office and Tony Parsons that a vote was about to be taken in the Security Council and that the Japanese were voting against us. As theirs was the ninth vote required for the resolution to pass, this was particularly irritating. I tried hard to contact Mr Suzuki, the Japanese Prime Minister, to persuade him to at least abstain but I was told that he could not be reached.

Attention was, in fact, somewhat diverted from our problems by the extraordinary behaviour of the US Ambassador to the United Nations, Mrs Kirkpatrick. Having cast her veto alongside ours, she announced only minutes later that if the vote could be taken again she would, on instructions just received, abstain. Ironically, this rather helped us by distracting media attention from our veto. However, that had not been the intention. Apparently, succumbing to pressure from the Latin American countries, Al Haig had telephoned her from Versailles telling her to withdraw her vote of support from us but she had not received the message in time. There was a still more embarrassing sequel to this event for the United States. Just before lunch in the Palace of Versailles, the television cameras were allowed in and an American journalist asked President Reagan what had lain behind the US confusion at the United Nations the previous evening. To my amazement, he said that he did not know anything about it. The journalist then turned to me. I had no intention of rubbing salt into a friend's wounds, so all I said was that I did not give interviews over lunch.

That same morning the Japanese Prime Minister gave me an extremely lame explanation of Japan's vote in support of the resolution, claiming that he believed that it would lead to Argentine withdrawal. However, President Mitterrand's summing up at his press conference after the conclusion of the G7 was excellent and totally supportive.

Neither Tony Parsons nor I was particularly surprised that we had finally had to use our veto. In retrospect, we were very lucky – and it was a tribute also to Tony Parsons's skill – that we had not had to veto such a resolution much earlier.

By now, my thoughts were again on what was happening in the Falklands. The landing ships, *Sir Tristram* and *Sir Galahad*, full of men, equipment and munitions, had been sent round to Bluff Cove and Fitzroy in preparation for the final assault on Port Stanley. The clouds cleared while the ships were still unloading the Rapier missiles which would protect them from air attack and the Argentinians scored hits on both. *Sir Galahad* had not discharged its troops and the result was great loss of life and many survivors were left with terrible burns. The Welsh Guards took the brunt of it. As on all these occasions, the natural reaction was 'if only' – above all, if only the men had been taken off and dispersed as soon as they arrived then nothing like this number of casualties would have been suffered. But the losses would have been even greater were it not for the heroism of the helicopter pilots. They hovered close to the burning oil slicks around the ship and used the draught from their rotors to blow life rafts full of survivors away from the inferno into which they were being drawn.

Again, there were almost insuperable problems in releasing news of casualties. Rumours of very large numbers were spread by the Argentinians. Families were frantically worried. But we decided to hold up details of the numbers lost – although of course (as always) relatives were individually informed. We knew from intelligence that the Argentinians thought that our casualties were several times worse than they were and that they believed this would hold up our attack on Port Stanley. The attack on Mount Longdon, Two Sisters and Wireless Ridge was due to begin on Friday night. Surprise was vital.

I hoped against hope that our worst losses were behind us. But early on the morning of Saturday 12 June the No. 10 duty clerk came up to the flat with a note. I all but seized it from him, expecting it to say that the attack on the mountains around Port Stanley had begun. But the news was very different. I kept the note, which reads:

> HMS *Glamorgan* struck by suspected Exocet missile. Ship is in
> position 51/58 South. Large fire in vicinity of hangar and in gas
> turbine and gear room. Power still available. Ship making ten
> knots to the South.
>
> – MoD as yet have no details of casualties and wouldn't expect
> them for several hours. They will keep us informed.

Glamorgan had been bombarding the Argentine positions in Port
Stanley and on the hills around before the forthcoming battle. She had in
fact been hit by a land-based Exocet while on her way out of the area.

How bitterly depressed I was. At moments like this I felt almost guilty
at the comfort, protection and safety in No. 10 while there was so much
danger and death in the South Atlantic. That day was the Trooping of the
Colour for the Queen's birthday. For the only time that I can remember
the ceremony was marred by a downpour of rain. It was unpleasant for
the Guards, but with the news so bad and the uncertainty so great, it
seemed appropriate. I wore black, for I felt that there was much to mourn.
John Nott arrived shortly before I was to take my place on the stand. He
had no further news. But he thought he would have been told if the attack
had not started. Afterwards, dripping wet, the guests, including Rex and
Mrs Hunt, dried out before the fires in No. 10 as best we could.

Shortly before 1 o'clock we heard that all our military objectives had
been achieved. But there had been a stiff battle. Two Sisters, Mount
Harriet and Mount Longdon had been secured. The plan had been to
press on that night to take Mount Tumbledown, still closer to Port
Stanley, but the troops were tired and more time was needed to bring up
ammunition, so it was decided to wait. I went up to Northwood that
afternoon to hear precisely what was happening. There was better news
there about *Glamorgan*; her fires were under control and she was steam-
ing at 20 knots.

More than ever, the outcome now lay in the hands of our soldiers on
the Falklands, not with the politicians. Like everyone else in Britain, I was
glued to the radio for news – strictly keeping to my self-imposed rule not
to telephone while the conflict was under way. On my way back from
Chequers to No. 10 that Sunday (13 June), I went via Northwood to learn
what I could. What was to turn out to be the final assault was bitterly
fought, particularly at Mount Tumbledown. But Tumbledown, Mount
William and Wireless Ridge fell to our forces, who were soon on the
outskirts of Stanley.

I visited the islands seven months later and saw the terrain for myself, walking the ground at first light in driving wind and rain, wending my way around those grim outcrops of rock which made natural fortifications for the Argentine defenders. Our boys had to cover the ground and take the positions in thick darkness. It could only have been done by the most professional and disciplined of forces.

When the War Cabinet met on Monday morning, all that we knew was that the battle was still in progress. The speed with which the end came took all of us by surprise. The Argentinians were weary, demoralized and very badly led – as ample evidence at the time and later showed. They threw down their arms and could be seen retreating through their own minefields into Stanley.

That evening I went to the House of Commons to announce the victory. I could not get into my own room; it was locked and the Chief Whip's assistant had to search for the key. I then wrote out on a scrap of paper which I found somewhere on my desk the short statement which, there being no other procedural means, I would have to make on a Point of Order to the House. At 10 p.m. I rose and told them that it had been reported that there were white flags flying over Port Stanley. The war was over. We all felt the same and the cheers showed it. Right had prevailed. And when I went to sleep very late that night I realized how great the burden was which had been lifted from my shoulders.

CHAPTER TWENTY-ONE

Generals, Commissars and Mandarins

Meeting the military and political challenge of communism
from the autumn of 1979 to the spring of 1983

W ELL BEFORE I ENTERED DOWNING STREET I was preoccupied with the balance of military power between the NATO alliance and the Warsaw Pact. NATO was founded in April 1949 in response to the growing aggression of Soviet policy. Although the United States is the leading power in NATO, ultimately it can only seek to persuade not coerce. In such a relationship the danger of dissension always exists. The Soviet aim, only thinly disguised, right up until the time when a united Germany remained in NATO, was to drive a wedge between America and her European allies. I always regarded it as one of Britain's most important roles to see that such a strategy failed.

By the time we took office the Soviets were ruthlessly pressing ahead to gain military advantage. Soviet military spending, believed to be some five times the published figures, took between 12 and 14 per cent of the Soviet Union's GNP.* The Warsaw Pact outnumbered NATO by three-to-one in main battle tanks and artillery and by more than two-to-one in tactical aircraft. Moreover, the Soviets were rapidly improving the quality of their tanks, submarines, surface ships and aircraft. The build-up of the Soviet Navy enabled them to project their power across the world. Improvements in Soviet anti-ballistic missile defences threatened the credibility of the alliance's nuclear deterrent – not least the British independent deterrent – at the same time as the Soviets were approaching parity in strategic missiles with the United States.

* * *

---

* By the end of the decade 25–30 per cent of GNP was commonly estimated.

It was, however, in what in the jargon are known as long-range theatre nuclear forces (LRTNF) – usually called intermediate-range nuclear forces (INF) – that the most pressing and difficult decisions were required. The so-called 'dual-track' agreement to modernize NATO's medium-range nuclear weapons, while engaging in talks with the Soviet Union on arms control, had been taken in principle by the previous Labour Government; whether they would have seen the decision through to deployment I somewhat doubt.

This agreement was needed to deal with the threat from new Soviet nuclear weapons. The Soviet SS-20 mobile ballistic missiles and their new supersonic Backfire bomber could strike western European targets from the territory of the Soviet Union. But the Americans had no equivalent weapons stationed on European soil. The only NATO weapons able to strike the USSR from Europe were those carried by the ageing UK Vulcan bombers and the F1-11s stationed in Britain. Both forces could be vulnerable to a Soviet first strike. Of course, the United States could be expected by an attacking Soviet army at some point to have recourse to its own strategic nuclear weapons. But the essence of deterrence is its credibility. Now that the Soviet Union had achieved a broad parity in strategic nuclear weapons, some thought that this reduced the likelihood of the United States taking such action. In any case, there were many in Europe who suggested that the United States would not risk its own cities in defence of Europe.

Why would the Soviets wish to acquire this new capability to win nuclear war in Europe? The answer was that they hoped ultimately to split the alliance.

NATO's strategy was based on having a range of conventional and nuclear weapons so that the USSR could never be confident of overcoming NATO at one level of weaponry without triggering a response at a higher level. This strategy of 'flexible response' would not be effective if there were no Europe-based nuclear weapons as a link between the conventional and strategic nuclear response. NATO knew that the Warsaw Pact forces would never be held for more than a short time if they attacked with all the strength at their disposal in central Europe. That is why NATO repeatedly pledged that although it would never use military force first, it could not play into the Soviet hands of renouncing first use of nuclear weapons once it had been attacked. So only by modernizing its intermediate-range nuclear weapons in Europe could NATO's strategy retain its credibility.

In an act of remarkable courage in the face of so much domestic and Soviet opposition, the NATO ministers made the required decision in Brussels on 12 December 1979. The arms control proposals, including the American offer to withdraw 1,000 nuclear warheads from Europe, were agreed. Most important, the alliance agreed to the deployment in Europe of all the 572 new American missiles which had been envisaged. The Belgians agreed to accept a share of these missiles, subject to reconsideration after six months in the light of the progress of arms control negotiations. The Dutch Government accepted the proposals as a whole but postponed the decision to take a share of the missiles in Holland until the end of 1981.

Of course, this was not the end of the matter. In June the following year we announced the sites of the Cruise missiles in Britain – Greenham Common in Berkshire and Molesworth in Cambridgeshire. From that time on Greenham was to be the focus for an increasingly strident unilateralist campaign.

Another early decision which we had to take related to our independent nuclear deterrent. Britain had four nuclear-armed Polaris submarines. The previous Conservative and Labour Governments had pressed ahead with a programme of improvement to our Polaris missiles. The programme, code-named Chevaline, had been paid for and managed by the United Kingdom in co-operation with the United States. The upgraded Polaris system would maintain the full effectiveness of our strategic deterrent into the 1990s, though at a cost which had alarmingly escalated as the development continued. However, for a variety of technical and operational reasons we could not responsibly plan for the continuance of this system much into the 1990s. If Britain was to retain its deterrent a decision would shortly have to be made about Polaris's ultimate replacement.

We began to look at the options from almost the first days in government. These quickly proved a good deal narrower than they at first appeared, though inevitably they seemed wider to those without access to all the information. By late September 1979 we had discarded the option of a successor force of air-launched Cruise missiles because they would be too vulnerable to attack. The possibility of co-operation with France, which retained its own independent deterrent, was rejected for technological reasons. From an early stage the American Trident looked the most promising option.

We had received firm assurances that the SALT II Agreement, reached between Presidents Carter and Brezhnev in June 1979, would not affect the situation regarding our own deterrent. But our aim was, if possible, to conclude an agreement with the Americans on purchasing Trident before the end of that year, so that it could not get caught up in the argument in the run-up to the expected ratification by the US Senate of the treaty. The Trident missile included the advanced and very important technology of multiple nuclear warheads, each separately targeted (MIRVs). Not only was this the most up-to-date and therefore credible system – as measured against Soviet anti-submarine warfare capability and anti-ballistic missile defences – but by purchasing it from the Americans we could hope to avoid immensely expensive improvement programmes like Chevaline. On 6 December 1979 the ministers concerned agreed that the best system to replace Polaris was the Trident I (C4) MIRV system if it could be purchased from the US, less the warheads and the submarines carrying the system which would be produced in Britain. The decision was later confirmed by Cabinet.

But at this point, although President Carter told me that he would supply us with whatever we needed, he was desperately worried that news of his decision would cause him political difficulties in the SALT II Agreement whose chances of being ratified by the Senate were already in doubt. The Americans were also keen to ensure that the announcement on Trident did not occur before the scheduled 12 December meeting of NATO to decide on deploying Cruise and Pershing. I could see the sense of this. But in view of the problems which SALT II was facing I began to be anxious lest the decision on Trident be postponed well into 1980.

With the Soviet invasion of Afghanistan at the end of the year the prospect of ratifying SALT II immediately sharply receded. But at this point the US Administration said that it was reluctant to announce the Trident decision because it could be seen as an overreaction to events in Afghanistan. The Americans were similarly unduly worried about the attitude of Chancellor Schmidt to the Trident decision. More hard-headedly, the Carter Administration also pressed strongly for both political and financial returns on the decision to supply us with Trident. They wanted us to agree to a form of words which would commit us to expanding our defence efforts. They were also keen to develop their defence facilities at our island of Diego Garcia in the Indian Ocean – something for which I had a good deal of sympathy. There was the matter of a substantial levy which we would be charged for American research and development costs which they were not prepared to waive.

On the afternoon of Monday 2 June 1980 I finalized the terms in discussion with Dr Harold Brown, the able US Defense Secretary, in Downing Street. I said that Britain wanted to purchase the Trident I missile on the same terms as regards research and development as Polaris, that is, paying a 5 per cent levy. Dr Brown would not agree to this – but he would accept it providing the British Government bore the cost of manning the Rapier Air Defence Systems which the US intended to purchase for their bases in Britain. I agreed. I also agreed with the objective of extending and increasing US use of the base at Diego Garcia; but this made sense on its own merits and had nothing to do with the Trident decision. Dr Brown accepted this. At last the decision was effectively made and I wrote formally to President Carter requesting purchase of Trident, simultaneously informing President Giscard, Chancellor Schmidt and Italy's Prime Minister Cossiga. The decision was announced to the House by Francis Pym on 15 July and at Francis's suggestion fully debated and endorsed on 3 March 1981.

In the summer of 1980 we thought that we had made our final decision on the independent nuclear deterrent. But it was not to be. President Reagan came into office in 1981 with a programme of modernizing US strategic nuclear forces, including Trident. On 24 August the new US Defense Secretary, Caspar Weinberger, wrote to me to confirm that President Reagan had now decided to use the Trident II (D5) missile in the Trident submarines. The US Administration would make this missile available to us if we wished to buy it. On 1 October President Reagan formally told me of his decision.

I well understood and indeed supported President Reagan's decision to improve the US strategic nuclear capability. However, we now faced a new situation. If we were still to go ahead with Trident I we risked spending huge sums on a system that would be outdated and increasingly difficult to maintain as the Americans went over to Trident II. But if we were to accept President Reagan's generous offer of the new technology represented by Trident II we risked the increasing costs of any new project. Moreover, a number of political difficulties arose.

In November 1981 a group of ministers met to discuss what we should do. We argued out all the questions between us; and all the arguments which would be raised in the outside world were discussed, including some feeble and unrealistic ones.

In January 1982 we had a further and fuller discussion based on a presentation. The more we considered the question the more it seemed that we must indeed have the Trident II. But we must get it on the best possible terms. The issue was put to Cabinet later that month and on 1 February I sent a message to President Reagan saying that I would send officials to Washington to discuss terms.

In the end, we concluded an agreement to buy Trident II on more advantageous terms than Trident I. The missile was to be purchased at the same price as the United States Navy's own requirements in accordance with the Polaris Sales Agreement. But the additional overheads and levies would be lower than would have been the case under the 1980 Agreement to purchase Trident I. In particular, the so-called R & D levy would be a fixed sum in real terms and there would be a complete waiver of the facilities charge which was part of the Trident I deal. The terms protected us completely from the escalation of the development cost. The United States would set up a liaison office in London to advise British industry on how to compete on equal terms with US industry for sub-contracts for the Trident II programme as a whole, including the American programme. We also decided to improve and increase the size of the submarines which would carry Trident, making them more efficient and less detectable, and by running longer between refits make them more available for patrol. The total cost of Trident II and the other changes over the whole period would be £7.5 billion, just over 3 per cent of the total defence budget over the same period. When I learned of the terms now being offered I was delighted and I gladly authorized their acceptance.

No matter how effectively Britain managed its defence effort it was on the unity, strength and credibility of NATO that our security ultimately depended. It was of the utmost importance that American public opinion remained committed to western Europe. So the tensions and divisions which arose in the alliance at this time were of great concern to me. My view was that ultimately we must support American leadership: but that did not mean that the Americans could pursue their interests regardless of the opinion of their European allies.

The need to decide how to react to the imposition of martial law by General Jaruzelski's Government in Poland on 13 December 1981 highlighted problems which had been growing throughout 1981. Some European countries, most importantly the Germans, were hostile to President Reagan's economic policy and mistrustful of his rhetoric on defence and arms control. I did not share these attitudes, though I wanted tougher action to control the widening US budget deficit. What I found irritating was the way in which the actions the Americans preferred inflicted a good deal more pain on their allies than on themselves and, one might argue, the communists in Poland and the Soviet Union. The first such issue was the Polish Government's crackdown on Solidarity.

Martial law was declared in Poland from midnight on 12–13 December 1981 and a 'Military Council for National Salvation' consisting of military leaders was set up under the Prime Minister, General Jaruzelski. The borders were sealed, telex and telephone links severed, a curfew imposed, strikes and assemblies banned, the broadcasting system brought under tight control. There was no doubt in my mind that all of this was morally unacceptable but that did not make it easier to gauge the correct response. After all, in order to ward off Soviet intervention, we had consistently said that the Poles must be allowed to decide on their own internal affairs. Were the Soviets themselves behind it, intending to use the crackdown as a means of turning the clock back to hardline communism and subordination to Moscow? Or was this really a temporary decision, as the Jaruzelski Government claimed, forced upon them to bring some kind of order to Poland, with the implication that this would prevent a Soviet takeover?

The more we learned of the background to what had happened, however, the worse it appeared. President Reagan was personally outraged by what had occurred, believed that the Soviet Union was behind it and was determined to take swift action. I received a message from him on 19 December to this effect. Al Haig sent a parallel message to Peter Carrington pointing out that the Americans were not proposing that the West should now implement the far-reaching measures to meet Soviet military intervention that had already been agreed in NATO. What they wanted were some political and economic measures at once and others in reserve if the situation worsened. Without any further reference to us, the Americans would be announcing sanctions against the Soviet Union later that day. These, we were glad to note, rightly did not include abandonment of the disarmament talks going on in Geneva. But they did include measures such as the cancellation of Aeroflot landing rights, a halt to negotiations on a new long-term grain agreement and a halt to the export of material for the construction of the planned natural gas pipelines on which work had already begun.

It was this last point which was to be the cause of great anger in Britain and other European countries. British, German and Italian firms had legally binding contracts to provide equipment for the West Siberian Gas

Pipeline, which involved components made in the United States or under United States licence. If the ban extended to existing contracts this would deprive British firms of over £200 million of business with the Soviet Union. Worst affected would be a contract of John Brown Engineering for pump equipment for the pipeline project on which large numbers of jobs depended.

While pressing the Americans on this particular point, I ensured that we gave them the strongest possible backing both in NATO and the European Community for the general line they wanted to take. This was by no means easy. Initially, the Germans were reluctant to take any measures against the Polish Government. The French were pressing hard for continuing the sale of food at special subsidized prices by the European Community to the Soviet Union. But I still felt that if we could persuade the Americans to take a more reasonable line over the pipeline project we would be able to demonstrate a fairly impressive western unity. The trouble was that there were those in the American Administration whose opposition to the pipeline project had nothing much to do with events in Poland. These people believed that if it went ahead the Germans and the French would be dangerously dependent on Soviet energy supplies, which would have damaging strategic implications. There was some force in this argument; but although Russia would be providing just over a quarter of Germany's and just under a third of France's gas, this would be no more than 5 per cent of either country's total energy consumption. In any case, neither the Germans nor the French were going to accede to American pressure. Such pressure would therefore be counter-productive as well as irrelevant to the specific problem we faced in Poland. There was also American talk, which seriously worried the Bank of England, of forcing Poland to default on her international debts, which would have had severe effects on European banks.

Al Haig joined me for a late lunch at Downing Street on Friday 29 January. I told him that the single most important aim must be to keep the western alliance together. The most recent meeting of the NATO Council had gone well. But the measures now being proposed by the United States were causing concern. I said that whatever the Americans felt about the matter we had to face the fact that the French and the Germans were never going to abandon their contracts for the Siberian Gas Pipeline. Nearer the bone, I noted that the Americans had not included a grain embargo which would hurt their own people. Indeed, few of the measures adopted by the United States would have any serious effect at home – but they would hurt Europe. I gained the strong impression that Mr Haig basically agreed with my analysis.

Out of the blue, however, the Americans announced on 18 June that the ban on the supply of oil and gas technology to the Soviet Union was to apply not only to US companies but also to their foreign subsidiaries and to foreign companies manufacturing American-designed components under licence. I was appalled. The reaction of the Europeans generally was still more hostile.

Britain took legislative action under the Protection of Trading Interests Act to resist what was in effect the extension of US extra-territorial authority. Then European irritation was increased still further by the news that the Americans were intending to renew grain sales to the USSR on the pretext that this would drain the USSR of hard currency – but transparently because it was in the interests of American farmers to sell their grain. It was left to America's excellent new Secretary of State, George Shultz, to find a way out of the difficulties, which he did later in the year, allowing the existing contracts for the pipeline to go ahead. But it had all been a lesson in how not to conduct alliance business.

The summer of 1982 saw some useful international diplomacy. Between 4 and 6 June the heads of government of the G7 countries met amid the splendid opulence of Versailles and my most vivid recollection of the proceedings is of the impression made by President Reagan. At one point he spoke for twenty minutes or so without notes, outlining his economic vision. His quiet but powerful words provided those who did not yet know him with some insight into the qualities which made him such a remarkable political leader. After he had finished, President Mitterrand acknowledged that no one would criticize President Reagan for being true to his beliefs. Given President Mitterrand's socialist policies, that was almost a compliment.

From Paris President Reagan flew to London for an official visit where he addressed both Houses of Parliament in the Royal Gallery of the Palace of Westminster. The speech itself was a remarkable one. It marked a decisive stage in the battle of ideas which he and I wished to wage against socialism, above all the socialism of the Soviet Union. Both of us were convinced that strong defence was a necessary, but not sufficient, means of overcoming the communist threat. Instead of seeking merely to contain communism, we wished to put freedom on the offensive. In his speech President Reagan proposed a worldwide campaign for democracy to support 'the democratic revolution [which was] gathering new strength'. In retrospect, however, that speech had a larger significance. It marked a new direction in the West's battle against communism. It was the manifesto of the Reagan doctrine under which the West would not abandon those countries which had had communism forced upon them.

By the time I visited the Far East in September 1982 Britain's standing in the world, and my own, had been transformed as a result of victory in the Falklands. But one issue on which this was, if anything, a drawback was in talking to the Chinese over Hong Kong. The Chinese leaders were out to demonstrate that the Falklands was no precedent for dealing with the Colony.

On the morning of Wednesday 22 September my party and I took off from Tokyo, where I had been visiting, for Peking. Fifteen years remained of the lease to Britain of the New Territories which constitute over 90 per cent of the land of the Colony of Hong Kong. The island of Hong Kong itself is British sovereign territory, but, like the rest of the Colony, dependent on the mainland for water and other supplies. The People's Republic of China refused to recognize the Treaty of Nanking, signed in 1842, by which the island of Hong Kong had been acquired by Britain. Consequently, our negotiating aim was to exchange sovereignty over the island of Hong Kong in return for continued British administration of the entire Colony well into the future. This I knew from my many consultations with politicians and business leaders of Hong Kong was the solution which would suit them best.

The immediate danger was that financial confidence would evaporate and that money and in due course key personnel would flee the Colony, impoverishing and destabilizing it well before the lease of the New Territories came to an end. Moreover, it was necessary to act now if new investment was to be made, since investors would be looking some fifteen years or so ahead in judging what decisions to make.

I had visited Peking in April 1977 as Leader of the Opposition. The 'Gang of Four' had been deposed a few months before and Hua Guo Feng was Chairman. Deng Xiaoping, who had suffered so much during the Cultural Revolution, had been ousted by the 'Gang of Four' the previous year and was still in detention. But on the occasion of this, my first visit as Prime Minister – indeed the first visit of any Prime Minister while still in office – Deng Xiaoping was indisputably in charge.

On the afternoon of Wednesday 22 September I had my first meeting with the Chinese Prime Minister, Zhao Ziyang – whose moderation and reasonableness proved to be a great handicap to him in his subsequent career. We had a discussion of the world scene in which, because of the Chinese hostility to Soviet hegemony, we found much to agree about. However, we were aware that the following morning's meeting on Hong Kong would be a very different matter.

I began that meeting with a prepared statement setting out the British position. I said that Hong Kong was a unique example of successful Sino-British co-operation. I noted that the two main elements of the Chinese view concerned sovereignty and the continued prosperity of Hong Kong. Prosperity depended on confidence. If drastic changes in the administrative control of Hong Kong were to be introduced or even announced now there would certainly be a wholesale flight of capital. This was not something which Britain would prompt – far from it. But nor was it something we could prevent. A collapse of Hong Kong would be to the discredit of both our countries. Confidence and prosperity depended on British administration. If our two governments could agree on arrangements for the future administration of Hong Kong; if those arrangements would work and command confidence among the people of the Colony; and if they satisfied the British Parliament – we would then consider the question of sovereignty.

I had hoped that this practical and realistic line of argument would prove persuasive.

However, it was quite clear from the Chinese Prime Minister's opening remarks that they would not compromise on sovereignty and that they intended to recover their sovereignty over the whole of Hong Kong – the island as well as the New Territories – in 1997 and no later. The people of Hong Kong could become a special administrative zone administered by local people with its existing economic and social system unchanged. The capitalist system in Hong Kong would remain, as would its free port and its function as an international financial centre. The Hong Kong dollar would continue to be used and to be convertible. In answer to my vigorous intervention about the loss of confidence which such a position, if announced, would bring, he said that if it came to a choice between sovereignty on the one hand and prosperity and stability on the other, China would put sovereignty first. The meeting was courteous enough. But the Chinese refused to budge an inch.

I knew that the substance of what had been said would be conveyed to Deng Xiaoping whom I met the next day. Mr Deng was known as a realist, but on this occasion he was obdurate. He reiterated that the Chinese were not prepared to discuss sovereignty. He said that the decision that Hong Kong would return to Chinese sovereignty need not be announced now, but that in one or two years' time the Chinese Government would formally announce their decision to recover it. At one point he said that the Chinese could walk in and take Hong Kong later today if they wanted to. I retorted that they could indeed do so, I could not stop them, but this would bring about Hong Kong's collapse. The world would then see what followed a change from British to Chinese rule.

For the first time he seemed taken aback: his mood became more accommodating, but he had still not grasped the essential point, going on to insist that the British should stop money leaving Hong Kong. I tried to explain that as soon as you stop money going out you effectively end the prospect of new money coming in. Investors lose all confidence and that would be the end of Hong Kong. It was becoming very clear to me that the Chinese had little understanding of the legal and political conditions for capitalism. They would need to be educated slowly and thoroughly in how it worked if they were to keep Hong Kong prosperous and stable. I also felt throughout these discussions that the Chinese, believing their own slogans about the evils of capitalism, just did not realize that we in Britain considered we had a moral duty to do our best to protect the free way of life of the people of Hong Kong.

For all the difficulties, however, the talks were not the damaging failure which they might have been. I managed to get Deng Xiaoping to agree to a short statement which, while not pretending that we had reached agreement, announced the beginning of talks with the common aim of maintaining the stability and prosperity of Hong Kong. Neither the people of the Colony nor I had secured all that we wanted, but I felt that we had at least laid the basis for reasonable negotiations. We each knew where the other stood.

CHAPTER TWENTY-TWO

Disarming the Left

Winning the argument and formulating the
policies for a second term 1982–1983

I T IS NO EXAGGERATION to say that the outcome of the Falklands War
transformed the British political scene. In fact, the Conservative Party
had begun to recover its position in the opinion polls before the conflict,
as people began to realize that economic recovery was under way. But the
so-called 'Falklands factor' was real enough. I could feel the impact of the
victory wherever I went. It is often said that elections are won and lost on
the issue of the economy, and though there is some truth in this, it is
plainly an oversimplification. Without any prompting from us, people
saw the connection between the resolution we had shown in economic
policy and that demonstrated in the handling of the Falklands crisis.
Reversing our economic decline was one part of the task of restoring
Britain's reputation; demonstrating that we were not the sort of people to
bow before dictators was another. I found that people were starting to
appreciate what had been achieved during the last three years. I drew
attention in my speeches to the record and to the fact that none of it
would have happened if we had followed the policies pressed upon us by
the Opposition.

The Opposition itself was divided between Labour and the new
'Alliance' of the Liberal and Social Democratic parties. Though we were
not to know it at the time, Alliance support had peaked and it would
never be able to recapture the heady atmosphere of late 1981 when it had
led in the opinion polls and its supporters had claimed they had truly
'broken the mould' of British two-party politics. In fact, of course, the
one thing you never get from parties which deliberately seek the middle

way between left and right is new ideas and radical initiatives. The SDP
and Liberals hankered after all the failed policies of the past and though
the SDP's instincts on defence were sound – as opposed to the Liberals,
perpetually tempted by unilateralism – and they were contemptuous of
Marxist dogma, I always felt – and still do – that the leaders of the SDP
would have done better to stay in the Labour Party and drive out the Left.
The risk was that by abandoning the Labour Party they might actually let
into power the very people they were seeking to keep out.

As for Labour, the Party continued an apparently inexorable leftward
shift. Michael Foot is a highly principled and cultivated man, invariably
courteous in our dealings. In debate and on the platform he has a kind of
genius. But the policies he espoused, including unilateral disarmament,
withdrawal from the European Community, sweeping nationalization of
industry and much greater powers for trade unions, were not only catastrophically unsuitable for Britain: they also constituted an umbrella
beneath which sinister revolutionaries, intent on destroying the institutions of the state and the values of society, were able to shelter. The more
the general public learned of Labour's policies and personnel the less they
liked them.

The opinion polls and by-election results confirmed what my own
instincts told me – that the Falklands had strengthened our standing in
the country. On the eve of the war we had already moved just ahead of the
Alliance parties in the polls. Between April and May our support rose ten
percentage points to 41.5 per cent, well ahead of all the other parties. It
rose again in the wake of the recapture of the islands and then fell back a
little during the second half of the year. However, on only one occasion
between then and the election did it dip below 40 per cent. I never took
much notice of what the polls said about me personally. Too much
concentration on this sort of thing can be a distraction. But it was also
true that my own standing in the polls had gone up substantially.

Inevitably, defence was the political issue on which the Falklands War had
the greatest bearing. During the Falklands campaign itself the nuclear
issue was almost entirely edged out of public debate, though my speech at
the UN Special Session on disarmament in June 1982 was an attempt to
show how the same fundamental principles underlay the whole of
defence policy. However, in the autumn of that year, I began to be more
concerned about the presentation of our nuclear strategy. Although
public opinion was with us on the principle of the nuclear deterrent and

opposed to unilateralism, there was a good deal of opposition to Trident II, mainly on grounds of cost, and to the stationing of Cruise missiles. Underlying both was a disagreeable streak of anti-Americanism. Accordingly, on 20 October and 24 November I chaired meetings of the Liaison Committee of Ministers and Central Office officials to explore the facts and refine the arguments.

Unilateralism became the official policy of the Labour Party at the 1982 Party Conference, when the necessary two-thirds majority was secured. Michael Foot personally had long been committed to the unilateralist position. It had an appeal in the universities and among some intellectuals and received a good deal of covert support from those in the media, especially the BBC. Labour councils had adopted the gimmick of declaring their areas 'nuclear free zones'. Although the Campaign for Nuclear Disarmament (CND) had begun to lose support from the high point it had reached in 1981, it remained dangerously strong.

Ultimate control of Cruise missiles was the most tricky issue. The decision to modernize medium-range nuclear missiles in Europe had been made under pressure from the Europeans, particularly the Germans, anxious to prevent any 'decoupling' of the American and European wings of NATO. The Americans had developed and paid for the missiles, and therefore owned them, massively reducing the cost to European governments. There was a strong feeling in the US Congress that any US-owned missiles should be subject to US control. However, American ownership obviously carried implications if it ever came to decisions about use.

In Britain, distrust of the United States surfaced on the question of whether there should be a 'dual key' – that is, whether there should be a technical arrangement to ensure that the US could not fire these weapons without the consent of the British Government. That would go beyond the existing agreement that the US would not use nuclear weapons based in Britain without an Anglo-American 'joint decision'.

The United States had offered us the possibility of dual key right at the start, but to exercise that option we would have had to buy the weapons ourselves, which would have been hugely expensive. John Nott, before he left his post as Defence Secretary, had been attracted by the dual key option. But neither Michael Heseltine, his successor, nor I shared his view. The UK had never exercised *physical* control over systems owned and manned by the US. It was in my view neither fair nor necessary to ask the US to break with that precedent now. Also, the more the Soviets were told about how and in what conditions Cruise missiles would be fired, the less credible they would be as a deterrent. The Soviets might be persuaded that at the last moment a British Government might not agree to their use. Finally, the use of a dual key in the United Kingdom would have raised the whole question of arrangements elsewhere in Europe. In West Germany both government and public opinion would only agree to deploying Cruise and Pershing II missiles if there was no German finger on the trigger.

So for all these reasons I satisfied myself through discussions with Washington that the position was satisfactory from the point of view of British security and defence, and on 1 May 1983 I cleared personally with President Reagan the precise formula we should use to describe it. But I knew that it would be difficult to defend our line: not only anti-nuclear protesters but a sizeable number of our own supporters in and out of Parliament had their doubts. Moreover, most of the newspapers were opposed to us on the question of dual key.

We were anxious to avoid very visible signs of deployment in the run-up to or during the 1983 general election campaign, with demonstrations stretching police resources. Until almost the last moment we had been planning an autumn election. But as events happened we had an election in June, so this was not the problem which it might have been. (The launchers and warheads duly arrived in November.)

Elsewhere in Europe the situation was still more difficult. There was already a good deal of public criticism in Germany and Italy of NATO's offer of the zero-option, which was widely felt to be unrealistic. And the Soviets were mounting a major public relations campaign.

It was crucial that NATO's policy on arms control be well presented and that the alliance should stick together. On Wednesday 9 February I had a meeting at Downing Street with George Bush to discuss these matters. The Vice-President had a special remit from President Reagan to keep in touch with European governments and he did this with great skill. He was always very well briefed and had a friendly, straightforward manner, the proof that this reflected personality rather than artifice being that his staff were well known to be devoted to him. I now urged the Vice-President that the American Administration should take a new initiative in the INF negotiations. The aim should be to seek an interim agreement whereby limited reductions on the Soviet side would be balanced by reduced deployments on the part of the United States, without abandoning the zero-option as our ultimate goal – that is the complete elimination of intermediate-range nuclear weapons.

Mr Bush reported my views back to President Reagan who replied in a message to me on Wednesday 16 February. The President was at this stage somewhat noncommittal about a new initiative but said that he would be willing to consider seriously any reasonable alternative idea for producing the same result as the zero-option. This did not seem to me to be sufficient. I replied two days later on the hotline. I stressed the success of Vice-President Bush's visit to Europe, but pointed out that one of its effects had been to raise expectations. I hoped that the speech which President Reagan was due to make shortly on these matters would go beyond a restatement of the US position and begin to indicate how it might be developed. As things turned out, the President's statement contained nothing new. So I continued the private pressure for further movement, while remaining in public totally supportive of the American position.

Then on Monday 14 March President Reagan sent me another message. He said that he had directed that a prompt review of the US position on INF negotiations should be made as a basis for new instructions to the US arms negotiating team. In the meantime, he asked that there should be no European calls for US flexibility and specifically asked me to express confidence in the very close co-ordination of our policies. I replied warmly, welcoming his decision. On Wednesday 23 March the President told me the results of his review. While sticking to the ultimate objective of the zero-option, the chief US negotiator, Paul Nitze, would tell the Soviets at Geneva before the end of the current round of negotiations that the US was indeed prepared to negotiate an interim agreement. The Americans would stop deployment of a (still to be specified) number of warheads, on condition that the USSR reduced the number of warheads on its mobile long-range INF missiles to one equal with the US on a global basis. Again, I welcomed his decision, but argued that he should consider giving specific figures. In fact the President's proposal announced on 30 March did not do so. But his modest flexibility did have a beneficial effect on public opinion and incidentally helped us in Britain fighting the general election campaign soon to be upon us.

In that election campaign, defence would be of great political importance. Yet I had no doubt that the result would ultimately depend on the economy. Our economic course had already been set in the 1981 budget. We now had to see the strategy through. It was a remarkable testament to the soundness of public finances by this stage that we managed to pay for the Falklands War out of the Contingency Reserve without a penny of extra taxation and with barely a tremor in the financial markets. The economy was already beginning to recover and would have done so more rapidly but for sluggish world conditions.

The black spot in the record was, of course, unemployment, which was still well over three million. It would be vital in the campaign to explain why this was so and what we were doing about it. Our ability to deal with this issue successfully would be a test not only of our eloquence and credibility but also of the maturity and understanding of the British electorate.

Unlike some of my colleagues, I never ceased to believe that, other things being equal, the level of unemployment was related to the extent of trade union power. The unions had priced many of their members out of jobs by demanding excessive wages for insufficient output, making British goods uncompetitive. So both Norman Tebbit, my new Secretary of State for Employment, and I were impatient to press ahead with further reforms in trade union law, which we knew to be necessary and popular, not least among trade unionists.

Towards the end of October 1981 Norman sought Cabinet agreement for what was to become the Employment Act, 1982.

By far the most important of Norman's proposals related to the immunity currently extended to trade union funds. By virtue of Section 14 of Labour's Trade Union and Labour Relations Act, 1974, trade unions enjoyed virtually unlimited immunity from actions for damages, even if industrial action was not taken in contemplation or furtherance of a trade dispute. They could not be sued for their unlawful acts or for unlawful acts done on their behalf by their officials. This breadth of immunity was quite indefensible. As long as unions were able to shelter behind it they had no incentive to ensure that industrial action was restricted to legitimate trade disputes and that it was lawful in other ways. Norman therefore proposed that this immunity should be reduced to that enjoyed by individuals under our 1980 legislation. Both of those immunities would be restricted further by our proposals which removed that immunity for disputes not mainly about pay and conditions and for disputes between trade unions.

There was at first some opposition in Cabinet to Norman's proposals, but most of us were full of admiration for his boldness. He went away to consider some of the points made in discussion, but the package agreed by Cabinet in November was more or less on the lines he wanted. Norman announced our intentions to the House of Commons later that month. The Bill was introduced the following February and the Act's main provisions finally came into force on 1 December 1982.

Far from being unpopular, these proposals were soon being criticized on the grounds that they did not go far enough. The SDP were trying to outflank us by urging greater use of mandatory secret ballots. Many of our own supporters wanted to see action to stop the abuses connected with the 'political levy', a substantial sum extracted from trade unionists largely for the benefit of the Labour Party. There was continuing pressure to do something to prevent strikes in essential services. But it would not have been practical to deal with all of these issues at once in a single Bill: each raised complicated questions and we could not afford to make mistakes in this vital area. I was glad, however, that the atmosphere had changed and that the dangers of trade union power were now so much more widely understood. We were winning that battle, too.

In September Norman came forward with a paper containing his thoughts for new industrial relations legislation which would be formally submitted to 'E' Committee, the Economic Committee of the Cabinet, with a view to inclusion in the manifesto. Norman had already announced that we would undertake consultations with interested parties on legislation that would require trade unions to use secret ballots for the election of their leaders. There was strong support in both Houses for mandatory secret ballots before industrial action. But we were divided on this.

Ministers now discussed what should be the priorities for the forth-coming consultative Green Paper. We agreed to concentrate on ballots for the election of trade union leaders, mandatory strike ballots, and the political levy. Norman had reservations about the use of compulsory ballots before strikes. We had previously concluded that these should be voluntary. Moreover, there were doubts whether or not the use of ballots would actually reduce the frequency and length of strikes. But I was very aware of the great advantages of linking trade union reform to the unas-sailable principle of democracy, and I was keen to see that the proposals on strike ballots were expressed in a positive way in the Green Paper.

We published the Green Paper under the title *Democracy in Trade Unions*, in January 1983. Ministers discussed in April where we should go from there. We had no difficulty deciding in favour of proposals relating to trade union elections and strike ballots. Two other issues proved much more difficult: the prevention of strikes in essential services and the political levy.

Public sector strikes and consequent disruption to the lives of the general public had been a feature of life in post-war Britain, but the practical difficulties of tackling the problem were immense. How should one define an 'essential service'? How much would it cost the taxpayer in extra pay to secure 'no strike' agreements? What should be the penalty for failure to observe a 'no strike' agreement?

The political levy was a second difficult subject. It was paid by trade unionists into political funds held by their unions, the principal use of which was, in fact, to support the Labour Party. Payment was on the basis of 'contracting out': that is, trade unionists contributed automatically unless they specified otherwise. On the face of it, it would have been fairer to base the system on a principle of 'contracting in' and some argued for the change. But 'contracting in' would have wreaked havoc with the Labour Party's finances. Had we introduced such a measure, there would undoubtedly have been pressure to change the system by which some companies donated to political parties, from which, of course, the Conservative Party heavily benefited. I never believed that the cases were parallel: after all, trade unionists in a closed shop could find it very difficult to avoid paying the political levy. By contrast, shareholders who did not approve of company donations to a political party could either hold the Board to account for their decisions or simply sell their shares. But the funding of political parties was a sensitive topic. If we brought forward radical proposals on the eve of a general election, we would be accused both of attempting to crush the Labour Party financially and of unfairness on the matter of corporate donations.

On Tuesday 10 May I held a meeting of ministers at which we decided our manifesto commitment. On essential services, the introduction of strike ballots would clearly help reduce the risk of strikes in these areas. But we would also consult further about the need for industrial relations in specified essential services to be governed by adequate procedure agreements, breach of which would deprive industrial action of immunity. On the question of the political levy, we had evidence from the consultations on the Green Paper that there was widespread disquiet about the operation of the system and we proposed to consult with the TUC to see what action they were prepared to take, failing which we would act ourselves. These were matters to which we would have to return after the election. But we had made substantial progress in reducing the overbearing power of trade unions – much more than the faint-hearted had ever believed possible. And far from proving a political incubus it was one of our strongest appeals to the voters.

For all sorts of reasons it is much easier to prepare for an election when you are in government than in Opposition. You have more information available about forthcoming events and more power to shape them. But parties in government face two risks in particular. First, ministers can get out of the habit of thinking politically and become cocooned in their departments. Having to face, as I did, rigorous cross-questioning from an often hostile House of Commons twice a week, there was little danger that I personally would succumb to this: but others might. The second risk is that having implemented its manifesto, a government may run out of ideas. It is part of the job of ministers to see that this does not happen in their own areas of responsibility, and the job of the Prime Minister to prevent it happening to the Government as a whole.

One of the main obstacles to the kind of forward thinking which all governments should do is unauthorized disclosure of information by disaffected ministers or civil servants. A particularly serious problem arose in the last half of the 1979–83 Parliament. In March 1982 Geoffrey Howe asked officials to undertake an examination of long-term public expenditure up to and including 1990 and its implications for levels of taxation: their report was presented to me on 28 July. It was intended to get us all to examine how the long-term momentum for the expansion of the state and public spending might be curbed and reversed. As it turned out the paper was excessively gloomy and its most likely scenario under-estimated very substantially the economic growth rate for the 1980s. To make matters worse, the CPRS prepared its own paper, which contained a number of very radical options that had never been seriously consid-ered by ministers or by me. These included, for example, sweeping changes in the financing of the National Health Service and extensions of the use of charging. I was horrified. As soon as I saw the paper, I pointed out that it would almost certainly be leaked and give a totally false impression. That is exactly what happened.

When the papers were discussed at Cabinet in early September, they made no great impact on our thinking. Our main conclusions could have been reached without any such exercise: that there should be no major new expenditure commitments pending further consideration, and that we should generally examine the scope for changing policies in ways which would bring public spending under proper control. But that failed to stop the media frenzy. A fairly full account of the CPRS paper duly appeared in the *Economist*. The *Observer* developed the story. The *Economist* later gave a blow-by-blow account of discussions at Cabinet. The *Observer* and then *The Times* revealed still more information. Of course, the Opposition had a field day. We were to be plagued by talk of secret proposals and hidden manifestos up to polling day and beyond. It was all the greatest nonsense.

There were two lessons from this incident which I never forgot. The first was that we had political opponents about us who would stop at nothing to distort and thereby prevent our forward thinking on policy. The second lesson was of equal importance: it was unacceptable for highly controversial proposals to come before Cabinet without the prior knowledge and approval of the ministers responsible. This raised acutely what role there could be for the CPRS.

In earlier days, the CPRS had been a valuable source of sound long-range analysis and practical advice. But it had become a freelance 'Ministry of Bright Ideas', some of which were sound, some not. Moreover, as I have noted earlier, a government with a clear sense of direction does not need advice from first principles. Now, as this incident had shown, the CPRS could become a positive embarrassment. That was why, shortly after the election, I was to dissolve the 'Think-Tank', and ask two of its members to join the in-house Policy Unit which worked more closely with me.

Ferdy Mount was now head of my Policy Unit. I had long been a great admirer of Ferdy's witty and thoughtful articles even when, as over the Falklands, I did not agree with his views; and I was delighted when in April 1982 he agreed to succeed John Hoskyns. Ferdy was particularly interested in all that goes under the heading of social policy – education, criminal justice, housing, the family and so on, to which I was increasingly turning my attention. In late May he prepared for me a paper which contained the outline of an approach to 'renewing the values of society':

> This Government came to power asserting that it is the exercise of responsibility which teaches self-discipline. But in the early stages of life it is the experience of authority, when exerted fairly and consistently by adults, which teaches young people how to exercise responsibility themselves. We have to learn to take orders before we learn how to give them. This two-way relationship between

obedience and responsibility is what makes a free, self-governing society. And in the breakdown of that relationship we can trace the origins of so much that has gone wrong with Britain.

If we can rebuild this relationship, we might begin to restore also respect for law and order, respect for property, and respect for teachers and parents. But the rebuilding itself has to be a two-way business. On the one hand, we need to restore effective authority to teachers and parents. On the other hand, we need to offer young people a taste of responsibility and a useful role in society.

CHAPTER TWENTY-THREE

Home and Dry

The background to and course of the 1983 general election campaign

THE CENTRAL IMPORTANCE of the manifesto in British general elections often strikes foreign observers as slightly odd. In the United States and continental Europe, party 'platforms' have less authority and as a result they are not nearly as closely studied. Even in Britain it is only relatively recently that manifestos have been so full of detailed proposals.

The first Conservative manifesto was Sir Robert Peel's 1835 address to his electors in Tamworth. The 'Tamworth manifesto', for all the obvious differences, has one basic similarity with the Conservative manifesto today: it was then and is now very much the Party Leader's own statement of policies.

However, the rest of the Government and Parliamentary Party need to feel committed to the manifesto's proposals and consequently there has to be a good deal of consultation. I discussed the question with Cecil Parkinson and we agreed that Geoffrey Howe was the right person to oversee the manifesto-making process. As Chancellor of the Exchequer he had the seniority and experience to supervise the required policy work. Looking back, this arrangement was successful in one of its aims – that of reducing the burden on me – but it turned out to have significant drawbacks. In 1987 I decided to oversee the preparation of the manifesto myself.

The whole process began almost a year before the election. On Saturday 19 June 1982 I approved the setting up of Party policy groups with the remit of identifying 'tasks for Conservative administration during the rest of this decade; to make proposals for action where possible; where not possible, to identify subjects for further study'. The nine groups we set up covered unemployment, enterprise, family and women's affairs, education, the cities and law and order, the poverty trap, the European Community, nationalized industries and urban transport. We decided that the chairman of each group should be a parliamentarian who would help to select members for their group from among the Conservative-minded in the worlds of business, academia, voluntary service and local government. Special advisers to the relevant Cabinet ministers would sit in on the meetings. (Special advisers are political appointees, and so free from the constraints of political neutrality which prevent the use of civil servants in such roles.) Secretarial and research work was done by members of the Conservative Research Department.

Essentially, the policy groups had two purposes. The more important was to involve the Party as a whole in our thinking for the future. In this I believe they were successful. The second was to come up with fresh ideas for the manifesto, and unfortunately in this purpose they failed. For one reason or another it took too long to find appropriate chairmen and the right balance of group members. It was not until October or November 1982 that the groups actually got down to work. The groups were due to report only at the end of March 1983, but by then of course we in government were all well advanced on our own policy work. Another problem is the human vanity of wanting to demonstrate that you are on the inside track. All too often their proposals trickled out through the press.

The fact is that the really bold proposals in any manifesto can only be developed over a considerable period of time. Relying on bright ideas thought out at the last moment risks a manifesto that would be incoherent and impossible to carry out. So, in the end, the real work for the 1983 manifesto had to be done in No. 10 and by ministers in departments.

The most important pledges in the manifesto fell into three groups. First, we promised to accelerate privatization, which was fundamental to our whole economic approach. If elected, we committed ourselves to sell British Telecom, British Airways, substantial parts of British Steel, British Shipbuilders, British Leyland and as many as possible of Britain's airports. The offshore oil interests of British Gas would also be privatized and private capital would be introduced into the National Bus Company. This was an ambitious programme.

The second important group of pledges concerned trade union reform. Building on the consultations on our Trade Union Democracy Green Paper, we promised legislation to require ballots for the election of trade union governing bodies and ballots before strikes, failing which unions would lose their immunities. There was also a cautious pledge to consider legislation on the trade union political levy and on strikes in essential services. At a time when Labour was promising to repeal our earlier trade union reforms, we were moving ahead with new ones: the contrast was stark, and we were sure the voters would appreciate the fact.

The third significant group of manifesto proposals related to local government. In particular, we promised to abolish the Greater London Council (GLC) and the Metropolitan County Councils, returning their functions to councils closer to the people – the boroughs in London, and the districts in the other metropolitan areas. We also promised to introduce what came to be known as 'rate-capping' – legislation enabling us to curb the extravagance of high-spending councils, in the interests of local ratepayers and the wider economy.

Though the manifesto took our programme forward, it was somehow not an exciting document. The first years of Conservative administration had been dominated by the battle against inflation and by a different kind of warfare in the South Atlantic. Great as the achievements were, neither economics nor defence is the kind of issue that generates exciting material for manifestos. Social policy is very different, but we were only really starting to turn our attention to this area. And on this occasion at least, Geoffrey Howe may have been too safe a pair of hands.

Perhaps the most important feature of the manifesto was what it did not contain. It did not promise a change of direction or an easing of the pace. It gave no quarter to the advocates of socialism and corporatism.

On Wednesday 5 January 1983 I set aside a full day for discussion of our general election strategy. It was in the recess, so we held it at Chequers, always a relaxing place to think things out. The first half of the morning was spent with Cecil Parkinson, Michael Spicer (Deputy Chairman of the Party), Ian Gow and David Wolfson.

We discussed how to handle television: it was likely to be even more important than in earlier elections, though the new breakfast television would have less impact than had often been predicted. Gordon Reece had come over from the United States to help with this aspect of the campaign. Gordon was a former television producer with a unique insight into the medium. He had a much better grasp of popular taste than might have been expected from a man whose principal diet was champagne and cigars. He argued that we should be prepared to accept a series of televised debates between myself and Michael Foot, and (separately) with the Alliance leaders. This was an exceptional suggestion: British Prime Ministers have never accepted challenges to election debates of this kind. I rejected the idea. I disliked the way that elections were being turned into media circuses. And the arguments were too important to be reduced to a 'sound bite' or a gladiatorial sport.

One of our principal assets was the state of the Party's organization. Cecil Parkinson had done wonders for Central Office. He had brought the Party's finances into order since he had become Chairman: this was essential, because it is only by husbanding resources in mid-term that you can afford to spend as heavily as required in a general election campaign.

In the afternoon Tim Bell presented a paper summarizing the strengths and weaknesses of our position, based upon opinion polls. Tim could pick up quicker than anyone else a change in the national mood. And, unlike most advertising men, he understood that selling ideas is different from selling soap. Tim set out a communications strategy whose main theme was 'keep on with the change', an approach I welcomed. Its wisdom lay in the perception that it was the Conservative Government rather than the Opposition parties which was the radical force in British society.

At this meeting I made no secret of the fact that my own instincts were against an early election; I had in mind an election in October. I was convinced that we were now seeing sustainable economic recovery, which would continue to strengthen the longer we waited: clearly, the more solid economic good news we could show the better.

But, of course, the overriding consideration in choosing an election date is whether or not you think you are going to win. On Sunday 8 May I had a final Chequers meeting with Cecil Parkinson, Willie Whitelaw, Geoffrey Howe, Norman Tebbit, Michael Jopling, Ferdy Mount, David Wolfson and Ian Gow. There had been local government elections on Thursday 5 May and we knew that the results would tell us a good deal about our prospects. Central Office staff had worked furiously to provide a detailed computer analysis by the weekend. We also had the evidence provided by private and public opinion polls.

By long-established custom, elections take place on a Thursday: if we were to go in June, which Thursday should it be? It seemed that the second Thursday in June would be best, although this meant that the campaign would have to include a Bank Holiday – something electioneers prefer to avoid since it is almost impossible to campaign over that weekend. But Ascot began the following Monday and I did not like the idea of television screens during the final or penultimate week of the campaign filled with pictures of toffs and ladies in exotic hats while we stumped the country urging people to turn out and vote Conservative. Therefore, if we went in June it would have to be the 9th.

I did not make up my mind finally that day, returning to No. 10 only provisionally convinced. When I am making a big decision, I always prefer to sleep on it.

The following morning just before 7 o'clock I rang down to the duty clerk asking my principal private secretary, Robin Butler, to see me as soon as he came in: Robin would arrange for an Audience with the Queen later that morning. I had decided to seek a dissolution and go to the country on Thursday 9 June.

I saw the Chief Whip and the Party Chairman to tell them of my decision, summoned a special Cabinet for 11.15 a.m. and went on to the Palace at 12.25 p.m. The rest of the day was spent discussing final election campaign preparations and the manifesto, and recording interviews.

I also had to make some decisions about my future engagements as Prime Minister, particularly meetings already arranged with foreign visitors: which, if any, should I see? Another question was whether I should go to the United States for the forthcoming G7 summit at Williamsburg at the end of May. I decided immediately that I had to cancel my planned visit to Washington on 26 May for pre-summit talks with President Reagan. As for the Williamsburg summit itself, I was minded to go. The summit was important in its own right, not least because the President would be chairing it. Moreover, it would show Britain in a leading international role and lend international endorsement to the sort of policies we were pursuing.

Labour's manifesto, all over the newspapers shortly before the dissolution of Parliament, was an appalling document. It committed the Party to a non-nuclear defence, withdrawal from the European Community, enormously increased public spending and a host of other irresponsible policies and was dubbed by one of the wittier Shadow Cabinet ministers 'the longest suicide note ever written'. We were very keen to publicize it and I understand that Conservative Central Office placed the largest single order for copies. But at my customary address to the '22 that evening, I warned the Party against overconfidence: even a short election campaign is quite long enough for things to go badly wrong.

The next day I flew to Scotland to address the Scottish Conservative Party Conference in Perth. The hall in Perth is not large, but it has excel-

lent acoustics. In spite of a sore throat from the tail-end of a heavy cold, I
enjoyed myself.

That weekend I was also able to study the results of our first major
'state of battle' opinion poll survey. It showed that we had a 14 per cent
lead over Labour and that there had been a fall in support for the Alliance.
This was, of course, very satisfactory. I was glad to note that there was no
evidence that people thought I had been wrong to call the election;
indeed, the great majority thought it was the correct decision. But the poll
also showed that if the Alliance looked in with a chance there was considerable potential for an increase in its support from weakly committed
Conservative and Labour voters. Obviously this was something we would
have to guard against.

In 1983, as in 1979 and 1987, we usually began the morning with a press
conference on a prearranged topic. Before the press conference I was
briefed in Central Office – during this election by Stephen Sherbourne,
who would shortly join my team in Downing Street as political secretary.
This briefing took place at 8.30 a.m. in a cramped room at Central Office.
We would begin by approving the day's press release and go on to
consider questions likely to come up. Someone from the Conservative
Research Department would come in partway through the briefing to
report what had happened at Labour's press conference. It was convenient that Labour's daily schedule ran ahead of ours. Our press conference
would begin at 9.30 a.m. and was planned to last an hour. We had
arranged my tours so that I spent very few nights away from London, and
therefore I was nearly always available to chair it. I would field some of
the questions myself, but try to give whichever ministers were appearing
beside me that morning a chance to make their points.

Our main aim both in the press conferences and speeches was to deal
with the difficult question of unemployment by showing that we were
prepared to take it head-on and prove that our policies were the best to
provide jobs in the future. So successful were we in this that by the end of
the campaign the opinion polls showed that we were more trusted to deal
with this problem than Labour. People knew that the real reasons for the
high level of unemployment were not Conservative policies but rather
past overmanning and inefficiency, strikes, technological change, changes
in the pattern of world trade and the international recession. Labour lost
the argument when they tried to place the whole blame for this deep-
seated problem on the callous, uncaring Tories.

Then there were the speeches. During the campaign I used Sundays to work on speeches for the forthcoming week with Ferdy Mount and others at Chequers. Ferdy had prepared about half a dozen speech drafts on different topics before the campaign. The actual speeches I delivered consisted of extracts from these, with additional material often provided by Ronnie Millar and John Gummer, and topical comment addressing the issue of the day. I would put on the finishing touches in the campaign coach, trains, aeroplanes, cars and just about anywhere else you can imagine along the campaign trail. There were a few big speeches during this election but a large number of short speeches on 'whistle stops', often delivered off the back of a lorry on a small mobile platform, always off the cuff. I preferred the whistle stops, particularly when there were some hecklers. People tell me that I am an old-fashioned campaigner; I enjoy verbal combat, though it has to be said that neither I nor the crowds derived much intellectual challenge from the monotonous chants of the CND and Socialist Worker protesters who followed me round the country.

Third, there were the tours themselves. The basic principle, of course, is that you should concentrate the Leader's appearances in marginal seats. One day on the campaign bus David Wolfson chided me for waving too much to people watching us pass: 'only wave in marginals, Prime Minister'. As the importance of television and the 'photo-opportunity' increases, the Leader's physical location on a particular day is rather less important than it once was, but one thing you must do is to visit all the main regions of the country: nothing is more devastating to candidates and party workers than to think they have been written off.

Finally, there were the interviews. They came in quite different styles. Brian Walden on *Weekend World* would ask the most probing questions. Robin Day on *Panorama* was probably the most aggressive, though in this campaign he made the mistake of plunging into detail on the problem of calculating the impact of unemployment on the public finances – a gaffe when cross-examining a former Minister of National Insurance. I made a gaffe of my own calling Sir Robin 'Mr Day' throughout. Alistair Burnet specialized in short, subtle questions which sounded innocuous but contained hidden dangers. One needed all one's nimbleness of wit to make it unscathed through the minefields. Then there were the programmes on which members of the public asked questions. My favourite was always the *Granada 500* when a large audience quizzes you about the things which really matter to them.

Our manifesto was launched at the first Conservative press conference on Wednesday 18 May. The whole Cabinet was there. I ran through the main proposals, and then Geoffrey Howe, Norman Tebbit and Tom King made short statements on their sections of the manifesto. After that I invited questions. Manifestos rarely make the headlines unless, as on this occasion, something goes wrong. The press will consign carefully thought-out proposals for government to an inside page and concentrate on the slightest evidence of a 'split'. At the press conference a journalist asked Francis Pym about negotiations with Argentina. I felt that Francis's reply risked being ambiguous, so I interrupted to make clear that while we would negotiate on commercial and diplomatic links, we would not discuss sovereignty. The press highlighted this: but there was in fact no split. That's politics.

It was not Francis Pym's week. He told a questioner on BBC's *Question Time* that in his opinion 'landslides on the whole don't produce successful governments'. Naturally, people drew the inference that he did not want us to win a large majority. Of course, this was all very well for those with safe seats like Francis himself. But it was distinctly less good news for candidates in the Conservative marginals and those of our people hoping to win seats from other parties. And since complacency was likely to be our worst enemy in the campaign, this remark struck a wrong note.

The first regular press conference on the campaign took place on Friday 20 May. Geoffrey Howe challenged Labour on the cost of their manifesto proposals and said that if they did not publish them, we would. This was the first deployment of a very effective campaign theme. Patrick Jenkin, taking it up, drew attention to Labour's plans for nationalization and regulation of industry. There were a number of questions about the economy. But, inevitably, what the press really wanted to know was what I thought about Francis's remark. Francis had been Chief Whip under Ted Heath and I made that the basis of my reply:

> I think I could handle a landslide majority all right. I think the comment you're referring to was natural Chief Whip's caution. Ex-Chief Whip's caution. You know there's a club of Chief Whips. They're very unusual people.

It was on Monday 23 May that my campaign began in earnest. We started as usual with a briefing meeting for that morning's press conference where we spent some time discussing the Party's advertising. Saatchi

& Saatchi had devised some brilliant advertisements and posters in 1979. Most of those they produced in 1983 were not quite as good, although there were exceptions. One compared the Communist and Labour Party manifestos by printing side by side a list of identical commitments from each. It was a long list. A second poster set out 14 rights and freedoms that the voter would be signing away if Labour was elected and carried out its programme. Another poster, aimed at winning us support from ethnic minorities with the slogan 'Labour Think He's Black, Conservatives Think He's British', caused some controversy. But I thought it was perfectly fair. I did, however, veto one showing a particularly unflattering picture of Michael Foot with the slogan: 'Under The Conservatives All Pensioners Are Better Off'. Maybe that was a fair political point too: but I do not like personal attacks.

My speech that evening was at the Cardiff City Hall. It was a long speech, made a little longer but much more lively when I broke away from the text, which always seems to help the delivery. I covered all the main election issues – jobs, health, pensions, defence – but the lines I liked best related to Labour's plans for savings:

> Under a Labour Government, there's virtually nowhere you can put your savings where they would be safe from the state. They want your money for state socialism, and they mean to get it. Put your savings in the bank – and they'll nationalize it. Put your savings in a pension fund or a life assurance company – and a Labour Government would force them to invest the money in their own socialist schemes. If you put money in a sock they'd probably nationalize socks.

I had returned early to No. 10 from Tuesday's daily tour in order to prepare for a Question and Answer session with Sue Lawley on *Nationwide*. This unfortunately degenerated into an argument about the sinking of the *General Belgrano*.

The Left thought it was scoring points by keeping the public's attention focused on this, exploiting minor discrepancies to support its theory of a ruthless government intent on slaughter. This was not only odious; it was inept. The voters overwhelmingly accepted our view that protecting British lives came first. On the *Belgrano*, as on everything else, the Left's obsessions were at variance with their interests. But I found the whole episode distasteful.

The Labour Party was now in deep trouble. On Wednesday 25 May – the very day we had chosen to devote to defence – Jim Callaghan made a speech in Wales rejecting unilateral nuclear disarmament. The newspapers were full of contradictory statements about Labour's position on nuclear weapons. Even among Labour front-benchers there was disarray: you could choose between Michael Foot, Denis Healey and John Silkin – each seemed to have his own defence policy. Michael Heseltine at our press conference and throughout the campaign was devastating in his criticisms of Labour's policy.

I always realized that there were a few issues on which Labour was especially vulnerable – issues on which they had irresponsible policies but ones to which the public attached great importance. They were the 'gut issues'. Defence was one. Another was public spending. For that reason I was very keen that Geoffrey Howe do a more comprehensive costing of Labour's manifesto promises than usual. He produced a superb analysis that ran to twenty pages. It showed that Labour's plans implied additional spending in the life of a Parliament of between £36–43 billion – the latter figure almost equal to the total revenue of income tax at that time. Labour's economic credibility never recovered. Indeed, Labour's profligacy has been its Achilles heel in every election I have fought – all the more reason for a Conservative Government to manage the nation's economic affairs prudently.

On Thursday 26 May the opinion polls reported in the press gave us anything between a 13 and 19 per cent lead over Labour. The principal danger from now on would be complacency among Conservative voters rather than any desperate Labour attempts at a comeback.

Thursday was to be a pleasant day of traditional campaigning, this time in Yorkshire. One highlight was lunch in Harry Ramsden's Fish and Chip Shop – the 'biggest fish and chip shop in the Free World' – in Leeds. I thoroughly enjoyed myself.

That evening I spoke at the Royal Hall, Harrogate, dwelling on a theme which was central to my political strategy. The turbulence of politics in the 1970s and 1980s had overturned the set patterns of British politics. Labour's own drift to the left and the extremism of the trade unions had disillusioned and fractured its traditional support. They were benefiting from the opportunities we had made available, especially the sale of council houses; more important, they shared our values, including a strong belief in family life and an intense patriotism. We now had an opportunity to bring them into the Conservative fold, and I directed my speech at Harrogate to doing just that.

By the time that I arrived back in London on Friday there had been yet another extraordinary development in Labour's campaign. Labour's General Secretary, Jim Mortimer, reported to an astonished press corps that 'The unanimous view of the campaign committee is that Michael Foot is the Leader of the Labour Party.' With statements like that one wondered how long either of them would keep his job.

My own mind that evening was very much on the forthcoming G7 economic summit at Williamsburg, for which I would leave for the United States at midday on Saturday.

Whatever its electoral implications for me, there was no doubt that the Williamsburg summit was of real international importance. President Reagan was determined to make a success of it. At previous G7 summits the scope for genuine discussion had been somewhat limited by the fact that a draft communiqué had been drawn up even before the leaders met. This time the Americans had insisted that we should discuss first and draft later, which was far more sensible. But I took along a British draft just in case it was needed.

The atmosphere at Williamsburg was excellent, not just because of the President's own radiant good humour but because of the place itself. In the surroundings of this restored Virginian town each head of government stayed in a separate house. We were welcomed by friendly townspeople in old-style colonial dress. There was a complete contrast with the perhaps over-luxurious feel of Versailles.

The two main objectives which President Reagan and I shared for the summit were the reaffirmation of sound economic policies and a public demonstration of our unity behind NATO's position on arms control, especially as regards the deployment of Cruise and Pershing II missiles. I introduced the discussion on arms control at dinner on Saturday. In fact, by that morning we had what most of us considered a satisfactory draft communiqué. France's position – as a country outside the NATO command structure – required to be taken into account. But President Mitterrand said that he had no dispute with the substance of our proposal. In fact, he came up with an amendment that we were able to accept, because it strengthened it in the direction we wanted. It seems improbable that President Mitterrand realized this.

The text on the economy was pretty satisfactory as well, except for a little misty language on exchange rate co-ordination.

I came home by the overnight British Airways flight, confident that the outcome of the summit vindicated my approach to the crucial election issues of defence and the economy. This summit also marked a change in the relationship between President Reagan and the other heads of government. They had sometimes been dismissive of his grasp of detail. I, myself, had felt some concern about this earlier. Not so on this occasion. He had all the facts and figures at his fingertips. He steered the discussions with great skill and aplomb. He managed to get all he wanted from the summit, while allowing everyone to feel that they had got at least some of what *they* wanted, and he did all this with an immense geniality. What President Reagan demonstrated at Williamsburg was that he was a master politician.

Monday 30 May was a Bank Holiday. That day Denis Healey released what the Labour Party claimed was the 'real' Conservative manifesto, a fantastical affair, full of lies, half-truths and scares culled from reports of leaked documents, especially the CPRS long-term public expenditure document, the whole thing imaginatively embellished. I was not surprised. Labour had tried this tactic in 1979: it had not worked then either. Once again, Labour was catering not to the interests of the voter but to its own obsessions. They failed to realize that propaganda can never persuade people of the incredible.

I am not usually much affected either by pressure of work or by attacks from opponents. But on Wednesday 1 June Denis Healey made the tasteless remark that I had been 'glorying in slaughter' during the Falklands War. I was both angry and upset. We had deliberately decided not to raise the Falklands in the campaign and had done nothing whatsoever to make it an issue. The remark hurt and offended many people besides me – not all of them Conservatives – particularly the relatives of those who had fought and died in the war. Mr Healey later made a half-hearted retraction: he had meant to say 'conflict' rather than 'slaughter' – a distinction without a difference. Neil Kinnock returned to the subject a few days later, in an even more offensive form. These remarks were all the more revealing because they were politically stupid: indeed they did enormous harm to Labour. They were not made from political calculation, but can only have emerged from something coarse and brutal in the imagination.

One of the opinion polls on Sunday put the Alliance ahead of Labour for the first time. This gave the last days of the campaign a new feel and a new uncertainty. But personally I never believed that the Alliance would beat

Labour into third place – even though the Labour leaders were doing their best to ensure it did.

I chaired our last press conference of the campaign on Wednesday morning, accompanied by more or less the same team as had launched the manifesto. There was an end-of-term feeling among the journalists, which we felt confident enough to share. I said that the vital issues on which the voters must decide between the parties were defence, jobs, social services, home ownership and the rule of law. I was keen to answer the charge that a large Conservative majority would lead us to ditch our manifesto policies and pursue a 'hidden agenda' of an extreme kind. I argued that a large Conservative majority would in fact do something quite different: it would be a blow against extremism in the Labour Party. And that, I think, was the real underlying theme of the 1983 general election.

While waiting for my own count to finish I watched the national results coming in on television. It really was a landslide. We had won a majority of 144: the largest of any party since 1945.

I returned to Conservative Central Office in the early hours. I was greeted by cheering Party staff as I entered and gave a short speech of thanks to them for their efforts. After that I returned to No. 10. Crowds had gathered at the end of Downing Street and I went along to talk to them, as I had on the evening of the Argentine surrender. Then I went up to the flat. Over the previous weeks I had spent some time clearing things out, in case we lost the election. Now the clutter could build up again.

ABOVE The Grand Hotel in Brighton after it was bombed in October 1984.

LEFT Leaving the hotel with Denis, following the blast.

ABOVE Photocall at Chequers with the Gorbachevs during their first visit to Britain in December 1984.

BELOW Meeting Den Xiaoping in Peking in December 1984.

ABOVE With President Reagan at Camp David in December 1984.

BELOW Signing the Anglo-Irish Agreement at Hillsborough Castle,
15 November 1985, with Dr Garret FitzGerald, the Irish Taoiseach.

Greeting the Queen outside No. 10.

ABOVE Signing and exchanging the Channel Tunnel Agreement with President Mitterrand in 1986.

BELOW Some of the Commonwealth leaders who attended the Special Commonwealth Conference in London, August 1986. From l-r: *back row* Rajiv Gandhi, Brian Mulroney, Sonny Ramphal, Bob Hawke, Robert Mugabe; *front row* myself, Sir Lynden Pindling, Kenneth Kaunda.

ABOVE In the kitchen at No. 10, being filmed for a BBC series.

LEFT On holiday with Denis in Cornwall, 1987.

ABOVE Launching the 1987 general election manifesto with Willie Whitelaw and Norman Tebbit at Central Office.

BELOW Talking to the media from the Conservative Party 'battle bus' during the 1987 general election campaign.

Outside No. 10 with Denis after the historic third election victory.

ABOVE With Neil Kinnock at the State Opening of Parliament in June 1987.

BELOW Walking across a desolate urban landscape near Stockton-on-Tees in September 1987.

ABOVE With President Reagan outside No. 10 when he
visited Britain in June 1988.

BELOW At the dinner at No. 10 held in honour of
President Reagan; on the right is George Shultz.

*Dear Margaret – As you can see, I agree with every word you are
saying. I always do. Warmest Friendship.
Sincerely Ron*

ABOVE Test driving the new Challenger tank during a visit to Germany in September 1988.

BELOW Arriving at Camp David by helicopter for talks with President Bush, November 1989.

With Helmut Kohl at a press conference in February 1990.

With Boris Yeltsin at No. 10
in April 1990.

With Nelson Mandela during his
visit to Britain in July 1990.

Addressing the United Nations General Assembly in November 1989.

ABOVE Receiving a standing ovation at the Party Conference in October 1989.

BELOW With members of the Cabinet and Denis at the Carlton Club for a dinner to mark my tenth anniversary as Prime Minister, May 1989.

ABOVE Answering questions in the House of Commons in October 1990.

BELOW Driving away from Buckingham Palace having handed over the seals of office, 28 November 1990.

aving No. 10 for the last time.

CHAPTER TWENTY-FOUR

Back to Normalcy

Politics, the economy and foreign affairs from
the election to the end of 1983

THE 1983 MANIFESTO did not inspire the Government with the sort
of crusading spirit which would have got us off to a good start in the
new Parliament. Some of the main pledges were popular enough, such as
the abolition of the GLC and Metropolitan Counties and the introduction of rate-capping, but they ran into a difficulty with which any reforming administration must bear: that the generalized approval of the silent
majority is no match for the chorus of disapproval from the organized
minority. The left-wing municipal socialists and their subsidized front
organizations were astute campaigners. Much of the manifesto promised
'more of the same' – not the most inspiring of cries, although there is no
doubt that a lot more was needed. We had not yet cut taxes anything like
as much as we wished. There was more work to be done on trade union
law and the privatization programme was barely under way; the Bill to
privatize British Telecom, which had fallen with the election, had to be
reintroduced.

The second problem was that there was still too much socialism in
Britain. The fortunes of socialism do not depend on those of the Labour
Party: in fact, in the long run it would be truer to say that Labour's
fortunes depend on those of socialism. And socialism was still built into
the institutions and mentality of Britain. We had sold thousands of
council homes; but 29 per cent of the housing stock remained in the
public sector. We had increased parents' rights in the education system;
but the ethos in classrooms and teachers' training colleges remained stubbornly left wing. We had grappled with the problem of bringing more

efficiency into local government; but the Left's redoubts in the great cities still went virtually unchallenged. We had cut back trade union power; but still almost 50 per cent of the workforce in employment was unionized, and of them around 4 million were working in a union closed shop. Moreover, as the miners' strike would shortly demonstrate, the grip of the hard Left on union power was still unbroken. We had won a great victory in the Falklands War, reversing the years in which British influence seemed doomed to an inexorable retreat; but there was still a sour envy of American power and sometimes a deeper anti-Americanism, shared by too many across the political spectrum.

In all this, my problem was simple. There was a revolution still to be made, but too few revolutionaries. The appointment of the first Cabinet in the new Parliament, which took place incongruously to the background accompaniment of traditional military music and the Trooping of the Colour, seemed a chance to recruit some.

In following Peter Carrington with Francis Pym as Foreign Secretary I had exchanged an amusing Whig for a gloomy one. Francis and I disagreed on the direction of policy, in our approach to government and indeed about life in general. But he was liked in the House of Commons which always warms to a minister who is believed to be out of step with the Government, something which is often mistaken for independence of mind. I hoped he would consent to become Speaker and I still believe that he would have done the job well. (In fact, I am not at all clear that we would have been able to ensure Francis got the job for it is, of course, a decision for the House itself.)

But in any case he was having none of it. He preferred to go to the backbenches where he was a not very effective critic of the Government.

I also asked David Howell to leave the Cabinet. His shortcomings as an administrator had been exposed when he was at Energy and nothing I saw of his performance at Transport suggested to me that my judgement of him was wrong. He lacked the mixture of creative political imagination and practical drive to be a first-class Cabinet minister. And I asked Janet Young to make way for Willie Whitelaw as Leader of the Lords. She had turned out not to have the presence to lead the Lords effectively and she was perhaps too consistent an advocate of caution on all occasions. She stayed on in the Government outside the Cabinet as a Minister of State at the Foreign Office. I regretted the loss of both David and Janet on personal grounds, for they had been close to me in Opposition.

Willie Whitelaw clearly fitted the bill as Janet's successor. Willie had become, quite simply, indispensable to me in Cabinet. When it really mattered I knew he would be by my side and because of his background, personality and position in the Party he could sometimes sway colleagues when I could not. Yet Willie had not had an easy time as Home Secretary. In part, this is because Home Secretaries never do have an easy time; it is sometimes said that they possess a unique combination of responsibility without power, taking the blame for matters ranging from breaches of royal security, to the misdemeanours of police officers, prison break-outs and the occasional riot, when their power to prevent them is indirect or nonexistent. But there was more to it than that. Willie and I knew that we did not share the same instincts on Home Office matters. I believe that capital punishment for the worst murders is morally right as retribution and practically necessary as a deterrent: Willie does not. My views on sentencing in general and on immigration are a good deal tougher than his. And, flatteringly but often awkwardly, the great majority of the Conservative Party and the British public agreed with me and showed it regularly at our Party Conferences.

I chose Leon Brittan to be Willie's successor. I never appointed a Home Secretary who shared all my instincts on these matters, but I thought that at least Leon would bring a keen lawyer's mind and intellectual rigour to the job. He would have no time for the false sentimentality which surrounds so much discussion of the causes of crime. His was a powerful mind and I thought he should be given his chance.

With hindsight, I think that I should have promoted him to head another department first. He needed the experience of running his own ministry before moving to one of the three great offices of state. Too rapid promotion can jeopardize politicians' long-term future. It turns press and colleagues against them; they become touchy and uncertain about their standing; and all this makes them vulnerable. Leon suffered in this way, but he also had great strengths. For example, he proved extremely capable in devising the package of measures to tighten up the sentencing of violent criminals which we introduced after the rejection of capital punishment by the House of Commons on a free vote in July. He was to prove tough and competent during the miners' strike in 1984–85. Yet there were also weaknesses. He was better at mastering and expounding a brief than in drawing up his own. Moreover, everybody complained about his manner on television, which seemed aloof and uncomfortable. Of course, there have been plenty of complaints over the years about my manner too, so I had a good deal of sympathy with him. But that did not change the situation, particularly since I was shortly to lose from my Cabinet a really gifted presenter of policy.

I made Nigel Lawson Chancellor of the Exchequer – an enormous and to most people unexpected promotion. Whatever quarrels we were to have later, if it comes to drawing up a list of Conservative – even Thatcherite – revolutionaries I would never deny Nigel a leading place on it. He is imaginative, fearless and – on paper at least – eloquently persuasive. His mind is quick and he makes decisions easily. His first budget speech shows what good reading economics can make and I doubt whether any other Financial Secretary to the Treasury could have come up with the inspired clarity of the Medium Term Financial Strategy, which guided our economic policy until Nigel himself turned his back on it in later years. As Chancellor, Nigel's tax reforms had the same quality about them – a simplicity which makes everyone ask why no one thought to do this before.

But what to do with Geoffrey Howe? The time had come to move Geoffrey on. Four gruelling years in the Treasury was enough and it seems a kind of psychological law that Chancellors naturally incline towards the Foreign Office. Partly this is simply because that is the next logical step. But it is also because international finance is nowadays so important that Chancellors have to take a keen interest in the IMF, the G7 and the European Community and so the longing to tread the world stage naturally takes hold of them. I had doubts about Geoffrey's suitability for the Foreign Office. And, in retrospect, I was right. He fell under the spell of the Foreign Office where compromise and negotiation were ends in themselves. This magnified his faults and smothered his virtues. In his new department he fell into the habits which the Foreign Office seems to cultivate – a reluctance to subordinate diplomatic tactics to the national interest and an insatiable appetite for nuances and conditions which can blur the clearest vision. To the extent that Geoffrey did have a cause to guide him in foreign affairs it was one on which the two of us were far apart, though I did not give this much thought at the time. For Geoffrey harboured an almost romantic longing for Britain to become part of some grandiose European consensus. I never heard him define this misty Europeanism, even in the last turbulent days of my Premiership, but it was for him a touchstone of high-mindedness and civilized values. It was to bring us all no end of trouble.

My first choice for the job of Foreign Secretary had been Cecil Parkinson. He and I agreed on economic and domestic policy. Neither of us had the slightest doubt that Britain's interests must come first in foreign policy. He had served in the Falklands War Cabinet. He had just master-minded the most technically proficient general election campaign I have known. He seemed to me right for this most senior job.

However, in the early evening on election day, after I had returned from my own constituency, Cecil visited me in Downing Street and told me that he had been having an affair with his former secretary, Sara Keays. I did not immediately decide that it was an insuperable obstacle to his becoming Foreign Secretary. But the following day, shortly before Cecil was due for lunch at No. 10, I received a personal letter from Sara Keays's father. It revealed that she was pregnant with Cecil's child. When Cecil arrived I showed him the letter. It must have been one of the worst moments of his life.

It was immediately obvious that I could not send Cecil to the Foreign Office with such a cloud hanging over him. I urged him to discuss the personal questions with his family. Meanwhile I decided to make him Secretary of State for the newly combined Departments of Trade and Industry. It was a job I knew he would do well – and it was a less sensitive post than Foreign Secretary would have been.

In September I appointed John Gummer to succeed Cecil as Party Chairman (I would have appointed a new Chairman sooner or later in any case). John had been a Vice-Chairman of the Party under Ted Heath and so knew Central Office well. He is also a gifted speaker and writer. Unfortunately, John Gummer was not a born administrator and when we ran into political trouble he did not carry the weight to help us get out of it.

An appointment that strengthened the Party, however, was that of John Wakeham who became Chief Whip. John would probably not dissent from his reputation as a 'fixer'. He was on the right of the Party, a highly competent accountant, who had tried to make sense for me of British Leyland's elliptical accounts. He had a manner which exuded self-confidence, a good deal of which was deserved. These talents made him a highly effective party manager.

Within months I had to make further important changes. At the beginning of October Cecil Parkinson, with the agreement of Sara Keays, issued a statement to the press revealing their affair and the fact that she was pregnant. I wanted if possible to keep Cecil. At first, it seemed that I might succeed. There was no great pressure from within the Party for him to go. The Party Conference took place the week after Cecil's statement and his ministerial speech was well received. However, very late on Thursday evening, as I was completing my own speech for the following day, the Press Office at No. 10 rang my hotel suite. Sara Keays had given an interview to *The Times* and the story dominated Friday's front page. I called a meeting immediately, with Willie Whitelaw, John Gummer and Cecil himself. It was clear that the story was not going to die down and, though I asked Cecil to hold back from resigning that evening, we all knew that he would have to go.

Early next morning Cecil came in to see me and said that he and Ann had decided that he should resign. There was only one problem. He had a public engagement to open the new Blackpool Heliport and to unveil a commemorative plaque. Clearly, it was impossible for him to go ahead with this. Denis stepped into the breach and unveiled the plaque, which poignantly had Cecil's name on it.

Thankfully, this did not mean the end of Cecil's political career. But he had to endure four years in the political wilderness and lost whatever chance he might have had of climbing to the very top of the political ladder.

In everything but the short term, Cecil's resignation weakened the Government. He had proved an effective minister and, though he was only at the DTI a short time, had made a big impact. It was Cecil who took the difficult but correct decision to introduce legislation to exclude the Stock Exchange from the operation of the Restrictive Trade Practices Act and so to terminate the court case which had been brought against it by the Director-General of Fair Trading. In return the Stock Exchange made a commitment to dismantle long-standing restrictions on trading and the process was begun that led to the Financial Services Act (1986) and the 'Big Bang' in October of that year. These reforms allowed the City to adapt to the highly competitive international markets in which it now operates and have been crucial to its continued success.

I asked Norman Tebbit to move from Employment to take over the DTI and shifted Tom King from Transport as Norman's replacement. This enabled me to bring Nick Ridley into the Cabinet, as Transport Secretary. Nick's arrival in Cabinet was a silver lining to the cloud that hung over us following Cecil's departure. Like Keith Joseph, Nick was someone who wanted office in order to do what he believed was right. Although in my experience there are few politicians for whom doing the right thing is of no importance, there are fewer still for whom it is the only consideration. Nick and Keith were among them. At Transport Nick pressed ahead with privatization and deregulation. And in the later years of the Government he was someone I could rely upon for complete loyalty and honest dealing. Indeed, it was an excess of honesty that ultimately brought him down.

Such was the team on which the success of the Government's second term depended. I hoped that they would share the zeal and enthusiasm of their captain.

I spent most of August on holiday in Switzerland, getting over an awkward and painful eye operation that I had had at the beginning of the month. By the time I returned to England I felt fully recovered, which was all to the good since I had to make several important foreign visits in September, not least to the United States.

After visiting Canada I flew to Washington for a meeting with President Reagan. Overall, the President's domestic political position was strong. In spite of the difficulties which the US budget deficit was causing, the American economy was in remarkably good shape. It was growing faster with markedly less inflation than when he came into office and there was widespread appreciation of this. As he himself used to say: 'Now that it is working, how come they don't call it Reaganomics any more?' The President had also set his imprint on East-West relations. The Soviets were now definitely on the defensive in international relations. And they were in the dock as a result of the shooting down of a South Korean Airliner. In Central America the Government of El Salvador, which the United States had been backing against communist insurgency, was looking stronger. Perhaps only in the Middle East had the Administration's policy not proved even a qualified success. Arab-Israeli peace talks were unlikely to be resumed and there was a growing danger of the US and its allies becoming irrevocably sucked into the turbulent politics of the Lebanon. The President had yet to announce whether he would stand for a second term, but I thought and hoped that he would and it looked as if he would win.

Our discussion that morning and over the lunch which followed covered a wide canvas. I raised the question of the US resuming the supply of arms to Argentina, telling him that a decision to do this would simply not be understood in Britain. The President said that he was aware of that, but there would be great pressure for the resumption of arms supplies if a civilian regime were established in Buenos Aires.

I also took the opportunity to explain our opposition to the inclusion of the British and French independent nuclear deterrents in the arms talks between the United States and the Soviet Union. The Soviet insistence on the inclusion of our deterrents was simply a device to divert attention from the American proposal for deep reductions in strategic nuclear weapons. From the point of view of Britain, our deterrent constituted an irreducible minimum, but it was only 2.5 per cent of the Soviet strategic arsenal. I repeated what I had told the Senate Foreign Relations Committee that morning: the inclusion of the British deterrent would logically mean that the United States could not have parity with the Soviet Union. Would that really be acceptable to the United States? Or if, say, the French decided to increase their nuclear weapons, would the United States really be prepared to cut its own by an equivalent amount? The President seemed to take my point, which I found reassuring. I for my part was able to reassure him as regards the timetable for deployment of Cruise and Pershing missiles in Europe.

However, our discussion turned on the strategy we should pursue towards the Soviet Union generally over the years ahead. I had been giving a good deal of thought to this matter and had discussed it with the experts at a Chequers seminar. I began by saying that we had to make the most accurate assessment of the Soviet system and the Soviet leadership so as to establish a realistic relationship: whatever we thought of them, we all had to live on the same planet. I congratulated the President on his speech to the UN General Assembly after the shooting down of the Korean Airliner and said how right he was to insist that despite this outrage the arms control negotiations in Geneva should continue. The President agreed that now was not the time to isolate ourselves from the Soviet Union. When the USSR failed to prevent NATO's INF deployment they might start to negotiate seriously. Like me, he had clearly been considering the way in which we should deal with the Soviets once that happened.

The President argued that there were two points on which we had to form a judgement. First, the Russians seemed paranoid about their own security: did they really feel threatened by the West or were they merely trying to keep the offensive edge? The second question related to the control of Soviet power itself. He had always assumed that in the Soviet Union the Politburo controlled the military. But did the fact that the first public comments on the Korean Airliner incident had come from the military indicate that the Politburo was now dominated by the generals? As regards negotiation with the Soviets, we should never forget that the main reason why they were at the negotiating table in Geneva at all was the build-up of American defences. They would never be influenced by sweet reason. However, if they saw that the United States had the will and the determination to build up its defences as far as necessary, the Soviet attitude might change because they knew they could not keep up the pace. He believed that the Russians were now close to the limit in their expenditure on defence. The United States, on the other hand, had the capacity to double its military output. The task was to convince Moscow that the only way it could remain equal was by negotiations because they could not afford to compete in weaponry for very much longer. The President recalled a cartoon which had Mr Brezhnev saying to a Russian general, 'I liked the arms race better when we were the only ones in it.'

Now that the Soviet system has crumbled along the lines he envisaged, his words seem prophetic. It may be that one reason why President Reagan and I made such a good team was that, although we shared the same analysis of the way the world worked, we were very different people. He had an accurate grasp of the strategic picture but left the tactical detail to others. I was conscious that we must manage our relations with the communists on a day-to-day basis in such a way that events never got out of control. This was why, throughout my discussion with the President, I kept on coming back to the need to consider precisely how we should deal with the Soviets when they faced up to reality and returned to the negotiating table in a more reasonable frame of mind.

Unexpectedly, the autumn of 1983 turned out to be a testing time for Anglo-US relations. This was because we adopted different attitudes towards crises in the Lebanon and in Grenada.

These events took place against the background of great strategic decisions for the West. November 1983 was the time we had agreed for the deployment of intermediate-range missiles in Britain and West Germany: I had to ensure that nothing interfered with it. Doing so depended to a large degree on demonstrating that the United States could indeed be relied upon as a trustworthy ally.

I had wider objectives as well. I needed to ensure that whatever short-term difficulties we had with the United States, the long-term relationship between our two countries, on which I knew Britain's security and the free West's interests depended, would not be damaged. I was equally determined that international law should be respected and that relations between states should not be allowed to degenerate into a game of *realpolitik* played out between contesting power blocs.

Shortly before the end of the Falklands War Israel had launched a full-scale invasion of Lebanon, which led in August 1982 to the deployment of a mainly American Multi-National Force (MNF) in Beirut. The MNF was withdrawn after a brief period but returned in September following the massacres that took place in the Palestinian refugee camps in the suburbs of Beirut which shocked the world. At this point it consisted of American, French and Italian forces. The Lebanese Government asked Britain to make a contribution too. I explained that in my view we were overextended as it was. But they sent a special envoy to see me who told me that Britain held a unique position and that it was vital that it be represented in the Force. So I agreed, with the support of Michael Heseltine and Geoffrey Howe, that about 100 of our men currently stationed in Cyprus with the UN should join the MNF. In practice, the British contingent had a slightly different role from the others, manning no substantial fixed positions. The mandate of the MNF was to assist the Lebanese Government and the Lebanese Armed Forces to restore their authority over the Beirut area and so help to ensure the safety of the population there.

I am always uneasy about any commitment of British forces if it is made without very clear objectives. The original limited mandate of the MNF was indeed clear, at least on paper. But later in September we came under strong pressure from the Americans and the Italians to increase our commitment and to extend the mandate. The doubt in everyone's mind was whether the current force would be sufficient to allow the Lebanese Government and Army to restore their authority. But that fact was, of course, as much an argument for withdrawing the MNF as for expanding it. I held a meeting to discuss these matters with ministers and advisers at Chequers on Friday 9 September. I was alarmed by reports that the US seemed determined to take a much tougher line with the Syrians than seemed sensible. Syria's support for any solution to the Lebanese crisis would be essential.

In the Chouf mountains south of Beirut, the force of the Druze minority, historically friendly to Britain, were locked in a conflict with the Lebanese Army which neither side seemed able to win: it looked like a military stalemate. The Druze were under pressure from their Syrian backers to secure wider objectives than they themselves probably wanted. Certainly, they had no quarrel of their own with the British and sought to avoid firing on our position. On one occasion during a lunch party at Downing Street I was told that a Druze shell had fallen close to our troops. Michael Heseltine was at the lunch, so I asked him to telephone the Druze leader, Walid Jumblatt, to have the shelling stopped – and it was. Our force was small, exposed and isolated, and I was becoming increasingly concerned about what might happen. Three-quarters of the Lebanon was now occupied by the Syrians or the Israelis and the prospects for peace and stability for the remainder seemed bleak.

Then on Sunday 23 October a suicide bomber drove a lorry laden with explosives into the basement of the US Marine headquarters in Beirut. The building was totally destroyed. A second bomb shortly afterwards did the same to the headquarters of the French Paratroopers. Altogether 242 American and 58 French troops were killed – in total more than Britain had lost in the Falklands War. Responsibility was claimed by two militant Shia Muslim groups. My immediate reaction was one of shock at the carnage and disgust at the fanatics who had caused it. But I was also conscious of the impact it would have on the position and morale of the MNF. What had happened highlighted the enormous dangers of our continued presence and the question arose about whether we were justi-fied in continuing to risk the lives of our troops for what was increasingly no clear purpose.

At this point my attention was abruptly diverted by events on the other side of the world. The humiliation inflicted on the United States by the Beirut bombing undoubtedly influenced its reaction to the events which were taking place on the island of Grenada in the eastern Caribbean.

On Wednesday 19 October 1983 a pro-Soviet military coup had over-thrown the Government of Grenada. The new regime were certainly a vicious and unstable bunch. Maurice Bishop, the overthrown Prime Minister, and five of his close supporters were shot dead. Jamaica and Barbados wanted military intervention in which they would have liked the Americans and us to take part. My immediate reaction was that it would be most unwise of the Americans, let alone us, to accede to this suggestion. I was afraid that it would put foreign communities in Grenada at severe risk. There were some 200 British civilians there and many more Americans. The main organization of Caribbean States, CARICOM, was not prepared to agree to military intervention in Grenada. However, the Organization of Eastern Caribbean States, the OECS, decided unanimously to put together a force and called on other governments to help in restoring peace and order in the island. Clearly, the American reaction would be crucial.

The new 'hemispheric' strategy which President Reagan's Administra-tion was pursuing, combined with experience of living beside the Soviet satellite of Cuba, in our view led the United States to exaggerate the threat which a Marxist Grenada posed. Our intelligence suggested that the Soviets had only a peripheral interest in the island. By contrast, the Government of Cuba certainly was deeply involved. A new airfield was being constructed as an extension to the existing airport. It was due to open in March 1984, though aircraft would be able to land there from about January. The Americans saw this as having a military purpose. It did indeed seem likely that the Cubans, who were providing the workforce for the project, regarded it in this light. For them, it would be a way of managing more easily the traffic of their thousands of troops in Angola and Ethiopia back and forth to Cuba. It would also be useful if the Cubans wished to intervene closer to home. But our view remained that the Grenada Government's main purpose was, as they claimed, a commercial one, planning to cater for the undoubtedly exaggerated projections of their currently minimal tourist industry. The coup of 19 October 1983, morally objectionable as it was, was a change in degree rather than in kind.

On Saturday 22 October – the day before the Beirut bomb outrages – I received a report of the conclusions of the United States National Security Council meeting about Grenada. I was told that it had been decided that the Administration would proceed very cautiously. An American carrier group based on the USS *Independence* had been diverted south to the Caribbean; it was now east of the southern tip of Florida and due north of Puerto Rico. An amphibious group with 1,900 marines and two landing craft was 200 miles further east. The *Independence* would reach the area the following day but would remain well to the east of Dominica and well to the north of Grenada. The amphibious group would reach the same area later on the following day. The existence of this force would give the Americans the option to react if the situation warranted it. They had received a firm request from the east Caribbean heads of government to help them restore peace and order in Grenada. Jamaica and Barbados were supporting the request. If the Americans took action to evacuate US citizens they promised to evacuate British citizens as well. We were also assured that there would be consultation if they decided to take any further steps.

That evening I spoke with Richard Luce, now back in the Foreign Office as Minister of State (Geoffrey Howe was in Athens), Willie Whitelaw and Michael Heseltine. I approved the order that HMS *Antrim* should sail from Colombia to the area of Grenada, remaining beyond the horizon. In public it should be made clear that this was a precautionary move designed to help with the evacuation of British subjects from Grenada should this be required. In fact, it did not seem necessary. The Deputy High Commissioner in Bridgetown (Barbados) reported after a day's visit to Grenada that British citizens were safe, that the new regime in Grenada was willing to allow arrangements to be made for them to leave if they wished and that Sir Paul Scoon, the Governor-General (the Queen's representative on the island), was well and in reasonably good heart. He did not request our military intervention, either directly or indirectly.

Suddenly the whole position changed. What precisely happened in Washington I still do not know, but I find it hard to believe that outrage at the Beirut bombing had nothing to do with it. I am sure that this was not a matter of calculation, but rather of frustrated anger – yet that did not make it any easier for me to defend, not least to a British House of Commons in which anti-American feeling was increasing. The fact that Grenada was also a Commonwealth member, and that the Queen was Head of State, made it harder still.

At 7.15 in the evening of Monday 24 October I received a message from President Reagan while I was hosting a reception at Downing Street. The President wrote that he was giving serious consideration to the OECS request for military action. He asked for my thoughts and advice. I was strongly against intervention and asked that a draft reply be prepared at once on lines which I laid down. I then had to go to a farewell dinner given by Princess Alexandra and her husband, Angus Ogilvy, for the outgoing American Ambassador, J.J. Louis, Jnr. I said to him: 'Do you know what is happening about Grenada? Something is going on.' He knew nothing about it.

I received a telephone call during the dinner to return immediately to No. 10 and arrived back at 11.30 p.m. By then a second message had arrived from the President. In this he stated that he had decided to respond positively to the request for military action. I immediately called a meeting with Geoffrey Howe, Michael Heseltine and the military chiefs and we prepared my reply to the President's two messages, which was sent at 12.30 a.m. There was no difficulty in agreeing a common line. My message concluded:

> This action will be seen as intervention by a western country in the internal affairs of a small independent nation, however unattractive its regime. I ask you to consider this in the context of our

wider East-West relations and of the fact that we will be having in the next few days to present to our Parliament and people the siting of Cruise missiles in this country. I must ask you to think most carefully about these points. I cannot conceal that I am deeply disturbed by your latest communication. You asked for my advice. I have set it out and hope that even at this late stage you will take it into account before events are irrevocable.

I followed this up twenty minutes later by telephoning President Reagan on the hotline. I told him that I wanted him to consider very carefully the reply which I had just sent. He undertook to do so but said, 'We are already at zero.'

At 7.45 that morning a further message arrived, in which the President said that he had weighed very carefully the considerations that I had raised but believed them to be outweighed by other factors. In fact, the US military operation to invade Grenada began early that morning. After some fierce fighting the leaders of the regime were taken prisoner.

At the time I felt dismayed and let down by what had happened. At best, the British Government had been made to look impotent; at worst we looked deceitful. Only the previous afternoon Geoffrey had told the House of Commons that he had no knowledge of any American intention to intervene in Grenada.

The international reaction to American intervention was in general strongly adverse. It certainly gave a propaganda boost to the Soviet Union and the Cubans were portrayed as having played an heroic role in resisting the invasion. When I went to the Commonwealth Heads of Government Meeting in New Delhi the following month it was still Grenada which was the most controversial topic of discussion. My own public criticism of American action and refusal to become involved in it also led to temporarily bad relations with some of Britain's long-standing friends in the Caribbean. It was an unhappy time.

In Britain we had to face strong pressure, not least in the House of Commons, to renegotiate the arrangement for the deployment of Cruise missiles. The argument was that if the Americans had not consulted us about Grenada, why should they do so as regards the use of Cruise missiles.

So when President Reagan telephoned me on the evening of Wednesday 26 October during an emergency House of Commons debate on the American action, I was not in the sunniest of moods. The President said he very much regretted the embarrassment that had been caused and wanted to explain how it had happened. It was the need to avoid leaks of what was intended which had been at the root of the problem. He had been woken at 3 o'clock in the morning with an urgent plea from the OECS. A group had then convened in Washington to study the matter and there was already fear of a leak. By the time he had received my message setting out my concerns the zero hour had passed and American forces were on their way. The military action had gone well and the aim was now to secure democracy.

There was not much I felt able to say and so I more or less held my peace, but I was glad to have received the telephone call.

Just as events in the Lebanon had affected American action in Grenada, so what I had seen in the crisis over Grenada affected my attitude to the Lebanon. I was concerned that American lack of consultation and unpredictability might be repeated there with very damaging consequences.

Naturally, I understood that the United States wanted to strike back after the terrorist outrage against its servicemen in Beirut. But whatever military action now took place, I wanted it to be a lawful, measured and effective response. I sent a message to President Reagan on 4 November welcoming assurances which Geoffrey Howe had received from George Shultz that there would be no hasty reaction by the Americans in retaliation and urging that a more broadly based Lebanese Government be constructed. The President replied to me on 7 November, emphasizing that any action would be a matter of self-defence, not of revenge, but adding that those who committed the atrocity must not be allowed to strike again if it was possible to prevent them. A week later he sent me a further message saying that although he was inclined to take decisive but carefully limited military action, the US had reports of planning for other terrorist acts against the MNF and he intended to deter these. He added that, because of the need for absolute secrecy, knowledge of his current thinking was being severely limited within the US Government.

I quickly replied. I said that I well understood all the pressures upon him to take action but any action must, in my view, be clearly limited to legitimate self-defence. It would be necessary to ensure the avoidance of civilian casualties and minimize the opportunities for hostile propaganda. I was glad that he did not envisage involving Israel or targeting Syria or Iran, action against either of which would be very dangerous. I did not believe that retaliatory action was advisable. However, in the end

France did launch air strikes – at American urging, as President Mitterrand told me later. And in response to attacks on its aircraft, the United
States struck at Syrian positions in central Lebanon in December.

These retaliations failed to have any effect. The position there continued to deteriorate. The real question was no longer whether there should
be a withdrawal but how to effect one. In February 1984 the Lebanese
Army lost control of West Beirut and the Lebanese Government
collapsed. The time had clearly come to get out and a firm joint decision
with the United States and other members of the MNF was accordingly
made to do so. I left it to the British commander on the ground to make
the final decision as to what time of the day to move. He decided that it
should be done by night. But I suddenly learned that President Reagan
would be making a broadcast that evening to tell the American people
what would be happening and why. Obviously it became necessary to
alert our men to be ready to move as soon as they could. Then, at the last
minute, while I was at Buckingham Palace for an Audience with the
Queen, I received a message that the President was reconsidering the
decision and would not after all broadcast. As it turned out the postponement decision promptly leaked and the President had to make his broadcast in any case. Clearly, we could not carry on like this, putting the safety
of British troops at risk: so I refused to countermand the planned withdrawal of our men to British naval vessels lying offshore, which was duly
effected with the British Army's usual professionalism. In fact, all the
MNF forces were shortly withdrawn to ships away from the perils they
would have faced on shore. Nothing could now be done to save the
Lebanon; the reconstituted Lebanese Government increasingly fell under
the control of a Syria whose hostility to the West was now reinforced; and
in March the MNF force returned home.

The American intervention in the Lebanon – well intentioned as it
was – was clearly a failure. It seemed to me that what happened there
contained important lessons which we should heed. First, it is unwise to
intervene in such situations unless you have a clear, agreed objective
and are prepared and able to commit the means to secure it. Second,
there is no point in indulging in retaliatory action which changes
nothing on the ground. Third, one must avoid taking on a major
regional power, like Syria, unless one is prepared to face up to the full
consequences of doing so.

By contrast, American intervention in Grenada was, in fact, a success.
Democracy was restored, to the advantage not only of the islanders but

also of their neighbours who could look forward to a more secure and prosperous future. Yet even governments acting on the best of motives are wise to respect legal forms. Above all, democracies have to show their superiority to totalitarian governments which know no law. Admittedly, the law on these matters is by no means clear, as was confirmed for me during a seminar I held after the Grenada affair to consider the legal basis for military intervention in another country. Indeed, to my surprise, I found that the lawyers at the seminar were more inclined to argue on grounds of *realpolitik* and the politicians were more concerned with the issue of legitimacy. My own instinct was – and is – always to found military action on the right of self-defence, which ultimately no outside body has the authority to question.

Grenada was still very much on my mind when I went to Bonn for one of my regular Anglo-German summits with Chancellor Kohl on Tuesday 8 November.* Like me, Chancellor Kohl was worried about the impact of the American action on European public opinion in the run-up to the deployment of Cruise and Pershing missiles later that month.

The main purpose of my visit, however, was to seek German support for the line I would take at the European Council in Athens, just a few weeks away. I began by making what I hoped would be the welcome suggestion that the next President of the European Commission should come from Germany, if the German Government wished to put forward a candidate. It appeared that they did not. Chancellor Kohl said that he agreed with me that the Commission was too big and tended to create unnecessary work. Then a little more diplomacy: I said that our aim was to build on the excellent foundation laid under the German presidency. After this we got down to business. I stressed the need for firm control of spending on the CAP if there was to be anything left of the Community's 'own resources' for other purposes, such as the development of the electronics industry, which the Germans wanted. I also warned against allowing protectionism to create another area of disagreement with the United States. The Germans were most interested in the future level of MCAs,† which affected German farmers' incomes, and the steel industry where they considered that they were receiving a raw deal and that the Italians

---

* Helmut Kohl had succeeded Helmut Schmidt as West German Chancellor in 1982.
† Monetary Compensatory Amounts (MCAs) were a system of border taxes and levies on CAP products.

were using subsidies to undercut German producers. I hoped that at the end of this discussion each side had understood the areas on which we would stand firm and those where compromise was possible. In particular, I hoped that the Germans realized how serious I was about achieving my objectives on the budget question at Athens.

The Community heads of government met in the magnificent Zappeion Hall, a classical Greek building adapted to the needs of a modern conference centre. At the first sessions of the Council that afternoon I was sitting opposite President Mitterrand and Chancellor Kohl. I noticed that whereas my own table was covered with piles of heavily annotated briefing on different complex agricultural and financial issues, no such encumbrance appeared in front of my French and German counterparts. This doubtless made for an impression of appropriately Olympian detachment, but it also suggested that they had not mastered the detail. And this turned out to be the case. Throughout the meeting Chancellor Kohl seemed unwilling or unable to make much effective contribution. Worse, President Mitterrand appeared not only badly briefed on the issues but strangely – I think genuinely – misinformed about his own Government's position.

The Greek presidency did not assist much either. Mr Papandreou always proved remarkably effective in gaining Community subsidies for Greece but he was less skilful in his present role as President of the European Council.

On Tuesday I had a working breakfast with President Mitterrand. We were so far apart that there was no point in spending much time discussing Community issues at all and we largely concentrated on the Lebanon. The French President said jokingly that unless we demonstrated that discussions between Britain and France were continuing, the press would soon be talking about a return to the Hundred Years' War. So in what I hoped was a suitably non-belligerent way I told him how his attitude at the Council had taken me by surprise, given the fact that I was going along with the proposals on the budget which the French Finance minister, M. Jacques Delors, had been advancing. The President asked me precisely what I meant and I explained. But I received no very satisfactory or clear response.

Where we did see eye to eye – at least in private – was about Germany. I said that even though the Germans were willing to be generous because they received other political benefits from the Community, a new generation of Germans might arise who would refuse to make such a large contribution. This would risk a revival of German neutralism – a temptation which, as President Mitterrand rightly said, was already present.

The meeting had been an amicable one and I tried to keep the atmosphere relatively friendly after the Council broke up, as in press interviews I avoided being too harsh about France's performance. After all, M. Mitterrand was to be the next President of the Council and so it would fall to him to chair the crucial meetings as we at last approached the time when the Community's money ran out. It did cross my mind that he might have wished to delay a settlement until he could take credit for it in his own presidency.

CHAPTER TWENTY-FIVE

Mr Scargill's Insurrection

The background to and course of the year-long
miners' strike of 1984–1985

T HE 1983 GENERAL ELECTION RESULT was the single most devastating defeat ever inflicted upon democratic socialism in Britain. But there was also undemocratic socialism, and it too would need to be beaten. I had never had any doubt about the true aim of the hard Left: they were revolutionaries who sought to impose a Marxist system on Britain whatever the means and whatever the cost. For them, the institutions of democracy were no more than tiresome obstacles on the long march to a Marxist Utopia. While the electoral battle was still being fought their hands had been tied by the need to woo more moderate opinion, but in the aftermath of defeat they were free from constraint and thirsting for battle.

The hard Left's power was entrenched in three institutions: the Labour Party, local government and the trade unions. Predictably, it was the National Union of Mineworkers, led by its Marxist president, Arthur Scargill, who were destined to provide the shock troops for the Left's attack. Within a month of the 1983 election Mr Scargill was saying openly that he did not 'accept that we are landed for the next four years with this Government'. And this would be an attack directed not only against the Government, but against anyone and anything standing in the way of the Left, including fellow miners and their families, the police, the courts, the rule of law and Parliament itself.

From the time of Mr Scargill's election to the leadership of the NUM in 1981 I knew we would have to face another miners' strike. The National Coal Board, the Government and the great majority of miners wanted a thriving, successful, competitive coal industry. But coal mining in Britain had become an industry where reason simply did not apply. Britain's industrial revolution was to a large extent based on the easy availability of coal. At the industry's height on the eve of the First World War it employed more than a million men to work over 3,000 mines. Production was 292 million tons. Thereafter decline was continuous, and relations between miners and owners frequently bitter. Conflict in the coal industry precipitated Britain's only general strike in 1926. (Prefiguring later developments, the miners' union split during the year-long coal strike that followed the general strike, and a separate union was set up in Nottinghamshire.) Successive governments found themselves dragged ever deeper into the task of rationalizing and regulating the industry, and in 1946 the post-war Labour Government finally nationalized it outright. By that time production was down to 187 million tons at 980 pits, with a workforce of just over 700,000.

Government now began setting targets for coal production and investment in a series of documents inaugurated by the 'Plan for Coal' in 1950. These consistently overestimated both the demand for coal and the prospects for improvements in productivity within the industry. The only targets that were met were those for investment. Public money was poured in, but two problems proved insoluble: overcapacity and union resistance to the closure of uneconomic pits.

By the 1970s the coal mining industry had come to symbolize everything that was wrong with Britain. In February 1972 mass pickets led by Arthur Scargill forced the closure of the Saltley Coke Depot in Birmingham by sheer weight of numbers. It was a frightening demonstration of the impotence of the police in the face of such disorder. The fall of Ted Heath's Government after the 1973–74 miners' strike lent substance to the myth that the NUM had the power to make or break British Governments, or at the very least the power to veto any policy threatening their interests by preventing coal getting to the power stations.

I have already described the threat of a miners' strike which we faced in February 1981. From then on it was really only a question of time. Would we be sufficiently prepared to win the fight when the inevitable challenge came?

It fell mainly to Nigel Lawson who became Secretary of State for Energy in September 1981 to build up – steadily and unprovocatively – the stocks of coal which would allow the country to endure a coal strike. To maximize endurance it was vital that coal stocks be in place at the power stations and not at the pit heads, from which miners' pickets could make movement impossible. But coal stocks were not the only element determining power station endurance. Some Central Electricity Generating Board (CEGB) power stations were oil fired. Ordinarily they were used only part of the time, to meet peak demand, but if needed they could be run continuously to help meet the 'base load' – that element of electricity demand that is more or less constant. 'Oilburn' was expensive, but would add significantly to the system's ability to withstand a strike. Nuclear-powered stations, providing about 14 per cent of supply, were mostly some distance away from the coalfields and their primary fuel supply was also secure. Over the next few years more Advanced Gas-cooled Reactors (AGRs) would be coming on stream and would steadily reduce our dependence on coal-fired power. We were still building a cross-Channel link which would allow us to buy power from France, though we already had a link in operation between the English and Scottish systems. We also did our best to encourage industry to hold more stocks.

Danger began to loom in the autumn of 1983. Peter Walker was now Secretary of State for Energy. As he had shown at Agriculture in our first Parliament, he was a tough negotiator. He was also a skilled communicator, something which I knew would be important if we were to retain public support in the coal strike which the militants would some day force upon us. Unfortunately, Peter Walker never really got on with Ian MacGregor, and this sometimes created tensions.

Ian MacGregor took over as Chairman of the NCB on 1 September. He had been an excellent Chairman of the British Steel Corporation, turning the Corporation around after the damaging three-month steel strike in 1980. Unlike the militant miners' leaders, Ian MacGregor genuinely wanted to see a thriving coal industry making good use of investment, technology and human resources. Perhaps his greatest quality was courage. Within the NCB itself he often found himself surrounded by people who had made their careers in an atmosphere of appeasement and collaboration with the NUM and who greatly resented the changed atmosphere he brought with him. Yet it transpired that Ian MacGregor was strangely lacking in guile. He was quite used to dealing with financial difficulties and hard bargaining. But he had no experience of dealing with trade union leaders intent on using the process of negotiation to score political points. Time and again he and his colleagues were outmanoeuvred by Arthur Scargill and the NUM leadership.

On Friday 21 October 1983 an NUM delegate conference voted for a ban on overtime in protest at the Board's 5.2 per cent pay offer and at prospective pit closures. In itself, an overtime ban was unlikely to have much effect. It probably had an ulterior purpose: to increase tension among the miners and so make them more prepared for a strike when the NUM leadership thought that one could successfully be engineered. We always knew that it was pit closures that were more likely to ignite a strike than a dispute about pay. The case for closures on economic grounds remained overwhelming. Even Labour had acknowledged it: thirty-two pits had been closed under the Labour Government between 1974 and 1979. Mr Scargill's line was that no pit should be closed unless it was physically exhausted. In his view a pit that made a loss – and there were many – simply required further investment. Called to give evidence before a Select Committee, he had been asked whether there was any level of loss that he would deem intolerable. He replied memorably: 'As far as I am concerned, the loss is without limit.'

The Monopolies and Mergers Commission had produced a report on the coal industry in 1983 which showed that some 75 per cent of the pits were making a loss. In September 1983 Mr MacGregor told Government that he intended to cut the workforce by some 64,000 over three years, reducing capacity by 25 million tons. There was, though, never any secret 'hit list' of pits due for closure: decisions as to which pits were to be closed would be made on a pit-by-pit basis. He came back to us in December 1983 indicating that he had decided to accelerate the programme, aiming to cut the workforce by 44,000 over the next two years; to achieve this he urged us to extend the existing redundancy scheme to include miners under the age of fifty. The terms we agreed in January 1984 were extremely generous: £1,000 for each year of service, paid as a lump sum, the scheme to operate for two years only, so that a man who had been in the pits all his working life would get over £30,000. In the coming year, 1984–85, Mr MacGregor proposed 20,000 redundancies. We were confident that this figure could be achieved without anyone being forced to leave the industry against their will. Around twenty pits would close and annual capacity would be reduced by 4 million tons a year.

As discussions continued, accusations began to fly about a 'hit list' of pits. The rhetoric of the NUM leadership took ever greater leave of reality – in particular, of the economic reality that the industry was receiving £1.3 billion of subsidies from the taxpayer in 1983–84. At the end of February there was an early intimation of the violence which would characterize the strike when Ian MacGregor – then seventy years old – was knocked to the ground at a Northumberland colliery by demonstrating miners. Far worse was to come.

We doubted whether the strike would happen before the end of 1984, when winter set in and the demand for coal was at its annual peak. To begin a strike in the spring would be the worst possible tactic for the NUM. But this was a point on which Mr Scargill misled his own members: in February he was making wild claims, saying that the CEGB had only eight weeks of coal stocks. In fact stocks were far higher – something that could have been deduced from figures in the public domain. However, the union had a tradition of balloting its members before strike action took place, and there was good reason to think that Mr Scargill would not get the necessary majority (55 per cent) to call a national strike at any point in the immediate future. Since he had become President the NUM membership had voted against strike action three times already. We could not have foreseen the desperate and self-destructive tactics he chose to adopt.

On Thursday 1 March the NCB announced the closure of the Yorkshire colliery Cortonwood. The announcement was not particularly well handled by the local NCB: the impression was given that the colliery review procedure was being bypassed, whereas in fact the NCB had no such intention. But the executive of the radical Yorkshire area of the NUM – Mr Scargill's home ground – announced a strike in protest at the decision, relying on a local ballot held two years previously to provide authority for their action.

Cortonwood may have triggered the strike, but it was not the cause. Even if Cortonwood had never happened, a meeting between the NCB and the mining unions on 6 March might have had the same result. Ian MacGregor outlined his plans for the coming year and confirmed the figure of twenty closures. That same day the Scottish NUM called a strike from 12 March. Two days later, on Thursday 8 March, the national executive of the NUM met and gave official support to the Yorkshire and Scottish strikes.

Under rule 43 of the NUM constitution a national strike could only be called if the union held a national ballot and a majority of 55 per cent voted in favour. The militant majority on the executive doubted whether they could win such a national ballot, but they found a procedural way round the problem. Under rule 41 of the constitution, the national executive could give official sanction to strikes declared by the constituent areas that made up the union. If all the areas could be pushed into action individually, this would have the effect of a national strike without the need for the national ballot. If any proved difficult, pickets could be sent from striking areas to intimidate them into joining the dispute. This ruthless strategy very nearly worked. But in the end it proved to be a disaster for its authors.

The strike began on Monday 12 March. Over the following two weeks the brutal weight of the militants' shock troops descended on the coalfields and for a moment it seemed as if rationality and decency would go under. At the beginning of the first day of the strike 83 pits were working and 81 were out. Ten of these, I was told, were not working due to heavy picketing rather than any positive desire to join the strike. By the end of the day the number of pits not working had risen to about 100. The police were fighting a losing battle to ensure that those who wished to work could do so. I was determined that the message should go out from Government loud and clear: there would be no surrender to the mob and the right to go to work would be upheld.

By Wednesday morning only twenty-nine pits were working normally. The police were by now drafting in officers from around the country to protect the miners who wanted to work: 3,000 police officers from seventeen forces were involved. At this point the violence centred on Nottinghamshire, where the flying pickets from Yorkshire were determined to secure a quick victory. However, the Nottinghamshire men went ahead with their ballot and the result that Friday showed 73 per cent against the strike. Area ballots the following day in the Midlands, the North-West and the North-East coalfields also gave heavy majorities against strike action. Of the 70,000 miners balloted, over 50,000 voted to work.

Early though it was, this was one of the turning points of the strike. The huge police operation was highly effective and together with the moral force of the ballot results it reversed the trend towards a shutdown of the pits. The first, crucial battle had been won. On Monday morning the latest information was telephoned through to me in Brussels, where I was attending a European Council. Forty-four pits were now working, compared with just eleven on Friday. The militants knew that if it had not been for the courage and competence of the police the result would have been very different and from now on they and their mouthpieces in the Labour Party began a campaign of vilification against them.

On the day the NUM executive met, I told Cabinet that I would set up a committee of ministers under my chairmanship to monitor the strike and to decide what action should be taken. Willie Whitelaw was a member, of course, and Peter Walker, as Energy Secretary, and Leon Brittan as Home Secretary, were crucial figures. The Chancellor, Nigel Lawson, was directly concerned as the issue was of vital importance to the economy; he also brought to bear his experience as former Energy Secretary. Norman Tebbit (Trade and Industry), Tom King (Employment) and Nick Ridley (Transport) all had obvious contributions to make. In Scotland, George Younger had responsibility both for Scottish mining and for Scotland's police. All these ministers or their deputies regularly attended. When issues of law arose the Attorney-General, Michael Havers, also joined us. The group met about once a week, but the large membership sometimes proved unwieldy and so Peter Walker and I made some important decisions in smaller meetings, called *ad hoc* to deal with developments as they arose, particularly when notice was short.

Mob violence can only be defeated if the police have the complete moral and practical support of government. We made it clear that the politicians would not let them down. We had already given them the equipment and the training they would need, learning the lessons of the 1981 inner-city riots. More recently the police had shown themselves skilled in tackling violence masquerading as picketing when pickets from the National Graphical Association (NGA) had tried to close down Eddie Shah's newspaper in Warrington in November 1983. On that occasion they had, for the first time, made effective use of powers to prevent a breach of the peace by turning back pickets before they arrived at their destination.

Another prerequisite of effective policing is that the law should be clear. Early in the strike Michael Havers made a lucid statement in a written answer to the Commons, setting out the scope of police powers to deal with mass picketing, including the power (mentioned above) to turn back pickets on their way to the picket line when there are reasonable grounds to expect a breach of the peace. These common law powers long predated our trade union legislation, and were matters of criminal rather than civil law. In the second week of the strike the Kent NUM challenged those powers in court, but they lost the case. The prevention of large numbers of pickets assembling to intimidate those who wished to work would be vital to the outcome of the dispute.

By the last week of March the situation was fairly clear. At the majority of pits Mr Scargill and his colleagues had a tight grip, which it would not be easy to break. But in our planning over the previous two years we had not allowed ourselves to assume that any coal would be mined during a strike, whereas in fact a substantial section of the industry was still working. If we could move this coal to the power stations then the prospects for endurance would be transformed. But we had to act so that at any one time we did not unite against us all the unions involved in the use and distribution of coal. This consideration meant that we all had to be very careful when and where the civil law was used, and the NCB suspended – though it did not withdraw – its civil action.

Although Mr Scargill had been very anxious to avoid a ballot before the strike began, it was clear to us that he wanted to keep the possibility open. Indeed the following month an NUM Special Delegate Conference voted to reduce the majority required for a strike from 55 per cent to 50 per cent. Also at the beginning of the strike we had hopes that moderates on the NUM executive might succeed in forcing a ballot. This made it even more important to keep the balance of opinion among miners favourable to our cause because it seemed that much of the opposition to the strike came from miners angry not to have been allowed to vote. Would a ballot held during a strike, with emotions raised, produce a majority for or against Mr Scargill? I was not entirely sure.

I received weekly reports from the Department of Energy setting out the position and I read them very carefully indeed. Early in the strike the power stations were consuming coal at the rate of about 1.7 million tons a week, though the net reduction in stocks was smaller because some deliveries were getting through. The CEGB estimated endurance at about six months but this assumed a build-up to maximum oilburn – that is, using oil-fired stations at full capacity – which had not yet begun. We had to judge when this should be set in train because it would certainly be described as provocative by the NUM leadership. However, I decided on Monday 26 March that this nettle must now be grasped.

Industrial stocks were, of course, much lower than those at the power stations: the cement industry was particularly vulnerable and important. But it was BSC whose problems were most immediate. Their integrated steel plants at Redcar and Scunthorpe would have to close in the next fortnight if supplies of coke and coal were not delivered and unloaded. Port Talbot, Ravenscraig and Llanwern had stocks sufficient for no more than three to five weeks. Not surprisingly, BSC was extremely concerned as the position changed from day to day.

This was the state of uncertainty as we ended the first month of the strike.

The stalemate continued during April. In spite of continuing heavy picketing, there were some signs of a drift back to work, particularly in Lancashire. The leaders of the rail unions and the seamen promised to support the miners in their struggle: there were many declarations of this kind during the strike, but their members were less enthusiastic. The first court cases against the NUM began: two coke hauliers began legal action against the South Wales NUM picketing of Port Talbot steelworks.

In May there were brief but revealing contacts between the NCB and the NUM leadership – the first since the strike began. The talks took place on Wednesday 23 May; I had a full report the next day. Mr Scargill would allow no one to speak for the NUM side but himself. The NCB had given two presentations, one on the marketing prospects of the coal industry and another on the physical condition of the pits, some of which were now in danger of becoming unworkable because of the strike. At the end of each presentation the NUM representatives declined to comment or to ask questions. Mr Scargill then made a prepared statement. He insisted that there could be no discussion of pit closures on grounds other than exhaustion – certainly no question of closing pits on economic grounds. Ian MacGregor made some brief remarks to the effect that he saw no purpose in continuing the meeting in the light of this, but nevertheless he suggested further talks between two senior members of the NCB and two senior representatives of the NUM. Mr Scargill again insisted that the withdrawal of all closure plans was a precondition for any talks. There the meeting ended. But at that point the NUM sprung a trap. They asked to be allowed to stay in the room in which the meeting had just taken place for a discussion among themselves. Ian MacGregor saw this as a perfectly innocent request and readily agreed. The NCB representatives left the room. But later we discovered that the NUM had managed to persuade the press that this was a 'walkout' by the NCB. Many people seized on the episode as evidence that Ian MacGregor was unwilling to talk. It was a classic example of the dangers of negotiating with people like Mr Scargill.

Week by week the strike grew more bitter. There was evidence that many miners were losing their early enthusiasm for it and questioning Mr Scargill's forecasts of limited power station endurance. The NUM leadership responded by increasing the allowances they paid to pickets – they paid nothing at all to strikers who did not turn out to picket – recruiting non-miners to the task. There was a general escalation of the level of violence. Perhaps the most shocking scenes of violence were those which took place outside Orgreave Coke Works in an attempt to prevent coke convoys reaching the Scunthorpe steelworks. On Tuesday 29 May over 5,000 pickets engaged in violent clashes with the police. The police were pelted with all kinds of missiles, including bricks and darts, and sixty-nine people were injured. Thank goodness they at least had proper protective riot gear, I thought, as, like so many millions of others, I watched the terrible scenes on television.

Over the next three weeks there were further violent clashes at Orgreave, but the pickets never succeeded in halting the road convoys. The battles at Orgreave did a great deal to turn public opinion against the miners.

It was at about this time that we had the first clear evidence of large-scale intimidation in the mining villages. Working miners were not the only targets: their wives and children were also at risk. The sheer vicious-ness of what was done provides a useful antidote to some of the more romantic talk about the spirit of the mining communities. In its very nature intimidation is extremely difficult for the police to combat, though as time went on officers in uniform and teams in plain clothes were specially deployed to tackle it.

As the violence continued and the problems of BSC in particular increased, the ministerial group frequently discussed whether to encour-age the use of the civil law against the NUM and other unions involved in secondary action. Failure to take civil action against the unions and their funds put all the pressure onto the criminal law and onto the police whose duty it was to uphold it. It was also pointed out that, if successful, legal action against union funds would restrict their ability to finance mass pickets and to engage in unlawful action. People were saying openly that our trade union reforms were being discredited by the failure of the nationalized industries involved to use the legal remedies. Instinctively, I had a good deal of sympathy with this view, as did my advisers.

However, Peter Walker persuaded us that use of the civil law might alienate the support we had among working miners or moderate trade unionists. The chairmen of the BSC, NCB, BR and CEGB met towards the end of June and decided that this was not the time to apply for an injunc-tion. Nor were the police convinced that civil action would make their job on the picket lines any easier. Of course, that did not prevent others – whether businessmen or working miners – making use of the new laws. The fact was that throughout this dispute there was much to be said for emphasizing the point that it was the basic criminal law of the country which was being flouted by the pickets and their leaders, rather than Thatcher's laws.

On Monday 9 July, almost out of the blue, the TGWU called a national dock strike over a supposed breach of the National Dock Labour Scheme (NDLS). The NDLS had been established by the Attlee Government with the aim of eliminating casual labour in the docks. Based on statute, it operated in the majority of British ports, establishing a closed shop and giving the union extraordinary powers. The occasion for the strike was BSC's use of contract labour to move iron ore by road from stockpiles in the docks at Immingham to the Scunthorpe steelworks. In fact, BSC were satisfied that neither the scheme nor local agreements had been breached. Under the scheme's absurd provisions 'shadow' labour consisting of registered dock workers was required to stand and watch the work as it was being done by contractors. This had been complied with in the 'normal way'. We hoped that the National Dock Labour Board, which included union representatives, would give an early ruling to this effect. But the TGWU leadership was strongly committed to supporting Mr Scargill and plainly welcomed the opportunity to call a strike.

We had already made an extensive study of the implications of a national dock strike in 1982. It seemed likely that the strike – which would probably only seriously affect those ports which were part of the NDLS – would have little direct impact on the outcome of the coal strike. We were not importing coal for the power stations, because it would have risked losing us the support of working miners. But a dock strike would have serious implications for BSC by disrupting its imports of coal and iron ore. Indeed, it looked as if a major motive for the strike had been the desire of the left-wing TGWU leadership to assist the miners by tightening their grip on the major steel plants. The general effect on trade would be very serious – particularly on imports of food – though about a third of non-bulk cargo was carried by roll-on-roll-off ships (known as 'RO-RO'), much of which was driver-accompanied and passed through 'non-scheme' ports such as Dover and Felixstowe.

Our regular meetings of the ministerial group on coal had to deal with two strikes rather than one. I told the group on the day after the dock strike began that it was vital to make a major effort to mobilize opinion over the next forty-eight hours. We should urge the port employers to adopt a resolute approach and use all available means to strengthen opposition to the strike among workers in industries likely to be damaged by it and, indeed, among the public. It must be clearly demonstrated that the pretext for the strike was false and that those taking this action already enjoyed extraordinary privileges. We should make the point that it was estimated that 4,000 out of the 13,000 dockers registered under the NDLS were surplus to the requirements of the industry. Of course, this was not the right time to abolish the NDLS – in the middle of a coal strike – but we should aim for the present to solve the dispute without ruling out future change.

In the event the dock strike proved far less of a problem than we had feared. Whatever the views of their leaders, the ordinary dockers were simply not prepared to support action which threatened their jobs: even those at the NDLS ports were less than enthusiastic, fearing that a strike would hasten the demise of the scheme itself. But the decisive role was played by the lorry drivers who had an even greater direct interest in getting goods through and were not prepared to be bullied and threatened. By 20 July the TGWU had no alternative but to call off the strike. It had lasted only ten days.

Following the fruitless meeting between the NCB and NUM on 23 May, talks had resumed at the beginning of July. Our hope was that they would end quickly but they had drifted on, and there were indications that the NCB was softening its negotiating position. One problem was that each new round of negotiations naturally discouraged a return to work: few would risk going back if a settlement seemed to be in the offing. More troubling still, there was a real danger that the talks would end by fudging the issue on the closure of uneconomic pits: a formula was being developed based upon the proposition that no pit should be closed if it was capable of being 'beneficially developed'. We were very alarmed.

But on 18 July negotiations collapsed. I have to say I was enormously relieved.

On Tuesday 31 July I spoke in a debate in the House of Commons on a Censure Motion which the Labour Party had been ill-advised enough to put down. The debate went far wider than the coal strike. But the strike was on everyone's minds and inevitably it was the exchanges on this matter which caught the public attention. I did not mince my words:

> The Labour Party is the party which supports every strike, no matter what its pretext, no matter how damaging. But above all, it is the Labour Party's support for the striking miners against the working miners which totally destroys all credibility for its claim to represent the true interests of working people in this country.

I went on to deal with Neil Kinnock:

> The Leader of the Opposition went silent on the question of a
> ballot until the NUM changed its rules to reduce the required
> majority. Then he told the House that a national ballot of the
> NUM was a clearer and closer prospect. That was on 12 April – the
> last time that we heard from him on the subject of a ballot. But on
> 14 July he appeared at an NUM rally and said, 'There is no alterna-
> tive but to fight: all other roads are shut off.' What happened to the
> ballot?

Answer came there none.

Neil Kinnock had succeeded Michael Foot as Leader of the Labour
Party in October 1983. Like Michael Foot, Neil Kinnock was a gifted
orator; but unlike Mr Foot he was no parliamentarian. His Commons
performances were marred by verbosity, a failure to master facts and
technical arguments and, above all, a lack of intellectual clarity. Mr
Kinnock was entirely a product of the modern Labour Party – left-wing,
close to the unions, skilful at party management and political manipulation, basically convinced that Labour's past defeats resulted from weaknesses of presentation rather than errors of policy. He regarded words as
a means of concealing his and the Labour Party's socialism rather than of
converting others to it. So he forcefully denounced Trotskyists and other
left-wing troublemakers, not for their brutal tactics or their extreme revolutionary objectives but because they were an embarrassment to his and
Labour's ambitions. Mr Kinnock was involved in what seemed to me a
fundamentally discreditable enterprise, that of making himself and his
party appear what they were not. The House of Commons and the electorate found him out. As Opposition Leader he was out of his depth. As
Prime Minister he would have been sunk.

As we entered August we had some reason to hope that the worst of the
strike was behind us. Although the return to work remained a trickle –
about 500 during July – there was no sign of any weakening of determination at the working pits. Finally, on Tuesday 7 August two Yorkshire
miners began a High Court action against the Yorkshire NUM for striking without a ballot. This proved to be a vital case and led eventually to
the sequestration of the whole of the NUM's assets.

One sign of the militants' frustration was an increase in violence
against working miners and their families.

There was also the threat of another dock strike. A tense situation had developed at Hunterston, the deep-water port in Scotland which supplied BSC's Ravenscraig plant. An important cargo of coal, of the kind necessary for Ravenscraig's coke ovens, was aboard the bulk carrier *Ostia*, presently moored in Belfast Lough. BSC told us that if it were not landed quickly they would have to start to run down Ravenscraig. Steel furnaces cannot be shut down fully without irreversible damage and there was every likelihood that the whole plant would have to close for good if coal supplies were halted. As with the earlier dock strike, absurd restrictive practices were the pretext for the strike threat. The normal operation at Hunterston for BSC-destined cargo was divided between work done aboard ship by TGWU registered dockers and work done on-shore by members of the steel union, the ISTC. But 90 per cent of the cargo could be unloaded even without 'trimming'. BSC wanted to use its employees to unload this coal, but the TGWU was likely to claim that such action was contrary to the National Dock Labour Board agreement in order to provoke a new docks dispute. BSC told us that they were prepared to go to court if the cargo could not be unloaded.

This was a very delicate question. The National Dock Labour Board was asked to offer a ruling but delayed and, finally, funked the issue altogether. BSC began the rundown of Ravenscraig on 17 August; unless the coal was landed by 23–24 August, their furnaces would have to be 'banked' on 28–29 August – that is, kept running at a minimum level, without production. Total closure would follow if coal supplies did not resume.

After putting off the decision as long as possible, BSC had its employees start unloading the *Ostia* on the morning of Thursday 23 August. TGWU dockers immediately walked out and the union called a second national dock strike.

But in Scotland public opinion was strongly opposed to any action that threatened the future of Ravenscraig. So we had doubts whether the union could sustain a strike across the whole of Scotland, let alone in the United Kingdom as a whole. And we were right. Though to begin with the strike received considerable support from registered dockers, a majority of ports remained open. Finally, the TGWU called it off on 18 September.

The most serious development, however, had been a circular issued on 15 August by the NCB to members of the National Association of Colliery Overmen, Deputies and Shotfirers (NACODS). By law, coal could only be mined in the presence of suitably qualified safety personnel – the great majority of whom were members of NACODS. In April, NACODS members voted to strike, but the margin was less than the two-thirds required by union rules. Up to mid-August the NCB had varied in its policy towards NACODS: in some areas members were being allowed to stay away from striking pits where no work was being done, in others they were being required to cross picket lines. The NCB circular now generalized the latter policy, threatening to withhold pay from NACODS members who refused to comply.

The NCB circular played into the hands of those leaders of NACODS, particularly its president, who were strongly sympathetic to the NUM. It was easy to understand why the NCB acted as they did. But it was a major error, subsequently compounded by their failure to perceive the swing in favour of a strike among NACODS members, and it almost precipitated disaster.

September and October were always likely to be difficult months. The miners would be looking forward to the winter when demand for electricity was at its highest and power cuts most likely. At the TUC Conference in early September a majority of trade unions – strongly opposed by the electricity and power workers – pledged support for the miners, though in most cases they had no intention of giving it. When the forthright electricians' leader Eric Hammond made a powerful speech pointing this out, he was heavily barracked. Neil Kinnock also spoke at the conference, coming as near as he ever did to outright condemnation of picket line violence, but without taking any action to expel from his party those who supported it. Meanwhile, Mr Scargill reaffirmed his view that there was no such thing as an uneconomic pit, only pits which had been starved of the necessary investment.

Negotiations between the NCB and the NUM were resumed on 9 September. I was always concerned that Ian MacGregor and the NCB team would unwittingly give away basic principles for which the strike was being fought. He was a businessman, not a politician, and thought in terms of reasonableness and reaching a deal. I suspect that Mr MacGregor's view was that once he got the miners back to work he would be able to restructure the industry as he wished, whatever the precise terms on which a settlement had been reached. The rest of us, from long experience, understood that Arthur Scargill and his friends would exploit a fudged formula and that we should be back where we started. It was crucial that the NUM's claim that uneconomic pits should never be closed should be defeated, and be seen to be defeated, and the use of strikes for political purposes discredited once and for all.

It was also in September that I first met in person members of the 'Miners' Wives Back to Work Campaign', whose representatives came to see me at 10 Downing Street. I was moved by the courage of these women, whose families were subject to abuse and intimidation. They said that the majority of miners still did not understand the full extent of the NCB's pay offer and plans for investment: more needed to be done to put across the NCB's case to striking miners, many of whom relied on the NUM for their information. They confirmed that while talks between the NCB and the NUM were going on, or were in prospect, it was extremely difficult to persuade men to return to work. They explained to me how small shops in the coalfields were being blackmailed into supplying food and goods for striking miners and withholding them from working miners. But perhaps the most shocking thing they had to say was that local NCB management in some areas were not anxious to promote a return to work and in one particular area were actively siding with the NUM to discourage it.

Of course, the vital thing for these women was that the NCB should do everything it could to protect miners who had led the return to work, if necessary transferring them to pits where there were fewer militants and giving them priority in applications for redundancies. I said that we would not let them down, and I think I kept my word. The whole country was in their debt.

One working miner's wife, Mrs McGibbon from Kent, spoke at the Conservative Party Conference, describing the harrowing experiences which she and her family had undergone. Even her small children were targets: they were told that their parents were going to be killed. Shortly after she had spoken the *Morning Star* published her address. A week later her home was attacked.

On 11 September the National Working Miners' Committee was formed. This was an important development in the history of the working miners' movement. Meanwhile the threat from NACODS crept up on us. A strike ballot was to be held on 28 September. At first the NCB was optimistic about the result of the ballot, but ominously, as the days went by, their assessments grew less and less hopeful and it was clear that a NACODS strike would make it even more difficult to bring about a return to work by miners in the more militant areas. NACODS men were not the only NCB employees with the necessary safety qualifications.

Many members of the British Association of Colliery Managers (BACM) were also qualified, but it would be difficult to persuade them to go underground and perform these tasks in the face of NACODS hostility. And while there were some NUM members who had passed the requisite examinations, they could provide only limited cover.

On Tuesday 25 September Peter Walker told the ministerial group on coal that it now looked likely that NACODS would vote for a strike. He was right: when the result came through on Friday we discovered that 82.5 per cent had voted in favour.

This was very bad news. Some in Whitehall feared that a bandwagon might begin to roll in Mr Scargill's favour. We were now approaching the autumn and the militants might gain new heart.

The NCB and NACODS held talks on Monday 1 October. Agreement was reached on pay and on guidelines as regards crossing picket lines. The following day there were discussions on machinery for the review of pit closures and the possibility of some form of arbitration in cases of disagreement. This was to remain the most difficult question. No matter how elaborate the process of consultation, the NCB could not concede to a third party the right of ultimate decision over pit closures. This, although generally understood, was best not set out too starkly.

All this time we were faced with hostile outside comment and pressure. The Labour Party Conference wholeheartedly backed the NUM and condemned the police. Worst of all, perhaps, was Neil Kinnock's speech in which, under pressure from the left wing and trade unions, he retreated from the tougher line he had taken at the TUC Conference. He took refuge in a general condemnation of violence which made no distinction between the use of violence with the aim of breaking the law and the use of force to uphold it.

Towards the end of October the situation changed sharply once again. Three events within a week were particularly hopeful for us and must have come as hammerblows to Mr Scargill. First, on Tuesday 24 October the NACODS executive agreed not to strike after all. Precisely what happened is unclear. In all probability the moderates on the executive convinced the hardliners that their members simply would not act as stooges for Mr Scargill.

Second, it was at this point that the civil law at last began to bite. I have already mentioned a case which had been brought against the NUM by two Yorkshire miners: the High Court had ruled in the two miners' favour that the strike in Yorkshire could not be described as 'official'. The NUM had ignored the ruling and as a result a writ had been served on an astonished Mr Scargill on the floor of the Labour Party Conference. On 10 October both he and the union had been found in contempt of court and fined £1,000 and £200,000 respectively. Mr Scargill's fine was paid anonymously, but the NUM refused to pay and the High Court ordered its assets to be sequestrated. It soon became evident that the NUM had prepared for this event, but the financial pressure on the union was now intense and its ability to organize was greatly hampered.

Finally, on Sunday 28 October – only three days after the sequestration order – the *Sunday Times* revealed that an official of the NUM had visited Libya and made a personal appeal to Colonel Gaddafi for his support. This was astonishing news and even Mr Scargill's friends were dismayed. At the beginning of October, Mr Scargill (travelling under an alias as 'Mr Smith') had visited Paris with his colleague Mr Roger Windsor to meet representatives of the French communist trade union, the CGT. Present at the meeting was a Libyan whom Mr Scargill later claimed to be a representative of Libyan trade unionists – a rare breed, in fact, since Colonel Gaddafi had dissolved all trade unions when he came to power in 1969. It seems likely that Colonel Gaddafi made a donation to the NUM, though the amount is uncertain. The sum of £150,000 has been suggested. Mr Windsor's visit to Libya was a follow-up to the Paris meeting.

A further sum was certainly received from an equally unlikely source: the nonexistent 'trade unions' of Soviet-controlled Afghanistan. And in September reports had begun to surface that the NUM was receiving assistance from Soviet miners – a group whose members would have looked with envy on the freedoms, incomes and working conditions of their British equivalents. It was quite clear that these initiatives had the support of the Soviet Government. Otherwise the Soviet miners would not have had access to convertible currency. Our displeasure was made very clear to the Soviet Ambassador and I raised the matter with Mr Gorbachev when he visited Britain for the first time in December, who claimed to be unaware of it.[*]

All this did the NUM's cause great harm, not least with other trade unionists. The British people have plenty of sympathy for someone fight-

---

[*] In fact, I have since seen documentary evidence suggesting that he knew full well and was among those who authorized payment.

ing for his job, but very little for anyone who seeks help from foreign powers out to destroy his country's freedom.

In November the NCB announced that miners who were back at work on Monday 19 November would qualify for a substantial Christmas bonus. The NCB mounted a direct mail campaign to draw the attention of striking miners to the offer. Combined with the growing disillusionment with Mr Scargill, this had an immediate effect. In the first week after the offer 2,203 miners returned to work, six times more than in the previous week. Our strategy was to let this trend continue without trying to take any explicit political credit for it, which could have been counterproductive.

The return to work continued. But so did the violence. Violence and intimidation well away from the pit heads were more difficult for the police to prevent and required fewer people to perpetrate: consequently it was on such tactics that the militant miners now concentrated. One incident that particularly struck me took place on Friday 23 November when Michael Fletcher, a working miner from Pontefract in Yorkshire, was attacked and beaten by a gang of miners in his own home. No fewer than nineteen men were arrested for the crime. Then a week later came one of the most appalling events of the strike: a three-foot concrete post was thrown from a motorway bridge onto a taxi carrying a South Wales miner to work. The driver, David Wilkie, was killed. I wondered whether there was any limit to the savagery of which these people were capable.

As the year ended, our main objective was to encourage a further return to work from 7 January, the first working Monday in the New Year. Though the NCB's bonus offer had expired, there was still a strong financial incentive for strikers to return to work in the near future because they would pay little, if any, income tax on their wages if they went back before the end of the tax year on 31 March. The great strategic prize would be to get more than 50 per cent of NUM members back to work: if we could secure that, it would be equivalent in practical and presentational terms to a vote in a national ballot to end the strike. This would require the return of a further 15,000 to work, which the NCB were busily preparing a new campaign of letters and press advertising to achieve.

It was also vital that the miners and the public at large should be told that there would be no power cuts that winter, contrary to Mr Scargill's ever more desperate and incredible predictions. We held off making such an announcement until we could be absolutely certain, but finally on 29 December Peter Walker was able to issue a statement saying that he had been informed by the Chairman of the CEGB that at the level of coal production that had now been achieved there would be no power cuts during the whole of 1985.

By the middle of January there were almost 75,000 NUM members not on strike and the rate of return was running at about 2,500 a week.

The one thing which could be relied upon to slow down the progress was further negotiations: and so it proved. When news broke of 'talks about talks', which were arranged between the NCB and the NUM on Monday 21 January, the effect was to cut the rate of return to rather less than half that of the previous week.

Meanwhile, public attention increasingly focused on the attempts of the sequestrators to trace and recover NUM funds which had been transferred abroad. In early December further legal action by working miners had led to the removal of the NUM's trustees and the appointment of an official receiver. These were, of course, principally questions for the courts. However, even with the full armoury of the law, there were such difficulties in tracing the funds that the sequestrators might not even have been able to cover their costs. Accordingly, Michael Havers told the Commons on Tuesday 11 December that the Government would indemnify them against the loss. We were also involved in trying to ensure maximum co-operation from foreign governments – Ireland and Luxemburg – in whose jurisdictions the NUM had lodged its money. Towards the end of January some £5 million was recovered.

The TUC leaders were anxious to save the militants from humiliating defeat. But Mr Scargill had no intention of budging: he had already stated publicly that he would prefer a return to work without an agreement to acceptance of the NCB's proposals. For its part, the NCB had told the TUC that there was no basis for negotiation on the terms still demanded by the NUM. I recognized that, although their motives were decidedly mixed, the TUC leaders and particularly the General Secretary had been acting in good faith. They must have realized by now that there was no possibility of doing business with Mr Scargill. Consequently, when a delegation from the TUC asked to see me, I agreed.

I met Norman Willis and other union leaders at No. 10 on the morning of Tuesday 19 February. Willie Whitelaw, Peter Walker and Tom King joined me on the Government side. The meeting was good-natured. Norman Willis put as fair a construction on the NUM's negotiating stance as anyone could. In reply I said that I appreciated the TUC's efforts. I too wanted to see the strike settled as soon as possible. But this required a clear resolution of the central issues of the dispute. It was in no one's interest to end the strike with an unclear formula: arguments about interpretation and accusations of bad faith could provide the basis for another dispute. I gave an assurance that the NACODS agreement would be fully honoured and that I saw no difficulties about implementing it. An effective settlement of the dispute required clear understandings about procedures for closure, acknowledgement of the NCB's right to manage and to make the final decisions, and an acknowledgement that the Board would take the economic performance of pits into account when those decisions were made.

It was now evident to the miners and to the public that the TUC were neither willing nor able to stop events taking their course. Large numbers of miners were going back to work and the rate of return was increasing. On Wednesday 27 February the magic figure was reached: more than half the members of the NUM were now not on strike. On Sunday 3 March an NUM Delegates' Conference voted for a return to work, against Mr Scargill's advice, and over the next few days even the most militant areas returned. That Sunday I gave an interview to reporters outside No. 10. I was asked who if anyone had won. I replied:

> If anyone has won, it has been the miners who stayed at work, the dockers who stayed at work, the power workers who stayed at work, the lorry drivers who stayed at work, the railwaymen who stayed at work, the managers who stayed at work. In other words, all of those people who kept the wheels of Britain turning and who, in spite of a strike, actually produced a record output in Britain last year. It is the whole working people of Britain who kept Britain going.

And so the strike ended. It had lasted almost exactly a year. Even now we could not be sure that the militants would not find some new excuse to call a strike the following winter. So we took steps to rebuild coal and oil stocks and continued to watch events in the coal industry with the closest attention. I was particularly concerned about the dangers faced by the working miners and their families now that the spotlight had moved away from the pit head villages. In May I met Ian MacGregor to emphasize how vital it was that they should receive the necessary consideration and support.

The strike certainly established the truth that the British coal industry could not remain immune to the economic forces which applied elsewhere in both the public and private sectors. In spite of heavy investment, British coal has proved unable to compete on world markets and as a result the British coal industry has now shrunk far more than any of us thought it would at the time of the strike.

Yet the coal strike was always about far more than uneconomic pits. It was a political strike. And so its outcome had a significance far beyond the economic sphere. From 1972 to 1985 the conventional wisdom was that Britain could only be governed with the consent of the trade unions. Even as we were reforming trade union law and overcoming lesser disputes, such as the steel strike, many on the left and outside it continued to believe that the miners had the ultimate veto and would one day use it. That day had now come and gone. Our determination to resist a strike emboldened the ordinary trade unionist to defy the militants. What the strike's defeat established was that Britain could not be made ungovernable by the Fascist Left. Marxists wanted to defy the law of the land in order to defy the laws of economics. They failed, and in doing so demonstrated just how mutually dependent the free economy and a free society really are. It is a lesson no one should forget.

CHAPTER TWENTY-SIX

Shadows of Gunmen

The political and security response to
IRA terrorism 1979–1990

A S USUAL, BY THE END OF THE WEEK of our 1984 Party Conference in Brighton I was becoming frantic about my speech. A good Conference speech cannot just be written in advance: you need to get the feel of the Conference in order to achieve the right tone. I spent as much time as I could working on the text with my speech writers on Thursday afternoon and evening, rushed away to look in at the Conservative Agents' Ball and returned to my suite at the Grand Hotel just after 11 o'clock.

By about 2.40 a.m. the speech – at least from my point of view – was finished. So while the speech writers themselves went to bed, my long-suffering staff typed in what I was (fairly) confident would be the final changes to the text and prepared the Autocue tape. Meanwhile, I got on with some government business.

At 2.54 a.m. a loud thud shook the room. There was a few seconds' silence and then there was a second slightly different noise, in fact created by falling masonry. I knew immediately that it was a bomb – but at this stage I did not know that the explosion had taken place inside the hotel. Glass from the windows of my sitting room was strewn across the carpet. But I thought that it might be a car bomb outside. (I only realized that the bomb had exploded above us when Penny, John Gummer's wife, appeared a little later from upstairs, still in her night clothes.) The adjoining bathroom was more severely damaged, though the worst I would have suffered had I been in there were minor cuts. Those who had sought to kill me had placed the bomb in the wrong place.

Apart from the broken glass and a ringing fire alarm, set off by the explosion, there was a strange and, as it turned out, deceptive normality. The lights, thankfully, remained on: the importance of this played on my mind for some time and for months afterwards I always kept a torch by my bed when I was staying the night in a strange house. Denis put his head round the bedroom door, saw that I was all right and went back inside to dress. For some reason neither of us quite understands he took a spare pair of shoes with him, subsequently worn by Charles Price, the American Ambassador, who had lost his in the confusion of leaving the hotel. While Crawfie gathered together my vanity case, blouses and two suits – one for the next day – Robin Butler came in to take charge of the government papers. I went across the landing to the secretaries' room to see if my staff were all right. One of the girls had received a nasty electric shock from the photocopier. But otherwise all was well. They were as concerned about my still only partly typed-up speech as they were for themselves. 'It's all right,' they assured me, 'we've got the speech.'

By now more and more people were appearing in the secretaries' room with me – the Gummers, the Howes, David Wolfson, Michael Alison and others, unkempt, anxious but quite calm. While we talked, my detectives had been checking out as best they could our immediate security. There is always a fear of a second device, carefully timed to catch and kill those fleeing from the first explosion. It was also necessary for them to find a way out of the hotel which was both unblocked and safe.

At 3.10 a.m., in groups, we began to leave. It turned out that the first route suggested was impassable and we were turned back. So we went back and waited in the office. Later we were told that it was safe to leave and we went down by the main staircase. It was now that I first saw from the rubble in the entrance and foyer something of the seriousness of the blast. I hoped that the porter had not been injured. The air was full of thick cement dust: it was in my mouth and covered my clothes as I clambered over discarded belongings and broken furniture towards the back entrance of the hotel. It still never occurred to me that anyone would have died.

Ten minutes later Denis, Crawfie and I arrived in a police car at Brighton Police Station. We were given tea in the Chief Constable's room. Willie Whitelaw came in. So did the Howes, accompanied by their little dog 'Budget'. But it was Leon Brittan, as Home Secretary, and John Gummer, as Party Chairman, with whom I had most to discuss. At this stage none of us knew whether the Conference could continue. I was already determined that if it was physically possible to do so I would deliver my speech. It was eventually decided that I would spend the rest of the night at Lewes Police College. I changed out of evening dress into a navy suit and, as I left the Police Station with Denis and Crawfie, I made a brief statement to the press.

Whether by chance or arrangement, there was no one staying at the College. I was given a small sitting room with a television and a twin-bedded room with its own bathroom. Denis and the detectives shared rooms further down the corridor. Crawfie and I shared too. We sat on our beds and speculated about what had happened. By now I was convinced that there must have been casualties. But we could get no news.

I could only think of one thing to do. Crawfie and I knelt by the side of our beds and prayed for some time in silence.

I had brought no nightclothes and so I lay down fully clothed and slept fitfully for perhaps an hour and a half. I awoke to the sound of the break-fast television news at 6.30 a.m. The news was much worse than I had feared. I saw pictures of Norman Tebbit being pulled out of the rubble. Then came the news that Roberta Wakeham and Anthony Berry MP were dead. I knew that I could not afford to let my emotions get control of me. I had to be mentally and physically fit for the day ahead. I tried not to watch the harrowing pictures. But it did not seem to do much good. I had to know each detail of what had happened – and every detail seemed worse than the last.

It was a perfect autumn day and as we drove back into Brighton the sky was clear and the sea completely calm. I now had my first sight of the front of the Grand Hotel, a whole vertical section of which had collapsed.

Then we went on to the Conference Centre itself, where at 9.20 a.m. the Conference opened; and at 9.30 a.m. precisely I and the officers of the National Union* walked onto the platform. (Many of them had had to leave clothes in the hotel, but Alistair McAlpine had persuaded the local Marks & Spencer to open early and by now they were smartly dressed.) The body of the hall was only about half full, because the rigorous secu-rity checks held up the crowds trying to get in. But the ovation was colos-sal. All of us were relieved to be alive, saddened by the tragedy and determined to show the terrorists that they could not break our spirit.

By chance, but how appropriately, the first debate was on Northern Ireland. I stayed to listen to this but then left to work on my speech which

---

* The National Union of Conservative and Unionist Associations – the voluntary wing of the Party.

had to be completely revised. All the while, and in spite of attempts by my staff to minimize the interruptions, I was receiving messages and fleeting visits from colleagues and friends. I knew that John Wakeham had not yet been freed from the rubble and several people were still missing. A steady stream of flowers arrived which were sent on to the hospital where the injured had been taken.

As in earlier days, I delivered the speech from a text rather than Autocue and ad-libbed a good deal as well. But I knew that far more important than what I said was the fact that I, as Prime Minister, was still able to say it. I did not dwell long in the speech on what had happened. But I tried to sum up the feelings of all of us.

> The bomb attack . . . was an attempt not only to disrupt and terminate our conference. It was an attempt to cripple Her Majesty's democratically elected government. That is the scale of the outrage in which we have all shared. And the fact that we are gathered here now, shocked but composed and determined, is a sign not only that this attack has failed, but that all attempts to destroy democracy by terrorism will fail.

I did not linger after my speech but went immediately to the Royal Sussex County Hospital to visit the injured. Four people had already died. Muriel McLean was on a drip feed: she would die later. John Wakeham was still unconscious and remained so for several days. He had to be operated on daily for some time to save his legs which had been terribly crushed. By chance we all knew the consultant in charge, Tony Trafford, who had been a Conservative MP. I spent hours on the telephone trying to get the best advice possible from experts in dealing with crush injuries. In the end it turned out that there was a doctor in the hospital from El Salvador who had the expertise required. Between them they managed to save John's legs. Norman Tebbit regained consciousness while I was at the hospital and we managed a few words. I also talked to Margaret Tebbit who was in the intensive care unit. She told me she had no feeling below the neck. As a former nurse, she knew well enough what that meant.

I left the hospital overcome by such bravery and suffering. I was driven back to Chequers that afternoon faster than I have ever been driven before, with a full motorcycle escort. As I spent that night in what had become my home I could not stop thinking about those unable to return to theirs.

* * *

What happened in Brighton shocked the world. But the people of Northern Ireland and the security forces face the ruthless reality of terrorism day after day. There is no excuse for the IRA's reign of terror. If their violence were, as the misleading phrase often has it, 'mindless' it would be easier to grasp as the manifestation of a disordered psyche. But that is not what terrorism is, however many psychopaths may be attracted to it. Terrorism is the calculated use of violence – and the threat of it – to achieve political ends.

There are terrorists in both the Catholic and Protestant communities, and all too many people prepared to give them support or at least to acquiesce in their activities. Indeed, for a person to stand out against the terrorists carries great personal risk. The result is that it is impossible to separate entirely the security policy, required to prevent terrorist outrages and bring the perpetrators to book, from the wider political approach to the long-standing 'Northern Ireland problem'. For some people that connection implies that you should make concessions to the terrorist, in particular by weakening the Union between Ulster and Britain. But it never did so for me. My policy towards Northern Ireland was always one aimed above all at upholding democracy and the law.

The IRA are the core of the terrorist problem; their counterparts on the Protestant side would probably disappear if the IRA could be beaten. But the best chance of beating them is if three conditions are met. First, the IRA have to be rejected by the nationalist minority on whom they depend for shelter and support.* This requires that the minority should be led to support or at least acquiesce in the constitutional framework of the state in which they live. Second, the IRA have to be deprived of international support, whether from well-meaning but naive Irish Americans, or from Arab revolutionary regimes like that of Colonel Gaddafi. This requires constant attention to foreign policy aimed at explaining the facts to the misinformed and cutting off the weapons from the mischievous. Third, relations between Britain and the Republic of Ireland have to be carefully managed. Although the IRA have plenty of support in areas like West

---

* In this chapter and elsewhere nationalist is generally used as an alternative to 'Catholic' and Unionist to 'Protestant'. While it is true that the political and ethnic division in Northern Ireland is largely (though not always) consistent with and sometimes worsened by religious division, it is misleading to describe it in essentially religious terms. The IRA gunmen who murder and the hunger strikers who committed suicide are not in any proper sense 'Catholic' nor are 'loyalist' sectarian killers 'Protestant'. They are not even in any meaningful sense Christians.

Belfast within Northern Ireland, very often it is to the South that they go to be trained, to receive money and arms and to escape capture after crimes committed within the United Kingdom. The border, long and difficult to patrol, is of crucial significance to the security problem. Much depends on the willingness and ability of the political leaders of the Republic to co-operate effectively with our intelligence, security forces and courts.

My own instincts are profoundly Unionist and our Party has always, throughout its history, been committed to the defence of the Union: indeed, on the eve of the First World War, the Conservatives were not far short of provoking civil disorder to support it. That is why I could never understand why leading Unionists – apparently sincerely – suggested that in my dealings with the South and above all in the Anglo-Irish Agreement, which I shall discuss shortly, I was contemplating selling them out to the Republic.

But what British politician will ever fully understand Northern Ireland? In the history of Ireland – both North and South – which I tried to read up when I could, reality and myth from the seventeenth century to the 1920s take on an almost Balkan immediacy. Distrust mounting to hatred and revenge is never far beneath the political surface. And those who step onto it must do so gingerly.

I started from the need for greater security, which was imperative. If this meant making limited political concessions to the South, I had to contemplate it. But the results in terms of security must come through. In Northern Ireland itself my first choice would have been a system of majority rule with strong guarantees for the human rights of the minority, and indeed everyone else. That is broadly the approach which Airey Neave and I had in mind when the 1979 manifesto was drafted. But it was not long before it became clear to me that this model was not going to work, at least for the present. The nationalist minority were not prepared to believe that majority rule would secure their rights – whether it took the form of an assembly in Belfast, or more powerful local government. They insisted on some kind of 'power sharing' as well as demanding a role for the Republic in Northern Ireland, both of which proposals were anathema to the Unionists.

I had always had a good deal of respect for the old Stormont system.* When I was Education Secretary I was impressed by the efficiency of the

---

* A system of majority rule had existed in the province from the creation of Northern Ireland in the partition of 1920 until 1972, known as 'Stormont' (from the location of government buildings on the edge of Belfast).

Northern Ireland education service. The province has kept its grammar schools and so has consistently achieved some of the best academic results in the United Kingdom. But majority rule meant permanent power for the Protestants, and there was no getting away from the fact that, with some justice, the long years of Unionist rule were associated with discrimination against the Catholics. I believe the defects were exaggerated, but Catholic resentment gave rise to the civil rights movement at the end of the 1960s, which the IRA was able to exploit. By early 1972 civil disorder existed on such a scale that Stormont was suspended and replaced by direct rule from London. At the same time the British Government gave a guarantee that Northern Ireland would remain a part of the United Kingdom so long as the majority of its people wished, and this has remained the cornerstone of policy under governments of both parties.

The political realities of Northern Ireland prevented a return to majority rule. This was something that many Unionists refused to accept, but since 1974 they had been joined in the House of Commons by Enoch Powell, who helped to convert some of them to an altogether different approach. His aim was that of 'integration'. Essentially, this would have meant eliminating any difference between the government of Northern Ireland and that of the rest of the UK, ruling out a return to devolution (whether majority rule or power sharing) and any special role for the Republic. Enoch's view was that the terrorists thrived on uncertainty about Ulster's constitutional position: that uncertainty would, he argued, be ended by full integration combined with a tough security policy. I disagreed with this for two reasons. First, I did not believe that security could be disentangled from other wider political issues. Second, I never saw devolved government and an assembly for Northern Ireland as weakening, but rather strengthening the Union. Like Stormont before it, it would provide a clear alternative focus to Dublin – without undermining the sovereignty of the Westminster Parliament.

Such were my views about Northern Ireland's future on entering office. My conviction that further efforts must be made on both the political and security fronts had been strengthened by the events of the second half of 1979. In the course of that October we discussed in government the need for an initiative designed to achieve devolution in Northern Ireland. I was not very optimistic about the prospects but I agreed to the issue of a discussion document setting out the options. A conference would be called of the main political parties in Northern Ireland to see what agreement could be reached.

On Monday 7 January 1980 the conference opened in Belfast. On this occasion the largest Unionist group, the Official Unionist Party (OUP), refused to attend. Dr Paisley's more militant Democratic Unionist Party (DUP), the mainly Catholic nationalist Social Democratic and Labour Party (SDLP) and the moderate middle-class Alliance Party did attend, but there was no real common ground.

We adjourned the conference later in March and began to consider putting forward more specific proposals ourselves in the form of a White Paper. Ministers discussed a draft paper from Northern Ireland Secretary Humphrey Atkins in June. I had various changes made in the text in order to take account of Unionist sensitivities. I was no more optimistic than earlier that the initiative would succeed, but I agreed that the White Paper should be published in early July. It described areas – not including security – in which powers might be transferred to an executive chosen by an assembly in the province. It also spelt out two ways of choosing that executive, one inclining towards majority rule and the other towards power sharing. By November it was clear that there would not be sufficient agreement among the Northern Irish parties to go ahead with the assembly.

In any case, by now Republican prisoners inside the Maze Prison had begun the first of their two hunger strikes. I decided that no major political initiative should be made while the hunger strike was continuing: we must not appear to be bowing to terrorist demands. I was also cautious about any high-profile contacts with the Irish Government at such a time for the same reason.

Charles Haughey had been elected leader of his Fianna Fáil Party and Taoiseach in mid-December 1979. Mr Haughey had throughout his career been associated with the most Republican strand in respectable Irish politics. How 'respectable' was a subject of some controversy: in a famous case in 1970 he had been acquitted of involvement while an Irish minister in the importing of arms for the IRA. I found him easy to get on with, less talkative and more realistic than Garret FitzGerald, the leader of Fine Gael. He had come to see me in May at No. 10 and we had had a general and friendly discussion of the scene in Northern Ireland. He left me a gift of a beautiful Georgian silver teapot, which was kind of him. (It was worth more than the limit allowed for official gifts and I had to leave it behind at No. 10 when I left office.) By the time that I had my next talk with Mr Haughey when we were attending the European Council in

Luxemburg on Monday 1 December 1980 it was the hunger strike which was the Irish main concern.

To understand the background to the hunger strikes it is necessary to refer back to the 'special category' status for convicted terrorist prisoners in Northern Ireland which had been introduced, as a concession to the IRA, in 1972.* This was a bad mistake. It was ended in 1976. Prisoners convicted of such offences after that date were treated as ordinary prisoners – with no greater privileges than anyone else. But the policy was not retrospective. So some 'special category' prisoners continued being held apart and under a different regime from other terrorists. Within the so-called 'H blocks' of the Maze Prison where the terrorist prisoners were housed, protests had been more or less constant, including the revolting 'dirty protest'. On 10 October a number of prisoners announced their intention of beginning a hunger strike on Monday 27 October unless certain demands were met. The most significant were that they should be able to wear their own clothes, associate freely with other 'political' prisoners and refrain from prison work.

All my instincts were against bending to such pressure, and certainly there could be no changes in the prison regime once the strike had begun. There was never any question of conceding political status. But the RUC Chief Constable believed that some concessions before the strike would be helpful in dealing with the threatened public disorder which such a strike might lead to and, though we did not believe that they could prevent the hunger strike, we were anxious to win the battle for public opinion. Accordingly, we agreed that all prisoners – not just those who had committed terrorist crimes – might be permitted to wear 'civilian type' clothing – but not their own clothes – as long as they obeyed the prison rules. As I had foreseen, these concessions did not prevent the hunger strike.

As the hunger strike continued and the prospect approached of one or more of the prisoners dying we came under a good deal of pressure. When I met Mr Haughey in the margins of the Luxemburg European Council on Monday 1 December 1980 he urged me to find some face-

---

* Convicted criminals sentenced to more than nine months' imprisonment who claimed political motivation and were acceptable to the paramilitary leaders in the jails were accorded special category status – allowed to wear their own clothes, exempted from work, and segregated in compounds.

saving device which would allow the strikers to end their fast, though he said that he fully accepted that political status was out of the question. I replied that there was nothing left to give. Nor was I convinced, then or later, that the hunger strikers were able to abandon the strike, even if they had wanted to, against the wishes of the IRA leadership.

We met again exactly a week later for our second Anglo-Irish summit in Dublin. This meeting did more harm than good because, unusually, I did not involve myself closely enough in the drafting of the communiqué and, as a result, allowed through the statement that Mr Haughey and I would devote our next meeting in London 'to special consideration of the totality of relationships within these islands'. Mr Haughey then gave a press briefing which led journalists to write of a breakthrough on the constitutional question. There had of course been no such thing. But the damage had been done and it was a red rag to the Unionist bull.

The Catholic Church was also a factor in dealing with the hunger strike. I explained the circumstances personally to the Pope on a visit to Rome on 24 November. He had as little sympathy for terrorists as I did, as he had made very clear on his visit to the Republic the previous year. After the Vatican brought pressure on the Irish Catholic hierarchy, they issued a statement calling on the prisoners to end their fast, though urging the Government to show 'flexibility'.

Talk of concessions and compromises continued and intensified and then, on Thursday 18 December, one of the prisoners began to lose consciousness and the strike was abruptly called off. The IRA claimed later that they had done this because we had made concessions, but this was wholly false.

I had hoped that this would see the end of the hunger strike tactic, and indeed of all the prison protests. But it was not to be so. Another hunger strike was begun on 1 March 1981 by the IRA leader in the Maze, Bobby Sands, and he was joined at intervals by others. Simultaneously the 'dirty protest' was finally ended, ostensibly to concentrate attention on the hunger strike.

This was the beginning of a time of troubles. The IRA were on the advance politically: Sands himself, *in absentia*, won the parliamentary seat of Fermanagh and South Tyrone at a by-election caused by the death of an Independent Republican MP. More generally, the SDLP was losing ground to the Republicans. There was some suggestion, to which even some of my advisers gave credence, that the IRA were contemplating ending their terrorist compaign and seeking power through the ballot box. I never believed this. But it indicated how successful their propaganda could be.

Bobby Sands died on Tuesday 5 May. From this time forward I became the IRA's top target for assassination.

Sands's death provoked rioting and violence, mainly in Londonderry and Belfast, and the security forces came under increasing strain. It was possible to admire the courage of Sands and the other hunger strikers who died, but not to sympathize with their murderous cause. We had done everything in our power to persuade them to give up their fast.

So had the Catholic Church. I went as far as I could to involve an organization connected with the Catholic hierarchy, the Irish Commission for Justice and Peace (ICJP), hoping that the strikers would listen to them – though our reward was to be denounced by the ICJP for going back on undertakings we had allegedly made in the talks we had with them. This false allegation was supported by Garret FitzGerald who became Taoiseach at the beginning of July 1981.

In striving to end the crisis, I had stopped short of force-feeding, a degrading and dangerous practice which I could not support. At all times hunger strikers were offered three meals a day, had constant medical attention and, of course, took water. When the hunger strikers fell into unconsciousness it became possible for their next of kin to instruct the doctors to feed them through a drip. My hope was that the families would use this power to bring an end to the strike. Eventually, after ten prisoners had died, a group of families announced that they would intervene to prevent the deaths of their relatives and the IRA called off the strike on Saturday 3 October. With the strike now over, I authorized some further concessions on clothing, association and loss of remission. But the outcome was a significant defeat for the IRA.

However, the IRA now turned to violence on a larger scale, especially on the mainland. The worst incident was caused by an IRA bomb outside Chelsea Barracks on Monday 10 October. A coach carrying Irish Guardsmen was blown up, killing one bystander and injuring many soldiers. The bomb was filled with six-inch nails, intended to inflict as much pain and suffering as possible.

After Garret FitzGerald had overcome his initial inclination to play up to Irish opinion at the British Government's expense I had quite friendly dealings with him – all too friendly, to judge by Unionist reaction to our agreement after a summit in November 1981 to set up the rather grand sounding 'Anglo-Irish Inter-Governmental Council', which really continued the existing ministerial and official contacts under a new name. How Garret FitzGerald would have reacted to the new proposals we made in the spring of 1982 for 'rolling devolution' of powers to a Northern Ireland Assembly it is difficult to know. But in fact by now the whirligig of Irish politics had brought Charles Haughey back as Taoiseach and Anglo-Irish relations cooled to freezing. The new Taoiseach denounced our proposals for devolution as an 'unworkable mistake' in which he was also joined by the SDLP. But what angered me most was the thoroughly unhelpful stance taken by the Irish Government during the Falklands War, which I have mentioned earlier.

Jim Prior, who succeeded Humphrey Atkins as Secretary of State for Northern Ireland shortly before the end of the second hunger strike, was a good deal more optimistic about the proposals in our White Paper than I was. Ian Gow, my PPS, was against the whole idea and I shared a number of his reservations. Before publication, I had the text of the White Paper substantially changed in order to cut out a chapter dealing with relations with the Irish Republic and, I hoped, minimize Unionist objections: although Ian Paisley's DUP went along with the proposals, many integrationists in the Official Unionist Party were critical. Twenty Conservative MPs voted against the Bill when it came forward in May and three junior members of the Government resigned.

In the elections that October to the Northern Ireland Assembly Sinn Fein won 10 per cent of the total, over half of the vote won by the SDLP. For this, of course, the SDLP's own tactics and negative attitudes were heavily to blame: but they continued them by refusing to take their seats in the assembly when it opened the following month. The campaign itself had been marked by a sharp increase in sectarian murders.

The IRA were still at work on the mainland too. I was chairing a meeting of 'E' Committee in the Cabinet Room on the morning of Tuesday 20 July 1982 when I heard (and felt) the unmistakable sound of a bomb exploding in the middle distance. I immediately asked that enquiries be made, but continued the meeting. When the news finally came through it was even worse than I feared. Two bombs had exploded, one two hours after the other, in Hyde Park and Regent's Park, the intended victims being in the first case the Household Cavalry and in the second the band of the Royal Green Jackets. Eight people were killed and 53 injured. The carnage was truly terrible. I heard about it first hand from some of the victims when I went to the hospital the next day.

The return of Garret FitzGerald as Taoiseach in December 1982 provided us with an opportunity to improve the climate of Anglo-Irish relations with a view to pressing the South for more action on security. I had a meeting with Dr FitzGerald at the European Council at Stuttgart in June 1983. I shared the worry he expressed about the erosion of SDLP support by Sinn Fein. However uninspiring SDLP politicians might be – at least since the departure of the courageous Gerry Fitt – they were the minority's main representatives and an alternative to the IRA. They had to be wooed. But Dr FitzGerald had no suggestions to make about how to get the SDLP to take part in the Northern Ireland Assembly, which was pointless without their participation. He pressed me to agree talks between officials on future co-operation.

I did not think there was much to talk about, but I accepted the proposal. Robert Armstrong, head of the civil service and Cabinet Secretary, and his opposite number in the Republic, Dermot Nally, became the main channels of communication. Over the summer and autumn of 1983 we received a number of informal approaches from the Irish, by no means consistent or clear in content.

I allowed the talks between the two sides to continue. I also had in mind the political danger of seeming to adopt a negative reaction to new proposals. This in turn meant that I had, within limits, to treat seriously the Republic's so-called 'New Ireland Forum'. This had originally been set up mainly as a way of helping the SDLP at the 1983 general election but Garret FitzGerald was now using it as a sounding board for 'ideas' about the future of Northern Ireland. Since the Unionist parties would take no part in it the outcome was bound to be skewed towards a united Ireland. For my part I was anxious that this collection of nationalists, North and South, might attract international respectability for moves to weaken the Union, so I was intensely wary of them.

The need for Irish help on security was again evident after the appalling murder by the Irish National Liberation Army (INLA) of worshippers at the Pentecostal Gospel Hall at Darkley in County Armagh on Sunday 20 November. In spite of all the fine words about the need to defeat terrorism which I had been hearing from the Taoiseach, the Irish Justice minister refused to meet Jim Prior to review security co-operation and the Garda Commissioner similarly refused to meet the Chief Constable of the RUC.

Then the IRA struck again on the mainland. On Saturday 17 December I was attending a carol concert in the Royal Festival Hall. While I was there I received news that a car bomb had exploded just outside Harrods. I left at the first opportunity and went to the scene. By the time I arrived most of the dead and injured had been removed but I shall never forget the sight of the charred body of a teenage girl lying where she had been blown against the store window. Even by the IRA's own standards this was a particularly callous attack. Five people including two police officers died. The fact that one of the dead was an American should have brought home to US sympathizers with the IRA the real nature of Irish terrorism.

The Harrods bomb was designed to intimidate not just the Government but the British people as a whole. The IRA had chosen the country's most prestigious store at a time when the streets of London were full of shoppers in festive mood looking forward to Christmas. There was an instinctive feeling – in reaction to the outrage – that everyone must go about their business normally. Denis was among those who went to shop in Harrods the following Monday to do just that.

By the end of the year the prospects for some kind of negotiation seemed reasonable, but the acid test for me would be the question of security.

In January and February 1984 I held meetings to run through the options. The Irish were keen to pursue possibilities of joint policing and even mixed courts (with British and Irish judges sitting on the same bench). The idea, favoured by Dr FitzGerald, of the Garda policing nationalist areas like West Belfast seemed quite impractical: not only would the Unionists have been outraged, the Garda officers would probably have been shot on sight by the IRA. As for joint Anglo-Irish courts – majority decisions in terrorist cases by a mixed court would have been disastrous.

There was an important development over the summer: the Irish for the first time explicitly put forward the idea of amending Articles 2 and 3 of their constitution to make Irish unity an aspiration rather than a legal claim. This was attractive to me, in that I thought it should reassure the Unionists. But it was clear that the Irish would expect a good deal in return, and I still doubted their capacity to deliver the referendum vote. So the net effect of their proposal was actually to make me more pessimistic and suspicious. Also they were trying to go too far too fast. The Irish still hankered after joint authority (indeed this lay behind the subsequent contrary interpretations we and they placed on the provisions of the Anglo-Irish Agreement).

Jim Prior resigned as Northern Ireland Secretary in September 1984 to become Chairman of GEC. I brought Douglas Hurd, a former Foreign

Office mandarin and a talented political novelist, who had been Ted Heath's political secretary at No. 10, into the Cabinet as his replacement. Shortly afterwards I widened the circle of those involved on our side of the talks to include senior officials in the Northern Ireland Office (NIO). We held a meeting of ministers and officials in early October which brought out the likely extent of Unionist objections, and in particular the fact that amendment of Articles 2 and 3 might cut little ice with them; indeed, I was told that 'an aspiration to unity' was scarcely less offensive to the Unionists than an outright claim.

It was at this point that the IRA bombed the Grand Hotel in Brighton. I was not going to appear to be bombed to the negotiating table; the incident confirmed my feeling that we should go slowly, and I feared too that it might be the first of a series which might poison the atmosphere so much that an agreement would prove impossible.

We toughened our negotiating position.

On Wednesday 14 November 1984 I held a meeting of ministers and officials to review the position. I was to meet Garret FitzGerald at our regular Anglo-Irish summit the following week and I was alarmed by the lack of realism which still seemed evident in the Irish proposals. I decided that while I would go to the summit willing to make progress on co-operation I would disabuse him in no uncertain terms of the possibility of joint authority.

In our discussions with the Irish of a joint Anglo-Irish body as a framework for consultation there was a succession of misunderstandings and disagreements. Although the idea of amending Articles 2 and 3 was clearly now off the agenda, we pressed the Irish for some kind of firm declaration committing them to the principle that unification could only come about with the consent of the majority in Northern Ireland. We hoped that such a declaration would reassure the Unionists. The Irish wanted the proposed joint body to have a much bigger say over economic and social matters in the North than we were prepared to concede. Nor did the gains we could hope for on security become any clearer. I found myself constantly toning down the commitments which were put before me in our own draft proposals, let alone being prepared to accept those emanating from Dublin. In early June I insisted that there should be a review mechanism built into the Anglo-Irish Agreement. I also continued to resist Irish pressure for joint courts and SDLP demands for radical changes in the Ulster Defence Regiment (UDR) and the RUC.

When I met Dr FitzGerald at the Milan European Council on the morning of Saturday 29 June 1985 he said that he was prepared to have the Irish Government state publicly that there could be no change in the status of Northern Ireland without the consent of the majority of the people and acknowledge the fact that this consent did not exist. He was prepared to have a special Irish task force sent to the south side of the border to strengthen security. He was also prepared to have Ireland ratify the European Convention on the Suppression of Terrorism (ECST). But he was still pressing for joint courts, changes in the RUC and the UDR, and now added the proposal for a major review of sentences for terrorist prisoners if the violence was brought to an end. It remained to be seen whether he could deliver on his promises. But the demands were still unrealistic, as I told him. I could go no further than considering the possibility of joint courts: I was certainly not going to give an assurance in advance that they would be established. I considered a review of sentences quite out of the question and he did not press the point. I warned him that announcing measures on policing at the same time as the Anglo-Irish Agreement would cause a sharp Unionist reaction and jeopardize the whole position.

At this point Dr FitzGerald became very agitated. He declared that unless the minority in Northern Ireland could be turned against the IRA, Sinn Fein would gain the upper hand in the North and provoke a civil war which would drag the Republic down as well, with Colonel Gaddafi providing millions to help this happen. A sensible point was being exaggerated to the level of absurdity. I said that of course I shared his aim of preventing Ireland falling under hostile and tyrannical forces. But that was not an argument for taking measures which would simply provoke the Unionists and cause unnecessary trouble.

By the time our meeting ended, however, I felt that we were some way towards an agreement, though there were still points to resolve. I also knew that a lot of progress had been made in the official talks, so I had good reason to believe that a successful conclusion was possible. Dr FitzGerald and I even discussed the timing and place of the signing ceremony.

At 2 o'clock on the afternoon of Friday 15 November Garret FitzGerald and I signed the Anglo-Irish Agreement at Hillsborough Castle in Northern Ireland. It was not perfect from either side's point of view. Article 1 affirmed that any change in the status of Northern Ireland would only

come about with the consent of a majority of the people of Northern
Ireland and recognized that the present wish of that majority was for no
change in the status of the province. I believed that this major concession
by the Irish would reassure the Unionists that the Union itself was not in
doubt. I thought that given my own well-known attitude towards Irish
terrorism they would have confidence in my intentions. I was wrong
about that. But the Unionists miscalculated too. The tactics which they
used to oppose the agreement – a general strike, intimidation, flirting
with civil disobedience – worsened the security situation and weakened
their standing in the eyes of the rest of the United Kingdom.

The agreement allowed the Irish Government to put forward views
and proposals on matters relating to Northern Ireland in a wide range of
areas, including security. But it was made clear that there was no deroga-
tion from the sovereignty of the United Kingdom. It was for us, not the
Irish, to make the decisions. If there was devolution in Northern Ireland,
which the agreement committed us to work for, those areas of policy
devolved would be taken out of the hands of the Anglo-Irish Inter-
Governmental Conference. (Garret FitzGerald, showing some courage,
publicly accepted this implication of the agreement at the press conference which followed the signing.) The agreement itself would be subject
to review at the end of three years or earlier if either government
requested.

The real question now was whether the agreement would result in
better security. The strong opposition of the Unionists would be a major
obstacle. By contrast, international – most importantly American – reaction was very favourable. Above all, however, we hoped for a more co-
operative attitude from the Irish Government, security forces and courts.
If we got this, the agreement would be successful. We would have to wait
and see.

One person who was not going to wait was Ian Gow. I spent some
time trying to persuade him not to go but he insisted on resigning as a
Treasury minister. This was a personal blow to me, though I am glad to
say that the friendship between the two of us and our families was
barely affected. Ian was one of the very few who resigned from my
Government on a point of principle. I respected him as much as I
disagreed with him.

By the end of the year, however, I had become very worried about the
Unionist reaction. It was worse than anyone had predicted to me. Of the
legitimate political leaders, Ian Paisley was in the forefront of the mass

campaign against the agreement. But far more worrying was the fact that behind him and other leaders stood harder and more sinister figures who might all too easily cross the line from civil disobedience to violence.

Shortly before the agreement, Tom King had taken over as Secretary of State for Northern Ireland. Tom was initially highly sceptical about the value of the agreement though he later became more enthusiastic. Both of us agreed that the political priority was to win over the support of at least some Unionist leaders and that wider Unionist opinion which I felt was probably more understanding of what we were trying to achieve. I was convinced that the people who met me on my visits to Northern Ireland could harbour no doubts about my commitment to their safety and freedom. Indeed, this was confirmed for me when I invited non-political representatives of the majority community from business and the professions to lunch at No. 10 on Wednesday 5 February 1986. Their view was that for many people the real concerns in Northern Ireland were with jobs, housing, education – in short, the sort of issues which are at the centre of politics on the mainland. I was also confirmed in my impression that one of the problems of Northern Irish politics was that it no longer attracted enough people of high calibre.

I invited Jim Molyneaux and Ian Paisley to Downing Street on the morning of Tuesday 25 February. I told them that I believed that they underestimated the advantages which the agreement offered. I recognized that they were bitter at not having been consulted during the negotiation of the agreement. I offered to devise a system which would allow full consultation with them in future and which would not just be confined to matters discussed in the Anglo-Irish Inter-Governmental Conference. Security, for example, could be included. I also said that we were prepared in principle to sit down at a round-table conference with the parties in Northern Ireland to consider, without any preconditions, the scope for devolution. Third, we were ready for consultations with the Unionist parties on the future of the existing Northern Ireland Assembly and on the handling of Northern Ireland business at Westminster. I made it plain that I would not agree to even temporary suspension of the Anglo-Irish Agreement, but the agreement would be operated 'sensitively'. At the time this seemed to go down well. I went on to warn of the damage which would be done if the proposed general strike in Northern Ireland on 3 March took place. Ian Paisley said that he and Jim Molyneaux knew nothing of the plans. They would reach their decisions when they had considered the outcome of the present meeting. The following day after they had consulted their supporters in Northern Ireland they came out in support of the strike.

Nor did I find the SDLP any more co-operative. I saw John Hume on the afternoon of Thursday 27 February. I urged that the SDLP should give more open support to the security forces, but to no avail. He seemed more interested to score points at the expense of the Unionists. A few days later I wrote to Garret FitzGerald urging him to get the SDLP to adopt a more sensible and statesmanlike approach.

But by now Dr FitzGerald and his colleagues in Dublin were adding their own fuel to the flames, publicly exaggerating the powers which the Irish had obtained through the agreement, a tactic which was of course entirely self-defeating. Nor, in spite of detailed criticisms and suggestions, could we get the Irish to make the required improvements in their own security. The Irish judicial authorities were proving no more co-operative either, having sent back warrants for the arrest and extradition of Evelyn Glenholmes from the Irish Republic on suspicion of involvement in terrorism because, among other things, they claimed that a full stop was missing.

In any case, Garret FitzGerald's Government's own position was weakening and he was backtracking on his commitment to get the European Convention on the Suppression of Terrorism though the Dáil. His Government was now in a minority and he told us that he was under pressure to accept the requirement that we should make a *prima facie* case before extradition to the United Kingdom was granted. This would actually have worsened the situation on extradition, reviving past difficulties which recent Irish judge-made law had overcome. Dr FitzGerald told us that he was resisting the pressure, but it soon became clear that he was seeking a *quid pro quo*. He wanted us to introduce three-judge courts for terrorist trials in Northern Ireland. Tom King brought forward a paper supporting the idea, which Geoffrey Howe and Douglas Hurd also backed. But the lawyers were outraged and my sympathies lay with them. The proposal was turned down at a ministerial meeting at the beginning of October 1986.

In the end Dr FitzGerald managed to pass his legislation, but with the proviso that it would not come into effect unless the Dáil passed a further resolution a year later, which stored up trouble for the future. Shortly afterwards, in January 1987, his Coalition Government collapsed and the subsequent election brought Charles Haughey back to the office of Taoiseach. This heralded more difficulties. Mr Haughey and his Party had opposed the agreement, though his formal position was now that he would be prepared to make it work. But I suspected that he would be prepared to play up to Republican opinion in the South more than had his predecessor.

The security position in the province had also worsened. I received a report from George Younger on the strength of the IRA north and south of the border which convinced me that a new drive against them was necessary. The scale of the supplies of arms being received by the IRA, on which we already had a good deal of intelligence, was confirmed by the interception of the *Eksund* – with its hoard of Libyan arms – by French customs in October.

I was at the reception which follows the Remembrance Day Service at the Cenotaph when I received news that a bomb had exploded at Enniskillen in County Fermanagh. It had been planted yards away from the town War Memorial in an old school building, part of which collapsed on the crowd which had assembled for the service. Eleven people were killed, and more than sixty injured. No warning was given.

From now on the requirements for practical improvements in security, reviewed after each new tragedy, increasingly dominated my policy towards both Northern Ireland and the Republic. It slowly became clear that the wider gains for which I had hoped from greater support by the nationalist minority in Northern Ireland or the Irish Government and people for the fight against terrorism were not going to be forthcoming. Only the international dimension became noticeably easier to deal with as a result of the agreement.

On Sunday 6 March three Irish terrorists were shot dead by our security forces in Gibraltar. There was not the slightest doubt about the terrorists' identity or intentions. Contrary to later reports, the Spanish authorities had been extremely co-operative. The funeral of the terrorists was held in Milltown Cemetery, Belfast. From the thousands attending you would imagine that these people were martyrs not would-be murderers. The spiral of violence now accelerated. A gunman attacked the mourners, three of whom were killed and 68 injured. It was at the funeral of two of these mourners that what was to remain in my mind as the single most horrifying event in Northern Ireland during my term of office occurred.

No one who saw the film of the lynching of the two young soldiers trapped by that frenzied Republican mob, pulled from their car, stripped and murdered, will believe that reason or goodwill can ever be a substitute for force when dealing with Irish Republican terrorism. I went to be with the relatives of our murdered soldiers when the bodies were brought back to Northolt; I shall not forget the remark of Gerry Adams, the Sinn Fein leader, that I would have many more bodies to meet in that way. I could hardly believe it when the BBC initially refused to supply to the RUC film which might have been useful in bringing to justice the perpetrators of this crime, though they later complied. But I knew that the most important task was for us to use every means available to beat the IRA. On the same day as the news came in of what had happened I told Tom King that there must be a paper brought forward setting out all the options. I was determined that nothing should be ruled out.

On the afternoon of Tuesday 22 March I held an initial meeting and this far-reaching security review continued during the spring.

Mr Haughey added to the problem of restoring confidence and stability in Northern Ireland by an astonishing speech which he made in the United States in April. This listed all of his objections to British policy, lumping together the Attorney-General's decision not to initiate prosecutions following the Stalker-Sampson Report into the RUC,* the Court of Appeal's rejection of the appeal of the so-called 'Birmingham Six'† (as if it was for the British Government to tell British courts how to administer justice), the killing of the terrorists in Gibraltar and other matters. There was no mention in his speech of IRA violence, no acknowledgement of the need for cross-border co-operation and no commitment to the Anglo-Irish Agreement. It was a shabby case of playing to the American Irish gallery.

I wrote to Mr Haughey on Wednesday 27 April to protest in the most vigorous terms.

At the next European Council in Hanover I took up the question of security co-operation, which was of far more importance to me than any personal differences. I said that though Mr Haughey had affirmed that he had difficulties with Irish public opinion about this, I had difficulty myself about bombs, guns, explosions, people being beaten to death and

---

* The Stalker-Sampson Report was the outcome of a police inquiry into a series of fatal incidents in 1982 in which the RUC was alleged to have operated a 'shoot-to-kill' policy in dealing with terrorist suspects.

† The 'Birmingham Six' were six Irishmen convicted of multiple murders resulting from the IRA bombing of two pubs in Birmingham in 1974. A long campaign was undertaken to prove the convictions unsafe, eventually resulting in their release. At this time, however, their latest appeal had just been rejected by the Court of Appeal.

naked hatred. I had had to see ever more young men in the security forces killed. We knew that the terrorists went over the border to the Republic to plan their operations and to store their weapons. We got no satisfactory intelligence of their movements. Once they crossed the border they were lost. Indeed, we received far better intelligence co-operation from virtually all other European countries than from the Republic. If it was a question of resources, then we were ready to offer equipment and training. Or if this were politically difficult, there were other countries who could offer such help. There was no room for amateurism.

Mr Haughey defended the Irish Government's and security forces' record. But I was not convinced. I said that I wondered whether Mr Haughey realized that the biggest concentration of terrorists anywhere in the world save Lebanon was to be found in Ireland. I accepted that the Republic's resources were limited, but I was not satisfied that they were using them to best effect. I said that the results of the Anglo-Irish Agreement so far had been disappointing. Nor was I any less disappointed by the attitude of the SDLP. As for the suggestion that all would be peace and light if there were a united Ireland, as Mr Haughey's recent message had suggested, the reality was that there would be the worst civil war ever. In any case, most nationalists in the North would prefer to continue to live there because they were much better provided for than in the Republic. Indeed, there continued to be a substantial flow of Irish immigrants to the UK, who were a significant burden on the welfare system.

There was a surge in IRA violence from early August. It began with an IRA bomb at an Army Communications Centre in Mill Hill in North London. One soldier was killed. This was the first mainland bomb since 1984.

I was on holiday in Cornwall when I was woken very early on Saturday 20 August to be told of an attack at Ballygawley in County Tyrone on a bus carrying British soldiers travelling from Belfast back from a fortnight's leave. Seven were dead and twenty-eight injured. I immediately decided to return to London and helicptered into the Wellington Barracks at 9.20 a.m. Archie Hamilton (my former PPS, who was now Armed Forces minister) came straight in to No. 10 to brief me. He told me that the bus had not been on its designated route at the time of the explosion but on a parallel road some three miles away. A very large bomb, wire-controlled, had been laid in wait for the bus and then detonated.

Ken Maginnis MP, whose constituency was yet again the scene of this tragedy, came in to see me over lunch, accompanied by a local farmer who had been first on the scene and a surgeon at the local hospital who had operated on some of the wounded. Then that evening I held a long meeting with Tom King, Archie, and the security forces chiefs for the province.

Although the bus had been travelling on a forbidden route this did not seem to be material to what had happened. The IRA had from 1986 acquired access to Semtex explosive material, produced in Czechoslovakia and probably supplied through Libya. This substance was extremely powerful, light and relatively safe to use and as a result had given the terrorists a new technical advantage. The device could, therefore, have been planted very quickly and so the attack could have occurred on either route. It was also clear that the IRA had been planning their campaign for some time.

More and more in the struggle to bring peace and order to Northern Ireland, we were being forced back on our own resources. Because of the professionalism and experience of our security forces, those resources were adequate to contain, but not as yet to defeat the IRA. Terrible tragedies continued to occur. Yet the terrorists did not manage to make even parts of the province ungovernable, nor were they successful in undermining the self-confidence of Ulster's majority community or the will of the Government to maintain the Union.

The contribution which the Anglo-Irish Agreement was making to all this was very limited. But it never seemed worth pulling out of the agreement altogether because this would have created problems not only with the Republic but, more importantly, with broader international opinion as well.

The Patrick Ryan case demonstrated just how little we could seriously hope for from the Irish. Ryan, a non-practising Catholic priest, was well known in security service circles as a terrorist; for some time he had played a significant role in the Provisional IRA's links with Libya. The charges against Ryan were of the utmost seriousness, including conspiracy to murder and explosives offences. In June 1988 we had asked the Belgians to place him under surveillance. They, in turn, pressed us strongly to apply for extradition. So the application was made and the Belgian court which considered the extradition request gave an advisory opinion, which we knew to have been favourable, to the Minister of Justice. The latter then took the decision to the Belgian Cabinet. The Cabinet decided to ignore the court's opinion and to fly Ryan to Ireland, only telling us afterwards. Presumably this political decision was prompted by fear of terrorist retaliation if the Belgians co-operated with us.

We now sought the extradition of Ryan from the Republic; but this was refused. I wrote a vigorous protest to Mr Haughey. I had already taken up the matter personally with him and with the Belgian Prime Minister, M. Martens, at the European Council in Rhodes on Friday 2 and Saturday 3 December 1988. I told both of them how appalled I was. I was particularly angry with M. Martens. I reminded him how his Government's attitude contrasted with all the co-operation we had given Belgium over those British people charged in relation to the Heysel Football Stadium riot.* As I warned him I would, I then told the press of my views in very similar terms. But as a Belgian government under the same M. Martens later showed at the time of the Gulf War, it would take more than this to provide them with a spine. And Patrick Ryan is still at large.

I had moved Peter Brooke to become Northern Ireland Secretary in the reshuffle of July 1989. Peter's family connections with the province and his deep interest in Ulster affairs made him seem an ideal choice. His unflappable good humour also meant that no one would be better suited for trying to bring the parties of Northern Ireland together for talks. Soon after his appointment I authorized him to do so: these talks were still continuing at the time I left office.

Meanwhile, the struggle to maintain security continued. So did the IRA's murderous campaign. On Friday 22 September ten bandsmen were killed in a blast at the Royal Marines School of Music at Deal. June 1990 saw bombs explode outside Alistair McAlpine's former home and then at the Conservative Party's Carlton Club. But it was the following month that I experienced again something of that deep personal grief I had felt when Airey was killed and when I learned, early on the Friday morning at Brighton in 1984, of the losses in the Grand Hotel bomb attack.

Ian Gow was singled out to be murdered by the IRA because they knew that he was their unflinching enemy. Even though he held no government office, Ian was a danger to them because of his total commitment to the Union. No amount of terror can succeed in its aim if even a few outspoken men and women of integrity and courage dare to call terrorism murder and any compromise with it treachery. Nor, tragically, was Ian

---

* British football fans had attacked Italian fans at the Heysel Stadium in Brussels in 1985, crushing thirty-eight of them to death when a wall collapsed. Twenty-six were later extradited from Britain to face charges in Belgium.

someone who took his own security precautions seriously. And so the IRA's bomb killed him that Monday morning, 30 July, as he started up his car in the drive of his house. I could not help thinking, when I heard what had happened, that my daughter Carol had travelled with Ian in his car the previous weekend to take the Gows' dog out for a walk: it might have been her too.

The IRA will not give up their campaign unless they are convinced that there is no possibility of forcing the majority of the people of Northern Ireland against their will into the Republic. That is why our policy must never give the impression that we are trying to lead the Unionists into a united Ireland either against their will or without their knowledge. Moreover, it is not enough to decry individual acts of terrorism but then refuse to endorse the measures required to defeat it. That applies to American Irish who supply NORAID with money to kill British citizens; to Irish politicians who withhold co-operation in clamping down on border security; and to the Labour Party that for years has withheld its support from the Prevention of Terrorism Act which has saved countless lives.

Ian Gow and I had our disagreements, above all about the Anglo-Irish Agreement: but for the right of those whose loyalties are to the United Kingdom to remain its citizens and enjoy its protection I believe, as did Ian, that no price is too high to pay.

CHAPTER TWENTY-SEVEN

Keeps Raining All the Time

The mid-term political difficulties of 1985–1986

WHATEVER LONG-TERM POLITICAL GAINS might accrue from the successful outcome of the miners' strike, from the spring of 1985 onwards we faced accumulating political difficulties. Matters of no great importance in themselves were invested within the hyperactive and incestuous world of Westminster with huge significance.

Generally, a political malaise spreads because underlying economic conditions are bad or worsening. But this was not the case on this occasion. It became clear to me that the root of our problems was presentation and therefore personnel. A reshuffle was required.

My first discussion about the 1985 reshuffle was with Willie Whitelaw and John Wakeham, now Chief Whip, over supper in the flat at No. 10 in late May.

Planning a reshuffle is immensely complex. There is never a perfect outcome. It is necessary to get the main decisions about the big offices of state right and then work outward and downward from these.

Nigel Lawson was turning out to be an effective tax-reforming Chancellor. Geoffrey Howe seemed a competent Foreign Secretary; I had not yet taken the full measure of our disagreements. Leon Brittan was the obvious candidate to be moved: however unfairly, he just did not carry conviction with the public.

I asked Leon to come to Chequers on Sunday afternoon 1 September where Willie, John and I were putting the final touches to the decisions. Willie told me that the first thing Leon would ask when I broke the news to him was whether he would keep his order of precedence in the Cabinet list. To my surprise, this was indeed what he asked. Forewarned, I was able to reassure him. I was also able to say – and mean it – that with complex Financial Services legislation coming up to provide a framework of regulation for the City Leon's talents would be well employed at the Department of Trade and Industry to which I was moving him.

I replaced Leon at the Home Office with Douglas Hurd, who looked more the part, was immensely reassuring to the police, and, though no one could call him a natural media performer, inspired a good deal of confidence in the Parliamentary Party. He also knew the department, having earlier been Leon's number two there. By and large, it was a successful appointment.

I had to move Leon; but was I right to move him to the DTI? He was obviously shaken – friends later described him as somewhat demoralized – and determined to make his political mark. As a result he proved oversensitive about his position when the Westland affair blew up.

I had brought David Young into the Cabinet as minister without portfolio the previous year and I now had him succeed Tom King, who went to be Secretary of State for Northern Ireland. I had started off with a wrong view of Tom King, inherited from Opposition. I had thought that he was a man with a taste for detail who, when I made Michael Heseltine Secretary of State for the Environment in 1979, would complement Michael's very broad-brush approach. I then made the uncomfortable discovery that detail was not at all Tom's forte. At Employment he had not shown himself to best effect. At Northern Ireland, Tom subsequently demonstrated the other side of his character, which was a robust, manly good sense that won even hardened opponents to his point of view, at least as far as is possible in Northern Ireland.

David Young did not claim to understand politics: but he understood how to make things happen. He had revolutionized the working of the Manpower Services Commission (MSC) and at the Department of Employment his schemes for getting the unemployed back into work made a major contribution to our winning the 1987 general election. He shared Keith Joseph's and my view about how the economy worked and how jobs were created – not by government but by enterprise. And he had that sureness of touch in devising practical projects which make sense in the marketplace that few but successful businessmen ever acquire. The 'Action for Jobs' programme was the single most effective economic programme we launched in my term in office. As a general rule I did not bring outsiders directly into Cabinet. David Young was an exception and proved eminently worthy of being so.

If the Government's presentation was to be improved something had to be done about Conservative Central Office. John Gummer just did not have the political clout or credibility to rally the troops. It was time for a figure of weight and authority to succeed him and provide the required leadership. In many ways, the ideal man seemed to be Norman Tebbit. Norman is one of the bravest men I have ever met. He will never deviate on a point of principle – and those principles are ones which even the least articulate Tory knows he shares.

So I appointed him Chairman of the Party; he remained a member of the Cabinet as Chancellor of the Duchy of Lancaster. At least for the moment, Party morale soared.

Norman needed a Deputy Chairman who would be able to make those visits to the Party around the country which Norman's health precluded him from doing. Only someone with a high profile already could do this successfully and I decided that Jeffrey Archer was the right choice. He was the extrovert's extrovert. He had prodigious energy; he was and remains the most popular speaker the Party has ever had. Unfortunately, as it turned out, Jeffrey's political judgement did not always match his enormous energy and fund-raising ability.

Two future Cabinet ministers came into the Government – Michael Howard at the DTI and John Major who moved from the Whips' Office to the DHSS. John Major was certainly not known to be on the right of the Party during his first days as an MP. When as a whip he came to the annual whips' lunch at Downing Street he disagreed with me about the importance of getting taxation down. He argued that there was no evidence that people would rather pay lower taxes than have better social services. I did not treat him or his argument kindly and some people, I later heard, thought that he had ruined his chances of promotion. But in fact I enjoy an argument and when the Whips' Office suggested he become a junior minister I gave him the job which I myself had done first, dealing with the complex area of pensions and national insurance. If that did not alert him to the realities of social security and the dependency culture, nothing would.

There are differing views even now of what the Westland affair was really about. At various times Michael Heseltine claimed that it was about Britain's future as a technologically advanced country, the role of government in industry, Britain's relationship with Europe and the United States and the proprieties of constitutional government. Of course, these are all interesting points for discussion. But Westland was really about none of these things. Michael Heseltine's own personality alone provides a kind of explanation for what arose.

My relations with Michael Heseltine had never been easy, but when John Nott told me that he did not intend to stand again for the next Parliament, I decided to give Michael his big chance and put him into Defence. There Michael's strengths and weaknesses were both apparent. He defended our approach to nuclear arms with great panache and inflicted a series of defeats on CND and the Labour Left. He reorganized the MoD, rationalizing its traditional federal structure. Supported by me in the face of departmental obstruction, he brought in Peter Levene to run defence procurement on sound business lines.

These were real achievements. But Michael's sense of priorities was gravely distorted by his personal ambitions and political obsessions. For while Michael Heseltine was becoming increasingly obsessed with a small West Country helicopter company with a turnover of something over £300 million, far more important issues escaped his interest. In particular, the Nimrod Airborne Early Warning System project which would have to be cancelled by George Younger in December 1986 after £660 million had been spent was running into grave difficulties while Michael Heseltine was at Defence. The Nimrod affair constituted a unique – and uniquely costly – lesson in how not to monitor and manage defence procurement. A minister has to be prepared to work through the details if he is going to come to the right decisions and this Michael was always unwilling to do.

The basic issue at stake in Westland was clear enough. It was whether the directors and shareholders of a private sector firm, heavily but not exclusively dependent on government orders, should be free to decide its future, or whether government should do so. In this sense an important issue was indeed at stake in Westland. If government manipulates its purchasing power, if it arbitrarily changes the rules under which a particular company's financial decisions have to be made, and if it then goes on to lobby directly for a particular commercial option – these things are abuses of power. Once the state plays fast and loose with economic freedom, political freedom risks being the next casualty.

The Westland helicopter company was small by international aerospace standards but it was Britain's only helicopter manufacturer. It was never nationalized by the Labour Government and was reasonably profitable into the early 1980s. It then began to run into financial trouble. Mr Alan Bristow bid for the company in April 1985 and it was in the light of this that on 30 April Michael Heseltine informed me and other members of the Cabinet's Overseas and Defence Committee of the Ministry of Defence's view of Westland. Westland hoped to obtain an order from the Indian Government for helicopters partly financed from our Overseas Aid budget. But they were also looking to the MoD for crucial new orders: from Michael's minute it was clear that they would look in vain. He made no suggestion at this stage that Westland was of strategic significance to Britain. Indeed, he emphasized that he would not wish to give the company extra orders for which there was no defence need. He added that even with the best will in the world it was difficult to see a single British specialist helicopter company competing in worldwide markets in the longer term.

In mid-June we learned that Mr Bristow was threatening to withdraw his bid unless the Government provided assurances of future MoD orders and agreed to waive its right to repayment of over £40 million of launch aid provided by the DTI for Westland's latest helicopter. I held a series of meetings with Michael Heseltine, Norman Tebbit, Nigel Lawson and others. At the meeting on Wednesday 19 June Michael suggested a scheme by which we could provide £30 million in aid to the company, but explained that what was important to the defence programme was not the existing Westland company but rather Britain's capability to service existing helicopters and to develop the EH 101 large helicopter project. In spite of that, we all agreed that it was desirable to avoid Westland going into receivership, which appeared likely if the Bristow bid was withdrawn. In the end we decided that Norman Tebbit should encourage the Bank of England to bring together the main creditors with the object of putting in new management and developing a recovery strategy as an alternative to receivership.

As a result Mr Bristow withdrew his bid and in due course Sir John Cuckney took over as Chairman. Shortly afterwards it emerged that a large privately owned American company was considering making a bid for Westland. The new Westland management opposed this particular bid. Norman Tebbit and Michael Heseltine were also against it. But I made it clear that a different American offer would have to be judged on its merits.

The situation of Westland was one of the first difficult issues which Leon Brittan had to face when he took over at the DTI in September. On

Friday 4 October Leon sent me a thorough assessment of the position. The matter was urgent. It seemed likely that the company would have to go into receivership if a solution could not be found before the end of November. Leon urged me to take up the issue of India's proposed helicopter order with Rajiv Gandhi when he visited Britain in October. As part of the proposed financial reconstruction of the company the Government was asked to underwrite some helicopter sales. We would also have to decide what to do about the launch aid, which seemed unlikely to be recovered. What would be the most controversial aspect of the package put forward by Sir John Cuckney, however, was the introduction of a new large minority shareholder to raise new capital. No British company was prepared to take such a shareholding. The most likely candidate was the large American company, Sikorsky. Westland were in contact with their European counterparts, but the prospects of a European solution within the timetable did not look good.

It was from a note of a meeting on Wednesday 16 October between Leon Brittan and Michael Heseltine that I first read about Michael's concern that Sikorsky would turn Westland into 'merely a metal bashing operation'. Michael did not wish to go so far as to oppose Sikorsky's taking the 29.9 per cent in any circumstances, but he did think it important to make every effort to find an acceptable European shareholder instead. More ominously, he apparently did not think that Sir John Cuckney was the right person to deal with negotiations with the European companies. Michael argued that the approaches needed to be made at a political level by the Ministry of Defence.

It was now becoming clear that the preference of the Westland board was likely to be for Sikorsky, while Michael Heseltine's preference was very different. Other things being equal, we would all have preferred a European solution. Since 1978, European governments had agreed to make every effort to meet their needs with helicopters made in Europe.

I still do not understand why anyone later imagined that the Westland board, Leon Brittan and I were all biased against a European option. In fact, the Government bent over backwards to give that option and Michael Heseltine every opportunity to advance their arguments and interests. Yet in the frenzy which followed there was almost no limit to the deviousness and manipulation we were accused of employing to secure Sikorsky its minority holding.

At the end of November the opposition between the Westland board's views and Michael Heseltine came out into the open. Sikorsky made an offer for a substantial stake in Westland which the Westland board was inclined to accept. But entirely off his own bat Michael now called together a meeting of the National Armaments Directors (NADs) of France, Italy and Germany as well as the United Kingdom to agree a document under which the respective governments would refrain from buying helicopters other than those designed and built in Europe. This was more than a blatant departure from the Government's policy of maximizing competition to get the best value for money: it also placed Westland in an almost impossible position. There was now an obvious risk that if Westland concluded its deal with Sikorsky it would not be deemed to meet the NADs criterion and would be excluded from all further orders from the four governments, including the UK. It was my view – and Leon Brittan's – that the Government must not seek to prevent any particular solution to Westland's problems: it must be for the company to decide what to do. Yet by a stroke of a pen Michael Heseltine was effectively ruling out the company's preferred option for its future. If Westland were to be able to make a free decision it would be necessary for the Government to overrule the NADs decision. This, of course, meant overruling Michael.

Although these were essentially matters for the company, the closer that we looked at the European option the less substantial did it seem. The three European companies concerned – Aérospatiale (France), MBB (West Germany) and Agusta (Italy) – were, as Michael certainly knew, subject to pressure from their own governments. All the European companies were short of work and promises of more work for Westland from Europe seemed likely to remain just promises. By contrast, Westland had been collaborating with Sikorsky for several decades and had produced a number of models under licence from them. Indeed, most of not just Westland's but Agusta's existing helicopter designs were of American origin. Michael Heseltine argued that if Sikorsky took even a minority stake in Westland they would use their position to put pressure on the Ministry of Defence to order American-designed Blackhawk helicopters. In fact, it was widely rumoured that the armed services would have liked the MoD to do just that. I could well understand, as would anyone else conversant with the facts, why Westland had their preference for the American option and how angry they and Sikorsky were with Michael Heseltine's manoeuvrings.

Nor, by now, was the 'American' option American only. Sikorsky had been joined by Fiat in their bid. Not to be outdone, Michael Heseltine suddenly revealed that British Aerospace would be ready to join the European consortium, thus making it less 'foreign'. There were several accounts of how precisely this had occurred: I had my own opinions.

I held two meetings with Michael Heseltine, Leon Brittan, Willie Whitelaw, Geoffrey Howe, Norman Tebbit and Nigel Lawson to discuss Westland on Thursday 5 December and the following day. (British Aerospace entered the field between the first and second meetings.) By the time of the second meeting Michael had totally changed his line from the one he had pursued in April. Suddenly the issue had become whether it was right to allow a significant British defence contractor to come under foreign control. But the real issue was whether the Government should reject the recommendation from the NADs, thus leaving Westland to reach their decision whether to accept the Sikorsky offer or that from the European consortium on straightforward commercial grounds. By the end of the second meeting it was clear that for most of us the argument had been won by Leon Brittan: the NADs decision should be set aside. But Geoffrey, Norman and, of course, Michael strongly dissented and so I decided that a decision should be reached in a formal Cabinet committee. 'E'(A)* enlarged as appropriate would meet on Monday 9 December.

Over the weekend the pace quickened and tempers frayed. Michael Heseltine blocked a joint MoD and DTI paper on Westland and had it redrafted to emphasize the risks of a Sikorsky bid. Leon Brittan was furious, but allowed it to go forward to 'E'(A). This was a mistake. Michael said that the French Defence minister also telephoned over the weekend to place unspecified sub-contract work on the 'Super Puma' helicopter with Westland provided it was not sold to Sikorsky. Monday morning's newspapers covered the row between Michael and Leon.

The main argument of substance which Michael Heseltine advanced was that the attitude of the Europeans to a Sikorsky deal would jeopardize future collaboration between Westland and the European defence companies. But the real sleight of hand was Michael's suggestion that as a result of the recommendations of NADs two projected European battlefield helicopters – an Anglo-Italian model and a Franco-German one – could be rationalized and that the savings in development costs which for the UK might amount to £25 million over the next five years would become available for extra work for Westland. This would enable additional helicopter orders to be placed by the MoD to help fill the gap in

---

* The principal sub-committee of 'E'.

production work. Whether or not one thought this £25 million was in fact likely to be saved or whether this was the best way to spend it seemed almost beside the point. It appeared that for Michael Heseltine the procurement budget of the MoD and arrangements with other govern-ments were to be manipulated in whatever way necessary to secure his own preferred future for this modest helicopter company. What small sense of proportion Michael possessed had vanished entirely.

At the 'E'(A) meeting on 9 December Sir John Cuckney brought matters down to earth: Westland needed fundamental reconstruction and an improved product range and it was the view of his board that this was best met by Sikorsky. The longer it took to make the decision the greater would be the pressure on the share price. Westland's accounts were due to be published on 11 December and the company would not maintain market confidence if publication was delayed much beyond that.

There was a majority at the meeting in favour of overturning the NADs recommendation, but instead of terminating the discussion and summing up the feeling of the meeting in favour of that, I gave Michael Heseltine (and Leon Brittan) permission to explore urgently the possibil-ity of developing a European package which the Westland board could finally accept. If this had not been done and a package which the West-land board could recommend had not been produced by 4 p.m. on Friday 13 December, we would be obliged to reject the NADs recommendation.

In fact, the Westland board did not accept the European bid and chose to recommend that from Sikorsky-Fiat. But Michael had now developed another fixation or perhaps tactic. At the 'E'(A) meeting it was recognized that the timetable would allow for another meeting of ministers before the Friday deadline. But there was no decision to call a meeting; and indeed none was necessary. What was the point? Westland's board knew precisely where they stood: it was up to them and the shareholders. Michael urged John Wakeham to get me to call another meeting, saying it was a constitutional necessity under Cabinet government. It so happened that officials had rung round to see whether people would be available if a further meeting was called: but that was very definitely not a summons to a meeting, because no meeting had been arranged. This was of little consequence, however, because from this point on Michael became convinced that he was the victim of a plot in which more and more people seemed to be involved.

The next twist came soon. Without any warning Michael raised the issue of Westland in Cabinet on Thursday 12 December. This provoked a short, ill-tempered discussion, which I cut short on the grounds that we could not discuss the issue without papers. Nor was it on the agenda. The full account of what was said was not circulated, though a summary record should have been sent round in the minutes. Unfortunately, by an oversight this was not done. The Cabinet Secretary noticed the omission himself and rectified it without prompting. However, Michael Heseltine was not satisfied with the brief record, complaining that it did not record his 'protest'. For Michael the plot was thickening fast.

Michael lobbied backbenchers. He lobbied the press. He lobbied bankers. He lobbied industrialists. GEC, of which Jim Prior was chairman, mysteriously developed an interest in joining the European consortium. The consortium itself came forward with a new firm bid. Each new development was adduced as a reason to review the Government's policy. The battle was fought out in the press. There was an increasingly farcical air about the affair, which was making the Government look ridiculous. There was even a completely contrived 'Libyan scare'. Michael Heseltine suggested that the long-standing involvement of the Libyan Government in Fiat raised security questions about the Sikorsky bid. In fact, Fiat would have owned 14.9 per cent of Westland and Libya owned 14 per cent of Fiat. Fiat already supplied many important components for European defence equipment. The Americans, who were even more sensitive than we were about both security and Libya, seemed quite content for Fiat to be involved with Sikorsky.

I rejected Michael's argument that we needed now to come down in favour of the European bid. But the public row between Michael and Leon continued over Christmas.

Westland's board were still extremely anxious about whether they could look forward to British and European government business. In answer to John Cuckney, I wrote to say that 'As long as Westland continues to carry on business in the UK, the Government will of course continue to regard it as a British and therefore European company and will support it in pursuing British interests in Europe.' Michael had wanted to include a good deal of other less reassuring material in my reply but I rejected this. Imagine, therefore, my admiration when I found early in the New Year that Lloyds Merchant Bank had sent him a letter which enabled him to make all the points in his published reply about what – in Michael's view – would happen if Westland chose Sikorsky rather than the bid of the European consortium. It was in response to

Michael's letter that Patrick Mayhew, the Solicitor-General, wrote to him of 'material inaccuracies'. The leaking of the Solicitor-General's letter to the press magnified the Westland crisis and eventually led to Leon Brittan's resignation; but all that lay in the future.

I now knew from Michael's behaviour that unless he were checked there were no limits to what he would do to secure his objectives at Westland. This had to stop.

Westland was placed on the agenda for the Cabinet of Thursday 9 January. At that meeting I began by rehearsing the decisions which had been made by the Government. I then ran over the damaging press comment which there had been in the New Year. I said that if the situation continued, the Government would have no credibility left. I had never seen a clearer demonstration of the damage done to the coherence and standing of a government when the principle of collective responsibility was ignored. Leon Brittan and then Michael Heseltine put their respective cases. After some discussion, I began to sum up by pointing out that the time was approaching when the company and its bankers at a shareholders' meeting had to decide between the two consortia. It was legally as well as politically important that they should come to their decision without further intervention by ministers and there must be no lobbying or briefing directly or indirectly. Because of the risks of misinterpretation during this period of sensitive commercial negotiations and decisions, answers to questions should be cleared interdepartmentally through the Cabinet Office so as to ensure that all answers given were fully consistent with the policy of the Government.

Everyone else accepted this. But Michael Heseltine said that it would be impossible to clear every answer through the Cabinet Office and that he must be able to confirm statements already made and answer questions of fact about procurement requirements without any delay. I suspect that no one present saw this as anything other than a ruse. No one sided with Michael. He was quite isolated. I again summed up, repeating my earlier remarks and adding that consideration should also be given to the preparation under Cabinet Office auspices of an interdepartmentally agreed fact sheet which could be drawn upon as a source of answers to questions. I then emphasized the importance of observing collective responsibility in this and in all matters. At this Michael Heseltine erupted. He claimed that there had been no collective responsibility in the discussion of Westland. He alleged a breakdown in the propriety of Cabinet discussions. He could not accept the decision recorded in my summing up. He must therefore leave the Cabinet. He gathered his papers together and left a Cabinet united against him.

I have learnt that other colleagues at the meeting were stunned by what had happened. I was not. Michael had made his decision and that was that. I already knew whom I wanted to succeed him at Defence: George Younger.

I called a short break and walked through to the Private Office. Nigel Wicks, my principal private secretary, brought George Younger out; I offered him, and he accepted, the Defence post. I asked my office to telephone Malcolm Rifkind to offer him George's former post of Scottish Secretary, which he too subsequently accepted. We contacted the Queen to ask her approval of these appointments. Then I returned to Cabinet, continued the business and by the end of the meeting I was able to announce George Younger's appointment. Within the Cabinet at least all had been settled.

When the House reassembled on Monday 13 January, at a meeting that morning Willie, Leon, George, the Chief Whip and others discussed with me what should be done. It was decided that Leon, rather than I, would make a statement on Westland in the House that afternoon. It went disastrously wrong. Michael Heseltine trapped Leon with a question about whether any letters from British Aerospace had been received bearing on a meeting which Leon had with Sir Raymond Lygo, the Chief Executive of British Aerospace. It was suggested (as it transpired quite falsely) that at his meeting with Sir Raymond Lygo Leon had said that British Aerospace's involvement in the European consortium was against the national interest and that they should withdraw. The letter in question, which had arrived at No. 10 and which I saw just before coming over to the House to listen to Leon's statement, had been marked 'Private and Strictly Confidential'. Leon felt that he had to respect that confidence, but in doing so he used a lawyer's formulation which opened him to the charge of misleading the House of Commons. He had to return to the House later that night to make an apology. In itself it was a small matter; but in the atmosphere of suspicion and conspiracy fostered by Michael Heseltine – who mysteriously knew all about this confidential missive – it did great harm to Leon's credibility. The letter was subsequently published with the permission of its author, Sir Austin Pearce, but it contributed little to the debate since the day after that Sir Raymond withdrew his allegations as having been based on a misunderstanding. By then, however, Leon's political position was all but irrecoverable.

But none of this made my life any easier when I had to reply to Neil Kinnock in the debate on Westland on Wednesday 15 January.

My speech was strictly factual. It demonstrated that we had reached our decisions on Westland in a proper and responsible way. Indeed, as I listed all the meetings of ministers, including Cabinet committees and Cabinets which had discussed Westland, I half felt that I had been guilty of wasting too much of ministers' time on an issue of relative unimportance. Although it set out all the facts, my speech was not well received.

Michael Heseltine spoke, criticizing the way in which collective responsibility had been discharged over Westland and quite ignoring the fact that he had walked out of a Cabinet meeting on Westland because he was the only minister unwilling to abide by a Cabinet decision.

Leon summed up for the Government in a speech which I hoped would restore his standing in the House and which seemed a modest success. The press, however, still kept up the pressure on him and there was plenty of criticism of me as well. It seemed, though, that given time, we were over the worst. It was not to be. On Thursday 23 January I had to make a difficult statement to the House. It outlined the results of the leak inquiry into the disclosure of the Solicitor-General's letter of 6 January. The tension was great, speculation at fever pitch. The inquiry concluded that civil servants at the Department of Trade and Industry had acted in good faith in the knowledge that they had the authority of Leon Brittan, their Secretary of State, and cover from my office at No. 10 for proceeding to reveal the contents of Patrick Mayhew's letter. For their part, Leon Brittan and the DTI believed that they had the agreement of No. 10 to do this. In fact I was not consulted. It is true that, like Leon, I would have liked the fact that Michael Heseltine's letter was thought by Patrick Mayhew to contain material inaccuracies needing correction to become public knowledge as soon as possible. Sir John Cuckney was to hold a press conference to announce the Westland board's recommendation to its shareholders that afternoon. But I would not have approved of the leaking of a law office's letter as a way of achieving this.

In my statement I had to defend my own integrity, the professional conduct of civil servants who could not answer for themselves and, as far as I could, my embattled Trade and Industry Secretary. I never doubted that as long as the truth was known and believed all would ultimately be well. Yet it is never easy to persuade those who think that they know how government works, but in fact do not, that misunderstandings and errors of judgement do happen, particularly when ministers and civil servants are placed under almost impossible pressure day after day after day, as they were by Michael Heseltine's antics.

Alas, Leon's days were numbered. It was a meeting of the '22 Committee, not any decision of mine, which sealed his fate. He came to see me on the afternoon of Friday 24 January and told me that he was going to resign. I tried to persuade him not to; I hated to see the better man lose. His departure from the Cabinet meant the loss of one of our best brains and cut short what would have been, in other circumstances, a successful career in British politics. But I was by now thinking hard about my own position. I had lost two Cabinet ministers and I had no illusions that, as always when the critics sense weakness, there were those in my own Party and Government who would like to take the opportunity of getting rid of me as well.

I knew that the big test would come in the House of Commons the following Monday when I was to answer Neil Kinnock in an emergency debate on Westland. I spent the whole of Sunday with officials and speech writers. I went through all of the papers relating to the Westland affair from the beginning, clarifying in my own mind what had been said and done, by whom and when. It was time well spent.

Neil Kinnock opened the debate that Monday afternoon with a long-winded and ill-considered speech which certainly did him more harm than it did me. But I knew as I rose to speak that it was my performance which the House was waiting for. Once again, I went over all the details of the leaked letter. It was a noisy occasion and there were plenty of interruptions. But the adrenalin flowed and I gave as good as I got. The speech does not now read as anything exceptional. But it undoubtedly turned the tide. I suspect that Conservative MPs had by now woken up to the terrible damage which had been done to the Party. They would have found in their constituencies that weekend that people were incredulous that something of such little importance could be magnified into an issue which threatened the Government itself. So, by the time I spoke, what Tory MPs really wanted was leadership, frankness and a touch of humility, all of which I tried to provide. Even Michael Heseltine deemed it expedient to protest his loyalty.

But the most damaging effect of the Westland affair was the fuel which had been poured on the flames of anti-Americanism.

On the heels of Westland came the question of privatizing British Leyland. Paul Channon, whom I appointed to succeed Leon, was faced within days of taking office with a fresh crisis and one which affected the jobs of many thousands of people and concerned a significant number of Conservative MPs, including ministers.

I had not always seen eye to eye with Norman Tebbit over BL. I felt that the company was continuing to perform badly and wanted to take a tougher line with it. There had certainly been improvements, but the management was still poor.

There must, I felt, be a new management and new Chairman at BL, tighter financial discipline and, above all, a renewed drive for privatization. From October 1985 Leon Brittan concentrated closely on all these aspects but it was privatization which increasingly took centre stage. Jaguar had already been successfully sold off. Unipart, which handled BL's spare parts, should have been privatized too, though BL seemed to be reluctant to move ahead with this. But, most important, we had secretly been in contact with General Motors (GM) which was interested in acquiring Land Rover, including Range Rover, Freight Rover (vans) and Leyland Trucks (heavy vehicles). These negotiations too seemed to drag on and on; so I was pleased when Leon sent me on 25 November his proposals for moving ahead with the deal.

Apart from (though having a bearing upon) the price, there were three tricky questions which required attention.

- First, we had to consider the consequences for jobs of the rationalization of the GM (Bedford) and BL (Leyland) truck businesses, which was undoubtedly one of the attractions for GM of their proposal. We thought that up to 3,000 jobs might go: but the choice in an industry where there was great overcapacity was not between job losses and no job losses but between some jobs going and a possible collapse of one or other – or conceivably both – truck producers.
- Second, we had to consider the position of the rest of BL's operations: the volume car business of Austin Rover, which would be left to pay off the accumulated debt, and which GM had no intention themselves of taking on.
- Third, the thorniest issue would be the future control of Land Rover, which GM were determined to acquire but on which public opinion would require safeguards that it should in some sense 'stay British'.

Suddenly, however, we were facing an *embarras de richesses*. Before we had fully come to grips with the GM offer, code-named 'Salton', the still more intriguingly code-named 'Maverick' put in an appearance. At the end of November the Chairman of Ford in Europe came to see Leon Brittan to say that Ford were considering making an offer for Austin Rover and Unipart. The company fully recognized the political sensitivity of this and so wanted the green light from the Government first. Leon Brittan, Nigel Lawson and I discussed what should be done at a meeting on the afternoon of Wednesday 4 December. There was no doubt in our minds of the political difficulties involved. Although Ford said that they intended to keep the main BL and Ford plants open there would be opposition from MPs fearful of job losses in the areas affected. Ford's productivity was worse than BL's, their newest models were not selling well and they were worried about Japanese penetration of their European markets. There might be problems about collaboration with Honda on which BL had come to depend. But for all that the Ford offer was certainly worth pursuing.

To Paul Channon's horror – and mine – at the start of February the weekend press was full of details of what was planned. BL had almost certainly leaked it. All hope of confidential commercial discussion had been destroyed. Irrationality swept through the debate.

I chaired an extremely difficult meeting of the Cabinet on Thursday 6 February in the course of which it became clear to me that there was no way in which the Ford deal could be put through. Paul Channon told the House that afternoon that in order to end the uncertainty we would not pursue the possibility of the sale of Austin Rover to Ford. It was humiliating and did less than justice to Ford, which had provided so many jobs in Britain. But in politics you have to know when to cut your losses.

The question now was whether we could still strike a satisfactory deal with GM. And now the news was out, we were faced with a rash of alternative bids. Few of them were serious and all of them were an embarrassment rather than a help. Most politically sensitive was the proposal for a management buy-out of Land Rover. GM remained – in our and BL's view – by far the best option because that company was interested in all, not just some, divisions; because of its financial strength; and because of the access to its distribution network.

GM in the end were not willing to proceed with a deal for Leyland Trucks and Freight Rover which excluded Land Rover and so the talks ended. When this was announced by Paul to the House of Commons on

Tuesday 25 March, one after another of our backbenchers stood up to say that a great opportunity had been lost and that the GM deal should have gone through. I told several later that they should have spoken up when the going was rough.

This whole sorry episode had harmed not just the Government but Britain. Time and again I had drawn attention to the benefits Britain received as a result of American investment. The idea that Ford was foreign and therefore bad was plainly absurd. Their European headquarters was located in Britain, as was their largest European Research and Development Centre. All of the trucks and most of the tractors that Ford sold in Europe were made in Britain. Ford's exports from the UK were 40 per cent more by value than those of BL. But it was not just a matter of Ford. Over half the investment coming into Britain from abroad was from the United States. Both Ford and GM were offended and annoyed by the campaign waged against them. Britain just could not afford to indulge in self-destructive anti-Americanism of this sort. Yet it would continue and was shortly to be raised to fever pitch – not just in the area of industrial policy but that of defence and foreign affairs, where passions ignite more easily.

I was at Chequers on Friday 27 December 1985 when I learned that terrorists had opened fire on passengers waiting on the concourses at the Rome and Vienna airports, killing seventeen people. The gunmen were Palestinian terrorists from the Abu Nidal group. They had apparently been trained in the Lebanon, but evidence soon emerged of a Libyan connection.

On Tuesday 7 January the United States unilaterally imposed sanctions on Libya with little or no consultation and expected the rest of us to follow. I was not prepared to go along with this. I made it clear in public that I did not believe that economic sanctions against Libya would work.

In late January, February and March tension between the United States and Libya rose as US naval forces started manoeuvres in an area of the Gulf of Sirte which Libya, in violation of international law, claimed as its own territorial waters. On Monday 24 March US aircraft were attacked by Libyan missiles fired from the shore. US forces struck back at the Libyan missile sites and sank a Libyan fast patrol boat.

I had to consider what our reaction would be. I was conscious that we had 5,000 British subjects in Libya. I was also aware of the possibility of Libyan action against our base in Cyprus. But I told Cabinet that in spite of this we must endorse the right of the United States to maintain freedom of movement in international waters and air space and its right to self-defence under the UN Charter.

Meanwhile, the Americans may have started to see who their true friends were. I learned that the French were expressing reservations about any policy of confrontation with Colonel Gaddafi, arguing that any US military action would win Libya Arab support and urging the need to avoid 'provocation'.

Then in the early hours of Saturday 5 April a bomb exploded in a discotheque frequented by US servicemen in West Berlin. Two people – one a US soldier – were killed and some 200 others – including 60 Americans – were injured. US intelligence, confirmed by ours, pointed to a Libyan involvement. For the Americans this was the final straw.

Just before 11 p.m. on the night of Tuesday 8 April I received a message from President Reagan. He requested our support for the use of the American F1-11s and support aircraft based in Britain in strikes against Libya, and he asked for an answer by noon the following day. I immediately called in Geoffrey Howe and George Younger to discuss what should be done. At 1 a.m. I sent an interim reply to the President. Its main purpose was to support the United States but I also expressed very considerable anxiety. I wanted more information on the targets in Libya. I was worried that US action might begin a cycle of revenge. I was concerned that there must be the right public justification for the action which was taken, otherwise we might just strengthen Gaddafi's standing. I was also worried about the implications for British hostages in the Lebanon – and, as events were to turn out, rightly so.

Looking back, I think that this initial response was probably too negative. But it had the practical benefit of making the Americans think through precisely what their objectives were and how they were to justify them. Two other considerations influenced me. First, I felt that there was an inclination to precipitate action in the United States, which was doubtless mirrored there by a perception of lethargy in Europe. Second, I knew that the political cost to me of giving permission for the use of US bases by the United States in their strikes against Libya would be high. I could not take this decision lightly.

Some time after midnight President Reagan's response came through on the hotline. It was a powerful and not uncritical answer to the points I had raised. He stressed that the action he planned would not set off a new cycle of revenge: for the cycle of violence began a long time ago, as the story of Gaddafi's terrorist actions demonstrated. He drew attention to what we knew from intelligence about Libyan direction of terrorist violence. He argued that it was the lack of a firm western response which had encouraged this. He felt that the legal justification for such action was clear. The US action would be aimed at Gaddafi's primary headquarters and immediate security forces, rather than the Libyan people. The strikes would be at limited targets. I was particularly impressed by the President's sober assessment of the likely effect of what was planned. He wrote:

> I have no illusion that these actions will eliminate entirely the terrorist threat. But it will show that officially sponsored terrorist actions by a government – such as Libya has repeatedly perpe-trated – will not be without cost. The loss of such state sponsor-ship will inevitably weaken the ability of terrorist organizations to carry out their criminal attacks even as we work through diplo-matic, political, and economic channels to alleviate the more fundamental cause of such terrorism.

The more I considered the matter, the clearer the justification for America's approach to Libya seemed.

That afternoon I sent a further message to President Reagan. I pledged 'our unqualified support for action directed against specific Libyan targets demonstrably involved in the conduct and support of terrorist activities'. I pledged support for the use of US aircraft from their bases in the UK, as long as that criterion was met. But I questioned some of the proposed targets and warned that if there ensued more wide-ranging action the Americans should recognize that even those most keen to give them all possible support would then find themselves in a difficult position.

Now that America was actually asking the Europeans for assistance which involved a political price they showed themselves in a less than glorious light. Chancellor Kohl apparently told the Americans that the US should not expect the wholehearted support of its European allies and said that everything would turn on whether the action succeeded. The French refused to allow the F1-11s to cross French air space. The Spanish said that the American aircraft could fly over Spain, but only if it was done in a way which would not be noticed. Since this condition could not be met, they had to fly through the Straits of Gibraltar.

Speculation was now rife. We could not confirm or deny our exchanges with the Americans. The Labour and Liberal Parties insisted that we should rule out the use of American bases in the UK for the action which everyone now seemed to expect. It was important to ensure that senior members of the Cabinet had my decision. At midday on Monday (14 April) I told the Cabinet's Overseas and Defence Committee what had been happening in recent days. I said that it was clear that the US was justified in acting in self-defence under Article 51 of the UN Treaty. Finally, I stressed that we had to stand by the Americans as they had stood by us over the Falklands.

That afternoon it was confirmed from Washington that American aircraft would soon take off from their British bases.

Late that night I received a message from President Reagan saying that the US aircraft would shortly strike at five named terrorist-associated targets in Libya. The President confirmed that the text of his televised statement to the American people took into account our advice to stress the element of self-defence to get the legal position right. My own statement to the House of Commons on the raid for the following day was already being drafted.

The American attack was carried out principally by sixteen F1-11s based in the UK, though a number of other aircraft were also used. The attack lasted forty minutes. Libyan missiles and guns were fired but their air defence radars were successfully jammed. The raid was undoubtedly a success, though sadly there were civilian casualties and one aircraft was lost. Television reports, however, concentrated all but exclusively not on the strategic importance of the targets but on weeping mothers and children.

The initial impact on public opinion in Britain was even worse than I had feared. Public sympathy for Libyan civilians was mixed with fear of terrorist retaliation by Libya.

I was to speak in the emergency debate on the Libyan raid in the House on Wednesday afternoon. It was intellectually and technically the most difficult speech to prepare because it depended heavily on describing the intelligence on Libya's terrorist activities and we had to marshal the arguments for self-defence in such circumstances. Every word of the speech had to be checked by the relevant intelligence services to see that it was accurate and that it did not place sources at risk.

The debate was rank with anti-American prejudice but my speech steadied the Party and the debate was a success. There was still a large measure of incomprehension even among our supporters. Yet the Libyan raid was also a turning point; and three direct benefits flowed from it.

First, it turned out to be a more decisive blow against Libyan-sponsored terrorism than I could ever have imagined. We are all too inclined to forget that tyrants rule by force and fear and are kept in check in the same way. There were revenge killings of British hostages organized by Libya, which I bitterly regretted. But the much-vaunted Libyan counter-attack did not take place. Gaddafi had not been destroyed but he had been humbled. There was a marked decline in Libyan-sponsored terrorism in succeeding years.

Second, there was a wave of gratitude from the United States which is still serving this country well. The *Wall Street Journal* flatteringly described me as 'magnificent'. Senators wrote to thank me. Our Washington embassy's switchboard was jammed with congratulatory telephone calls. And it was made quite clear by the Administration that Britain's voice would be accorded special weight in arms control negotiations. The Extradition Treaty, which we regarded as vital in bringing IRA terrorists back from America, was to receive stronger Administration support against filibustering opposition. The fact that so few had stuck by America in her time of trial strengthened the 'special relationship', which will always be special because of the cultural and historical links between our two countries, but which had a particular closeness for as long as President Reagan was in the White House.

The third benefit, oddly enough, was domestic, though it was by no means immediate. However unpopular, no one could doubt that our action had been strong and decisive. I had set my course and stuck to it.

As the spring of 1986 moved into summer the political climate began slowly, but unmistakably, to improve.

CHAPTER TWENTY-EIGHT

Men to Do Business With

East-West relations during the second term 1983–1987

A S 1983 DREW ON, the Soviets must have begun to realize that their game of manipulation and intimidation would soon be up. European governments were not prepared to fall into the trap opened by the Soviet proposal of a 'nuclear-free zone' for Europe. In March President Reagan announced American plans for a Strategic Defence Initiative (SDI) whose technological and financial implications for the USSR were devastating. Then, at the beginning of September the Soviets shot down a South Korean civilian airliner, killing 269 passengers. Not just the callousness but the incompetence of the Soviet regime, which could not even bring itself to apologize, was exposed. Perhaps for the first time since the Second World War, the Soviet Union started to be described, even in liberal western circles, as sick and on the defensive.

We had entered a dangerous phase. Both Ronald Reagan and I knew that the strategy of matching the Soviets in military strength and beating them on the battlefield of ideas was succeeding and that it must go on. But we had to win the Cold War without running unnecessary risks in the meantime.

Such was the thinking which lay behind my decision to arrange a seminar at Chequers on Thursday 8 September 1983 to pick the brains of experts on the Soviet Union. We discussed the Soviet economy, its technological inertia and the consequences of that, the impact of religious issues, Soviet military doctrine and expenditure on defence, and the benefits and costs to the Soviet Union of their control over eastern Europe. The purpose of this seminar was to provide me with the information on which to shape policy towards the Soviet Union and the eastern bloc in the months and years ahead. There were always two oppo-site outlooks among the Sovietologists.

At the risk of oversimplification, these were as follows. On the one hand, there were those who played down the differences between the western and Soviet systems and who were generally drawn from political analysis and systems analysis. They were the people who appeared on our television screens, analysing the Soviet Union in terms borrowed from liberal democracies. These were the optimists, confident that somehow, somewhere, within the Soviet totalitarian system rationality and compro-mise were about to break out. I remember a remark of Bob Conquest's that the trouble with systems analysis is that if you analyse the systems of a horse and a tiger, you find them pretty much the same: but it would be a great mistake to treat a tiger like a horse. On the other hand, there were those – mainly the historians – who grasped that totalitarian systems are different in kind, not just degree, from liberal democracies and that approaches relevant to the one are irrelevant to the other. These analysts argued that a totalitarian system generates a different kind of political leader from a democratic one and that the ability of any one individual to change that system is almost negligible.

My own view was much closer to the second, but with one very impor-tant difference. I always believed that our western system would ulti-mately triumph, if we did not throw our advantages away, because it rested on the unique, almost limitless, creativity and vitality of individu-als. Even a system like that of the Soviets, which set out to crush the indi-vidual, could never totally succeed in doing so, as was shown by the Solzhenitsyns, Sakharovs, Bukovskys, Ratushinskayas and thousands of other dissidents and *refuseniks*. This also implied that at some time the right individual could challenge even the system which he had used to attain power. For this reason I was convinced that we must seek out the most likely person in the rising generation of Soviet leaders and then cultivate and sustain him, while recognizing the clear limits of our power to do so. That is why those who subsequently considered that I was led astray from my original approach to the Soviet Union because I was dazzled by Mr Gorbachev were wrong. I spotted him because I was searching for someone like him.

At the time of my Chequers seminar it did seem that there would soon be important changes in the Soviet leadership. Mr Andropov, though he was no liberal, did undoubtedly want to revive the Soviet economy, which was in fact in a far worse state than any of us realized at the time. In order to do this he wanted to cut back bureaucracy and improve efficiency. Although he had inherited a top leadership which he could not instantly change, the high average age of the Politburo would present him with the opportunity of filling vacancies with those amenable to his objective. There were already doubts about Andropov's health. If he lived for just a few more years, however, it seemed likely that the leadership would pass to a new generation. The two main contenders appeared to be Grigory Romanov and Mikhail Gorbachev. I asked for all the information we had about these two.

It was soon obvious to me that – attractive as was the idea of seeing a Romanov back in the Kremlin – there would probably be unpleasant consequences. Romanov as First Secretary of the Communist Party in Leningrad had won a reputation for efficiency but also as a hardline Marxist which, like many of the sort, he combined with an extravagant lifestyle. And I confess that when I read about those priceless crystal glasses from the Hermitage being smashed at the celebration of his daughter's wedding some of the attraction of the name was lost as well.

Of Mr Gorbachev what little we knew seemed modestly encouraging. He was clearly the best educated member of the Politburo, not that anybody would have described this group as intellectuals. He had acquired a reputation for being open-minded; but of course this might be just a matter of style. He had risen steadily through the Party under Khrushchev, Brezhnev and now Andropov, of whom he was clearly a special protégé; but that might well be a sign of conformity rather than talent. Nevertheless, I heard favourable reports of him from Pierre Trudeau in Canada later that month. I began to take special notice when his name was mentioned in reports on the Soviet Union.

For the moment, however, relations with the Soviets were so bad that direct contact with them was almost impossible. It seemed to me that it was through eastern Europe that we would have to work.

Hungary was the choice for my first visit as Prime Minister to a Warsaw Pact country for several reasons. The Hungarians had gone furthest along the path of economic reform and a certain amount of liberalization had occurred, though outright dissent was punished. János Kádár, officially First Secretary of the Hungarian Communist Party but in fact unchallenged leader, used economic links with the West to provide his people with a tolerable standard of living while constantly asserting Hungary's loyalty to the Warsaw Pact, socialism and the Soviet Union: a necessary consideration, given that some 60,000 Soviet troops had been 'temporarily' stationed in Hungary since 1948.

I stepped off the plane at 10 o'clock on the night of Thursday 2 February 1984 to be met by the Hungarian Prime Minister, Mr Lázár. My first official engagement the next morning was a private discussion with him. He gave every sign of loyalty to the communist system. But what he had to say showed the roots of that loyalty. He warned me that the worst possible thing I could do on my visit was to cast doubt on Hungary's remaining part of the socialist bloc. The Hungarians had been concerned at what Vice-President George Bush had said to this effect in Vienna after making a successful visit to the country. I realized that formal adherence to the Soviet system was the price of the limted reforms they had been able to make. I immediately said that I understood and I was careful to keep my word.

Later that morning I saw Mr Kádár. He was a square-faced, large-boned, healthy-complexioned man with an air of easy authority and an apparently reasonable frame of mind in discussion. I hoped to gain from him a clear picture of the situation in the USSR.

The one surprise – and disappointment – of my visit was how far even Hungary was from a free economy. There were some small businesses, but they were not allowed to grow beyond a certain size. The main emphasis of Hungary's economic reforms was not on increasing private ownership of land or investment but rather on private or co-operative use of state-owned facilities.

In retrospect, my Hungarian visit was the first foray in what became a distinctive British diplomacy towards the captive nations of eastern Europe. The first step was to open greater economic and commercial links with the existing regimes, making them less dependent upon the closed COMECON system. Later we were to put more stress on human rights. And, finally, as the Soviet control of eastern Europe began to decay, we made internal political reforms the condition of western help.

Just a few days after my return from Hungary Mr Andropov was dead. His funeral would give me the opportunity to meet the man who to our surprise emerged as the new Soviet leader, Mr Konstantin Chernenko. We had thought that Mr Chernenko was too old, too ill and too closely connected with Mr Brezhnev and his era to succeed to the leadership – and, as events turned out, we were more astute than his colleagues in the Politburo.

My party landed at Moscow Airport at 9.30 p.m. on Monday 13 February. I spent the night at our embassy – a magnificent house, facing the Kremlin across the Moskva river. (Later, when we would otherwise have had to give it up at the end of the lease, I did a deal with Mr Gorbachev for us to keep our splendid building in exchange for the Soviets keeping their current embassy in Britain when that lease expired. One of the few points on which the Foreign Office and I agreed was the need for British embassies to be architecturally imposing and provided with fine pictures and furniture).

The day of the funeral was bright, clear and even colder than when I arrived. At these occasions visiting dignitaries do not have seats: we had to stand for several hours in a specially reserved enclosure. Later I met the new Soviet leader for a short private meeting which was a formal affair, covering all the old ground of disarmament issues. I was unimpressed.

With long hours of standing I was glad that Robin Butler had persuaded me that I should wear fur-lined boots, rather than my usual high heels. They had been expensive. But when I met Mr Chernenko the thought crossed my mind that they would probably come in useful again soon.

I now had to consider the next step in my strategy of gaining closer relations – on the right terms – with the Soviet Union. Clearly, there must be more personal contact with the Soviet leaders. Geoffrey Howe wanted us to extend an invitation to Mr Chernenko to come to Britain. I said that it was too early to do this. We needed to see more about where the new Soviet leader was heading first. But I was keen to invite others and invitations went to several senior Soviet figures, including Mr Gorbachev. It quickly appeared that Mr Gorbachev was indeed keen to come on what would be his first visit to a European capitalist country and wanted to do so soon. By now we had learned more about his background and that of his wife, Raisa, who, unlike the wives of other leading Soviet politicians, was often seen in public and was an articulate, highly educated and attractive woman. I decided that the Gorbachevs should both come to Chequers, which has just the right country house atmosphere conducive to good conversation. I regarded the meeting as potentially of great significance.

The Gorbachevs drove down from London on the morning of Sunday 16 December, arriving in time for lunch. Over drinks in the Great Hall Mr Gorbachev told me how interested he had been to see the farmland on the way to Chequers. Agriculture had been his responsibility for a number of years and he had apparently achieved some modest progress in reforming the collective farms, but up to 30 per cent of the crops were lost because of failures of distribution.

Raisa Gorbachev knew only a little English – as far as I could tell her husband knew none: but she was dressed in a smart western-style outfit, a well-tailored grey suit – just the sort I could have worn myself, I thought. She had a philosophy degree and had indeed been an academic. Our advice at this time was that she was a committed hardline Marxist; her obvious interest in Hobbes's *Leviathan*, which she took down from the shelf in the library, might possibly have confirmed that. But I later learned from her – after I had left office – that her grandfather had been one of those millions of kulaks killed during the forced collectivization of agriculture under Stalin. Her family had no good reason for illusions about communism.

We went in to lunch – I was accompanied by a rather large team of Willie Whitelaw, Geoffrey Howe, Michael Heseltine, Michael Jopling, Malcolm Rifkind (Minister of State at the Foreign office), Paul Channon and advisers; he and Raisa by Mr Zamyatin, the Soviet Ambassador, and the quietly impressive Mr Alexander Yakovlev, the adviser who was to play a large part in the reforms of the 'Gorbachev years'. It was not long before the conversation turned from trivialities – for which neither Mr Gorbachev nor I had any taste – to a vigorous two-way debate. In a sense, the argument has continued ever since and is taken up whenever we meet; and as it goes to the heart of what politics is really about, I never tire of it.

He told me about the economic programmes of the Soviet system, the switch from big industrial plant to smaller projects and 'businesses'; the ambitious irrigation schemes and the way in which the industrial planners adapted industrial capacity to the labour force to avoid unemployment. I asked whether this might not all be easier if reform were attempted on a free enterprise basis, with the provision of incentives and a free hand for local enterprise to run their own show, rather than everything being directed from the centre. Mr Gorbachev denied indignantly that everything in the USSR was run from the centre. I took another tack. I explained that in the western system everyone – including the poorest – ultimately received more than they would from a system which depended simply on redistribution. Indeed, in Britain we were attempting to cut taxes in order to increase incentives so that we could create wealth, competing in world markets. I said I had no wish to have power to direct everyone where he should work and what he or she should receive.

Mr Gorbachev insisted on the superiority of the Soviet system. Not only did it produce higher growth rates, but if I came to the USSR I would see how the Soviet people lived – 'joyfully'. If this was so, I countered, why did the Soviet authorities not allow people to leave the country as easily as they could leave Britain?

In particular, I criticized the constraints placed on Jewish emigration to Israel. He claimed that 80 per cent of those who had expressed the wish to leave the Soviet Union had been able to do so and repeated the Soviet line, which I did not believe, that those forbidden to leave had been working in areas relating to national security. I knew there was no purpose in persisting now; but the point had been registered. The Soviets had to know that every time we met their treatment of the *refuseniks* would be thrown back at them.

We had coffee in the main sitting room. All of my team except Geoffrey Howe, my private secretary Charles Powell, and the interpreter left. Denis showed Mrs Gorbachev around the house.

If at this stage I had paid attention only to the content of Mr Gorbachev's remarks I would have to conclude that he was cast in the usual communist mould. But his personality could not been more different from the wooden ventriloquism of the average Soviet *apparatchik*. He smiled, laughed, used his hands for emphasis, modulated his voice, followed an argument through and was a sharp debater. He was self-confident and though he larded his remarks with respectful references to Mr Chernenko, he did not seem in the least uneasy about entering into controversial areas of high politics. He never read from a prepared brief, but referred to a small notebook of manuscript jottings. Only on matters of pronunciation of foreign names did he refer to his colleagues for advice. As the day wore on I came to understand that it was the style, far more than the Marxist rhetoric, which expressed the substance of the personality beneath. I found myself liking him.

The most practical piece of business I had to discuss on this occasion was arms control. I had found in talking to the Hungarians that the best basis on which to discuss arms control in a relatively serene atmosphere was to state that our two opposing systems must live side by side, with less hostility and lower levels of armaments. I did the same again now.

Two things quickly became clear. The first was just how well briefed Mr Gorbachev was about the West. He commented on my speeches, which he had clearly read. He quoted Lord Palmerston's dictum that Britain had no eternal friends or enemies but only eternal interests. He had been closely following leaked conversations from the American press, to the effect that the US had an interest in not allowing the Soviet economy to emerge from stagnation.

At one point, with a touch of theatre, he pulled out a full-page diagram from the *New York Times*, illustrating the explosive power of the weapons of the superpowers compared with the explosive power available in the Second World War. He was well versed in the fashionable arguments then raging about the prospect of a 'nuclear winter' resulting from a nuclear exchange. I was not much moved by all this. I said that what interested me more than the concept of the nuclear winter was avoiding the incineration, death and destruction which would precede it. But the purpose of nuclear weapons was, in any case, to deter war not to wage it. Yet this must now be achieved at a lower level of weaponry. Mr Gorbachev argued that if both sides continued to pile up weapons this could lead to accidents or unforeseen circumstances, and with the present generation of weapons the time for decision-making could be counted in minutes. As he put it, in one of the more obscure Russian proverbs, 'Once a year even an unloaded gun can go off.'

The other point which emerged was the Soviets' distrust of the Reagan Administration in general and of their plans for a Strategic Defence Initiative in particular. I emphasized on more than one occasion that President Reagan could be trusted and that the last thing he would ever want was war, that the United States had never shown any desire for world domination.

As the discussion wore on it was clear that the Soviets were indeed very concerned about SDI. They wanted it stopped at almost any price. I knew that to some degree I was being used as a stalking horse for President Reagan. I was also aware that I was dealing with a wily opponent who would ruthlessly exploit any divisions between me and the Americans. So I bluntly stated that he should understand that there was no question of dividing us: we would remain staunch allies of the United States. My frankness on this was particularly important because of my equal frankness about what I saw as the President's unrealistic dream of a nuclear-free world.

The talks were due to end at 4.30 p.m. to allow Mr Gorbachev to be back for a reception at the Soviet Embassy, but he said that he wanted to continue. It was 5.50 p.m. when he left, having introduced me to another pearl of Russian popular wisdom to the effect that, 'Mountain folk cannot live without guests any more than they can live without air. But if the guests stay longer than necessary, they choke.' As he took his leave, I hoped that I had been talking to the next Soviet leader. For, as I subsequently told the press, this was a man with whom I could do business.

President Reagan's Strategic Defence Initiative was to prove central to the West's victory in the Cold War. Although I differed sharply from the President's view that SDI was a major step towards a nuclear-weapon-free world – something which I believed was neither attainable nor even desirable – I had no doubt about the rightness of his commitment to press ahead with the programme. Looking back, it is now clear to me that Ronald Reagan's original decision on SDI was the single most important of his presidency.

In Britain, I kept tight personal control over decisions relating to SDI and our reactions to it. This was one of those areas in which only a firm grasp of the scientific concepts involved allows the right policy decisions to be made. Laid-back generalists from the Foreign Office – let alone the ministerial muddlers in charge of them – could not be relied upon. By contrast, I was in my element.

In formulating our approach to SDI, there were four distinct elements which I bore in mind. The first was the science itself. The American aim in SDI was to develop a new and much more effective defence against ballistic missiles. This would be what was called a 'multi-layered' Ballistic Missile Defence (BMD), using both ground and space-based weapons. This concept of defence rested on the ability to attack incoming ballistic missiles at all stages of their flight, right up to the point of re-entry of the earth's atmosphere on its way to the target. Scientific advances opened up new possibilities to make such defence far more effective than the existing Anti-Ballistic Missile (ABM) defence. The main advances which appeared likely were in the use of kinetic energy weapons (which were non-nuclear and which, when launched at high speed against the nuclear missile, would smash it) and in the use of laser weapons. Even more challenging, however, was the requirement for an enormously powerful and sophisticated computer capability to direct and co-ordinate the system as a whole. Such an undertaking would not only require huge sums of money but also test the ultimate creative abilities of the western and communist systems competing for it.

The second element was the existing international agreement limiting the deployment of weapons in space and ABM systems. The 1972 ABM Treaty, as amended by a 1974 Protocol, allowed the United States and the

Soviet Union to deploy one static ABM system with up to one hundred launchers in defence of either an Inter-Continental Ballistic Missile (ICBM) silo field or the national capital. The precise implications of the treaty for the research, testing, development and deployment of new kinds of ABM system were subject to heated legalistic dispute. The Soviets had started out with a 'broad interpretation' of the treaty which they narrowed when it later suited them. Within the American Administration there were those who pressed for a 'broader than broad' interpretation which would have placed almost no effective constraint on the development and deployment of SDI. The Foreign Office and the Ministry of Defence always sought to urge the narrowest possible interpretation, which the Americans – rightly in my view – believed would have meant that SDI was stillborn. I made it clear in private and public that research on whether a system was viable could not be said to have been completed until it had been successfully tested. This apparently technical point was really a matter of common sense. But it was to become the issue dividing the United States and the USSR at the Reykjavik summit and so assumed great importance.

The third element in the calculation was the relative strength of the two sides in Ballistic Missile Defence. Only the Soviet Union possessed a working ABM system (known as GALOSH) around Moscow, which they were currently upgrading. The Americans had never deployed an equivalent system. The United States assessed that the Soviets were spending in the order of $1 billion a year on their research programme of defence against ballistic missiles. Also the Soviets were further advanced in anti-satellite weapons. There was, therefore, a strong argument that the Soviets had already acquired an unacceptable advantage in this whole area.

The fourth element was the implications of SDI for deterrence. I started off with a good deal of sympathy for the thinking behind the ABM Treaty. This was that the more sophisticated and effective the defence against nuclear missiles, the greater the pressure to seek hugely expensive advances in nuclear weapons technology. I was always a believer in a slightly qualified version of the doctrine known as MAD – 'mutually assured destruction'. The threat of (what I preferred to call) 'unacceptable destruction' which would follow from a nuclear exchange was such that nuclear weapons were an effective deterrent against not just nuclear but also conventional war. I had to consider whether SDI was likely to undermine that. On one argument, of course, it would. If any power believed that it had a completely effective shield against nuclear weapons it had, in

theory, a greater temptation to use them. I knew – and post-war experience demonstrated beyond doubt – that the United States would never
start a war by launching a first strike against the Soviet Union, whether it
believed that it was secure from retaliation or not. The Soviets, by
contrast, claimed to have no such confidence.

But I soon began to see that SDI would strengthen not weaken the
nuclear deterrent. I never believed that SDI could offer one hundred per
cent protection, but it would allow sufficient United States missiles to
survive a first strike by the Soviets. Theoretically, the US would then be in
a position to launch its own nuclear weapons against the Soviet Union. It
follows that the Soviets would be far less likely to yield to the temptation
to use nuclear weapons in the first place.

The decisive argument for me, however, was precisely the one which
made me reject President Reagan's vision of a nuclear-weapon-free
world. It was that you could not ultimately hold back research on SDI any
more than you could prevent research into new kinds of offensive
weapons. We had to be the first to go for it. Science is unstoppable: it will
not be stopped for being ignored. The deployment of SDI, just like the
deployment of nuclear weapons, must be carefully controlled and nego-
tiated. But research, which necessarily involved testing, must go ahead.

It was the subject of SDI which dominated my talks with President
Reagan and members of his Administration when I went to Camp David
on Saturday 22 December 1984 to brief the Americans on my talks with
Mr Gorbachev. This was the first occasion on which I had heard President
Reagan speaking about SDI. He did so with passion. He was at his most
idealistic. He stressed that SDI would be a defensive system and that it was
not his intention to obtain for the United States a unilateral advantage.
Indeed, he said that if SDI succeeded he would be ready to international-
ize it so that it was at the service of all countries, and he had told Mr
Gromyko, the Soviet Foreign minister, as much. He reaffirmed his long-
term goal of getting rid of nuclear weapons entirely.

I was horrified to think that the United States would be prepared to
throw away a hard-won lead in technology by making it internationally
available. (Fortunately the Soviets never believed that he would.) But I
did not raise this directly. Instead, I concentrated on my areas of agreement with the President. I said that it was essential to pursue the research,
but that if this reached the point where decisions had to be made to
produce and deploy weapons in space a very different situation would

arise. Deployment would not be consistent either with the 1972 ABM Treaty or the 1967 Outer Space Treaty. Both of these would have to be renegotiated. I also explained my concern about the possible intermediate effect of SDI on the doctrine of deterrence. I was worried that deployment of a Ballistic Missile Defence system would be destabilizing and that while it was being constructed a pre-emptive first strike against it would become an attractive option. But I acknowledged that I might well not be fully informed of all the technical aspects and wanted to hear more. In all this I was keen to probe the Americans, not just in order to learn more of their intentions but to ensure that they had clearly thought through the implications of the steps they were now taking.

What I heard was reassuring. President Reagan did not pretend that they yet knew where the research could finally lead. But he emphasized that keeping up with the United States would impose an economic strain on the Soviet Union. He argued that there had to be a practical limit as to how far the Soviet Government could push their people down the road of austerity. As so often, he had instinctively grasped the key to the whole question. What would the effects be of SDI on the Soviet Union? In fact, as he foresaw, the Soviets did recoil in the face of the challenge of SDI, finally renouncing the goal of military superiority which alone had given them the confidence to resist the demands for reform in their own system. But of course this still lay in the future.

What I wanted now was an agreed position on SDI to which both the President and I could lend our support, even though our long-term view of its potential was different. I now jotted down, while talking to National Security Adviser Bud McFarlane, the four points which seemed to me to be crucial.

My officials then filled in the details. The President and I agreed a text which set out the policy.

The main section of my statement reads:

> I told the President of my firm conviction that the SDI research programme should go ahead. Research is, of course, permitted under existing US/Soviet treaties; and we, of course, know that the Russians already have their research programme and, in the US view, have already gone beyond research. We agreed on four points: (1) the US, and western, aim was not to achieve superiority, but to maintain balance, taking account of Soviet development; (2) SDI-related deployment would, in view of treaty obligations,

have to be a matter for negotiation; (3) the overall aim is to enhance, not undercut, deterrence; (4) East-West negotiation should aim to achieve security with reduced levels of offensive systems on both sides. This will be the purpose of the resumed US-Soviet negotiations on arms control, which I warmly welcome.

I subsequently learnt that George Shultz thought that I had secured too great a concession on the Americans' part in the wording; but in fact it gave them and us a clear and defensible line and helped reassure the European members of NATO. A good day's work.

March 1985 saw the death of Mr Chernenko and the succession of Mr Gorbachev to the Soviet leadership. Once again I attended a Moscow funeral: the weather was, if anything, even colder than at Yuri Andropov's. I had almost an hour's talk with Mr Gorbachev that evening in the Kremlin. The atmosphere was more formal than at Chequers and the silent, sardonic presence of Mr Gromyko did not help. But I was able to explain to them the implications of the policy I had agreed with President Reagan the previous December at Camp David. It was clear that SDI was now the main preoccupation of the Soviets in arms control.

Mr Gorbachev brought, as we had expected, a new style to the Soviet Government. He spoke openly of the terrible state of the Soviet economy, though at this stage he was still relying on the methods associated with Mr Andropov's drive for greater efficiency rather than radical reform. As the year wore on, there was no evidence of improvement in conditions in the Soviet Union. Indeed, as our new – and first-class – ambassador to Moscow, Bryan Cartledge, pointed out in one of his first dispatches, it was a matter of, 'jam tomorrow and meanwhile, no vodka today'.

A distinct chill entered into Britain's relations with the Soviet Union as a result of expulsions which I authorized of Soviet officials who had been spying. The defection of Oleg Gordievsky, a former top KGB officer, meant that the Soviets knew how well informed we were about their activities. I had several meetings with Mr Gordievsky and repeatedly tried to have the Soviets release his family to join him in the West. (They eventually came after the failed coup in August 1991.)

In November President Reagan and Mr Gorbachev had their first meeting in Geneva. Not much of substance came out of it but a good personal rapport quickly developed between the two leaders (though not, sadly, between their wives).

During 1986 Mr Gorbachev showed great subtlety in playing on western public opinion by bringing forward tempting, but unacceptable, proposals on arms control. Late in the year it was agreed that President Reagan and Mr Gorbachev – with their Foreign ministers – should meet in Reykjavik, Iceland, to discuss substantive proposals.

In retrospect, the Reykjavik summit on that weekend of 11 and 12 October can be seen to have a quite different significance than most of the commentators at the time realized. Ever greater Soviet concessions were made during the summit: they agreed for the first time that the British and French deterrents should be excluded from the INF negotiations; and that cuts in strategic nuclear weapons should leave each side with equal numbers. They also made significant concessions on INF numbers. As the summit drew to an end President Reagan was proposing an agreement by which the whole arsenal of strategic nuclear weapons – bombers, long-range Cruise and ballistic missiles – would be halved within five years and the most powerful of these weapons, strategic ballistic missiles, eliminated altogether within ten. Mr Gorbachev was even more ambitious: he wanted the elimination of all strategic nuclear weapons by the end of the ten-year period.

But then suddenly, at the very end, the trap was sprung. President Reagan had conceded that during the ten-year period both sides would agree not to withdraw from the ABM Treaty, though development and testing compatible with the treaty would be allowed. Mr Gorbachev said that the whole thing depended on confining SDI to the laboratory – a much higher restriction that was likely to kill the prospect of an effective SDI. The President rejected the deal and the summit broke up. Its failure was widely portrayed as the result of the foolish intransigence of an elderly American President, obsessed with an unrealizable dream. In fact, President Reagan's refusal to trade away SDI for the apparent near fulfilment of his dream of a nuclear-free world was crucial to the victory over communism. He called the Soviets' bluff. The Russians may have scored an immediate propaganda victory when the talks broke down. But they had lost the game and I have no doubt that they knew it.* For they must have realized by now that they could not hope to match the United States in the competition for military technological supremacy and many of the concessions they made at Reykjavik proved impossible for them to retrieve.

---

* In February 1993 former senior Soviet officials confirmed precisely this point at a conference at Princeton University on the end of the Cold War.

My own reaction when I heard how far the Americans had been prepared to go was as if there had been an earthquake beneath my feet. The whole system of nuclear deterrence which had kept the peace for forty years was close to being abandoned. Had the President's proposals gone through, they would also have effectively killed off the Trident missile, forcing us to acquire a different system if we were to keep an independent nuclear deterrent. Somehow I had to get the Americans back onto the firm ground of a credible policy of nuclear deterrence. I arranged to fly to the United States to see President Reagan.

I have never felt more conscious than in the preparation for this visit of how much hung on my relationship with the President. I received the fullest briefing from the military about the implications of a defence strategy involving the elimination of all ballistic missiles.

I flew into Washington on the afternoon of Friday 14 November. That evening I practised my arguments in meetings with George Shultz and Cap Weinberger. I saw George Bush for breakfast the following morning and then left for Camp David where I was met by President Reagan.

To my great relief I found that the President quickly understood why I was so deeply concerned about what had happened in Reykjavik. He agreed the draft statement which we had finalized after talking to George Shultz the previous day and which I subsequently issued at my press conference. This stated our policy on arms control after Reykjavik. It ran as follows:

> We agreed that priority should be given to: an INF agreement, with restraints on shorter range systems; a 50 per cent cut over 5 years in the US and Soviet strategic offensive weapons; and a ban on chemical weapons. In all three cases, effective verification would be an essential element. We also agreed on the need to press ahead with the SDI research programme which is permitted by the ABM Treaty. We confirmed that NATO's strategy of forward defence and flexible response would continue to require effective nuclear deterrence, based on a mix of systems. At the same time, reductions in nuclear weapons would increase the importance of eliminating conventional disparities. Nuclear weapons cannot be dealt with in isolation, given the need for stable overall balance at all times. We were also in agreement that these matters should continue to be the subject of close consultation within the alliance.

The President reaffirmed the United States' intention to proceed with its strategic modernization programme, including Trident. He also confirmed his full support for the arrangements made to modernize Britain's independent nuclear deterrent, with Trident.

I had reason to be well pleased.

It is easy to imagine what the effect of the Camp David statement must have been in Moscow. It meant the end of the Soviets' hope of using SDI and President Reagan's dream of a nuclear-weapons-free world to advance their strategy of denuclearizing Europe, leaving us vulnerable to military blackmail. It also demonstrated that, whether they liked it or not, I was able to have some influence on President Reagan on fundamental issues of alliance policy. Mr Gorbachev, therefore, had as much reason to do business with me as I with him, and it is no surprise that I was soon invited to Moscow.

I prepared myself very thoroughly. On Friday 27 February 1987 I held an all-day seminar on the Soviet Union at Chequers. I also read through in detail the – usually long and indigestible – speeches which Mr Gorbachev had been making and I felt that something new was emerging from them.

I was not going to Moscow as the representative of the West, but it was clearly very important that other western leaders should know the line I intended to take and that I should gauge their sentiments beforehand. I knew President Reagan's mind and therefore limited myself to sending him a lengthy message.

I also arranged to meet President Mitterrand and then Chancellor Kohl on Monday 23 March. President Mitterrand believed, as I did, that Mr Gorbachev was prepared to go a long way to change the system. But the French President knew too that the Soviets respected toughness. He said that we must resist the attempt to denuclearize Europe. I warmly agreed.

Nor did I find any disagreement with Chancellor Kohl.

My last public pronouncement about the Soviet Union before I left had been my speech to the Conservative Central Council in Torquay on Saturday 21 March. It would have been easy to tone down my criticism of the Soviet regime. But I was not prepared to do so. Too often in the past western leaders had placed the search for trouble-free relations with foreign autocrats above plain speaking of the truth. I said:

We have seen in Mr Gorbachev's speeches a clear admission that the communist system is not working. Far from enabling the Soviet Union to catch up with the West it is falling further behind. We hear new language being used by their leaders. Words which we recognize, like 'openness' and 'democratization'. But do they have the same meaning for them as they do for us? Some of those who have been imprisoned for their political and religious beliefs have been released. We welcome that. But many more remain in prison or are refused permission to emigrate. We want to see them free, or reunited with their families abroad, if that is what they choose . . . When I go to Moscow to meet Mr Gorbachev next week, the goal will be a peace based not on illusion or surrender, but on realism and strength . . . Peace needs confidence and trust between countries and peoples. Peace means an end to the killing in Cambodia, an end to the slaughter in Afghanistan. It means honouring the obligations which the Soviet Union freely accepted in the Helsinki Final Act in 1975 to allow free movement of people and ideas and other basic human rights . . . We shall reach our judgements not on words, not on intentions, not on promises, but on actions and results.

I sat across the table from Mr Gorbachev in the Kremlin, a long flower vase between us. I was accompanied by just one member of my staff and an interpreter. It was soon clear that he intended to take me to task for my Central Council speech. He said that when the Soviet leaders had studied it they had felt the breeze of the 1940s and '50s. It reminded them of Winston Churchill's speech at Fulton, Missouri (about the 'Iron Curtain') and the Truman doctrine.

I did not apologize. I said that there was one point which I did not make in my speech but which I would make now. This was that I knew of no evidence that the Soviet Union had given up the Brezhnev doctrine or the goal of securing world domination for communism. We were ready to fight the battle of ideas: indeed this was the right way to fight. But instead we in the West saw Soviet subversion in South Yemen, in Ethiopia, in Mozambique, in Angola and in Nicaragua. We saw Vietnam being supported by the Soviet Union in its conquest of Cambodia. We saw Afghanistan occupied by Soviet troops. We naturally drew the conclusion that the goal of worldwide communism was still being pursued. This was a crucial consideration for the West. We recognized that Mr Gorbachev was committed to internal reforms in the Soviet Union. But we had to ask ourselves whether this would lead to changes in external policies.

I went on to show that I had read Mr Gorbachev's speeches with as much care as he seemed to have read mine. I told him that I had found his January Central Committee speech fascinating. But I wanted to know whether the internal changes he was making would lead to changes in the Soviet Union's foreign policies as well. I added that I had not expected that we would have generated quite so much heat so early in the discussion. Mr Gorbachev replied with a roar of laughter that he welcomed 'acceleration' and was pleased we were speaking frankly.

The conversation went back and forth, not just covering regional conflicts but going right to the heart of what differentiated the western and communist systems. This I described as being a distinction between societies in which power was dispersed and societies based on central control and coercion.

The afternoon discussion was less contentious and more informative. He explained to me the economic reforms he was making and the problems still to be faced. This led on to technology. He claimed to be confident about the Soviet Union's capacity for developing computers in competition with the United States. But I was not convinced. And that led back to SDI which Mr Gorbachev promised the Soviets would match – in some way that he would not disclose. I tried to interest him in my proposal for greater 'predictability' as regards the progress of the American SDI programme, but apparently to no avail.

Then I pressed Mr Gorbachev on human rights in general and the treatment of the Jews in particular. I also raised the question of Afghanistan, where I had the impression that he was searching for some way out. Finally, I listed the points which I thought we could agree on for a public account of our discussion which, he agreed, had contributed to better relations and greater confidence between us. But it was now very late. Guests were already assembling for the formal banquet at which I was to speak. Putting diplomacy ahead of fashion, I abandoned my plans to return to the embassy and change: I attended the banquet in the short wool dress I had been wearing all day. I felt rather like Ninotchka in reverse.

Tuesday began with a rather dull meeting with Prime Minister Ryzhkov and other Soviet ministers. I had hoped to learn more about the Soviet economic reforms, but we got bogged down once again in arms control and then in bilateral trade issues.

Far more exciting and worthwhile for all concerned was the interview which I gave to three journalists from Soviet Television. I learned afterwards that this had an enormous impact on Soviet opinion. Most of the questions related to nuclear weapons. I defended the West's line and indeed the retention of the nuclear deterrent. I reminded them of their huge superiority in conventional and chemical weapons. I pointed out that the Soviet Union was ahead of the United States in ABM defences. Nobody had ever told ordinary Russians these facts. They learned them from my interview for the first time. The interview was allowed to go out uncut from Soviet Television, which I afterwards regarded as proof that my confidence in Mr Gorbachev's basic integrity was not misplaced.

That evening the Gorbachevs gave me dinner in an old mansion, converted many years before for entertaining foreign guests. The atmosphere was as close to that of Chequers as I ever found in the Soviet Union. In the rooms around which Mr Gorbachev showed us, Churchill, Eden, Stalin and Molotov had smoked, drunk, and argued. We were a small group, the Gorbachevs being joined by just the Ryzhkovs, who did not take a very active part in the conversation. A brightly burning log fire – again like Chequers – illumined the room to which we later withdrew to put right the world's problems over coffee and liqueurs. I saw two interesting examples of the way in which old Marxist certainties were being challenged. There was a lively argument between the Gorbachevs, which I provoked, about the definition of the 'working class' about which we heard so much in Soviet propaganda. I wanted to know how they defined this in the Soviet Union – a point of some substance in a system in which, as the old Polish saying goes, 'we pretend to work and they pretend to pay us'. Mrs Gorbachev thought that anyone who worked, whatever his job or profession, was a worker. Her husband argued initially that only the blue-collar workers counted. But he then reconsidered and said that this was largely an historical or 'scientific' (that is Marxist) term which did not do justice to the diversity of today's society.

The second indication of a break with old socialist certainties was when he told me – with tantalizingly little detail – of plans which were being discussed for increasing people's incomes and then having them make some payment for public services like health and education. Not surprisingly, such plans, whatever they were, came to nothing.

The following morning I had breakfast with *refuseniks* at the British Embassy. Theirs was a disturbing tale of heroism under mainly petty but continual persecution. Later that morning I left Moscow for Tbilisi in

Georgia. I had wanted to see a Soviet republic other than Russia and I knew that Georgia would present a great cultural and geographical contrast.

It had been, quite simply, the most fascinating and most important foreign visit I had made. I could sense in the days I spent in the Soviet Union that the ground was shifting underneath the communist system. De Tocqueville's insight that 'experience shows that the most dangerous moment for a bad government is generally that in which it sets about reform' sprang to my mind. The welcome I had received – both the warm affection from the Russian crowds, and the respect of the Soviet authorities in long hours of negotiations – suggested that something fundamental was happening under the surface. The West's system of liberty which Ronald Reagan and I personified in the eastern bloc was increasingly in the ascendant. I sensed that great changes were at hand – but I could never have guessed how quickly they would come.

CHAPTER TWENTY-NINE

Putting the World to Rights

Diplomacy towards and visits to the Far East,
the Middle East and Africa 1984–1990

W HEN I WAS IN OPPOSITION I was very doubtful of the value of high-profile public diplomacy. To some extent I remain so. My political philosophy in domestic affairs is founded on a deep scepticism about the ability of politicians to change the fundamentals of the economy or society: the best they can do is to create a framework in which people's talents and virtues are mobilized not crushed. Similarly, in foreign affairs, the underlying realities of power are not transformed by meetings and understandings between heads of government. A country with a weak economy, an unstable social base or an ineffective administration cannot compensate for these – at least for long – with an ambitious diplomatic programme. That said, my experience as Prime Minister did convince me that a skilfully conducted foreign policy based on strength can magnify a country's influence and allow progress to be made in dealing with thorny problems around the world. As the years went by, I put increasing effort into international diplomacy.

Foreign visits allowed me to meet, talk to and seek to influence heads of government on their own ground. These visits gave me insights into the way those I dealt with in the clinical atmosphere of great international conferences actually lived and felt.

In the Far East, the dominant long-term questions concerned the future role and development of a political and military super-power, the People's Republic of China, and an economic super-power, Japan; for Britain, it was the future of Hong Kong which had to take precedence over everything else.

In the Middle East, it was the Iran-Iraq War, with its undercurrent of destabilizing Muslim fundamentalism, which cost most lives and threatened most economic harm. But I always felt that the Arab-Israeli dispute was of even more abiding importance. For it was this which time and again prevented the emergence – at least until the Gulf War – of a solid bloc of more or less self-confident pro-western Arab states, no longer having to look over their shoulders at what their critics would make of the plight of the landless Palestinians.

Finally, in Africa – where, as in the Middle East, Britain was not just another player in the great game, but a country with historic links and a distinct, if not always favourable, image – it was the future of South Africa which dominated all discussion. For reasons which will become clear, no one had a better opportunity – or a more thankless task – than I did in resolving an issue which had poisoned the West's relations with black Africa, left isolated the most advanced economic power in that continent and been used, incidentally, to justify more hypocrisy and hyperbole than I heard on any other subject.

China

My visit to China in September 1982 and my talks with Zhao Ziyang and Deng Xiaoping had had three beneficial effects. First, confidence in Hong Kong about the future had been restored. Second, I now had a very clear idea of what the Chinese would and would not accept. Third, we had a form of words which both we and the Chinese could use about the future of Hong Kong which would provide a basis for continuing discussion between us. But there was a real risk that each of these gains would be transitory. And – what I found most worrying – the Chinese proved very reluctant to get on with the talks which I had envisaged when I left Peking.

On the morning of Friday 28 January 1983 I held a meeting with ministers, officials and the Governor of Hong Kong to review the position. We had learnt that in June the Chinese were proposing unilaterally to announce their own plan for Hong Kong's future. We were all agreed that we must try to prevent this happening. I proposed that in the absence of progress in the talks we should now develop the democratic structure in Hong Kong as though it were our aim to achieve independence or self-government, as we had done with Singapore. This would involve building up a more Chinese government and administration in Hong Kong, with the Chinese members increasingly taking their own decisions and with

Britain in an increasingly subordinate position. We might also consider using referenda as an accepted institution there. Since then legislative elections have demonstrated a strong appetite for democracy among the Hong Kong Chinese, to which the Government has had to respond. At that time, however, nobody else seemed much attracted by my ideas, but I could not just leave things as they were, so in March 1983 I sent a private letter to Zhao Ziyang which broke the deadlock and got Anglo-Chinese talks off the ground again. In Peking I had told Mr Deng that I would be prepared to consider making recommendations to Parliament about Hong Kong's sovereignty if suitable arrangements could be made to preserve its stability and prosperity. I now subtly strengthened the formulation:

> Provided that agreement could be reached between the British and Chinese Government on administrative arrangements for Hong Kong which would guarantee the future prosperity and stability of Hong Kong, and would be acceptable to the British Parliament and to the people of Hong Kong as well as to the Chinese Government, I *would be prepared to recommend* to Parliament that sovereignty over the whole of Hong Kong should revert to China. [my italics]

Geoffrey Howe and the Foreign Office argued strongly that I should concede early in the talks that British administration would not continue. I saw no reason to make such a concession. I wanted to use every bargaining card we had to maximum effect. Just how few such cards there were, however, quickly became apparent.

There were three rounds of talks over the summer and when we took stock of the situation at a meeting on Monday 5 September it was clear that the talks would break down when they resumed on 22 September unless we conceded administration as well as sovereignty to the Chinese. One particular problem was that the timing of the talks was publicly known and it had become the practice at the end of each session to announce the date of the next. If the Chinese decided to hold up progress or break off altogether it would immediately become apparent and damage would be done to confidence in Hong Kong.

This is indeed what happened after the 22–23 September talks. Intensified Chinese propaganda and anxiety at the absence of any reassuring element in the official communiqué caused a massive capital flight out of the Hong Kong dollar and a sharp fall in its value on the foreign exchanges.

Early on Sunday morning, 25 September, I received a telephone call from Alan Walters, who was then in Washington and had been unable to track down either Nigel Lawson or the Governor of the Bank of England. Alan was convinced that the only way to prevent a complete collapse of the currency and all the serious political consequences that entailed was to restore the currency board system – backing the Hong Kong dollar at a par value with the United States dollar. Although I was largely convinced and accepted the urgent need for action, I still had some concerns – mainly whether our exchange reserves would be put at risk. But I informed the Treasury of what I considered was a dangerous crisis that needed immediate defusing, and they got in touch with Nigel and the Governor of the Bank. The following Tuesday I met Nigel, the Governor and Alan at the Washington embassy. Although Nigel was at first reluctant and the Governor had reservations, they eventually agreed with me that a restoration of the currency board was the only solution. As always this news soon leaked out to financial markets, confidence was restored and the crisis of the Hong Kong dollar was over.

On 14 October I sent a message to Zhao Ziyang expressing our willingness to explore Chinese ideas for the future of Hong Kong and holding out the possibility of a settlement on those lines. I had by now reluctantly decided that we would have to concede not just sovereignty but administration to the Chinese. On 19 October the talks were accordingly resumed and in November I authorized that working papers on the legal system, financial system and external economic relations of Hong Kong be handed over to the Chinese. But their position hardened. They now made it clear that they were not prepared to sign a treaty with us at all but rather to declare 'policy objectives' for Hong Kong themselves. By now I had abandoned any hope of turning Hong Kong into a self-governing territory. The overriding objective had to be to avoid a breakdown in the negotiations, so I authorized our ambassador in Peking to spell out more clearly the implications of my 14 October letter: that we envisaged no link of authority or accountability between Britain and Hong Kong after 1997. But I felt depressed.

The single most difficult issue which we now faced in negotiations with the Chinese was the location of the 'Joint Liaison Group' which would be established after the planned Anglo-Chinese Agreement had been signed to make provision for the transition. I was worried that during the transition this body would become an alternative power centre to the Governor or, worse, that it would create the impression of some kind of Anglo-Chinese 'Condominium' which would have destroyed confidence. But I also insisted that it should continue for three years after 1997 so as to maintain confidence after the handover of administration had taken place. Geoffrey Howe had visited Peking in April and now returned in July. He successfully reached a compromise on the Joint Liaison Group, which would not operate in Hong Kong before 1988.

The terms had three main advantages. First, they constituted what would be an unequivocally binding international agreement. Second, they were sufficiently clear and detailed about what would happen in Hong Kong after 1997 to command the confidence of the people of Hong Kong. Third, there was a provision that the terms of the proposed Anglo-Chinese Agreement would be stipulated in the Basic Law to be passed by the Chinese People's Congress: this would in effect be the constitution of Hong Kong after 1997.

My visit to China in December to sign the Joint Agreement on Hong Kong was a much less tense occasion than my visit two years earlier, but the crucial meeting was with Deng Xiaoping. The most important immediate guarantee of Hong Kong's future was Mr Deng's goodwill. I told him that the 'stroke of genius' in the negotiations had been his concept of 'one country, two systems'. He, with becoming modesty, attributed the credit for this to Marxist historical dialectics, or to use what appeared to be the appropriate slogan, 'seeking truth from the facts'.

The Chinese had set out in the agreement a fifty-year period after 1997 for its duration. I was intrigued by this and asked why fifty years. Mr Deng said that China hoped to approach the economic level of advanced countries by the end of that time. If China wanted to develop herself, she had to be open to the outside world for the whole of that period. The maintenance of Hong Kong's stability and prosperity accorded with China's interest in modernizing its economy. This did not mean that in fifty years China would be a capitalist country. Far from it. The one billion Chinese on the mainland would pursue socialism firmly. If Taiwan and Hong Kong practised capitalism that would not affect the socialist orientation of the bulk of the country. Indeed, the practice of capitalism in some small areas would benefit socialism. (Since then, it has become clear that Chinese socialism is whatever the Chinese Government does; and what it has been doing amounts to a thoroughgoing embrace of capitalism. In economic policy, at least, Mr Deng has indeed sought truth from facts.)

I found his analysis basically reassuring, if not persuasive. It was reassuring because it suggested that the Chinese would for their own self-interest seek to keep Hong Kong prosperous. It was unpersuasive for quite different reasons. The Chinese belief that the benefits of a liberal economic system can be had without a liberal political system seems to me false in the long term. The crackdown after the Tiananmen Square massacre in June 1989 convinced many outside observers that in China political and economic liberty were not interdependent. Certainly, after those terrible events we reassessed what needed to be done to secure Hong Kong's future. I was reinforced in my determination to honour Britain's obligations to those on whom British administration and Hong Kong's prosperity depended up to 1997. In any case, I always felt Britain would benefit economically from talented, entrepreneurial Hong Kong people coming here.

So in 1990 we legislated to give British citizenship to 50,000 key people in the Colony and their dependants – though the essential purpose of the scheme was to provide sufficient reassurance to persuade them to stay at their posts in Hong Kong where they were vitally needed. We were also brought under strong pressure immediately to accelerate the process of democratization in Hong Kong. But all my instincts told me that this was the wrong time. The Chinese leadership was feeling acutely apprehensive. Such a step at that moment could have provoked a strong defensive reaction that might have undermined the Hong Kong Agreement. We needed to wait for calmer times before considering moves towards democratization within the scope of the agreement.

At some point the increasing momentum of economic change in China will lead to political change. Keeping open the channels of trade and communication, while firmly pressing for human rights in China to be upheld, are the best means of ensuring that this great military power, on the verge of becoming a great economic power, becomes also a reliable and predictable member of the international community.

The Middle East

Little progress was made during my time as Prime Minister in solving the Arab-Israeli dispute. It is important, though, to be clear about what such a 'solution' can and cannot be. The likelihood of a total change of heart among those concerned is minimal. Nor will outside influences ever be entirely removed from the region. The United States, which was the power most responsible for the establishment of the state of Israel, will and must always stand behind Israel's security. It is equally right that the Palestinians should be restored in their land and dignity: and, as often happens in my experience, what is morally right eventually turns out to be politically expedient. Removing the Palestinian grievance is a necessary condition for cutting the cancer of Middle East terrorism out by the roots. The only way this can happen is for Israel to exchange 'land for peace', returning occupied territories to the Palestinians in exchange for credible undertakings to respect Israel's security. During my time as Prime Minister all initiatives eventually foundered on the fact that the two sides ultimately saw no need to adjust their stance. But that did not mean that we could simply sit back and let events take their course.

In September 1985 I visited the two key moderate Arab states, Egypt and Jordan. President Mubarak of Egypt had continued to pursue, though with greater circumspection, the policies of his assassinated predecessor, Anwar Sadat. King Hussein of Jordan had put forward a proposal for an international peace conference, as a prelude to which US Ambassador Murphy was to meet a joint Jordanian-Palestinian delegation. The Egyptians were keen to see the Jordanian initiative succeed. But the sticking point was which Palestinian representatives would be acceptable to the Americans, who would have nothing directly to do with the PLO. President Mubarak felt that the Americans were not being sufficiently positive. I had some sympathy for this point of view, though I restated what I said was a cardinal principle for the US, as for Britain, that we would not agree to talks with those who practised terrorism. I felt that President Mubarak and I understood one another. He was a large personality, persuasive and direct – the sort of man who could be one of the key players in a settlement.

We arrived on the evening of Wednesday 18 September in Amman. I already knew King Hussein well and liked him. Like President Mubarak, but more so, King Hussein was vexed with the Americans, believing that, having encouraged him to take a peace initiative, they were now drawing back under domestic Jewish pressure. I understood what he felt. He had been taking a real risk in trying to promote his initiative and I thought he deserved more support. I wanted to do what I could to help. So when the King told me that two leading PLO supporters would be prepared publicly to renounce terrorism and accept UNSCR 242 I said that if they would do this, I would meet them in London. I announced this at my press conference. It would have been the first meeting between a British minister and representatives of the PLO. When they arrived in London, I checked to see if they were still prepared to adhere to these conditions. One did. But the other could not: he was afraid for his life. So I could not see them. I am glad to say that King Hussein supported me in that decision. But it demonstrated how treacherous these waters were.

Before leaving Jordan I was taken out to see a Palestinian refugee camp. Denis used to say to me that these camps always tore his heart out. This was no exception. It was clean, well organized, orderly – and utterly hopeless. It was in effect run by the PLO who had, of course, a vested interest in making such camps a permanent recruiting ground for their revolutionary struggle. The most talented and educated Palestinians would not remain long there, preferring to join the Palestinian diaspora all over the Arab world.

I had been to Israel several times before I became Prime Minister; and each time I visited what for the world's three great religions is 'the Holy Land' it made an indelible impression. Anyone who has been to Jerusalem will understand why General Allenby, on taking the city from the Turks, dismounted to enter it on foot, as a mark of respect.

I have enormous admiration for the Jewish people, inside or outside Israel. There have always been Jewish members of my staff and indeed my Cabinet. In fact I just wanted a Cabinet of clever, energetic people – and frequently that turned out to be the same thing. My old constituency of Finchley has a large Jewish population. In the thirty-three years I represented it I never had a Jew come in poverty and desperation to one of my constituency surgeries. They had always been looked after by their own community.

I believe in what are often referred to as 'Judaeo-Christian' values: indeed, my whole political philosophy is based on them. But I have always been wary of falling into the trap of equating in some way the Jewish and Christian faiths. I do not, as a Christian, believe that the Old Testament – the history of the Law – can be fully understood without the New Testament – the history of Mercy. But I often wished that Christian leaders would take a leaf out of the teaching of Britain's wonderful former Chief Rabbi, Immanuel Jakobovits, and indeed that Christians themselves would take closer note of the Jewish emphasis on self-help and acceptance of personal responsibility. On top of all that, the political and economic construction of Israel against huge odds and bitter adversaries is one of the heroic sagas of our age. They really made 'the desert bloom'. I only wished that Israeli emphasis on the human rights of the Russian *refuseniks* was matched by proper appreciation of the plight of landless and stateless Palestinians.

The Israelis knew when I arrived in May 1986 that they were dealing with someone who harboured no lurking hostility towards them, who understood their anxieties, but who was not going to pursue an unqualified Zionist approach. Above all, I could be assured of respect for having stood up to terrorism at home and abroad. So if anyone was in a good position to speak some home truths without too much fear of being misunderstood it was I.

I was looking forward to seeing Prime Minister Shimon Peres again. I knew him to be sincere, intelligent and reasonable. It was a great pity that he would shortly hand over the premiership to the hardline Yitzhak Shamir. Both Mr Peres and I wondered in the light of past history how people would react to seeing the Union Jack and the Star of David flying side by side. But we need not have worried. I arrived to be greeted by welcoming crowds at Tel Aviv, and was driven up to Jerusalem to stay at the King David Hotel – so full of associations for all British people.* Outside the hotel even larger crowds were cheering in the darkness. I insisted on getting out of the car to see them, which threw the security men into a fit of agitation. But it was worth it: the people were delighted.

I breakfasted the following morning with Teddy Kollek, the Mayor of Jerusalem who combined a warm humanity with formidable administrative zeal and – a still more valuable combination – loyalty to his own people with a sympathetic understanding of the problems of the Arabs. The whole day – Sunday 25 May – was full of evocative demonstrations of Israel's history and identity. Naturally, I attended the Yad Vashem Memorial to the Holocaust: as on every occasion, I came out numb with shock that human beings could sink to such depravity.

I went on to a meeting with Mr Shamir. This was a hard man, though undoubtedly a man of principle, whose past had left scars on his personality. There was no hostility between us: but it was clear that there was no possibility of Mr Shamir giving up 'land for peace' and the Jewish settlements on the West Bank would continue to go ahead.

I believed that the real challenge was to strengthen moderate Palestinians, probably in association with Jordan, who would eventually push aside the PLO extremists. But this would never happen if Israel did not encourage it. I also believed that there should be local elections on the West Bank. But at that time one of the strongest opponents of conces-

---

* On 22 July 1946 91 people were killed when the hotel was bombed by Jewish terrorists from a group led by Menachem Begin.

sions on this – or anything else it seemed – was the then Defence minister, Mr Rabin, with whom I had breakfast on Monday. He proceeded to read out his views to me for forty minutes with barely time for a bite of toast.

But I was not to be put off. I repeated my proposals for local elections in a speech that afternoon to a group of Israeli MPs at the Knesset – the Israeli Parliament – chaired by the eloquent and respected Abba Eban.

Later I went to a dinner with carefully selected moderate Palestinians – mostly businessmen and academics – of precisely the sort I felt the Israelis should be prepared to deal with. They poured out their complaints, particularly about their treatment on the West Bank and especially in Gaza, where conditions were worst, partly because of insensitive security policing and partly, it seemed, because of economic discrimination in favour of Jewish business. I promised to take these matters up with Mr Peres – and did so in detail the following day – but I also made clear to them the need to reject terrorism and those who practised it. Although the general view was that only the PLO were able to represent the Palestinians, I also detected in conversations with smaller groups that this did not mean that there was any great love for that organization.

During my visit I had two long discussions with Mr Peres. He was conscious of the need to keep King Hussein's now faltering peace initiative in play, not least so as to avoid destabilizing Jordan itself. But he was obviously highly sceptical about the proposal for an international peace conference and I did not come away with any real optimism. In fact, the succession of Mr Shamir as Prime Minister would soon seal off even these few shafts of light.

On Tuesday on my way to the airport for my return flight I stopped at Ramat Gan, a suburb of Tel Aviv that was twinned with Finchley. I had expected that I would be meeting the mayor and a few other dignitaries, perhaps some old acquaintances. Instead, 25,000 people were awaiting me. I was plunged into – at times, to the horror of my detectives and staff, almost sank into – a huge crowd of cheering residents, before being squeezed through and onto a large platform from which I had to give an unscripted speech – always the best. Later, during the Gulf War, scud missiles from Iraq fell on Ramat Gan. The people of Finchley raised money to rebuild the houses that had been destroyed. This, I thought, was what 'twinning' should be all about.

South Africa

I no more shared the established Foreign Office view of Africa than I did of the Middle East. The basic, if usually unstated, assumption seemed to be that Britain's national interests required that we should ultimately be prepared to go along with the opinions of the radical black African states in the Commonwealth. In fact, a clear-sighted analysis suggested something rather different.

Admitted that fundamental changes must be made in South Africa's system, the question was of how best to achieve them. It seemed to me that the worst approach was to isolate South Africa further. It was absurd to believe that the governing Afrikaner class would be prepared to relinquish power suddenly or without acceptable safeguards. Indeed, had that occurred the result would have been anarchy in which black South Africans would have suffered most. Nor could the latter be considered a homogeneous group. Tribal loyalties were of great importance. Any new political framework for South Africa had to take account of such differences. Not least because of these complexities, I did not believe that it was for outsiders to impose a particular solution. What I wanted to achieve was step-by-step reform – with more democracy, secure human rights, and a flourishing free enterprise economy able to generate the wealth to improve black living standards. I wanted to see a South Africa which was fully reintegrated into the international community.

It was also true that Britain had important trading interests in the continent and that these were more or less equal in black Africa on the one hand and South Africa on the other. South Africa had by far the richest and most varied range of natural resources of any African country. It was the world's largest supplier of gold, platinum, gem diamonds, chrome, vanadium, manganese and other vital materials. Moreover, in a number of these cases South Africa's only real rival was the Soviet Union. Even if it had been morally acceptable to pursue a policy which would have led to the collapse of South Africa, it would not therefore have made strategic sense.

South Africa was rich not just because of natural resources but because its economy was at least mainly run on free enterprise lines. Other African countries, well endowed with natural resources, were still poor because their economies were socialist and centrally controlled. Consequently, the blacks in South Africa had higher incomes and were generally better educated than elsewhere in Africa: that was why the South Africans erected security fences to keep intended immigrants out, unlike the

Berlin Wall which kept those blessed with a socialist system in. But simply because I recognized these facts did not mean that I held any brief for apartheid. The colour of someone's skin should not determine his or her political rights.

President P.W. Botha was to visit Europe on the occasion of the fortieth anniversary of the Normandy Landings and I sent him an invitation to come to see me at Chequers. He had a whole programme of visits in Europe, made possible by an agreement that he had reached earlier in the year with President Machel of Mozambique which seemed a promising development to many European states. Nevertheless, my invitation provoked accusations that I was 'soft' on apartheid. On Wednesday 30 May Bishop Trevor Huddleston, the veteran anti-apartheid campaigner, came to Downing Street to put the case against my seeing Mr Botha. His argument was that the South African President should not be accorded credibility as a man of peace and that South Africa should not be allowed to re-enter the international community until it changed its internal policies. This seemed to me to miss the point. It was South Africa's isolation which was an obstacle to reform. Before his European trip, the only country that Mr Botha had visited in recent years was Taiwan.

President Botha came to Chequers on the morning of Saturday 2 June. I had a private conversation with him which lasted some forty minutes and then I was joined over lunch by Geoffrey Howe, Malcolm Rifkind and officials – the South African President by his Foreign minister R.F. ('Pik') Botha. President Botha told me that South Africa never received any credit for the improvements which had been made in the conditions of the blacks. Although there was some truth in this, I had to tell him also how appalled we were by the forced removal of blacks from areas which had been designated for white residents only. I went on to raise the case of the imprisoned Nelson Mandela whose freedom we had persistently sought. It was my view, moreover, that no long-term solution to South Africa's problems could be achieved without his co-operation. But the main discussion concentrated on Namibia, the former South African colony, where South Africa had reimposed direct rule the previous year. Our policy was to support Namibian independence. There was little progress here: South Africa had no intention of allowing Namibia to become independent while Cuban troops remained in Angola, but there was no prospect of Cuban withdrawal until civil war ended in Angola – which at the time seemed a forlorn hope.

The year 1985 was one of mounting crisis for South Africa. There was widespread rioting. A state of emergency was declared in many parts of the country. Foreign banks refused to renew South African credit and the South African Government declared a four-month freeze on the repayment of the principal of foreign debt. The international pressure on South Africa continued to mount. President Reagan, who was as opposed to economic sanctions as I was, introduced a limited package of sanctions to forestall pressure from Congress. It was clear that the Commonwealth Heads of Government Meeting in the Bahamas at Nassau that October would be a difficult one for me.

Bob Hawke, the Australian Prime Minister, opened the conference debate on South Africa, obviously seeking a compromise. Kenneth Kaunda, the President of Zambia, followed with an emotional call for sanctions. I tried to meet both points of view in my reply. I began by detailing the evidence of social and economic change in South Africa. I carefully cited the number of black South Africans who had professional qualifications, who had cars, who were in business. Of course, there was a long way to go. But we were not faced with a static situation. The speech had an effect, as I saw from the reactions of those around the table. But natural caution had led me to have a fall-back position prepared which I would take with me to the heads of government retreat over the weekend at Lyford Cay, where I knew that the real business would be done.

Lyford Cay is a beautiful spot with interesting historical associations. Private houses in the estate had been made available for the delegations. In a rather nice touch the Prime Minister of the Bahamas had seen that the house allocated to me and my delegation was the one where the Polaris agreement had been signed by Harold Macmillan and John Kennedy in 1962. At Lyford Cay a drafting committee of heads of government was formed and in the course of Saturday morning drew up a draft communiqué on South Africa. Meanwhile I got on with other work. At 2 o'clock Brian Mulroney, Prime Minister of Canada, and Rajiv Gandhi, the Prime Minister of India, arrived at the house to show me their best efforts. I spent the best part of two hours explaining why their proposals were unacceptable. I suggested that the text should include a firm call for an end to violence in South Africa as a condition for further dialogue: but this they considered far too controversial.

After dinner I was invited to join a wider group and put under great pressure to agree to the line they wanted. Bob Hawke bitterly attacked me.

I replied with vigour. In a steadily worsening atmosphere, the argument went on for some three hours. Fortunately, I can never be defeated by attrition.

Overnight, I had officials prepare an alternative text to be presented at the plenary session due to begin at 10.30 next morning, before which a dejected Sonny Ramphal, the Commonwealth Secretary-General, begged me to compromise and show goodwill. There was certainly not much goodwill evident when the meeting began. The British text was not even considered. I was lectured on my political morality, on my preferring British jobs to black lives, on my lack of concern for human rights. One after the other, their accusations became more vitriolic and personal until I could stand it no longer.

To their palpable alarm I began to tell my African critics a few home truths. I noted that they were busily trading with South Africa at the same time as they were attacking me for refusing to apply sanctions. I wondered when they intended to show similar concern about abuses in the Soviet Union, with which of course they often had not just trade but close political links. I wondered when I was going to hear them attack terrorism. I reminded them of their own less than impressive record on human rights. And when the representative from Uganda took me to task for racial discrimination, I turned on him and reminded him of the Asians which Uganda had thrown out on racial grounds, many of whom had come to settle in my constituency in North London, where they were model citizens and doing very well. No one spoke for my position, though President Jayewardene of Sri Lanka caused something of a ripple when he said that in any case he had no intention of ending trade links with South Africa because it would throw the Sri Lankan tea planters out of work. The heads of government of some of the smaller states also told me privately that they agreed with me.

Over the lunch break I made a tactical decision as to which of the prepared options I would concede. My modest choice was to take unilateral action against the import of krugerrands and withdraw official support for trade promotion with South Africa. I would only do this, however, if there was a clear reference in the communiqué to the need to stop the violence. Then, at 3.30 p.m. I went to join the 'drafting committee' in the library.

As I entered the room they all glared at me. It was extraordinary how the pack instinct of politicians could change a group of normally courteous people into a gang of bullies. I had never been treated like this and I was not going to stand for it. So I began by saying that I had never been so insulted as I had been by the people in that room and that it was an entirely unacceptable way of conducting international business. At once the murmurs of surprise and regret rose: one by one they protested that it was not 'personal'. I answered that it clearly was personal and I wasn't having it. The atmosphere immediately became more subdued. They asked me what I would accept. I announced the concessions I was prepared to make. I said that this was as far as I was going: if my proposals were not accepted I would withdraw and the United Kingdom would issue its own statement. The 'draftsmen' went into a huddle. Ten minutes later it was all over. I suddenly became a stateswoman for having accepted a 'compromise'. A text was agreed and at a plenary session later that evening was accepted without amendment.

Though I was genuinely hurt and dismayed by the behaviour I had witnessed, I was not displeased with the outcome. In particular, I was glad that the Commonwealth heads of government endorsed an idea with which several of us had been toying – the sending of a group of 'eminent persons' to South Africa to report back on the situation to a future conference. This had the great merit of giving us time – both to press the South Africans for further reform and to fight the diplomatic battle. I sought to persuade Geoffrey Howe to be an 'eminent person' but he was most reluctant to do so. He probably rated its chances of success as poor, and events proved him right. I may, myself, have been less than tactful. For when he protested that he was Foreign Secretary and could not do both jobs, I said that I could just about cope with his as well while he was away. Since by now I was firmly in charge of our approach to South Africa, making the main decisions directly from No. 10, that may have been close to the bone. One advantage of those eventually chosen as members of the 'Eminent Persons Group' was that a distinguished black African, the Nigerian General Obasanjo, would act as chairman of the group and would see for himself what the reality of life in South Africa was. But this advantage was more than cancelled out by the problems created by Malcolm Fraser, still full of rancour at his election defeat by Bob Hawke, longing to achieve a high international profile once more and consequently making a thoroughly 'eminent person' of himself.

At the press conference after the summit I described, with complete accuracy, the concessions I had made on sanctions as 'tiny', which enraged the Left and undoubtedly irritated the Foreign Office. But I did not believe in sanctions and I was not prepared to justify them. I was able to leave the shores of Nassau with my policy intact, albeit with my personal relations with Commonwealth leaders somewhat bruised: but that, after all, was not entirely my fault. And there were thousands of black Africans who would keep their jobs because of the battle I had fought.

The 'eminent persons' visit to southern Africa was an unmitigated disaster. Whether to scupper the initiative or for quite unconnected reasons, the South African armed forces launched raids against African National Congress (ANC) bases in Botswana, Zambia and Zimbabwe and the EPG cut short their visit.

This gave me a very difficult hand to play at the European Council meeting at The Hague in June 1986 – and because the actions of European Community countries, unlike most Commonwealth members, could have a real impact on the South African economy this was at least as important a forum for the sanctions issue as was CHOGM. The Dutch themselves – the Netherlands having been the original home of the Afrikaners – suffered from a pervasive guilt complex about South Africa, which did not make them ideal chairmen. In the end we agreed to consider introducing later in the year a ban on new investment and sanctions on imports of South African coal, iron, steel and krugerrands. But it was also agreed that Geoffrey Howe should, as a sort of lone 'eminent person' and in view of the fact that Britain would shortly be taking on the presidency of the Community, visit South Africa to press for reform and the release of Nelson Mandela.

Geoffrey was extremely reluctant to go and it must be said that his reluctance proved justified since he was insulted by President Kaunda and brushed off by President Botha. I later learned that he thought I had set him up for an impossible mission and was deeply angry about it. I can only say that I had no such intention. I had a real admiration for Geoffrey's talent for quiet diplomacy. If anyone could have made a breakthrough he would have done it.

Shortly after Geoffrey's return I had to face the Special Commonwealth Conference on South Africa which we had agreed at Lyford Cay to review progress. It had been decided that seven Commonwealth heads of government would meet in London in August. The worst aspect was that because of President P.W. Botha's obstinacy we did not have enough to show by way of progress since the Nassau CHOGM. There had been some significant reforms and the partial state of emergency had been lifted in March. But a nationwide state of emergency had been imposed in June,

Mr Mandela was still in prison, and the ANC and other similar organizations were still banned.

The media and the Opposition were by now quite obsessive about South Africa. There was talk of the Commonwealth breaking up if Britain did not change its position on sanctions, though there was never any likelihood of either event. I was always convinced – and my postbag showed – that the views and priorities of these commentators were quite unrepresentative of what the general public felt.

My meetings with heads of government before the official opening filled me with gloom. Brian Mulroney urged me to have Britain 'give a lead' and seemed to want me to reveal my negotiating hand to him in advance: but this I had no intention of doing. Kenneth Kaunda was in a thoroughly self-righteous and uncooperative frame of mind when I dropped in to see him at his hotel. He predicted that if sanctions were not applied, South Africa would go up in flames. Later I told Rajiv Gandhi that I would be prepared to move 'a little' at the conference. He seemed rather more amenable than he had been at Nassau, as indeed he usually was in private.

In fact, the formal discussions were every bit as unpleasant as at Lyford Cay. My refusal to go along with the sanctions they wanted was attacked by Messrs Kaunda, Mugabe, Mulroney and Hawke. I found no support. Their proposals went well beyond what had been proposed the previous year. At Nassau they had wanted to cut off air links with South Africa, to introduce a ban on investment, agricultural imports, the promotion of tourism and other measures. Now they were demanding a whole raft of additional measures: a ban on new bank loans, imports of uranium, coal, iron and steel and the withdrawal of consular facilities. Such a package sacrificed the living standards of South Africa's black population to the posturing of South Africa's critics and the interests of their domestic industries. I was simply not prepared to endorse it. Instead, I had a separate paragraph inserted into the communiqué detailing our own approach which noted our willingness to go along with a ban on South African coal, iron and steel imports, if the European Community decided on it, and to introduce straight away voluntary bans on new investment and the promotion of tourism in South Africa. In the event we in the Community decided against the sanctions on coal, to which the Germans were particularly strongly opposed, though the other sanctions proposed at The Hague were introduced in September 1986.

Perhaps the most extraordinary feature of these discussions was that they seemed to be carried on without regard to what was happening in

South Africa itself. As I was informed by our excellent new ambassador, Robin Renwick, and by others who had dealings with the real rather than the bogus South Africa, fundamental changes were taking place. Black trade unions had been legalized, the Mixed Marriages Act had been repealed, influx controls had been abolished and the general policy (though not without exceptions) of forced removals of blacks had ended. So had job reservation for whites and the very unpopular pass laws. Still more important, there was a practical breakdown of apartheid at the workplace, in hotels, in offices and in city centres. The repeal of the Separate Amenities Act had been proposed and seemed likely to be implemented. In all these ways 'apartheid', as the Left continued to describe it, was rapidly dying. Yet South Africa received no credit for this, only unthinking hostility.

I was less prepared than ever to go along with measures which would weaken the South African economy and thus slow down reform. So as the 1987 CHOGM at Vancouver approached I was still in no mood for compromise. In some respects the position was easier for me than it had been at Nassau and in London. Events in Fiji and in Sri Lanka were likely to occupy a good deal of attention at the conference. My line on sanctions was well known and the domestic pressure on me had decreased: I had made headway in winning the sanctions argument at home during the London conference.

In January 1989 Mr Botha suffered a stroke and was succeeded as National Party Leader by F.W. de Klerk, who became President in August. It was surely right to give the new South African leader the opportunity to make his mark without ham-fisted outside intervention.

The 1989 CHOGM was due to take place in October in Kuala Lumpur, hosted by Dr Mahathir. I went there with a new Foreign Secretary, John Major, and a renewed determination not to go further down the path of sanctions. Introducing the session on the 'World Political Scene' I drew attention to the momentous changes occurring in the Soviet Union and their implications for all of us. I said that there was now the prospect of settling regional conflicts – not least those in Africa – which had been aggravated by the international subversion of communism. Throughout the world we must now ardently advocate democracy and a much freer economic system. I secretly hoped that the message would not be lost on the many illiberal, collectivist Commonwealth countries whose representatives were present.

But the debate on South Africa brought out all the old venom. Bob Hawke and Kenneth Kaunda argued the case for sanctions.

By now I was quite used to the vicious, personal attacks in which my Commonwealth colleagues liked to indulge. John Major was not: he found their behaviour quite shocking. I left him back in Kuala Lumpur with the other Foreign ministers to draft the communiqué while I and the other heads of government went off to our retreat in Langkawi. While I was there my officials faxed through a text which the Foreign ministers apparently thought we could all 'live with'. But I could only live with it if I also put out a separate unambiguous statement of our own views. I had it drafted and sent back to John Major in Kuala Lumpur. Contrary to what the press – almost as eager for 'splits' as they were for describing Britain's 'isolation' – subsequently alleged, John was quite happy to go along with issuing a separate British document and made some changes to it, which I agreed. The issue, however, of our separate document prompted howls of anger from the other heads of government.

In South Africa, as 1990 opened, the movement which I had hoped and worked for began. There were indications that Nelson Mandela would shortly be released. I told the Foreign Office – who did not like it one bit – that as soon as Mr Mandela was freed I wanted us to respond rapidly by rescinding or relaxing the measures we had taken against South Africa, starting with the relatively minor ones which rested with us alone and did not have to be discussed with the European Community.

On 2 February 1990 President de Klerk made a speech which announced Mr Mandela's and other black leaders' imminent release, the unbanning of the ANC and other black political organizations and promised an end to the state of emergency as soon as possible. I immediately went back to the Foreign Office and said that once the promises were fulfilled we should end the 'voluntary' ban on investment and encourage the other European Community countries to do likewise. I asked Douglas Hurd – now Foreign Secretary – to propose to other Community Foreign ministers at his forthcoming meeting with them an end to the restrictions on purchase of krugerrands and iron and steel. I also decided to send messages to other heads of government urging practical recognition of what was happening in South Africa.

In April I was briefed by Dr Gerrit Viljoen, the South African Minister for Constitutional Development, on the contacts between the South African Government and the ANC, now effectively led once more by Mr Mandela. I was disappointed by the fact that Mr Mandela kept repeating the old ritual phrases, arguably suitable for a movement refused recognition, but not for one aspiring to a leading and perhaps dominant role in government. The South African Government was formulating its own ideas for the constitution and was moving towards a combination of a lower house elected by one-man one-vote with an upper chamber with special minority representation. This would help to accommodate the great ethnic diversity which characterizes South Africa, although in the long run some sort of cantonal system may be needed to do this efficiently.

By the time that President de Klerk set off for his talks with European leaders in May, discussions with the ANC had begun in earnest. I was also glad that the South African Government was paying due regard to Chief Buthelezi, who had been such a stalwart opponent of violent uprising in South Africa while the ANC had been endorsing the Marxist revolution, to which some of its members are still attached.

President de Klerk, Pik Botha and their wives came to talks and lunch at Chequers on Saturday 19 May. My talks with Mr de Klerk focused on his plans for the next steps in bringing the ANC to accept a political and economic system which would secure South Africa's future as a liberal, free enterprise country. The violence between blacks, which was to get worse, was already the single biggest obstacle to progress. But he was optimistic about the prospects for agreement with the ANC on a new constitution; and he thought that the ANC wanted this too.

We discussed what should be done about sanctions. He said that he was not like a dog begging for a biscuit, seeking specific rewards for actions he took. What he wanted was the widest possible international recognition of and support for what he was doing, leading to a fundamental revision of attitudes towards South Africa. This seemed to me very sensible. Mr de Klerk also invited me to South Africa. I said that I would love to come but I did not want to make things more difficult for him at this particular moment. There was, I knew, nothing more likely to sour his dealings with other governments who had been proved wrong about South Africa than for me to arrive in his country as a kind of proclamation that I had been right. (In fact, it is a disappointment to me that I was never to go to South Africa as Prime Minister and I only finally accepted his invitation after I left office.)

On Wednesday 4 July I held talks and had lunch at Downing Street with the other main player in South African politics, Nelson Mandela.

The Left were rather offended that he was prepared to see me at all. But then he, unlike them, had a shrewd view as to what kind of pressure for his release had been more successful. I found Mr Mandela supremely courteous, with a genuine nobility of bearing and – most remarkable after all he had suffered – without any bitterness. I warmed to him. But I also found him very outdated in his attitudes, stuck in a kind of socialist timewarp in which nothing had moved on, not least in economic think-ing, since the 1940s. Perhaps this was not surprising in view of his long years of imprisonment: but it was a disadvantage in the first few months of his freedom because he tended to repeat these outdated platitudes which in turn confirmed his followers in their exaggerated expectations.

It was only shortly before I left office that President de Klerk again came to see me at Chequers – on Sunday 14 October. There had been some progress since I had seen Mr Mandela in July. The ANC had agreed to suspend the 'armed struggle' and the two sides had agreed in principle on the arrangements for the return of South African exiles and the release of the rest of the political prisoners. The remaining features of the old apartheid system were being dismantled. The Land Acts were due to be repealed and the Population Registration Act – the last remaining legisla-tive pillar of apartheid – would go when a new constitution was agreed. Only state education remained segregated but movement on this – for the whites – very sensitive matter had begun. However, violence between blacks had sharply worsened and this was poisoning the atmosphere for negotiations.

The South Africans were being careful about pressing for the lifting of the remaining sanctions. The most important contribution to this would have been that of the ANC: but they stubbornly refused to recognize that the case for sanctions – to the extent it had ever existed – was dead. Within the European Community, the key to a formal change of policy now was Germany, but for domestic political reasons Chancellor Kohl was still unwilling to act. The Americans held back for similar reasons. (In fact, sanctions were gradually dismantled over the next few years: indeed the international community began to prepare financial aid for South Africa to undo the damage that sanctions had wrought.)

President de Klerk was clearly frustrated that the further round of informal talks with the ANC on the constitution for which he had been pressing had still not occurred. The main principle to which he held was that there must be power sharing in the Executive. In the new South Africa no one must have as much power as he himself had now. In some respects he thought that the Swiss Federal Cabinet was a guide to what was needed. This seemed to me to be very much on the right lines – not that either hybrid constitutions or federal systems have much inherent appeal, but in states where allegiances are at least as much to subordinate groups as to the overarching institutions of the state itself these things may constitute the least bad approach.

———◆◆◆———

CHAPTER THIRTY

Jeux Sans Frontières

Relations with the European Community 1984–1987

T HE WISDOM OF HINDSIGHT, so useful to historians and indeed to authors of memoirs, is sadly denied to practising politicians. Looking back, it is now possible to see the period of my second term as Prime Minister as that in which the European Community subtly but surely shifted its direction away from being a Community of open trade, light regulation and freely co-operating sovereign nation-states towards statism and centralism. I can only say that it did not seem like that at the time.

Now I see that the underlying forces of federalism and bureaucracy were gaining in strength as a coalition of Socialist and Christian Democrat governments in France, Spain, Italy and Germany forced the pace of integration and a commission, equipped with extra powers, began to manipulate them to advance its own agenda. It was only in my last days in office and under my successor that the true scale of the challenge had become clear. At this time I genuinely believed that once our budget contribution had been sorted out and we had set in place a framework of financial order, Britain would be able to play a strong positive role in the Community.

Crucial to this was the European Council to be held at Fontainebleau, outside Paris, on Monday 25 and Tuesday 26 June 1984. On the short flight to Orly I finalized our tactics. Geoffrey Howe and I shared the same analysis. We wanted an agreement on the budget at this meeting but only if it was close enough to our terms. I was prepared to accept, if necessary, a different formula from that which we advanced, but the money rebated must be enough and the arrangement had to be lasting.

I arrived at lunchtime at the Château of Fontainebleau to be met by President Mitterrand and a full guard of honour. The French know how to do these things properly. Lunch took place in the Château's Hall of Columns and then we went through into the Ballroom, which was heavily disguised by interpreters' booths, for the first session of the Council. Without any warning, President Mitterrand asked me to open the proceedings by summing up the results of the recent economic summit in London. Others then joined in to give their own views and two hours elapsed. I started to fidget. Were these just delaying tactics? At last we got on to the budget. Again I opened, demonstrating what I thought unsatisfactory about the other schemes which had been put forward to provide a solution, and argued for our own ideas of a formula. There was further discussion. Then President Mitterrand remitted the matter to the Foreign ministers to discuss later in the evening. Our meeting now returned to generalities, in particular President Mitterrand's lively account of his recent visit to Moscow.

That evening we drove back through the forest to our hotel at Barbizon. This little village attracts artists and gastronomes. Anyone who has eaten at the local Hôtellerie du Bas-Bréau will know why: the food was simply delicious.* As we drank our coffee, we saw that the Foreign ministers were taking theirs outside onto the terrace and naturally concluded that they had done their work. Far from it. President Mitterrand did not conceal his displeasure and the Foreign ministers quickly went inside again to get down to discussing the budget.

At about 11.30 p.m. M. Cheysson emerged to tell us that the Foreign ministers had 'clarified the points of difference'. In fact, the French had apparently managed to persuade the Foreign ministers to favour a rebate system giving us back a simple percentage of our net contribution. On such a percentage system there would be no link between net contributions and relative prosperity – unlike the 'threshold' system we had been arguing for.

But a percentage of what? The French proposed in calculating our contributions to take into account only those payments to the Community that Britain made under VAT. That formula, however, ignored the

---

* I am a great collector of menus. For the connoisseur I reproduce the menu for dinner on 25 June: *Assortiment de foie gras d'oie; Homard breton rôti, beurre Cancalais; Carré d'agneau aux petites girolles; Asperges tièdes; Fromages de la Brie et de Fontainebleau; Soufflé chaud aux framboises; Mignardises et fours frais.* All washed down with the finest wines.

considerable sums we also contributed through tariffs and levies. But in the end we had to accept the calculation.

And, finally, how big a percentage would the rebate be? I had in mind a figure of well over 70 per cent. But it seemed from the Foreign ministers' meeting that we were now likely to be offered at most something between 50 and 60 per cent with a temporary two-year sweetener that would bring the refund up to 1,000 million ecus a year for the first two years. How Geoffrey had allowed the Foreign ministers to reach such a conclusion I could not understand.

I was in despair. I told the heads of government I was not prepared to go back to talking about a temporary sum: if this was the best they had to offer the Fontainebleau Council would be a disaster.

Geoffrey, civil servants and I then met to discuss what should be done. Our officials set to work with their opposite numbers all through the night and into the early morning. As a result of their efforts, the next day began a great deal better than the previous one had ended.

President Mitterrand's and Chancellor Kohl's breakfast the following morning probably cleared the way for a settlement. President Mitterrand opened the formal session by saying that we must try for an agreement on the budget, but if we had not succeeded by lunchtime we should go on to other things. I made it clear that I was now ready to negotiate on the basis of a percentage agreement, but I held my ground for a figure of over 70 per cent. Quite soon, and sensibly, President Mitterrand adjourned the main session so that bilateral meetings could take place.

How hard should I hold out on the figure? I saw President Mitterrand and Chancellor Kohl separately. At this stage the French President would not move above 60 per cent. Chancellor Kohl would go as far as 65 per cent. I came to the conclusion that I could obtain a deal on the basis of a two-thirds refund. But I was determined to get the full 66 per cent. It was only when the full session resumed that I managed to do so. I said that it would be absurd to deny me my 1 percentage point. The French President smiled and said: 'Of course, Madame Prime Minister, you must have it.' And so the agreement was reached. Or almost. When the agreement was being drafted an attempt was made to exclude the costs of enlargement from this refund arrangement. I resisted this fiercely and won. The heads of government also agreed to release our 1983 refund.

At my press conference and at the time of my later statement to the House of Commons on the outcome of Fontainebleau there was some criticism that I had not got more. But the crucial achievement was to have gained a settlement which would last as long as the increased 'own resources' from the new 1.4 per cent VAT ceiling itself lasted. Of course, in a sense that was not 'permanent': but it meant that I would not have to go back every year to renegotiate the rebate until the new VAT limit ran out, and that when it did so I would be in just as strong a position as I had been at Fontainebleau to veto any extra 'own resources' unless I had a satisfactory deal on Britain's budget contribution. More generally, the resolution of this dispute meant that the Community could now press ahead both with the enlargement and with the Single Market measures which I wanted to see. In every negotiation there comes the best possible time to settle: this was it.

It had generally been expected that once we and the Germans had agreed to increase the Community's 'own resources' the admission of Spain and Portugal would run fairly smoothly. In fact it took two European Councils at Dublin and at Brussels to sort it out. The Irish having assumed the Community presidency, the Dublin Council was set for Monday 3 and Tuesday 4 December. I was always the odd 'man' out on such occasions simply because as the IRA's prime political target I had to be surrounded by especially tight security. I could barely venture out of Dublin Castle, where I would stay, helicoptering back and forth only as strictly necessary.

At least on this occasion it was not Britain but Greece which was marked out as the villain of the piece. The two outstanding issues as regards the terms for Spain's and Portugal's entry had turned out to be wine and fish, on both of which the Iberian countries were heavily dependent. The negotiations seemed to be nearing a mutually satisfactory conclusion. It was at this point that Mr Papandreou, the left-wing Greek Prime Minister, now intervened, effectively vetoing enlargement unless he received an undertaking that Greece should be given huge sums over the next six years. The occasion for this arose as a result of discussions which had been going on for some time about an 'Integrated Mediterranean Programme' of assistance, from which Greece would be the main beneficiary. It seems that the Greeks' appetite had been further whetted by unauthorized discussion of large sums within the Commission. Mr Papandreou's statement threw the Council into disarray. Everyone resented not just the fact that Greece was holding us to ransom, but still more the fact that, though Greece had been accepted into the Community precisely to entrench its restored democracy, the Greeks would not now allow the Community to do exactly the same for the former dictatorships of Spain and Portugal.

As it happened I talked to Sr Felipe González, the Spanish Prime Minister, when we were both in Moscow for Mr Chernenko's funeral the following March. Sr González, whom I liked personally however much I disagreed with his socialism, was indignant about the terms being offered Spain for entry into the Community. I had a good deal of sympathy with him but I cautioned Sr González against holding out for better terms, which I doubted he would get. I said it was better to argue the case from within. For whatever reason, he accepted the advice and at the otherwise fairly uneventful Brussels Council the following month, chaired by Italy, negotiations for the entry of Spain and Portugal were effectively completed. There would be a special bonus to Britain in having Spain in because she would over time have to dismantle discriminatory tariffs against our car imports, which had long been a source of irritation in the motor industry.

But the Greek Danegeld had to be paid. I was alone in Brussels in arguing vigorously against the size of the bill we were presented for the 'Integrated Mediterranean Programmes'.

At Brussels I also launched an initiative on deregulation designed to provide impetus to the Community's development as a free trade and free enterprise area. It was intended to fit in with our own economic policy: I have never understood why some Conservatives seem to accept that free markets are right for Britain but are prepared to accept *dirigisme* when it comes wrapped in the European flag. I noted that the Treaty of Rome was a charter for economic liberty and we must not allow ourselves to change it into a charter for thousands of minor regulations. We should seek to cut the bureaucracy on business and see that labour markets worked properly so as to create jobs. Some Community legislation had been amended up to forty times: we should think what this meant for the small trader. I pointed to a large pile of directives in front of me on VAT and company law. There had been fifty-nine new regulations in 1984. Of these my three favourites were: a draft directive on sludge in agriculture; a draft directive on trade in mincemeat; and a draft directive amending the main regulation on the common organization of the market in goat meat.

I received a good deal of support for the initiative; but of course it was for the Commission – the source of the problem – to follow it through.

It was at Brussels that the new Commission was approved with M. Delors as its President. At the time, all that I knew was that M. Delors was extremely intelligent and energetic and had, as French Finance minister, been credited with reining back the initial left-wing socialist policies of President Mitterrand's Government and with putting French finances on a sounder footing.

I nominated Lord Cockfield as the new British European Commissioner. I was no longer able to find a place for him in the Cabinet and I thought that he would be effective in Brussels. He was. Arthur Cockfield was a natural technocrat of great ability and problem-solving outlook. Unfortunately, he tended to disregard the larger questions of politics – constitutional sovereignty, national sentiment and the promptings of liberty. He was the prisoner as well as the master of his subject. It was all too easy for him, therefore, to go native and to move from deregulating the market to re-regulating it under the rubric of harmonization. Alas, it was not long before my old friend and I were at odds.

In retrospect, the Dublin and Brussels summits had been an interlude between the two great issues which dominated Community politics in these years – the budget and the Single Market. The Single Market – which Britain pioneered – was intended to give real substance to the Treaty of Rome and to revive its liberal, free trade, deregulatory purpose. I realized how important it was to lay the groundwork in advance for this new stage in the Community's development. I hoped that a significant first step would be the paper which Geoffrey Howe and I worked up for the Milan Council, hosted and chaired by Italy, on Friday 28 and Saturday 29 June 1985. It covered four areas: the completion of the Common Market, strengthened political co-operation, improvements in decision-making and better exploitation of high technology. The most significant element was that dealing with 'political co-operation', which in normal English means foreign policy. The aim was closer co-operation between Community member states, which would nonetheless reserve the right of states to go their own way.

I was keen to secure agreement for our approach well before the Milan Council. So when Chancellor Kohl came to see me for an afternoon's talks at Chequers on Saturday 18 May I showed him the paper on political co-operation and said that we were thinking of tabling it for Milan. I said that what I wanted was something quite separate from the Treaty of Rome, basing co-operation on an intergovernmental agreement. Chancellor Kohl seemed pleased with our approach and in due course I also sent a copy to France. Imagine my surprise, then, when just before I was to go to Milan I learned that Germany and France had tabled their own paper, almost identical to ours. Such were the consequences of prior consultation.

The ill-feeling this created was an extraordinary achievement, given the fact that nearly all of us had come there with a view to proceeding in roughly the same direction. Matters were not helped by the chairmanship of the Italian Prime Minister, Bettino Craxi. Sig. Craxi, a socialist, and his Foreign minister, the Christian Democrat Sig. Andreotti, were political rivals but they shared a joint determination to call an Inter-Governmental Conference (IGC). Such a conference, which could be called by a simple majority vote, would be necessary if there were to be changes in the Treaty of Rome, which themselves, however, would have to be agreed by unanimity. An IGC seemed to me unnecessary (as I said) and dangerous (as I thought). Quite what the French and Germans wanted was unclear – beyond their desire for a separate treaty on political co-operation. They certainly wanted more moves towards European 'integration' in general and it had to be likely that they would want an IGC if one were attainable as – for reasons I shall explain shortly – it was. It is also possible that some kind of secret agreement had been reached on this before the Council began. Certainly when I had a bilateral meeting with Sig. Craxi early on Friday morning he could not have been more sweetly reasonable; an IGC was indeed mentioned as a possibility, but I made it very clear that I thought that the relevant decisions could largely be taken at the present Council without the postponement inevitable if a full IGC were to be called. I came away thinking how easy it had been to get my points across.

It was, in fact, Sig. Craxi himself as President who suggested at the Council that we should have an IGC. I argued that the Community had demonstrated that it did have the capacity to take decisions under the present arrangements and that we should now at the Milan Council agree upon the measures needed to make progress on the completion of the Common Market internally and political co-operation externally. There would, I granted, be a need for improved methods of decision-taking if these ends were to be met. I proposed that we agree now to greater use of the existing majority voting articles of the Rome Treaty, while requiring any member state which asked for a vote to be deferred to justify its decision publicly. I called for a reduction in the size of the Commission to twelve members. I also circulated a paper suggesting some modest ways in which the European Assembly might be made more effective. I suggested that the Luxemburg European Council, due to meet in December, should as necessary constitute itself as an IGC. There agreements could be signed and conclusions endorsed. But I did not see any case for a special IGC working away at treaty changes in the meantime.

But it was to no avail. I found myself being bulldozed by a majority which included a highly partisan chairman. I was not alone: Greece and Denmark joined me in opposing an IGC. Geoffrey Howe would have agreed to it. His willingness to compromise reflected partly his temperament, partly the Foreign Office's *déformation professionelle*. But it may also have reflected the fact that Britain's membership of the European Community gave the Foreign Office a voice in every aspect of policy that came under the Community. And the more the Community moved in a centralized direction the more influential the Foreign Office became in Whitehall. Inevitably, perhaps, Geoffrey had a slightly more accommodating view of federalism than I did.

To my astonishment and anger Sig. Craxi suddenly now called a vote and by a majority the Council resolved to establish an IGC. My time had been wasted. I would have to return to the House of Commons and explain why all of the high hopes which had been held of Milan had been dashed. And I had not even had an opportunity while there to go to the opera. Annoyed as I was with what had happened, I realized that we must make the best of it. I made it clear that we would take part in the IGC: I saw no merit in the alternative policy – practised for a time in earlier years by France – of the so-called 'empty chair'.

I had one overriding positive goal. This was to create a single Common Market. The price which we would have to pay to achieve a Single Market, with all its economic benefits, though, was more majority voting in the Community. There was no escape from that, because otherwise particular countries would succumb to domestic pressures and prevent the opening up of their markets. It also required more power for the European Commission: but that power must be used in order to create and maintain a Single Market, rather than to advance other objectives.

I knew that I would have to fight a strong rear-guard action against attempts to weaken Britain's own control over areas of vital national interest to us. I was not going to have majority voting applying, for example, to taxation which the Commission would have liked us to 'harmonize'. Competition between tax regimes is far healthier than the imposition of a single system. It forces governments to hold down government spending and taxation, and to limit the burden of regulations; and when they fail to do these things, it allows companies and taxpayers to move elsewhere. In any event, the ability to set one's own levels of taxation is a crucial element of national sovereignty. I was not prepared to give up our powers to control immigration (from non-EC countries), to combat terrorism, crime, and drug trafficking and to take measures on human, animal and plant health, keeping out carriers of dangerous diseases – all of which required proper frontier controls. There was, I felt, a perfectly practical argument for this: as an island – and one quite unused to the more authoritarian continental systems of identity cards and policing – it was natural that we should apply the necessary controls at our ports and airports rather than internally. Again, this was an essential matter of national sovereignty. I was prepared to go along with some modest increase in the powers of the European Assembly, which would shortly and somewhat inaccurately be described as a Parliament: but the Council of Ministers, representing governments answerable to national Parliaments, must always have the final say. Finally, I was going to resist any attempt to make treaty changes which would allow the Commission – and by majority vote the Council – to pile extra burdens on British businesses.

Right up to the beginning of the Luxemburg Council I thought that we could rely on the Germans to support us in opposing any mention of the European Monetary System (EMS) and economic and monetary union in the revisions of the treaty. Then, as now, however, there was an inherent tension between, on the one hand, the German desire to retain control over their own monetary policy to keep down inflation and, on the other, to demonstrate their European credentials by pressing further towards economic and monetary union.

I arrived in Luxemburg at 10 o'clock on Monday morning, 2 December 1985. The first session of the Council began soon afterwards. The heads of government went through the draft treaty – what would become the Single European Act – which the presidency and the Commission had drawn up. The ability of those present to argue at great length and with much repetition about matters of little interest was, as ever, astonishing. It would have been far better to have agreed on the principles and then let others deal with the details, referring back to us.

I was also dismayed that the Germans shifted their ground and said that they were now prepared to include monetary matters in the treaty. I was, however, able in a side discussion with Chancellor Kohl to reduce the formula to what I considered insignificant proportions which merely described the status quo, rather than set out new goals. This added to the phrase 'Economic and Monetary Union' the important gloss 'co-opera- tion in economic and monetary policy'. The former had been the official objective, unfortunately, since October 1972: the latter, I hoped, would signal the limits the act placed on it. But this formulation delayed M. Delors's drive to monetary union only briefly.

Tuesday's discussions, though long and intense, were far more produc- tive. It was midnight when I gave my press conference on the conclusions of the Council. I was pleased with what had been achieved. We were on course for the Single Market by 1992. I had had to make relatively few compromises as regards wording; I had surrendered no important British interest; I had had to place a reservation on just one aspect of social policy in the treaty.* Italy, which had insisted on the IGC in the first place, had not only applied the most reservations on it but also demanded that it must be agreed by the European Assembly.

Perhaps I derived most satisfaction from the inclusion in the official record of the conference of a 'general statement' recording that:

> Nothing in these provisions shall affect the right of member states
> to take such measures as they consider necessary for the purpose
> of controlling immigration from third countries, and to combat
> terrorism, crime, the traffic in drugs and illicit trading in works of
> art and antiques.

I had insisted on the insertion of this statement. I said that otherwise terrorists, drug dealers and criminals would exploit the provisions of the act to their own advantage and to the danger of the public. Without it I would not have agreed the Single European Act. In fact, neither the Commission, nor the Council nor the European Court would in the long run be prepared to uphold what had been agreed in this statement any more than they would honour the limits on majority voting set out in the treaty itself. But this is to anticipate.

The first fruits of what would be called the Single European Act were good for Britain. At last, I felt, we were going to get the Community back on course, concentrating on its role as a huge market, with all the oppor- tunities that would bring to our industries. Advantages will indeed flow

---

* Britain and Ireland – as island countries – were permitted to retain or take new meas- ures on grounds of health, safety, environment and consumer protection.

from that achievement well into the future. The trouble was – and I must give full credit to those Tories who warned of this at the time – that the new powers the Commission received only seemed to whet its appetite.

European affairs took second place for me during the rest of this Parliament. The main decisions had been made and even the Commission's search for new 'initiatives' had been slowed for the moment by the need to work out and implement the Single Market programme. The Community was overspending its resources, but had not yet reached the new limits of VAT revenue which had been set. Enlargement had to be carried out. There was plenty to be getting on with.

CHAPTER THIRTY-ONE

Hat Trick

The preparations for and course of the
1987 general election campaign

A LL ELECTION VICTORIES look inevitable in retrospect; none in prospect. The wounds which Westland, BL and reaction to the US raid on Libya inflicted on the Government and the Conservative Party would take some time to heal. Economic recovery would in time provide an effective salve. But Labour had moderated their image and gained a lead in the opinion polls. It was important that I should unify the Party around my authority and vision of Conservatism. This would not be easy.

So I set in train a series of steps to make plain that the Government encompassed – and was receptive to – a wide range of views. My first concern was to deal with the impression that the Government was unaware of people's worries. I could do this without diluting the Thatcherite philosophy because, whatever commentators imagined, the hopes and aspirations of the great majority were in tune with my beliefs.

A step towards getting the Government and Party off to a new start was provided by the reshuffle. Keith Joseph had decided that he now wished to leave the Cabinet. The departure of my oldest political friend and ally saddened me. But Keith's departure gave rise to important changes. What I needed was ministers who could fight battles in the media as well as in Whitehall.

Any analysis of the opinion polls revealed that where we were strong was on economic management; where we were weak was on the so-called 'caring issues'. In Health I felt that the best answer was to set out the record: but it was widely disbelieved. In Education, however, the Conser-

vatives were trusted because people rightly understood that we were
interested in standards – academic and non-academic – parental choice
and value for money; and they knew that Labour's 'loony Left' had a
hidden agenda of social engineering and sexual liberation. Ken Baker
(successor to Patrick Jenkin) had won hands-down the propaganda battle
against the Left in the local authorities and he and William Waldegrave,
stimulated by the advice of Lord Rothschild, had set out what I had long
been looking for – an alternative to the rates. But I felt that a first-class
communicator like Ken Baker was now needed at Education.

John Moore, highly regarded by Nigel Lawson, now entered the
Cabinet as Transport Secretary. I had high hopes of John. He was consci-
entious, charming, soft spoken and in some ways he had the strengths of
Cecil Parkinson – that is, he was right-wing but not hard or aggressive. He
came across very well on television. I had no doubt that John Moore
would be an asset to the Government and a loyal supporter to me.

I moved Nick Ridley to the Department of the Environment. Nick
could not match Ken or John in presentation. But we still needed to come
up with some radical policies for our manifesto and the third term. No
one was better suited to find the right answers to the complicated issues
which faced us in Nick's new field of responsibility. Housing was certainly
one area which required the application of a penetrating intellect. The
sale of council houses had led to a real revolution in ownership. But the
vast, soulless high-rise council estates remained ghettos of deprivation,
poor education and unemployment. The private rented sector had
continued to shrink, holding back labour mobility. Housing benefit and
housing finance generally was a jungle. The community charge had to be
thought through in detail and implemented in England and Wales. And
further ahead lay the vexed question of pollution of the environment.

On the evening of Thursday 24 July 1986 I spoke to the '22 Committee to give the traditional 'end of term' address. My task was to ensure
that the Parliamentary Party left in the past all the agonized debates
about Westland, BL and Libya and came back in the autumn determined to demonstrate the unity and self-confidence required to fight
and win the arguments – and then a general election. In an unvarnished
speech I told them that they had had to take a lot of difficulties on the
chin in the last year, but those difficulties had nothing to do with our
fundamental approach, which was correct. They had resulted from
throwing away the precious virtue of unity and also because, as over
Libya, we had had to do genuinely difficult things which were right. I

was glad to get warm and noisy applause for this, because such a warm response to such a strong speech meant that the Party was recovering its nerve.

The summer of 1986 was important too in another regard. At Conservative Central Office Norman Tebbit, the Chairman of the Party, had been having a very hard time. A good deal of criticism of Norman found its way into the press and at one point he believed that it was coming from me or my staff. Norman arrived one day at Downing Street armed with a sheaf of critical press cuttings, asking where these rumours came from. I reassured Norman that they certainly did not come from me, or my staff, nor – I emphasized strongly – did they reflect my views. These tensions build up when people do not see one another frequently enough to give vent to tensions and clear up misunderstandings. Relations improved, I am glad to say, when Stephen Sherbourne, my political secretary, whose shrewdness never failed me, ensured that Norman and I had regular weekly meetings.

A further step was to involve senior Cabinet ministers in the strategy for the next election. In June Willie Whitelaw and John Wakeham, the Chief Whip, sent me a memorandum urging me to set up the group of ministers which was to be officially known as the Strategy Group and, no doubt to the great pleasure of its male members, was soon known by the press as the 'A-Team'. I agreed that, apart from Willie and John, the group should consist of Geoffrey Howe, Nigel Lawson, Douglas Hurd and Norman Tebbit.

At about the same time as the Strategy Group was established I set up eleven Party policy groups. On this occasion I made the chairman of each group the Cabinet minister whose responsibilities covered its area of interest. Apart from the obvious areas – the economy, jobs, foreign affairs and defence, agriculture, the NHS – there were separate groups on the family (under Nicholas Edwards, Welsh Secretary) and young people (under John Moore – the nearest we had in Cabinet to a young person). At least on this occasion, unlike 1983, the groups were set up promptly and for the most part managed to send in their reports on time.

When Parliament reassembled the Party was in a quite different frame of mind than it had been just a few months earlier. We had a brief legislative programme on the advice of David Young, so crucial legislation would not be abandoned if we went for an early election the following summer. And our position in the opinion polls had begun to improve.

The compilation of documents which constitute the Party's plans for an election campaign is traditionally called the 'War Book'. On 23 December Norman sent me the first draft 'as a Christmas present'. I felt a new enthusiasm as I considered the fresh policies and the battle for them which would be required in 1987.

On Thursday 8 January I discussed with Norman and others the papers he had sent me about the election campaign. We met at Alistair McAlpine's house in order to escape detection by the press, which had already started to speculate about election dates. Many details of the campaign had not been worked out as yet, but I found myself largely in agreement with the suggestions. I did, however, have one continuing worry; this was about the advertising. Several months earlier I had asked whether Tim Bell, who had worked with me on previous elections, could do so again now. I understood that he was a consultant to Saatchis. But in fact the rift between them was greater than I had imagined and the suggestion was never taken up. I might have been prepared to insist, but this would have caused more important problems with Norman and Central Office. In any case I continued to see Tim socially. At this stage in January, though, I still hoped that Saatchis would exhibit the political nous and creativity we had had from them in the past.

I regarded the manifesto as my main responsibility. Brian Griffiths and Robin Harris, from my Policy Unit, brought together in a single paper the proposals which had come in from ministers and policy groups. We discussed this at Chequers on Sunday 1 February. Nigel Lawson, Norman Tebbit and Nick Ridley were there. It was as important at this stage to rule out as to rule in different proposals. It was at this meeting that the main shape of the manifesto proposals became clear.

We agreed to include the aim of a 25 per cent basic rate of income tax and I kept out of the manifesto any commitment to transferable tax allowances between husband and wife which, if they had been implemented along the lines of the earlier Green Paper, would have been extremely expensive. I commissioned further work on candidates for privatization which I wanted to be spelt out clearly in the manifesto itself. Education would, we all agreed, be one of the crucial areas for new proposals in the manifesto. There must be a core curriculum to ensure that the basic subjects were taught to all children. There must be graded tests or benchmarks against which children's knowledge should be judged. All schools should have greater financial autonomy. There must be a new *per capita* funding system which, along with 'open enrolment', would mean that successful, popular schools were financially rewarded and enabled to expand. There must be more powers for head teachers. Finally, and most controversially, schools must be given the power to apply for what at this stage we were describing as 'direct grant' status, by which we meant that they could become in effect 'independent state schools' – a phrase that the DES kept trying to remove from my speeches in favour of the bureaucratically flavoured 'grant-maintained schools' – outside the control of Local Education Authorities.

Housing was another area in which radical proposals were being considered: Nick Ridley's main ideas – all of which eventually found their way into the manifesto – were to give groups of tenants the right to form tenants' co-operatives and individual tenants the right to transfer owner-ship of their house (or flat) to a housing association or other approved institution – in other words to swap landlords. We would also reform local authority housing accounts to stop housing rents being used to subsidize the rate fund when they should have gone towards repairs and renovation.

We were by now under a good deal of political pressure on the Health Service and discussed at our meeting how to respond. Norman Fowler at the 1986 Party Conference had set out a number of targets, backed up by special allocations of public spending, for increases in the number of particular sorts of operation. This announcement had gone well. I was reluctant to add the Health Service to the list of areas in which we were proposing fundamental reform – not least because not enough work had yet been done on it. The direction of reform which I wanted to see was one towards bringing down waiting lists by ensuring that money moved with the patient, rather than got lost within the bureaucratic maze of the NHS. But that left so many questions still unanswered that I eventually ruled out any substantial new proposals on Health for the manifesto.

After the meeting I wrote to Cabinet ministers asking them to bring forward any proposals which required policy approval for implementa-tion in the next Parliament. To knock all these submissions into a coher-ent whole I established a small Manifesto Committee that reported directly to me. Chaired by John MacGregor, Chief Secretary to the Treas-ury, its other members were Brian Griffiths, Stephen Sherbourne, Robin Harris and John O'Sullivan, a former Associate Editor of *The Times*, who drafted the manifesto.

As a party which had been in government for eight years, we had to dispel any idea that we were stale and running out of ideas. We therefore had to advance a number of clear, specific, new and well-worked-out reforms. At the same time we had to protect ourselves against the gibe: if these ideas are so good, why haven't you introduced them before? We did so by presenting our reforms as the third stage of a rolling Thatcherite programme. Looking back, once the manifesto was published, we heard no more about the Government running out of steam.

Because a good deal of misleading comment has been made about the background to and course of the 1987 general election campaign it is worth setting some matters straight at the outset. According to some versions of events this was all about a battle between rival Tory advertising agencies; according to other accounts the main participants – particularly myself – behaved in such an unbalanced way that it is difficult to see why we were all not carried off to one of our new NHS hospitals by the men in white coats. This was not to be a happy campaign; but it was a successful one and that is what counts. There were disagreements – but good old-fashioned stand-up rows, in which most of us regret what we have said and try to forget about it without bearing grudges, feature in all election campaigns.

While the manifesto was being drafted, I was discussing with Norman Tebbit what I hoped would be the final shape of the campaign and my own role in it. At our meeting on Thursday 16 April we went over press conference themes, advertising and Party Election Broadcasts. By now I was in a mood for an early – June – election. I felt in my bones that the popular mood was with us and that Labour's public relations gimmicks were starting to look just a little tired.

As is the way of these things, the most appropriate date eventually wrote itself into our programme – Thursday 11 June. By then we would have seen the results of the local elections which, as in 1983, would be run through the number-crunchers of Central Office to make it into a useful guide for a general election. It would be supplemented by other private polls Norman had commissioned: this was particularly necessary for Scotland and London where there were no local elections that year. Some polling in individual key constituencies would also be done: though such are the problems of sampling in constituency polls that no one would attach too much weight to these. I saw this analysis and heard senior colleagues' views at Chequers on Sunday: I knew by then that the manifesto was in almost final form. I had been through the final text with the draftsmen and with Nigel and Norman on that Saturday.

We had one last disagreement. Nigel wished to include a commitment to zero inflation in the next Parliament. I thought this was a hostage to fortune. Events unfortunately proved my caution right.

As always, I slept on the decision about whether to go to the country, and then on Monday 11 May I arranged to see the Queen at 12.25 p.m. to seek a dissolution of Parliament for an election on 11 June.

In my case, preparation for the election involved more than politics. I also had to be dressed for the occasion. I had already commissioned from Aquascutum suits, jackets and skirts – 'working clothes' for the campaign.

I took a close interest in clothes, as most women do: but it was also extremely important that the impression I gave was right for the political occasion.

From the time of my arrival in Downing Street, Crawfie helped me choose my wardrobe. Together we would discuss style, colour and cloth. Everything had to do duty on many occasions so tailored suits seemed right. On foreign visits, it was, of course, particularly important to be appropriately dressed. We always paid attention to the colours of the national flag when deciding on what I should wear. The biggest change, however, was the new style I adopted when I visited the Soviet Union in the spring of 1987, for which I wore a black coat with shoulder pads, that Crawfie had seen in the Aquascutum window, and a marvellous fox fur hat. (Aquascutum have provided me with most of my suits ever since.)

With the televising of the House of Commons after November 1989 new considerations arose. Stripes and checks looked attractive and cheerful in the flesh but they could dazzle the television viewer. People watching television would also notice whether I had worn the same suit on successive occasions and even wrote in about it. So from now on Crawfie always kept a note of what I wore each week for Prime Minister's Questions. Out of these notes a diary emerged and each outfit received its own name, usually denoting the occasion it was first worn. The pages read something like a travel diary: Paris Opera, Washington Pink, Reagan Navy, Toronto Turquoise, Tokyo Blue, Kremlin Silver, Peking Black and last but not least English Garden. But now my mind was on the forthcoming campaign: it was time to lay out my navy and white check suit, to be known as 'Election '87'.

On Tuesday 19 May, I chaired the first press conference of the campaign to launch our manifesto: the Alliance's had already appeared, and disappeared, and Labour's, which would be more notable for omissions than contents, would be launched the same day. Our manifesto launch was not quite all that I had wished. The press conference room at Central Office was far too crowded, hot and noisy. Cabinet ministers were crowded in too, so much so that the television shots of the conference looked truly awful. Nick Ridley explained our housing policy and I hoped that the journalists might be tempted actually to read the detailed policies of the manifesto. I was certainly determined that our candidates should do so and I took them through it in my speech to their conference in Central Hall, Westminster, the following morning.

But I also used the speech for another purpose. Our political weak point was the social services, especially Health, so I went out of my way to tell the candidates, and through them the voters, that the Government was committed to the principle of a National Health Service which I said was 'safe only in our hands'. That done, I devoted most of the campaign to stressing our strong points on the economy and defence. This did not prevent Health emerging later in the campaign as an issue; but it meant that we had armed ourselves against Labour's attack and done our best to soothe the voters' anxieties.

Our first regular press conference of the campaign was on Friday (22 May). The subject was officially defence and George Younger made the opening statement. We had suddenly been given a great opportunity to sink the Alliance parties which some Tory strategists – but not I – thought were the principal electoral threat to us. Instead, the two Davids sank themselves. The passage in our manifesto claimed that their joint defence policy, because it amounted to unilateral nuclear disarmament by degrees, would just as surely as Labour's eventually produce a 'frightened and fellow-travelling Britain' vulnerable to Soviet blackmail. This was not, of course, an allegation of a lack of patriotism, but a forecast of what weakness would inevitably lead to. David Owen, however, failed to make this distinction and took enormous offence. We could hardly believe our luck when, for several days, he concentrated the public's attention on our strongest card, defence, and his weakest one, his connection with the Liberal Party's sandal-wearing unilateralists. The Alliance never recovered from this misjudgement.

But we were not without our difficulties. I was questioned on education, on which it was suggested that there were contradictions between my and Ken Baker's line on 'opted-out', grant-maintained schools. In fact, we were not suggesting that the new schools would be fee paying in the sense of being private schools: they would remain in the public sector. Moreover, the Secretary of State for Education has to give his approval if a school – whether grant-maintained or not – wishes to change from being a comprehensive school to becoming a grammar school.

That said, I was saddened that we had had to give all these assurances. It is my passionate belief that what above all has gone wrong with British education is that since the war we have 'strangled the middle way'. Direct grant schools and grammar schools provided the means for people like me to get on equal terms with those who came from well-off backgrounds. I would have liked grant-maintained schools – combined with the other changes we were making – to move us back to that 'middle way'. I also wanted a return to selection – not of the old eleven-plus kind but a development of specialization and competition so that some schools would become centres of excellence in music, others in technology, others in science, others in the arts etc. This would have given specially gifted children the chance to develop their talents, regardless of their background.

At Monday's press conference we took the economy as the subject of the day and Nigel Lawson made the opening statement. This was a good campaign for Nigel. Not only did he demonstrate complete command of the issues, he also spotted the implications of Labour's tax and national insurance proposals – especially their planned abolition of the married man's tax allowance and of the upper limit on employees' national insurance contributions – for people on quite modest incomes. This threw Labour into total disarray in the last week of the campaign and revealed that they did not understand their own policies. Nigel had earlier published costings of the Labour Party's manifesto at some £35 billion over and above the Government's spending plans. As I was to say later in a speech: 'Nigel's favourite bedside reading is Labour policy documents: he likes a good mystery.'

At this stage, however, defence continued to dominate the headlines, mainly because of Neil Kinnock's extraordinary gaffe in a television interview in which he suggested that Labour's response to armed aggression would be to take to the hills for guerrilla warfare. We gleefully leapt upon this and it provided the inspiration for the only good advertisement of our campaign, depicting 'Labour's Policy on Arms' with a British soldier, his hands held up in surrender. On Tuesday evening, after a day's campaigning in Wales, I told a big rally in Cardiff:

> Labour's non-nuclear defence policy is in fact a policy for defeat,
> surrender, occupation, and finally, prolonged guerrilla fighting
> ... I do not understand how anyone who aspires to government
> can treat the defence of our country so lightly.

Wednesday's press conference was of particular importance to the campaign because we took education as the theme, with Ken Baker and me together, in order to allay the doubts our early confusion had generated and to regain the initiative on the subject, which I regarded as central to our manifesto. It went well.

But my tours, by general agreement, did not. Neil Kinnock was gaining more and better television coverage. He was portrayed – as I had specifically requested at the beginning of the campaign that I should be – against the background of cheering crowds, or doing something which fitted in with the theme of the day. The media were entranced by the highly polished Party Election Broadcast showing Neil and Glenys walking hand in hand, bathed in a warm glow of summer sunlight, to strains of patriotic music, looking rather like an advertisement for early retirement. This probably encouraged them to give favourable coverage to the Kinnock tours.

In spite of our difficulties the political situation was still favourable. Our lead in the polls was holding up. There had been a big erosion of support for the Alliance, whose campaign was marred by splits and that basic incoherence which is the nemesis of people who eschew principle in politics. Neil Kinnock kept away from the main London-based journalists and Bryan Gould took most of the press conferences. By the second week, however, this tactic was beginning to rebound. The Fleet Street press were able to cross-question me day after day and they expected to enjoy a similar sport with the Leader of the Opposition. In this they were enthusiastically encouraged by Norman Tebbit, who by temperament and talent was perfectly suited to maul Neil Kinnock and did so effectively in successive speeches as the campaign wore on.

That Thursday's press conference was on the NHS. Norman Fowler had devised a splendid illustration of new hospitals built throughout Britain, marked by lights on a map which were lit up when he pressed a switch. Like the Kinnocks' Election Broadcast, I had him repeat the performance by popular demand. But what was worrying me, as usual, was my speech that evening in Solihull.

We had worked on the draft late until 3.30 a.m. but I was still not happy with it. I continued to break away to work on it whenever I could during the day – that is when I was not meeting candidates, talking to regional editors, admiring Jaguars at the factory and then meeting crowds at the Home and Garden exhibition at the Birmingham NEC. As soon as we arrived at Dame Joan Seccombe's house – she is one of the Party's most committed volunteers – I left the others to enjoy her hospitality and closeted myself away with my speech writers, working frantically on the text right up to the last moment. For some mysterious reason the more you all suffer in preparing a speech, the better it turns out to be and this speech was very good indeed. It contained one wounding passage which drew a roar of approval from the audience:

> Never before has the Labour Party offered the country a defence policy of such recklessness. It has talked of occupation – a defence policy of the white flag. During my time in government white flags have only once entered into our vocabulary. That was the night, when at the end of the Falklands War, I went to the House of Commons to report: 'The white flags are flying over Port Stanley.'

And so to the final week. After voting myself, I spent the Thursday morning of June 11 and the early afternoon in Finchley visiting our Committee Rooms and then, as the time for getting late voters out to the poll approached, I returned to No. 10. Norman Tebbit came over and we had a long talk over drinks, not just about the campaign and the likely result, but also about Norman's own plans. He had already told me that he intended to leave the Government after the election because he felt that he should spend more time with Margaret. There was not much I could say to try to persuade him otherwise, because his reasons were as personal as they were admirable. But I did bitterly regret his decision.

I had supper in the flat and listened to the television comment and speculation about the result. Before I left for Finchley at 10.30 p.m. I heard Vincent Hanna on the BBC forecasting a hung Parliament. ITV was talking about a Conservative majority of about 40. I felt reasonably confident that we would have a majority, but I was not at all confident how large it would be. My own result would be one of the later ones; but the first results began to come in just after 11 p.m. We held Torbay with a larger than predicted majority. Then we held Hyndburn, the second most marginal seat, then Cheltenham, a seat targeted by the Liberals, and then

Basildon. At about 2.15 a.m. we had passed the winning post. My own majority was down by 400, though I secured a slightly higher percentage of the vote (53.9 per cent).

I was driven back into town, arriving at 2.45 a.m. at Conservative Central Office to celebrate the victory and thank those who had helped achieve it. Then I returned to Downing Street where I was met by my personal staff. I remember Denis saying to Stephen Sherbourne, as we went down the line: 'You have done as much as anyone else to win the election. We could not have done it without you.' Stephen may have been less pleased by my next remark. It was to ask him to come up to the study to begin work on making the next Cabinet. A new day had begun.

CHAPTER THIRTY-TWO

————≫•◇•≪————

An Improving Disposition

Reforms in education, housing
and the Health Service

THE FIRST PRIORITY after the 1987 election victory was to see that I
had the right team of ministers to implement the reforms set out in
our manifesto. The reshuffle was a limited one: five Cabinet ministers left
the Government, two at their own request. The general balance of the
new Cabinet made it clear that 'consolidation' was no more my preferred
option after the election than before it. John Biffen left the Cabinet: this
was a loss in some ways, for he agreed with me about Europe and had
sound instincts on economic matters too, but he had come to prefer
commentary to collective responsibility. I lost Norman Tebbit for reasons
I have explained. But Cecil Parkinson, a radical of my way of thinking,
rejoined the Cabinet as Energy Secretary. I made no change at Education
where Ken Baker would make up in presentational flair whatever he
lacked in attention to detail, nor Environment where Nick Ridley was
obviously the right man to implement the housing reforms which he had
conceived. These two areas – schools and housing – were those in which
we were proposing the most far-reaching changes. But it was not long
before I decided that there must be a major reform of the National Health
Service too. In John Moore, whom I had promoted to be Secretary of
State for Health and Social Services, I had another radical, anxious to
reform the ossified system he had inherited. So the Government soon
found itself embarked on even more far-reaching social reforms than we
had originally intended.

* * *

The starting point for the education reforms outlined in our general election manifesto was a deep dissatisfaction (which I fully shared) with Britain's standard of education.

I had come to the conclusion that there had to be some consistency in the curriculum, at least in the core subjects. Alongside the national curriculum should be a nationally recognized and reliably monitored system of testing at various stages of the child's school career, which would allow parents, teachers, local authorities and central government to know what was going right and wrong and take remedial action if necessary. The fact that since 1944 the only compulsory subject in the curriculum in Britain had been religious education reflected a healthy distrust of the state using central control of the syllabus as a means of propaganda. But that was hardly the risk now: the propaganda was coming from left-wing local authorities, teachers and pressure groups, not us. What I never believed, though, was that the state should try to regiment every detail of what happened in schools. Some people argued that the French centralized system worked: but such arrangements would not be acceptable in Britain. Here even the strictly limited objectives I set for the national curriculum were immediately seen by the vested interests in education as an opportunity to impose their own agenda.

The other possibility was to go much further in the direction of decentralization by giving power and choice to parents. Keith Joseph and I had always been attracted by the education voucher, which would give parents a fixed – perhaps means-tested – sum, so that they could shop around in the public and private sectors of education for the school which was best for their children. By means testing a voucher one could even reduce the 'dead weight' cost – that is the amount lost to the Exchequer in the form of subsidy for parents who would otherwise have sent their children to private schools anyway.

However, Keith Joseph recommended and I accepted that we could not bring in a straightforward education voucher scheme. In the event, we were, through our education reforms, able to realize the objectives of parental choice and educational variety in other ways. Through the assisted places scheme and the rights of parental choice of school under our 1980 Parents' Charter we were moving some way towards this objective without mentioning the word 'voucher'.

In the 1988 Education Reform Act we now made further strides in that direction. We introduced open enrolment – that is allowing popular schools to expand to their physical capacity. This significantly widened choice further and prevented local authorities setting arbitrary limits on good schools just to keep unsuccessful schools full. An essential element in the same reforms was *per capita* funding, which meant that state money followed the child to whatever school he attended. Parents would vote with their children's feet and schools actually gained resources when they gained pupils. The worse schools in these circumstances would either have to improve or close. In effect we had gone as far as we could towards a 'public sector voucher'. I would have liked to go further still and decided that we must work up a possible full-scale voucher scheme – I hinted at this in my final Party Conference speech – but did not have the time to take the idea further. It was Brian Griffiths who devised the extremely successful model of the 'grant-maintained' (GM) schools, which are free from local education authority (LEA) control entirely and are directly funded from the DES. With a healthy range of GM schools, City Technology Colleges, denominational schools and private schools (known as 'public' schools, much to the confusion of American visitors to Britain) parents would have a much wider choice. But, even more vital, the very fact of having all the important decisions taken at the level closest to parents and teachers, not by a distant and insensitive bureaucracy, would make for better education. This would be true of all schools, which was why we had introduced the Local Management of Schools Initiative (LMS) to give schools more control of their own budgets. But GM schools took it a giant step further.

The governors of a GM school were empowered to manage its budget (receiving their money directly without a service charge deducted by the LEA). They appointed the staff including the head teacher, agreed policy as regards admissions with the Secretary of State, decided the curriculum (subject to the core requirements) and owned the school and its assets. The schools most likely to opt out of LEA control and become GM schools were those which had a distinctive identity, which wished to specialize in some particular subject or which wanted to escape from the clutches of some left-wing local authority keen to impose its own ideological priorities.

The vested interests working against the success of GM schools were strong. The DES, reluctant to endorse a reform that did not extend central control, would have liked to impose all manner of checks and controls on their operation. Local authority officials sometimes campaigned fiercely to prevent opting out by particular schools. And, unexpectedly, the churches also mounted an opposition. In the face of so much hostility I had the Grant-Maintained Schools Trust set up to publicize the GM scheme and advise those interested in making use of it. In fact, GM schools proved increasingly popular, not least with head teachers who were now, in consultation with the governors, able to set their own priorities.

The decentralizing features of our policy were extraordinarily successful. By contrast, the national curriculum – the most important centralizing measure – soon ran into difficulties. I wanted the DES to concentrate on establishing a basic syllabus for English, Mathematics and Science with simple tests to show what pupils knew. It always seemed to me that a small committee of good teachers ought to be able to pool their experience and write down a list of the topics and sources to be covered without too much difficulty. There ought then to be plenty of scope left for the individual teacher to concentrate with children on the particular aspects of the subject in which he or she felt a special enthusiasm or interest. I had no wish to put good teachers in a strait jacket. As for testing, I always recognized that no snapshot of a child's, a class's or a school's performance on a particular day was going to tell the whole truth. But tests did provide an independent outside check on what was happening. Nor did it seem to me that the fact that some children would know more than others was something to be shied away from. The purpose of testing was not to measure merit but knowledge and the capacity to apply it. Unfortunately, my philosophy turned out to be different from that of those to whom Ken Baker entrusted the drawing up of the national curriculum and the formulation of the tests alongside it.

There was a basic dilemma. As Ken emphasized in our meetings, it was necessary to take as many as possible of the teachers and Her Majesty's Inspectorate (HMI) with us in the reforms we were making. After all, it was teachers not politicians who would be implementing them. On the other hand, the educational establishment's terms for accepting the national curriculum and testing could well prove unacceptable. For them, the new national curriculum would be expected to give legitimacy and universal application to the changes which had been made over the last twenty years or so in the content and methods of teaching. Similarly, testing should in their eyes be 'diagnostic' rather than 'summative' – and this was only the tip of the jargon iceberg – and should be heavily weighted towards assessment by teachers themselves, rather than by objective outsiders. So by mid-July the papers I was receiving from the DES were proposing a national curriculum of ten subjects which would account for 80–90 per cent of school time. They wanted different 'attainment targets', stressing that assessments should not denote 'passing' or 'failing': much of this assessment would be internal to the school. Two new bodies – the National Curriculum Council and the Schools Examination and Assessment Council – were to be set up. The original simplicity of the scheme had been lost and the influence of HMI and the teachers' unions was manifest.

All this was bad enough. But then in September I received a further proposal from Ken Baker for comprehensive monitoring of the national curriculum by the recruitment of 800 extra LEA Inspectors, who themselves would be monitored and controlled by the HMI, which would doubtless have to be expanded as well. I noted: 'It is utterly ridiculous. The results will come through in the tests and exams.' I stressed to the DES that all of these proposals would alienate teachers, hold back individual initiative at school level and centralize education to an unacceptable degree. The Cabinet sub-committee which I chaired to oversee the education reforms decided that all of the core and foundation subjects taken together should absorb no more than 70 per cent of the curriculum. But, at Ken Baker's insistence, I agreed that this figure should not be publicly released – presumably it would have caused offence with the education bureaucrats who were by now planning how each hour of school time should properly be spent.

Perhaps the hardest battle I fought on the national curriculum was about history. I had a very clear – and I had naively imagined uncontroversial – idea of what history was. History is an account of what happened in the past. Learning history, therefore, requires knowledge of events. It is impossible to make sense of such events without being able to place matters in a clear chronological framework – which means knowing dates. No amount of imaginative sympathy for historical characters or situations can be a substitute for the initially tedious but ultimately rewarding business of memorizing what actually happened. I was, therefore, very concerned when in December 1988 I received Ken Baker's written proposals for the teaching of history and the composition of the History Working Group on the curriculum. There was too much emphasis given to 'cross-curricular' learning: I felt that history must be taught as a separate subject. Nor was I happy at the list of people Ken Baker was suggesting. His initial names contained no major historian of repute but included the author of the definitive work on the 'New History', which, with its emphasis on concepts rather than chronology and empathy rather than facts, was at the root of so much that was going wrong. Ken saw my point and made some changes. But this was only the beginning of the argument.

In July 1989 the History Working Group produced its interim report. I was appalled. It put the emphasis on interpretation and enquiry as against content and knowledge. There was insufficient weight given to British history. There was not enough emphasis on history as chronological study. I considered the document comprehensively flawed and told Ken that there must be major, not just minor, changes. In particular, I wanted to see a clearly set out chronological framework for the whole history curriculum. But the test would of course be the final report.

By the time this arrived in March 1990 John MacGregor had gone to Education. I thought that he would prove more effective than Ken Baker in keeping a grip on how our education reform proposals were implemented. On this occasion, however, John MacGregor was far more inclined to welcome the report than I had expected. It did now put greater emphasis on British history. But the attainment targets it set out did not specifically include knowledge of historical facts, which seemed to me extraordinary. However, the coverage of some subjects – for example twentieth-century British history – was too skewed to social, religious, cultural and aesthetic matters rather than political events. John defended the report's proposals. But I insisted that it would not be right to impose the sort of approach which it contained. It should go out to consultation but no guidance should at present be issued.

There was no need for the national curriculum proposals and the testing which accompanied them to have developed as they did. Ken Baker paid too much attention to the DES, the HMI and progressive educational theorists in his appointments and early decisions; and once the bureaucratic momentum had begun it was difficult to stop. John MacGregor did what he could. He made changes to the history curriculum which reinforced the position of British history and reduced some of the unnecessary interference. He insisted that the sciences could be taught separately, not just as one integrated subject. He stipulated that at least 30 per cent of GCSE English should be tested by written examination. Yet the whole system was very different from that which I originally envisaged. By the time I left office I was convinced that there would have to be a new drive to simplify the national curriculum and testing.

*   *   *

Education policy was one of the areas in which my Policy Unit and I had begun radical thinking about proposals for the next election manifesto – some of which we envisaged announcing in advance, perhaps at the March 1991 Central Council meeting. Brian Griffiths and I were concentrating on three questions at the time I left office.

First, there was the need to go much further with 'opting out' of LEA control. I authorized John MacGregor to announce to the October 1990 Party Conference the extension of the GM schools scheme to cover smaller primary schools as well. But I had much more radical options in mind. Brian Griffiths had written me a paper which envisaged the transfer of many more schools to GM status and the transfer of other schools to the management of special trusts, set up for the purpose. Essentially, this would have meant the unbundling of many of the LEAs' powers, leaving them with a monitoring and advisory role. It would have been a way to ease the state still further out of education, thus reversing the worst aspects of post-war education policy.

Second, there was the need radically to improve teacher training. Unusually, I had sent a personal minute to Ken Baker in November 1988 expressing my concerns. I said we must go much further in this area and asked him to bring forward proposals. The effective monopoly exercised by the existing teacher-training routes had to be broken. Ken Baker devised two schemes – that of 'licensed teachers' to attract those who wished to enter teaching as a second career and that of 'articled teachers' which was essentially an apprenticeship scheme of 'on the job' training for younger graduates. These were good proposals. But there was no evidence that there would be a large enough inflow of teachers from these sources to significantly change the ethos and raise the standards of the profession. So I had Brian Griffiths begin work on how to increase the numbers: we wanted to see at least half of the new teachers come through these or similar schemes, as opposed to teacher-training institutions.

The third educational policy issue on which work was being done was the universities. By exerting financial pressure we had increased administrative efficiency and provoked overdue rationalization. Universities were developing closer links with business and becoming more entrepreneurial. Student loans (which topped up grants) had also been introduced: these would make students more discriminating about the courses they chose. A shift of support from university grants to the payment of tuition fees would lead in the same direction of greater sensitivity to the market. Limits placed on the security of tenure enjoyed by university staff also encouraged dons to pay closer attention to satisfying the teaching requirements made of them. All this encountered strong political opposition from within the universities. Some of it was predictable. But undoubtedly other critics were genuinely concerned about the future autonomy and academic integrity of universities.

I had to concede that these critics had a stronger case than I would have liked. It made me concerned that many distinguished academics thought that Thatcherism in education meant a philistine subordination of scholarship to the immediate requirements of vocational training. That was certainly no part of my kind of Thatcherism. That was why, before I left office, Brian Griffiths, with my encouragement, had started working on a scheme to give the leading universities much more independence. The idea was to allow them to opt out of Treasury financial rules and raise and keep capital, owning their assets as a trust. It would have represented a radical decentralization of the whole system.

Of the three major social services – Education, the Health Service and Housing – it was, in my view, over the last of these that the most significant question mark hung.

State intervention to control rents and give tenants security of tenure in the private rented sector had been disastrous in reducing the supply of rented properties. The state in the form of local authorities had frequently proved an insensitive, incompetent and corrupt landlord. And insofar as there were shortages in specific categories of housing, these were in the private rented sector where rent control and security of tenure had reduced the supply. Moreover, new forms of housing had emerged. Housing Associations and the Housing Corporation which financed them offered alternative ways of providing 'social housing' without the state as landlord. Similarly, tenant involvement in the form of co-operatives and the different kinds of trusts being pioneered in the United States offered new ways of pulling government out of housing management. I believed that the state must continue to provide mortgage tax relief in order to encourage home ownership, which was socially desirable. The state also had to provide assistance for poorer people with housing costs through housing benefit. But as regards the traditional post-war role of government in housing – that is building, ownership, management, and regulation – the state should be withdrawn from these areas as far and as fast as possible.

This was the philosophical starting point for the housing reforms on which Nick Ridley was working from the autumn of 1986, which he submitted for collective discussion at the end of January 1987, and which after several meetings under my chairmanship were included in the 1987 general election manifesto. The beauty of the package which Nick devised was that it combined a judicious mixture of central government intervention, local authority financial discipline, deregulation and wider choice for tenants. In so doing it achieved a major shift away from the ossified system which had grown up under socialism.

Central government would play a role through Housing Action Trusts (HATs) in redeveloping badly run down council estates and passing them on to other forms of ownership and management – including home ownership, ownership by housing associations and transfer to a private landlord – with no loss of tenant rights. Second, the new 'ring-fenced' framework for local authority housing accounts would force councils to raise rents to levels which provided money for repairs. It would also increase the pressure on councils for the disposal of part or all of their housing stock to housing associations, other landlords or indeed home ownership. Third, deregulation of new lets – through development of shorthold and assured tenancies – should at least arrest the decline of the private rented sector: Nick rightly insisted that there should be stronger legal provisions enacted against harassment to balance this deregulation. Finally, opening up the possibility of council tenants changing their landlords, or groups of tenants running their estates through co-operatives under our 'tenants' choice' proposals, could reduce the role of local authority landlords still further.

The most difficult aspect of the package seemed likely to be the higher council rents, which would also mean much higher state spending on housing benefit. But it seemed better to provide help with housing costs through benefit than through subsidizing the rents of local authority tenants indiscriminately. Moreover, the higher rents paid by those not on benefit would provide an added incentive for them to buy their homes and escape from the net altogether.

These reforms will need time to produce results. But the new arrangements for housing revenue accounts are applying a beneficial new discipline to local authorities. And deregulation of the private rented sector will increase the supply of rented housing gradually, as ideological hostility to private landlordism recedes. But I have to say that I had expected more from 'tenants' choice' and from HATs. The obstacle to both was the deep-rooted hostility of the Left to the improvement and enfranchisement of those who lived in the ghettos of dependency which they controlled. The propaganda against 'tenants' choice', however, was as nothing compared with that directed against HATs and, sadly, the House of Lords gave the Left the opportunity they needed.

Their Lordships amended our legislation to require that a HAT could only go ahead if a majority of eligible tenants voted for it. This would have been an impossibly high hurdle, given the apathy of many tenants and the intimidation of the Left. We finished up by accepting the principle of a ballot, limiting it to the requirement of a majority of those voting. In the summer of 1988 Nick Ridley announced proposals to set up six HATs, of which – after receiving consultants' reports – he decided to go ahead with four in Lambeth, Southwark, Sunderland and Leeds. I later saw some of the propaganda by left-wing tenants' groups – strongly backed by the trade unions – which showed how effective their campaigns had been to spread alarm among tenants who were now worried about what would happen when they moved out as their flats were refurbished and about levels of rents and security of tenure. One would never have guessed that we were offering huge sums of taxpayers' money to improve the conditions of people living in some of the worst housing in the country. As a result, no HATs were set up while I was Prime Minister, though three have been since I left office.

Housing, like Education, had been at the top of the list for reform in 1987. But I had reserved Health for detailed consideration later. I believed that the NHS was a service of which we could genuinely be proud. It delivered a high quality of care at a reasonably modest unit cost, at least compared with some insurance-based systems. Yet there were large and on the face of it unjustifiable differences between performance in one area and another. Consequently, I was much more reluctant to envisage *fundamental* changes than I was in the nation's schools. Although I wanted to see a flourishing private sector of health alongside the National Health Service, I always regarded the NHS and its basic principles as a fixed point in our policies. And so I peppered my speeches and interviews with the figures for extra doctors, dentists and midwives, patients treated, operations performed and new hospitals built. I felt that on this record we ought to be able to stand our ground.

Some of the political difficulties we faced on the Health Service could be put down to exploitation of hard cases by Opposition politicians and the press. But there was more to it than that. There was bound to be a potentially limitless demand for health care (in the broadest sense) for as long as it was provided free at the point of delivery. The number of elderly people – the group who made greatest call on the NHS – was increasing; advances in medicine opened up the possibility of – and demand for – new and often expensive forms of treatment.

In significant ways, the NHS lacked the right economic signals to respond to these pressures. Dedicated its staff generally were; cost conscious they were not. Indeed, there was no reason why doctors, nurses or patients should be in a monolithic state-provided system. Moreover, although people who were seriously ill could usually rely on first-class treatment, in other ways there was too little sensitivity to the preferences and convenience of patients.

If one were to recreate the National Health Service, starting from fundamentals, one would have allowed for a bigger private sector and one would have given much closer consideration to additional sources of finance for health, apart from general taxation. But we were not faced by an empty slate and any reforms must not undermine public confidence.

I had had several long-range discussions with Norman Fowler, then Secretary of State at the DHSS, in the summer and autumn of 1986 about the future of the National Health Service. It was a time of renewed inter-est in the economics of health care so there was much to talk about. Norman provided a paper at the end of January 1987. The objective of reform, which we even now distinguished as central, was that we should work towards a new way of allocating money within the NHS, so that hospitals treating more patients received more income. There also needed to be a closer, clearer connection between the demand for health care, its cost and the method for paying for it. We discussed whether the NHS might be funded by a 'health stamp' rather than through general taxation. Yet these were very theoretical debates. I did not believe that we were yet in a position to advance significant proposals for the manifesto. Even the possibility of a Royal Commission – not a device which I would generally have preferred but one which had been used by the previous Labour Government in considering the Health Service – held some attractions for me.

Norman Fowler was much better at publicly defending the NHS than he would have been at reforming it. But his successor, John Moore, was very keen to have a fundamental review. John and I had our first general discussion on the subject at the end of July 1987. At this stage I still wanted him to concentrate on trying to ensure better value for money from the existing system. But as the year went on it became clear to me also that we needed to have a proper long-term review. During the winter of 1987–8 the press began serving up horror stories about the NHS on a daily basis. I asked for a note from the DHSS on where the extra money the Government had provided was actually going. Instead, I received a report on all of the extra pressures which the NHS was facing – not at all the same thing. I said that the DHSS must make a real effort to respond quickly to the attacks on our record and the performance of the NHS. After all, we had increased real spending on the NHS by 40 per cent in less than a decade.

There was another strong reason for favouring a review at this time. There was good evidence that public opinion accepted that the NHS's problems went far deeper than a need for more cash. If we acted quickly we could take the initiative, put reforms in place and see benefits flowing from them before the next election.

There was a setback, however, before the review had even been decided on. John Moore fell seriously ill with pneumonia in November. With characteristic gallantry, John insisted on returning to work as soon as he could – in my view too soon. Not fully recovered, he could never bring enough energy to bear on the complex process of reform. The tragedy of this was that his ideas for reform were in general the right ones, and he deserves much more of the credit for the final package than he has ever been given.

I made the final decision to go ahead with a Health review at the end of January 1988: we would set up a ministerial group, which I would chair. I made it clear from the start that medical care should continue to be readily available to all who needed it and free at the point of consumption, and I set out four principles which should inform its work. First, there must be a high standard of medical care available to all, regardless of income. Second, the arrangements agreed must be such as to give the users of health services, whether in the private or the public sectors, the greatest possible choice. Third, any changes must be made in such a way that they led to genuine improvements in health care. Fourth, responsibility, whether for medical decisions or for budgets, should be exercised at the lowest appropriate level closest to the patient.

For intellectual completeness all such reviews list virtually every conceivable bright idea for reform. This contained, if I recall aright, about eighteen. But the serious possibilities boiled down to two broad approaches in John Moore's paper. On the one hand we could attempt to reform the way the NHS was financed, perhaps by wholly replacing the existing tax-based system with insurance or, less radically, by providing tax incentives to individuals who wished to take out cover privately. On the other hand, we could concentrate on reforming the structure of the NHS, leaving the existing system of finance more or less unchanged. Or we could seek to combine changes of both kinds. I decided that the emphasis should be on changing the structure of the NHS rather than its finance.

On reforming the structure of the NHS, two possibilities seemed to have most appeal. The first was the possible setting up of 'Local Health Funds' (LHFs). People would be free to decide to which LHF they subscribed. LHFs would offer comprehensive health care services for their subscribers – whether provided by the LHF itself, purchased from other LHFs, or purchased from independent suppliers. The advantage of this system was that it had built-in incentives for efficiency and so for keeping down the costs which would otherwise escalate as they had in some health insurance systems. What was not so clear was whether if they were public sector bodies there would be any obvious advantage over a reformed structure of the District Health Authorities (DHAs).

So I was impressed by a suggestion in John's paper that we should make NHS hospitals self-governing and independent of DHA control. This was a proposal by which all hospitals would (perhaps with limited exceptions) be contracted out individually or in groups through charities, privatization or management buy-outs, or perhaps leased to operating companies formed by the staff. This would loosen the excessively rigid control of the hospital service from the centre and introduce greater diversity in the provision of health care. But, most important, it would create a clear distinction between buyers and providers. The DHAs would become buyers, placing contracts with the most efficient hospitals to provide care for their patients.

This buyer/provider distinction was designed to eliminate the worst features of the existing system: the absence of incentives to improve performance and indeed of simple information. There was at that time virtually no information about costs within the NHS. We had already begun to remedy this. But when I asked the DHSS at one review meeting how long it would be before we had a fully working information flow and was told six years, I exploded involuntarily: 'Good heavens! We won the Second World War in six years!'

Within the NHS money was allocated from regions to districts and then to hospitals by complicated formulas based on theoretical measures of need. A hospital which treated more patients received no extra money for doing so; it would be likely to spend over budget and be forced to cut services. The financial mechanism for reimbursing DHAs when they treated patients from other areas was to adjust their future spending allocations several years after the event – a hopelessly unresponsive system. But with DHAs acting as buyers money could follow the patient and patients from one area treated in another would be paid for straight away. Hospitals treating more patients would generate a higher income and thus improve their services rather than having to cut back. The resulting competition between hospitals – both within the NHS and between the public and private sectors – would increase efficiency and benefit patients.

I held two seminars on the NHS at Chequers – one in March with doctors and the other in April with administrators – to brief myself more fully. Then in May we began our next round of discussions with papers from John Moore and Nigel Lawson.

Nigel took a critical view of John Moore's ideas. By now, the Treasury had become thoroughly alarmed that opening up the existing NHS structure might lead to much higher public expenditure. Despite apparent Treasury interest earlier in the idea of an 'internal market', at the end of May Nigel sent me a paper questioning the whole direction of our thinking. John Major followed up with a proposal for a system of 'top-slicing' by which the existing system of allocating funds to health authorities would continue, but the extra element provided for growth in the health budget each year would be held back ('top-sliced') and allocated separately to hospitals which fulfilled performance targets set down from the centre.

In the face of these challenges John Moore did not defend his approach very robustly and I too began to doubt whether it had been properly thought through. We had a particularly difficult meeting on Wednesday 25 May. Meanwhile, the Treasury did not have it all their own way. I asked them for a paper on possible new tax incentives for the private sector – an idea which Nigel fiercely opposed.

Nigel's objection to tax relief for private medical insurance was essentially twofold. First, tax reliefs in his view distorted the system and should be eroded and if possible removed. Second, he argued that tax relief for private health insurance would in many cases help those who could already afford private cover and so fail to deliver a net increase in private sector provision. In those cases where it did provide an incentive, it would increase the demand for health care, but without corresponding efforts to improve supply the result would just be higher prices. Neither of these objections was trivial – but both objections missed the point that unless we achieved a growth in private sector health care, all the extra demands would fail to be met by the NHS. In the long term it would be impossible to resist that pressure and public expenditure would have to rise much further than it otherwise would. I was not arguing for across the board tax relief for private health insurance premiums but rather for a targeted measure. If we could encourage people over sixty to maintain the health insurance which they had subscribed to before their retirement, that would reduce the demand on the NHS from the limited group which put most pressure on its services.

Nor, of course, were we neglecting the 'supply side'. The whole approach we were taking in the review was designed to remove obstacles to supply. And in addition the review was considering a significant increase in the number of consultants' posts, which would have an impact on the private sector as well as the NHS. We had further plans to tackle restrictive practices and other inefficiencies in the medical profession, directing the system of merit awards more to merit and less to retirement bonuses, and we planned the general introduction of 'medical audit'.*

Nigel fought hard even against these limited tax reliefs but I got it through with John Moore's help in the first part of July. In other areas I was less happy. The DHSS had been shaken by the Treasury's criticisms and responded by seeking to obtain Treasury support for their proposals before they presented the review. This gave the Treasury an effective power of veto. Accordingly, the DHSS put forward, with Treasury agreement, a much more evolutionary approach. Though money following the patient and self-governing hospitals remained goals of policy, they were relegated to the indefinite future and 'top-slicing' took centre stage in the short term.

I had no objection, in principle, to an evolutionary approach to the introduction of self-governing hospitals. But I was suspicious of the distinction that was emerging between short- and long-term changes, generally worried about the slow pace of the review and thought we were losing our way.

At the end of July 1988, I made the difficult decision to replace John Moore on the review. I took this opportunity to split the unwieldy DHSS

---

* 'Medical audit' is a process by which the quality of medical care provided by individual doctors is assessed by their peers.

into separate Health and Social Security departments, leaving John in charge of the latter and bringing in Ken Clarke as Health Secretary. As he was to demonstrate during the short period in which he was my Secretary of State for Education (when he publicly discounted my advocacy of education vouchers), Ken Clarke was a firm believer in state provision. But whatever the philosophical differences between us, Ken's arrival at the Department of Health undoubtedly helped our deliberations. He was an extremely effective Health minister – tough in dealing with vested interests and trade unions, direct and persuasive in his exposition of government policy.

Ken Clarke now revived an idea which my Policy Unit had been urging: that GPs should be given budgets. In Ken's version GPs would hold budgets to buy from hospitals 'elective acute services' – surgery for non-life-threatening conditions such as hip replacements and cataract operations. These were the services for which the patient had (in theory at least) some choice as to timing, location and consultant and for which GPs could advise between competing providers in the public and private sector. This approach had a number of advantages. It would bring the choice of services nearer to patients and make GPs more responsive to their wishes. It would maintain the traditional freedom of GPs to decide to which hospitals and consultants they wanted to refer their patients. It also improved the prospects for hospitals which had opted to leave DHA control and become self-governing: otherwise it was all too likely that if District Health Authorities were the only buyers they would discriminate against any of their own hospitals which opted out.

By the autumn of 1988 it was clear to me that the moves to self-governing hospitals and GPs' budgets, the buyer/provider distinction with the DHA as buyer, and money following the patient were the pillars on which the NHS could be transformed in the future. They were the means to provide better and more cost-effective treatment.

A good deal of work had by now been done on the self-governing hospitals. I wanted to see the simplest possible procedure for hospitals to change their status and become independent – what I preferred to call 'trust' – hospitals. They should also own their assets, though I agreed with the Treasury that there should be some overall limits on borrowing. It was also important that the system should be got under way soon and that we had a significant number of trust hospitals by the time of the next election. At the end of January 1989 – after the twenty-fourth ministerial meeting I had chaired on the subject – the White Paper was finally published.

The White Paper proposals essentially simulated within the NHS as many as possible of the advantages which the private sector and market choice offered but without privatization, without large-scale extra charging and without going against those basic principles which I had set down just before Christmas 1987 as essential to a satisfactory result. But there was an outcry from the British Medical Association, health trade unions and the Opposition, based squarely on a deliberate and self-interested distortion of what we were doing. In the face of this Ken Clarke was the best possible advocate we would have. Not being a right-winger himself, he was unlikely to talk the kind of free market language which might alarm the general public and play into the hands of the trade unions. But he had the energy and enthusiasm to argue, explain and defend what we were doing night after night on television.

In their different ways, the White Paper reforms will lead to a fundamental change in the culture of the NHS to the benefit of patients, taxpayers and those who work in the service. By the time I left office the results were starting to come through.

CHAPTER THIRTY-THREE

Not So Much a Programme, More a Way of Life

Family policy, science and the environment

THE SURGE OF PROSPERITY – most of it soundly based but some of it unsustainable – which occurred from 1986 to 1989 had one paradoxical effect: the Left turned their attention to non-economic issues. Was the price of capitalist prosperity too high? Was it not resulting in a gross and offensive materialism, traffic congestion and pollution? Were not the attitudes required to get on in Thatcher's Britain causing the weak to be marginalized, homelessness to grow, communities to break down?

I found all this misguided and hypocritical. Socialism had failed. And it was the poorer, weaker members of society who had suffered worst as a result of that failure. More than that, socialism, in spite of the high-minded rhetoric in which its arguments were framed, had literally demoralized communities and families, offering dependency in place of independence as well as subjecting traditional values to sustained derision. It was a cynical ploy for the Left to start talking as if they were old-fashioned Tories, fighting to preserve decency amid social disintegration.

But nor could the arguments be ignored. Some Conservatives were always tempted to appease the Left's social arguments on the grounds that we ourselves were very nearly as socialist in practice. These were the people who thought that the answer to every criticism was for the state to spend and intervene more. I could not accept this. There was a case for the state to intervene in specific instances – for example to protect children in real danger from malign parents. The state must uphold the law and ensure that criminals were punished – an area in which I was deeply uneasy, for our streets were becoming more, not less violent. But the root cause of our contemporary social problems – to the extent that these did not reflect the timeless influence and bottomless resources of old-fashioned human wickedness – was that the state had been doing too much. A Conservative social policy had to recognize this. If individuals were discouraged and communities disorientated by the state stepping in to take decisions which should properly be made by people, families and neighbourhoods then society's problems would grow not diminish.

This belief was what lay behind my remarks in an interview with a woman's magazine – which caused a storm of abuse at the time – about there being 'no such thing as society'. But people never quoted the rest. I went on to say:

> There are individual men and women, and there are families. And no government can do anything except through people, and people must look to themselves first. It's our duty to look after ourselves and then also to help look after our neighbour.

My meaning, distorted beyond recognition, was that society was not an abstraction, separate from the men and women who composed it, but a living structure of individuals, families, neighbours and voluntary associations. The error to which I was objecting was the confusion of society with the state as the helper of first resort. Whenever I heard people complain that 'society' should not permit some particular misfortune, I would retort, 'And what are you doing about it, then?' Society for me was not an excuse, it was a source of obligation.

I was an individualist in the sense that I believed that individuals are ultimately accountable for their actions and must behave like it. But I always refused to accept that there was a conflict between this kind of individualism and social responsibility. If irresponsible behaviour does not involve penalty of some kind, irresponsibility will, for a large number of people, become the norm. More important still, the attitudes may be passed on to their children, setting them off in the wrong direction.

I never felt uneasy about praising 'Victorian values' or – the phrase I originally used – 'Victorian virtues', not least because they were by no means just Victorian. But the Victorians also had a way of talking which summed up what we were now rediscovering – they distinguished between the 'deserving' and the 'undeserving' poor. Both groups should be given help: but it must be help of very different kinds if public spending is not just going to reinforce the dependency culture. The problem with our welfare state was that we had failed to remember that distinction and so we provided the same 'help' to those who had genuinely fallen into difficulties and needed some support till they could get out of them, as to those who had simply lost the will or habit of work and self-improvement. The purpose of help must not be to allow people merely to live a half-life, but to restore their self-discipline and through that their self-esteem.

I was also impressed by the writing of the American theologian and social scientist Michael Novak who put into new and striking language what I had always believed about individuals and communities. Mr Novak stressed the fact that what he called 'democratic capitalism' was a moral and social, not just an economic system, that it encouraged a range of virtues and that it depended upon co-operation not just 'going it alone'. These were important insights which, along with our thinking about the effects of the dependency culture, provided the intellectual basis for my approach to those great questions brought together in political parlance as 'the quality of life'.

The fact that the arguments deployed against the kind of economy and society which my policies were designed to foster were muddled and half-baked did not, of course, detract from the fact that there *were* social ills and that in some respects these were becoming more serious. I have mentioned the rise in crime. The Home Office and liberal opinion more generally were inclined to cast doubt on this. Certainly, it was possible to point to similar trends throughout the West and to worse criminality in American cities. It was also arguable that the rise in the number of recorded crimes reflected a greater willingness to report crimes – rape for example – which would previously have not come to the attention of the police. But I was never greatly impressed by arguments which minimized the extent and significance of crime. I shared the view of the general public that more must be done to apprehend and punish those who committed it and that violent criminals must be given exemplary sentences. In this regard the measure we introduced in which I took greatest satisfaction was the provision in the 1988 Criminal Justice Act which empowered the Attorney-General to appeal against overlenient sentences passed by the Crown Court.

The fact that the level of crime rose in times of recession and of prosperity alike gave the lie to the notion that poverty explained – or even justified – criminal behaviour. Arguably, the opposite might have been true: greater prosperity led to more opportunities to steal. In any case, the rise in violent crime and the alarming levels of juvenile delinquency had their origins deeper in society.

I became increasingly convinced during the last two or three years of my time in office that we could only get to the roots of crime and much else besides by concentrating on strengthening the traditional family. The statistics told their own story. One in four children were born to unmarried parents. No fewer than one in five children experienced a parental divorce before they were sixteen. Of course, family breakdown and single parenthood did not mean that juvenile delinquency would inevitably follow. But all the evidence pointed to the breakdown of families as the starting point for a range of social ills of which getting into trouble with the police was only one. Boys who lack the guidance of a father are more likely to suffer social problems of all kinds. Single parents are more likely to live in relative poverty and poorer housing. Children can be traumatized by divorce far more than their parents realize. Children from unstable family backgrounds are more likely to have learning difficulties. They are at greater risk of abuse in the home from men who are not the real father. They are also more likely to run away to our cities and join the ranks of the young homeless where, in turn, they fall prey to all kinds of evil.

The most important – and most difficult – aspect of what needed to be done was to reduce the positive incentives to irresponsible conduct. Young girls were tempted to become pregnant because that brought them a council flat and an income from the state. My advisers and I were considering whether there was some way of providing less attractive – but correspondingly more secure and supervised – housing for these young people. Similarly, young people who ran away from home needed help. But I firmly resisted the argument that poverty was the basic cause – rather than the result – of their plight and felt that it was the voluntary bodies which could provide not just hostel places (which were often in surplus) but guidance and friendship of the sort the state never could.

We were feeling our way towards a new ethos for welfare policy: one comprising the discouragement of state dependency and the encouragement of self-reliance; greater use of voluntary bodies including religious and charitable organizations like the Salvation Army; and, most controversially, built-in incentives towards decent and responsible behaviour. But our attempts to rethink welfare along these lines met a number of objections. Some were strictly practical and we had to respect them.

Others, though, were rooted in the attitude that it was not for the state to make moral distinctions in its social policy.

In spite of all the difficulties, by the time I left office my advisers and I were assembling a package of measures to strengthen the traditional family whose disintegration was the common source of so much suffering. We had not the slightest illusion that the effects of what could be done would be more than marginal. Nor, in a sense, would I have wanted them to be. For while the stability of the family is a condition for social order and economic progress the independence of the family is also a powerful check on the authority of the state. There are limits beyond which 'family policy' should not seek to go.

I preferred if at all possible that direct help should come from someone other than professional social workers. Of course, professionals have a vital role in the most difficult cases – for example, where access to the home has to be gained to prevent tragedy. In recent years, however, some social workers have exaggerated their expertise and magnified their role, in effect substituting themselves for the parents with insufficient cause.

I was also appalled by the way in which men fathered a child and then absconded, leaving the single mother – and the taxpayer – to foot the bill for their irresponsibility and condemning the child to a lower standard of living. So – against considerable opposition from Tony Newton, the Social Security Secretary, and from the Lord Chancellor's department – I insisted that a new Child Support Agency be set up, and the maintenance be based not just on the cost of bringing up a child but on that child's right to share in its parents' rising living standards. This was the background to the Child Support Act, 1991.

As for divorce itself, I did not accept that we should follow the Law Commission's recommendation in November 1990 that this should just become a 'process' in which 'fault' was not at issue. In some cases – for example where there is violence – I considered that divorce was not just permissible but unavoidable. Yet I also felt strongly that if all the remaining culpability was removed from marital desertion, divorce would be that much more common.

The question of how best – through the tax and social security system – to support families with children was a vexed one to which I and my advisers were giving much thought when I left office. There was great pressure, which I had to fight hard to resist, to provide tax reliefs or subsidies for child care. This would, of course, have swung the emphasis further towards discouraging mothers from staying at home. I believed that it was possible – as I had – to bring up a family while working, as long as one was willing to make a great effort to organize one's time properly and with some extra help. But I did not believe that it was fair to those mothers who chose to stay at home and bring up their families on the one income to give tax reliefs to those who went out to work and had two incomes.* It always seemed odd to me that the feminists – so keenly sensitive to being patronized by men but without any such sensitivity to the patronage of the state – could not grasp that.

More generally, there was the question of how to treat children within the tax and benefit system. At one extreme were those 'libertarians' who believed that children no more merited recognition within the tax and benefit systems than a consumer durable. At the other were those who would have liked a fully fledged 'natalist policy' to increase the birth rate. I rejected both views. But I accepted the long-standing idea that the tax someone paid on his income should take into account his family responsibilities. This starting point was important in deciding what to do about child benefit. This sum was paid – tax free – to many families whose incomes were such that they did not really need it and was very expensive. But it had been introduced partly as an equivalent of the (now abolished) child tax allowances, so there was an argument on grounds of fairness that its real value should be sustained. As a compromise, we eventually decided in the autumn of 1990 that it should be uprated for the first child but not the others. I would have liked to return to a system including child tax allowances, which I believed would have been fairer, clearer and – incidentally – extremely popular. But the fiscal purists in the Treasury were still fighting a strong action against me on this at the time I left Downing Street.

All that family policy can do is to create a framework in which families are encouraged to stay together and provide properly for their children. But so much hung on what happened to the structure of the nation's families that only the most myopic libertarian would regard it as outside the purview of the state: for my part, I felt that over the years the state had done so much harm that the opportunity to do some remedial work was not to be missed.

*   *   *

---

* I was, though, content to make one minor adjustment. This was to provide tax relief for workplace nurseries.

In 1988 and 1989 there was a great burst of public interest in the environment. Unfortunately, under the green environmental umbrella sheltered a number of only slightly connected issues. At the lowest but not any means least important level, there was concern for the local environment, which I too always felt strongly about. But this was essentially and necessarily a matter for the local community, though the privatizing of badly run municipal cleaning services often helped.

Then there was the concern about planning – or rather the alleged lack of it – and overdevelopment of the countryside. Here there was, as Nick Ridley became somewhat unpopular for robustly pointing out, a straightforward choice. If people were to be able to afford houses there must be sufficient amounts of building land available. Tighter planning meant less development land and fewer opportunities for home ownership.

There was also widespread public concern about the standard of Britain's drinking water, rivers and sea. The European Commission found this a fruitful area into which to extend its 'competence' whenever possible. In fact, a hugely expensive and highly successful programme was under way to clean up our rivers and the results were already evident – for example the return of healthy and abundant fish to the Thames, Tyne, Wear and Tees.

I always drew a clear distinction between these 'environmental' concerns and the quite separate question of atmospheric pollution. For me, the proper starting point in formulating policy towards this latter problem was science. But the closer I examined what was happening to Britain's scientific effort, the less happy I was about it.

There were two problems. First, too high a proportion of government funding for science was directed towards the Defence budget. Second, too much emphasis was being given to the development of products for the market rather than to pure science. Government was funding research which could and should have been left to industry and, as a result, there was a tendency for the research effort in the universities and in scientific institutes to lose out. I was convinced that this was wrong. As someone with a scientific background, I knew that the greatest economic benefits of scientific research had always resulted from advances in fundamental knowledge rather than the search for specific applications. For example, transistors were not discovered by the entertainment industry seeking new ways of marketing pop music but rather by people working on wave mechanics and solid-state physics.

In the summer of 1987 I instituted a new approach to government funding of science. I set up 'E'(ST) as a new sub-committee of the

Economic Committee of the Cabinet which I now chaired. My ideal was to search out the brightest and best scientists and back them rather than try to provide support for work in particular sectors.

At every stage scientific discovery and knowledge set the requirements and the limits for the approach we should pursue towards the problems of the global environment. It was, for example, the British Antarctic Survey which discovered a large hole in the ozone layer which protects life from ultra-violet radiation. Similarly, it was scientific research which proved that chlorofluorocarbons (CFCs) were responsible for ozone depletion. Convinced by this evidence, governments agreed first to cut and then to phase out the use of CFCs – for example in refrigerators, aerosols and air conditioning systems.

'Global warming' was another atmospheric threat which required the application of hard-headed scientific principles. The relationship between the industrial emission of carbon dioxide – the most significant though not the only 'greenhouse gas' – and climatic change was a good deal less certain than the relationship between CFCs and ozone depletion. Nuclear power production did not produce carbon dioxide – nor did it produce the gases which led to acid rain. It was a far cleaner source of power than coal. However, this did not attract the environmental lobby towards it: instead, they used the concern about global warming to attack capitalism, growth and industry. I sought to employ the authority which I had gained in the whole environmental debate, mainly as a result of my speech to the Royal Society in September 1988, to ensure a sense of proportion.

That speech was the fruit of much thought and a great deal of work and broke quite new political ground. But it is an extraordinary commentary on the lack of media interest in the subject that, contrary to my expectations, the television companies did not even bother to send film crews to cover the occasion. In fact, I had been relying on the television lights to enable me to read my script in the gloom of the Fishmongers' Hall, where it was to be delivered; in the event, candelabra had to be passed up along the table to allow me to do so. The speech itself triggered much debate and discussion, particularly one passage:

> For generations, we have assumed that the efforts of mankind would leave the fundamental equilibrium of the world's systems and atmosphere stable. But it is possible that with all these enormous changes (population, agricultural, use of fossil fuels)

concentrated into such a short period of time, we have unwittingly
begun a massive experiment with the system of this planet
itself . . . In studying the system of the earth and its atmosphere we
have no laboratory in which to carry out controlled experiments.
We have to rely on observations of natural systems. We need to
identify particular areas of research which will help to establish
cause and effect. We need to consider in more detail the likely
effects of change within precise timescales. And to consider the
wider implications for policy – for energy production, for fuel efficiency, for reforestation . . . We must ensure that what we do is
founded on good science to establish cause and effect.

The relationship between scientific research and policy towards the
global environment went to the heart of what differentiated my approach
from that of the socialists. For me, the economic progress, scientific
advance and public debate which occur in free societies *themselves* offered
the means to overcome threats to individual and collective well-being.
For the socialist, each new discovery revealed a 'problem' for which the
repression of human activity by the state was the only 'solution' and state-
planned production targets must always take precedence. The scarred
landscape, dying forests, poisoned rivers and sick children of the former
communist states bear tragic testimony to which system worked better,
both for people and the environment.

CHAPTER THIRTY-FOUR

A Little Local Difficulty

The replacement of the rating system
with the community charge

THE INTRODUCTION OF THE COMMUNITY CHARGE to replace the domestic rates turned out to be by far the most controversial of the changes promised in our 1987 general election manifesto. Whereas the other elements of those reforms – in education, housing and trade union law – took root, the community charge has since been abolished by a government consisting largely of those who framed and implemented it.

The charge became a rallying point for those who opposed me, both within the Conservative Party and on the far Left. Had I not been facing problems on other fronts – above all, had the Cabinet and Party held their nerve – I could have ridden through the difficulties. Indeed, the community charge was beginning to work at the very time it was abandoned. Given time, it would have been seen as one of the most far-reaching and beneficial reforms ever made in the working of local government. Its abandonment will mean that more and more powers will pass to central government, that upward pressures on public spending and taxation will increase accordingly, and that still fewer people of ability will become local councillors.

We did not enter lightly upon the path of radical reform of local government finance. If it had been possible to carry on as before I would have been quite prepared to do so. But by almost universal agreement it was not. The person who knew this best was Michael Heseltine – in fact, the most vocal Conservative opponent of the community charge. Michael, as Environment Secretary in the early 1980s, had tried to make the old system work by taking on a whole battery of new powers in an attempt to deal with the problem: that we lacked the means to control local government spending, though it made up a large fraction of overall public expenditure. He brought in the block grant system and 'grant-related expenditure assessments' (GREAs), 'targets' and 'holdback', limits on local authority capital expenditure, and the Audit Commission, as well as beginning a general squeeze on the central government grant – all designed to hold down local spending and to give ratepayers an incentive to think twice before re-electing high-spending councils.*

The system became so complicated that scarcely anyone understood it. It was like the 'Schleswig-Holstein question' of the last century: Palmerston joked once that only three people ever had a real grasp of it – one of them was dead, one was mad and he himself had forgotten it. The system was also highly unpopular, wayward in its application and inexplicably unfair to historically low-spending authorities, many of whom were set targets below their GREAs. Worse still, it did not work. Local government spending grew inexorably in real terms, year after year.

So in 1981 Michael proposed that if local authorities spent more than a certain amount over and above their GREAs all the extra would have to be paid for by domestic ratepayers. The Government also agreed that a local referendum should be held before a council could go ahead with the extra spending. This proposal had something new and important to be said for it because it at least marginally reinforced local accountability. But, in spite or even because of that, it drew howls of protest from local authorities and the Tory backbenchers whom they so easily influenced. The proposal had to be withdrawn.

---

* Central government grant contributes a large proportion of local authority spending. GREAs were an attempt to allocate grants to authorities on the basis of their 'need to spend', as defined by central government on the basis of dozens of indicators covering everything from an authority's population to the state of its roads. The block grant system altered the distribution of central government grant so that it provided a lower proportion of local authorities' expenditure if they spent significantly more than their GREAs – in other words, the more a council overspent, the higher the proportion of its spending ratepayers would have to meet. 'Targets' for individual local authorities (based on past spending) were introduced later in an attempt to secure year-on-year reductions in local authority spending: local authorities exceeding their targets actually lost grant ('holdback'). The Audit Commission was established in 1982 with responsibility for auditing the accounts of local authorities in England and Wales and with powers to undertake or promote work on value for money and efficiency.

Michael's successors at the Department of the Environment – Tom King and then Patrick Jenkin – were left no alternative but to apply more and more complex central controls, while the local authorities went on spending. In 1984 we took powers to limit directly the rates of selected local authorities, with powers in reserve to limit them all. This procedure – known as 'rate-capping' – was one of the most effective weapons at our disposal. Much of the overspending was concentrated in a small number of authorities, so that capping fewer than twenty could make a considerable difference. It allowed us to offer some protection from very high rates to businesses and families who were trying to make their own way in profligate Labour authorities. But rate-capping stretched the capacity of the Department of the Environment and could be challenged in the courts. The fundamental problem remained.

I had always disliked the rates intensely. Any property tax is essentially a tax on improving one's own home. It was manifestly unfair and un-Conservative. In letters received from people all over the country I witnessed a chorus of complaints from people living alone – widows for example – who consumed far less of local authority services than the large family next door with several working sons, but who were expected to pay the same rates bills, regardless of their income. I had witnessed the anger and distress caused by the 1973 rate revaluation and believed strongly that something new must replace the existing discredited system.* When I became Prime Minister I stopped any further rate revaluations in England. (In Scotland a domestic rate revaluation was required by law every five years, though extensions were possible, and we took powers to put off for two years a revaluation due in 1983.) But the counterpart of this decision was that the potential disruption which a rate revaluation would have caused in England grew by the year. And we could not put it off for ever.

The reliance on property taxes as a principal source of income for local government went back centuries. Rates made sense, perhaps, when the bulk of local authority services were supplied to property – roads, water and drains, and so on – but in the course of the present century local

---

* Rates were levied at so many pence in the pound (the 'poundage') on the basis of the rental value of the property, which was assessed by a general valuation carried out by the Inland Revenue. Since the rental market in domestic property was small and shrinking the valuations were often very artificial. In addition, obviously, their accuracy deteriorated over time; hence the need for periodic revaluations.

authorities have increasingly become providers of services for people, such as education, libraries and personal social services.

Moreover, the franchise for local election has been widened dramatically. Originally, it was limited to property holders: now it is almost identical to that for parliamentary elections. Of the 35 million local electors in England, 17 million were not themselves liable for rates, and of the 18 million liable, 3 million paid less than full rates and 3 million paid nothing at all. Though some of those not liable contributed to the rates paid by others (for example, spouses and working children living at home), many people had no direct reason to be concerned about their council's overspending, because somebody else picked up all or most of the bill. Worse still, people lacked the information they needed to hold their local authority to account: the whole system of local government finance worked to obscure the performance of individual authorities. It is not surprising that many councillors felt free to pursue policies which no properly operating democratic discipline would have permitted.

Higher rates were ruinous for businesses. And in the summer of 1985 when we began seriously to look at the alternatives to the rating system, some 60 per cent of the rate income of local authorities in England was coming from business rates. In some areas it was a far higher percentage. For example, in the Labour-controlled London borough of Camden it reached 75 per cent. Socialist councils were thus able to squeeze local businesses dry and the latter had no recourse except to press central government to cap the council concerned or to move out of the area.

Popular discontent with the rates surfaced strongly in the motions submitted by constituencies for our 1984 Party Conference. Accordingly, in September 1984 Patrick Jenkin sought my agreement to announce to the Party Conference a major review of local government finance. The Party Chairman, John Gummer, gave him strong support. But I was cautious. There was a danger of raising expectations that we could not meet. I authorized Patrick to say no more than that we would undertake studies of the most serious inequities and deficiencies of the present system. There would be no publicly announced 'review' and no hint that we might go as far as abolishing the rates.

I discussed the proposed studies with the junior Local Government minister, William Waldegrave, and suggested that Lord Rothschild – for whom I had the highest regard, having worked with him on science policy when I was Education Secretary – should be brought into it.

William jumped at the idea. Much of the radical thinking which resulted was Victor Rothschild's,

By the time that the studies were complete, the political imperative for change had been dramatically demonstrated by a disastrous rate revaluation in Scotland. The Scottish Conservative Party Chairman, Jim Goold, came to see me in the middle of February 1985 to describe the fury which had broken out north of the border when the new rateable values became known. The revaluation had led to a large shift in the burden from industry to domestic ratepayers and – with the high level of spending of Scottish local authorities – this was combined with large overall increases in the poundage. By the time I chaired a proper ministerial discussion on the evening of Thursday 28 February to see what could be done about the problem, it was really too late. Scottish ministers, businessmen and Tory supporters began with one voice to call for an immediate end to the rating system.

For us, south of the border, it was powerful evidence of what would happen if we ever had a rate revaluation in England. There was no legal obligation to undertake a revaluation in England by a particular year, but it could fairly be argued that without any revaluation the rates would contain more and more anomalies.

So it was that when Ken Baker, the DoE minister responsible for local government, his junior, William Waldegrave, and Lord Rothschild made their presentation to a seminar I held at Chequers at the end of March 1985, I was very open to new ideas. It was at the Chequers meeting that the community charge was born. They convinced me that we should abolish domestic rates and replace them with a community charge levied at a flat rate on all resident adults. There would be rebates for those on low incomes – though rebates should be less than 100 per cent so that everyone should contribute something, and therefore have something to lose from electing a spendthrift council. This principle of accountability underlay the whole reform.

The second element of the approach was that business rates would be charged at a single nationally set level and the revenue redistributed to all authorities on a *per capita* basis. The reform of business rates would also make it possible to end one of the most unsatisfactory features of the old system: 'resource equalization'. One problem with the rating system was that taxable capacity varied enormously from one authority to another, since the value and amount of property itself varied – particularly commercial and business property. 'Resource equalization' was the name given to the process by which central government redistributed income between authorities to even out the effect. As a result there were major variations across the country in the amount of rates paid on similar properties for a given standard of service, generally to the disadvantage of the South, where properties were usually valued much more highly. Such a system, of course, made it still harder for voters to judge whether they were getting value for money from their authority. But with the abolition of domestic rates and the distribution of the national business rate on a *per capita* basis, taxable capacity would no longer vary between authorities and so the need for 'resource equalization' disappeared. Obviously some authorities had greater needs than others, but this would be compensated for by giving them more in central grant.

In the discussion which followed there was a lot of tough questioning, but general support for the DoE approach and in particular a commitment to the strengthening of local accountability.

Of the ideas now put forward by the DoE team, the only proposal which I rejected was that we should consider changing the whole of local government to single-tier authorities. Then and later I was to be attracted by this on the grounds of the transparency it would have brought to the community charge figures. But we could not do everything at once.

William Waldegrave and the DoE officials went away to prepare more detailed proposals. Nigel Lawson had already expressed reservations through his Chief Secretary, Peter Rees, at the seminar. But it was only afterwards that it became clear just how deeply opposed he was. The DoE proposals were to come before a Cabinet committee at the end of May. A few days before the meeting Nigel sent in a Cabinet memorandum strongly challenging the community charge and urging the consideration of alternatives.

Nigel's dissenting Cabinet memorandum showed prescience in one crucial respect: he foresaw that local authorities would use the introduction of the new tax as an excuse to increase spending, knowing that they stood a good chance of persuading the voters that the Government was to blame for higher bills. I, too, had worries on this score, and the main aspect of the DoE's early thinking of which I was doubtful was their optimistic suggestion that enhanced accountability would make it possible to abandon 'capping' altogether. In an ideal world perhaps this would have been true. But the world which years of socialism in our inner cities had created was far from ideal. I was determined that capping powers would

remain and, indeed, I would find myself pressing for much more extensive community charge capping than was ever envisaged for the rates.

When the committee met I asked Nigel to work up his alternative
proposals quickly: I had it in mind – if we went ahead – to get a Green
Paper published by the autumn of 1985, with a view to legislating in the
1986–87 session, which was a tight timetable. But his idea for a 'Modified
Property Tax' was not to win any support from colleagues outside the
Treasury when it was circulated in August 1985. It had most of the defects
of the existing system and some more as well.

In September 1985 I promoted Ken Baker to Secretary of State for the
Environment, with responsibility for refining and then presenting the
proposals. During autumn and winter that year we slogged away in
Cabinet committee.

The problem of limiting individual losses raised the question of
whether the community charge itself should be phased in, and if so, how.
Ken Baker – always canny and cautious – wanted a very long transition
period during which the rates and community charge would run alongside each other (known in the jargon as 'dual running'). The final position, which Ken Baker announced to the House of Commons on Tuesday
28 January 1986, was that the community charge would start at a low level,
with a corresponding cut in the rates. But the whole burden of any
increased spending would fall on the community charge from the start so
that there was a clear link between higher spending and higher community charges. In subsequent years there would be further shifts from the
rates to the charge. In some areas the rates would disappear within three
years: they would be eliminated in all areas within ten. The Green Paper
made it clear that we were retaining capping. On the strong advice of
Scottish ministers, who reminded us continually how much the Scottish
people loathed the rates, we also accepted that we should legislate to bring
in the community charge in Scotland in advance of England and Wales.

In May 1986 I moved Ken Baker to Education and brought in Nick Ridley
to replace him at the Department of the Environment. Nick brought a
combination of clarity of thought, political courage and imagination to
the questions surrounding the implementation of the new system. His
vision was that local authorities should enable services to be provided
but, unless it was truly necessary, local authorities should not provide
those services themselves. Nick's 1988 Local Government Act required
that refuse collection, street cleaning, the cleaning of buildings, ground

maintenance, vehicle maintenance and repair and catering services (including school meals) be put out to tender.

It was entirely consistent with this rigorous approach that Nick considered it illogical to retain capping powers, except perhaps during the transition to the new system. But I felt we needed this safeguard. He also wanted to introduce the community charge more quickly than Ken Baker had envisaged, believing that the sooner local authorities could be made truly accountable the faster we could go in bringing local government back onto the right lines. Nick had always opposed dual running and in the end he persuaded the rest of us to abandon it – though, as I shall explain, not without a little help from the Party in the country.

During the winter of 1986–87 Parliament legislated to introduce the community charge in Scotland from April 1989. In February 1987 Malcolm Rifkind won our agreement to drop dual running in Scotland, though a safety net was retained, and it was on this basis that the Party north of border fought the 1987 election. The community charge was an important issue during the campaign there. Our results were disappointing but Malcolm Rifkind wrote to me afterwards that the community charge had been 'neutral' in its effect and that it had at least defused the rates problem. In England and Wales the community charge was hardly an election issue at all.

Nevertheless, when the new Parliament met it became clear that many of our backbenchers had got the jitters. On 1 July the whips estimated that while over 150 were clear supporters, there were nearly 100 'doubters', with 24 outright opponents. There was a real danger that over the summer recess many of the doubters would commit themselves against the charge altogether. Nick's response was characteristically robust: to propose that we drop dual running, drastically cut down the safety net and attack the London problem by direct action to reduce the Inner London Education Authority's costs. But he met strong opposition from colleagues, particularly Nigel, and in the end we compromised on dual running for four years with a full safety net phased out over the same period.*

It quickly became clear that this had not done the trick. At the Party Conference in October speaker after speaker attacked dual running and backbench opinion was also very strongly opposed to it. We argued it out at a ministerial meeting on 17 November, and decided that dual running

---

* A 'full' safety net was one that ensured there would be no losses or gains from the abolition of 'resource equalization' during the first year of the charge.

should be abandoned except for a very few councils, all but one of them in inner London. We also ended the full safety net, setting a maximum contribution of £75 per person from the gaining authorities, so that their gains came through more quickly. (In June 1988 we abandoned dual running altogether: by that time we had made the decision to abolish ILEA, which seemed likely to reduce community charge bills in London significantly in the long term. There were serious doubts too whether the authorities scheduled for dual running were administratively competent to do the job.)

It is worth noting that the changes we made in local government finance originated in and continued to reflect opinion in the Conservative Party, notwithstanding these arguments about transitional arrangements. Both the English and the Scottish Party demanded fundamental changes in the rates. It was the Scottish Party which insisted upon the early introduction of the community charge in Scotland: and if, as the Scots subsequently claimed, they were guinea pigs for a great experiment in local government finance, they were the most vociferous and influential guinea pigs which the world has ever seen.

It is true that in April 1988 we had to fight off an amendment put forward by Michael Mates MP, a lieutenant of Michael Heseltine, which would have introduced a 'banding' of the community charge – that is, income would be taken into account in setting the charge. This would have defeated the whole purpose of the flat-rate charge. The proper way to help the less well off was through community charge rebates, and Nick Ridley won round many of the rebels by announcing improvements in these. But the most consistent pressure was from Tory MPs anxious to see that the benefits of the new system came through faster to their constituents.

The Bill received its Royal Assent in July 1988. The new system would come into operation in England and Wales on 1 April 1990.

It was very important that the first year's community charge in England (1990–91) was not so high as to discredit the whole system. In particular it was crucial that good authorities be able to announce community charges at or below the level we deemed necessary to achieve the standard level of service (known as the Community Charge for Standard Spending, or CCSS).

In May 1989 Nick Ridley, Nigel Lawson and John Major (as Chief Secretary) began discussions on the level of the local authority grant settlement for 1990–91. There was a wide gap between the DoE and the Treasury. The figures suggested by Nick Ridley were, he argued, the only ones which would lead to actual community charges below £300 (a far higher figure than we had envisaged a year before). The Treasury view, with which I agreed, was that the 1989–90 settlement had been very generous – deliberately so to pave the way for the community charge. But the only result had been to lead to greatly increased local authority spending. Local authorities had kept down the rates themselves in 1989–90 through the use of reserves, merely deferring increases. The lesson, the Treasury argued, was that providing more money from the Exchequer did not mean lower rates (or a lower community charge). On 25 May I summed up the discussion at a ministerial meeting by rejecting both Nick Ridley's and John Major's preferred options and going for something in the middle, which I thought would still give us a tolerable community charge while not validating the large increase in local authority spending in 1989–90. But I said that I wanted to see exemplifications of the likely community charge in each local authority area.

We were not to know it at the time, but these decisions contributed to the undoing of the community charge. At this time the Treasury was still using an inflation measure (the GDP deflator) of just 4 per cent. In fact, inflation and – most important – wage settlements were turning sharply upwards. Combined with a pretty tight grant settlement and with the determination of many local authorities to push up spending for political reasons, we were now on course for much higher levels of community charge in 1990–91 than any of us foresaw.

I moved Chris Patten to become Secretary of State for the Environment later that summer and in early September Chris, with my approval, began a review of the operation of the charge. A couple of days before, Ken Baker (now the Party Chairman) had sent me in great secrecy research conducted by Central Office in ten Conservative marginal seats. This confirmed the scale of the political problem we faced. On the assumption of a 7 per cent increase in local spending the following year, 73 per cent of households and 82 per cent of individuals would lose from the introduction of the charge in 1990 compared with the rates in the previous year. If spending increased by 11 per cent the figures would rise to 79 per cent and 89 per cent respectively. On any calculation these figures were pretty bad.

Now that dual running had been dropped, the only way in which we could limit the losses of individuals or households generally was by a new scheme altogether. Chris Patten and the Treasury accordingly worked up a proposal for 'transitional relief'.

Chris favoured a massive programme of transitional relief for households to limit losses to £2 a week – that is, £2 a week on the basis of what we thought local authorities should spend (the CCSS), which many of them of course would exceed. Even in this limited form the scheme might cost as much as £1,500 million. Ken Baker wanted a very costly scheme too. The Treasury argued for something much more modest, targeted on the worst losers. All of this was against a difficult public expenditure round and a worsening economic situation with rising inflation. I told Chris Patten that transitional relief on the scale he was proposing was out of the question, but I also pressed the Treasury hard to take a positive and co-operative attitude. I held a meeting at the end of September to try to get agreement and concluded by saying that it was essential that the scheme should be sufficiently generous to defuse genuine criticism but that it must be clear that this was indeed the last word and that the Government would not make further money available for 1990–91.

Discussions continued up to the eve of the Party Conference where David Hunt, the Local Government minister, announced a scheme costing £1.2 billion over three years. The scheme would ensure that former ratepayers (and ratepayer couples) need pay in community charges no more than £3 a week extra, over and above their 1989–90 rate bills, provided that their local authority spent in line with the Government's assumptions. Pensioners and disabled people would be entitled to the same level of help even if they had not previously paid the rates (and of course many of them were entitled to rebates as well). At the same time David Hunt announced that the taxpayer would finance the safety net in England and Wales after the first year and that all gains would therefore come through in full from 1 April 1991. In spite of this, backbench pressure increased. There was even doubt as to whether we could win the crucial Commons votes in January 1990 to authorize payment of the 1990–91 Revenue Support Grant. And I was under no illusion that victory in the House of Commons would be sufficient to convince public opinion, which had now turned strongly against the community charge.

By January 1990 the DoE had yet again raised its estimate of the average community charge to £340. We were heading for double the original estimate. That had been bad enough. Now, in February, the latest indications were that it could be £20 or more higher.

Another piece of bad news was that the Retail Price Index Advisory Committee had decided that the community charge should be included in the RPI – treating it like the rates, but unlike other direct taxes. But the massive reliefs to individual charge payers should not be taken into account. This administrative fiction gave another expensive upward twist to the RPI and greatly increased the political damage which we were sustaining.

The political atmosphere was becoming grim. All my instincts told me that we could not continue as we were. On Thursday 22 March we sustained a very bad by-election defeat in Mid-Staffordshire where we had had a majority of over 19,000. The press was full of outraged criticism of the community charge from Conservative supporters. What hurt me was that the very people who had always looked to me for protection from exploitation by the socialist state were those who were suffering most. These were the people who were just above the level at which community charge benefit stopped but who were by no means well off and who had scrimped and saved to buy their homes. Our new scheme of transitional relief did not protect them against overspending councils. Something more must be done.

There was widespread support for the principle that everyone should pay something towards the cost of local government, which only the community charge could ensure. When people complained about its fairness they were not usually rehearsing the hackneyed – and spurious – point about the hypothetical duke and dustman paying the same. Unless the duke was very poor or the dustman very wealthy this could not be so, because about half of local authority expenditure was met out of general taxation which did reflect 'ability to pay'. The problem was the levels at which the charge was now being levied and the fact that it was sudden and unexpected in its impact. But what could now be done?

The essential point, I felt, was to ensure that central government stepped in to protect the victims of what was essentially an arbitrary abuse of power by irresponsible local authorities.

The main option seemed to be the introduction of a direct central control over levels of local authority spending; for example, laying down that expenditure by each authority could be no more than a certain percentage above a Standard Spending Assessment (SSA) – that is, the level at which the authority needed to spend to deliver a certain nationally uniform standard of service. That, however, would need to be matched by a substantial increase in the level of government grant to local authorities, perhaps with a larger proportion of the total in the form of specific grants for particular services. We would then have to consider whether to continue with the community charge as the sole means of financing expenditure above the level allowed for, given that at present all the extra expenditure fell on the charge. An alternative would be to place some of the burden of higher spending on the business rate. All this pointed to the need for a major internal review.

John Major, as Chancellor, did not dissent from my judgement that a radical review was necessary. He also agreed that the changes we came up with must control total public expenditure.

But the most public opposition to the community charge came not from the respectable Tory lower-middle classes for whom I felt so deeply, but rather from the Left. From 1988 a number of Labour MPs, mostly in Scotland, had proclaimed their determination to break the law and refuse to pay the community charge and the far Left were agitating effectively in England too. On Saturday 31 March, the day before the introduction of the community charge in England and Wales, a demonstration against the charge degenerated into rioting in and around Trafalgar Square. There was good evidence that a group of troublemakers had deliberately fomented the violence. Scaffolding on a building site in the square was dismantled and used as missiles; fires were started and cars destroyed. Almost 400 policemen were injured and 339 people were arrested. It was a mercy that no one was killed. I was appalled at such wickedness.

For the first time a government had declared that anyone who could reasonably afford to do so should at least pay something towards the upkeep of the facilities and the provision of the services from which they benefited. A whole class of people had been dragged back into the ranks of responsible society and asked to become not just dependants but citizens. The violent riots of 31 March was their and the Left's response. And the eventual abandonment of the charge represented one of the greatest victories for these people ever conceded by a Conservative Government.

The trouble was that, because of the size of the bills now being sent out, the new system had the very same law-abiding, decent people, on whom we depended for support in defeating the mob, protesting themselves. The riot did not, therefore, shift me from my determination to continue with the community charge itself or to see the criminals of that day brought to justice.

In fact, unbeknown to me, the rioters were on their way up to Whitehall as I was addressing the Central Council in Cheltenham.

I began my speech with what was to be the first of a number of increasingly risky jokes about the political threat to my leadership. Cheltenham's reputation as the traditional retirement centre for those who governed our former empire provided the peg. I began:

> It's a very great pleasure to be in Cheltenham once again. To avoid any possible misunderstanding, and at the risk of disappointing a few gallant colonels, let me make one thing absolutely clear: I haven't come to Cheltenham to retire.

I then went almost immediately to the heart of the issue about which the Party was agonizing:

> Many of the bills for the community charge which people are now receiving are far too high. I share the outrage they feel. But let's be clear: it's not the way the money is raised, it's the amount of money that local government is spending. That's the real problem. No scheme, no matter how ingenious, could pay for high spending with low charges.

But I did go on to announce a number of limited special reliefs. Even this modest package had necessitated my tearing up a feeble draft from the Treasury and writing it myself. Given the weak draft, the absence of colleagues and the late hour, however, I was not able to write into my speech assurances of the weight and substance I would have liked. So I had to content myself with hinting at my ideas about further capping powers to deal with overspenders.

My main message, therefore, had to be that the way to have low community charge bills was to vote Conservative in the forthcoming local elections.

The reception was good. But for them and for me the worries remained. Now I had to ensure that my colleagues threw themselves as wholeheartedly as I would into the job of protecting our people from the kind of problems we were experiencing in 1990–91.

Chris Patten was strongly opposed to any kind of comprehensive capping of local authorities but I insisted that the DoE should work up the options. I wanted to see cuts in expenditure in some local authorities. The local election results on Thursday 3 May 1990 strongly suggested that where Conservative councillors and candidates used the community charge in order to point up the differences between them and the Labour Party and then worked to get out the Conservative vote – rather than indulge in recrimination against the Government – they could do very well. (Indeed, some of our councillors opposed wider capping in 1990–91 on the ground that it would protect profligate Labour councils from the electoral *coup de grâce*.) Conservative successes in Wandsworth and Westminster were the results of that approach. Where the Conservatives were in control of an authority, the lower the charge it set, the better we did. The reverse was true where Labour was in office. In this respect the community charge was already transforming local government. There was the prospect that, even in a bad year for the Conservative Party nationally, local government elections could now be fought and won on genuinely local issues and the local record, rather than the political control of councils swinging according to national trends.

These successes, however, did not diminish the urgency of ensuring that next year's charge levels throughout the country were kept down. Throughout May and early June papers were produced and discussions between ministers and officials held. Chris Patten and I were still at odds over the question of a general capping power. I put some pressure on him by refusing to allow any discussion about the level of next year's central grant until we had reached a decision on spending controls. John Major was in two minds. On the one hand, as Chancellor, he wanted to see effective controls on public spending. On the other, he was worried about getting the Parliamentary Party to pass the necessary new legislation for stronger capping powers.

But suddenly the whole basis of our discussions was changed by new legal advice. When we had met on the morning of Thursday 17 May the lawyers advised that even new legislation on capping could be undermined by judicial review. This seemed to me to be extraordinary. It suggested that Parliament would not be allowed by the courts to fulfil its duty to protect the citizen from unreasonable levels of taxation: it cast doubt on our ability to control public expenditure and manage the economy. At that point I asked for urgent advice about how these difficulties could be overcome.

It is easy to imagine my surprise – and initial scepticism – when, as I worked through my boxes overnight on Wednesday 13 June, I came across a note from my private secretary reporting a telephone conversation with government lawyers earlier that evening. Their view now was that the present legislation – let alone any future legislation – might be more robust than their earlier advice had indicated.* They told us that we would be in a position to cap large numbers of authorities as long as we made clear at an early stage in the budgetary cycle what we would regard as an excessive increase in spending – and we could achieve this without the difficulties which new legislation would have brought. This legal advice was strengthened as a result of the Government's victory in a court case several days later against a number of local authorities appealing against capping.

On the evening of Tuesday 26 June I held a meeting of ministers to sort out exactly where we stood. The lawyers confirmed their advice that it was unlikely that we could have any greater certainty about capping under new legislation than under the present. I was reluctant to drop the idea of introducing a general capping power. I would have liked to combine this with the use of local referenda, so that an authority which wanted to spend more than the limit set by central government would have first to win the agreement of its electorate. This would have done a good deal to defuse the accusation that new spending controls would undermine local democracy. In the light of the revised legal advice, though, I accepted that unless the courts came up with some new judgment which changed the position it would be best to cap in 1991–92 under the existing law. It was crucial, however, to achieve the greatest possible deterrent effect and so Chris Patten had to announce in July – well before local authorities set their budgets – how he intended to use his powers. The other aspect we had to discuss was the extra money which was needed to be put in in order to limit the burden on individuals. Chris was authorized to announce to the House certain extensions to the transitional relief scheme and other changes.

The system of local authority finance which I bequeathed to my successor remained unpopular. At the end of March 1991 Michael Heseltine, once again Environment Secretary, announced that the Government had decided to abandon the community charge and to return to a property tax, supplemented by a sharp rise in VAT from 15 to 17.5 per cent.

Few episodes of my period in government have generated more myths than the community charge. It is generally presented as a doctrinaire

---

* The capping legislation allowed us to act on a number of different criteria. The lawyers now advised that we could be much more rigorous than we had thought in capping authorities which had made excessive increases of the charge year-on-year (as opposed to capping those which had an excessive level of spending in a particular year).

scheme forced on reluctant ministers by an authoritarian Prime Minister and eventually rejected by popular opinion as unworkable. This picture is a tissue of nonsenses. As Nigel Lawson has generously conceded, few pieces of legislation have ever received such a thorough and scrupulous examination by ministers and officials in the relevant Cabinet committees as did the charge. The conclusion I draw is that whatever reform was chosen, we should have accompanied it with draconian restraints on local government spending from the centre in order to prevent local authorities – Conservative as well as Labour – from using the transition to jack up spending and blame it on the Government.

The fact remains that the defects in our system of local government finance were largely remedied by the charge, and its benefits had just started to become apparent when it was abandoned. The fundamental problems of local government – badly administered services, an obscure relationship with central government, lack of effective local accountability – not only remain: they will get worse.

CHAPTER THIRTY-FIVE

To Cut and to Please

Tax cuts, tax reform and privatization

THE 1980S SAW THE REBIRTH in Britain of an enterprise economy. This was, by and large, a decade of great prosperity, when our economic performance astonished the world. From 1987 there were classic signs of 'overheating' and initial confusion about what monetary indicators were showing. Nigel Lawson's shadowing the deutschmark meant that we did not take action early enough to tighten monetary policy. That is not to say that the surge of prosperity in these years was just or even mainly the result of an artificial consumer boom. It was more soundly based than that. The current account deficit which became a real problem must not obscure the fact that industry was investing in the future during these years: in the 1980s British business investment grew faster than in any other major industrial country, with the exception of Japan. Profitability rose, and so did productivity. New firms grew and expanded. New jobs followed – 3,320,000 of them created between March 1983 and March 1990.

It is, therefore, as important to understand what went right in these years as what went wrong. Where the problem arose was on the 'demand side' as money and credit expanded too rapidly and sent the prices of assets soaring, particularly non-internationally traded goods like houses. This spiral was clearly unsustainable. By contrast the 'supply side' reforms were highly successful. These were the changes which made for greater efficiency and flexibility and so enabled British business to meet the demands of foreign and domestic markets. Without them, the economy would not have been able to deliver such improvements in profits, living standards and employment: in short, the country would have been poorer.

Trade union reform was crucial. The most important changes were those made between 1982 and 1984, but the process continued right up to the time I left office. The 1988 Employment Act, based on our manifesto pledges, strengthened rights of individual trade unionists against industrial action organized by their unions without a ballot and against the unions' attempts to 'discipline' them if they refused to go out on strike. It also instituted a special commissioner to help individual union members exercise their rights and opened up trade union accounts for inspection. The 1990 Employment Act concluded the long process of whittling away at the closed shop, which had held so many in its vicious thrall. The abolition of that monument to modern Luddism – the National Dock Labour Scheme – was another blow to restrictive practices.

Such reforms not only allowed management to manage and so ensured that investment was once again regarded as the first call on profits rather than the last; they also helped change the attitudes of employees to the businesses for which they worked, and in which they increasingly held shares. So in my last year in office there were fewer industrial stoppages than in any year since 1935: under two million working days were lost in this way, compared with approaching thirteen million a year on average during the 1970s. Still too many, by the way.

But there were other changes aimed at improving the quality of the workforce by helping people to obtain the right qualifications and experience. In my last year as Prime Minister some two and a half times as much – in real terms – was being spent by government on training as under the last Labour Government. Of course, there is always a danger that 'training' becomes an end in itself, with its own bureaucracy and momentum, particularly when public funds on this scale are involved. So I was keen that as much as possible of the administration and decision-taking in these great state-funded programmes should be decentralized. Training and Enterprise Councils (TECs) were set up from 1988 to take over responsibility for the delivery of these programmes. They consisted of groups of local employers, who knew more than any 'expert' what skills were actually going to be needed.

Another innovation in which I took a keen interest was the use of Training Vouchers – which, because of the corporatist sensibilities of the training establishment, I was always being urged to describe as 'Credits'.

Housing is vital to a properly working labour market. If people cannot move to regions where there are jobs – 'getting on their bike', to quote Norman Tebbit's immortal phrase – there will remain pockets of intractable unemployment. And the less willing or able they are to move, the greater call there will be for state intervention to force or bribe firms to go to commercially unsuitable locations to provide the jobs. The private rented sector of housing would be the ideal source of cheap, often temporary, accommodation of the sort that those seeking work are likely to want. After decades of rent control, however, private landlordism – almost uniquely in Britain – is popularly associated with exploitation and bad conditions. This meant that it was never possible to take the radical action needed to reverse the shrinkage in rented housing which has got steadily worse since the First World War.

In our 1988 Housing Act we introduced some measures to revive the private rented sector. We further developed the two schemes – originally introduced in 1980 – of the shorthold tenancy (short lets at market rents, after which the landlord can regain possession) and the assured tenancy (also market rents but with security of tenure). These measures had some effect, but there will need to be a sea change in attitudes towards private rented housing if it is ever to grow to make a major contribution to labour mobility.

By contrast, council housing is the worst source of immobility. Many large council estates bring together people who are out of work but enjoy security of tenure at subsidized rents. They not only have every incentive to stay where they are: they mutually reinforce each other's passivity and undermine each other's initiative. Thus a culture grows up in which the unemployed are content to remain living mainly on the state with little will to move and find work.

So the great increase in private home ownership in my years as Prime Minister and the corresponding reduction of the public sector's share of the housing stock was an important benefit to the economy. Attempts were made to deny this on narrow financial grounds. In particular, it was said that through mortgage tax relief too much of the nation's saving has been channelled into bricks and mortar, too little into industry. This I never found convincing. First, it overlooks the fact that many people whose main means of saving is by buying their house on a mortgage would probably not otherwise invest their money in shares or set up businesses. Indeed, buying a house *is* for many people the gateway to other investments. Second, the idea that British industry has fallen behind in recent decades because of a lack of investment is at best a half-truth. The fact is that much of the investment has been of the wrong sort and wrongly directed. What Britain lacked in the past was the right opportunities to make use of the investment available – because of low productivity, poor labour relations, low profits and bad management. What is true is that a high level of home ownership does need to be complemented by a sufficiently large private rented sector, as ours is not. On this score we were only half successful and the private rented sector is an area in which, given time, I would have liked to do more.

It was a different story with deregulation of business. Year after year – and with a further boost from David Young when he went to the Department of Trade and Industry in June 1987 – unnecessary regulations on business were identified and duly scrapped. David Young also shifted the emphasis of the assistance received from the DTI towards job creation, small firms and innovation. It was not just a piece of gimmickry when what had principally been a sponsoring Department for state-owned industries and heavy manufacturing was rechristened the 'Department for Enterprise'. The importance of a continuing drive for deregulation is that otherwise reregulation is never far behind. More regulation means higher costs, less competitiveness, fewer jobs and thus less wealth to raise the real quality of life in the long run.

All of these areas – trade union power, training, housing and business regulation – were ones in which in varying degrees we made progress in strengthening the 'supply side' of the economy. But the most important and far-reaching changes were in tax reform and privatization.

Nigel Lawson's tax reforms mark him out as a Chancellor of rare technical grasp and constructive imagination. We had some differences – not least about mortgage tax relief which he would probably have liked to abolish and whose threshold I would certainly have liked to raise. But Nigel did not generally like to seek or take advice. Doubtless he felt he did not need to. He liked to take me through his budget proposals when he already had them well worked out, and without any private secretary present to take notes, over dinner at No. 11 one Sunday towards the end of January. Had I restricted informing myself of his plans to these informal occasions it would have been difficult for me to have any real influence, but Treasury spies, realizing that this was an impossibly secretive way of proceeding with someone who after all was 'First Lord of the Treasury', furtively filled me in – with the strictest instructions not to divulge what I knew – before Nigel proudly announced to me his budget strategy. This at least put me in a better position to question the proposed fiscal stance or to object to individual measures.

But the fact remains that Nigel's budgets were essentially his. And just as I hold him largely responsible for the errors of policy which threw away our success on inflation, so I have no hesitation in giving him the lion's share of the credit for the ingenious measures in his budgets.

Whereas Geoffrey Howe was instinctively a Chancellor who liked well-balanced packages of measures, Nigel Lawson liked a budget with everything based on one central theme and purpose. Geoffrey was always one to go for the prudent course, whereas Nigel's search for the brilliant solution to a fiscal problem could lead him to risk all on a winning streak. He was, indeed, a natural gambler.

The 1984 budget showed Nigel at his brilliant best. He abolished the Investment Income Surcharge, a grossly unfair charge on often elderly savers, and got rid of the National Insurance Surcharge, which Geoffrey had already cut. But his most important reform was the phasing out of tax reliefs for business at the same time as he cut Corporation Tax rates, so improving the direction and quality of business investment and greatly increasing incentives for business success. Nineteen eighty-five was a less remarkable budget, but like that of 1984 raised personal income tax allowances well above inflation. In 1986 he made what I considered just the right political judgement by cutting the basic rate of income tax by one penny, which was in effect a statement that we would not ignore the basic rate in future budgets when there was more fiscal leeway. He also introduced Personal Equity Plans (PEPs) to encourage personal investment in shares as a way of encouraging popular capitalism. In 1987 he cut two pence more off the basic rate, but balanced what might have seemed a pre-election 'give away' with the incorporation within the MTFS of the objective of a PSBR of 1 per cent of GDP, as a standard of fiscal prudence.

More controversial was Nigel's 1988 budget. I certainly had my doubts at the time. I felt – rightly – that the overall financial conditions had become too loose.

I began by questioning the size of tax cuts Nigel now proposed, partly because I felt that big income tax cuts in a climate of excessive consumer and business confidence may have a psychological effect, not directly predictable by the dubious science of economics, but real nonetheless. They might fire up what already seemed to be overheating. In fact, the figures which I saw on the eve of the budget for the very large public sector debt repayment (PSDR) or budget surplus – forecast in the budget at £3 billion (though the figure was distorted by privatization proceeds) – considerably reassured me. Moreover the budget surplus out-turn for

1988–89 was some £14 billion. I therefore believe that – with one apparently technical but in fact significant qualification – Nigel's 1988 budget was a success. The cuts in the basic rate of income tax to 25 pence and the top rates to 40 pence provided a huge boost to incentives, particularly for those talented, internationally mobile people so essential to economic success.

The technical point which had such practical consequences was a change in the system of mortgage tax relief, by which the £30,000 limit would no longer apply to each individual purchasing a property but rather to the house itself. This removed the discrimination in favour of unmarried cohabiting couples. Though announced in April, however, it only took effect from August. This gave a huge immediate boost to the housing market as people took out mortgages before the loophole ended, and it happened at just the wrong time, when the housing market was already overheating.

By 1989 even Nigel's usual apparently limitless confidence about our economic prospects had become dented. Monetary policy had been tightened sharply to cut back inflation. But what about fiscal policy? It was clear that the budget surplus was a reflection at least as much of the runaway pace of economic growth raising tax revenues as of underlying financial soundness; even so it was difficult to argue that such a large budget surplus should be increased still further.

And indeed, I found less difficulty than usual in persuading Nigel to see things my way. I urged him to revise his Cabinet paper, to be less complacent, to drop the idea of a further one-penny cut in income tax (which I said would look wrong psychologically), to forget his proposal to remove the tax on the basic retirement pension and to scrap the earnings rule instead.* I also said that there must be no loosening of monetary policy. He went along with all this: he then used some of the revenue in hand to make sensible changes in the structure of employees' national insurance contributions.

But Nigel decided not to raise the excise duties with inflation, giving an artificial downward twist to the inflation figure, which enabled him to predict that inflation would rise to about 8 per cent before falling back in the second half of the year to 5.5 per cent and perhaps 4.5 per cent in the second quarter of 1990. However, by the second quarter of 1990 it was to

---

* The earnings rule limited in the early years of retirement the amount a pensioner could earn without reducing his pension.

reach not 4.5 per cent but approaching 10 per cent. The degree of inflation that shadowing the deutschmark had injected into the system was greater than anyone, including Nigel, had realized. But by 1990 Mr 10 per cent had departed and others were left to deal with the consequences.

John Major was in some ways all too different from Nigel Lawson as Chancellor. It seemed strange to me that, having been a competent Chief Secretary, he did not feel more at home with tackling the difficult issues he now faced when he returned to the Treasury. As preparation for the 1990 budget, we had a seminar attended by John and me, Richard Ryder, the Economic Secretary to the Treasury, and officials. It did not get us very far, which was not John's fault: the problem was that by now none of us had any faith in the forecasts. I found myself in disagreement with John on only one issue: I stopped consideration being given to a new tax on credit. I had a good deal of sympathy with the proposition that banks and building societies had made credit too easily available and that this was leading feckless or just inexperienced borrowers into debt. But I never doubted that if we once tried to stop this by imposing a tax on it, all that general support which puritanical policies evoke in principle would soon turn into a hedonistic outcry as video recorders, expensive lunches, sports cars and foreign holidays moved out of financial reach. The tax would also have put up the RPI. In fact, within the little room for manoeuvre available in these circumstances, John Major's only budget was a modest success, containing several eye-catching proposals to boost the woefully low level of savings. But by then it would take more than a sound budget – more even than a Prime Minister and Chancellor who subscribed to the same policies – to avert the political and economic consequences of allowing inflation to rise.

The fact that the return of inflation and then recession obscured the benefits of the tax changes Nigel Lawson's budgets made does not mean that those benefits had evaporated. Inflation distorts; but, once tamed again, it turns out not to have destroyed the improvements in economic performance which lower and simpler taxes bring. Only one thing can undermine these supply side benefits: that is letting public expenditure get out of control, which puts up borrowing and which eventually requires tax increases that destroy incentives. When I left office both public spending and borrowing were under tight control. Indeed, we were still budgeting for a surplus. And during my period of office public spending fell as a share of GDP from 44 per cent in 1979–80 to 40.5 per cent in 1990–91. It has since risen to 45.5 per cent of GDP (1993–94) and public sector borrowing to around £50 billion, some 8 per cent of GDP. These figures bring strange echoes of the past. In politics there are no final victories.

Privatization, no less than the tax structure, was fundamental to improving Britain's economic performance. But for me it was also far more than that: it was one of the central means of reversing the corrosive and corrupting effects of socialism. Through privatization – particularly the kind which leads to the widest possible share ownership by members of the public – the state's power is reduced and the power of the people enhanced. Just as nationalization was at the heart of the collectivist programme by which Labour Governments sought to remodel British society, so privatization is at the centre of any programme of reclaiming territory for freedom. Whatever arguments there may – and should – be about means of sale, the competitive structures or the regulatory frameworks adopted in different cases, this fundamental purpose of privatization must not be overlooked. That consideration was of practical relevance. For it meant that in some cases if it was a choice between having the ideal circumstances for privatization, which might take years to achieve, and going for a sale within a particular politically determined timescale, the second was the preferable option.

But, of course, the narrower economic arguments for privatization were also overwhelming. The state should not be in business. State ownership effectively removes – or at least radically reduces – the threat of bankruptcy which is a discipline on privately owned firms. As a result, decisions about investment are made according to criteria quite different from those which would apply to a business in the private sector. Nor, in spite of valiant attempts to do so (not least under Conservative Governments), can one find an even moderately satisfactory framework for making decisions about the future of state-owned industries. Targets can be set; warnings given; performance monitored; new chairmen appointed. But state-owned businesses can never function as proper businesses. The very fact that the state is ultimately accountable for them to Parliament rather than management to the shareholders means that they cannot be. The spur is just not there.

Privatization itself does not solve every problem. Monopolies or quasi-monopolies which are transferred to the private sector need careful regulation to ensure against abuses of market power, whether at the expense of competitors or of customers. But on regulatory grounds there are good arguments for private ownership as well: regulation which had, when in the public sector, been covert now had to be overt and specific. This provides a clearer and better discipline. And more generally, of course, the evidence of the lamentable performance of government in running any business – or indeed administering any service – is so overwhelming that the onus should always be on statists to demonstrate why government should perform a particular function rather than why the private sector should not.

The depth of the recession meant that there was not much prospect of successful privatization in the early years, due to low market confidence and large nationalized industry losses. But, for all that, by the time of the 1983 election British Aerospace and the (now) National Freight Consortium were flourishing in the private sector; Cable and Wireless, Associated British Ports, Britoil (a nationalized North Sea oil exploration and production company set up by Labour in 1975), British Rail Hotels and Amersham International (which manufactured radioactive materials for industrial, medical and research uses) had also in whole or in part been moved back to private ownership.

The huge losses of British Shipbuilding and the massive restructuring required of British Airways prevented their sale for the moment; though in both cases the prospect of privatization was an important factor in asserting tighter financial discipline and attracting good management. The British Telecom Bill – to privatize BT – had only fallen with the old Parliament and would be introduced with the new. The 1983 manifesto mentioned all of these as candidates for privatization as well as Rolls-Royce, substantial parts of British Steel and of British Leyland and Britain's airports. Substantial private capital would also be introduced into the National Bus Company. And there was the repeated promise of shares offered to employees in the companies concerned. Perhaps the most far-reaching pledge, though, was that we would seek to 'increase competition in, and [attract] private capital into the gas and electricity industries'. Gas was indeed privatized in 1986. The more complicated and ambitious privatization of electricity had to wait for the next Parliament. In the 1987 manifesto both electricity and the water industry were the main candidates for privatization. So over these years privatization had leapt from fairly low down to somewhere near the top of our political and economic agenda. This continued to be so for the rest of my time in office.

I was always especially pleased to see businesses which had absorbed huge sums of taxpayers' money and been regarded as synonyms for

Britain's industrial failure pass out of state ownership and thrive in the private sector. The very prospect of privatization compelled such companies to make themselves competitive and profitable. Lord King turned round British Airways by a bold policy of slimming it down, improving its service to the customer and giving its employees a stake in success. It was sold as a thriving concern in 1987. British Steel, which had absorbed vast subsidies in the 1970s and early '80s, re-entered the private sector as a profitable company in 1988. But it was perhaps BL (now known as the Rover Group) whose return to private ownership caused me most satisfaction – in spite of the almost endless arguments about how much its private sector purchaser, the once state-owned British Aerospace, had received.

I was not immediately clear that British Aerospace's offer just before Christmas 1987 was serious. But it soon turned out that it was. There was an industrial logic in the acquisition. Aerospace depends on gaining a few huge contracts at inevitably irregular intervals; cars satisfy a steadier market. And, of course, the sale to BAe would have one marked political advantage: the company would stay British.

The special financial provisions of the deal only reflected the poor state of BL after years of state ownership and wasted investment. That the terms had to be revised reflected the new interest of the European Commission in probing the details of state aid to industry, rather than being a reflection on the basic soundness of the deal itself.

Only satisfied customers can ultimately guarantee the future of a business or the jobs depending on it and Rover could not be an exception to that rule. But the effects of the disastrous socialist experiment to which the company had been subject had now been overcome; and Rover was back in the private sector where it belonged.

British Telecom was the first utility to be privatized. Its sale did more than anything else to lay the basis for a share-owning popular capitalism in Britain. Some two million people bought shares, about half of whom had never been shareholders before. But the relationship between privatization and liberalization was a complex one. The first steps of liberalization had begun under Keith Joseph who split British Telecom from the Post Office, removed its monopoly over telephone sales and licensed Mercury to provide a competing network. Further liberalization took place at the time of privatization.

But if we had wanted to go further and break up BT into separate businesses, which would have been better on competition grounds, we would have had to wait many years before privatization could take place. This was because its accounting and management systems were, by modern standards, almost nonexistent. There was no way in which the sort of figures which investors would want to see could have been speedily or reliably produced. So I was well satisfied when, after the delay which had been caused by the need to withdraw the original Bill with the advent of the 1983 general election, British Telecom was eventually successfully privatized in November 1984.

The consequences of privatization for BT were seen in a doubling of its level of investment, now no longer constrained by the Treasury rules applying in the public sector. The consequences for customers were just as good. Prices fell sharply in real terms, the waiting list for telephones shrank and the number of telephone boxes in operation at any particular time increased. It was a convincing demonstration that utilities were better run in the private sector.

Many of the same issues arose in the privatization of British Gas, which had been a nationalized industry for nearly forty years. BGC had five main businesses. These were: the purchase of gas from the oil companies which produced it; the supply of gas, involving the transmission and distribution of gas from the beach-head landing points to the customer; its own exploration for and production of gas, mostly from offshore fields; the sale of gas appliances through its showrooms; and the installation and servicing of those appliances. Of these functions only the second – the supply of gas to consumers – could be described as a natural monopoly. Both the BGC and Energy Secretary, Peter Walker, were determined to privatize BGC as a whole and their full co-operation was essential if it were to be achieved as I wanted during our second term.

Accordingly, at a meeting I held with Peter Walker, Nigel Lawson and John Moore on Tuesday 26 March 1985 I agreed that we should go for a sale of the whole business. The formula for regulation and the issue of liberalizing imports and exports of gas became the focus of much argument between Peter Walker who was prepared to accept a degree of monopoly as the price of early privatization on the one hand, and the Treasury and the DTI on the other who would have preferred stronger competition from the first. We were able to liberalize gas exports but I went along with most of Peter Walker's arguments in order to achieve privatization in the available timescale. I still think I was right to do so because the privatization was a resounding success.

The privatization of the water industry was a more politically sensitive issue. Much emotive nonsense was talked along the lines of, 'Look, she's even privatizing the rain which falls from the heavens.' I used to retort that the rain may come from the Almighty but he did not send the pipes, plumbing and engineering to go with it. And about a quarter of the water industry in England and Wales had long been in the private sector. Of more significance was the fact that the water authorities did not just supply water: they also safeguarded the quality of rivers, controlled water pollution and had important responsibilities for fisheries, conservation, recreation and navigation. It was Nick Ridley – a countryman – who, when he became Environment Secretary, grasped that what was wrong was that the water authorities combined both regulatory and supply functions. It made no sense that those who were responsible for the treatment and disposal of sewage, for example, should also be responsible for regulating pollution. So the Bill which Nick introduced also established a new National Rivers Authority. Privatization also meant that the companies would be able to raise money from capital markets for the investment needed to improve the water quality.

The most technically and politically difficult privatization was that of the electricity supply industry. The industry had two main components. First, there was the Central Electricity Generating Board (CEGB) which ran the power stations and the National Grid (the transmission system). Second, there were the twelve Area Boards which distributed the power to customers. (In Scotland there were two companies running the industry – the South of Scotland Electricity Board and the North of Scotland Hydro Board.) The CEGB had a monopoly nationally and the Area Boards monopolies regionally. The challenge for us would be to privatize as much as possible of the industry while introducing the maximum amount of competition.

I had an initial discussion about electricity privatization with Peter Walker and Nigel Lawson on the eve of the 1987 general election. I did not intend to keep Peter at Energy so there was no point in going into detail. But we did agree that the pledge of privatization should be included in the manifesto and be given effect in the next Parliament.

When Cecil Parkinson took over as Energy Secretary after the election he found that the department's thinking had been strongly influenced by Peter Walker's corporatist instincts – and by their recognition that Walter Marshall would be passionately opposed to the break-up of the CEGB of which he was chairman. The prevailing idea seemed to be that the CEGB and the National Grid would be floated as one company and the twelve Area Boards would be combined into another. This would have done no more than change a monopoly into a duopoly; but Cecil changed all this. He was subsequently the butt of much malicious and unjust criticism because of the changes which his successor, John Wakeham, had to make in his original privatization strategy, particularly in connection with the nuclear power stations. In fact, it was Cecil who took the bold and right decision to reject both corporatist thinking and vested interests by breaking up the CEGB and – most crucially – removing from its control the National Grid. The grid would now be owned jointly by the twelve distribution companies created from the old Area Boards. Whereas under the old system the controller of the grid was also its near monopoly supplier, control would now be with those who had the strongest interest in ensuring that as much competition as possible be allowed to develop in power generation.

Cecil Parkinson was working towards this model over the summer of 1987 and in September we had a seminar at Chequers to look at the options. Cecil continued to work up the plans and discussed them again with me and other ministers in mid-December. No one was attracted by solutions which retained a monopoly of generation for the CEGB or its continued ownership of the grid. The real question was whether the CEGB should be divided up into just two or as many as four or five competing generating companies. Nigel Lawson favoured the more radical option. The trouble was that it was difficult to see any of these companies being large enough to keep up the very costly development of nuclear power, which I regarded as essential to ensure security of power supply and for environmental reasons.

There was also Walter Marshall to consider. Not only did I like and admire him. I also felt that we all owed him a great debt for having kept the power stations working during the miners' strike. He might just be willing to go along with a two-way split in which the larger company retained the nuclear power stations. I could not, of course, allow his views to be decisive: nor did I do so. But I hoped to obtain his and his colleagues' co-operation in the difficult transition to the new privatized and competitive system. So at a meeting in mid-January I came down on the side of the solution that Cecil favoured. But I added that this did not preclude moving at some future time to the more competitive model which Nigel Lawson would have preferred.

Later that month I agreed that the split in capacity between the two new proposed generating companies should be 70/30. This was the plan which I tried to sell to Walter Marshall. Walter – never averse to blunt speaking – did not conceal his disagreement with the approach we favoured. I agreed with him about the great importance of nuclear power. But I did not think that its prospects would be damaged by our plans. Again and again I insisted that whatever structure we created must provide genuine competition. I often found that straight talking pays dividends. On further consideration and after further discussions with Cecil, Walter Marshall said that though the CEGB would express regret at what we had decided he was prepared to make the system work. Cecil Parkinson's plans were also strongly opposed by Peter Walker who suggested that it would take at least eight years before there was any chance of completing this competitive model of privatization. None of us was convinced by this. So on Thursday 25 February Cecil could make his statement to the House of Commons setting out how we intended to privatize electricity.

As always, the prospect of privatization meant that the finances of the industry were subject to searching scrutiny, and what came to light was extremely unwelcome. For environmental reasons and to ensure security of supply, I felt it was essential to keep up the development of nuclear power. But in the autumn of 1988 the figures for the cost of decommissioning the now ageing power stations were suddenly revised sharply upwards by the Department of Energy. These had been consistently underestimated or perhaps even concealed. And the more closely the figures were scrutinized the higher they appeared. By the summer of 1989 the whole prospect for privatizing the main generating company which would have the nuclear power stations started to look in jeopardy. So I agreed that the older Magnox power stations should remain under government control. This was one of Cecil's last actions at Energy and it fell to his successor, John Wakeham, to deal with the rest of the nuclear problem.

Alan Walters had been urging from the previous autumn that all the nuclear power stations should be removed from the privatization. As so often, he turned out to be right. The figures for decommissioning the other power stations started to look uncertain and then to escalate, just as those for Magnox had done. John Wakeham recommended and I agreed that all nuclear power in England and Wales should be retained in state control. One consequence of this was that Walter Marshall, who naturally wanted to retain the nuclear provinces in his empire, decided to resign, about which I was very sad. But the other consequence was that privatization could now proceed, as it did, with great success, to the benefit of customers, shareholders and the Exchequer.

The result of Cecil Parkinson's ingenious reorganization of that industry on competitive lines is that Britain now has perhaps the most efficient electricity supply industry in the world. And as a result of the transparency required by privatization we also became the first country in the world to investigate the full costs of nuclear power – and then to make proper financial provision for them.

There was still much I would have liked to do. But by the time I left office, the state-owned sector of industry had been reduced by some 60 per cent. Around one in four of the population owned shares. Over six hundred thousand jobs had passed from the public to the private sector. It constituted the greatest shift of ownership and power away from the state to individuals and their families in any country outside the former communist bloc. Indeed, Britain set a worldwide trend in privatization. Some £400 billion of assets have been or are being privatized worldwide. And privatization is not only one of Britain's most successful exports: it has re-established our reputation as a nation of innovators and entrepreneurs. Not a bad record for something we were constantly told was 'just not on'.

CHAPTER THIRTY-SIX

Floaters and Fixers

Monetary policy, interest rates and the exchange rate

A CORRECT ECONOMIC POLICY depends crucially upon a correct judgement of what activities properly fall to the state and what to people. After a long struggle during my first term, from 1979 to 1983, like-minded ministers and I had largely converted the Cabinet, the Conservative Party and opinion in the worlds of finance, business and even the media to a more restrictive view of what the state's role in the economy should be. Moreover, as regards the regulatory framework within which business could run its affairs, there was a general understanding that lower taxes, fewer controls and less interference should be the goal. But as regards setting the overall financial framework there was less common ground. Whereas Nigel Lawson and I agreed strongly about the role of the state in general, we came sharply to differ about monetary and exchange rate policy.

Our success in bringing down inflation in our first term from a rate of 10 per cent (and rising) to under 4 per cent (and falling) had been achieved by controlling the money supply. 'Monetarism' – or the belief that inflation is a monetary phenomenon, i.e., 'too much money chasing too few goods' – had been buttressed by a fiscal policy which reduced government borrowing, freeing resources for private investment and getting the interest rate down. This combined approach had been expressed through the Medium Term Financial Strategy – in large measure Nigel Lawson's brainchild. Its implementation depended heavily on monitoring the monetary indicators. These, as I have noted, were often distorted, confusing and volatile. So, before the end of Geoffrey Howe's Chancellorship, the value of the pound against other currencies – the exchange rate – was also being taken into account.

It is important to understand what the relationship between the exchange rate and the money supply is – and what it is not. First consider the effect of an increase in the exchange rate; that is, one pound sterling is worth more in foreign currency. Because most import and export prices are fixed in foreign currencies, the sterling prices of these tradeable goods will fall. But this only applies to goods and services which are readily imported and exported, like oil or textiles. Many of the goods and services that comprise our national income are not of this sort: for example, we cannot export our houses or the services provided in our restaurants. The prices of these things are not directly affected by the exchange rate, and the indirect effect – passed on via wages – will be limited. What does more or less determine the prices of houses and other 'non-tradeables', however, is the money supply.

If the money supply rises too fast, the prices of non-tradeable domestic goods will rise accordingly, and a strong pound will not prevent that. But the interaction of a strong pound and a loose money supply causes the export sector to be depressed, resources to flow to houses, restaurants and the like. The balance of trade will then go into larger and larger deficits, which have to be financed by borrowing from foreigners. This kind of distortion just cannot last. Either the exchange rate has to come down, or monetary growth has to be curtailed, or both.

This result is of the utmost importance. Either one chooses to hold an exchange rate to a particular level, whatever monetary policy is needed to maintain that rate. Or one sets a monetary target, allowing the exchange rate to be determined by market forces. It is, therefore, quite impossible to control both the exchange rate *and* monetary policy.

A free exchange rate, however, is fundamentally *influenced* by monetary policy. The reason is simple. If a lot more pounds are put into circulation, then the value of the pound will tend to fall – just as a glut of strawberries will cause their value to go down. So a falling pound may indicate that monetary policy has been too loose.

But it may not. There are many factors other than the money supply which have a great influence on a free exchange rate. The most important of these are international capital flows. If a country reforms its tax, regulatory and trade union arrangements so that its after-tax rate of return on capital rises well above that of other countries, then there will be a net inflow of capital and its currency will be in considerable demand. Under a free exchange rate, it would appreciate. But this would not be a sign of monetary stringency: indeed, as in Britain in 1987 to mid-1988, a high exchange rate may well be associated with a considerable monetary expansion.

It follows from this that if the exchange rate becomes an objective in itself, 'monetarism' itself has been abandoned.

The only effective way to control inflation is by using interest rates to control the money supply. If, on the contrary, you set interest rates in order to stick at a particular exchange rate you are steering by a different and potentially more wayward star. As we have now seen twice – once when, during my time, Nigel shadowed the deutschmark outside the ERM and interest rates stayed too low; once when, under John Major, we tried to hold to an unrealistic parity inside the ERM and interest rates stayed too high – the result of plotting a course by this particular star is that you steer straight onto the reefs.

These questions went to the very heart of economic policy, which itself lies at the heart of democratic politics. But there was an even more important issue which was raised first by argument about whether sterling should join the ERM and then, in a more acute form, about whether we should accept European Community proposals for Economic and Monetary Union (EMU). This was the issue of sovereignty. Sterling's participation in the ERM was seen partly as proof that we were 'good Europeans'. But it was also seen as a way of abdicating control over our own monetary policy, in order to have it determined by the German Bundesbank. This was what was meant when people said we would gain credibility for our policies if we were 'anchored' to the deutschmark. Actually, if the tide changes and you *are* anchored, the only option to letting out more chain as your ship rises is to sink by the bows; and in an ERM where revaluations were ever more frowned upon there was no more chain to let out. Which leads on to EMU.

EMU – which involves the loss of the power to issue your own currency and acceptance of one European currency, one central bank and one set of interest rates – means the end of a country's economic independence and thus the increasing irrelevance of its parliamentary democracy. Control of its economy is transferred from the elected government, answerable to Parliament and the electorate, to unaccountable supranational institutions. In our opposition to EMU, Nigel Lawson and I were at one. But, alas, by his pursuit of a policy that allowed British inflation to rise, which itself almost certainly flowed from his passionate wish to take sterling into the ERM, Nigel so undermined confidence in my government that EMU was brought that much nearer.

I made Nigel Lawson Chancellor in 1983. At this time the exchange rate was just one factor being taken into account in order to assess monetary conditions. It was the monetary aggregates which were crucial. The wider measure of money – £M3 – which we had originally chosen in the MTFS had become heavily distorted. A large proportion of it was in reality a form of savings, invested for the interest it earned. In Nigel's first budget (1984) he set out different target ranges for narrow as well as broad money. The former – Mo – had been moving upward a good deal more slowly and this was taken into account in plotting the future course. But at this stage M3 and Mo were formally given equal importance in the conduct of policy. Other monetary indicators, including the exchange rate, were also taken into account. Our critics, who had until now denounced our policy as a rigid adherence to a statistical formula, began to denounce our rootless and arbitrary pragmatism. And indeed this was to mark the beginning of a process by which the clarity of the MTFS became muddied. This in turn, I suspect, caused Nigel, as the years went by, to search with increasing desperation for an alternative standard which he finally thought he had found in the exchange rate.

Events in January 1985 brought the ERM back into discussion. The dollar was soaring and there was intense pressure on sterling. I agreed with Nigel that our interest rates should be raised sharply. I also agreed with Nigel's view that there should be co-ordinated international intervention in the exchange rates to achieve greater stability, and I sent a message to this effect to President Reagan. This policy was formalized by Nigel and other Finance ministers under the so-called 'Plaza Agreement' in September. In retrospect, I believe that this was a mistake. The Plaza Agreement gave Finance ministers – Nigel above all perhaps – the mistaken idea that they had it in their power to defy the markets indefinitely. This was to have serious consequences for all of us.

Sterling's problems prompted Nigel to raise with me in February the issue of the ERM. He said that in his view controlling inflation required acceptance of a financial discipline which could be provided either by monetary targets or by a fixed exchange rate. New factors, argued Nigel, favoured the ERM. First, it was proving difficult to get financial markets to understand what the Government's policy towards the exchange rate really was: the ERM would provide much clearer rules of the game. There was also a political consideration. Many Conservative MPs were in favour of joining. Entry into the ERM would also move the focus of attention away from the value of the pound against the dollar – where, of course, the problem at this particular moment lay. Finally, £M3 was becoming increasingly suspect as a monetary indicator because its control depended increasingly on 'overfunding', with the resulting rise in the so-called 'bill mountain'.* I was not convinced on any of these counts, with the possible exception of the last. But I agreed that there should be a seminar involving the Treasury, the Bank of England and the Foreign Office to discuss it all.

Alan Walters could not attend the seminar and let me have his views separately. He put his finger on the key issue. Would membership of the ERM reduce the speculative pressure on sterling? In fact, it would proba-bly make it worse. That was the lesson to be drawn from what had happened to other ERM currencies.

At my seminar Nigel repeated the general argument in favour of joining which he had put to me earlier. Perhaps the most significant inter-vention, however, was that of Geoffrey Howe who had now been converted to the Foreign Office's departmental enthusiasm for the ERM and thought that we should be looking for an appropriate opportunity to join – though he, like Nigel, did not think the circumstances at the moment were right. It became clear that we would need to build up foreign exchange reserves if we wanted to be in a position to enter. I agreed that the Treasury and the Bank of England should consider how this should be done and the meeting ended amicably enough.

During the summer of 1985 I started to become concerned about the inflation prospect. £M3 was rising rather fast. Property prices were increasing, always a dangerous sign. The 'bill mountain' was worrying too – not because it suggested anything about inflation (indeed, the over-funding which led to it was in part the result of the Bank's attempt to control £M3). Rather, since we had decided against a policy of overfund-ing as far back as 1981, the fact that it had been resumed on such a scale without authorization did not increase my confidence in the way policy in general was being implemented.

---

* Overfunding was the practice by which the Government sought to reduce private bank deposits – and hence £M3 – by selling greater amounts of public debt than were required merely to finance its own deficit. The 'bill mountain' arose from the use of the proceeds to buy back Treasury bills from the market.

Even now it is unclear whether my misgivings were justified. Some analysts – notably the perceptive Tim Congdon – would argue that the rise in £M3 now and later did cause inflationary problems. By contrast, Alan Walters reckoned that monetary policy was sufficiently tight, as did the rest of my advisers. The important thing is that when clear evidence appears that things are slipping you take action fast. Certainly, I do not believe that monetary policy in 1985 – or 1986 – was the main cause of the problems we were later to face.

Nigel now returned to the charge on the ERM. I agreed to hold a further seminar at the end of September though by now I was more convinced than ever of the disadvantages of the ERM. I could see no particular reason to allow British monetary policy to be determined largely by the Bundesbank rather than by the British Treasury, unless we had no confidence in our own ability to control inflation. I was extremely sceptical about whether the industrial lobby, which was pressing us so hard to join the ERM, would maintain its enthusiasm once they came to see that it was making their goods uncompetitive. I doubted whether the public would welcome what might turn out to be the huge cost of defending sterling within the ERM – which, indeed, might well prove to be impossible in the run-up to a general election and so be compounded by a forced devaluation. Looking back over the last few years it was clear that sterling had not tracked other European currencies in a stable way. In 1980, sterling rose 20 per cent against the European Currency Unit (ecu). In 1981 it fell by 15 per cent from peak to trough. In 1982 it did the same. In 1983 it rose by as much as 10 per cent. In 1984 it was somewhat more stable. But in 1985 it had risen by more than 10 per cent. To control such movements, we would have needed recourse to huge quantities of international reserves and to a very tough interest rate policy.

There was nothing secret about these facts. But nothing is more obstinate than a fashionable consensus. Nor is it without influence on Cabinet committees. I had no support at the seminar at the end of September.

Nor did my arguments budge Nigel and Geoffrey. There was no point in continuing the discussion. I said that I was not convinced that the balance of argument had shifted in favour of joining.

Until 1987, when Nigel made the exchange rate the overriding objective of policy, there was no fundamental difference between us, although Nigel apparently now thinks I was 'soft' on interest rates. Anyone who recalls our decisions from 1979 to 1981 will find that implausible. It would also surprise anyone who considers that one of the main arguments advanced for joining the ERM, which Nigel so passionately wanted, was that it would lead to *lower* interest rates. And, as I shall show subsequently, there were occasions when I thought that *he* was soft on interest rates and wanted to raise them more quickly. The two of us were equally opposed to inflation but it was my constant refrain that much as I might admire his fiscal reforms, he had made no further progress in getting down the underlying inflation rate.

But we did have rather different starting points. I was always more sensitive to the political implications of interest rate rises – particularly their timing – than was Nigel. Prime Ministers have to be. I was also acutely conscious of what interest rate changes meant for those with mortgages whose prospects – even lives – can be shattered overnight by higher interest rates. My economic policy was also intended to be a social policy. It was a way to a property-owning democracy. And so the needs of home owners must never be forgotten. A low interest rate economy is far healthier than a high interest rate economy.

High real interest rates* do ensure that there is a high real reward for saving. But they discourage risk-taking and self-improvement. In the long run, they are a force for stagnation rather than enterprise. For these reasons I was cautious about putting up interest rates unless it was necessary.

Another reason for caution was the difficulty of judging precisely what the monetary and fiscal position was. The Mo figures were volatile from month to month. The other aggregates were worse. In these circumstances, making the right judgement about when and whether to cut or raise interest rates was indeed difficult. So at the meetings I had with Nigel, the Bank and Treasury officials to decide on what must be done I would generally cross-examine those involved, give my own reaction and then – when I was sure all the factors had been considered – go along with what Nigel wanted. There were exceptions. But they were very few.

It was only from March 1987 – though I did not know it at the time – that Nigel began to follow a new policy, different from mine, different

---

* In all this, it is always necessary to distinguish between nominal and real interest rates. High money interest rates are predominantly a consequence of the market's expectations of high inflation. If inflation is expected to be high, say at 10 per cent, then, even if one ignores taxes, interest rates of 10 per cent are required just to offset the inflationary erosion of a family's savings. In fact it is real interest rates – the excess of the percentage interest rate above the expected inflation – which affects the thrift and investment of families and businesses.

from that to which the Cabinet had agreed, and different from that to which the Government was publicly committed. Its origins lay in the ambitious policy of international exchange rate stabilization. In February Nigel and other Finance ministers agreed on intervention to stabilize the dollar against the deutschmark and the yen by the 'Louvre Accord' agreed in Paris. I received reports of the massive intervention this required which made me uneasy.

In July Nigel raised again with me the question of whether sterling should join the ERM. I was not unprepared for this and had earlier talked the subject through with Alan Walters and Brian Griffiths, the head of my Policy Unit who in an earlier incarnation had been Director of the Centre for Banking and International Finance at the City University. I said to Nigel that the Government had built up over the last eight years a well-founded reputation for prudence. By joining the ERM we would in effect be saying that we could not discipline ourselves. ERM membership would reduce the room for manoeuvre on interest rates which would, at times of pressure, be higher than they would be if we were outside. Overall, when things were going smoothly membership of the ERM would add nothing to our economic policy-making, and when things were going badly membership would make things worse. Nigel completely rejected this. He said he would want to discuss it all again with me in the autumn. I said that I would not wish to hold a further discussion on the subject until the New Year.

By now there was some evidence that the economy might be growing at a rate too strong to be sustainable. In August 1987 Nigel proposed a 1 per cent rise in interest rates on the grounds that this was required to defeat inflation by the next election. I accepted the proposal. That was the position when on 'Black Monday' (19 October 1987) there was a sharp fall in the Stock Market, precipitated by a fall in Wall Street. These developments were, in retrospect, no more than a market correction of overvalued stocks, made worse by 'programmed selling'. But they raised the question of whether, far from overheating, we might now be facing a recession.

I was in the United States when I learned about the Stock Market collapse. I dined that evening with some of America's leading businessmen and they put what had happened in perspective, saying that, contrary to some of the more alarmist reports, we were not about to see a meltdown of the world economy. Still, I thought it best to make assurance doubly sure, and I agreed to Nigel's request for two successive half percentage point cuts in interest rates in response to help restore business confidence.

What I did not know was that Nigel was setting interest rates according to the exchange rate so as to keep the pound at or below DM3. It may be asked how he could have pursued this policy since March without it becoming clear to me. But the fact that sterling tracks the deutschmark (or the dollar) over a particular period does not necessarily mean that the pursuit of a particular exchange rate is determining policy. There are so many factors involved in making judgements about interest rates and intervention that it is almost impossible at any particular time to know which factor has been decisive for whoever is in day-to-day charge.

Extraordinarily enough, I only learned that Nigel had been shadowing the deutschmark when I was interviewed by journalists from the *Financial Times* on Friday 20 November 1987. They asked me why we were shadowing the deutschmark at 3 to the pound. I vigorously denied it. But the chart they brought with them bore out what they said. The implications of this were, of course, very serious at several levels. First, Nigel had pursued a personal economic policy without reference to the rest of the Government. How could I possibly trust him again? Second, our heavy intervention in the exchange markets might well have inflationary consequences. Third, perhaps I had allowed interest rates to be taken too low in order that Nigel's undisclosed policy of keeping the pound below DM3 should continue.

I brought together as much information as I could about what had been happening to sterling and the extent of intervention. Then I tackled Nigel. At our meeting on Tuesday 8 December I expressed very strong concern about the size of the intervention needed to hold sterling below DM3. Nigel argued that the intervention had been 'sterilized' by the usual market operations and that it would not lead to inflation. I understood sterilization to mean that the Bank sold Treasury bills and gilts to ensure that the intervention funds did not affect short-term interest rates. But the large inflow of capital, even if sterilized in this sense, had its own effect, on the one hand in increasing monetary growth and on the other in putting additional downward pressure on market interest rates. This was an environment where Nigel superficially could justify lower base rates than domestic pressures warranted. As a result, inflation was stoked up.

In the early months of 1988 my relations with Nigel worsened. It seemed to me contradictory to raise interest rates – as we did by half a percentage point in February – while at the same time intervening to hold down sterling. But, equally, I knew that once I exerted my authority to forbid intervention on this scale it would be at the cost of my already damaged working relationship with Nigel. He had boxed himself into a situation where his own standing as Chancellor would be weakened if the pound went above DM3.

By the beginning of March, however, I had no option. On 2 and 3 March 1988 over £1 billion of intervention took place. The Bank of England was deeply anxious about the policy. So, I knew, were senior Treasury officials.

I had the matter out with Nigel at two meetings on Friday 4 March. I again complained about the level of exchange rate intervention. For his part, Nigel said it would be sterilized. But he did accept that intervention at the present rate could not continue indefinitely. I asked him to consult the Bank of England and report back later that day on whether the DM3 'cap' should be removed and, if so, when. When he returned he accepted that if on Monday there was still strong demand for sterling the rate should be allowed to go above DM3. He was keen to have some further intervention to break the speed at which the exchange rate might rise. I expressed my concern about this and said that my strong preference would be to allow time for the rate to find its own level without any intervention. But I was prepared to go along with some limited intervention if necessary. The pound accordingly rose through the DM3 limit.

Immediately, the Opposition and the media sought to make capital out of divisions between Nigel and me. I set out the policy accurately and the thinking behind it in the House of Commons on Thursday 10 March at Prime Minister's Questions:

> My Rt Hon. Friend the Chancellor and I are absolutely agreed that the paramount objective is to keep inflation down. The Chancellor never said that aiming for greater exchange rate stability meant total immobility. Adjustments are needed, as we learnt when we had a Bretton Woods system, as those in the EMS have learnt that they must have revaluation and devaluation from time to time. There is no way in which one can buck the market.

This last remark however provoked a flurry of press comment to which truth was no defence. The trouble was that it appeared to contrast with Nigel's continuing public statements that he did not want to see the exchange rate appreciate further.

The question arises whether at some point now or later I should have sacked Nigel. I would have been fully justified in doing so. He had pursued a policy without my knowledge or consent and he continued to adopt a different approach from that which he knew I wanted. On the other hand, he was widely – and rightly – credited with helping us win the 1987 election. He had complete intellectual mastery of his brief. He had the strong support of Conservative backbenchers and much of the Conservative press who had convinced themselves that I was in the wrong. Whatever had happened, I felt that if Nigel and I – supported by the rest of the Cabinet – pulled together we could avert or at least overcome the consequences of past mistakes and get the economy back on course for the next general election.

But this was not to be. Whatever I said in the House in answer to questions about interest rates and the exchange rate was given a construction to suggest that either I was not endorsing Nigel's views or that I was protesting too much my adherence to them. In these situations you just cannot win. Nigel was extremely upset over my remarks at Prime Minister's Questions on Thursday 12 May. Though I warmly supported him and his public statements I had not repeated Nigel's view that further exchange rate appreciation would be 'unsustainable'.

Geoffrey Howe was now also making mischief. From this time on it became clear to me that Nigel and he were in cahoots, and that of the two Geoffrey was the more ill-disposed to me personally. Earlier – in March – Geoffrey had made a speech in Zurich which was widely taken as siding with Nigel against me on the question of the exchange rate. Then on Friday 13 May he quite gratuitously slipped into his speech to the Scottish Party Conference in Perth the remark, apropos of our commitment to join the ERM 'when the time is right', that: 'We cannot forever go on adding that qualification to the underlying commitment.' This led the press to widen the perceived rift between me and Nigel over the ERM once more. I was not best pleased. When Geoffrey imprudently telephoned me the morning after his speech to ask for a meeting at which he and the Chancellor should come to see me later in the day to 'settle the semi-public dispute', I told him that I would be seeing Nigel later in the day to discuss the markets – which Geoffrey's own remarks had unsettled. But I was not seeing them together. I told him three times – since he persisted in his attempt to contrive a meeting at which he and Nigel could get their way – that the best thing he could do now was to keep quiet. We were not going into the ERM at present and that was that.

I spent Sunday at Chequers working on a speech I was to deliver to the General Assembly of the Church of Scotland: there was some mirth when my speech writers and I were discovered down on our knees in an appropriate posture, though drawing on the resources of Sellotape rather than the Holy Spirit. But, following the news reports during the day, I was also aware of just how damaging the constant media reports of splits and disagreements on the exchange rate were becoming.

Nigel arranged to see me on the Monday. He wanted to agree a detailed formulation for use by me in the House to describe our policy. I had been told by the Treasury in advance of the meeting that Nigel wanted a further interest rate cut. For my part, I had become appalled at the size of our intervention in the money markets which was clearly still failing to hold sterling at the level Nigel wanted and which, in spite of assurances from Nigel, I feared might prove inflationary. But I had got part of what I wanted – which would ideally have been a pound which found its own level in the markets – in that sterling had been allowed to rise to DM3.18. So I was not unhappy to have the suggested interest rate cut I knew he wanted. I was also aware that the speculators were beginning to consider sterling a one-way bet and that allowing them to burn their fingers a little would do no end of good.

Above all, however, this reduction of the interest rate on Tuesday 17 May by half a point to 7.5 per cent was the price of tolerable relations with my Chancellor, who believed that his whole standing was at stake if the pound appreciated outside any 'band' to which he might have semi-publicly consigned it. If I had refused both intervention and an interest rate cut and sterling had drifted up to find its proper level there was little doubt in my mind that Nigel would have resigned – and done so at a time when both the majority of the Parliamentary Party and the press supported his line rather than mine. Yet the economic price of accepting this political constraint now seems to me to have been too high. For the whole of this period the interest rate was too low. It should have been a good deal higher, whatever the effect on the level of sterling – or the level of the Chancellor's blood pressure.

I also agreed to use in the House a detailed endorsement of the line which Nigel and I had agreed at our Monday meeting on the place of the exchange rate as an element in economic policy. I had to go further than I would have liked, saying:

We have taken interest rates down three times in the last two months. That was clearly intended to affect the exchange rate. We use the available levers, both interest rates and intervention as seems right in the circumstances and ... it would be a great mistake for any speculator to think at any time that sterling was a one-way bet.

In fact from June 1988 onwards interest rates rose steadily.

Nigel insisted on raising them only half a per cent at a time. I would have preferred something sharper to convince the markets how seriously we took the latest indicator that the economy was growing too fast and that monetary policy had been too lax – namely the balance of payments figures. Nigel took a more laid-back view of these than I did. He thought that the current account balance of payments deficit, which was growing ever larger, was more important as an indicator that other things were going wrong than in its own right. But the deficit worried me because it confirmed that as a nation we were living beyond our means – as well as suggesting that higher inflation was on the way.

House prices were rising sharply. Mo was still growing too fast – outside its target range. The forecasts of inflation were constantly being revised upwards, though they still turned out to be too low. For example, in the September 1988 monthly Treasury Monetary Assessment inflation in March 1989 was forecast at 5.4 per cent. In October's note the forecast was 7 per cent. (In fact it turned out to be 7.9 per cent.) So as 1988 drew to a close – and although unemployment was down and growth and incomes were well up – there was trouble ahead.

It is on the face of it extraordinary that at such a time – November 1988 – Nigel should have sent me a paper proposing an independent Bank of England. My reaction was dismissive. Here we were wrestling with the consequences of his diversion from our tried-and-tested strategy which had worked so well in the first Parliament; and now we were expected to turn our policy upside down again. I minuted, 'It would be seen as an abdication by the Chancellor when he is at his most vulnerable.' I added that 'It would be an admission of a failure of resolve on our part.'

The year 1989 – Nigel's last as Chancellor – was a time of increasing political difficulty for me. It was also a time of very high interest rates – 13 per cent in January, 15 per cent from October – and with inflation still rising and the forecast figures apparently inexorably rising too. Alan Walters's view was that there was now too tight a monetary squeeze which would push the economy into a serious recession. In particular, he strongly advised against raising interest rates to 15 per cent, as Nigel wanted in response to a rise in interest rates in Germany. Alan was right. But I went along with Nigel's judgement and up went interest rates again. It is perhaps sufficient comment on the later allegation that I was undermining the Chancellor's position by not dismissing Alan Walters, that I backed Nigel against Alan's advice and against my own instincts just days before Nigel walked out.

Apart from the conduct of monetary policy, there were two economic issues of substance which concerned us during this period. On the first – the ERM – Nigel and I were sharply at odds. On the second – European Economic and Monetary Union – we were in complete agreement.

As a result of the Hanover European Council in June 1988 a Committee of European Community central bank heads – serving in a personal capacity – had been set up under the chairmanship of Jacques Delors to report on EMU. Nigel and I hoped that together Robin Leigh-Pemberton, Governor of the Bank of England, and Karl Otto Pohl, President of the Bundesbank, would prevent the emergence of a report which would give momentum to EMU. Herr Pohl we considered strongly hostile to any serious loss of monetary autonomy for the Bundesbank and Robin Leigh-Pemberton was in no doubt about the strength of our views – and indeed those (at this stage) of the great majority of the Parliamentary Conservative Party and of the House of Commons. Our line was that the report should be limited to a descriptive not a prescriptive document. But we hoped that paragraphs would be inserted which would make it clear that EMU was in no way necessary to the completion of the Single Market and which would enlarge upon the full implications of EMU for the transfer of power and authority from national institutions to a central bureaucracy.

Nigel and I had met the Governor on the evening of Wednesday 14 December 1988 and urged him to make all these points in the discussions on the text which ensued. We saw the Governor again on the afternoon of Wednesday 15 February. What we had seen of the draft report seemed thoroughly unsatisfactory, along lines known to be favoured by M. Delors who was clearly making the running. Nigel and I wanted the Governor to circulate his own document; but when this appeared it was something of a mouse. Most damaging of all was that Herr Pohl's known opposition to the Delors approach simply was not expressed.

When the Delors Report finally appeared in April 1989 it confirmed our worst fears. From the beginning there had been discussion of a 'three-stage' approach, which might at least have allowed us to slow the pace and refuse to 'advance' further than the first or second stage. But the report now insisted that by embarking on the first stage the Community committed itself irrevocably to the eventual achievement of full economic and monetary union. There was a requirement for a new treaty and for work on it to start immediately. There was also plenty of material in the treaty about regional and social policy – costly, Delorsian socialism on a continental scale. None of these was acceptable to me.

Nigel and then Geoffrey used the Delors Report to reopen the argument about the ERM. But I did not believe that the Delors Report on EMU altered the balance of argument on the ERM. On the contrary, we should certainly not be drawn further into a European system that would almost certainly change following the Delors Report. I did not accept that it was necessary to join the ERM in order to prevent developments in the Community which we did not like.

This did not mean that I was giving no thought to it. Alan Walters sent me a paper entitled 'When the Time will be Ripe', spelling out the conditions which must be met before we would join. He suggested that all the constituent countries must have abolished all foreign exchange controls and the legal machinery through which they were imposed. All domestic banking systems and financial and capital markets must be deregulated and open to competitive entry from EC countries. Any institution, corporation, partnership or individual must be free to enter any banking or financial business, subject only to minimum prudential conditions.

These were bold suggestions. The difficulty of Alan's approach, of course, was that it did not remove the fundamental objections which both he and I had to the system of semi-fixed exchange rates which the ERM constituted. But I knew that Alan's ingenious suggestion might be the only way in which I could resist the pressure from Nigel, Geoffrey and the European Community for early entry.

My relations with Nigel went through another difficult patch in May when an interview I gave to the World Service came indiscreetly close to admitting that the reason why our inflation rate had increased was because we had been shadowing the deutschmark. This, of course, was true, but it was a departure from the convenient answer that it was because we cut interest rates in the wake of the 'Black Monday' Stock Market crash and held them down too long that inflation had begun to rise. Nigel was at a European Finance ministers' meeting in Spain and became very upset. So I authorized a line for the press which reverted to the less accurate but more mutually acceptable explanation. But I did at this time ask the Treasury to provide me with a paper giving their explanation as to why inflation had risen. I was subsequently interested to learn that Nigel had asked that the first draft of this paper, which had focused almost exclusively on the shadowing of the ERM, should be revised to extend the analysis to cover the earlier 1985–86 period as well.* Not surprisingly under these circumstances, I found the finished product less sharp and persuasive than some other Treasury papers.

There was worse to come. On Wednesday 14 June 1989, just twelve days before the European Council in Madrid, Geoffrey Howe and Nigel Lawson mounted an ambush. Geoffrey, I soon learned, was the moving force. They sent me a joint minute arguing that in order to strike an acceptable compromise on the Delors EMU proposals – agreeing to Stage 1 but with no commitment to Stages 2 and 3 or an Inter-Governmental Conference – I should say that I would accept a 'non-legally binding reference' to sterling joining the ERM by the end of 1992, provided that certain conditions were fulfilled by then. The alternative was – as usual – 'isolation'. It was a typical Foreign Office paper which Nigel Lawson in his better days would have scornfully eviscerated.

However, I saw Nigel and Geoffrey on the evening of Tuesday 20 June to discuss their minute and its contents. At the end I said that I would reflect further on the way in which this issue should be handled at Madrid. I remained sceptical whether a concession on membership of the ERM would really achieve our agreed aim of blocking an IGC and Stages 2 and 3 of Delors. But this could only be judged on the spot at Madrid. In any event, I remained very wary of setting a date for sterling's membership.

I had not liked this way of proceeding – by joint minutes, pressure and cabals. But I was more than angry about what happened next. I received a further joint minute. In this Nigel and Geoffrey said that just spelling out in greater detail the conditions which would have to be fulfilled before we joined – widening these to include for example Single Market measures –

---

* The suggestion that the inflation, which began at the end of 1988 and lasted until mid-1991, could be explained by decisions on interest rates and monetary policy in 1985 assumed almost a four-year lag in the effect of monetary expansion on inflation. We know that lags, in Milton Friedman's words, are 'long and variable' with an average of about eighteen months. So three to four years is possible, but hardly plausible.

would be 'counter-productive'. There must be a date. And they wanted another meeting before Madrid.

I read their minute on Saturday morning at Chequers and almost immediately received a telephone call from my office to ask about the time for a meeting. This was extremely inconvenient. On Sunday afternoon I was due in Madrid. But they could not be deterred. I could have seen them late on Saturday night or early on Sunday morning at No. 10. They chose the latter.

I knew that Geoffrey had put Nigel up to this. He had been in a great state about the European election campaign which had not gone well for us. I knew that he had always thought that he might one day become Leader of the Conservative Party and Prime Minister – an ambition which became more passionate as it was slipping away from him. He considered himself – with some justice – as an important contributor to our past successes. This quiet, gentle, but deeply ambitious man with his insatiable appetite for compromise was now out to make trouble for me if he possibly could. Above all, I suspect, he thought that he had become indispensable – a dangerous illusion for a politician. There is no other explanation for what he now did and put Nigel up to doing.

Geoffrey and Nigel came to see me at 8.15 on Sunday morning, as arranged. They had clearly worked out precisely what they were to say. Geoffrey began. He urged that I should speak first at the Madrid Council setting out the conditions on which I would have sterling join and announcing a date for entry into the ERM. He and Nigel even insisted on the precise formula, which I took down: 'It is our firm intention to join not later than —' (a date to be specified). They said that if I did this I would stop the whole Delors process from going to Stages 2 and 3. And if I did not agree to their terms and their formulation they would both resign.

Three things jostled together in my mind. First, I was not prepared to be blackmailed into a policy which I felt was wrong. Second, I must keep them on board if I could, at least for the moment. Third, I would never, never allow this to happen again. I told them that I already had a paragraph spelling out in more detail the conditions under which sterling could enter the ERM and I would be using this in my opening speech. But I refused to give them any undertaking that I would set a date. Indeed, I told them that I could not believe that a Chancellor and a former Chancellor could seriously argue that I should set a date in advance: it would be a field day for the speculators, as they should have known. I said that I would reflect further on what to say at Madrid. They left, Geoffrey looking insufferably smug. And so the nasty little meeting ended.

I shall explain shortly the rest of what happened at the Madrid Council. Suffice it to say here that on the basis of what Alan had already suggested, and with some modification, I spelt out what became known as the 'Madrid conditions' for sterling's entry into the ERM. I reaffirmed our intention to join once inflation was down and there was satisfactory implementation of the first phase of the Delors Report, including free movement of capital and abolition of foreign exchange controls. But I did not set a date for entry, nor was I put under any pressure at Madrid to do so.

In fact, the Madrid conditions did allow me to rally the Conservative Party around our negotiating position and got us away from the tired and faintly ridiculous formula of 'when the time was right'. The outcome of Madrid was widely praised back at home. Unfortunately, in a sense the time would never be 'right' – because the ERM, particularly now that the Delors objective of EMU had come out into the open, would never be 'right'. But that was something I could do little about.

Back home, Cabinet began as usual at 10.30 on Thursday 29 June. Normally, I would sit at my place with my back to the door as Cabinet ministers trooped in. This time, however, I stood in the doorway – waiting. But there were no resignations. The condition that there must be a date for our joining the ERM might never have been mentioned. Nigel Lawson even managed the remark that Madrid had gone rather well, hadn't it? He certainly had a nerve, I thought: but then Nigel always did. That was one of his engaging characteristics.

It was from this time that tension between myself and Nigel Lawson arose over the independent economic advice that I was receiving from Alan Walters. Alan had returned to No. 10 in May 1989. I have already described his contribution to the 'Madrid conditions' for ERM entry. While the Treasury, thoroughly alarmed by the inflationary effects of Nigel's policy of shadowing the ERM, kept urging ever higher interest rates, Alan now drew my attention to the danger that excessively high interest rates might drive the economy into recession.[*] He was doing precisely what a Prime Minister's adviser should. He also had the merit of being right.

---

[*] Interest rates had gone up to 13 per cent in November 1988 and to 14 per cent in May 1989.

However, during his five-year absence from No. 10, he had been asked to give his views in all sorts of different forums and Alan's views were always trenchant. Various reports, articles and lectures containing his thoughts about economic policy issues in general and the ERM in particular kept on surfacing. Partly because these were exploited by the press to point up divisions between Nigel and me and partly because Nigel himself, knowing that he was being blamed for the return of inflation, was becoming hypersensitive, they became a major problem.

The important point, however, was that all this press speculation reflected an underlying reality. This was that Nigel and I no longer had that broad identity of views or mutual trust which a Chancellor and Prime Minister should. Nor was there any way that commentators were not going to hold Nigel to blame for the worsening economic outlook.

The *Financial Times* published on 18 October an article in which Alan was quoted, among other things, as describing the ERM as 'half-baked'. This article was based on an essay to be published in the *American Economist*. But what the *FT* did not say was that the latter was written by Alan in 1988, long before he returned as my economic adviser. I felt that he had nothing to apologize for and minuted:

> As the article was written well before Madrid (in which Alan also advised), I don't see the difficulty. Moreover, advisers ADVISE, ministers decide policy.

At 4.30 in the morning on Wednesday 25 October the VC10 which brought me back from the Commonwealth Conference at Kuala Lumpur arrived at Heathrow. Back at No. 10 I sorted out my personal belongings, discussed my diary with Amanda Ponsonby (my indispensable diary secretary), had lunch in the flat and then saw Nigel Lawson for one of our regular bilaterals. He was exercised about Alan Walters, having been repeatedly questioned in interviews about whether Alan should be sacked. But there were many other things we had to think about. In particular, we had to agree the line which Nigel would take at the forthcoming meeting of European Community Finance ministers on EMU. Nigel had devised an ingenious alternative approach, based on Friedrich Hayek's idea of competing currencies, in which the market rather than governments would provide the momentum for monetary union. (Unfortunately, this proposal did not get very far, not least because it was not at all in the statist, centralist model which our European Community partners preferred.) After seeing Nigel, I held a wider discussion of EMU which also included John Major (Foreign Secretary) and Nick Ridley (Trade and Industry Secretary) at which we endorsed Nigel's proposed approach in his paper, while accepting that its purpose was mainly tactical in order to slow down discussion of EMU within the Community.

The next day, Thursday, was bound to hold its difficulties. Not only were there Prime Minister's Questions: I also had to make a statement and answer questions on the outcome of the Kuala Lumpur CHOGM and, inevitably, on South Africa. I was under the hairdryer shortly after 8 o'clock in the morning when I received a message from my Private Office via Crawfie that Nigel Lawson wanted to see me at 8.50. Crawfie said something to me about it all being quite serious and that Nigel might be going to resign. But I said: 'Oh no, dear, you've got it all wrong. He's going to Germany this afternoon for a meeting and I expect he wants to see me about that.' So when I came downstairs to see Nigel I was quite unprepared for what he had to say. He told me that either Alan Walters must go or he – Nigel – would resign.

I told him not to be ridiculous. He was holder of a great office of state. He was demeaning himself even by talking in such terms. As for Alan, he was a devoted and loyal member of my staff who had always acted within the proprieties. If others, including the media, had attempted to exaggerate legitimate differences of opinion, that was no responsibility of his. There was no question of my sacking him. I asked Nigel to think again. I thought he accepted this advice. But there was little time to talk since I had to discuss the briefing for Parliamentary Questions and my statement at a meeting due to begin at 9.00 a.m.

An hour later Nigel came into a meeting with other ministers on the future of the Atomic Weapons Establishment at Aldermaston. He seemed on good form and made several acute interventions in the discussion. Then we met again – this time at Cabinet. I opened Cabinet by saying that we must be businesslike and get through the agenda promptly because two ministers had to leave for meetings in Europe. Nigel was one of them.

I was, therefore, doubly surprised when I was told over lunch that Nigel again wanted to see me. I had thought he was not even in the country. We again met in my study where he repeated his demand and said that he wanted to resign. There was nothing much new I could say and not much time to say it since I had soon to be in the House of Commons. But I made it clear that Alan Walters was not going and hoped that Nigel would reflect further. I said that I would see him after I had finished with Questions and my statement.

Over in my room in the House of Commons I was having a last look through my briefing when at 3.05 p.m. – a bare ten minutes before I was due to answer Questions in the House – Andrew Turnbull, my private secretary, came in to tell me that Nigel Lawson had decided to resign and that he wanted an announcement out by 3.30 p.m. This was out of the question. We had not told the Queen. We had no successor arranged. The London financial markets would still be open. I was about to face an hour on my feet answering questions and making a statement on the Commonwealth Conference. I repeated that I would see Nigel some time between 5.00 p.m. and 5.30 p.m. back in No. 10.

I only got through Questions and the Statement by relegating the crisis of Nigel's departure to the back of my mind. About an hour later, on my way out of the Chamber, I asked John Major, who had been sitting beside me for my Statement, to follow me to my room: 'I have a problem.'

Ideally, I would have liked to make Nick Ridley Chancellor. But Nick's scorn for presentational niceties might well have compounded the problem. John Major, who knew the Treasury from his days as Chief Secretary, looked the obvious choice. I had already thought that John might succeed me. But I would have liked him to gain more experience. He had only been at the Foreign Office for a few weeks and had not yet fully mastered this department. He would have liked to stay as Foreign Secretary rather than return to pick up the pieces after Nigel. When he expressed some reluctance I told him that we all have to accept second best occasionally. That applied to me just as much as to him. So he agreed with good grace.

I dashed back to No. 10 to see Nigel, who was still insisting that his resignation should be announced immediately. On reflection there seems to me just one explanation for Nigel's indecent haste. I think that he feared that I might telephone Alan Walters, who was in America, and that Alan would resign. This would have deprived him of the excuse he wanted. I now told Nigel that John Major was succeeding him. There was nothing left to discuss and it was a short meeting. I was sorry that our long and generally fruitful association should end in that way. I then telephoned Alan to tell him what happened. He told me that Nigel's resignation had put him in an impossible situation and so he insisted, against all my attempts to persuade him, on resigning too.

* * *

Nigel's departure was a blow to me – and one which Geoffrey Howe used to stir up more trouble when, the following weekend, in a speech of calculated malice, he praised Nigel as a Chancellor of great courage and insisted on entry into the ERM on the terms outlined at Madrid. But Nigel's going was also a boon in one respect. At least in John Major I had a Chancellor who, though he lacked Nigel's grasp of economics, had not got personal capital sunk in past policy errors. He was psychologically more able to deal with their consequences.

John – perhaps because he had made his name as a whip, or perhaps because he is unexcited by the sort of concepts which people like Nigel and I saw as central to politics – had one great objective: this was to keep the Party together. To him that meant that we must enter the ERM as soon as possible to relieve the political strains. This primacy of politics over economics – an odd attribute in a Treasury minister – also meant that John was attracted by a fudge on EMU which would assuage the anxieties of the timorous Europhiles in the Party that we would otherwise be 'isolated'. On ERM, I had agreed the principle at Madrid subject to the conditions expressed. Eventually, I was to go along with what John wanted. On EMU, which for me went to the very heart not just of the debate about Europe's future but about Britain's future as a democratic, sovereign state, I was not prepared to compromise.

Unlike Geoffrey and Nigel, John Major realized that to set an advance date for joining the ERM would leave us at the mercy of the markets. But by the morning of Thursday 29 March, it was increasingly clear that he wanted us to join soon. He said that bearing in mind the likely favourable impact of entry into the ERM on political sentiment and in turn on sentiment in the markets, it would be easier to bring interest rates down and maintain a firm exchange rate if we were inside rather than outside the ERM. That sounded all too like Nigel's cracked record to the effect that you should steer by the exchange rate rather than by the money supply. Alas, that policy had steered us into inflation. John's approach was that if the Party and the Government united around the policy and we looked like winning the next election, the economic prospect would improve as well. But I knew full well that whenever you take economic decisions for political purposes, you run considerable risks.

A few days later I discussed EMU and the Delors Report with John. He said that he would be minuting me with his conclusions on the best way forward. He said that the strategy must be to slow down the advance towards Stages 2 and 3 of Delors and the erosion of national sovereignty they entailed, but to ensure all the while that the UK was not excluded from the negotiating process. This had an India rubber feel to it. So I said that there were serious dangers if we adopted a posture which implied that moves beyond ERM membership towards further economic and monetary integration could be contemplated. If other member states wanted to take such steps that was up to them. But the UK would not participate in that process. If we made that absolutely clear, I thought it was likely that, under pressure from the Bundesbank, Germany would also decline to move to the next stages of EMU. I sought to get John to view all this in a wider context and talked to him about the need to develop free trade relations with the USA and other countries, pointing out that centrally controlled blocs of countries – such as a federal Europe looked like being – must not be allowed to stand in the way of this.

John Major became increasingly worked up about both ERM membership and EMU. On 9 April 1990 he minuted me that he had been startled by the determination of other European Community Finance ministers to agree a treaty for full EMU. He had found little support for our new alternative approach – a 'hard ecu' circulating alongside existing currencies, managed by a European Monetary Fund – which we had advanced as an 'evolutionary approach' to EMU.* He therefore set out a number of options as to how we might proceed. One – which was ultimately to be developed further at Maastricht – was to work for a treaty which gave a full definition of EMU and the institutions necessary for its final stage, but then allowed an 'opting-in' mechanism for member states. This would allow them to join in the new Stage 3 arrangements – that is, the single currency – at their own pace. He believed that this should be the goal we should work for as the outcome to the IGC. At a meeting with me on Wednesday 18 April, John rehearsed the arguments of his paper, emphasizing that the goal of full EMU as described by Delors was shared by all except the United Kingdom.

I agreed neither with John's analysis nor his conclusion. I said that the Government could not subscribe to a treaty amendment containing the full Delors definition of EMU. Further work should be done to develop our proposal for a European Monetary Fund which we could put forward

---

* Following the negative reception accorded to our original proposal for competing currencies, we began to develop this new hard ecu approach based on the suggestions made by Sir Michael Butler, Britain's former Ambassador to the Community, now working in the City.

as the most that it was necessary for the Community to agree upon for now. I was extremely disturbed to find that the Chancellor had swallowed so quickly the slogans of the European lobby. At this point, however, I felt that I should hold my fire. John was new to the job. He was right to be searching for a way forward which would attract allies in Europe as well as convince Conservative MPs of our reasonableness. But it was already clear that he was thinking in terms of compromises which would not be acceptable to me and that intellectually he was drifting with the tide.

Had Nigel Lawson managed to persuade me to have sterling enter the ERM in November 1985 the sterling/deutschmark rate would have been about DM3.75. A year later the pound was down to DM2.88. In November 1987 it was up to DM2.98. In November 1988 it was right up to DM3.16. In November 1989 it was back down to DM2.87. When we entered it was at a central parity of DM2.95, which was the rate at which the London market closed that day. What this shows on even a cursory glance is that revaluations and/or heavy intervention and very large shifts in interest rates would have been necessary to keep sterling in the mechanism throughout this period. It is, in fact, a demonstration that Alan Walters had been right in his view that the ERM ensured not stability, but rather the kind of instability which comes from movement in large leaps rather than by the more gradual accommodation of the market.

Only at my meeting with John Major on Wednesday 13 June did I eventually say that I would not resist sterling joining the ERM. Although the terms I had laid down had not been fully met, I had too few allies to continue to resist and win the day.

But my willingness to join the ERM was qualified by a crucial condition. I insisted that we enter the wide band – 6 per cent on either side. Even then I made it very clear that, if sterling came under pressure, I was not going to use massive intervention, either pouring in pounds and cutting interest rates to keep sterling down or raising interest rates to damaging levels and using precious reserves to keep sterling up. This makes nonsense of the claim, sometimes heard from ERM proponents justifying the subsequent collapse, that we were right to go in, but wrong to do so at that rate. In fact, a rate that is right today can be wrong tomorrow and vice versa. Until now, the ERM had never been a rigid system. I did not need to spell this out to our European partners because, whatever the fine points of detail, a country which wished to realign had always been able to do so in practice. Now that the UK was inside the ERM, other countries would have been so anxious to keep us in that they would have made little or no difficulty about realignment.

I resisted John Major's wish to go into the ERM in July. The monetary signals, indicating that inflation was starting to turn down so that we could enter the ERM with some confidence that the parity could be sustained, were not yet in place.

By the autumn, however, the high interest rates were clearly doing their work. The money supply fell sharply. It was clear that interest rates should now be reduced, quite apart from the question of the ERM. As regards ERM entry, the Madrid conditions had not been fully met. But the most important consideration was inflation. It was not till the end of the year that inflation as measured by the RPI (heavily distorted by mortgage interest rates and the way the community charge figured in it) began to fall. Other indicators, however – CBI surveys, car sales, retail sales and above all the money supply – showed that we were getting on top of inflation. I insisted against the Treasury and the Bank on a simultaneous announcement of a 1 per cent cut in interest rates. They had not disputed that the monetary and other figures warranted this; but they had wanted to delay. But I for my part was determined to demonstrate that we would be looking more to monetary conditions than to the exchange rate in setting interest rates. So on Friday 5 October we announced that we were seeking entry into the ERM, and I placed heavy emphasis on the interest rate cut and the reasons for it in presenting that day's decision.

CHAPTER THIRTY-SEVEN

The Babel Express

Relations with the European Community 1987–1990

I HAVE ALREADY DESCRIBED how during my second term of office as Prime Minister certain harmful features and tendencies in the European Community started to become evident. Against the notable gains constituted by the securing of Britain's budget rebate and progress towards a real Common – or 'Single' – Market had to be set a more powerful Commission ambitious for power, an inclination towards bureaucratic rather than market solutions to economic problems and the re-emergence of a Franco-German axis with its own covert federalist and protectionist agenda. As yet, however, the full implications of all this were unclear – even to me, distrustful as I always was of that un-British combination of high-flown rhetoric and pork-barrel politics which passed for European statesmanship.

It is fair to say that from early 1988 the agenda in Europe began to take an increasingly unwelcome shape. It also began to deviate sharply from that being pursued in the wider international community.

At the G7 summit in Toronto in June 1988, I had an hour's meeting with Chancellor Kohl. Much of it focused on the forthcoming Hanover summit. Chancellor Kohl, supported by the German Finance Ministry and the Bundesbank, seemed ready now to plump for a committee of central bankers rather than academic experts – as the French and the German Foreign Minister Hans-Dietrich Genscher wanted – to report on EMU. This I welcomed. But I restated my unbending hostility to setting up a European Central Bank. By now I was having to recognize that the chance of stopping the committee being set up at all was ebbing away; but

I was determined to try to minimize the harm it would do. I also had to recognize that we were saddled with M. Delors as President of the Commission for another two years, since my own favoured candidate, Ruud Lubbers, was not going to stand and the French and Germans supported M. Delors. (In the end I bit the bullet and seconded M. Delors's reappointment myself.)

The Hanover Council turned out to be a fairly good-humoured if disputatious affair. The most important discussion took place on the first evening over dinner. Jacques Delors introduced the discussion of EMU. Chancellor Kohl suggested that a committee of Central Bank governors with a few outsiders be set up under M. Delors's chairmanship. In the ensuing discussion most of the heads of government wanted the report to centre on a European Central Bank. Poul Schlüter, the Danish Prime Minister, opposed this and I supported him strongly. We succeeded in getting mention of the Central Bank removed. The Delors Group was to report back to the June 1989 European Council – that is, in a year's time.

My problem throughout these discussions of EMU was twofold. First, of course, was the fact that I had so few allies; only Denmark, a small country with plenty of spirit but less weight, was with me. But I was fighting with one hand tied behind my back for another reason. As a 'future member' of the EEC, the UK had agreed a communiqué in Paris following a conference of heads of government in October 1972. This reaffirmed 'the resolve of the member states of the enlarged Community to move irrevocably [towards] Economic and Monetary Union, by confirming all the details of the acts passed by the Council and by the member states' representatives on 22 March 1971 and 21 March 1972'. Such language may have reflected Ted Heath's wishes. It certainly did not reflect mine. But there was no point in picking a quarrel which we would have lost. I preferred to let sleeping dogs lie.

Then, of course, they woke up and started barking in the course of the negotiation of the Single European Act of 1985–86. I had not wanted any reference to EMU in at all. The Germans failed to support me and so the reference to EMU was inserted. But I had Article 20 of the Single European Act give my interpretation of what EMU meant; its title read: 'Co-operation in Economic and Monetary Policy (Economic and Monetary Union)'. This enabled me to claim at subsequent forums that EMU now meant economic and monetary co-operation, not moving towards a single currency. There was a studied ambiguity about all this. Councils at Hanover in June 1988 and then at Madrid in 1989 referred back to the

Single European Act's 'objective of progressive realization of economic and monetary union'. I was more or less happy with this, because it meant no more than co-operation. The rest of the European heads of government were equally happy, because they interpreted it as progress towards a European Central Bank and a single currency. At some point, of course, these two interpretations would clash. And when they did I was bound to be fighting on ground not of my choosing.

The fact was that the more I saw of how the Community operated, the less I was attracted by any further steps on the road towards monetary integration. We advanced our proposals for a 'hard ecu'. We issued Treasury bills denominated in ecu terms. And (though this was done because it was in our own interests, not in order to please our European partners) we had swept away exchange controls before anyone else. All this was very *communautaire* in its way, as I never ceased to point out when criticized for resisting entry into the ERM. But my own preference was always for open markets, floating exchange rates and strong political and economic transatlantic links. In arguing for that alternative approach I was bound to be handicapped by the formal commitment to European 'economic and monetary union' – or indeed that of 'ever closer union' contained in the preamble to the original Treaty of Rome. These phrases predetermined many decisions which we thought we had reserved for future consideration. This gave a psychological advantage to my opponents, who never let an opportunity go by of making use of it.

Not the least of those opponents was Jacques Delors. By the summer of 1988 he had become a fully fledged political spokesman for federalism. The blurring of the roles of civil servants and elected representatives was more in the continental tradition than in ours. It proceeded from the widespread distrust which their voters had for politicians in countries like France and Italy. That same distrust also fuelled the federalist express. If you have no real confidence in the political system or political leaders of your own country you are bound to be more tolerant of foreigners of manifest intelligence, ability and integrity like M. Delors telling you how to run your affairs. Or to put it more bluntly, if I were an Italian I might prefer rule from Brussels too. But the mood in Britain was different. I sensed it. More than that, I shared it and I decided that the time had come to strike out against what I saw as the erosion of democracy by centralization and bureaucracy, and to set out an alternative view of Europe's future.

It was high time. It was clear that the momentum towards full-blooded EMU, which I always recognized must mean political union too, was building. In July M. Delors told the European Parliament that 'We are not going to manage to take all the decisions needed between now and 1995 unless we see the beginnings of European government in one form or another,' and predicted that within ten years the Community would be the source of '80 per cent of our economic legislation and perhaps even our fiscal and social legislation as well'. In September he addressed the TUC in Bournemouth, calling for measures to be taken on collective bargaining at the European level.

But there were also more subtle, less easily detectable, but perhaps even more important signs of the way things were going. That summer I commissioned a paper from officials which spelt out in precise detail how the Commission was pushing forward the frontiers of its 'competence' into new areas – culture, education, health and social security. It used a whole range of techniques. It set up 'advisory committees' whose membership was neither appointed by, nor answerable to, member states and which tended therefore to reach *communautaire* decisions. It carefully built up a library of declaratory language, largely drawn from the sort of vacuous nonsense which found its way into Council conclusions, in order to justify subsequent proposals. It used a special budgetary procedure, known as *'actions ponctuelles',* which enabled it to finance new projects without a legal base for doing so. But, most seriously of all, it consistently misemployed treaty articles requiring only a qualified majority to issue directives which it could not pass under articles which required unanimity.

Often, it was difficult to explain to the general public precisely why we opposed the specific measure the Commission wanted. This made it politically difficult to resist the creeping expansion of the Commission's authority. In theory, it would have been possible to fight all this in the courts; for time after time the Commission were twisting the words and intentions of the European Council to its own ends. We did indeed fight, and won a number of cases on these grounds before the European Court of Justice (ECJ). But the advice from the lawyers was that in relation to questions of Community and Commission competence the ECJ would favour 'dynamic and expansive' interpretations of the treaty over restrictive ones. The dice were loaded against us.

The more I considered all this, the greater my frustration and the deeper my anger became. Were British democracy, parliamentary sovereignty, the common law, our traditional sense of fairness, our ability to run our own affairs in our own way to be subordinated to the demands of a remote European bureaucracy, resting on very different traditions? Because Britain was the most stable and developed democracy in Europe we had perhaps most to lose from these developments. But Frenchmen who wanted to see France free to decide her own destiny would be losers too. So would Germans, who wished to retain their own currency, the deutschmark, which they had made the most credible in the world.

I was no less conscious of those millions of eastern Europeans living under communism. How could a tightly centralized, highly regulated, supra-national European Community meet their aspirations and needs?

This wider Europe, stretching perhaps to the Urals and certainly to include that New Europe across the Atlantic, was an entity which made at least historical and cultural sense. And in economic terms, only a truly global approach would do. This then was my thinking as I turned my mind to what would be the 'Bruges Speech'.

The hall in which I made my speech was oddly arranged. The platform from which I spoke was placed in the middle of the long side so that the audience stretched far to my left and right, with only a few rows in front of me. But the message got across well enough. And it was not only my hosts at the College of Europe in Bruges who got more than they bargained for. The Foreign Office had been pressing me for several years to accept an invitation to speak there to set out our European credentials.

I began by doing what the Foreign Office wished. I pointed out just how much Britain had contributed to Europe over the centuries and how much we still contributed, with 70,000 British servicemen stationed there. But what was Europe? I went on to remind my audience that, contrary to the pretensions of the European Community, it was not the only manifestation of European identity. 'We shall always look on Warsaw, Prague and Budapest as great European cities.' I went on to argue that western Europe had something to learn from the admittedly dreadful experience of its eastern neighbours and their strong and principled reaction to it:

> It is ironic that just when those countries, such as the Soviet Union, which have tried to run everything from the centre, are learning that success depends on dispersing power and decisions away from the centre, some in the Community seem to want to move in the opposite direction. We have not successfully rolled back the frontiers of the state in Britain only to see them reimposed at a European level, with a European super-state exercising a new dominance from Brussels.

There were, moreover, powerful non-economic reasons for the retention of sovereignty and, as far as possible, of power, by nation-states. Not only were such nations functioning democracies, but they also represented intractable political realities which it would be folly to seek to override or suppress in favour of a wider but as yet theoretical European nationhood. I pointed out:

> Willing and active co-operation between independent sovereign states is the best way to build a successful European Community ... Europe will be stronger precisely because it has France as France, Spain as Spain, Britain as Britain, each with its own customs, traditions and identity. It would be folly to try to fit them into some sort of identikit European personality.

I set out other guidelines for the future. Problems must be tackled practically: and there was plenty in the CAP which still needed tackling. We must have a European Single Market with the minimum of regulations – a Europe of enterprise. Europe must not be protectionist: and that must be reflected in our approach to the GATT. Finally, I stressed the great importance of NATO and warned against any development (as a result of Franco-German initiatives) of the Western European Union as an alternative to it.*

Not even I would have predicted the furore the Bruges speech unleashed. In Britain, to the horror of the Euro-enthusiasts, there was a great wave of popular support for what I had said. But the reaction in polite European circles – or at least the official reaction – was one of stunned outrage.

By now attention in British politics was turning to two issues which, much as I sought to disentangle them, became entwined: the elections to the European Parliament and the occasion of my tenth anniversary. On the second of these, I had given strict instructions to Central Office and the Party that it should be handled with as little fuss as possible. I gave one or two interviews; I received a commemorative vase from the National Union; and a rather attractive publication was issued by the

---

* The WEU was formed in 1948, principally for the purpose of military co-operation between Britain, France and the Benelux countries. Germany and Italy joined it in the 1950s. The WEU predated NATO, which has entirely overshadowed it.

Party, which was a modest success without being exactly a bestseller. But, of course, there were plenty of journalists anxious to write 'reflective' pieces on ten years of Thatcher and to conclude, as I knew they would, that a decade of this woman was quite enough.

In such an atmosphere it was natural that the Labour Party would claim that the 1989 European elections were a 'referendum' on Thatcherism in general and the Bruges approach in particular. I might have accepted that the European elections were a sort of judgement on Bruges if we had had European candidates who were Brugesist rather than federalist. With a few notable exceptions that was not the case.

The overall strategy was simple. It was to bring Conservative voters – so many of whom were thoroughly disillusioned with the Community – out to vote. Perhaps it might have worked if the message had been got across with greater conviction and vigour by the candidates themselves and if we had been free of highly publicized attacks from Ted Heath and others. In fact, at the very last moment there was a late surge to the Green Party which undercut our vote. People had treated the European elections rather as they would a by-election, voting not to effect real changes in their lives but to make a protest against the sitting government. Labour were the beneficiaries and gained thirteen seats from us. For all the mitigating factors, I was not happy. The result would encourage all those who were out to undermine me and my approach to Europe.

This did not take long to occur. I have already described how Geoffrey Howe and Nigel Lawson tried to hustle me into setting a date for sterling's entry into the ERM and how I avoided this at the Madrid Council in June 1989. In fact, the ERM was something of an irrelevance at Madrid. The two real issues were the handling of the Delors Report on EMU and the question of whether the Community should have its own Social Charter.

I was, of course, opposed root and branch to the whole approach of the Delors Report. But I was not in a position to prevent some kind of action being taken upon it. Consequently, I decided to stress three points. First, the Delors Report must not be the only basis for further work on EMU. Second, there must be nothing automatic about the process of moving towards EMU either as regards timing or content. In particular, we would not be bound now to what might be in Stage 2 or when it would be implemented. Third, there should be no decision now to go ahead with an Inter-Governmental Conference on the Report. A fall-back position would be that any such IGC must receive proper – and as lengthy as possible – preparation.

As regards the Social Charter, the issue was simpler. I considered it quite inappropriate for rules and regulations about working practices or welfare benefits to be set at Community level. The Social Charter was quite simply a socialist charter – devised by socialists in the Commission and favoured predominantly by socialist member states.

Most of the first day's discussions in Madrid were taken up with EMU. Late in the afternoon we turned to the Single Market and the 'social dimension'. I have already described how I used my first speech to spell out my conditions for entering the ERM. But I also backed Poul Schlüter who challenged paragraph 39 of the Delors Report, which essentially spelt out the 'in for a penny, in for a pound approach' which the federalists favoured. The other extreme was represented by France. President Mitterrand insisted on setting deadlines for an IGC and for completion of Stages 2 and 3, which at one point he suggested should be 31 December 1992.

The argument then turned to the Social Charter. I was sitting next to Sr Cavaco Silva, the rather sound Portuguese Prime Minister who would doubtless have been sounder still if his country was not so poor and the Germans quite so rich.

'Don't you see', I said, 'that the Social Charter is intended to stop Portugal attracting investment from Germany because of your lower wage costs? This is German protectionism. There will be directives based on it and your jobs will be lost.' But he seemed unconvinced that the charter would be anything other than a general declaration. And perhaps he thought that if the Germans were prepared to pay enough in 'cohesion' money the deal would not be too bad. So I was alone in opposing the charter.

The European election results had no particular significance in themselves. But they had revealed a groundswell of discontent which could not be ignored. A minority of Conservative MPs were uneasy about the line I was taking on Europe. But more important was the fact that there was a widespread restlessness because avenues of promotion into the ranks of the Government seemed blocked. I too felt that changes were required. When a Prime Minister has been in power for ten years he or she must be that much more aware of the dangers of the Government as a whole appearing to be tired or stale. I decided to make some changes in the Cabinet to free up posts at every level and bring on some new faces.

I had also been thinking about my own future. I knew that I had a good few more years of active service left in me and I intended to see through to the end the restoration of our economic strength, the fulfilment of our radical social reforms and that remodelling of Europe on which I had embarked with the Bruges speech. I wanted to leave behind me when I went, perhaps halfway into the next Parliament, several candidates with proven character and experience from whom the choice of my successor could be made. For various reasons I did not believe that any of my own political generation were suitable. If one considers the possibilities – first among those who were of my own way of thinking: Norman Tebbit was now concentrating on looking after Margaret and on his business interests; Nick Ridley who never suffered fools gladly would not have been acceptable to Tory MPs; Cecil Parkinson had been damaged in the eyes of the old guard. Geoffrey Howe I shall come to shortly. Nigel Lawson had no interest in the job – and I had no interest in encouraging him. Michael Heseltine was not a team player and certainly not a team captain. Anyway, I saw no reason to hand over to anyone of roughly my age while I was fit and active. In the next generation, by contrast, there was a variety of possible candidates: John Major, Douglas Hurd, Ken Baker, Ken Clarke, Chris Patten and perhaps Norman Lamont and Michael Howard. I felt it was not for me to select my successor. But I did have the obligation to see that there were several proven candidates from whom to choose.

I was, however, wrong on one important matter. Of course, I understood that some of my Cabinet colleagues and other ministers were more to the left, some more to the right. But I believed that they had generally become convinced of the rightness of the basic principles as I had. Orthodox finance, low levels of regulation and taxation, a minimal bureaucracy, strong defence, a willingness to stand up for British interests wherever and whenever threatened – the arguments for them seemed to me to have been won. I now know that such arguments are never finally won.

A little earlier I left aside Geoffrey Howe from my discussion of possible leadership candidates. Something had happened to Geoffrey. His clarity of purpose and analysis had dimmed. I did not think he was any longer a possible leader. But worse than that, I could not have him as Foreign Secretary – at least while Nigel Lawson was Chancellor – after his behaviour on the eve of the Madrid Council. I was determined to move him aside for a younger man.

I decided that two ministers should leave the Cabinet altogether. Paul Channon was loyal and likeable. But Transport was becoming a very important department in which public presentation was at a premium – what with the appalling disasters which seemed to plague us at this time and in the light of the traffic congestion which Britain's new prosperity brought with it. I asked Paul to leave and he did so with perfect good humour. I appointed Cecil Parkinson to his place. Deciding to ask John Moore to go was even more of a wrench. He was of my way of thinking. At Health it was he – rather than his successor Ken Clarke – who had really got the Health review under way. At Social Security, after I split the DHSS into two departments, he had been courageous and radical in his thinking about dependency and poverty. But John had never fully recovered, at least psychologically, from the debilitating illness he suffered while Secretary of State at the old combined DHSS. So I asked him to make way and appointed Tony Newton, a stolid, left-inclining figure but one with a good command of the House and of his brief. I also brought into the Cabinet Peter Brooke who had been a much-loved and utterly dependable Party Chairman. He wanted to be Ulster Secretary and I gave him the job, moving Tom King to the Defence Ministry, vacated by George Younger who wanted to leave the Government to concentrate on his business interests. George's departure was a blow. I valued his common sense, trusted his judgement and relied on his loyalty. His career is proof of the fact that, contrary to myth, gentlemen still have a place in politics.

But there were three main changes which determined the shape of the reshuffle and the reception it received. In reverse order of importance: I moved Chris Patten to the Environment Department to succeed Nick Ridley, who went to the DTI (David Young left the Cabinet at his request and became Deputy Chairman of the Party); I moved Ken Baker to become Party Chairman from the Department of Education, where he was succeeded by John MacGregor. And John was succeeded by John Gummer who entered the Cabinet as Minister for Agriculture.

But first, and crucially, I called in Geoffrey Howe and said that I wanted him to leave the Foreign Office where I intended to put John Major. It was predictable that Geoffrey would be displeased. He had come to enjoy the trappings of his office and his two houses, in Carlton Gardens in London and Chevening in Kent. I offered him the Leadership of the House of Commons at a time when the House was shortly to be televised for the first time. It was a big job and I hoped he would recognize the fact. But he just looked rather sullen and said that he would have to talk to Elspeth first. This, of course, held up the whole process. I could see no other ministers until this matter was decided. Geoffrey also, I believe, saw David Waddington, the Chief Whip, who had advised me to keep Geoffrey in the Cabinet in some capacity. Back and forth to Downing Street messages passed in the course of which I offered Geoffrey the Home Office – knowing in advance that he would almost certainly not accept – then, after conferring with Nigel Lawson, Dorneywood, the Chancellor's country house which I rightly thought that he would accept, and finally, with some reluctance and at his insistence, the title of Deputy Prime Minister which I had held in reserve as a final sweetener. This is a title with no constitutional significance but which Willie Whitelaw (until his stroke in December 1987 and subsequent resignation) had almost made his own because of his stature and seniority. But because Geoffrey had bargained for the job, it never conferred the status which he hoped. In practical terms it just meant that Geoffrey sat on my immediate left at Cabinet meetings – a position he may well have come to regret.

The delay in concluding the reshuffle was bound to prompt speculation. But it was, I am told, Geoffrey's partisans who leaked the content of our discussions in a singularly inept attempt to damage me. As a result he received a very bad press about the houses, which he doubtless blamed on me.

John Major was not at first very keen on becoming Foreign Secretary. A modest man, aware of his inexperience, he would probably have preferred a less grand appointment. But I knew that if he was to have a hope of becoming Party Leader, it would be better if he had held one of the three great offices of state. I should add that I had not, contrary to much speculation, reached a firm decision that John was my preferred successor. I had simply concluded that he must be given wider public recognition and greater experience if he was to compete with the talented self-publicists who would be among his rivals. Unfortunately, because of Nigel Lawson's resignation, he had no opportunity to show what he was made of at the Foreign Office before returning to the Treasury.

In moving Nick Ridley to the DTI I was generally seen to be responding to the criticisms of him by the environmental lobby. This was not so. I knew he wanted a change. I was, of course, quite aware of the fact that the romantics and cranks of the movement did not like it when he insisted on basing policy on science rather than prejudice. I also suspected that from Chris Patten they would get a more emollient approach. Certainly, I subsequently found myself repeatedly at odds with Chris, for with him presentation on environmental matters always seemed to be at the expense of substance. But I also wanted Nick in the second most important economic department because of the need to have his support on the key issues of industry and Europe.

Ken Baker's appointment as Party Chairman was an attempt to improve the Government's presentation. Ken – like Chris Patten – had started off on the left of the Party. But unlike Chris, Ken had genuinely moved to the centre. In any case his great skills were in publicity. And I never forgot that for every few Thatchers, Josephs and Ridleys you need at least one Ken Baker to concentrate on communicating the message. My appointment of Ken Baker to the chairmanship was a success. He served me with vigour and enthusiasm right to the end, however hot the political kitchen became. We had never been close political allies, so I was doubly indebted to him for this.

After Spain the European Community presidency passed to France. Partly in order to ensure that eastern Europe did not dominate the European Council scheduled for December at Strasbourg, President Mitterrand called a special Council in November in Paris specifically to discuss the consequences of events in the East and the fall of the Berlin Wall. He was also pressing hard for the creation of a European Bank of Reconstruction and Development (EBRD) in order to channel investment and assistance to the emerging democracies. I was sceptical about whether such an institution was really necessary. The case had not been made that aid of this dimension had to go through a European institution, as opposed to national or wider international ones. I conceded the point in Strasbourg; but my wishes were eventually met because the EBRD now sensibly involves the Americans and Japanese, not just the Europeans.

To some extent the French strategy of holding an 'unofficial' Paris Council on East-West relations worked because the Strasbourg Council concentrated – at least in its official sessions – heavily on the more narrowly European matters of EMU and the Social Charter. The French aim was to set a date for the IGC and this I still hoped to stave off. Until a few days before the start of the Council we were optimistic that the Germans would support us in calling for 'further preparation' before the IGC met. But in a classic demonstration of the way in which the Franco-German axis always seemed to re-form in time to dominate the proceedings, Chancellor Kohl went along with President Mitterrand's wishes. By the time I arrived in Strasbourg I knew that I would be more or less on my own. I decided to be sweetly reasonable throughout, since there was no point in causing gratuitous offence when I could not secure what I really wanted. It was agreed that the IGC would meet under the Italian presidency before the end of 1990, but after the German elections. As for the Social Charter at which I had directed my fire at Madrid, I reaffirmed that I was not prepared to endorse the text, my determination having been if anything strengthened by the fact that the Commission was now proposing to bring forward no fewer than forty-three separate proposals, including seventeen legally binding directives, in the areas which the charter covered. That effectively ended the discussion of the charter from our point of view. On EMU I would return to the fray in Rome.

In the first half of 1990, however, there was the Irish presidency to contend with. The unwelcome habit of calling extra 'informal' Councils proved catching. Charles Haughey decided that another one was needed in order to consider events in eastern Europe and the implications for the Community of German unification. For others this was just an opportunity to keep up the federalist momentum.

'Political union' was now envisaged alongside 'monetary union'. In a sense, of course, this was only logical. But behind the concept of 'political union' there lay a special Franco-German agenda. The French wanted to curb German power. To this end, they envisaged a stronger European Council with more majority voting: but they did not want to see the powers of the Commission or the European Parliament increased. The French were federalists on grounds of tactics rather than conviction. The Germans wanted 'political union' for different reasons and by different means. For them it was partly the price of achieving quick reunification with East Germany on their own terms and with all the benefits which would come from Community membership, partly a demonstration that the new Germany would not behave like the old Germany from Bismarck to Hitler.

For my part I was opposed to political union of either kind. But the only way that I could hope to stop it was by getting away from the standard Community approach whereby a combination of high-flown statements of principle and various procedural devices prevented substantive discussion of what was at stake until it was too late. Within the Community I must aim to open up the divisions between the French and the Germans. At home I must point out in striking language just what 'political union' would and would not mean if it was taken at all seriously. Far too much of the Community's history had consisted of including nebulous phrases in treaties and communiqués, then later clothing them with federal meaning which we had been assured they never possessed. Consequently, I decided that I would go to Dublin with a speech which would set out what political union was not and should never be.

There was no doubt about how determined the French and Germans were in their federalist intentions. Shortly before the Council met in Dublin at the end of April President Mitterrand and Chancellor Kohl issued a joint public statement calling for the Dublin Council to 'initiate preparations for an Inter-Governmental Conference on political union'. They also called on the Community to 'define and implement a common foreign and security policy'. President Mitterrand and Chancellor Kohl chose at about the same time to send a joint letter to the President of Lithuania urging temporary suspension of that country's declaration of independence in order to ease the way for talks with Moscow. As I took some pleasure in pointing out in my subsequent speech at the Council, this was done without any consultation with the rest of the Community, let alone NATO – it demonstrated that the likelihood of a common 'foreign and security policy' was somewhat remote.

I made my speech early on in the proceedings over a working lunch. I said that the way to dispel fears was to make clear what we did not mean when we were talking about political union. We did not mean that there would be a loss of national identity. Nor did we mean giving up separate heads of state, either the monarchies to which six of us were devoted or the presidencies which the other six member states favoured. We did not intend to suppress national parliaments; the European Parliament must have no role at the expense of national parliaments. We did not intend to change countries' electoral systems. We would not be altering the role of the Council of Ministers. Political union must not mean any greater centralization of powers in Europe at the expense of national governments and parliaments. There must be no weakening of the role of NATO and no attempt to turn foreign policy co-operation into a restriction on the rights of states to conduct their own foreign policy.

To deliver a ten-minute speech with one's tongue in one's cheek is as much a physical as a rhetorical achievement. For of course this was precisely the route which political union, if taken seriously, would go.

At the end of June we were back in Dublin again. The Community Foreign ministers had been told to go away and produce a paper on political union for the European Council's consideration. I hoped that I had at least put down a marker against the sort of proposals which were likely to come before us at some future stage. But I was in no position to stop an IGC being called.

Of the two, it was EMU rather than political union which posed the more immediate threat. What was so frustrating was that others who shared my views had a variety of reasons for not expressing them and preferring to let me receive the criticism for doing so. The weaker economies would have been devastated by a single currency, but they hoped to receive sufficient subsidies to make their acquiescence worthwhile.

To get away from the often parochial atmosphere of the European Councils to a meeting of the G7 was always a relief. That at Houston in July was the first chaired by President Bush, who was by now imposing very much his own style on the US Administration. These economic summits were by no means just 'economic' any longer: nor could they be when the economic and political world order was changing so radically and rapidly. In the forefront of all our minds was what needed to happen to ensure order, stability and tolerable prosperity in the lands of the crumbling USSR. But no less important was that at the G7 I could argue much more effectively for free trade and recruit allies for my cause than I could within the narrower framework of the Community.

I now strongly supported Brian Mulroney who argued that the biggest losers if the GATT failed would be the less developed countries. I also reminded those present of the huge amounts still being spent by the European Community, the United States and Japan on agricultural support. In fact, the section of the Houston communiqué which dealt with trade constituted the best and toughest statement ever made by the major economies on the subject. The tragedy was that the European Community's commitment to trade liberalization was only skin deep, as subsequent events were to show.

I flew into Rome at midday on Saturday 27 October knowing that this would be a difficult occasion. I did not realize how difficult. This time the excuse for holding an 'informal' Council before the formal Council in December was allegedly to take stock of preparations for the forthcoming CSCE summit and to discuss relations with the Soviet Union. In fact, the Italians wanted to pre-empt the outcome of the two IGCs on EMU and political union.

As always with the Italians, it was difficult throughout to distinguish confusion from guile: but plenty of both was evident. In his 'bidding letter' to the Council Sig. Andreotti made no mention of the need to discuss the GATT Uruguay round trade negotiation. I wrote back insisting that if the Community Trade and Agriculture ministers had not reached agreement on the Community offer on agriculture beforehand we must discuss the matter at Rome because time was running out.

More of a clue to the Italians' intentions was perhaps given by the Italian Foreign minister's letter which went so far as to suggest a provision for future transfer of powers from member states to the Community without treaty amendment. The Italians gave out that they would be taking a moderate line, not pressing for a specific date for the start of Stage 2 of EMU and noting that Britain's hard ecu proposal must be taken seriously. A long and often contradictory list of proposals on political union had been drawn up by the presidency, including plans for a common foreign policy, extended Community competence, more majority voting, greater powers for the European Parliament and other matters. The precise purpose of this paper remained unclear. What I did not know was that behind the scenes the Italians had agreed with a proposal emanating from Germany and endorsed by Christian Democrat leaders from several European countries at an earlier caucus meeting that the GATT should not be discussed at the Council. Had there been such a discussion, of course, they would have found it more difficult to portray me as the odd one out and themselves as sea-green internationalists.

Chancellor Kohl had spoken publicly of the need to set deadlines for the work of the IGCs and for Stage 2 of EMU. But on the eve of the Rome Council he took a surprisingly soft line with Douglas Hurd, now Foreign Secretary, about his intentions. Herr Kohl suggested that perhaps the conclusions of the special Council could say something about a 'consensus building around the idea' of a specified starting date for Stage 2. But Douglas recorded his impression that the German Chancellor was not set on seeking even this much, and that he might be open to persuasion to drop references to any date. Moreover, Chancellor Kohl said that he did not oppose discussion of GATT in Rome. What he would not get into was negotiation of the Community position. He said that he recognized the importance of the Community's offer on agriculture in the GATT and accepted that December was a real deadline for the Uruguay round. He also recognized that Germany would have to compromise. He would be prepared to say tough things to the German farmers in due course – but not yet. Apparently he implied to Douglas that there could be a trade-off. If I was prepared to help him during the discussion of the GATT, he might be able to help me during the discussion on the EMU IGC. This, of course, turned out to be far from his real position.

I myself lunched with President Mitterrand at our embassy residence in Rome on the Saturday. He could not have been more friendly or amenable. I said that I was very disturbed at the Community's failure to agree a negotiating position on agriculture for the GATT negotiations. I understood that agreement had very nearly been reached after some sixteen hours of negotiations at the meeting of Agriculture and Trade ministers the previous day but had been blocked by the French. President Mitterrand said that this was all very difficult, that agriculture must not be looked at in isolation and that Europe – or more exactly France – should not be expected to make all the concessions at the GATT talks. He asked me when I proposed to raise the issue at the Council. I said that I would bring it up right at the beginning. I would demand that the Council make clear that the Community would table proposals within the next few days. Failure to do so would be a signal to the world that Europe was protectionist. President Mitterrand interjected that of course the Community was protectionist: that was the point of it.

The French President did, however, agree with me – or so he claimed – about the political union proposals. Indeed, he was highly critical of some of M. Delors's remarks and had no time at all for the European Parliament. He claimed that France, like Britain, wanted a common currency, not a single currency. This was not true. But let me be charitable – there may have been some confusion in translation. In any case, I detected no wish to force me into a corner.

I was too well versed in the ways of the Community to take all this *bonhomie* at face value. But even I was unprepared for the way things went once the Council formally opened. Sig. Andreotti made clear right at the beginning that there was no intention of discussing the GATT. I spoke briefly and took them to task for ignoring this crucial issue at such a time. I had hoped that someone other than me would intervene. But only Ruud Lubbers did and he raised a mild protest. No one else was prepared to speak up for these imminent and crucial negotiations.

Then M. Delors reported on his recent meeting with Mr Gorbachev. To my surprise, he proposed that the Council should issue a statement saying that the outer border of the Soviet Union must remain intact. I waited. But no one spoke. I just could not leave matters like this. I said that this was not for us in the Community to decide but for the peoples and Government of the Soviet Union. I pointed out that the Baltic States had in any case been illegally seized and incorporated in the USSR. In effect, we were denying them their claim to independence. M. Delors said that he had received an assurance from Mr Gorbachev that the Baltic States would be freed. I came back at him, saying that we had heard this sort of reassurance before from the Soviets; and, in any case, what about the other nations of the Soviet Union who might wish to leave it as well? At this point first Sr González, then President Mitterrand and finally Chancellor Kohl intervened on my side and this ill-judged initiative foundered.

But the atmosphere went from bad to worse. The others were determined to insert in the communiqué provisions on political union, none of which I was prepared to accept. I said that I would not pre-empt the debate in the IGC and had a unilateral observation to this effect incorporated in the text. They also insisted on following the German proposal that Stage 2 of monetary union should begin on 1 January 1994. I would not accept this either. I had inserted in the communiqué the sentence:

> The United Kingdom, while ready to move beyond Stage 1 through the creation of a new monetary institution and a common Community currency, believes that decisions on the substance of that move should precede decisions on its timing.

They were not interested in compromise. My objections were heard in stony silence. I now had no support. I just had to say no.

In three years the European Community had gone from practical discussions about restoring order to the Community's finances to grandiose schemes of monetary and political union with firm timetables but no agreed substance – all without open, principled public debate on these questions either nationally or in European forums. Now at Rome the ultimate battle for the future of the Community had been joined. But I would have to return to London to win another battle on which the outcome in Europe would depend – that for the soul of the Parliamentary Conservative Party.

CHAPTER THIRTY-EIGHT

The World Turned Right Side Up

The fall of communism in eastern Europe,
the reunification of Germany and the debate
about the future of NATO 1987–1990

I HAD BREATHED A SIGH OF RELIEF when George Bush defeated his
Democrat opponent in the US presidential election, for I felt that it
ensured continuity. But with the new team's arrival in the White House I
found myself dealing with an Administration which saw Germany as its
main European partner in leadership, which encouraged the integration
of Europe without seeming to understand fully what it meant and which
sometimes seemed to underestimate the need for a strong nuclear
defence. I felt I could not always rely as before on American co-operation.
This was of great importance at such a time. For by now – 1989 – the
cracks in the eastern European communist system were widening into
crevices and soon, wing by wing, the whole edifice fell away.

This welcome revolution of freedom which swept eastern Europe
raised great strategic issues, above all in the West's relations with the
Soviet Union. (Indeed, what now was 'the West'?) But I also saw at once
that it had profound implications for the balance of power in Europe,
where a reunified Germany would be dominant. There was a new and
different kind of 'German Question' which had to be addressed openly
and formally: I did so.

History teaches that dangers are never greater than when empires
break up and so I favoured caution in our defence and security policy.
Decisions about our security must, I argued, be made only after careful
reflection and analysis of the nature and direction of future threats.
Above all, they must be determined not by the desire to make a political

impression by arms control 'initiatives' but by the need credibly to deter aggression.

For thinking and speaking like this I was mocked as the last Cold Warrior – and an unreconstructed Germanophobe to boot. In fact, they said, I was a tiresome woman who might once have served a purpose but who just could not or would not move with the times. I could live with this caricature; there had been worse; but I also had no doubt that I was right, and that sooner or later events would prove it. And I did find my basic approach vindicated as 1990 wore on. This occurred in several ways.

First, Anglo-American relations suddenly lost their chill; indeed by the end they had hardly been warmer. The protectionism of that 'integrated' Europe, dominated by Germany, which the Americans had cheerfully accepted, suddenly started to arouse American fears and threaten to cost American jobs. But this change of heart was confirmed by the aggression of Saddam Hussein against Kuwait which shattered any illusion that tyranny had been everywhere defeated. Suddenly a Britain with armed forces which had the skills, and a government which had the resolve, to fight alongside America, seemed to be the real European 'partner in leadership'.

Then again the full significance of the changes in eastern Europe began to be better understood. Having democratic states with market economies, which were just as 'European' as those of the existing Community, lining up as potential EC members made my vision of a looser, more open Community seem timely rather than backward. It also became clear that the courageous reforming leaders in eastern Europe looked to Britain – and to me because of my anti-socialist credentials – as a friend who genuinely wanted to help them, rather than exclude them from markets (like the French) or seek economic domination (like the Germans). These eastern European states were – and are – Britain's natural allies.

Further east in the USSR more disturbing developments made for a reassessment of earlier euphoric judgements about the prospects for the peaceful, orderly entrenchment of democracy and free enterprise. In the Soviet Union I had won the respect both of the embattled Mr Gorbachev and of his anti-communist opponents. Events now increasingly suggested that a far-reaching political crisis in the USSR might soon be reached. The implications of this for control over nuclear weapons and indeed the whole arsenal which the Soviet military machine had accumulated could not be ignored even by the most enthusiastic western disarmers. In short, the world of the 'new world order' was turning out to be a dangerous and uncertain place in which the conservative virtues of hardened Cold Warriors were again in demand. And so, while domestic political pressures mounted, I found myself once more at the centre of great international events with renewed ability to influence them in Britain's interests and in accord with my beliefs.

On Thursday 16 July 1987 I flew into Washington to see President Reagan. I had just won an election with a decisive majority, enhancing my authority in international affairs. By contrast my old friend and his Administration were reeling under the continuing 'Irangate' revelations. I found the President hurt and bemused by what was happening. Nothing wounds a man of integrity more than to find his basic honesty questioned. It made me very angry. I was determined to do what I could to help President Reagan ride out the storm. It was not just a matter of personal loyalty – though it was that too, of course: he also had eighteen months to serve as leader of the most powerful country in the world and it was in all our interests that his authority be undiminished. So I set about using my interviews and public statements in Washington to get across this message. For example, I told the interviewer on CBS's *Face the Nation*:

> Cheer up. Cheer up. Be more upbeat. America is a strong country with a great president, a great people and a great future.

Our embassy was besieged by telephone calls of congratulation. My remarks also touched another grateful audience. On Monday evening – after I arrived back in London – I received a telephone call from the President who wanted to thank me for what I had said. He was in a Cabinet meeting and at one point he put down the receiver and told me to listen. I heard loud and long applause from the Cabinet members.

My main business in Washington, though, had been to discuss the implications for our future defence of the INF treaty which would be signed by Presidents Reagan and Gorbachev in December. I had always had mixed feelings about the INF 'zero-option'. On the one hand, it was a great success to have forced the Soviets to withdraw their SS-20 missiles by deploying our Cruise and Pershing. But, on the other, the removal of our intermediate-range land-based missiles would have two undesirable effects. First, it threatened precisely what Helmut Schmidt had wanted to avoid when he originally urged NATO to deploy them: namely the decoupling of Europe from NATO. It could then be argued that in the last resort the United States would not use nuclear weapons to deter a conventional Warsaw Pact attack on Europe. This argument would boost the always-present tendency to German neutralism – a tendency which it had been the long-standing Soviet objective to magnify wherever possible. Second, the INF 'zero-option' also cast doubt on – though as I always argued it did not in fact undermine – the NATO strategy of 'flexible response'. That strategy depended on the ability of the West to escalate its response to Soviet aggression through each stage of conventional and nuclear weapons. The removal of the intermediate-range missiles might be argued to create a gap in that capability. It followed that NATO must have other nuclear weapons, stationed on German soil, which would be a credible deterrent, and that those weapons be modernized and strengthened where necessary. It was this question – the avoidance of another 'zero' on Short-Range Nuclear Forces (SNF) – which was to divide the alliance so seriously in 1988–89.

The main points I now made to the President were the need to allocate submarine-launched Cruise missiles and additional F1-11 aircraft to the Supreme Allied Commander in Europe to compensate for the withdrawal of Cruise and Pershing, and the need to resist pressure from the Germans for early discussion of reductions of SNF in Europe. I also wanted to see an upgraded and longer-range Follow-On to LANCE missile (FOTL) developed by the Americans and deployed by the mid-1990s, and a Tactical Air to Surface Missile (TASM) to replace our free-fall bombs. On these matters the President and I saw eye to eye. Where I did agree with the Germans – but found myself unable to convince the Americans – was that I would have liked to retain the old German Pershing ballistic missiles for the rest of their natural life (a few years), not including them as part of the INF package. But it was the future of SNF that to my mind was the most crucial element in our nuclear deterrence; and it certainly proved the most controversial.

Britain's own security interests were closely bound up with US-Soviet arms negotiations, so I was delighted when Mr Gorbachev accepted my invitation to stop over at Brize Norton on his way to the United States to sign the INF Treaty.

Within the Soviet Union there were mixed signs. Mr Gorbachev had brought his ally Mr Yakovlev into the Politburo; but his one-time protégé, Boris Yeltsin, who had been brought in as head of the Moscow Party as an incorruptible radical reformer, had been publicly humiliated. Within the Soviet leadership, apart from Mr Gorbachev himself, it still seemed that probably only Foreign Minister Shevardnadze and Mr Yakovlev were fully committed to the Gorbachev reforms.

We got down to the detailed discussions on arms control. There was not much to say now about INF and it was the projected START Agreement,* which would lead to cuts in strategic nuclear weapons, on which we focused. There were still large differences between the two sides as regards definition and verification. I also repeated my determination to keep nuclear weapons, which Mr Gorbachev described as my preferring to 'sit on a powder keg rather than an easy chair'. I countered by reminding him of the large superiority which the Soviets enjoyed in conventional and chemical forces. Then I raised Soviet withdrawal from Afghanistan and the human rights issue, suggesting that any action he took on these would be likely to assist the US Administration in overcoming opposition in the Senate to the INF Treaty. But I made no headway: he said that a solution in Afghanistan would be easier if we stopped supplying the rebels with arms and that human rights was a matter for the particular country involved. (It was this sort of attitude which had already created a very bad impression in the United States as a result of Mr Gorbachev's remarks about human rights in an interview with NBC.)

In spite of his tetchiness over human rights, it was a vigorous, enjoyable and even rather jolly occasion.

When I got back to London I telephoned President Reagan to let him know about our discussions. I told him what I had said on Afghanistan and arms control. I also said that though the President must be prepared to tackle Mr Gorbachev on human rights he should also be prepared for a sharp reaction. President Reagan said that he expected some tough sessions with Mr Gorbachev. He also asked me if I thought that he should try to get on first name terms with the Soviet leader. I advised him to go carefully on this, because although I found Mr Gorbachev friendly and open he was also quite formal, something which the whole rigid Soviet system encouraged.

In fact, the Reagan-Gorbachev summit in Washington was a success. The INF Treaty was agreed and a further summit in Moscow in the first half of 1988 was arranged in principle at which the treaty would be signed

---

* The US-Soviet Strategic Arms Reduction Talks, which had begun in the first year of the Reagan Administration.

and possibly agreement reached on a START Treaty as well. In February 1988 Mr Gorbachev announced that Soviet withdrawal from Afghanistan would begin in May. We were clearly moving into new territory and it seemed to me the right time to take our bearings at a NATO summit. The first NATO heads of government summit for six years – incidentally, the first attended by a French president for twenty-two years – was scheduled for March in Brussels.

It was clear from the start that the West Germans were likely to be the main source of difficulty. Mr Gorbachev had launched a very successful propaganda drive to win over German opinion to a denuclearized Germany. Within the Federal German Government, I knew that Chancellor Kohl was still fundamentally sound on the need to avoid a 'third zero' and denuclearization. Herr Genscher, the Federal Foreign minister, by contrast, was not. Chancellor Kohl insisted on NATO adherence to what was called its 'comprehensive concept' – that is, regarding the different elements of defence strategy, of which SNF was one, as a whole. Within this 'comprehensive concept' he was prepared to support measures agreed, after proper study by the alliance as necessary, to maintain flexible response; but he had said publicly in Washington that there was no present need to make a decision on SNF modernization. It was possible for the Americans and us to take account of German sensitivities in the NATO communiqué while still maintaining the right stance both on the military doctrine and modernization of nuclear weapons. Consequently, I was not at all displeased by the wording which resulted. The heads of government agreed on: 'a strategy of deterrence based on an appropriate mix of adequate and effective nuclear and conventional forces which will continue to be kept up to date where necessary'. That was enough.

After the Brussels summit officially broke up I met President Reagan to discuss the outcome. I told him that I thought the summit had been a great success because Britain and the United States had stood together. I left Brussels reassured that the President and I were at one as we faced up to all the difficult and complicated arms control negotiations which would now ensue.

President Reagan was as good as his word when he went to Moscow. Although the INF Treaty was signed there was tough negotiation and no compromise on START, where the Soviets wanted the United States to have Sea-Launched Cruise Missiles (SLCMs) included in the agreement. But, as with my own visit in 1987, it was the opportunity for President

Reagan and the Russian people to meet one another face to face which was probably of greatest importance. He told me when he came to London on Thursday 2 June, on his way back from Moscow, how moved he had been by the huge, welcoming crowds there. The only thing which had upset him was the brutal way in which the KGB had dealt with the people who wanted to approach him. He had given high prominence to human rights matters – particularly to freedom of worship – when he was in the Soviet Union and I said how right I thought he had been to do this. The President also told me about the difficult arms control talks. He said he had been determined not to give an inch on SDI and he was not going to be rushed on START. In the meantime, NATO must move ahead with modernization of its short-range nuclear forces and the West Germans must be persuaded to approach this in a positive way.

The President spoke to a large City and diplomatic audience at Guildhall the next day. It was a vintage performance and one of some significance in the light of later events. He harked back to the speech he had made to Members of Parliament in 1982 in which he had enunciated what came to be called the 'Reagan Doctrine'. Neither he nor I knew how close we were to its triumphant vindication; but what was clear was that great advances had been made in the 'crusade for freedom' we had been fighting. It was now time to restate the cause, which was as much spiritual as political or economic. As the President put it:

> Our faith is in a higher law . . . we hold that humanity was meant, not to be dishonoured by the all-powerful state, but to live in the image and likeness of Him who made us.

Just five months later – in November 1988 – I visited Poland. My aim was to continue that strategy towards the eastern bloc countries which I had first begun in Hungary in 1984. I wanted to open up these countries – their governments and peoples – to western influence and to exert pressure for respect for human rights and for political and economic reform. But Poland's recent past demonstrated how dependent events in such countries were on the intentions of the Soviet Union. Whether one regarded General Jaruzelski as a patriot stepping in to prevent worse things befalling his fellow countrymen or just as a Soviet puppet, the circumstances under which martial law was imposed and Solidarity crushed in 1981 were an unforgettable lesson in the reality of power politics. Now the political and economic bankruptcy of the Jaruzelski

Government was again apparent and its authority challenged by a revived Solidarity. The role of the West – above all of a visiting western leader – was to give heart to the anti-communists, while urging on them a carefully calculated response to the opportunities they had to improve conditions and increase their influence; and in dealings with the Government it must be to combine straight talking about the need for change with an attitude which avoided outright and counter-productive conflict. It would not be an easy task.

For their part, the authorities were determined to make it harder still. On the eve of my visit the Government announced their intention to close the Lenin Shipyard at Gdansk, the home of Solidarity. It was a trap. The communists hoped that I would be forced to welcome the closure of uneconomic plant and to condemn Solidarity's resistance to it on the grounds of 'Thatcherite' economics. Some commentators fully expected me to fall for this.

In the light of these manoeuvrings I was glad that I had insisted that there should be an unofficial as well as an official side to my visit. I was not prepared to be prevented from meeting Lech Walesa and the leading opponents of the regime. To his credit, I felt, General Jaruzelski did not raise objections to my doing so.

In planning my visit I had consulted the Pope whose own visit there in June 1987 had provided the main impetus for the revival of Solidarity and the pressure for reform. It was clear that the Vatican thought my visit could do good but also that the Church was proceeding with great caution.

In preparing my Polish trip there was another matter on which I felt I must consult a wise authority and that was what I should wear. A Polish lady who served me at Aquascutum said that green was the colour which represented hope in Poland. So green was the colour of the suit I chose.

My first official meeting in Warsaw on the evening of Wednesday 2 November was with the recently appointed Polish Prime Minister, Mr Rakowski. He was not an impressive or persuasive advocate of the line the Polish Government was taking about the Lenin Shipyard, though he did his best. He said how much he agreed with my public statements about the need for economic reform and portrayed closure of the shipyard as part of this process. In somewhat forced 'Thatcherite' tones he told me that rationalization was the only way to extricate Poland from its crisis and that Poland's great weakness historically had been lack of consistency, which was something he was determined to change.

Later that evening I met a number of opponents of the regime and learned a little more about its shortcomings.

On Thursday afternoon I had my first real taste of the Poland which the communists had tried and failed to destroy. I visited the church of St Stanislaw Kostka in the north of Warsaw where Father Jerzy Popieluszko had preached his anti-communist sermons until in 1984 he was abducted and murdered by members of the Polish Security Services. The church itself was overflowing with people of every age who had come out to see me, and on my arrival they broke into a Polish hymn. In Father Popieluszko they had evidently found a martyr, and I came away in little doubt that it was his creed rather than that of his murderers which would prevail in Poland.

I said as much to General Jaruzelski when I met him for talks later. The General had spoken for one and three-quarter hours without interruption about his plans for Poland. In this, at least, he was a typical communist. He even said that he admired the trade union reforms I had put through in Britain. When he finished I pointed out that people in Britain did not have to rely on trade unions as a means of expressing their political views because we had free elections. I had just experienced the power of the Solidarity movement in that church in northern Warsaw. I said that, as a politician, all my instincts told me that this was far more than a trade union – it was a political movement whose power could not be denied.

The next day, Friday, was one I shall never forget. I flew up to Gdansk in the early morning to join General Jaruzelski in laying a wreath at the Westerplatte, which saw the first fighting between the Poles and the invading Germans in 1939. It was a bleak peninsula above the bay of Gdansk and the wind was bitter; the ceremony lasted half an hour. I was pleased to get aboard and into the cabin of the small naval ship which was to take me down the river to Gdansk itself. I changed out of my black hat and coat into emerald green and then went back up on deck. The scenes at the arrival of our boat at Gdansk shipyard were unbelievable. Every inch of it seemed taken up with shipyard workers waving and cheering.

After a walkabout in old Gdansk itself I was driven to the hotel where Lech Walesa and his colleagues came up to see me in my room. He was under a sort of liberal house arrest and had been brought to the hotel, ironically enough, by Polish Security Police. I gave him the present I had brought with me – some fishing tackle, for he was a great fisherman – and we departed again for the shipyard. Again there were thousands of shipyard workers waiting for me, cheering and waving Solidarity banners. I laid flowers on the memorial to shipyard workers shot by the police and army in 1970, and then went to the house of Father Jankowski, Mr Walesa's confessor and adviser, for a meeting followed by lunch.

The Solidarity leaders were a mixture of workers and intellectuals. Mr Walesa was in the former group, but he had a large physical presence as well as a symbolic importance, which allowed him to dominate. He told me that Solidarity was disinclined to accept the Government's invitation to join in round-table talks, believing that the purpose was to divide and if possible discredit the opposition. Solidarity's goal he described as 'pluralism', that is a state of affairs in which the Communist Party was not the sole legitimate authority. What struck me, though, was that they did not have a specific plan of action with immediate practical objectives. Indeed, when I said that I thought that Solidarity should attend the talks and submit its own proposals in the form of a detailed agenda with supporting papers my hosts looked quite astonished.

Over lunch – one of the best game stews I have ever tasted – we argued through together what their negotiating stance might be and how in my final discussions with the Polish Government I could help. We decided that the most important point I could make to General Jaruzelski was that Solidarity must be legalized. Throughout I was repeatedly impressed by the moderation and eloquence of Mr Walesa and his colleagues. At one point I said: 'You really must see that the Government hears all this.' 'No problem', replied Mr Walesa, pointing up to the ceiling; 'our meetings are bugged anyway.'

After lunch it was suggested that I might like to look around the nearby church of St Brygida. To my delighted astonishment, when Mr Walesa and I entered I found the whole church packed with Polish families who rose and sang the Solidarity anthem 'God give us back our free Poland': I could not keep the tears from my eyes. I seemed to have shaken hundreds of hands as I walked around the church. I gave a short emotional speech and Lech Walesa spoke too. As I left, there were people in the streets crying with emotion and shouting 'Thank you, thank you' over and over again. I returned to Warsaw with greater determination than ever to do battle with the communist authorities.

In my final meeting with General Jaruzelski I kept my word to Solidarity. I told him that I was grateful that he had put no obstacle in the way of my visit to Gdansk – though it has to be said that the authorities had put on a total news blackout about it both before and afterwards. I said how impressed I had been by Solidarity's moderation. If they were good enough to attend round-table discussions, they were also good enough to be legalized. General Jaruzelski gave no impression of being prepared to budge.

A fortnight later I was back in Washington as President Reagan's last official guest. This gave me the chance of discussions with President-elect Bush.

I later learned that President Bush was sometimes exasperated by my habit of talking nonstop about issues which fascinated me and felt that he ought to have been leading the discussion. More important than all of this, perhaps, was the fact that, as President, George Bush felt the need to distance himself from his predecessor: turning his back fairly publicly on the special position I had enjoyed in the Reagan Administration's counsels and confidence was a way of doing that. This was understandable; and by the time of my last year in office we had established a better relationship. By then I had learned that I had to defer to him in conversation and not to stint the praise. If that was what was necessary to secure Britain's interests and influence, I had no hesitation in eating a little humble pie.

Unfortunately, even then the US State Department continued to put out briefings against me and my policies – particularly on Europe – until the onset of the Gulf crisis made them hastily change their stance. To some extent the relative tilt of American foreign policy against Britain in this period may have been the result of the influence of Secretary of State James Baker. Although he was always very courteous to me, we were not close. Yet that was not crucial. Rather, it was the fact that Jim Baker's many abilities lay in the area of 'fixing'. He had had a mixed record of this, having as US Treasury Secretary been responsible for the ill-judged Plaza and Louvre Accords which brought 'exchange rate stability' back to the centre of the West's economic policies with highly deleterious effects. Now at the State Department Jim Baker and his team brought a similar, allegedly 'pragmatic' problem-solving approach to bear on US foreign policy.

The main results of this approach as far as I was concerned were to put the relationship with Germany – rather than the 'special relationship' with Britain – at the centre.

* * *

At the end of 1988 I could foresee neither the way in which Anglo-American relations would develop nor the scale of the difficulties with the Germans over SNF. My basic position on short-range nuclear weapons was that they were essential to NATO's strategy of flexible response. Any potential aggressor must know that if he were to cross the NATO line he might be met with a nuclear response. If that fear was removed he might calculate that he could mount a conventional attack that would reach the Atlantic seaboard within a few days. And this, of course, was the existing position. But once land-based intermediate-range nuclear weapons were removed, as the INF Treaty signed in Washington in December 1987 took effect, the land-based short-range missiles became all the more vital. So, of course, did the sea-based intermediate missiles.

At the Rhodes European Council in early December 1988 I discussed arms control with Chancellor Kohl. He was keen for an early NATO summit which would help him push through agreement within his Government on the 'comprehensive concept' for arms control. I agreed that the sooner the better. We must take decisions on the modernization of NATO's nuclear weapons by the middle of the year, in particular on the replacement of LANCE. Chancellor Kohl said that he wanted both of these questions out of the way before the June 1989 European elections.

By the time of the next Anglo-German summit in Frankfurt the political pressure on the German Chancellor had increased further and he had begun to argue that a decision on SNF was not really necessary until 1991–92.

Certainly, the Soviets were in no doubt about the strategic importance of the decisions which would have to be made about SNF. Mr and Mrs Gorbachev arrived at 11 o'clock at night on Wednesday 5 April in London for the visit which had had to be postponed the previous December as a result of an earthquake in Armenia. I met them at the airport and returned to the Soviet Embassy where the number of toasts drunk suggested that the Soviet leader's early crackdown on vodka was not universally applicable. In my talks with Mr Gorbachev I found him frustrated by – and surprisingly suspicious of – the Bush Administration. I defended the new President's performance and stressed the continuity with the Reagan Administration. But the real substance of our discussions related to arms control. I raised directly with Mr Gorbachev the evidence which we had that the Soviets had not been telling us the truth about the quantity and types of chemical weapons which they held. He stoutly maintained that they had. He then brought up the issue of SNF modernization. I said that obsolete weapons did not deter and that NATO's SNF would certainly have to be modernized. The forthcoming NATO summit would confirm this intention. Mr Gorbachev returned to the subject in his speech at Guildhall which contained a somewhat menacing section about the effect on East-West relations and arms control talks more generally if NATO went ahead with SNF modernization.

All this pressure was by now having an effect. In particular, Chancellor Kohl was retreating. In April a new German position on SNF modernization and negotiation was extensively leaked before any of the allies – other than the Americans – were informed. The German position paper did not rule out a 'third zero', did not call on the Soviet Union unilaterally to reduce its SNF levels to those of NATO, and cast doubt on SNF modernization.

I had acrimonious discussions with Chancellor Kohl behind the stage-managed friendliness of our meeting at Deidesheim at the end of April. Chancellor Kohl said that it was simply not sustainable politically in Germany to argue that those nuclear weapons which most directly affected Germany should be the only category not subject to negotiation. I repeated that Britain and the United States were absolutely opposed to negotiations on SNF and would remain so. Even if a decision to deploy the Follow-On to LANCE were postponed, there must be clear evidence at the forthcoming summit of NATO support for the US development programme. In fact, the German Government's actions had put NATO under severe strain. Chancellor Kohl said he did not need any lectures about NATO, that he believed in flexible response and repeated his opposition to a 'third zero'.

In the run-up to the NATO summit the newspapers continued to focus on splits in the alliance. This was particularly galling because we should have been celebrating NATO's fortieth anniversary and highlighting the success of our strategy of securing peace through strength. Apart from the Americans only the French fully agreed with my line on SNF and in any case, not being part of the NATO integrated command structure, they would not be of great importance in the final decision. I minuted on Tuesday 16 May: 'If we get a "no negotiations" SNF section this will be reasonable, combined with a supportive piece on SNF research.' I was still quite optimistic.

Then on Friday 19 May I suddenly learned that the American line had shifted. They were now prepared to concede the principle of negotiations on SNF. Jim Baker claimed in public that we had been consulted about this US change of tack, but in fact we had not. Without in any way endorsing the American text, which I considered wrong-headed, I sent two main comments to the Americans. It should be amended to make the opening of SNF negotiations dependent upon a decision to deploy a successor to LANCE. It should include a requirement of substantial reductions in Soviet SNF towards NATO levels. Jim Baker replied that he doubted whether the Germans would accept this. The attitude of Brent Scowcroft – the President's National Security Adviser – was sounder. But I could not tell what the President's own view would be. In any case, I now found myself going to Brussels as the odd man out.

In fact, at the last minute the Americans brought forward proposals calling for conventional forces reductions and for not just further deep cuts but accelerated progress in the CFE talks in Vienna, so that those reductions could be accomplished by 1992 or 1993. This sleight of hand permitted a compromise on SNF by enabling the Germans to argue that the prospect of 'early' SNF negotiations was preserved. However, I emphasized in my subsequent statement to the House of Commons the fact that only after agreement had been reached on conventional force reductions, and implementation of that agreement was under way, would the United States be authorized to enter into negotiations to achieve partial reductions in short-range missiles. No reductions would be made in NATO's SNF until after the agreement on conventional force reductions had been fully implemented.

I felt that I had done as much as was humanly possible to stop our sliding into another 'zero'. I could live with the text which resulted from the tough negotiations which took place in Brussels. But I had seen for myself that the new American approach was to subordinate clear statements of intention about the alliance's defence to the political sensibilities of the Germans. I did not think that this boded well.

In the late summer of 1989 the first signs appeared of the imminent collapse of communism in eastern Europe. Solidarity won the elections in early June in Poland and General Jaruzelski accepted the result. Liberalization proceeded in Hungary, which opened its borders to Austria in September across which flooded East German refugees. The haemorrhage of population from East Germany and demonstrations at the beginning of October in Leipzig led to the fall of Erich Honecker. The demolition of the Berlin Wall began on 10 November. The following month it was the turn of Czechoslovakia. By the end of the year Václav Havel, the dissident playwright who had been jailed in February, had been elected President of Czechoslovakia and the evil Ceausescus had been overthrown in Romania.

These events marked the most welcome political change of my lifetime. But I was not going to allow euphoria to extinguish either reason or prudence. I did not believe that it would be easy or painless to entrench democracy and free enterprise. It was too soon to be sure precisely what sort of regimes would emerge. Moreover, central and eastern Europe – still more the Soviet Union – was a complicated patchwork of nations. Political freedom would also bring ethnic disputes and challenges to frontiers, which might have moved several times in living memory. War could not be ruled out.

The welcome changes had come about because the West had remained strong and resolute – but also because Mr Gorbachev and the Soviet Union had renounced the Brezhnev doctrine. On the continued survival of a moderate, reforming government in the USSR would depend the future of the new democracies. It was too early to assume that the captive nations were permanently free from captivity: their Soviet captors could still turn ugly. It was therefore essential to go carefully and avoid actions which would be deemed provocative by either the Soviet political leadership or the military.

And nothing was more likely to stir up old fears in the Soviet Union – fears which the hardliners would be anxious to exploit – than the prospect of a reunited, powerful Germany.

There was – and still is – a tendency to regard the 'German problem' as something too delicate for well-brought-up politicians to discuss. This always seemed to me a mistake. The problem had several elements which could only be addressed if non-Germans considered them openly and constructively. I do not believe in collective guilt: it is individuals who are morally accountable for their actions. But I do believe in national character, which is moulded by a range of complex factors: the fact that national caricatures are often absurd and inaccurate does not detract from that. Since the unification of Germany under Bismarck Germany has veered unpredictably between aggression and self-doubt. Germany's immediate neighbours, such as the French and the Poles, are more deeply aware of this than the British, let alone the Americans; though the same concern often leads Germany's immediate neighbours to refrain from comments which might appear insensitive. The Russians are acutely conscious of all this too, though in their case the need for German credit and investment has so far had a quiescent effect. But perhaps the first people to recognize the 'German problem' are the modern Germans, the vast majority of whom are determined that Germany should not be a great power able to exert itself at others' expense. The true origin of German *angst* is the agony of self-knowledge.

As I have already argued, that is one reason why so many Germans genuinely – I believe wrongly – want to see Germany locked in to a federal Europe. In fact, Germany is more rather than less likely to dominate within that framework; for a reunited Germany is simply too big and powerful to be just another player. Moreover, Germany has always looked east as well as west, though it is economic expansion rather than territorial aggression which is the modern manifestation of this tendency. Germany is thus by its very nature a destabilizing force in Europe. Only the military and political engagement of the United States in Europe and close relations between the other two strongest sovereign states in Europe – Britain and France – are sufficient to balance German power: and nothing of the sort would be possible within a European super-state.

One obstacle to achieving such a balance of power when I was in office was the refusal of France under President Mitterrand to follow his and French instincts and challenge German interests. This would have required abandoning the Franco-German axis on which he had been relying and, as I shall describe, the wrench proved just too difficult for him.

Initially, it also seemed likely that the Soviets would be strongly opposed to the re-emergence of a powerful Germany. Of course, the Soviets might have calculated that a reunited Germany would return a left-of-centre government which would achieve their long-term objective of neutralizing and denuclearizing West Germany. (As it turned out – and perhaps with a clearer idea than we had of the true feelings of the East German people – the Soviets were prepared to sell reunification for a modest financial boost from Germany to their crumbling economy.)

These matters were at the forefront of my mind when I decided to arrange a stopover visit in Moscow for talks with Mr Gorbachev on my way back from the IDU Conference in Tokyo in September 1989.

In Moscow Mr Gorbachev and I talked frankly about Germany. I explained to him that although NATO had traditionally made statements supporting Germany's aspiration to be reunited, in practice we were rather apprehensive. Nor was I speaking for myself alone – I had discussed it with at least one other western leader, meaning but not mentioning President Mitterrand. Mr Gorbachev confirmed that the Soviet Union did not want German reunification either. This reinforced me in my resolve to slow up the already heady pace of developments. Of course, I did not want East Germans to have to live under communism. But it seemed to me that a truly democratic East Germany would soon emerge and that the question of reunification was a separate one on which the wishes and interests of Germany's neighbours and other powers must be fully taken into account.

To begin with the West Germans seemed to be willing to do this. Chancellor Kohl telephoned me on the evening of Friday 10 November after his visit to Berlin and as demolition of the Berlin Wall began. He was clearly buoyed up by the scenes he had witnessed: what German would not have been? I advised him to keep in touch with Mr Gorbachev who would obviously be very concerned with what was happening. He promised to do so. Later that night the Soviet Ambassador came to see me with a message from Mr Gorbachev who was worried that there might occur some incident – perhaps an attack on Soviet soldiers in East Germany or Berlin – which could have momentous consequences.

However, instead of seeking to rein back expectations, Chancellor Kohl was soon busily raising them. In a statement to the Bundestag he said that the core of the German question was freedom and that the people of East Germany must be given the chance to decide their own future and needed no advice from others. That went for the 'question of reunification and for German unity too'. The tone had already begun to change and it would change further.

This was the background to President Mitterrand's calling a special meeting of Community heads of government in Paris to consider what was happening in Germany – where Egon Krenz, the new East German leader who was, the Soviets had told me, a protégé of Mr Gorbachev, was looking precarious. Before I went I sent a message to President Bush reiterating my view that the priority should be to see genuine democracy established in East Germany and that German reunification was not something to be addressed at present. The President later telephoned me to thank me for my message with which he agreed and to say how much he was looking forward to the two of us 'putting our feet up at Camp David for a really good talk'.

Almost equally amiable was the Paris meeting on the evening of Saturday 18 November. President Mitterrand opened by posing a number of questions, including whether the issue of borders in Europe should be open for discussion. Then Chancellor Kohl began. He said that people wanted 'to hear Europe's voice'. He then obliged by speaking for forty minutes. He concluded by saying that there should be no discussion of borders but that the people of Germany must be allowed to decide their future for themselves. After Sr González had intervened to no great effect, I spoke.

I said that though the changes taking place were historic we must not succumb to euphoria. It would take several years to get genuine democracy and economic reform in eastern Europe. There must be no question of changing borders. The Helsinki Final Act must apply.* Any attempt to talk about either border changes or German reunification would undermine Mr Gorbachev and open up a Pandora's box of border claims right through central Europe. I said that we must keep both NATO and the Warsaw Pact intact to create a background of stability.

The following Friday – 24 November – I was discussing the same issues at Camp David with President Bush – though not exactly 'with my feet up'. Although friendly enough, the President seemed uneasy. I reiterated much of what I had said in Paris about borders and reunification and of the need to support the Soviet leader on whose continuance in power so much depended. The President asked me pointedly whether my line had given rise to difficulties with Chancellor Kohl and about my attitude to the European Community. It was also clear that we differed on the priority which still needed to be given to defence spending. The President told me about the budgetary difficulties he faced and argued that if conditions in eastern Europe and the Soviet Union had really changed, there must surely be scope for the West to cut its defence spending. I said that there would always remain the unknown threat which must be guarded against. Defence spending was like home insurance in this respect. You did not stop paying the premiums because your street was free from burglaries for a time. I thought that the US defence budget should be driven not by Mr Gorbachev and his initiatives but by the United States'

---

* The Helsinki Final Act of 1975 contained the following commitment: 'The participating States regard as inviolable all one another's frontiers as well as the frontiers of all States in Europe and therefore they will refrain now and in the future from assaulting these frontiers. Accordingly, they will also refrain from any demand for, or act of, seizure and usurpation of part or all of the territory of any participating State.' However, the Final Act also provided that 'frontiers can be changed, in accordance with international law, by peaceful means and by agreement'.

defence interests. The atmosphere did not improve as a result of our discussions.

Shortly after my return to Britain I learned that, in clear breach of at least the spirit of the Paris summit, Chancellor Kohl had set out in a speech to the Bundestag a 'ten-point' plan about Germany's future. The fifth point was the proposal of the development of 'confederative structures between the two states in Germany with the goal of creating a federation'. The tenth point was that his Government was working towards 'unity, reunification, the reattainment of German state unity'.

The real question now was how the Americans would react. I did not have to wait long to find out. In a press conference briefing Jim Baker spelt out the American approach to German reunification which, he said, would be based on four principles. Self-determination would be pursued 'without prejudice to its outcome'. Another element was that Germany should not only remain in NATO – with which I heartily agreed – but that it should be part of 'an increasingly integrated European Community' – with which I did not. The third point was that moves to unification should be peaceful, gradual and part of a step-by-step process. I entirely agreed with the final point – that the principles of the Helsinki Final Act, particularly as they related to borders, must be supported. What remained to be seen, however, was whether the Americans were going to give most weight to the notion of Germany's future in an 'integrated' Europe or to the thought that reunification must only come about slowly and gradually.

It was left to President Bush himself to provide the answer in his speech at the NATO heads of government meeting staged at Brussels in early December to hear his report on his talks with Mr Gorbachev in Malta. He made a carefully prepared statement on Europe's 'future architecture', calling for a 'new, more mature relationship' with Europe. He also restated the principles Jim Baker had laid out as regards reunification. But the fact that the President placed such emphasis on 'European integration' was immediately taken as a signal that he was aligning America with the federalist rather than my 'Bruges' goal of European development. There was no reason for journalists to take the President's remarks otherwise. The President telephoned me to explain his remarks and say that they just related to the Single Market rather than wider political integration. I hoped that they did – or that at least from now on they would. The fact remained that there was nothing I could expect from the Americans as regards slowing down German reunification – and possibly much I would wish to avoid as regards the drive towards European unity.

If there was any hope now of stopping or slowing down reunification it would only come from an Anglo-French initiative. Yet even were President Mitterrand to try to give practical effect to what I knew were his secret fears, we would not find many ways open to us.

At the Strasbourg European Council in December 1989 President Mitterrand and I had two private meetings to discuss the German problem. He was very critical of Chancellor Kohl's 'ten-point' plan. He observed that in history the Germans were a people in constant movement and flux. At this I produced from my handbag a map showing the various configurations of Germany in the past, which were not altogether reassuring about the future. We talked through what precisely we might do. I said that at the meeting he had chaired in Paris we had come up with the right answer on borders and reunification. But President Mitterrand observed that Chancellor Kohl had already gone far beyond that. He said that at moments of great danger in the past France had always established special relations with Britain and he felt that such a time had come again. We must draw together and stay in touch. It seemed to me that although we had not discovered the means, at least we both had the will to check the German juggernaut. That was a start.

Almost all the discussion I had with President Mitterrand at the Elysée Palace on Saturday 20 January 1990 concerned Germany. Picking up the President's remarks in the margins of Strasbourg I said that it was very important for Britain and France to work out jointly how to handle what was happening in Germany. East Germany seemed close to collapse and it was by no means impossible that we would be confronted in the course of this year with the decision in principle in favour of reunification. The President was clearly irked by German attitudes and behaviour. He accepted that the Germans had the right to self-determination but they did not have the right to upset the political realities of Europe; nor could he accept that German reunification should take priority over everything else. He complained that the Germans treated any talk of caution as criticism of themselves. Unless you were whole-heartedly for reunification, you were described as an enemy of Germany. The trouble was that in reality there was no force in Europe which could stop reunification happening. He was at a loss as to what we could do. I argued that we should at least make use of all the means available to slow down reunification. The trouble was that other governments were not ready to speak up openly – nor, I might have added but did not, were the French. President Mitterrand went on to say that he shared my worries about the

Germans' so-called 'mission' in central Europe. The Czechs, Poles and Hungarians would not want to be under Germany's exclusive influence, but they would need German aid and investment. I said that we must not just accept that the Germans had a particular hold over these countries, but rather do everything possible to expand our own links there. We agreed that our Foreign and Defence ministers should get together to talk over the issue of reunification and also examine the scope for closer Franco-British defence co-operation.

In February Chancellor Kohl – again without any consultation with his allies – went to Moscow and won from Mr Gorbachev agreement that 'the unity of the German nation must be decided by the Germans themselves'. (The *quid pro quo* would soon become clear. In July, at a meeting in the Crimea, the West German Chancellor agreed to provide what must have seemed to the Soviets a huge sum, though they could have extracted much more, to cover the costs of providing for the Soviet troops who would be withdrawn from East Germany. For his part, Mr Gorbachev now finally agreed in public that the reunified Germany should be part of NATO.)

On Saturday 24 February I had a three-quarters-of-an-hour telephone conversation with President Bush. I broke with my usual habit of trying to avoid detailed factual discussions over the telephone and tried to explain to the President how I thought we should be thinking about the future of a western alliance and a Europe which contained a reunified Germany. I stressed the importance of ensuring that a united Germany stayed within NATO and that United States troops remained there. However, if all Soviet forces had to leave East Germany that would cause difficulties for Mr Gorbachev and I thought it best to allow some to stay for a transitional period without any specific terminal date. I also said that we must strengthen the CSCE framework, which would not only help avoid Soviet isolation but would help balance German dominance in Europe. One had to remember that Germany was surrounded by countries most of which it had attacked or occupied in the course of this century. Looking well into the future, only the Soviet Union – or its successor – could provide such a balance. President Bush, as I afterwards learnt, failed to understand that I was discussing a long-term balance of power in Europe rather than proposing an alternative alliance to NATO. It was the last time that I relied on a telephone conversation to explain such matters.

* * *

Throughout my last year in office doubts were increasingly raised about the wisdom of supporting Mr Gorbachev in his reforms. But I continued to do so and have no regrets. First, I am not someone who throws over those I like and have shown themselves my friends simply because their fortunes change. And though this may have immediate disadvantages, in my experience it increases the respect in which one is held: respect is a powerful asset, as those in politics who fail to inspire it might secretly agree. But second, and more important, it did not seem to me that at the time anyone was better able than Mr Gorbachev to push ahead with reform. I wanted to see the fall of communism, but I wanted to see this achieved peacefully. The two obvious threats to peace were a takeover – covert or overt – by hardliners in the Soviet military or the violent break-up of the Soviet Union. Throughout the summer of 1990 there were disturbing reports of possible rebellious activities within the Soviet military. But it was the nationalities question – that is, the future of the Soviet Union itself – which was most difficult for outsiders to assess.

I now believe that all of us in the West overestimated the degree to which a Soviet Empire whose core was provided by Marxist ideology and a communist *nomenklatura* – an empire constructed and bound together by force – could survive the onset of political liberty. Perhaps we listened too much to the diplomats and western experts and too little to the émigrés. That said, I did not go along with much of the thinking which characterized the British Foreign Office and US State Department on the issue of nationalities or nationhood.

We were all quite clear, as it happens, about the special legal status of the Baltic States: it was not a question of whether but of when they must be allowed to go free. I warned the Soviets about the severe consequences of the use of force against the Baltic States when I saw Mr Gorbachev in June. But I urged the greatest caution on President Landsbergis (of Lithuania) when I saw him in November. And I pressed both sides to negotiate throughout – though only on the clear understanding that the final destination of the Baltic States was freedom.

The emergence of Boris Yeltsin as a radical proponent of reform – both political and economic – ought perhaps to have strengthened Mr Gorbachev's position. If the two of them had been able to sink their differences and if Mr Gorbachev had been prepared to cut his links with the Communist Party perhaps the impetus of reform might have been renewed. But these were two 'ifs' too many. Their relations remained bad and Mr Gorbachev remained a communist to the end.

There was a strong tendency in western circles to write off Mr Yeltsin as nothing more than a buffoon. I could not believe that this judgement was correct. But I wanted to see for myself. Consequently, although I was careful to notify Mr Gorbachev in advance and to make it clear that I was receiving Mr Yeltsin in the way that I would a Leader of the Opposition, I enthusiastically agreed to meet him when he came to London on the morning of Friday 27 April 1990.

I only spoke with Mr Yeltsin for three-quarters of an hour. At first I was not quite sure what to make of him. He was far more my idea of the typical Russian than was Mr Gorbachev – tall, burly, square Slavic face and shock of white hair. He was self-confident without being self-assertive, courteous, with a smile full of good humour and a touch of self-mockery. But what impressed me most was that he had obviously thought through some of the fundamental problems much more clearly than had Mr Gorbachev. I began by saying that I supported Mr Gorbachev and wanted that to be clear from the outset. Mr Yeltsin replied that he knew I supported the Soviet leader and *perestroika* and on some of these matters our opinions differed, but basically he too supported Mr Gorbachev and the cause of reform. Mr Gorbachev should, though, have paid more attention to some of the things being said by the supporters of reform three or four years earlier. *Perestroika* had originally been intended to make communism more efficient. But that was impossible. The only serious option was for far-reaching political and economic reform, including the introduction of a market economy. But it was all getting very late.

I totally agreed with this. What struck me was that Mr Yeltsin, unlike President Gorbachev, had escaped from the communist mindset and language. He it was who also first alerted me to the relationship between economic reform and the question of what powers should be devolved to the individual republics. He explained just how little autonomy the governments of the republics really had. As a result of this discussion I looked not just at Boris Yeltsin but at the fundamental problems of the Soviet Union in a new light. When I reported later in Bermuda to President Bush on my favourable impressions of Mr Yeltsin he made it clear that the Americans did not share them. This was a serious mistake.

I shall always be glad that I was able to visit two former communist countries while I was still Prime Minister. In Czechoslovakia and Hungary in September 1990 I found myself speaking with people who not long before had been totally excluded from power by the communists and who were coming to grips with the communist legacy of economic failure, pollution and despondency.

I had been greatly impressed by the inaugural speech of President Havel of Czechoslovakia. He had spoken of 'living in a decayed moral environment . . . [in which] notions such as love, friendship, compassion, humility and forgiveness have lost their depth and dimension'. He had described the demoralization which communism brought about, how 'the previous regime, armed with its arrogant and intolerant ideology, demeaned man into a production force and nature into a production tool. In this way they attacked their very essence and the mutual relationship between them.'

Czechoslovakia was lucky to have President Havel as an inspiration, but no less lucky to have Václav Klaus as a dynamic, convinced free enterprise economist for its Finance minister. Together they were rebuilding the social and economic foundations of the country. Apart from the obvious problems which confronted them, there was also the tension between the Czech and Slovak elements of the Federal Republic.

Then I went on to Hungary. Among the eastern European countries Hungary had three important advantages. First, substantial economic and a large amount of political reform had occurred under the previous communist regime. So the transition was less difficult and painful. Second, in Jozsef Antall, the Hungarian Prime Minister, the country was in the safe hands of a genuine Conservative. He and I shared very much the same political approach. Third, the Hungarians had held together their governing coalition rather than splitting up in divisions on minor points. Mr Antall had the skills – and was quickly developing the authority – to give Hungary the leadership and continuity it needed.

Yet the task of economic reform was still daunting. The Hungarians were tackling the key questions relating to property – both the ownership of land, which exiles and their families wanted back, and the privatization of industry. There was also a wider strategic issue. Even more than Czechoslovakia and Poland, the Hungarians were keen to break free from Soviet influence. Mr Antall had announced that Hungary would leave the Warsaw Pact and wanted closer relations with NATO or at least the Western European Union (WEU). Poland and Czechoslovakia were toying with the same idea. He assured me that the Warsaw Pact was indeed on its last legs. When it finally expired I favoured a special associate membership of NATO being offered to the eastern Europeans.

*   *   *

However fascinated I was by events in the Soviet Union and eastern Europe, I could not forget that the strength and security of the West ultimately depended upon the Anglo-American relationship. For reasons I have explained that relationship had become somewhat strained. I regarded it, therefore, as essential that the talks I was due to have with President Bush in Bermuda in April 1990 should be a success. This would be as much a matter of tone as substance. Generally speaking, I now waited for the President to set out his views before explaining mine. In Bermuda we deliberately sought to create the kind of relaxed atmosphere which I now knew he preferred. It was almost a 'family' affair and concluded with the President and Denis playing eighteen holes of golf in the pouring rain – a very British occasion.

It was the future of NATO and decisions about the defence of Europe which were in the forefront of my and the President's minds. I sought to leave him in no doubt about my strong commitment to NATO. The President was keen to have an early NATO summit. So, it seemed, was the NATO Secretary-General, Dr Woerner. I would have preferred one in the autumn in order to allow for more preparation. But it was clear that the President wanted a June summit and would like Britain to host it. (In fact it took place in early July.) He had also concluded that Congress was going to withhold funds for the development of a Follow-On to LANCE. He therefore wanted to announce its cancellation. I accepted that there was very little which could be done about this, but I thought it crucial to secure firm assurances about the future stationing of nuclear weapons in Germany, in particular TASM. The real question was how we were most likely to achieve this. In fact, this approach turned out to be a key to the Americans' thinking in the run-up to the NATO summit. Their aim was to make it a public relations success, so that we could win German support for SNF and Soviet acceptance that Germany should remain in NATO. When I got back to London I set in hand the arrangements for us to host a NATO summit. There was only one complication, which was that a meeting of the North Atlantic Council – that is, NATO Foreign ministers – was scheduled for June at Turnberry, a few miles south of Ayr on the west coast of Scotland. I wanted this to go ahead because it was where the more significant decisions were likely to be made about how NATO's forces might be reshaped.

Not for the first time, I found myself at odds with the Americans and indeed with the NATO Secretary-General about how we should approach the NATO summit. The Americans were keen to announce a range of initiatives, proposing deep cuts in conventional forces and still deeper cuts in the nuclear stockpile. Messages flew back and forth between me and President Bush and some of the more eye-catching and less considered proposals were dropped. Not that I disagreed with everything the Americans wanted from the summit. In particular, I was strongly in favour of Jim Baker's ideas about strengthening political consultation as one of the functions of NATO. I believed – as did the Americans – that the importance of NATO as a means of avoiding friction between America and Europe was greater than ever.

What I was unhappy about was the American proposal formally to change in the communiqué the traditional NATO strategy of flexible response. They were insistent on the insertion of the phrase that nuclear weapons were 'weapons of last resort'. This, I felt, would undermine the credibility of NATO's SNF. We should continue to resist any qualification of the role of nuclear weapons in NATO, just as we had always done. We were slipping towards – though we had not reached – that fatal position of undertaking that there would be 'no first use of nuclear weapons', on which Soviet propaganda had always insisted. Such an undertaking would leave our conventional forces vulnerable to attack by their superior numbers. In the end the first phrase did appear hedged around in the following form:

> Finally, with the total withdrawal of Soviet-stationed forces and the implementation of a CFE Agreement, the allies concerned can reduce their reliance on nuclear weapons. These will continue to fulfil an essential role in the overall strategy of the alliance to prevent war by ensuring that there are no circumstances in which nuclear retaliation in response to military action might be discounted. However, in the transformed Europe, they will be able to adopt *a new NATO strategy making nuclear forces truly weapons of last resort.* [my italics]

I cannot say that I was satisfied with this unwieldy compromise. But in the end military strategy is not dependent upon pieces of paper but on the commitment of resources to practical military objectives. The review which was begun at Turnberry and which in Britain's case would be put into effect through the 'Options for Change' exercise that Tom King conducted as Defence Secretary had to concentrate on where the priorities for inevitably decreased expenditure would now be.

A month before the NATO summit I set out in my speech to the North Atlantic Council my own views on the matter. The stress I placed on preservation of the United States' military presence in Europe and the continuing role of updated nuclear weapons would not have surprised my audience. But I also emphasized that NATO must consider an 'out of area' role. I asked the question:

> Ought NATO to give more thought to possible threats to our security from other directions? There is no guarantee that threats to our security will stop at some imaginary line across the mid-Atlantic. It is not long since some of us had to go to the Arabian Gulf to keep oil supplies flowing. We shall become very heavily dependent on Middle Eastern oil once again in the next century. With the spread of sophisticated weapons and military technology to areas like the Middle East, potential threats to NATO territory may originate more from outside Europe. Against that background, it would be only prudent for NATO countries to retain a capacity to carry out multiple roles, with more flexible and versatile forces.

This passage reflected my thinking over a number of years. I had seen for myself how important a western presence could be in securing western interests in far-flung areas of the world. I did not believe that even if the military threat from the Soviets had diminished, that from other dictators would not arise. But of course I could not know that within two months we would be confronted by an explosive crisis in the Gulf.

CHAPTER THIRTY-NINE

—————❖—————

No Time to Go Wobbly

The response to Iraq's invasion of Kuwait in 1990

O N THE MORNING OF WEDNESDAY 1 August 1990 the VC10 left Heathrow with me and my party aboard bound for Aspen, Colorado. The President was due to open the Aspen Institute Conference on the Thursday and I was to close it on the Sunday. At the time I left I already knew that the Iraqis were sending troops down to the border with Kuwait. The negotiations between Iraq and Kuwait, which had been taking place in Jeddah, had broken for the day but we understood that they were to be resumed. It therefore seemed that the Iraqi military action was a case of sabre rattling. We soon learned that it was not. At 2 a.m. Kuwaiti time on Thursday 2 August Iraq carried out a full-scale military invasion – though claiming that it was an internal coup – and assumed total control.

An hour later – early evening on Wednesday, Colorado time – Charles Powell telephoned me to tell me the news and I decided at once to instruct two ships in Penang and Mombasa, both about a week's sailing time away, to make for the Gulf while the situation developed. We already had one ship of the Armilla patrol in the Gulf – HMS *York*, at Dubai. First thing the following morning I learned in a note from Charles about the latest situation. Other Arab governments had evidently been caught off balance. The Arab League of Foreign Ministers meeting in Cairo had failed to agree a statement. King Hussein was trying to excuse the Iraqi action on the grounds that the Kuwaitis had been unnecessarily difficult. The ruling families in the Gulf were alarmed. With strong British support the UN Security Council had passed a resolution condemning Iraq for its action and calling for total withdrawal and immediate negotiations. Back in London, Douglas Hurd – competent professional that he was – had ordered the freezing of Kuwaiti assets in Britain, the Iraqis unfortunately having only debts. An immediate question now was whether Saddam Hussein would go over the border and seize Saudi Arabia's oil fields.

I was staying at the guesthouse to Ambassador Henry Catto's ranch while all this was going on. I read Charles's note, listened to the news and then went for a walk to sort things out in my own mind. By the time I got back Charles and Sir Antony Acland, our ambassador, were waiting for me. We established from the White House that President Bush was still coming to Aspen and would arrive later that morning. As is my wont, I set about arguing through the whole problem with them and by the end had defined the two main points. By the time I was due to meet him at the main ranch I was quite clear what we must do.

Fortunately, the President began by asking me what I thought. I told him my conclusions in the most straightforward terms. First, aggressors must never be appeased. Second, if Saddam Hussein were to cross the border into Saudi Arabia he could go right down the Gulf in a matter of days. He would then control 65 per cent of the world's oil reserves and could blackmail us all. Not only did we have to move to stop the aggression, therefore, we had to stop it quickly. In making these two points I felt that experience as well as instinct enabled me to trust my judgement. There was, of course, the enormously valuable experience of having been Prime Minister through the Falklands War. My visits to the Gulf had also allowed me to establish bonds of trust with the rulers of many of these states. I understood their problems and could gauge their reactions. At this point President Bush was told that the President of Yemen wanted to speak to him on the telephone. Before the President left to take the call, I reminded him that Yemen, a temporary member of the Security Council, had not voted on the resolution demanding the withdrawal of Iraqi forces from Kuwait. It turned out that the President of Yemen too wanted time to come up with an Arab solution. President Bush told him that such a 'solution' must involve the withdrawal of Iraqi forces and return of the proper Government of Kuwait if it was to be accepted. The President of Yemen then apparently compared what had happened in Kuwait to US intervention in Grenada, at which George Bush rightly bridled. When he returned President Bush and I agreed that all this did not seem very encouraging. We then went out to give a press conference. The President was asked if he ruled out the use of force. He replied that he did not – a statement the press took to be a strengthening of his position against Saddam Hussein. But I had never found any weakness in it from the first.

Understandably, I now had only half my mind on the programme of events which had been arranged for me. That said, I was fascinated by what I saw. Friday was a day of presentations and discussions about science, environment and defence – punctuated by news about what was happening in the crisis which now gripped the international community. I was talking to the young scientists working at the SDI National Test Facility at Falcon when I was called away to speak to President Bush on the telephone. He gave me the good news that President Ozal of Turkey had said he would take action to cut off the Iraqi oil which was going through the Turkish pipeline. As a secular but predominantly Muslim state with a large army, looking westwards to Europe but also on the fringe of the Middle East, Turkey would be a vital bulwark against aggressive Islamic fundamentalism or other brands of revolutionary Arab nationalism like that of Saddam Hussein.

After lunch I went by helicopter to the Strategic Air Defense Monitoring Center at Cheyenne Mountain which keeps a watch on every satellite launched. Again I felt awed by the sophistication of America's scientific and technological achievement. From within this hollowed-out mountain the United States could observe deep into space for military and scientific purposes. Two days later I was told by the general in charge of the operation that they had observed that the Soviets had now put up two satellites over the northern end of the Gulf. It was a useful indication of their concern.

On Saturday morning I spoke with President Mitterrand on the telephone. As over the Falklands, he was taking a robust position: in spite of a misconceived speech at the United Nations which tried to link a solution of the Gulf crisis with other Middle Eastern issues, President Mitterrand and France showed throughout the crisis that the French were the only European country, apart from ourselves, with the stomach for a fight.

Though the speech I gave on Sunday morning to the Aspen Institute addressed broader international issues, I inserted a section on the Gulf. It read:

> Iraq's invasion of Kuwait defies every principle for which the United Nations stands. If we let it succeed, no small country can ever feel safe again. The law of the jungle would take over from the rule of law.

The United Nations must assert its authority and apply a total economic embargo unless Iraq withdraws without delay. The United States and Europe both support this. But to be fully effective it will need the collective support of all the United Nations' members. They must stand up and be counted because a vital principle is at stake: an aggressor must never be allowed to get his way.

My mind was now turning to the next practical steps we could take to exert pressure on Iraq. The EC countries had agreed to support a complete economic and trade embargo of Iraq. But it was the Iraqi oil exports and the willingness of Turkey and Saudi Arabia to block them which would be crucial. I instructed the Foreign Office to prepare plans to implement a naval blockade in the north-east Mediterranean, the Red Sea and the north of the Gulf to intercept shipments of Iraqi and Kuwaiti oil. I also asked that more thought be given to precise military guarantees for Saudi Arabia and for details of what aircraft we could send to the Gulf area immediately. I had planned to take a few days' holiday with my family, but after an invitation from the White House decided instead to fly to Washington and resume my talks with the President. For all the friendship and co-operation I had had from President Reagan, I was never taken into the Americans' confidence more than I was during the two hours or so I spent that afternoon at the White House. The meeting began in a very restricted session with just the President, Brent Scowcroft, myself and Charles Powell. Half an hour later we were joined by Vice-President Dan Quayle, Jim Baker and Chief of Staff John Sununu. The last twenty minutes were attended by the Secretary-General of NATO.

The President that day was firm, cool, showing the decisive qualities which the Commander-in-Chief of the greatest world power must possess. Any hesitation fell away. I had always liked George Bush. Now my respect for him soared.

The President began by reporting what was known about the situation and US plans to deal with it. Saddam Hussein had sworn that if American forces moved into Saudi Arabia he would liberate the kingdom from the Saudi royal family. There were now clear photographs showing that Iraqi tanks had moved right up to the border with Saudi Arabia. I said that it was vital to bolster the Saudis. The main danger was that Iraq would attack Saudi Arabia before the King formally asked the United States for help.

In fact, part of the way through our discussions, Defense Secretary Dick Cheney telephoned the President from Saudi Arabia. He reported that King Fahd was fully behind the United States plan to move the 82nd Airborne Division together with forty-eight F-15 fighters to Saudi Arabia. The King's only condition was that there should be no announcement until the forces were actually in place. This was excellent news.

This meeting also saw the beginning of an almost interminable argument between the Americans – particularly Jim Baker – and me about whether and in what form United Nations authority was needed for measures against Saddam Hussein. I felt that the Security Council Resolution which had already been passed, combined with our ability to invoke Article 51 of the UN Charter on self-defence, was sufficient. Although I did not spell this out on the present occasion my attitude, which had been reinforced as a result of our difficulties with the UN over the Falklands, was based on two considerations. First, there was no certainty that the wording of a resolution, which was always open to amendment, would finish up by being satisfactory. If not, it might tie our hands unacceptably. Of course, with the end of the Cold War the Soviet Union was likely to be more co-operative. Communist China, fearful of isolation, was also disinclined to create too many problems. But the fact remained that if one could achieve an objective without UN authority there was no point in running the risks attached to seeking it.

Second, I did not like unnecessary resort to the UN, because it suggested that sovereign states lacked the moral authority to act on their own behalf. If it became accepted that force could only be used – even in self-defence – when the United Nations approved, neither Britain's interests nor those of international justice and order would be served. The UN was a useful – for some matters vital – forum. But it was hardly the nucleus of a new world order. There was still no substitute for the leadership of the United States.

I returned to London on the Tuesday. The following day I had an hour's telephone conversation with King Fahd to receive his formal request for our own planes and (if necessary) armed forces to be stationed in Saudi Arabia. He expressed incredulity that King Hussein should have sided with Saddam Hussein, whose party had murdered King Hussein's relatives. But King Fahd was as strong as ever in his determination to stand up against aggression.

Later that day I also had the sad duty of attending Ian Gow's funeral. One of my most loyal and candid advisers, there were to be many times when I missed his shrewd counsel and his deadpan wit.

* * *

I was not allowed by the Conservative Party to see through the campaign to throw Saddam Hussein out of Kuwait. But in the months which now followed – and in spite of the other difficulties I faced – my attention was rarely away from the Gulf for long. I set up a small Cabinet sub-committee – Douglas Hurd (Foreign Secretary), Tom King (Defence Secretary), John Wakeham (Energy Secretary), Patrick Mayhew (Attorney-General), William Waldegrave (Minister of State at the Foreign Office), Archie Hamilton (Minister of State for the Armed Forces) and the Chief of the Defence Staff. It was this group, which met regularly, rather than the wider Cabinet Committee OD, which took the main decisions.

One of our first tasks was to provide the promised support for Saudi Arabia. On Thursday 9 August Tom King announced the dispatch of two squadrons of aircraft – one made up of Tornado F3 air defence fighters and the other of Jaguar ground attack planes, 24 aircraft in all. They were in place and operational two days later. Nimrod maritime reconnaissance and VC10 tanker aircraft were also sent. We reinforced them at the end of August with a further squadron of Tornados – but this time the GRI ground-attack version – which were sent to Bahrain to provide a day-and-night anti-armour capability. Rapier air defence detachments were deployed in support.

Of course, I kept in frequent touch with President Bush over the telephone. We regularly discussed the latest information about Saddam Hussein's intentions. The general view seemed to be that whatever he had originally planned, he would not attack Saudi Arabia once American forces were there. But it seemed to me that the important lesson for us was that Saddam Hussein was simply not predictable. As I put it in a minute to the Ministry of Defence on Sunday 12 August:

> We thought that Iraq would not move into Kuwait, although their forces were massing on the border. Let us not make the same mistake again. They may move into Saudi Arabia. We must be ready.

These were weeks of vigorous telephone diplomacy. I encouraged Turkey in its steadfast opposition to Iraq. The Turkish economy was badly hit because – unlike Jordan – Turkey was applying UN sanctions effectively. I never failed to remind the Saudis and the governments of the Gulf States how much they owed to Turkey and urged them to offer generous financial compensation.

A less savoury ally was Syria, with which we still had no formal diplomatic relations. I disliked the regime and had no illusion about its continued willingness to employ terrorism and violence if they suited its purposes. But the fact remained that the rivalry between Syria and Iraq gave us an opportunity which must not be missed. Moreover, it made no sense to have our forces fighting alongside the Syrians if we still had no diplomatic channels for discussion. Reluctantly, therefore, I agreed to the reopening of diplomatic relations, though the formal announcement came a few days after I left office in November.

In the evening of 26 August President Bush telephoned me from Kennebunkport. I told him how pleased I was with Security Council Resolution 665 which had been passed the day before, enabling us to enforce the embargo. We must use our powers to stop Iraqi shipping. This was no time to go wobbly. Information we had gleaned from secret sources must be published to show up sanctions busting. The President agreed. I told him that the only area in which I thought we were not doing well was in the propaganda battle. We were now probably going into a longish period to see whether sanctions would work and we must not let the faint hearts grow in strength. The President was worried also about the use of the port of Aqaba in Jordan to evade sanctions and I told him that I would raise the question when I saw King Hussein in a few days' time.

I was saddened that one of Britain's most long-standing friends appeared to be siding with the enemy. I had been on the friendliest of terms with King Hussein of Jordan but there could be no question of just allowing him to continue to flout sanctions and justify the Iraqi invasion. So when he came to see me for lunch on Friday 31 August I could not conceal my feelings.

He began by making a forty-minute statement which yet again justified what the Iraqis had done. I said that I was amazed at his account of what was in fact a blatant act of aggression. Iraq was a country which had used chemical weapons against its own people. Saddam Hussein was not only an international brigand, he had done immense damage both to the Palestinian cause and to the Arabs and, over eight years, had vainly thrown wave after wave of young Iraqis into the war against Iran. I said that the King should not be attempting to negotiate on Iraq's behalf but rather to implement sanctions against it. But no amount of pressure was likely to alter the calculation which the King had made: that he could not come out openly against Saddam Hussein and survive.

On Thursday 6 September the House of Commons was recalled to debate the position in the Gulf. Unlike the US Congress, Parliament firmly supported the stance taken by the Government: the voting when the debate ended the following day was 437:35. I was also turning my mind to the military campaign which I believed would have to be fought. Later that same afternoon I discussed the situation with Douglas Hurd. I said that I was ever more certain that Saddam Hussein would not leave Kuwait unless he was thrown out. I did not want to see a firm deadline, but we must start to look at the dates which would narrow the options for military action. I also said that we must not be under any illusion: if the sanctions against Iraq did not work, and the Americans and the Multi-National Force failed to take action, Israel would strike.

It was very difficult to know how effective the Iraqi army would be. I had some doubts about their soldiers' spirit, based on the assessment of their preference for high-level bombing and chemical weapons over infantry fighting in the war against Iran. But the Republican Guard was thought to be more formidable. The Americans were extremely cautious, wanting very large amounts of armour in the Gulf before they would be prepared to move. By contrast, some of Iraq's neighbours thought that the Iraqis would crumble quickly; and as it turned out they were proved right.

In any case, as with the Falklands, I was determined to ensure that our forces had the best possible equipment and plenty of it. The Americans wanted us to reinforce our troops in the Gulf and had suggested that we should send an armoured brigade equipped with Challenger I tanks to join the Allied Forces there. I knew that the Challenger had a good reputation for manoeuvrability, but a bad one for reliability. So on Thursday 13 September I called a meeting with Tom King, the Chief of the Defence Staff, the Chief of the General Staff and representatives of Vickers. I cross-questioned them about all the possible weaknesses. I could not forget the way in which the earlier American attempt under President Jimmy Carter to rescue the Iranian hostages had failed because the helicopters used had been unable to cope with the desert conditions. After much discussion they convinced me. But I said that they must take all the spare parts they could possibly need with them, not wait for more to be sent out, and I also insisted upon receiving a written guarantee of 80 per cent availability – several times better than Challenger had achieved in Germany.

I also wanted the commander of our forces to be someone in whom I – and they – would have complete confidence. Only one man seemed to be right for the job – Sir Peter de la Billière. Tom King was reluctant to see him appointed: Peter de la Billière was within a week of retiring and the other candidates clearly had much to be said for them. But I wanted a fighting general. I knew the qualities of Sir Peter from his command of the SAS operation at the time of the 1980 Iranian Embassy siege and from the Falklands. I also knew that he spoke Arabic – of some importance when part of a large multi-national force with a crucial Arab element. So I told Tom King that Sir Peter was not retiring now if I had anything to do with it: and if he did not go to command our forces in the Gulf, he would be coming as personal adviser on the conduct of the war to Downing Street. He went to the Gulf.

I met the President again in New York on the evening of Sunday 30 September. We were officially there to attend the 'UN Children's Summit', an occasion at which the only high point was an inspiring speech from President Havel of Czechoslovakia. President Bush was very tired, having flown back to Washington from New York to complete negotiations with Congress on the fateful 1990 budget compromise, which was to undermine him politically, before returning for this meeting. But he was in good spirits. We discussed Jim Baker's wish for another UN Security Council Resolution specifically to endorse the use of force to bring about Iraq's withdrawal from Kuwait. As always, I was dubious. But what was clear to all of us was that the time for using force was now rapidly approaching. There was no evidence that sanctions were having any real effect on Iraq's decisions – and that was what counted. I was clearer than ever in my mind that there could be no weakening in our resolve to defeat – and be seen to defeat – Saddam Hussein's aggression.

On the evening of Tuesday 23 October I had a meeting with Tom King and Douglas Hurd. The main purpose was to give guidance to the Chief of the Defence Staff at his meetings with General Colin Powell, chairman of the US Joint Chiefs of Staff, in the United States over the next two days. I began by listing our strategic objectives. These were to provide the guidelines according to which British policy in the forthcoming war should be determined. Saddam Hussein must leave Kuwait and the latter's legitimate Government must be restored. All hostages must be released. Iraq must pay compensation. Those responsible for atrocities must be brought to account before an international court. Iraq's nuclear, biological and chemical capability must be eliminated in the event of hostilities and dismantled in the event of a peaceful withdrawal of Iraqi troops. To do this the widest possible alliance of Arab governments against Iraq must be maintained and Israeli involvement must be avoided. A regional security system must be established to constrain Iraq in the future.

As for Saddam Hussein himself, it would not be a specific objective to bring about his downfall, though that might be a desirable side-effect of our actions. I said that further work on targets in Iraq was needed. Purely civilian targets must be avoided. But it was for consideration whether power stations and dams should be regarded as legitimate targets. There was no intention that our forces should occupy any part of Iraqi territory, but they might need to enter Iraq in hot pursuit of Iraqi forces. I said that it was necessary to get the Americans to accept that military action would in all likelihood have to be initiated before the end of the year. I also said that we must try to continue to wean them away from seeking prior authorization for the use of force from the UN and to rely instead on Article 51.

I argued this last point through with Jim Baker when he came to see me on the evening of Friday 9 November. But I was not able to sway him. He said that UN authority was crucial to sustain the support of American public opinion for military action. I also raised my worries about delaying the military option until the extra American forces now being sent had arrived in the Gulf. I said that it was vital not to miss the window of opportunity which would close in early March. He was able to reassure me on this point. But by now time was running out for me as well as for Saddam Hussein.

In response to Jim Baker's request and at my last Cabinet on Thursday 22 November – to which I announced my resignation as Prime Minister – the decision was made to double Britain's military commitment and to deploy an extra brigade to the Gulf. We would send the 4th Brigade from Germany, comprising a regiment of Challenger tanks, two armoured infantry battalions and a regiment of Royal Artillery, with reconnaissance and supporting services. Together the two brigades would form the 1st Armoured Division. The total number of UK forces committed would amount to more than 30,000.

Since the morning of Thursday 2 August hardly a day had passed without my involvement in diplomatic and military moves to isolate and defeat Iraq. One of my very few abiding regrets is that I was not there to see the issue through. The failure to disarm Saddam Hussein and to follow through the victory so that he was publicly humiliated in the eyes of his subjects and Islamic neighbours was a mistake which stemmed from the excessive emphasis placed right from the start on international consensus. The opinion of the UN counted for too much and the military objective of defeat for too little. And so Saddam Hussein was left with the standing and the means to terrorize his people and foment more trouble. In war there is much to be said for magnanimity in victory. But not before victory.

CHAPTER FORTY

Men in Lifeboats

The background to and course of the 1990 Conservative
Party leadership campaign – and resignation

I N 1975 I WAS THE FIRST CANDIDATE for the leadership of the Conservative Party to challenge an existing leader under the rules which had been instituted by Sir Alec Douglas-Home a decade earlier. Having entered the field as a rank outsider, I won the leadership in an open contest. So I am the last person to complain about having to meet a challenge to my own leadership. But the circumstances of 1990, when Michael Heseltine challenged me, were very different. I had won three general elections and lost none, whereas Ted Heath had lost three out of four. I was a sitting Prime Minister of eleven and a half years in office, whereas Ted was a newly defeated Opposition leader. The beliefs and policies which I had pioneered in Britain were helping to remould world affairs. And our country was at that moment on the verge of war in the Gulf.

Of course, democracy is no respecter of persons, as my great predecessor, Winston Churchill, learned when having led Britain through her supreme struggle against the Nazi tyranny and in the midst of negotiations crucial to the post-war world order, he was defeated in the 1945 general election. At least, however, it was the British people who dismissed him from office. I was not given the opportunity to meet the voters – and they were not able to pronounce on my final term of office, except by proxy.

The 1965 procedure for electing the Tory Leader was, by unwritten convention, not intended for use when the Party was in office. Theoretically, I had to be re-elected every year; but since no one else stood, this was a formality.

I have already described the growth of political discontent in the summer and autumn of 1989. Of its causes, the most important was the economy. High interest rates aggravated what would otherwise have been more manageable problems, such as the agitation over the community charge – a running sore which would get much worse the following year. There was also a hard core of opposition to my approach to the European Community, though this was very much a minority view. And there was, of course, a range of backbenchers who for various idiosyncratic reasons, or because they had been denied or removed from office, would be happy to line up against me. There was even talk of one of them putting up for the leadership as a 'stalking horse' for the real contender, Michael Heseltine, lurking in the wings.

In fact, Sir Anthony Meyer decided to mount a challenge for reasons of his own in 1989, and there had to be a contest. Mark Lennox-Boyd, my PPS, George Younger, Ian Gow, Tristan Garel-Jones (a Foreign Office Minister of State), Richard Ryder (Economic Secretary) and Bill Shelton constituted my campaign team who quietly identified supporters, waverers and opponents. I did not myself campaign and no one seriously thought that I should. I won 314 votes, Sir Anthony Meyer 33. There were 24 spoilt ballots and 3 abstentions. But the contest had revealed, as George Younger told me, a certain amount of discontent.

Accordingly, I made more frequent visits to that fount of gossip, the Commons tearoom. I also began regular meetings with groups of backbenchers, usually recruited according to region so as to ensure a wide spectrum of views. At these meetings I would ask everyone around the table to speak their mind and then come in at the end to answer point by point. There was frank speaking on both sides – on one occasion a backbencher told me it was time for me to go. I may not have complied, but I did listen.

But no amount of discussion or attention to personal sensitivities could compensate for the political situation in the summer of 1990. High community charge bills made Conservative MPs anxious about their seats. Inflation and interest rates were still high. Divisions in the Parliamentary Party and the Government over Europe sharpened as the pace of the federalist programme accelerated. The rank and file of the Party was still with me, as they would show at the 1990 Party Conference, indeed perhaps stronger than ever in their support. But too many of my colleagues had an unspoken contempt for the Party faithful whom they regarded as organization fodder with no real right to hold political opinions. And in the event, no one would seriously listen to them – though they were formally consulted and pronounced heavily in my favour – when it came for my fate to be decided.

For my part, I remained confident that we could ride out these difficulties and win the next election. High interest rates were already doing their work in bringing down inflation, whatever the headline RPI figures showed. I was only waiting for signs that the money supply was firmly under control before cutting interest rates – and continuing to cut them even if that would entail a changed parity in the ERM. At the end of April I had my first serious discussion with the Policy Unit about policies that might be in the next manifesto. And that summer I had discussions with colleagues on setting up manifesto policy groups. My Party Conference speech in October 1990 raised the curtain on just a little of this, outlining proposals for privatization, training vouchers (and hinting at education vouchers), and increasing the number of grant-maintained schools. I wanted to be ready for the summer of 1991.

There was still much that I wanted to do. Most immediately, we had to defeat Saddam Hussein and establish a durable security framework for the Gulf. The economy was fundamentally strong, but I wanted to overcome inflation and recession and restore a stable framework for growth. I thought there was a good prospect of mopping up communism in central and eastern Europe and establishing limited government under law in the new democracies. Above all I hoped to win the battle for my kind of European Community – one in which a free and enterprising nation-state like Britain could comfortably flourish. But I also knew that the wider framework of international relations which was needed in the post-Cold War world – one in which international bodies like the UN, the GATT, the IMF, the World Bank, NATO and the CSCE held the ring, while nation-states and international commerce were left to their own proper spheres of activity – would not be built in a day. This was a substantial long-term programme. My problem was the lack of a successor whom I could trust both to keep my legacy secure and to build on it. I liked John Major and thought that he genuinely shared my approach. But he was relatively untested and his tendency to accept the conventional wisdom had given me pause for thought. Given time, John might grow in stature, or someone else might emerge. So, both because of the scale of the challenges and my uncertainty over the succession, I did not wish to step down before the next election.

Nor, however, did I seriously intend to go 'on and on'. I thought that about two years into the next Parliament would be the right time to leave.

Even then it would be a wrench. I felt as full of energy as ever. But I accepted that one day it would be my duty to leave No. 10, whether the electorate had demanded it or not.

What would not persuade me to depart, however, was the kind of argument put to me by Peter Carrington over dinner at his house one Sunday evening in April 1990. Denis was not there: he was away for the weekend. Peter argued that the Party wanted me to leave office both with dignity and at a time of my own choosing. I took this to be a coded message: dignity might suggest a rather earlier departure than I would otherwise choose. Peter was, I suspect, speaking on behalf of at least a section of the Tory establishment. My own feeling was that I would go 'when the time was ripe'. I reflected that if the great and the good of the Tory Party had had their way, I would never have become Party Leader, let alone Prime Minister. Nor had I the slightest interest in appearances nor in the trappings of office. I would fight – and, if necessary, go down fighting – for my beliefs as long as I could. 'Dignity' did not come into it.

The restiveness of Tory backbenchers was transformed into open panic by the Eastbourne by-election later in October. Ian Gow's old seat went to the Liberals with a swing of 20 per cent. The opinion polls also looked bad. Labour had a substantial lead. This was not a happy background to the Rome summit which I attended over the weekend of 27–28 October. Yet even as I was fighting a lone battle in Rome, Geoffrey Howe went on television and told Brian Walden that we did not in fact oppose the principle of a single currency, implying that I would probably be won round. This was either disloyal or remarkably stupid. At the first Prime Minister's Questions on my return, I was inevitably asked about his remarks. I countered Opposition taunts by saying that Geoffrey was 'too big a man to need a little man like [Neil Kinnock] to stand up for him'. But I could not endorse what he had said.

And my difficulties were just beginning. I now had to stand up in the House and make my statement on the outcome of the Rome summit. I duly stressed that 'a single currency is not the policy of this Government'. But this assertion had two important qualifications. The first was that our own proposal for a parallel or 'common' currency in the form of the hard ecu might evolve *towards* a single currency. The second was a form of words, which ministers had come to use, that we would not have a single currency 'imposed upon us'. And, inevitably, there were differing interpretations of precisely what that delphic expression meant. Such hypothetical qualifications could be used by someone like Geoffrey to keep open the possibility that we would at some point end up with a single currency. That was not our intention, and I felt there was a basic dishonesty in this interpretation. It was the removal of this camouflage which probably provided the reason for Geoffrey's resignation.

I said in reply to questions that 'in my view [the hard ecu] would not become widely used throughout the Community – possibly most widely used for commercial transactions. Many people would continue to prefer their own currency.' I also expressed firm agreement with Norman Tebbit when he made the vital point that 'The mark of a single currency is not only that all other currencies must be extinguished but that the capacity of other institutions to issue currencies must also be extinguished.' My reply was: 'This Government believes in the pound sterling.' And I vigorously rejected the Delors concept of a federal Europe in which the European Parliament would be the Community's House of Representatives, the Commission its Executive, and the Council of Ministers its Senate. 'No, no, no,' I said.

This performance set Geoffrey on the road to resignation. Exactly why is still unclear, perhaps to him, certainly to me. I do not know whether he actually wanted a single currency. Neither now or later, as far as I am aware, did he ever say where he stood – only where I should not stand. Perhaps the enthusiastic – indeed uproarious – support I received from the backbenchers convinced him that he had to strike at once, or I would win round the Parliamentary Party to the platform I earlier set out in Bruges.

No matter what I had said, however, Geoffrey would sooner or later have objected and gone. By this time the gap between us was as much a matter of personal antipathy as of policy difference. Geoffrey never put his heart into the Leadership of the House. In the Cabinet he was now a force for obstruction, in the Party a focus of resentment, in the country a source of division. On top of all that, we found each other's company almost intolerable. I was surprised at the immediate grounds of his resignation. But in some ways it is more surprising that he remained so long in a position which he clearly disliked and resented. I heard nothing of Geoffrey on Wednesday (31 October). On Thursday morning at Cabinet I took him to task, probably too sharply, about the preparation of the legislative programme. I was slightly curious that he had so little to say for himself. Afterwards, I had lunch in the flat, worked on my speech for the debate on the Loyal Address, had a short meeting with Douglas Hurd about the situation in the Gulf, and then went off to Marsham Street where, in the cellars beneath the DoE/Department of Transport complex, the Gulf Embargo Surveillance unit was operating. I had not been there long when a message came through that Geoffrey wanted urgently to see me back at No. 10.

I was back there at 5.50 p.m. for what turned out to be almost a rerun of Nigel Lawson's resignation. I asked Geoffrey to postpone his decision till the following morning: I already had so much to think about – surely a little more time was possible. But he insisted. He said that he had already cancelled the speech he was due to give that evening at the Royal Overseas League, and the news was bound to get out. So the letters were prepared and his resignation was announced. In a sense it was a relief he had gone. But I had no doubt of the political damage it would do. All the talk of a leadership bid by Michael Heseltine would start again. And it was impossible to know what Geoffrey himself planned to do. But presumably he would not remain silent. It was vital that the Cabinet reshuffle, made necessary by his departure, should reassert my authority and unite the Party. That would not be easy, and indeed the two objectives might by now be in conflict.

I could not discuss all this with my advisers immediately, however, because I had to host a reception at No. 10 for the Lord's Taverners, the charitable organization with which Denis was involved. But, as soon as I could, I broke away and went to my study where Ken Baker, John Wakeham and Alastair Goodlad, the Deputy Chief Whip, who was standing in for Tim Renton, got down to discussing what must be done.

I already knew my ideal solution: Norman Tebbit back in the Cabinet as Education Secretary. He was tough, articulate and trustworthy. He would have made a superb Education Secretary who could sell his programme to the country and wrong-foot the Labour Party. We could not reach him that night but made contact the following morning (Friday 2 November), and he agreed to come in and discuss it. As I feared, he would not be persuaded. He had left the Cabinet to look after his wife and that duty took precedence over all else. He would give me all the support he could from outside, but he could not come back into government.

When Norman left, Tim Renton, the Chief Whip, now back in London, came in. He argued strongly that William Waldegrave – who was on the left of the Party – should join the Cabinet. William was slim, cerebral and aloof – a sort of Norman St John Stevas without jokes – and he seemed likely to be even less of an ally. But I had never kept talented people out of my Cabinets just because they were not of my way of thinking, and I was not going to start even now. I asked him to take on the Department of Health.

But I still wanted a new face at Education, where John MacGregor's limitations as a public spokesman were costing us dear in an area of great importance. So I appointed Ken Clarke – again not someone on my wing of the Party, but an energetic and persuasive bruiser, very useful in a brawl or an election. John MacGregor I moved to Geoffrey's old post as Leader of the House. The appointments were well received and my objective of uniting the Party seemed to be succeeding.

Any prospect of a return to business as usual, however, was quickly dispelled. I spent Saturday 3 November at Chequers working with my advisers on my speech on the Address, which had, of course, assumed a new importance in the light of Geoffrey's resignation. That evening Bernard Ingham rang through to read me an open letter Michael Heseltine had written to his constituency chairman. It was ostensibly about the need for the Government to chart a new course on Europe. In fact, it was the first tentative public step in the Heseltine leadership bid. Sunday's papers (4 November) were accordingly full of stories about the leadership. They also contained the first opinion poll findings taken after Geoffrey's departure. Unsurprisingly, they were very bad. Labour was shown in one to be 21 per cent ahead. I spent the day working on another speech – on the environment – which I was to deliver on Tuesday in Geneva.

On as many Monday mornings as possible I used to meet Ken Baker and the Central Office team to look through the diary for the week ahead. Over lunch I would also discuss the political situation with Ken, the business managers and some other Cabinet colleagues. That Monday we talked about almost everything except what was on everyone's mind – whether or not there would be a leadership contest. A feeling was now evident in the British press that Michael had perhaps overplayed his hand in his open letter. If he did not now stand, he would be accused of cowardice. If he did stand, he would probably lose – despite the tremors over Geoffrey's departure.

This was the background to the discussion I had with Peter Morrison, my PPS, and Cranley Onslow, Chairman of the '22, on Tuesday afternoon (6 November) after a short visit to Geneva to address the World Climate Conference. We were all concerned that the speculation about the leadership was doing the Party and the Government great harm. It seemed best to try to bring matters to a head and get the leadership campaign – if there was to be one – out of the way quickly. The contest had to take place within twenty-eight days of the opening of the new parliamentary session, but it was up to the Leader of the Party, in consultation with the Chairman of the '22, to name the precise date. Accordingly, we agreed to bring forward the date for the closing of nominations to Thursday 15 November, with the first ballot on Tuesday 20 November. This meant that I would be away in Paris for the CSCE summit when the first ballot – if there was one – occurred. The disadvantage, of course, would be that I would not be at Westminster to rally support. But Peter Morrison and I did not in any case envisage that I would canvass on my own behalf. As things turned out, this may have been a wrong judgement. But it is important to understand why it was made.

First, it would have been absurd for a Prime Minister of eleven and a half years' standing to behave as if she were entering the lists for the first time. Tory MPs knew me, my record and my beliefs. If they were not already persuaded, there was not much left for me to persuade them with. I had been listening week after week to MPs' grumbles; but I could not now credibly tell an MP worried about the community charge that I had been convinced by what he said and intended to scrap the whole scheme. Nor would I have dreamt of doing so. Thus there were strict limits on any canvassing I could usefully do to maximize my vote. A challenger like Michael, however, could promise promotion to those out of office as well as security for those already in it; he would be the beneficiary of all the resentments of the backbenchers.

Second, I felt that, as in 1989, the most effective campaign would be carried out by others on my behalf. In Peter Morrison I considered that I had an experienced House of Commons man who could put together a good team to work for me. He had been one of the first backbenchers to urge me to stand in 1975. I knew that I could rely on his loyalty. Unfortunately, the same quality of serene optimism which made Peter so effective at cheering us all up was not necessarily so suitable for calculating the intentions of that most slippery of electorates – Conservative MPs. I also envisaged, of course, that Peter would have other heavyweights in my team, including George Younger who had done such a good job in 1989.

The debate on the Address would give me an opportunity to renew my authority and the Government's momentum. So I put extra effort into work on the speech. On the day itself (Wednesday 7 November), I was helped by yet another feeble attack from Neil Kinnock whose latest metamorphosis as a market socialist I mocked in the line: 'The Leader of the

Opposition is fond of talking about supply side socialism. We know what that means: whatever the unions demand, Labour will supply.' But I also had to deal with the more delicate issue of Geoffrey's resignation. And that had hidden traps.

In his resignation letter Geoffrey had not spelt out any significant policy differences between us. Instead, he had concentrated on what he described as 'the mood I had struck . . . in Rome last weekend and in the House of Commons this Tuesday'. I therefore felt entitled to point out in my speech that 'If the Leader of the Opposition reads my Rt Hon. and learned friend's letter, he will be very pressed indeed to find any significant policy difference on Europe between my Rt Hon. and learned friend and the rest of us on this side.'

The debate went quite well. But it soon became clear that Geoffrey was furious about what I had said. He apparently felt that there were substantial points of difference on policy between us, even if he had not so far managed to articulate what they were. We had reached nothing more than a lull before a political storm that was to rage ever more strongly.

At the end of Thursday's Cabinet (8 November), we took the unusual step of adjourning for a political session. Ken Baker warned of the likelihood of extremely bad results at the Bootle and Bradford North by-elections. Things turned out as he feared. The worst result was in Bradford, where we slumped to third place. Early the next morning (Friday 9 November), Ken telephoned me to discuss these results. I put on a brave face, saying it was no worse than I expected. But it was bad enough, and at the wrong time.

What really set the political commentators talking, however, was a statement that day by Geoffrey that he would 'be seeking an opportunity in the course of the next few days to explain in the House of Commons the reasons – of substance as well as style – which prompted [his] difficult decision'. The speculation that Michael Heseltine would stand naturally increased over the weekend. Indeed, politics entered one of those febrile, nervous phases in which events seem to be moving towards some momentous but unknowable climax almost independent of the wishes of the actors. And there was little I could do about any of this. I soldiered on with my arranged programme.

On Monday (12 November), as the previous week, there was only one subject on our minds at my morning 'Week Ahead' meeting with Ken Baker and at the subsequent lunch with colleagues – and again, significantly, none of us really wished to talk about it. No one knew as yet what

Geoffrey would say, or even when he would say it. But never had a speech by Geoffrey been so eagerly awaited.

I delivered my own speech at the Lord Mayor's Banquet in Guildhall that evening, striking a deliberately defiant note. But words now began to fail me. I employed a cricketing metaphor which that evening drew warm applause but which would later be turned to my disadvantage:

> I am still at the crease, though the bowling has been pretty hostile of late. And in case anyone doubted it, can I assure you there will be no ducking bouncers, no stonewalling, no playing for time. The bowling's going to get hit all round the ground.

I had now learned that Geoffrey would speak in the House the following day, Tuesday 13 November, about his resignation. I would, of course, stay on after Questions to hear him.

Geoffrey's speech was a powerful Commons performance – the most powerful of his career. If it failed in its ostensible purpose of explaining the policy differences that had provoked his resignation, it succeeded in its real purpose, which was to damage me. It was cool, forensic, light at points, and poisonous. His long-suppressed rancour gave Geoffrey's words more force than he had ever managed before. He turned the cricketing metaphor against me with a QC's skill, claiming that my earlier remarks about the hard ecu undermined the Chancellor and the Governor of the Bank of England: 'It is rather like sending your opening batsmen to the crease only for them to find, the moment the first balls are bowled, that their bats have been broken before the game by the team captain.' He persuasively caricatured my arguments of principle against Europe's drift to federalism as mere tics of temperamental obstinacy. And his final line – 'the time has come for others to consider their own response to the tragic conflict of loyalties with which I have myself wrestled for perhaps too long' – was an open invitation to Michael Heseltine to stand against me that electrified the House of Commons.

It was a peculiar experience listening to this bill of particulars, rather like being the accused during a prosecutor's summing up in a capital case. For I was as much the focus of attention as was Geoffrey. If the world was listening to him, it was watching me. And underneath the mask of composure, my emotions were turbulent. I had not the slightest doubt that the speech was deeply damaging to me. One part of my mind was making the usual political calculations of how I and my colleagues should react to it in the lobbies. Michael Heseltine had been handed more than an invitation to enter the lists; he had been given a weapon as well. How would we blunt it?

At a deeper level than calculation, however, I was hurt and shocked. Perhaps in view of the irritability that had been the coin of my relations with Geoffrey in recent years, I was foolish to be so pierced. But any ill-feeling between us had been expressed behind closed doors, even if news of it had sometimes leaked into political gossip columns. In public, I had been strongly supportive of him both as Chancellor and as Foreign Secretary. Indeed, the memory of the battles we had fought alongside each other in Opposition and in the early 1980s had persuaded me to keep him in the Cabinet as Deputy Prime Minister when a closer attention to my own political interests on Europe, exchange rates, and a host of other issues would have led me to replace him with someone more of my way of thinking.

Yet he had not been similarly swayed by those memories and he had deliberately set out to bring down a colleague in this brutal and public way. Geoffrey Howe, from this point on, would be remembered not for his staunchness as Chancellor, nor for his skilful diplomacy as Foreign Secretary, but for this final act of bile and treachery. The very brilliance with which he wielded the dagger ensured that the character he assassinated was in the end his own.

The following morning (Wednesday 14 November) Cranley Onslow telephoned to say that he had received formal notification of Michael Heseltine's intention to stand for the leadership. Douglas Hurd now proposed my nomination; John Major seconded it; this was intended as a demonstration of the Cabinet's united support for me. Peter Morrison quickly had my own leadership team up and running, though some people subsequently suggested that this was too energetic a metaphor. The key figures were to be George Younger, Michael Jopling, John Moore, Norman Tebbit and Gerry Neale. MPs would be discreetly asked their views so that we knew who were supporters, waverers and opponents. Michael Neubert was to keep the tally. Opponents would not be approached again, but waverers were to be called on by whichever member of the team seemed most likely to be persuasive.

It was agreed that I would use press interviews as the main platform for me to set out my case. So on Thursday evening (15 November) I was interviewed by Michael Jones of the *Sunday Times* and Charles Moore of the *Sunday Telegraph*. Nor did I back away from the European issue which

Geoffrey's speech had reopened. Indeed, I said that a referendum would be necessary before there was any question of our having a single currency. This was a constitutional issue, not just an economic one, and it would be wrong not to consult the people directly.

When the nuts and bolts of my campaign were explained to me, they sounded fine. Unfortunately, it was not clear how much time some of the main members of my team could give to the campaign. Norman Fowler had been approached by Peter and agreed to be part of it, but then dropped out immediately, claiming past friendship with Geoffrey Howe. George Younger, about to become Chairman of the Royal Bank of Scotland, was heavily involved in his business affairs. Michael Jopling too bowed out. John Moore was not always in the country. Subsequently, a number of my younger supporters in the 'No Turning Back Group' of MPs, alarmed at the way my campaign was going, drafted themselves as helpers and pulled out every stop. Their help was welcome; but why had it become necessary? This should have been a warning sign. But the campaign played on, and I carried on with the arrangements already in my diary, spending Friday 16 November on a visit to Northern Ireland.

Meanwhile, Michael Heseltine's campaign was in full swing. He had promised a fundamental review of the community charge and was talking about transferring the cost of services like education to central taxation. I had already noted in the House that this could mean an extra 5 pence on income tax or large cuts in other public spending – or a budget deficit just when we had enjoyed four years of surplus and had redeemed debt.

I now pressed home the attack on Michael's approach in a *Times* interview with Simon Jenkins where I drew attention to Michael's long-standing corporatist and interventionist views. This appeared on Monday and was promptly criticized in some circles as being too aggressive. But there was nothing remotely personal about it. Michael Heseltine and I disagreed fundamentally about all that is at the heart of politics. MPs should be reminded that this was a contest between two philosophies as well as between two personalities. It was a sign of the funk and frivolity of the whole exercise that they did not want to think anything was at stake apart from their seats.

On Saturday evening (17 November) Denis and I had friends and advisers to dinner at Chequers – Peter Morrison, the Bakers, the Wakehams, Alistair McAlpine, Gordon Reece, the Bells, the Neuberts, the Neales, John Whittingdale (my political secretary) and of course Mark and Carol. (George Younger could not attend because he had another engagement in Norfolk.) My team gave me a run down on the figures which seemed quite favourable. Peter Morrison told me he thought he had 220 votes for, 110 against and 40 abstentions, which would be an easy win. (To win in the first round I would need a majority of at least 15 per cent of those entitled to vote.) Even allowing for a 'lie factor', I would be all right. But I was not convinced, telling Peter: 'I remember Ted thought the same thing. Don't trust our figures – some people are on the books of both sides.' Everybody else seemed to be far more confident, and indeed spent their time discussing what should be done to unite the Party after my victory. I hoped they were right. Some instinct told me otherwise.

The next day (Sunday 18 November) I departed for the CSCE summit in Paris. It marked the formal – though sadly not the actual – beginning of that new era which was termed by President Bush a 'new world order'. In Paris far-reaching decisions were taken to shape the post-Cold War Europe. These included deep mutual cuts in conventional armed forces within the CFE framework, a European 'Magna Carta' guaranteeing political rights and economic freedom (an idea I had particularly championed), and the establishment of CSCE mechanisms to promote conciliation, to prevent conflict, to facilitate free elections, and to encourage consultations between governments and parliamentarians.

As usual, I had a series of bilateral meetings with heads of government. The Gulf was almost always at the forefront of our discussions, though my mind kept turning to what was happening back in Westminster. On Monday (19 November) I had breakfast with President Bush, signed on behalf of the United Kingdom the historic agreement to reduce conventional forces in Europe, attended the first plenary session of the CSCE, and lunched with the other leaders at the Elysée Palace. In the afternoon I made my own speech to the summit, looking back over the long-term benefits of the Helsinki process, emphasizing the continued importance of human rights and the rule of law, pointing to their connection with economic freedom, and warning against any attempt to downgrade NATO which was 'the core of western defence'. I later talked with the UN Secretary-General about the situation in the Gulf before entertaining Chancellor Kohl to dinner at the British Embassy.

It was characteristic of Helmut Kohl that he came straight to the point, namely the leadership election. He said it was good to talk about these difficult issues rather than bottle them up. He had been determined to devote this evening to me as a way of demonstrating his complete support. It was unimaginable that I should be deprived of office. Given that the Chancellor and I had strong differences on the future course of the European Community and that my departure would remove an obstacle to his plans – as, indeed, proved to be the case – this was big-hearted of him.

The following day I would know the results of the first ballot. Peter had spoken to me on the telephone on Monday evening, and he was still radiating confidence. It had already been arranged that he would come out to Paris to be there to give me 'the good news', which would be telephoned through to him from the Whips' Office. It had also been agreed precisely what I would do and say in the event of various eventualities – ranging from an overwhelming victory to a defeat on the first round. Knowing there was nothing more I could do, I threw all my energies on Tuesday into more meetings with heads of government and the CSCE proceedings. In the morning (Tuesday 20 November) I had talks with President Gorbachev, President Mitterrand and President Ozal, and lunch with the Dutch Prime Minister, Ruud Lubbers. After lunch I had a talk with President Zhelev of Bulgaria who said that President Reagan and I shared the responsibility for delivering freedom to eastern Europe and no one would ever forget that. Perhaps it took the leader of a country which had been crushed for decades under communist terror to understand just what had happened in the world and why.

The afternoon's session of the CSCE closed at 4.30. After tea and some discussion with my advisers of the day's events, I went upstairs to my room at the residence to have my hair done. Just after 6 o'clock I went up to a room set aside for me to await the results. Bernard Ingham, Charles Powell, our ambassador Sir Ewen Fergusson, Crawfie and Peter were there. Peter had a line open to the Chief Whip, and Charles had another to John Whittingdale back in London. I sat at a desk with my back to the room and got on with some work. Although I did not realize it then, Charles received the results first. Out of my sight, he gave a sad thumbs down to people in the room, but waited for Peter to get the news officially. Then I heard Peter Morrison receive the information from the Whips' Office. He read out the figures: I had 204 votes, Michael Heseltine 152, and there were 16 abstentions.

'Not quite as good as we had hoped,' said Peter, for once a master of understatement, and handed a note of the results to me. I quickly did the sums in my head. I had beaten Michael Heseltine and achieved a clear majority of the Parliamentary Party (indeed, I got more votes in defeat than John Major later won in victory); but I had not won by a margin sufficient to avoid a second ballot. A short silence followed.

It was broken by Peter Morrison's trying to telephone Douglas Hurd's room in the residence but finding that Douglas was on the line to John Major in Great Stukeley, where the Chancellor was recovering from an operation to remove his wisdom teeth. A few minutes later we got through to Douglas who at once came along to see me. I did not need to ask for his continued support. He declared that I should stand in the second ballot and promised his own, and John Major's, support. He proved as good as his word, and I was glad to have such a staunch friend by my side. Having thanked him and after a little more discussion I went down as previously planned to meet the press and make my statement.

> Good evening, gentlemen. I am naturally very pleased that I got more than half the Parliamentary Party and disappointed that it is not quite enough to win on the first ballot, so I confirm it is my intention to let my name go forward for the second ballot.

Douglas followed me and said:

> I would just like to make a brief comment on the ballot result. The Prime Minister continues to have my full support, and I am sorry that this destructive, unnecessary contest should be prolonged in this way.

I went back upstairs to my room and made a number of telephone calls, including one to Denis. There was little to be said. The dangers were all too obvious, and the telephone was not right for a heart-to-heart discussion of what to do. Anyway, everyone in London knew from my statement that I would carry on.

I changed out of the black wool suit with its tan and black collar which I was wearing when the bad news came through. Although somewhat stunned, I was perhaps less distressed than I might have expected. The evidence is that whereas other outfits which evoke sad memories never see the light of day again, I still wear that suit. But now I had to be in evening dress for dinner at the Palace of Versailles, before which a ballet was to be performed. I sent ahead to President Mitterrand warning him that I would be late and asking that they start without me.

Before leaving for Versailles, I went in to see my old friend Eleanor (the late Lady) Glover at whose Swiss home I had spent so many enjoyable hours on holiday and who had come round from her Paris flat to comfort me. We talked for just a few minutes in the ambassador's sitting room. Her maid, Marta, who was with her, had 'seen it in the cards'. I thought it might be useful to get Marta on the campaign team.

At 8 o'clock I left the embassy with Peter Morrison to be driven at break-neck speed through the empty Paris streets, cleared for Presidents Bush and Gorbachev. But my mind was in London. I knew that our only chance was if the campaign were to go into high gear and every potential supporter pressed to fight for my cause. Again and again, I stressed this to Peter; 'We have got to fight.' Some twenty minutes later we arrived at Versailles where President Mitterrand was waiting for me. 'Of course we would never have started without you,' the President said, and with the considerable charm at his command, he accompanied me inside as if I had just won an election instead of half-losing one.

It will be imagined that I could not give the whole of my attention to the ballet. Even the dinner afterwards, always a memorable event at President Mitterrand's table, was something of a strain. The press and photographers were waiting for us as we left, and they showed a special interest in me. Realizing this, George and Barbara Bush, who were just about to leave, swept me up to come out with them. It was one of those little acts of kindness which remind us that even power politics is not just about power.

From Paris the arrangements were now being made for my return to London. I would attend the signing ceremony for the Final Document of the summit but cut out the previously planned press conference so as to get back to London early. A meeting had been arranged with Norman Tebbit and John Wakeham and they would be joined later by Ken Baker, John MacGregor, Tim Renton and Cranley Onslow. Meanwhile, three trawls of opinion were being made. For my campaign team Norman Tebbit would assess my support in the Parliamentary Party; Tim Renton would do the same for the whips; and the Cabinet would be canvassed by John MacGregor. This last task was, in fact, meant to be the responsibility of John Wakeham, but because he was preparing for an announcement on electricity privatization, he delegated it to John MacGregor.

I now know that this was the time when other ministers back in London were preparing to abandon my cause. But my first inkling of what was taking place came the next morning when my Private Office told me that in accordance with my request they had telephoned Peter Lilley – a card-carrying Thatcherite whom I had appointed to succeed Nick Ridley at Trade and Industry in July 1990 – to ask him to help with the drafting of my speech for that Thursday's No Confidence debate. Peter had apparently replied that he saw no point in this because I was finished. Coming from such a source, this upset me more than I can say. It was going to be even more difficult than I had imagined in my worst nightmares.

I arrived at No. 10 just before midday (Wednesday 21 November). At Peter Morrison's suggestion, I had agreed that I should see members of the Cabinet one by one on my return. The arrangements were made as soon as I got back to London where first appearances were deceptive. The staff of No. 10 clapped and cheered as I arrived; a thousand red roses had arrived from one supporter; and as the long day wore on a constantly increasing flow of other bouquets lined every corridor and staircase.

I went straight up to the flat to see Denis. Affection never blunted honesty between us. His advice was that I should withdraw. 'Don't go on, love,' he said. But I felt in my bones that I should fight on. My friends and supporters expected me to fight, and I owed it to them to do so as long as there was a chance of victory. But was there?

After a few minutes I went down to the study with Peter Morrison where Norman Tebbit and John Wakeham soon joined us. Norman said that it was very difficult to know how my vote stood with MPs, but many would fight every inch of the way for me. My biggest area of weakness was among Cabinet ministers. The objective must be to stop Michael Heseltine, and Norman thought I had the best chance of doing so. I was quite frank with him in return. I said that if I could see the Gulf crisis through and inflation brought down, I would be able to choose the time of my departure. In retrospect, I can see this was a kind of code assuring them that I would resign not long after the next election.

But we had to consider other possibilities. If Michael Heseltine was unthinkable, who could best stop him? Neither Norman nor I believed that Douglas could beat Michael. Moreover, much though I admired Douglas's character and ability, I doubted whether he would carry on the policies in which I believed. And that was a vital consideration to me – it was, indeed, the consideration that prompted me to look favourably on John Major. What of him? If I withdrew, would he be able to win? His prospects were, at best, still uncertain. So I concluded that the right option was for me to stay in the fight.

John Wakeham said that we should think about the wider meeting just about to start. I should prepare myself for the argument that I would be humiliated if I fought. It was the first time I was to hear the argument that day; but not the last.

Norman, John, Peter and I then went down to the Cabinet Room where we were joined by Ken Baker, John MacGregor, Tim Renton, Cranley Onslow and John Moore. Ken opened the discussion by saying that the key issue was how to stop Michael Heseltine. In his view, I was the only person who could do this. Douglas Hurd did not want the job badly enough, and in any case he represented the old wing of the Party. John Major would attract more support: he was closer to my views and had few enemies, but he was short of experience. Ken said that two things were needed for my victory: my campaign needed a major overhaul and I must give an undertaking to look radically at the community charge. He advised against a high-profile media campaign.

John MacGregor then said that he had done his trawl of Cabinet ministers who in turn had consulted their junior ministers. He said that there were very few who were proposing to shift their allegiance, but the underlying problem was that they had no faith in my ultimate success. They were concerned that my support was eroding. In fact, I subsequently learned that this was not the full picture. John MacGregor had found a large minority of Cabinet ministers whose support was shaky – either because they actually wanted me out, or because they genuinely believed that I could not beat Michael Heseltine, or because they favoured an alternative candidate. He did not feel able to convey this information frankly in front of Tim Renton, or indeed of Cranley Onslow, and he had not managed to contact me with this information in advance. This was important, because if we had known the true picture earlier in the day, we might have thought twice about asking Cabinet ministers individually for their support.

The discussion continued. Tim Renton gave a characteristically dispiriting assessment. He said that the Whips' Office had received many messages from backbenchers and ministers saying that I should withdraw from the contest. They doubted if I could beat Michael Heseltine and they wanted a candidate around whom the Party could unite.

Then he said that Willie Whitelaw had asked to see him. Willie was worried that I might be humiliated in the second ballot – it was touching that so many people seemed to be worried about my humiliation – and feared that even if I won by a small margin, it would be difficult for me to unite the Party. He did not want to be cast in the role of a 'man in a grey suit'. But, if asked, he would come in and see me 'as a friend'.

Cranley Onslow said that he brought no message from the committee that I should stand down – the reverse, if anything, was true; but nor did they wish to convey any message to Michael Heseltine. In effect, with the ballot going ahead and the result uncertain, the '22 was declaring its neutrality. Cranley gave his own view that the quality of a Heseltine administration would be inferior to one led by me. As for issues, he did not believe that Europe was the main one. Most people were worried about the community charge and he hoped that something substantial could be done about that. I intervened to say that I could not pull rabbits out of a hat in five days. John MacGregor supported me; I could not now credibly promise a radical overhaul of the community charge, no matter how convenient it seemed.

John Wakeham said that the big issue was whether there was a candidate with a better chance of beating Michael Heseltine. He saw no sign of this. Everything, therefore, hung on strengthening my campaign. Both Ken Baker and John Moore gave their views about the people I needed to win over. Ken noted that those who feared I could not win were my strongest supporters – people like Norman Lamont, John Gummer, Michael Howard and Peter Lilley. John Moore stressed that I needed complete commitment from ministers, particularly junior ministers, in order to succeed. Norman Tebbit came in at the end. Like Cranley, he believed that Europe had faded as an issue in the leadership campaign: the only other major policy issue was the community charge where Michael's promise of action was proving particularly attractive to MPs from the North-West. In spite of this, Norman declared firmly that I could carry more votes against Michael, provided that most of my senior colleagues swung behind me.

I drew the meeting to a close, saying I would reflect on what I had heard. In retrospect, I can see that my resolve had been weakened by these meetings. As yet I was still inclined to fight on. But I felt that the decision would really be made at the meetings with my Cabinet colleagues that evening.

Before then I had to make my statement in the House on the outcome of the Paris summit. Leaving No. 10 I called out to the assembled journalists in Downing Street: 'I fight on, I fight to win,' and was interested to see later on the news that I looked a good deal more confident than I felt.

The statement was not an easy occasion, except for the Opposition. People were more interested in my intentions than in my words. Afterwards, I went back to my room in the House where I was met by Norman Tebbit. It was time – perhaps high time – for me to seek support for my leadership personally. Norman and I began to go round the tearoom. I had never experienced such an atmosphere before. Repeatedly I heard: 'Michael has asked me two or three times for my vote already. This is the first time we have seen you.' Members whom I had known well for many years seemed to have been bewitched by Michael's flattery and promises. That at least was my first reaction. Then I realized that many of these were supporters complaining that my campaign did not seem to be really fighting. They were in a kind of despair because we had apparently given up the ghost.

I returned to my room. I now had no illusion as to how bad the position was. If there was to be any hope, I had to put my whole campaign on a new footing even at this late stage.

I therefore asked John Wakeham, who I believed had the authority and knowledge to do this, to take charge. He agreed but said that he needed people to help him: physically, he had never entirely recovered from the Brighton bomb. So he went off to ask Tristan Garel-Jones and Richard Ryder – both of whom had been closely involved in the 1989 leadership campaign – to be his chief lieutenants.

I now saw Douglas Hurd and asked him formally to nominate me for the second ballot. This he agreed to do at once and with good grace. Then I telephoned John Major at home. I told him that I had decided to stand again and that Douglas was going to propose me. I asked John to second my nomination. There was a moment's silence. The hesitation was palpable. No doubt the operation on John's wisdom teeth was giving him trouble. Then he said that if that was what I wanted, yes. Later, when urging my supporters to vote for John for the leadership, I made play of the fact that he did not hesitate. But both of us knew otherwise.

I now went to the Palace for an Audience with the Queen at which I informed her that I would stand in the second ballot, as indeed I still intended to do. Then I returned to my room in the House to see the Cabinet one by one.

I could, of course, have concentrated my efforts for the second ballot on winning over the backbenchers directly. But the earlier meetings had persuaded me that it was essential to mobilize Cabinet ministers not just to give formal support, but also to go out and persuade junior ministers and backbenchers to back me. In asking for their support, however, I was also putting myself at their mercy. If a substantial number of Cabinet colleagues refused their backing, there could be no disguising the fact afterwards. I recalled a complaint from Churchill, then Prime Minister, to his Chief Whip that talk of his resignation in the Parliamentary Party – he would shortly be succeeded by Anthony Eden – was undermining his authority. Without that authority, he could not be an effective Prime Minister. Similarly, a Prime Minister who knows that his or her Cabinet has withheld its support is fatally weakened. I knew – and I am sure they knew – that I would not willingly remain an hour in 10 Downing Street without real authority to govern.

I had already seen Cecil Parkinson after returning from the tearoom. He told me that I should remain in the race, that I could count on his unequivocal support and that it would be a hard struggle but that I could win. Nick Ridley, no longer in the Cabinet but a figure of more than equivalent weight, also assured me of his complete support. Ken Baker had made clear his total commitment to me. The Lord Chancellor and Lord Belstead, Leader of the Lords, were not really significant players in the game. And John Wakeham was my campaign manager. But all the others I would see in my room in the House of Commons.

Over the next two hours or so, each Cabinet minister came in, sat down on the sofa in front of me and gave me his views. Almost to a man they used the same formula. This was that they themselves would back me, but that regretfully they did not believe I could win.

In fact, as I well realized, they had been feverishly discussing what they should say in the rooms off the Commons Cabinet corridor above my room. Like all politicians in a quandary, they had sorted out their 'line to take' and they would cling to it through thick and thin. After three or four interviews, I felt I could almost join in the chorus. Whatever the monotony of the song, however, the tone and human reactions of those who came into my room that evening offered dramatic contrasts.

My first ministerial visitor was not a member of the Cabinet at all. Francis Maude, Angus's son and Minister of State at the Foreign office, whom I regarded as a reliable ally, told me that he passionately supported the things I believed in, that he would back me as long as I went on, but that he did not believe I could win. He left in a state of some distress; nor had he cheered me up noticeably.

Ken Clarke now entered. His manner was robust in the brutalist style he has cultivated: the candid friend. He said that this method of changing

Prime Ministers was farcical, and that he personally would be happy to support me for another five or ten years. Most of the Cabinet, however, thought that I should stand down. Otherwise, not only would I lose; I would 'lose big' if that were to happen, the Party would go to Michael Heseltine and end up split. So Douglas and John should be released from their obligation to me and allowed to stand, since either had a better chance than I did. Then the solid part of the Party could get back together. Contrary to persistent rumours, Ken Clarke at no point threatened to resign.

Peter Lilley, obviously ill at ease, came in next. He duly announced that he would support me if I stood but that it was inconceivable that I would win. Michael Heseltine must not be allowed to get the leadership or all my achievements would be threatened. The only way to prevent this was to make way for John Major.

Of course, I had not been optimistic about Ken Clarke and Peter Lilley for quite different reasons. But I had written off my next visitor, Malcolm Rifkind, in advance. After Geoffrey's departure, Malcolm was probably my sharpest personal critic in the Cabinet and he did not soften his criticism on this occasion. He said bluntly that I could not win, and that either John or Douglas would do better. Still, even Malcolm did not declare against me. When I asked him whether I would have his support if I did stand, he said that he would have to think about it. Indeed, he gave the assurance that he would never campaign against me. Silently, I thanked God for small mercies.

After so much commiseration, it was a relief to talk to Peter Brooke. He was, as always, charming, thoughtful and loyal. He said he would fully support me whatever I chose to do. Being in Northern Ireland, he was not closely in touch with parliamentary opinion and could not himself offer an authoritative view of my prospects. But he believed I could win if I went ahead with all guns blazing. Could I win if all guns did *not* blaze? That was something I was myself beginning to doubt.

My next visitor was Michael Howard, another rising star who shared my convictions. Michael's version of the Cabinet theme was altogether stronger and more encouraging. Although he doubted my prospects, he himself would not only support me but would campaign vigorously for me.

William Waldegrave, my most recent Cabinet appointment, arrived next. William declared very straightforwardly that it would be dishonourable for someone to accept a place in my Cabinet one week and not support me three weeks later. He would vote for me as long as I was a candidate. But he had a sense of foreboding about the result. It would be a catastrophe if corporatist policies took over, which, of course, was another way of saying that Michael Heseltine should be held at bay.

At this point I received a note from John Wakeham who wanted an urgent word with me. Apparently, the position was much worse than he had thought. I was not surprised. It was hardly any better from where I was sitting.

John Gummer bounced in next. He reeled off the standard formula that he would support me if I decided to stand, but as a friend he should warn me that I could not win, and so I should move aside and let John and Douglas stand.

John Gummer was followed by Chris Patten. Chris was a man of the Left. So I could hardly complain when he told me that he would support me but that I could not win and so on.

Even melodramas have intervals, even *Macbeth* has the Porter's scene. I now had a short talk with Alan Clark, Minister of State at the Ministry of Defence, and a gallant friend, who came round to lift my spirits with the encouraging advice that I should fight on at all costs. Unfortunately, he went on to argue that I should fight on even though I was bound to lose because it was better to go out in a blaze of glorious defeat than to go gentle into that good night. Since I had no particular fondness for Wagnerian endings, this lifted my spirits only briefly. But I was glad to have someone unambiguously on my side even in defeat,

By now John Wakeham and Ken Baker had turned up to speak to me, and their news was not good. John said that he now doubted whether I could get the support of the Cabinet. What I had been hearing did not suggest that he was wrong. He added that he had tried to put together a campaign team but was not succeeding even at that. I had realized by now that I was not dealing with Polish Cavalrymen; but I was surprised that neither Tristan Garel-Jones nor Richard Ryder were prepared to serve as John's lieutenants because they believed I could not win. It was a personal as well as a political blow to learn that Richard, who had come with me to No. 10 all those years ago as my political secretary and whom I had moved up the ladder as quickly as I decently could, was deserting at the first whiff of grapeshot.

Ken Baker went on to report that the position had deteriorated since we had spoken that morning. He had found between ten and twelve members of the Cabinet who did not think I could win. And if they thought that, there would not be enough enthusiasm to carry the day. Even so he believed that I should carry on. But he floated Tom King's suggestion – that I should promise to stand down after Christmas if I won. The idea was that this would allow me to see through the Gulf War. I could not accept this: I would have no authority in the meantime and I would need all I could muster for forthcoming battles in the European Community.

After John and Ken had left, Norman Lamont came in and repeated the formula. The position, he said, was beyond repair. Everything we had achieved on industry and Europe would be jeopardized by a victory for Michael Heseltine. Everything but Robertson Hare's 'Oh Calamity'.

John MacGregor now appeared and somewhat belatedly gave me the news that I lacked support in the Cabinet which he had felt unable to convey to me earlier in the day. Tom King said the usual things, though more warmly than most. He added a suggestion trailed by Ken Baker that I should offer to stand down at a specific date in the future. I rejected this suggestion, but I was grateful for the diversion.

In all the circumstances, it was a relief to see David Waddington enter and sit down on the sofa. Here was a steadfast friend but, as I quickly saw, one in the deepest distress. David said that he wanted me to win and would support me but could not guarantee a victory. He left my room with tears in his eyes.

The last meeting was with Tony Newton who, though clearly nervous, just about managed to get out the agreed line. He did not think I could win, etc. Nor, by now, did I. John Wakeham came in again and elaborated further on what he had earlier told me. I had lost the Cabinet's support. I could not even muster a credible campaign team. It was the end.

I was sick at heart. I could have resisted the opposition of opponents and potential rivals and even respected them for it; but what grieved me was desertion of those I had always considered friends and allies and the weasel words whereby they had transmuted their betrayal into frank advice and concern for my fate. I dictated a brief statement of my resignation to be read out at Cabinet the following morning. But I said that I would return to No. 10 to talk to Denis before finally taking my decision.

I was preparing to return when Norman Tebbit arrived with Michael Portillo. Michael was Minister of State at the DoE with responsibility for local government and the community charge. He was beyond any questioning a passionate supporter of everything we stood for. He tried to convince me that Cabinet were misreading the situation, that I was being misled and that with a vigorous campaign it would still be possible to turn things round. With even a drop of this spirit in higher places, it might indeed have been possible. But this was just not there. Then another group of loyalists from the 92 Group of MPs arrived in my room – George Gardiner, John Townend, Edward Leigh, Chris Chope and a number of others. They had a similar message to Michael. I was immensely grateful for their support and warmth, and said that I would think about what to do. Then at last I returned to No. 10.

I went up to see Denis. There was not much to say, but he comforted me. He had given me his own verdict earlier and it had turned out to be right. After a few minutes I went down to the Cabinet Room to start work on the speech I was to deliver in the following day's No Confidence debate. My Private Office had already prepared a first draft, conceived under very different circumstances. Norman Tebbit and – for some reason – John Gummer came in to help. It was a mournful occasion. Every now and again I found I had to wipe away a tear as the enormity of what had happened crowded in.

While we worked on into the night, Michael Portillo returned with two other last-ditchers, Michael Forsyth and Michael Fallon. They were not allowed to see me as I was engrossed in the speech. But when I was told that they had been sent away, I said that I would naturally see them, and they were summoned back. They arrived about midnight and tried in vain to convince me that all was not lost. Before I went to bed that night I stressed how important it was to ensure that John Major's own nomination papers were ready to be submitted before the tight deadline if indeed I stood down. I said that I would sleep on my own resignation, as I always did with important matters, before making my final decision.

At 7.30 the next morning – Thursday 22 November – I telephoned down to Andrew Turnbull that I had finally resolved to resign. The Private Office put into action the plan already agreed for an Audience with the Queen. Peter Morrison telephoned Douglas Hurd and John Major to inform them of my decision. John Wakeham and Ken Baker were also told. I cleared the text of the press statement due to be issued later in the morning, spent half an hour of rather desultory briefing with Bernard, Charles and John for Questions in the House, and then just before 9 o'clock, went down to chair my last Cabinet.

Normally, in the Cabinet ante-room ministers would be standing around in groups, arguing and joking. On this occasion there was silence.

They stood with their backs against the wall looking in every direction except mine. There was a short delay: John MacGregor had been held up in the traffic. Then the Cabinet filed, still in silence, into the Cabinet Room.

I said that I had a statement to make. Then I read it out:

> Having consulted widely among my colleagues, I have concluded that the unity of the Party and the prospects of victory in a general election would be better served if I stood down to enable Cabinet colleagues to enter the ballot for the leadership. I should like to thank all those in the Cabinet and outside who have given me such dedicated support.

The Lord Chancellor then read out a statement of tribute to me, which ministers agreed should be written into the Cabinet minutes. Most of that day and the next few days, I felt as if I were sleepwalking rather than experiencing and feeling everything that happened. Every now and then, however, I would be overcome by the emotion of this occasion and give way to tears. The Lord Chancellor's reading of this tribute was just such a difficult moment. When he had finished and I had regained my composure, I said that it was vital that the Cabinet should stand together to safeguard all that we believed in. That was why I was standing down. The Cabinet should unite to back the person most likely to beat Michael Heseltine. By standing down I had enabled others to come forward who were not burdened by a legacy of bitterness from ex-ministers who had been sacked. Party unity was vital. Whether one, two or three colleagues stood, it was essential that Cabinet should remain united and support their favourites in that spirit.

Ken Baker on behalf of the Party and then Douglas Hurd as the senior member of the Cabinet made their own short tributes. I could bear no more of this, fearing I would lose my composure entirely, and concluded the discussion with the hope that I would be able to offer the new leader total and devoted support. There was then a ten-minute break for courtesy calls to be made to the offices of the Speaker, the Leader of the Opposition and the Leader of the Liberal Party (Jim Molyneaux of the Unionists could not be contacted) and a statement was accordingly issued at 9.25 a.m.

The Cabinet meeting then resumed. It was almost business as usual. This ranged from matters of the utmost triviality – an unsuccessful Fisheries Council ruined by incompetent Italian chairmanship – to matters of the greatest importance, the decision to increase our forces in the Gulf by sending a second armoured brigade. Somehow I got through it by concentrating on details, and the formal Cabinet ended at about 10.15 a.m. But I invited ministers to stay on. It was a relief to have more or less normal conversation on what was uppermost in our minds, namely the likely outcome of the second ballot, over coffee.

After Cabinet I signed personal messages to Presidents Bush and Gorbachev, European Community and G7 heads of government, and a number of Gulf leaders. Douglas and John were by now busily organizing their campaigns, both of them having decided to stand.

Later I worked on my speech for the afternoon debate. By this time I was beginning to feel that a great weight had been lifted from me. A No Confidence debate would have been a taxing ordeal if I had been fighting on with so many in the Cabinet, junior ministers and backbenchers against me. Now that I had announced my departure, however, I would again enjoy the united support of the Tory Party. Now it would be roses, roses, all the way. And since this would be my last major parliamentary performance as Prime Minister, I determined to defend the achievements of the last eleven years in the same spirit as I had fought for them.

After a brief Audience with the Queen I returned to No. 10 for lunch. I had a quick drink with members of my staff in the study. I was suddenly conscious that they too had their futures to think about, and I found myself now and later comforting them almost as much as they sought to comfort me. Crawfie had begun the packing. Joy was sorting out outstanding constituency business. Denis was clearing his desk. But I held my normal briefing meeting for Questions and then left for the House at just before 2.30 p.m.

No one will ever understand British politics who does not understand the House of Commons. The House is not just another legislative body. On special occasions it becomes in some almost mystical way the focus of national feeling. As newspaper comments and the reflections of those who were present will testify, I was not alone in sensing the concentrated emotion of that afternoon. And it seemed as if this very intensity, mingled with the feelings of relief that my great struggle against mounting odds had ended, lent wings to my words. As I answered Questions my confidence gradually rose.

Then I sat down to draw breath and listen to Neil Kinnock make his opening speech in the No Confidence Debate. Mr Kinnock, in all his years as Opposition leader, never let me down. Right to the end, he struck every wrong note. On this occasion he delivered a speech that might have served if I had announced my intention to stand for the second ballot. It was a standard, partisan rant. One concession to the generosity that the House feels on such occasions (and that his own backbencher, Dennis Skinner, no moderate and an old sparring partner of mine, was about to express in a memorable intervention) might have exploited the discomfiture that was palpably growing on the Tory benches. It might have disarmed me and eroded the control that was barely keeping my emotions in check. Instead, he managed to fill me and the benches behind me with his own partisan indignation and therefore intensified the newfound Tory unity – in the circumstances a remarkable, perverse, achievement.

The speech which I then rose to deliver does not read in Hansard as a particularly eloquent one. It is a fighting defence of the Government's record which replies point by point to the Opposition's attack, and which owes more to the Conservative Research Department than to Burke. For me at that moment, however, each sentence was my testimony at the bar of history. It was as if I were speaking for the last time, rather than merely for the last time as Prime Minister. And that power of conviction came through and impressed itself on the House.

After the usual partisan banter with Opposition hecklers, I restated my convictions on Europe and reflected on the great changes which had taken place in the world since I had entered No. 10. I said:

> Ten years ago, the eastern part of Europe lay under totalitarian rule, its people knowing neither rights nor liberties. Today, we have a Europe in which democracy, the rule of law and basic human rights are spreading ever more widely: where the threat to our security from the overwhelming conventional forces of the Warsaw Pact has been removed: where the Berlin Wall has been torn down and the Cold War is at an end.
>
> These immense changes did not come about by chance. They have been achieved by strength and resolution in defence, and by a refusal ever to be intimidated. No one in eastern Europe believes that their countries would be free had it not been for those western governments who were prepared to defend liberty, and who kept alive their hope that one day eastern Europe too would enjoy freedom.

My final reflection was on the Falklands and Gulf Wars, the second of which we were just then gearing up to fight.

> There is something else which one feels. That is a sense of this country's destiny: the centuries of history and experience which ensure that, when principles have to be defended, when good has to be upheld and when evil has to be overcome, Britain will take up arms. It is because we on this side have never flinched from difficult decisions that this House and this country can have confidence in this Government today.

Such was my defence of the record of the Government which I had headed for eleven and a half years, which I had led to victory in three elections, which had pioneered the new wave of economic freedom that was transforming countries from eastern Europe to Australasia, which had restored Britain's reputation as a force to be reckoned with in the world, and which, at the very moment when our historic victory in the Cold War was being ratified at the Paris conference, had decided to dispense with my services. I sat down with the cheers of colleagues, wets and dries, allies and opponents, stalwarts and faint hearts, ringing in my ears, and began to think of what I would do next.

But there was one more duty I had to perform, and that was to ensure that John Major was my successor. I wanted – perhaps I needed – to believe that he was the man to secure and safeguard my legacy. So it was with disquiet that I learned a number of my friends were thinking of voting for Michael Heseltine. They distrusted the role which John Major's supporters like Richard Ryder, Peter Lilley, Francis Maude and Norman Lamont had played in my downfall. They also felt that Michael Heseltine, for all his faults, was a heavyweight who could fill a room in the way a leader should. I did all I could to argue them out of this. In most cases I was successful.

Before then, however, I was to spend my last weekend at Chequers. I arrived there on Saturday evening, travelling down after quite a jolly little lunch with the family and friends at No. 10. On Sunday morning Denis and I went to church, while Crawfie filled a Range Rover with hats, books and a huge variety of personal odds and ends which were to be delivered to our house in Dulwich. Gersons took away our larger items. Denis and I entertained the Chequers staff for drinks before lunch to say farewell and thank you for all their kindness over the years. I had loved Chequers and I knew I would miss it. I decided that I would like to walk round the rooms one last time and did so with Denis as the light faded on that winter afternoon.

From the time that I had announced my resignation, the focus of public interest naturally switched to the question of who would be my successor. I did all that I could to rally support for John without publicly stating that I wanted him to win. From about this time, however, I became conscious that there was a certain ambiguity in his stance. On the one hand, he was understandably anxious to attract my supporters. On the other, his campaign wanted to emphasize that John was 'his own man'. A joke – made in the context of remarks on the Gulf – about my skills as a 'back-seat driver' provoked a flurry of anxiety in the Major camp. It was, unfortunately, the shape of things to come.

However, I was truly delighted when the results came through – John Major 185 votes, Michael Heseltine 131 and Douglas Hurd 56. Officially, John was two votes short; but within minutes Douglas and Michael had announced that they would support him in the third ballot. He was effectively the new Prime Minister. I congratulated him and joined in the celebrations at No. 11. But I did not stay long: this was his night, not mine.

Wednesday 28 November was my last day in office. The packing was now all but complete. Early that morning I went down from the flat to my study for the last time to check that nothing had been left behind. It was a shock to find that I could not get in because the key had already been taken off my keyring. At 9.10 I came down to the front hallway. (I was due shortly at the Palace for my final Audience with the Queen.) As on the day of my arrival, all the staff of No. 10 were there. I shook hands with my private secretaries and others whom I had come to know so well over the years. Some were in tears. I tried to hold back mine but they flowed freely as I walked down the hall past those applauding me on my way out of office, just as eleven and a half years earlier they had greeted me as I entered it.

Before going outside, and with Denis and Mark beside me, I paused to collect my thoughts. Crawfie wiped a trace of mascara off my cheek, evidence of a tear which I had been unable to check. The door opened onto press and photographers. I went out to the bank of microphones and read out a short statement which concluded:

> Now it is time for a new chapter to open and I wish John Major all
> the luck in the world. He will be splendidly served and he has the

makings of a great Prime Minister, which I am sure he will be in a very short time.

I waved and got into the car with Denis beside me, as he has always been; and the car took us past press, policemen and the tall black gates of Downing Street, away from red boxes and parliamentary questions, summits and party conferences, budgets and communiqués, situation room and scrambler telephones, out to whatever the future held.

CHRONOLOGY, 1955–1990

1955

5 April	Churchill resigned as Prime Minister; succeeded by Eden.
26 May	General election: Conservative majority sixty.

1956

26 July	Nasser nationalized the Suez Canal.
29 October	Israel invaded Sinai.
30 October	Joint Anglo-French ultimatum to Egypt and Israel; Soviet troops invaded Hungary.
5 November	British and French landings at Port Said; intervention aborted two days later under US pressure.

1957

9 January	Eden resigned as Prime Minister; Macmillan succeeded him.
25 March	Treaty of Rome signed, establishing EEC.
25 July	Macmillan: 'Most of our people have never had it so good.'
19 September	Thorneycroft increased Bank Rate from 5 to 7 per cent.

1958

6 January	Treasury Ministers (Thorneycroft, Powell and Birch) resigned from the Government over public expenditure plans; Macmillan left the following day for a Commonwealth tour, describing the resignations as 'little local difficulties'.
3 July	Credit squeeze relaxed.
31 August	Notting Hill and Nottingham riots.

1959

7 April	Budget: 9d reduction in income tax.
8 October	General election: Conservative majority 100; MT first elected MP for Finchley.
28 November	Gaitskell called for reform of Clause IV of Labour's constitution – forced to retreat the following year.

1960

3 February   Macmillan in South Africa: 'A wind of change is blowing through the continent.'

5 February   MT's maiden speech.

February–October   Parliamentary passage of MT's Public Bodies (Admission of the Press to Meetings) Bill.

1961

25 July   Deflationary emergency budget; 'Pay Pause' for government employees.

31 July   Macmillan announced beginning of negotiations for Britain to join EEC.

13 August   East Germany sealed the border with West Berlin; Berlin Wall begun.

9 October   Reshuffle: MT appointed to her first government post – Parliamentary Secretary, Ministry of Pensions and National Insurance.

1962

14 March   Orpington by-election: Liberals took Conservative seat, overturning a majority of 14,760.

13 July   'Night of the Long Knives' – seven of twenty-one Cabinet ministers fired by Macmillan.

October   Cuban missile crisis.

November   Vassall affair.

21 December   US agreement to sell Britain Polaris.

1963

14 January   De Gaulle rejected first British application to join the EEC.

14 February   Harold Wilson elected Labour Leader following death of Hugh Gaitskell.

4 June   Profumo resigned.

1 July   Philby named as 'the third man'.

10 October   Macmillan resigned as Prime Minister during Conservative Party Conference in Blackpool.

19 October   Douglas-Home became Prime Minister; Iain Macleod and Enoch Powell refused office.

1964

July   Legislation enacted to abolish Resale Price Maintenance.

15 October   General election: Labour won a majority of four; Wilson became Prime Minister.

28 October	MT became Opposition spokesman on Pensions.
November	Sterling crisis.

1965

24 January	Churchill died, aged ninety.
12 July	Crosland's circular 10/65 on comprehensive schools: LEAs to submit plans within a year to reorganize on comprehensive lines; Government's aim declared to be 'the complete elimination of selection and separatism in secondary education'.
22 July	Douglas-Home resigned as Conservative Leader; Heath elected to succeed him, defeating Maudling and Powell.
16 September	Labour's National Plan published.
5 October	Reshuffle of Opposition spokesmen: MT moved to Shadow Housing and Land.
8 November	Abolition of capital punishment.
11 November	Rhodesia: Unilateral Declaration of Independence (UDI).

1966

31 March	General election: Labour returned with an overall majority of ninety-seven.
19 April	Reshuffle of Opposition spokesmen: MT appointed Iain Macleod's deputy, shadowing the Treasury.
3 May	Budget introduced Selective Employment Tax (SET).
May–July	Seamen's strike.
15 June	Abortion Bill passed Second Reading.
July	Sterling crisis; deflation; wage freeze to be followed by a prices and incomes policy.
5 July	Sexual Offences Bill (legalizing homosexuality) passed Second Reading.
12 October	MT spoke against SET at the Conservative Conference.
10 November	Labour announced Britain to make a second application to join the EEC.

1967

11 April	Massive Conservative gains in local government elections.
10 October	Heath moved MT to Shadow Fuel and Power, with a place in the Shadow Cabinet.
18 November	Devaluation of sterling by 14 per cent ($2.80 to $2.40).
27 November	Britain's second EEC application vetoed by France.
29 November	Jenkins replaced Callaghan as Chancellor of the Exchequer; Callaghan succeeded Jenkins as Home Secretary.

1968

22 February	Callaghan announced emergency legislation to curb immigration of Asians expelled from Kenya; Shadow Cabinet divided.
17 March	Grosvenor Square riot – violent demonstration against Vietnam War.
19 March	Budget increased indirect taxes by almost £900 million – austerity under Jenkins.
20 April	Enoch Powell's 'River Tiber' speech in Birmingham; Heath dismissed him from the Shadow Cabinet the following day.
10 October	MT gave her CPC lecture *What's Wrong With Politics?*
14 November	MT moved by Heath to Shadow Transport.

1969

17 January	Barbara Castle introduced *In Place of Strife* – Labour's proposals to reform industrial relations law; opposition from within the Labour Party, led by Callaghan, forced their withdrawal in June.
14 August	British troops deployed on the streets of Londonderry.
21 October	MT appointed Opposition spokesman on Education in succession to Edward Boyle.

1970

30 January–1 February	Selsdon Park Conference – Shadow Cabinet discussion of Conservative policy for next manifesto.
18 June	General election: Conservatives won majority of thirty-one; Heath became Prime Minister; MT appointed Secretary of State for Education and Science.
30 June	MT issued Circular 10/70, withdrawing Labour's comprehensive education Circulars.
20 July	Iain Macleod died suddenly.
6–30 September	Leila Khalid affair.
27 October	Budget – ending free school milk for children over seven; increasing school meal charges; Open University reprieved.

1971

4 February	Nationalization of Rolls-Royce.
5 August	Industrial Relations Bill became law.
28 October	House of Commons on a free vote approved terms of entry to EEC.

1972

9 January	Miners went on strike.
20 January	Unemployment total passed one million.
10 February	Mass picketing closed Saltley Coke Depot.
19 February	Government conceded miners' demands to end the strike.
20 February	Government announced U-turn on Upper Clyde Shipbuilders.
March	Government began search for voluntary pay policy in talks with TUC and CBI.
21 March	Budget – reflation began in earnest.
22 March	Industry White Paper published.
24 March	Suspension of Northern Ireland Parliament at Stormont; direct rule began.
June–July	Industrial Relations Act badly damaged following court decisions leading to arrest of pickets in docks dispute.
23 June	Sterling floated after only six weeks' membership of the European currency 'snake'.
Summer–autumn	'Tripartite talks' between Government, TUC and CBI – Government attempted to negotiate a voluntary pay policy.
2 November	Collapse of 'Tripartite talks'.
6 November	Heath announced Stage 1 of statutory pay policy.
6 December	MT's White Paper *Education: A Framework for Expansion.*

1973

1 January	Britain joined EEC.
17 January	Heath announced Stage 2 of statutory pay policy.
16 March	End of Bretton Woods system – all major currencies floated.
May	Heath/Barber boom at its height; budget reduced spending plans.
6–24 October	Yom Kippur War; oil prices dramatically increased.
8 October	Heath announced Stage 3.
12 November	Miners began overtime ban, sharply cutting coal production.
2 December	Reshuffle – Whitelaw became Employment Secretary.
13 December	Heath announced three-day week.
17 December	Emergency budget cut £1,200 million from expenditure plans.

1974

9 January	NEDC meeting at which TUC suggested miners could be treated as a special case within government pay policy.

5 February	Miners voted to strike from 10 February.
7 February	General election called for 28 February.
21 February	Relativities Board leak suggesting that miners' claim could have been accommodated within Stage 3.
23 February	Enoch Powell announced that he would vote Labour.
28 February	General election: no single party won a majority; Labour won the largest number of seats.
1–3 March	Heath attempted to form a coalition with the Liberals.
4 March	Heath resigned following Liberal rejection of his proposals; Wilson became Prime Minister, leading a minority Labour Government.
11 March	Heath formed his Shadow Cabinet, giving MT responsibility for the Environment.
May	Centre for Policy Studies (CPS) founded.
22 June	Keith Joseph's speech at Upminster.
28 August	MT announced Conservative pledge to abolish domestic rates and hold down mortgage interest rates to maximum of 9½ per cent.
5 September	Keith Joseph's speech at Preston.
10 October	General election: Labour majority of three.
14 October	1922 Committee executive urged Heath to call a leadership election.
19 October	Keith Joseph's speech at Edgbaston.
7 November	Heath reshuffled Shadow Cabinet; MT became Robert Carr's assistant spokesman on Treasury questions.
14 November	Heath told 1922 that he would set up a committee to review leadership election procedure.
21 November	Keith Joseph told MT that he would not stand for the leadership against Heath; MT told him she would.
November– December	'Hoarding' story run against MT in the press.
17 December	Leadership election review reported.

1975

15 January	Airey Neave took over the organization of MT's leadership campaign, Edward du Cann having decided not to stand.
4 February	Leadership election first ballot: MT 130, Heath 119, Hugh Fraser 16; Heath resigned as leader.
11 February	Leadership election second ballot: MT elected leader.
12 February	MT called on Heath at Wilton Street; Heath refused to serve in the Shadow Cabinet.

18 February	Shadow Cabinet complete: Maudling, Foreign Affairs; Howe, Treasury; Joseph, Policy and Research; Thorneycroft, Chairman.
5 June	EEC referendum.
July	£6 a week quasi-statutory pay policy introduced; unemployment passed one million.

1976

2 March	Sterling fell below $2.
16 March	Wilson announced his resignation; Callaghan elected Labour Leader on 5 April.
7 April	Government lost its majority.
5 May	Stage 2 of pay policy agreed between Government and TUC.
10 May	Thorpe resigned as Liberal Leader over the Scott affair; Grimond interim Leader; Steel elected on 7 July.
7 June	Sterling under pressure – $5,300 million standby credit made available to UK for three months.
28 September	Healey forced to turn back from the airport as sterling fell to $1.63; spoke at the Labour Conference on 30 September.
4 October	*The Right Approach* published.
1 November	IMF team arrived in UK.
19 November	MT reshuffled Shadow Cabinet, dismissing Maudling and replacing him with John Davies.
1 December	Shadow Cabinet decision to oppose the Scotland and Wales Bill; Buchanan-Smith and Rifkind resigned.
15 December	Healey's mini-budget and IMF Letter of Intent 1977.

1977

22 February	Government defeated on Scotland and Wales Bill guillotine – Bill effectively lost; prospect that Government would fall.
23 March	'Lib-Lab Pact' saved the Government.
16 June	Government defeated over Rooker-Wise-Lawson amendments – tax allowances linked to RPI.
24 June	Grunwick dispute: mass picketing began.
18 September	MT interviewed by Brian Walden suggested referendum if a future Conservative Government met the kind of trade union challenge Heath faced in 1974.
8 October	*The Right Approach to the Economy* published.
16 October	Scotland Bill and Wales Bill successfully guillotined.

1978

25 January	Scotland Bill Committee – 'Cunningham amendment': 40 per cent hurdle for devolution in referendum.
30 January	MT on television referred to people's fears that they would be 'rather swamped' by immigration.
3 March	Rhodesia: 'internal settlement' – Muzorewa and others to join Ian Smith's Government.
25 May	Steel announced end of Lib-Lab Pact after current parliamentary session.
21 July	Incomes policy White Paper: Stage 3 – 5 per cent guideline for wage increases.
Summer	'Labour Isn't Working' – Saatchi & Saatchi's first campaign for the Conservative Party.
7 September	Callaghan announced there would be no autumn election.
21 September	Ford strike (ended 2 November): breached 5 per cent pay norm.
11 October	Heath spoke in favour of Stage 3 at the Conservative Party Conference.
8 November	114 Conservatives rebelled against leadership decision to abstain on motion to renew Rhodesian sanctions.

1979

3 January	Lorry drivers strike for 25 per cent pay claim: 'Winter of Discontent' reaching its height.
7 January	MT interviewed on *Weekend World*; suggested possible union reforms.
14 January	MT offered to co-operate in legislation on secondary picketing and no-strike agreements for essential services; Government made no direct reply but eased its pay guidelines and lorry drivers' strike settled locally over the following three weeks.
1 March	Scotland and Wales devolution referenda.
28 March	Government defeated on Motion of Confidence 311–310, forcing general election.
30 March	Airey Neave murdered by INLA bomb.
3 May	General election: Conservative majority of forty-three.
4 May	MT became Prime Minister.
7 June	European elections.
12 June	1979 budget. Standard rate of income tax cut to 30 per cent, top rate to 60 per cent.
28 June	Tokyo G7 summit.
1–8 August	Lusaka CHOGM.

27 August	Assassination of Lord Mountbatten/Warrenpoint bomb.
23 October	Geoffrey Howe announced abolition of remaining exchange controls.
29–30 November	Dublin European Council: budget arguments.
16 December	MT and Lord Carrington arrived in Washington for two-day visit.
25 December	Afghanistan: USSR began invasion.

1980

2 January	Steel strike began. Ended 3 April.
5 May	SAS stormed Iranian Embassy.
2 June	Cabinet endorsed EC budget agreement.
22 June	Venice G7 summit.
22 September	Iran-Iraq War began.
10 October	MT addressed Conservative Conference, Brighton: 'The lady's not for turning.'
27 October	First Maze hunger strike began. Ended 18 December.
4 November	USA: Ronald Reagan elected President.
8 December	Anglo-Irish summit in Dublin.

1981

5 January	Norman St John Stevas and Angus Maude left the Government. Francis Pym became Leader of House of Commons, John Nott to Defence, Leon Brittan joined Cabinet as Chief Secretary.
10 February	NCB announced pit closures. Government announced NCB plan withdrawn on 18 February.
1 March	Second IRA hunger strike begun by Bobby Sands. Ended 3 October after ten deaths; then Chelsea Barracks bomb.
10 March	1981 budget.
26 March	SDP formed. Alliance formed on 16 June.
30 March	364 economists' letter criticizing economic policy.
11–14 April	Brixton riots.
10 May	François Mitterrand elected French President.
3 July	Southall riot. Toxteth and Moss Side riots 4–8 July.
20 July	Ottawa G7 summit opened.
23 July	Argument at public spending cabinet.
14 September	Reshuffle: Ian Gilmour, Mark Carlisle and Lord Soames left the Government. Nigel Lawson, Norman Tebbit and Cecil Parkinson joined the Cabinet. Jim Prior appointed to Northern Ireland.
30 September	Melbourne CHOGM opened.
13 December	Poland: Martial law declared.

1982

25 March	Roy Jenkins won Glasgow, Hillhead by-election.
2 April	Argentina invaded Falkland Islands.
3 April	Saturday Commons debate on Falklands. Passage of UNSCR 502.
5 April	First naval units left Portsmouth. Lord Carrington and other Foreign Office ministers resigned. Francis Pym became Foreign Secretary, John Biffen Leader HC.
25 April	South Georgia recaptured.
2 May	*General Belgrano* sunk by HMS *Conqueror*.
4 May	HMS *Sheffield* hit by an Exocet.
21 May	British troops landed at San Carlos.
5 June	Versailles G7 summit opened.
14 June	Capture of Port Stanley. Argentinian surrender.
20 July	Hyde Park, then Regent's Park bombs.
26 July	St Paul's Thanksgiving Service.
17 September	West Germany: fall of Helmut Schmidt's Government. Helmut Kohl succeeded him as Chancellor.
20 September	MT began visit to Japan/China/Hong Kong.

1983

6 January	Reshuffle: John Nott resigned. Michael Heseltine to Defence; Tom King to Environment.
23 March	USA: President Reagan announced SDI.
28 May	Williamsburg G7 summit opened.
9 June	General election: Conservative majority of 144.
11 June	New Government formed: Nigel Lawson Chancellor; Leon Brittan Home Secretary; Geoffrey Howe Foreign Secretary; Francis Pym dropped.
14 October	Cecil Parkinson resigned.
25 October	US invasion of Grenada.
14 November	Cruise missiles arrived at Greenham.
December	Athens European Council.
17 December	Harrods bomb.

1984

9 February	USSR: death of Andropov. MT attended funeral.
8 March	Miners' strike began.
2 June	Fontainebleau European Council: budget settlement.
10 July	National dock strike (ended 20 July).
24 August	Second national dock strike (ended 18 September).
12 October	Brighton bomb.
25 October	High Court ordered sequestration of NUM.

31 October	India: Mrs Gandhi assassinated.
6 November	USA: President Reagan re-elected.
20 November	British Telecom flotation.
15 December	Mr and Mrs Gorbachev visited Chequers.
19 December	China: MT signed Hong Kong agreement in Peking.

1985

20 February	MT visited Washington and addressed a joint session of Congress.
5 March	Miners returned to work.
11 March	USSR: Mr Gorbachev new Soviet leader. MT visited Moscow for Chernenko's funeral.
4 April	MT began eleven-day tour of Far East.
2 May	Bonn G7 summit opened.
2 September	Reshuffle. Peter Rees, Patrick Jenkin and Lord Gowrie left the Government. Norman Tebbit new Party Chairman. Leon Brittan to DTI, Douglas Hurd to Home Office. Kenneth Clarke, John MacGregor and Kenneth Baker all joined the Cabinet.
9 September	Handsworth riots (continued 10 September). Brixton 28 September.
16–19 September	MT toured Egypt and Jordan.
25 September	Plaza Accord to reduce value of the dollar.
6–7 October	Broadwater Farm riot.
16–23 October	Nassau CHOGM: arguments about South Africa.
24 October	MT and President Reagan addressed UN General Assembly.
15 November	MT signed Anglo-Irish Agreement at Hillsborough.
3 December	Luxemburg European Council.

1986

9 January	Westland: Michael Heseltine resigned.
24 January	Westland: Leon Brittan resigned.
28 January	Publication of Community Charge Green Paper.
15 April	US raid on Libya.
3–6 May	MT visited South Korea and attended Tokyo G7 summit.
21 May	Reshuffle. Keith Joseph resigned. Kenneth Baker replaced him as Education Secretary.
24–27 May	MT visited Israel.
3 August	Special London Commonwealth summit on South Africa.
24 October	Britain broke off diplomatic relations with Syria following Hindawi affair.

15–16 November	MT visited Camp David, following Reykjavik summit.
5 December	London European Council.

1987

22 February	Louvre Accord to stabilize the dollar.
28 March	USSR: MT began five-day tour (ended 2 April).
8 June	Venice G7 summit opened.
11 June	General election: Conservative majority of 102.
17 June	USA: MT visited President Reagan in Washington.
6 October	Conservative Conference led to abandonment of decision to phase in community charge (dual running).
13 October	Vancouver CHOGM.
19 October	'Black Monday'.
8 November	Enniskillen bomb killed eleven, injured sixty.
7 December	MT held talks with Mr Gorbachev at Brize Norton.
8 December	INF Treaty signed in Washington.

1988

4–8 January	MT toured Africa.
10 January	Lord Whitelaw resigned due to ill-health.
7 March	Sterling 'uncapped'.
15 March	1988 budget. Standard rate of income tax cut to 25 per cent, top rate to 40 per cent.
March	NATO summit in Brussels.
6–8 April	MT visited Turkey.
18 April	Michael Mates's amendment to band community charge defeated.
21 May	MT spoke to General Assembly of Church of Scotland.
2 June	Interest rates increased from low of 7.5 per cent to 8 per cent.
19–21 June	Toronto G7 summit.
17 July	Alan Walters's return as economic adviser to MT announced.
25 July	Reshuffle. DHSS split between Kenneth Clarke and John Moore.
30 July	MT began eleven-day tour of the Far East and Australia.
20 August	IRA bomb at Ballygawley, Co. Tyrone. MT cut short Cornish holiday.
20 September	Bruges speech.
2 November	MT began three-day visit to Poland.
8 November	USA: George Bush elected President.
17 November	MT visited Washington: farewell to President Reagan and talks with President Bush.

21 December	Lockerbie bombing.

1989

31 January	Publication of NHS White Paper.
27 March	MT began six-day visit to Africa.
1 April	MT visited Namibia.
5 April	Mr Gorbachev began a three-day visit to UK.
29–30 May	NATO fortieth anniversary summit in Brussels.
3 June	China: Tiananmen Square massacre.
26 June	Madrid European Council.
14–16 July	French Revolution Bicentennial and Paris G7 summit.
24 July	Reshuffle: John Moore, Paul Channon, Lord Young and George Younger left the Government. Geoffrey Howe from FCO to Lord President and Leader HC. John Major succeeded him at FCO.
19–22 September	MT visited Japan.
18–24 October	Kuala Lumpur CHOGM.
26 October	Nigel Lawson resigned. John Major replaced him as Chancellor and Douglas Hurd became Foreign Secretary.
9 November	East Germany announced opening of its border with West Germany. Demolition of Berlin Wall began 10 November.
5 December	MT defeated Sir Anthony Meyer in leadership election 314:33. Twenty-seven abstained.
10 December	Czechoslovakia: end of communist rule.
22 December	Romania: Ceauşescu overthrown.

1990

2 February	South Africa: President de Klerk announced unbanning of ANC. Nelson Mandela released 11 February.
31 March	Trafalgar Square riot.
24–25 April	MT visited Turkey on seventy-fifth anniversary of Gallipoli landings.
6 July	NATO summit in London.
9 July	Houston G7 summit.
14 July	Nick Ridley resigned.
30 July	IRA murdered Ian Gow.
2 August	Gulf: Iraq invaded Kuwait. MT held talks in Aspen, Colorado with President Bush.
17–19 September	MT visited Czechoslovakia and Hungary.
3 October	German reunification.
27–28 October	Rome European Council.
1 November	Geoffrey Howe resigned.

19–21 November	CSCE summit in Paris.
20 November	Conservative leadership first ballot: MT 204, Heseltine 152, 16 abstentions.
22 November	MT announced decision not to contest second ballot. Final speech to the Commons as Prime Minister.
28 November	MT resigned as Prime Minister.

LIST OF ABBREVIATIONS

ABM	Anti-Ballistic Missile
ACAS	Advisory, Conciliation and Arbitration Service
ANC	African National Congress
AUEW	Amalgamated Union of Engineering Workers
BL	British Leyland (later Rover Group)
BMD	Ballistic Missile Defence
BR	British Rail
BSC	British Steel Corporation
CAP	Common Agricultural Policy
CBI	Confederation of British Industry
CEGB	Central Electricity Generating Board
CFCs	Chlorofluorocarbons
CFE	Conventional Forces in Europe
CHOGM	Commonwealth Heads of Government Meeting
CND	Campaign for Nuclear Disarmament
CPRS	Central Policy Review Staff
CPS	Centre for Policy Studies
CSCE	Conference on Security and Co-operation in Europe
DES	Department of Education and Science
DHA	District Health Authority
DHSS	Department of Health and Social Security (divided from 1988)
DoE	Department of the Environment
DTI	Department of Trade and Industry
DUP	Democratic Unionist Party
E	Economic Committee of the Cabinet
EBRD	European Bank for Reconstruction and Development
EC	European Community
ECJ	European Court of Justice
ECST	European Convention on the Suppression of Terrorism
Ecu	European Currency Unit
EFL	External Financing Limit
EFTA	European Free Trade Association
EMS	European Monetary System
EMU	Economic and Monetary Union

EPG	Eminent Persons Group (sent to South Africa)
ERM	Exchange Rate Mechanism (of the EMS)
FCO	Foreign and Commonwealth Office
FSBR	Financial Statement and Budget Report ('the Red Book')
G7	Group of Seven
GATT	General Agreement on Tariffs and Trade
GDP	Gross Domestic Product
GLC	Greater London Council
GM	General Motors
GM school	Grant-Maintained school
GNP	Gross National Product
H	Home Affairs Committee of the Cabinet
HAT	Housing Action Trust
HMI	Her Majesty's Inspectorate (of schools)
IDU	International Democratic Union
IEA	Institute of Economic Affairs
IGC	Inter-Governmental Conference
ILEA	Inner London Education Authority
IMF	International Monetary Fund
INF	Intermediate-range Nuclear Forces
INLA	Irish National Liberation Army
IRA	Irish Republican Army
ISTC	Iron and Steel Trades Confederation
LEA	Local Education Authority
MCAs	Monetary compensation amounts
MEZ	Maritime Exclusion Zone
MIRVs	Multiple Independently Targetable Re-entry Vehicles
MLR	Minimum Lending Rate
MNF	Multi-National Force
MoD	Ministry of Defence
MSC	Manpower Services Commission
MTFS	Medium Term Financial Strategy
M0	Monetary base
£M3	Sterling M3
NACODS	National Association of Colliery Overmen, Deputies and Shotfirers
NADs	National Armaments Directors
NATO	North Atlantic Treaty Organization
NCB	National Coal Board (later British Coal)
NDLS	National Dock Labour Scheme
NEB	National Enterprise Board
NEDC	National Economic Development Council ('Neddy')
NGA	National Graphical Association

NHS	National Health Service
NIO	Northern Ireland Office
NUM	National Union of Mineworkers
OAS	Organization of American States
OD	Overseas and Defence Committee of the Cabinet
OD(SA)	Sub-committee of OD which ran the Falklands War
OECS	Organization of Eastern Caribbean States
OPEC	Organization of Petroleum Exporting Countries
OUP	Official Unionist Party
PLO	Palestine Liberation Organization
PPS	Parliamentary Private Secretary
PSBR	Public Sector Borrowing Requirement
PSDR	Public Sector Debt Repayment
RPI	Retail Price Index
RUC	Royal Ulster Constabulary
SALT	Strategic Arms Limitation Treaty
SAS	Special Air Service
SDLP	Social Democratic and Labour Party
SDP	Social Democratic Party
SDI	Strategic Defence Initiative
SLCM	Sea-launched Cruise Missile
SNF	Short-range Nuclear Forces
SSA	Standard Spending Assessment
START	Strategic Arms Reduction Treaty
TASM	Tactical Air-to-Surface Missile
TEZ	Total Exclusion Zone
TGWU	Transport and General Workers' Union
TUC	Trades Union Congress
UDR	Ulster Defence Regiment
UNSCR	United Nations Security Council Resolution
VAT	Value Added Tax
WEU	Western European Union

INDEX